SOMETHING ABOUT THE AUTHOR®

Something about
the Author *was named
an "Outstanding
Reference Source"
the highest honor given
by the American
Library Association
Reference and Adult
Services Division.*

ISSN 0276-816X

something ABOUT THE AUThOR®

**Facts and Pictures about Authors
and Illustrators of Books for Young People**

EDITED BY
KEVIN S. HILE

VOLUME 84

Gale Research

An ITP Information/Reference Group Company

Changing the Way the World Learns

NEW YORK • LONDON • BONN • BOSTON • DETROIT
MADRID • MELBOURNE • MEXICO CITY • PARIS
SINGAPORE • TOKYO • TORONTO • WASHINGTON
ALBANY NY • BELMONT CA • CINCINNATI OH

STAFF

Editor: Kevin S. Hile
Managing Editor: Joyce Nakamura
Publisher: Hal May
Contributing Editor: Diane Telgen
Assistant Editor: Marilyn O'Connell Allen

Sketchwriters/Copyeditors: Linda R. Andres, Shelly Andrews, Joanna Brod,
Elizabeth A. Des Chenes, Ronie-Richele Garcia-Johnson, Mary Gillis, Alan Hedblad,
Janet L. Hile, Laurie Hillstrom, Motoko Fujishiro Huthwaite, David Johnson,
J. Sydney Jones, Julie Karmazin, Sharyn Kolberg, Thomas F. McMahon, and Susan Reicha

Research Manager: Victoria B. Cariappa
Project Coordinator: Donna Melnychenko
Research Assistant: Julia C. Daniel
Research Associates: Maria E. Bryson, Mary Beth McElmeel, Tamara C. Nott,
Michele P. Pica, and Amy Terese Steel

Permissions Manager: Marlene S. Hurst
Permissions Specialist: Margaret A. Chamberlain
Permissions Associates: Edna Hedblad and Arlene Johnson

Production Director: Mary Beth Trimper
Production Assistant: Shanna Heilveil

Graphic Services Manager: Barbara J. Yarrow
Image Database Supervisor: Randy Bassett
Macintosh Artist: Sherrell Hobbs
Scanner Operator: Robert Duncan
Photography Coordinator: Pamela A. Hayes

⊚™ This book is printed on acid-free paper that meets the minimum requirements of American National Standard for Information Sciences—Permanence Paper for Printed Library Materials, ANSI Z39.48-1984.

Library of Congress Catalog Card Number 72-27107

ISBN 0-8103-9370-0 ISSN 0276-816X

Printed in the United States of America

I(T)P™ Gale Research Inc., an International Thomson Publishing Company.
ITP logo is a trademark under license.

10 9 8 7 6 5 4 3 2 1

Contents

Authors in Forthcoming Volumes

Below are some of the authors and illustrators that will be featured in upcoming volumes of *SATA*. These include new entries on the swiftly-rising stars of the field, as well as completely revised and updated entries (indicated with *) on some of the most notable and best-loved creators of books for children.

*George Ancona: An award-winning photographer and author, Ancona has published numerous children's books that celebrate other cultures, especially that of his own Mexican heritage.

Robert D. Ballard: Ballard, renowned among oceanographers for his deep-sea discoveries, including the wreck of the *Titanic,* has written several nonfiction books for children.

David Drake: Well known as an author of military science fiction, Drake is the author of the ''Hammer's Slammers'' and ''Northworld'' series, as well as other sci-fi and fantasy novels.

Kathryn Galbraith: The author of novels, picture and chapter books for children, Galbraith has been especially praised for works like *Laura Charlotte,* the story of a toy elephant passed down through the generations.

William Horwood: After writing several novels in the ''Duncton'' series, which features anthropomorphized moles as the central characters, in 1993 Horwood completed a sequel to Kenneth Grahame's classic, *The Wind in the Willows,* entitled *The Willows in Winter.*

Roger Lea MacBride: The late MacBride, who served as the attorney to Laura Ingalls Wilder's daughter, Rose, for many years, wrote several books based on Wilder's characters, including *Little House on Rocky Ridge* and *Little Farm in the Ozarks.*

*Christobel Mattingley: The Australian author of such notable works as *The Miracle Tree* and *Windmill at Magpie Creek,* Mattingley proves that it is possible to write stories for middle-grade readers that feature serious issues like the war in Bosnia.

*Doris Orgel: A reteller and translator whose version of *Dwarf Long-Nose* won the 1960 Lewis Carroll Shelf Award, Orgel has also written original stories, such as *The Devil in Vienna* and *My War with Mrs. Galloway.*

Neal Shusterman: Since publishing his first novel in 1988, Shusterman has quickly gained recognition as an up-and-coming author of books for teenagers, winning awards for such books as *What Daddy Did* and *The Eyes of King Midas.*

*Jan Slepian: Having started as an author of picture books in the 1960s, Slepian has received many more awards since she began writing YA novels featuring characters who suffer from physical, mental, or social handicaps.

Ian Strachan: A prolific English author of novels for teens, Strachan has received honors for *The Flawed Glass, The Boy in the Bubble, Throwaways, Moses Beach,* and *Picking Up the Threads.*

Frances Temple: The author of thought-provoking novels for teenagers set in exotic locales like Haiti and medieval Europe, the late Temple was lauded for such books as *Taste of Salt* and *The Ramsay Scallop.* (Entry contains exclusive interview.)

Gloria Whelan: Whelan is a versatile writer of contemporary and historical fiction for children, including *A Time to Keep Silent, A Clearing in the Forest,* and *Goodbye, Vietnam.*

*Arthur Yorinks: Yorinks' successful partnership with Richard Egielski has resulted in many beloved picture books, the most recent of which have been *Oh, Brother,* about bickering twin brothers, and *Ugh,* which is about a caveboy and his bicycle.

Introduction

Something about the Author (*SATA*) is an ongoing reference series that deals with the lives and works of authors and illustrators of children's books. *SATA* includes not only well-known authors and illustrators whose books are widely read, but also those less prominent people whose works are just coming to be recognized. This series is often the only readily available information source on emerging writers and artists. You'll find *SATA* informative and entertaining, whether you are a student, a librarian, an English teacher, a parent, or simply an adult who enjoys children's literature for its own sake.

What's Inside SATA

SATA provides detailed information about authors and illustrators who span the full time range of children's literature, from early figures like John Newbery and L. Frank Baum to contemporary figures like Judy Blume and Richard Peck. Authors in the series represent primarily English-speaking countries, particularly the United States, Canada, and the United Kingdom. Also included, however, are authors from around the world whose works are available in English translation. The writings represented in *SATA* include those created intentionally for children and young adults as well as those written for a general audience and known to interest younger readers. These writings cover the entire spectrum of children's literature, including picture books, humor, folk and fairy tales, animal stories, mystery and adventure, science fiction and fantasy, historical fiction, poetry and nonsense verse, drama, biography, and nonfiction.

Obituaries are also included in *SATA* and are intended not only as death notices but also as concise overviews of people's lives and work. Additionally, each edition features newly revised and updated entries for a selection of *SATA* listees who remain of interest to today's readers and who have been active enough to require extensive revisions of their earlier biographies.

Two Convenient Indexes

In response to suggestions from librarians, *SATA* indexes no longer appear in every volume but are included in alternate (odd-numbered) volumes of the series, beginning with Volume 57.

SATA continues to include two indexes that cumulate with each alternate volume: the Illustrations Index, arranged by the name of the illustrator, gives the number of the volume and page where the illustrator's work appears in the current volume as well as all preceding volumes in the series; the Author Index gives the number of the volume in which a person's Biographical Sketch or Obituary appears in the current volume as well as all preceding volumes in the series.

These indexes also include references to authors and illustrators who appear in Gale's *Yesterday's Authors of Books for Children, Children's Literature Review,* and the *Something about the Author Autobiography Series.*

Easy-to-Use Entry Format

Whether you're already familiar with the *SATA* series or just getting acquainted, you will want to be aware of the kind of information that an entry provides. In every *SATA* entry the editors attempt to give as complete a picture of the person's life and work as possible. A typical entry in *SATA* includes the following clearly labeled information sections:

- *PERSONAL:* date and place of birth and death, parents' names and occupations, name of spouse, date of marriage, and names of children, educational institutions attended, degrees received, religious and political affiliations, hobbies and other interests.

- *ADDRESSES:* complete home, office, electronic mail, and agent addresses, whenever available.

• *CAREER:* name of employer, position, and dates for each career post; military service; memberships and offices held in professional and civic organizations.

• *AWARDS, HONORS:* literary and professional awards received.

• *WRITINGS:* title-by-title chronological bibliography of books written and/or illustrated, listed by genre when known; lists of other notable publications, such as plays, screenplays, and periodical contributions.

• *ADAPTATIONS:* a list of films, television programs, plays, CD ROMS, and other media presentations that have been adapted from the author's work.

• *WORK IN PROGRESS:* description of projects in progress.

• *SIDELIGHTS:* a biographical portrait of the author or illustrator's development, either directly from the person—and often written specifically for the *SATA* entry—or gathered from diaries, letters, interviews, or other published sources.

• *FOR MORE INFORMATION SEE:* references for further reading.

• *EXTENSIVE ILLUSTRATIONS:* photographs, movie stills, book illustrations, and other interesting visual materials supplement the text.

How a SATA Entry Is Compiled

A *SATA* entry progresses through a series of steps. If the biographee is living, the *SATA* editors try to secure information directly from him or her through a questionnaire. From the information that the biographee supplies, the editors prepare an entry, filling in any essential missing details with research and/or telephone interviews. When necessary, the author or illustrator is sent a copy of the entry to check for accuracy and completeness.

If the biographee is deceased or cannot be reached by questionnaire, the *SATA* editors examine a wide variety of published sources to gather information for an entry. Biographical and bibliographic sources are consulted, as are book reviews, feature articles, published interviews, and material sometimes obtained from the biographee's family, publishers, agent, or other associates.

Entries that have not been verified by the biographees or their representatives are marked with an asterisk (*).

We Welcome Your Suggestions

We invite you to examine the entire *SATA* series, starting with this volume. Please write and tell us if we can make *SATA* even more helpful to you. Send comments and suggestions to: The Editor, *Something about the Author,* Gale Research Inc., 835 Penobscot Bldg., 645 Griswold St., Detroit, MI 48226-4094.

Acknowledgments

Grateful acknowledgment is made to the following publishers, authors, and artists whose works appear in this volume.

ALMA FLOR ADA. Illustration from *The Gold Coin*, by Alma Flor Ada. Illustrations copyright © 1992 by Neil Waldman . Reprinted by permission of Macmillan Books for Young Readers, an imprint of Simon & Schuster Children's Publishing Division./ Illustration from *My Name Is Maria Isabel*, by Alma Flor Ada. Illustrations copyright © 1993 by K. Dyble Thompson. Reprinted by permission of Atheneum Books for Young Readers, an imprint of Simon & Schuster Children's Publishing Division./ Jacket of *The Rooster Who Went To His Uncle's Wedding*, by Alma Flor Ada. Jacket art copyright © 1993 by Kathleen Kuchera. Reprinted by permission of The Putnam Publishing Group./ Jacket of *Dear Peter Rabbit*, by Alma Flor Ada. Atheneum, 1994. Jacket illustration copyright © 1994 by Leslie Tryon. Jacket design by Kimberly M. Adlerman. Reprinted by permission of Atheneum Books for Young Readers, an imprint of Simon & Schuster Children's Publishing Division./ Jacket of *Where the Flame Trees Bloom*, by Alma Flor Ada. Atheneum, 1994. Jacket illustration copyright © 1994 by Antonio Martorell. Reprinted by permission of Atheneum Books for Young Readers, an imprint of Simon & Schuster Children's Publishing Division./ Photograph courtesy of Alma Flor Ada.

SALLY HOBART ALEXANDER. Photograph from *Mom's Best Friend*, by Sally Hobart Alexander. Photographs copyright © 1992 by George Ancona. Reprinted by permission of Macmillan Books for Young Readers, an imprint of Simon & Schuster Children's Publishing Division.

PEGGY PERRY ANDERSON. Photograph courtesy of Peggy Perry Anderson.

PIERS ANTHONY. Cover of *Chthon*, by Piers Anthony. Copyright © 1967 by Piers A. D. Jacob. Cover illustration by John Jude Palencar. Reprinted by permission of The Berkley Publishing Group./ Cover of *Var the Stick*, by Piers Anthony. Copyright © 1973 by Piers Anthony. Reprinted by permission of Bantam Books, a division of Bantam Doubleday Dell Publishing Group, Inc./ Cover of *A Spell for Chameleon*, by Piers Anthony. Copyright © 1977 by Piers Anthony. Cover art by Michael Whelan. Reprinted by permission of Ballantine Books, a division of Random House, Inc./ Cover of *Out of Phaze*, by Piers Anthony. Copyright © 1987 by Piers Anthony. Illustration by Darrell Sweet. Reprinted by permission of The Berkley Publishing Group./ Illustration from Piers Anthony's *Visual Guide to Xanith*, by Piers Anthony and Jody Lynn Nye. Copyright © 1989 by Bill Fawcett & Associates, Inc. Illustrations by Todd Cameron Hamilton and James Clouse. Reprinted by permission of Bill Fawcett & Associates, Inc./ Cover of *And Eternity*, by Piers Anthony. Copyright © 1990 by Piers Anthony Jacob. Cover art by Rowena Morrill. Reprinted by permission of Avon Books./ Jacket of *Mercycle*, by Piers Anthony. Copyright © 1991 by Piers Anthony. Jacket illustration by Ron & Val Lindahn. Reprinted by permission of Tafford Publishing, Inc./ Photograph courtesy of Piers Anthony.

PEGGY APPIAH. Jacket of *Ananse the Spider*, by Peggy Appiah, illustrated by Peggy Wilson. Copyright © 1966 by Peggy Appiah. Reprinted by permission of Pantheon Books, a division of Random House, Inc./ Cover of *Tales of an Ashanti Father*, by Peggy Appiah. Copyright © 1967 by Peggy Appiah. Illustrations by Mora Dickson. Reprinted by permission of Beacon Press./ Photograph courtesy of Peggy Appiah.

R. L. BACON. Cover of *The House of the People*, by R. L. Bacon. Illustrations © 1985 by Waiatarua Publishing. Illustrations by R. H. G. Jahnke.

SHEPARD BARBASH. Cover of *Oaxacan Woodcarving: The Magic in the Trees*, by Shepard Barbash. Photographs copyright © 1993 by Vicki Ragan. Reprinted by permission of Chronicle Books.

NANCY BARNET. Photograph courtesy of Nancy Barnet.

TRACY BARRETT. Cover of *Nat Turner and the Slave Revolt*, by Tracy Barrett. Copyright © 1993 by The Millbrook Press. Reprinted by permission of The Millbrook Press./ Photograph courtesy of Tracy Barrett.

REX BARRON. Photograph courtesy of Rex Barron.

SUSAN PROVOST BELLER. Cover of *Cadets at War*, by Susan Provost Beller. Copyright © 1991 by Susan Provost Beller. Cover photograph by Michael Latil. Cover painting, Charge of the New Market Cadets, by Benjamin West Clinedinst, VMI Class of 1880./ Photograph courtesy of Susan Provost Beller.

WILLIAM BENTLEY. Photograph courtesy of William Bentley.

MALCOLM J. BOSSE. Jacket of *Deep Dream of the Rainforest*, by Malcolm Bosse. Jacket art © 1993 by Tim Tanner. Reprinted by permission of Farrar, Straus & Giroux, Inc./ Jacket of *The Examination*, by Malcolm Bosse. Jacket art © 1994 by Richard Jordan. Reprinted by permission of Farrar, Straus & Giroux, Inc.

CARYL BROOKS. Photograph courtesy of Caryl Brooks.

JENNIFER BRUTSCHY. Jacket of *Winter Fox*, by Jennifer Brutschy, illustrated by Allen Garns. Jacket illustration copyright © 1993 by Allen Garns. Reprinted by permission of Alfred A. Knopf, Inc./ Photograph courtesy of Jennifer Brutschy.

THERESA BURNS. Photograph by Tony Gregory.

OCTAVIA E. BUTLER. Cover of *Kindred*, by Octavia E. Butler. Copyright © 1979 by Octavia E. Butler. Cover illustration by Laurence Schwinger. Reprinted by permission of Beacon Press./ Cover of *Wild Seed*, by Octavia E. Butler. Copyright © 1980 by Octavia E. Butler. Cover illustration by Wayne Barlowe. Reprinted by permission of Warner Books, Inc./ Cover of *Adulthood Rites*, by Octavia Butler. Copyright © 1988 by Octavia E. Butler. Reprinted by permission of Warner Books, Inc./ Cover of *Parable of the Sower*, by Octavia E. Butler. Copyright © 1993 by Octavia E. Butler. Cover illustration by John Jude Palencar. Reprinted by permission of Warner Books, Inc.

STEPHANIE CALMENSON. Cover of *The Principal's New Clothes*, by Stephanie Calmenson. Illustrations copyright © 1989 by Silverpin Studio. Reprinted by permission of Scholastic Inc./ Jacket of *Dinner at the Panda Palace*, by Stephanie Calmenson. Jacket art © 1991 by Nadine Bernard Westcott. Reprinted by permission of HarperCollins Publishers, Inc./ Cover of *It Begins with an A*, by Stephanie Calmenson. Illustrations © 1993 by Marisbina Russo. Reprinted by permission of Hyperion Books for Children./ Cover of *Hotter Than A Hot Dog*, by Stephanie Calmenson. Illustrations copyright © 1994 by Elivia Savadier. Reprinted by permission of Little, Brown and Company./ Photograph by Justin Sutcliffe, courtesy of Stephanie Calmenson.

SCOTT CAMERON. Photograph courtesy of Scott Cameron.

JOHN PAUL CAPONIGRO. Photograph courtesy of John Paul Caponigro.

MICHAEL CHANIN. Cover of *Grandfather Four Winds and Rising Moon*, by Michael Chanin. Copyright © 1994 by Michael Chanin. Illustrations copyright © 1994 by Sally J. Smith. All rights reserved. Reprinted by permission of H. J. Kramer Inc, P.O. Box 1082, Tiburon, CA.

EILEEN CHARBONNEAU. Cover of *In The Time of the Wolves*, by Eileen Charbonneau. Copyright © 1994 by Eileen Charbonneau. Cover art by Neil Waldman. Reprinted by permission of Tom Doherty Associates, Inc./ Photograph courtesy of Eileen Charbonneau.

CLARA GILLOW CLARK. Photograph of Clara Gillow Clark. Copyright © 1994 by Gene Tagle. Reprinted by permission of Boyds Mills Press.

WILLIAM R. CLEVENGER. Photograph courtesy of William R. Clevenger.

SNEED B. COLLARD III. Cover of *Sea Snakes*, by Sneed B. Collard III. Copyright © 1993 by Carl C. Hansen/Smithsonian Tropical Research Institute. Reprinted by permission of Boyds Mills Press, Inc./ Photograph courtesy of Sneed B. Collard III.

PETA COPLANS. Photograph courtesy of Peta Coplans.

PATRICIA BRENNAN DEMUTH. Cover of *The Onery Morning*, by Patricia Brennan Demuth. Illustrations copyright © 1991 by Craig McFarland Brown. Reprinted by permission of Dutton Children's Books, a division of Penguin Books USA Inc./ Photograph courtesy of Patricia Brennan Demuth.

ANNE LOUISE de ROO. Jacket of *Cinnamon and Nutmeg*, by Anne de Roo. Copyright © 1972, 1974 by Anne de Roo. Reprinted by permission of Anne de Roo./ Jacket of *Scrub Fire*, by Anne de Roo. Atheneum, 1980. Jacket painting copyright © 1980 by Pamela Carroll.

JEFFREY C. DOMM. Illustration by Jeff Domm from *Gray Wolf Pup*, by Doe Boyle. Copyright © 1993 by Trudy Management Corporation. Reprinted by permission of Soundprints.

JULIE DUNLAP. Cover of *Aldo Leopold: Living with the Land*, by Julie Dunlap. Illustrated by Antonio Castro. Illustrations copyright © 1993 by Twenty-First Century Books. Reprinted by permission of Henry Holt and Company, Inc./ Photograph courtesy of Julie Dunlap.

ANN E. ESKRIDGE. Jacket of *The Sanctuary*, by Ann E. Eskridge. Jacket painting copyright © 1994 by Nubia Owens. Used by permission of Cobblehill Books, an affiliate of Dutton Children's Books, a division of Penguin Books USA Inc./ Photograph courtesy of Ann E. Eskridge.

BILL FARNSWORTH. Photograph courtesy of Bill Farnsworth.

MAX FATCHEN. Jacket of *The Country Mail Is Coming: Poems from Down Under* by Max Fatchen. Illustrations copyright © 1990 by Catharine O'Neill. Reprinted by permission of Little, Brown and Company./ Movie still from *Chase through the Night*, story by Max Fatchen, filmed by Independant Productions./ Photograph courtesy of Max Fatchen.

JERI CHASE FERRIS. Cover of *Walking the Road to Freedom: A Story about Sojourner Truth*, by Jeri Ferris. Illustrations copyright © 1988 by Carolrhoda Books, Inc. Reprinted by permission of Carolrhoda Books, Inc./ Cover of *Arctic Explorer: The Story of Matthew Henson*, by Jeri Ferris. Text copyright © 1989 by Jeri Ferris. Cover photographs from the National Archives (black-and-white) and Steve McCutcheon (color). Reprinted by permission of Carolrhoda Books, Inc.

VIRGINIA FLEMING. Jacket from *Be Good to Eddie Lee*, by Virginia Fleming. Jacket illustration © 1993 by Floyd Cooper. Reprinted by permission of the Putnam Publishing Group./ Photograph courtesy of Virginia Fleming.

LISA ROWE FRAUSTINO. Jacket of *Ash: A Novel*, by Lisa Rowe Fraustino. Jacket art copyright © 1995 by Julie Granahan. Reprinted by permission of Orchard Books./ Photograph courtesy of Lisa Rowe Fraustino.

MARIE GARAFANO. Photograph courtesy of Marie Garafano.

THEODORE ROOSEVELT GARDNER III. Photograph courtesy of Audry Twining.

RITA GOLDEN GELMAN. Cover of *Why Can't I Fly?*, by Rita Golden Gelman. Illustrations copyright © 1976 by Jack Kent. Reprinted by permission of Scholastic Inc./ Jacket of *Dawn to Dusk in the Galapagos*, by Rita Golden Gelman. Photographs copyright © 1991 by Tui De Roy. Cover design reprinted by permission of Little, Brown and Company. Cover photograph reprinted by permission of Tui De Roy./ Jacket of *I Went to the Zoo*, by Rita Golden Gelman. Illustrations copyright © 1993 by Maryann Kovalski. Reprinted by permission of Scholastic Inc./ Photograph courtesy of Rita Golden Gelman.

DEBRA GOLDENTYER. Photograph by Mark Schaeffer, courtesy of Debra Goldentyer.

DIANE GOODE. Illustration by Diane Goode from *When I Was Young in the Mountains*, by Cynthia Rylant. Illustrations copyright © 1982 by Diane Goode. Reprinted by permission of Dutton Children's Books, a division of Penguin Books USA Inc.

JOHN GORDON. Jacket of *The Burning Baby and Other Ghosts*, by John Gordon. Jacket illustration copyright © 1992 by Robert Mason. Reprinted by permission of Walker Books Limited. Published in the United States by Candlewick Press, Cambridge, MA./ Photograph courtesy of John Gordon.

SUSAN GROHMANN. Cover by Susan Grohmann from her *The Dust under Mrs. Merriweather's Bed*. Copyright © 1994 by Susan Grohmann. Reprinted by permission of Whispering Coyote Press.

PHILIP GROSS. Photograph courtesy of Philip Gross.

ROBIN JONES GUNN. Cover of *A Promise Is Forever*, by Robin Jones Gunn. Copyright © 1994 by Robin Jones Gunn. Cover illustration by David R. Darrow. Reprinted by permission of Focus On The Family./ Photograph courtesy of Robin Jones Gunn.

PETER J. HAMLIN. Photograph by Tim Wilder, courtesy of Peter J. Hamlin.

CHERYL HANNA. Photograph courtesy of Cheryl Hanna.

MARK JONATHAN HARRIS. Jacket of *With a Wave of the Wand*, by Mark Jonathan Harris. Copyright © 1980 by Mark Jonathan Harris. Reprinted in the United States and Canada by permission of Lothrop, Lee & Shepard Books, a division of William Morrow & Company, Inc./ Jacket of *Come the Morning*, by Mark Jonathan Harris. Jacket illustration copyright © 1989 by Neil Waldman. Reprinted by permission of Neil Waldman./ Jacket of *Solay*, by Mark Jonathan Harris. Jacket illustration copyright © 1993 by Doron Ben-Ami./ Photograph by Alan Levenson, courtesy of Mark Jonathan Harris.

JAY HEALE. Photograph courtesy of Jay Heale.

SHARON E. HEISEL. Jacket of *A Little Magic*, by Sharon E. Heisel. Jacket art copyright © 1991 by Pat Grant Porter. Reprinted by permission of Houghton Mifflin Company./ Photograph courtesy of Sharon Heisel.

MARGARET HEWITT. Illustration by Margaret Hewitt from *Green Earings and a Felt Hat*, by Jerry Newman, copyright © 1993. Reprinted by permission of Henry Holt & Company, Inc./ Photograph courtesy of Margaret Hewitt.

WILL HILLENBRAND. Illustration by Will Hillenbrand from *Cat, Mouse and Moon*, by Roxanne Dyer Powell. Houghton Mifflin Company, 1994. Jacket art copyright © 1994 by Will Hillenbrand. Reprinted by permission of Houghton Mifflin Company./ Photograph courtesy of Will Hillenbrand.

SALLY HOBSON. Photograph courtesy of Sally Hobson.

HARRIET HODGSON. Photograph courtesy of Harriet Hodgson.

AMANDA HOPKINSON. Portrait of Amanda Hopkinson. Copyright © by Julio Etchart. Reprinted by permission of Julio Etchart.

JONATHAN HUNT. Cover of *Illuminations*, by Jonathan Hunt. Copyright © 1989 by Jonathan Hunt. Reprinted with the permission of Simon & Schuster Books for Young Readers, an imprint of Simon & Schuster Children's Publishing Division./ Photograph by David W. Behnke, courtesy of Jonathan Hunt.

GAIL JARROW. Photograph courtesy of Gail Jarrow.

STEPHEN T. JOHNSON. Photograph by Jeff Harris, courtesy of Stephen T. Johnson.

MARTIN GEORGE JORDAN. Illustration by Martin Jordan from *Jungle Days, Jungle Nights*, by Martin and Tanis Jordan.

Company./ Illustration by Susan Meddaugh from her *Tree of Birds*. Copyright © 1990 by Susan Meddaugh. Reprinted by permission of Houghton Mifflin Company./ Illustration by Susan Meddaugh from her *The Witches' Supermarket*. Houghton Mifflin Company, 1991. Copyright © 1991 by Susan Meddaugh. Reprinted by permission of Houghton Mifflin Company./ Illustration by Susan Meddaugh from her *Martha Speaks*. Houghton Mifflin Company, 1992. Copyright © 1992 by Susan Meddaugh. Reprinted by permission of Houghton Mifflin Company./ Photograph by Harry L. Foster, courtesy of Susan Meddaugh Foster.

THERESA ANN MILNE. Photograph courtesy of Theresa Ann Milne.

MARGAREE KING MITCHELL. Illustration from *Uncle Jed's Barbershop*, by Margaree King Mitchell. Illustrations copyright © 1993 by James Ransome. Reprinted by permission of Simon & Schuster Books for Young Readers, New York./ Photograph courtesy of Margaree King Mitchell.

JAMI MOFFETT. Photograph courtesy of Jami Moffett.

CHRISTINE MOLAN. Illustration by Chris Molan from *Growing Up In Ancient Greece*, by Chris Chelepi. Copyright © 1994 by Eagle Books. Reprinted by permission of Troll Associates.

HILARY MULLINS. Cover of *The Cat Came Back*, by Hilary Mullins. The Naiad Press, Inc., 1993. Copyright © 1993 by Hilary Mullins. Reprinted by permission of Naiad Press, Inc./ Photograph by April Evans, courtesy of Hilary Mullins.

CLAIRE A. NIVOLA. Photograph courtesy of Claire A. Nivola.

GRAHAM OAKLEY. Illustration by Graham Oakley from his *The Church Mice Adrift*. Copyright © 1976 by Graham Oakley. Reprinted by permission of Macmillan Children's Books. In the U. S. by Atheneum Books for Young Readers, an imprint of Simon & Schuster Children's Publishing Division./ Illustration by Graham Oakley from his *The Church Mice at Christmas*. Copyright © 1980 by Graham Oakley. Reprinted by permission of Macmillan Children's Books. In the U. S. by Atheneum Books for Young Readers, an imprint of Simon & Schuster Children's Publishing Division./ Jacket by Graham Oakley from his *Hetty and Harriet*. Copyright © 1981 by Graham Oakley. Reprinted by permission of Macmillan Children's Books. In the U. S. by Atheneum Books for Young Readers, an imprint of Simon & Schuster Children's Publishing Division./ Illustration by Graham Oakley from his *The Church Mice in Action*. Copyright © 1982 by Graham Oakley. Reprinted by permission of Macmillan Children's Books. In the U. S. by Atheneum Books for Young Readers, an imprint of Simon & Schuster Children's Publishing Division./ Jacket by Graham Oakley from his *The Foxbury Force*. Atheneum, 1994. Jacket illustration copyright © 1994 by Graham Oakley. Reprinted by permission of Macmillan Children's Books. In the U. S. by Atheneum Books for Young Readers, an imprint of Simon & Schuster Children's Publishing Division./ Photograph courtesy of Macmillan Children's Books.

ROBERT PATEMAN. Photograph courtesy of Robert Pateman.

PATRICIA PETERS. Photograph courtesy of Patricia Peters.

CRIS PETERSON. Jacket of *Extra Cheese, Please!: Mozzarella's Journey from Cow to Pizza*, by Cris Peterson. Jacket photographs copyright © 1994 by Alvis Upitis. Reprinted by permission of Boyds Mills Press, Inc./ Photograph courtesy of Cris Peterson.

PAT PFLIEGER. Jacket of *The Fog's Net*, by Pat Pflieger. Jacket art copyright © 1994 by Ruth Gamper. Reprinted by permission of Houghton Mifflin Company.

FELIX PITRE. Jacket of *Juan Bobo and the Pig*, retold by Felix Pitre. Illustrations copyright © 1993 by Christy Hale. Reprinted by permission of Lodestar Books, an affiliate of Dutton Children's Books, a division of Penguin Books USA Inc./ Photograph courtesy of Felix Pitre.

JENNIFER PLECAS. Jacket by Jennifer Plecas from *Peeping and Sleeping*, by Fran Manushkin. Jacket illustration copyright © 1994 by Jennifer Plecas. Reprinted by permission of Houghton Mifflin Company.

STATON RABIN. Jacket from *Casey Over There*, by Staton Rabin. Illustrations copyright © 1994 by Greg Shed. Reproduced by permission of Harcourt Brace and Company./ Photograph by Mike Griffin, courtesy of Staton Rabin.

BARBARA ROBINSON. Jacket of *The Best School Year Ever*, by Barbara Robinson. Jacket art copyright © 1994 by Michael Deas. Reprinted by permission of HarperCollins Publishers, Inc./ Photograph courtesy of Barbara Webb Robinson.

MICHAEL ROSEN. Illustration from *You Can't Catch Me!*, by Michael Rosen. Illustrations copyright © 1981 by Quentin Blake. Reprinted by permission of Andre Deutsch Children's Books, an imprint of Scholastic Publications Ltd./ Illustration from *Quick, Let's Get Out of Here*, by Michael Rosen. Copyright © 1983 by Quentin Blake. Reprinted by permission of Andre Deutsch Children's Books, an imprint of Scholastic Publications Ltd./ Jacket of *Smelly Jelly Smelly Fish*, by Michael Rosen. Illustrations copyright © 1986 by Quentin Blake. Reprinted by permission of Prentice-Hall Books for Young Readers, a division of Simon & Schuster, Inc./ Illustration from *We're Going on a Bear Hunt*, by Michael Rosen. Illustrations copyright © 1989 by Helen Oxenbury. Reprinted by permission of Macmillan Books for Young Readers, an imprint of Simon & Schuster Children's Publishing Division./ Jacket of *How Giraffe Got Such a Long Neck ... and Why Rhino Is So Grumpy*, by Michael Rosen. Pictures copyright © 1993 by John Clementson. Reprinted by permission of Dial Books for Young Readers, a division of Penguin Books USA Inc.

TOM ROSS. Photograph courtesy of Tom Ross.

LAURIE E. ROZAKIS. Cover of *Bill Hanna & Joe Barbera: Yabba-Dabba-Doo*, by Laurie E. Rozakis. Copyright © 1994 by Blackbirch Press, Inc. Illustrations by Dick Smolinski. Reprinted by permission of Blackbirch Press, Inc./ Photograph courtesy of Laurie E. Rozakis.

SUSAN GOLDMAN RUBIN. Cover of *Emily Good as Gold*, by Susan Goldman Rubin. Cover illustration copyright © 1993 by Ellen Thompson. Reprinted by permission of Ellen Thompson./ Photograph courtesy of Susan Goldman Rubin.

KAREN GRAY RUELLE. Photograph courtesy of Karen Gray Ruelle.

HENDLE RUMBAUT. Jacket of *Dove Dream*, by Hendle Rumbaut. Houghton Mifflin Company, 1994. Jacket art copyright © 1994 by Gwen Frankfeldt. Reprinted by permission of Houghton Mifflin Company./ Photograph courtesy of Hendle Rumbaut.

SARA ST. ANTOINE. Cover of *The Green Musketeers and the Incredible Energy Escapade*, by Sara St. Antoine. Cover art copyright © 1994 by Sara St. Antoine. Reprinted by permission of Bantam Books, a division of Bantam Doubleday Dell Publishing Group, Inc.

SYNTHIA SAINT JAMES. Photograph courtesy of Synthia Saint James.

KEM KNAPP SAWYER. Photograph courtesy of Kem Knapp Sawyer.

ELEANOR SCHMID. Cover by Eleonore Schmid from her *Wake Up, Dormouse*. Copyright © 1988 by Nord-Sud Verlag AG, Gossau Zurich, Switzerland. English translation copyright © 1989 by Elizabeth D. Crawford. Reprinted by permission of North-South Books./ Cover by Eleonore Schmid from her *The Water's Journey*. Copyright © 1989 by Nord-Sud Verlag AG, Gossau Zurich, Switzerland. Reprinted by permission of North-South Books, an imprint of Nord-Sud Verlag AG, Gossau Zurich, Switzerland.

JOE SHLICHTA. Photograph courtesy of Joe Shlichta.

HOPE SLAUGHTER. Photograph courtesy of Hope Slaughter.

DEVRA NEWBERGER SPEREGEN. Cover of *P.S. Friends Forever*, by Devra Newberger Speregen. Copyright © 1995 by Warner Bros., Inc. Reprinted by permission of Pocket Books, a division of Simon & Schuster Inc.

JANET TRAVELL STREET. Illustration by Janet Street from *Dinosaur Dress Up*. Illustrations copyright © 1992 by Janet Street. Reprinted in the United States and Canada by permission of Tambourine Books, a division of William Morrow & Company, Inc. Reprinted in the British Commonwealth by permission of Janet Street.

RUTH RICE SWANN. Photograph courtesy of Ruth Rice Swann.

HUDSON TALBOTT. Jacket by Hudson Talbott from his *Your Pet Dinosaur*. Jacket illustration © 1992 by Hudson Talbott. Reprinted in the United States and Canada by permission of Morrow Junior Books, a division of William Morrow & Company, Inc. Reprinted in the British Commonwealth by permission of Hudson Talbott./ Movie still from *We're Back!*, based on book of the same name illustrated by Hudson Talbott. Movie still courtesy of Universal Studios./ Photograph courtesy of Hudson Talbott.

HERBERT EATTON TODD. Illustration from *The Sick Cow*, by H. E. Todd. Illustrations copyright © 1974 by Val Biro. Reprinted by permission of Hodder & Stoughton Ltd./ Illustration from *Santa's Big Sneeze*, by H. E. Todd. Illustrations copyright © 1980 by Val Brio. Reprinted by permission of Hodder & Stoughton Ltd.

EUGENE TRIVIZAS. Illustration from *The Three Little Wolves and the Big Bad Pig*, by Eugene Trivizas. Illustrations copyright © 1993 by Helen Oxenbury. Reprinted by permission of Simon & Schuster Children's Publishing Division.

JODY WHEELER. Photograph courtesy of Jody Wheeler.

STANLEY WIATER. Photograph courtesy of Stanley Wiater.

LORI WIENER. Illustration from *Be a Friend: Children Who Live with HIV Speak*, art and writing compiled by Lori S. Wiener, Ph. D., Aprille Best, and Philip A. Pizzo, M. D. Developed during therapeutic sessions with Dr. Wiener. Copyright © 1994 by Albert Whitman & Company. All rights reserved. Reprinted by permission.

MARY HUISKAMP WILKINS. Jacket of *Wobble the Witch Cat*, by Mary Calhoun. Copyright © 1958 by Mary Calhoun. Reprinted by permission of Morrow Junior Books, a division of William Morrow & Company, Inc./ Jacket of *High-Wire Henry*, by Mary Calhoun. Jacket illustration © 1991 by Erick Ingraham. Reprinted by pemission of Morrow Junior Books, a division of William Morrow & Company, Inc./ Jacket of *Henry the Sailor Cat*, by Mary Calhoun. Jacket illustration © 1994 by Erick Ingraham. Reprinted by permission of Morrow Junior Books, a division of William Morrow & Company, Inc./ Photograph by James D. Steinberg, courtesy of Mary Calhoun.

JOYCE M. WILSON. Photograph by Joan Hague, courtesy of Derbyshire Canine Centre.

ADAM WOOG. Cover of *Poltergeists*, by Adam Woog. Copyright © 1995 by Greenhaven Press, Inc. Reprinted by permission of Greenhaven Press, Inc.

COURTNI C. WRIGHT. Photograph courtesy of Courtni C. Wright.

something about the author®

ADA, Alma Flor 1938-

■ Personal

Born January 3, 1938, in Camaguey, Cuba; daughter of Modesto A. (a professor) and Alma (a teacher; maiden name, Lafuente) Ada; married Armando Zubizarreta, 1961 (divorced, 1971); married Jorgen Voss, 1984 (divorced, 1995); children: Rosalma, Alfonso, Miguel, Gabriel Zubizarreta. *Education:* Universidad Complutense de Madrid, received diploma, 1959; Pontificia Universidad Catolica del Peru, M.A., 1963, Ph.D., 1965; Harvard University, post-doctoral study, 1965-67.

■ Addresses

Home—475 Connecticut, San Francisco, CA 94107.
Office—University of San Francisco, San Francisco, CA 94117.

■ Career

Colegio Alexander von Humboldt, Lima, Peru, instructor and head of Spanish department, 1963-65, 1967-69; Emory University, Atlanta, GA, associate professor of Romance languages, 1970-72; Mercy College of Detroit, Detroit, MI, professor of language and co-director of Institute for Bilingual Bicultural Services, 1973-75; University of San Francisco, San Francisco, CA, professor of education and director of doctoral studies, 1976—. University of Guam, Agana, visiting professor, summer, 1978; University of Texas, El Paso, TX, visiting professor, summer 1979, winter 1991; Universi-

ALMA FLOR ADA

dad Complutense, Madrid, Spain, visiting professor, summers 1989, 1990, 1991; St. Thomas University, Houston, TX, visiting professor, summers 1992, 1993. Member of selection committee, Fulbright Overseas

1

Fellowship Program, 1968-69, 1977-78; chairperson, National Seminar on Bilingual education, 1974, National Policy Conference on Bilingualism in Higher Education, 1978, International Congress of Children's Literature in Spanish, 1978, 1979, 1981; publishing house consultant, 1975-95; member of the board, Books for Youth and Children's Television Workshop's *Sesame Street* in Spanish. *Member:* International Association for Children's Literature in Spanish and Portuguese (founding member and president), International Reading Association, Friends of International Books for Young People, National Association for Bilingual Education (founding member of Michigan and Illinois branches), Teachers of English to Speakers of Other Languages, American Association of Teachers of Spanish and Portuguese, Modern Language Association of America, Mexican American Teachers Association.

■ Awards, Honors

Fulbright scholar, 1965-67; grants from Institute for International Education, 1965-67, Emory University, 1971, and Michigan Endowment for the Arts, 1974; Mary Bunting Institute scholar at Radcliffe College and Harvard University, 1966-68; University of San Francisco Distinguished Research Award from the School of Education, 1984; University of San Francisco Outstanding Teacher Award, 1985; Christopher Award (ages 8-10), 1992, and NCSS/CBC Notable Children's Trade Book in the Field of Social Studies, both for *The Gold Coin;* Parents' Choice Honor, 1995, for *Dear Peter Rabbit;* Marta Salotti Award (Argentina), for *Encaje de piedra;* California PTA Association Yearly Award.

■ Writings

FOR CHILDREN

(With Maria del Pilar de Olave) *El enanito de la pared y otras historias* (title means "The Wall's Dwarf and Other Tales"), Arica, 1974.

(With de Olave) *Las Pintas de la mariquitas* (title means "The Ladybug's Dots"), Arica, 1974.

(With de Olave) *Saltarin y sus dos amigas y otras historias* (title means "Springy and His Two Friends and Other Stories"), Arica, 1974.

(With de Olave) *La Gallinita Costurera y otras historias* (title means "The Little Hen Who Enjoyed Sewing and Other Stories"), Arica, 1974.

Amigos, illustrated by Barry Koch, Santillana Publishing Company, 1989.

Quien nacera aqui? ("Libros para Contar" series), illustrated by Vivi Escriva, Santillana Publishing Company, 1989 (also published as *Who's Hatching Here?*).

La moneda de oro, illustrated by Neil Waldman, translation by Bernice Randall published as *The Gold Coin,* Atheneum, 1991.

El papalote, illustrated by Escriva, Santillana Publishing Company, 1992 (also published as *The Kite*).

(Reteller) *The Rooster Who Went to His Uncle's Wedding: A Latin American Folktale,* illustrated by Kathleen Kuchera, Putnam, 1992.

Serafina's Birthday, illustrated by Louise Bates Satterfield, Atheneum, 1992.

Olmo y la mariposa azul, illustrated by Escriva, Laredo, 1992, translation by Rosalma Zubizarreta published as *Olmo and the Blue Butterfly,* Laredo, 1995.

(With Janet Thorne and Philip Wingeier-Rayo) *Choices and Other Stories from the Caribbean,* illustrated by Maria Antonia Ordonez, Friendship Press, 1993.

My Name Is Maria Isabel, illustrated by K. Dyble Thompson, translation by Ana M. Cerro published as *Me llamo Maria Isabel,* Macmillan, 1993.

El unicornio del oeste, illustrated by Abigail Pizer, translation by R. Zubizarreta published as *The Unicorn of the West,* Atheneum, 1993.

Barquitos de papel, illustrated by Pablo Torrecilla, Laredo, 1993, translation by R. Zubizarreta published as *Paper Boats,* Laredo, 1995.

Barriletes, illustrated by Torrecilla, Laredo, 1993, translation by R. Zubizarreta published as *Kites,* Laredo, 1995.

Dias de circo, Laredo, 1993, translation by R. Zubizarreta published as *Circus Time,* Laredo, 1995.

El panuelo de seda, illustrated by Escriva, Laredo, 1993, translation by R. Zubizarreta published as *The Silk Scarf,* Laredo, 1995.

Pin, pin, sarabin, illustrated by Torrecilla, Laredo, 1993, translated by R. Zubizarreta, Laredo, 1995.

Pregones, illustrated by Torrecilla, Laredo, 1993, translation by R. Zubizarreta published as *Vendor's Calls,* Laredo, 1995.

El reino de la geometria, illustrated by Jose Ramon Sanchez, Laredo, 1993, translation by R. Zubizarreta published as *The Kingdom of Geometry,* Laredo, 1995.

Dear Peter Rabbit: Querido Pedrin, illustrated by Leslie Tryon, translated into Spanish by R. Zubizarreta, Atheneum, 1994.

Where the Flame Trees Bloom, illustrated by Antonio Martorell, Atheneum, 1994 (also published as *Donde florecen los flamboyanes*).

I Love Saturdays y Domingos, illustrated by Michael Bryant, Atheneum, 1995.

Mediopollito: Half-Chicken: A New Version of a Traditional Story, illustrated by Kim Howard, translated by R. Zubizarreta, Doubleday, 1995.

Also author of *Abecedario de los animales* (also published as *Animal ABC*), also available on cassette; *La cancion del mosquito* (also published as *The Song of the Teeny Tiny Mosquito*), *Una extrana visita* (*Strange Visitors*), *Me gustaria tener* (*How Happy I Would Be*), *Pavo para la Cena de Gracias? No Gracias!* (*Turkey for Thanksgiving? No Thanks!*), *Rosa alada* (*A Rose with Wings*), *La hamaca de la vaca* (*In the Cow's Backyard*); *La pinata vacia* (*The Empty Pinata*); *No quiero derretirme* (*I Don't Want to Melt*); *Como nacio el arco iris* (*How the Rainbow Came to Be*); and *Despues de la tormenta* (*After the Storm*), all illustrated by Escriva. Author of *En el barrio,* illustrated by Liliana Wilson Grez; *No fui yo . . .* ("It Wasn't Me"); *Encaje de piedra* ("Stone Lace"), illustrated by Kitty Lorefice de Passalia; and *El vuelo de los colibries* (*The Flight of the Hummingbirds*), illustrated by Judith Jacobson, Laredo. Reteller of *La tataranieta de Cucarachita Martina* ("Martina's Great-grandaughter").

TEXTBOOKS AND EDUCATIONAL PUBLICATIONS

Sale el oso ("Big Book, Rimas y Risas Green" series), illustrated by Amy Myers, Hampton-Brown, 1988.

Los seis deseos de la jirafa ("Big Book, Rimas y Risas Green" series), illustrated by Doug Roy, Hampton-Brown, 1988.

Cassette Guide: Culture through Literature and Music (Spanish Elementary series), illustrated by Jan Mayer, Addison-Wesley, 1989.

Sol Kit, Addison-Wesley, 1989.

Una semilla nada mas ("Big Book" series), illustrated by Frank Remkiewicz, Hampton-Brown, 1990.

Cinco pollitos y otras poesias favoritas: Tan Small Book Set ("Dias y Dias de Poesia" series), Hampton-Brown, 1991.

Classroom Set: Tan Set ("Dias y Dias de Poesia" series), Hampton-Brown, 1991.

El patio de mi casa ("Early Learning Packs" series), illustrated by Liz Callen, Hampton-Brown, 1991.

Caballito blanco y otras poesias favoritas: Green Small Book Set ("Dias y Dias de Poesia" series), Hampton-Brown, 1992.

Chart Set: Green Set ("Dias y Dias de Poesia" series), Hampton-Brown, 1992.

Classroom Set: Green Set ("Dias y Dias de Poesia" series), Hampton-Brown, 1992.

Dias y dias de poesia: Complete Program (available with small books or tapes), Hampton-Brown, 1992.

Bear's Walk ("ESL Theme Links" series), illustrated by Myers, Hampton-Brown, 1993.

(With Violet J. Harris and Lee B. Hopkins) *A Chorus of Cultures: Developing Literacy Through Multicultural Poetry* (anthology), Hampton-Brown, 1993.

Giraffe's Sad Tale ("ESL Theme Links" series; teacher's guide), illustrated by Roy Doug, Hampton-Brown, 1993.

Hampton-Brown Pre-K Program, Hampton-Brown, 1993.

(Editor with Josefina Villamil Tinajero) *The Power of Two Languages: Literacy and Biliteracy for Spanish-Speaking Students*, Macmillan/McGraw-Hill, 1993.

(With Pam Schiller) *DLM Pre-Kindergarten and Kindergarten Early Childhood Programs*, McGraw-Hill, 1995.

Also author of *Whole Language and Literature: A Practical Guide*, 1989, and *A Magical Encounter*. Author of *Escribiendo desde el corazon/Writing from the Heart*, a video published in Spanish and English language versions, and the video, *Meeting an Author*. Author of cassettes, *Aprender cantando I y II* and *Como una flor*.

"HAGAMOS CAMINOS" SERIES; PUBLISHED BY ADDISON-WESLEY

(With de Olave) *Partimos* (title means "We Start"), illustrated by Ulises Wensell, 1986.

(With de Olave) *Andamos* (title means "We Walk"), illustrated by Wensell, 1986.

(With de Olave) *Corremos* (title means "We Run"), illustrated by Wensell, 1986.

(With de Olave) *Volamos* (title means "We Fly"), illustrated by Wensell, 1986.

(With de Olave) *Navegamos* (title means "We Sail"), illustrated by Wensell, 1986.

(With de Olave) *Exploramos* (title means "We Explore"), illustrated by Wensell, 1986.

COMPILER; PUBLISHED BY ARICA IN PERU

Poesia menuda (anthology; title means "Tiny Poetry"), 1970.

Poesia pequena (anthology; title means "Little Poetry"), 1973.

Poesia nina (anthology; title means "Child Poetry"), 1973.

Poesia infantil (anthology; title means "Poetry for Children"), 1974.

Fabulas de siempre (title means "Everlasting Fables"), 1974.

Cuentos en verso (title means "Stories in Verse"), 1974.

Vamos a leer (title means "Let's Read"), 1974.

Adivina adivinador (title means "A Collection of Traditional Riddles"), 1974.

El nacimiento del Imperio Incaico (history; title means "The Origins of the Inca Empire"), 1974.

El descubrimiento de America (history; title means "The Discovery of the New World"), 1974.

El sueno de San Martin (history; title means "San Martin's Dream"), 1974.

Las Aceitunas y La Cuchara (plays; title means "The Olives" and "The Wooden Spoon"), 1974.

La Condesita peregrina y La Desposada del rey (plays; title means "The Wandering Countess and The King's Bride"), 1974.

TRANSLATOR

Lucille Clifton, *El nino que no creia en la primavera*, illustrated by Birnton Turkle, Dutton, 1975 (originally published in English as *The Boy Who Didn't Believe in Spring*).

Evelyn Ness, *Tienes tiempo, Lidia?*, illustrated by E. Ness, Dutton, 1975 (originally published in English as *Do You Have Time, Lydia?*).

Norma Simon, *Cuando me enojo*, illustrated by Dora Leder, A. Whitman, 1976 (originally published in English as *When I Get Mad*).

Judith Vigna, *Gregorio y sus puntos*, illustrated by J. Vigna, A. Whitman, 1977 (originally published in English as *Gregory's Stitches*).

Barbara Williams, *El dolor de muelas de Alberto*, illustrated by Kay Chorao, Dutton, 1977 (originally published as *Albert's Toothache*).

Barbara Brenner, *Caras*, photographs by George Ancona, Dutton, 1977 (originally published as *Faces*).

Mary Garcia, *The Adventures of Connie and Diego/Las aventuras de Connie y Diego*, illustrated by Malaquis Montoya, Children's Book Press, 1978.

Lila Perl, *Pinatas and Paper Flowers/Pinatas y flores de papel: Holidays of the Americas in English and Spanish*, illustrated by Victori de Larrea, Clarion, 1982.

Harriet Rohmer, *The Legend of Food Mountain/La leyenda de la montana del alimento*, illustrated by Graciella Carrillo, Children's Book Press, 1982.

Judy Blume, *La ballena,* Bradbury, 1983 (originally published as *Blubber*).

Donald Charles, *El ano de gato Galano,* illustrated by D. Charles, Children's Book Press, 1985 (originally published as *Calico Cat's Year*).

Judith Viorst, *Alexander y el dia terrible, horrible, espantoso, horroso,* illustrated by Ray Cruz, Macmillan, 1989 (originally published as *Alexander and the Terrible, Horrible, No Good, Very Bad Day*).

Viorst, *Alexander, que era rico el domingo pasado,* illustrated by Cruz, Macmillan, 1989 (originally published as *Alexander, Who Was Rich Last Sunday*).

Manzano, Manzano! ("Big Book, Un Cuento Mas" series), illustrated by Sandra C. Kalthoff, Hampton-Brown, 1989.

El oso mas elegante ("Big Book, Un Cuento Mas" series), illustrated by Kalthoff, Hampton-Brown, 1989.

Robert Baden, *Y domingo, siete,* edited by Judith Mathews, illustrated by Michelle Edwards, A. Whitman, 1990.

La pequena locomotora que si pudo, illustrated by Doris Hauman, Putnam, 1992 (originally published as *The Little Engine That Could*).

(With R. Zubizarreta) *Uncle Nacho's Hat: El sombrero del tio Nacho,* edited by Harriet Rohmer, illustrated by Veg Reisberg, Children's Book Press, 1993.

Karen Ackerman, *Al amanecer,* illustrated by Katherine Stock, Macmillan, 1994 (originally published as *By the Dawn's Early Light*).

Keith Baker, *Quien es la bestia?,* Harcourt, 1994 (originally published as *Who Is the Beast?*).

Kristine L. Franklin, *El nino pastor,* illustrated by Jill Kastner, Macmillan, 1994 (originally published as *The Shepherd Boy*).

James Howe, *Hay un dragon en mi bolsa de dormir,* illustrated by David S. Rose, Atheneum, 1994 (originally published as *There's a Dragon in My Sleeping Bag*).

Nancy Luenn, *El cuento de Nessa,* illustrated by Neil Waldman, Atheneum, 1994 (originally published as *Nessa's Story*).

Lynne Cherry, *El gran capoquero,* Harcourt, 1994 (originally published as *The Great Kapok Tree*).

Luenn, *La pesca de Nessa,* illustrated by Waldman, Atheneum, 1995 (originally published as *Nessa's Fish*).

Carolyn S. Bailey, *El conejito que queria tener alas rojas,* illustrated by Jacqueline Rogers, Putnam, 1995 (originally published as *The Little Rabbit That Wanted to Have Red Wings*).

Margery Williams, *El conejito de pana,* illustrated by Florence Graham, Putnam, 1995 (originally published as *The Velveteen Rabbit*).

Ann Hayes, *Te presento a la orquesta,* illustrated by Karmen Thompson, Harcourt, 1995 (originally published as *Meet the Orchestra*).

Barbara Shook Hazen, *Adios! Hola!,* illustrated by Michael Bryant, Atheneum, 1995 (originally published as *Goodbye! Hello!*).

Carol Snyder, *Uno arriba, uno abajo,* Atheneum, 1995 (originally published as *One Up, One Down*).

Viorst, *Alexander se muda,* Atheneum, 1995 (originally published as *Alexander Moves*).

(Co-translator into Spanish) Lois Ehlert, *Feathers for Lunch,* Harcourt, 1995.

(Co-translator into Spanish) Ehlert, *Growing a Vegetable Soup,* Harcourt, 1995.

Julie Vivas, *La Natividad,* Harcourt, 1995 (originally published as *The Nativity*).

Hazen, *The Gorilla Did It,* Atheneum, 1995.

Sue Williams, *Sali de paseo,* Harcourt, 1995 (originally published as *I Went Walking*).

Also translator of Blume's *Are You There God? It's Me, Margaret* as *Estas ahi, Dias?;* Val Willis's *The Secret in the Matchbox* as *El secreto en la caja de fosforos,* Farrar, Straus; and Ruth Heller's *Chickens Aren't the Only Ones* as *Las gallinas no son las unicas,* Grosset & Dunlap.

OTHER

Author of *Aserrin Aserran.* Coauthor of "Cuentamundos" literature-based reading series, Macmillan/McGraw-Hill, 1993. Author of introduction, Mayra Fernandez, *Barrio Teacher,* Sandcastle Publishing, 1992. Founding editor-in-chief, *Journal of the National Association of Bilingual Education,* 1975-77, and board member; member of the board, International Reading Association's *Journal of Reading.*

■ Sidelights

Alma Flor Ada wrote in her 1994 Atheneum press release: "My grandmother taught me to read before I was three by writing the names of plants and flowers on the earth with a stick. Reading and nature became very intertwined for me." She continued, "My grandmother and one of my uncles were great storytellers. And every night, at bedtime, my father told me stories he invented to explain to me all that he knew about the history of the world. With all of these storytellers around me, it is not a surprise that I like to tell stories."

As an author and translator, Ada has made entertaining textbooks and storybooks available to Spanish-speaking children and speakers of English attempting to learn Spanish. Ada's efforts to promote bilingualism have resulted in storybooks that are published in both Spanish and English, so that readers may learn from and appreciate both languages. Through her books, Ada also serves as a cultural liaison: her books retell traditional Latin American tales (*The Rooster Who Went to His Uncle's Wedding; Half-Chicken*), present stories set in Latin America (*The Gold Coin*), offer perspectives of life in Latin American countries (*Where the Flame Trees Bloom*), and describe the feelings of children as they confront cultural misunderstanding and learn to take pride in their heritage (*My Name Is Maria Isabel*). "My vocation as a writer started as a young child," Ada once told *SATA*. "I couldn't accept the fact that we had to read such boring textbooks while my wonderful storybooks awaited at home. I made a firm commitment while in the fourth grade to devote my life to producing schoolbooks that would be fun—and since then I am having a lot of fun doing just that!"

Ada was born in Camaguey, Cuba, in 1938. After earning a degree from a university in Spain, she studied to earn a master's degree and a doctorate in Peru. After engaging in post-doctoral studies at Harvard University and at the Mary Bunting Institute at Radcliffe as an Institute fellow and a Fulbright scholar, she began a career as a university professor at Emory University. Within a few years, she began her writing career and published several stories for children and poetry compilations in Peru. Her translations of works from English into Spanish were published in the United States; later, she began to write original stories in Spanish and English.

While Ada's work as a scholar of romance languages and her active promotion of bilingualism influenced her work, Ada credits her children as a "constant source of inspiration." She once told *SATA,* "My childhood vocation was actualized when my daughter at age three complained that I was writing ugly books (I was in the midst of a very scholarly work). One of my greatest joys is that my daughter collaborates with me." Ada's daughter, Rosalma Zubizarreta, an author in her own right, has translated many of Ada's books into both English and Spanish.

Ada is the author of *The Rooster Who Went to His Uncle's Wedding,* an English retelling of a traditional Latin American folktale. A rooster spends so much time grooming himself in preparation for his Uncle's wed-

Intent on stealing Dona Josefa's gold, a thief instead finds her good qualities rubbing off on him, in Ada's *The Gold Coin.* (Illustration by Neil Waldman.)

On the way to his uncle's wedding, a rooster has trouble with a muddy beak, the grass, a lamb, and a dog in this classic folktale. (Cover illustration by Kathleen Kuchera.)

ding that he forgets to eat breakfast. On the way to the wedding, he can't resist pecking at the kernel of corn he finds in a mud puddle. The rooster asks the grass to clean his muddy beak, but the grass won't help. A lamb refuses to eat the grass, and a dog refuses to bite that lamb. The cumulative tale continues until the sun, who has always enjoyed the rooster's sunrise song, agrees to help the rooster. *School Library Journal* critic Lauralyn Persson recommended *The Rooster Who Went to His Uncle's Wedding* as a "solid addition to folklore collections." According to a *Kirkus Reviews* reviewer, it is an "unusually appealing readaloud."

Ada's *The Gold Coin* was honored with a Christopher Award in 1992 and was named a Notable Children's Trade Book. In this tale, Dona Josefa clutches her gold coin and tells herself that she is the richest woman in the world, as a thief greedily watches her through the window. Juan, the thief, decides he must possess the elderly woman's wealth. He does not find the gold coin when he searches Dona Josefa's home in her absence, so he follows her, hoping to snatch it. Instead of finding Dona Josefa's material riches, however, Juan encounters the people Dona Josefa has helped and is gradually transformed into a good person. As Ann Welton remarked in *School Library Journal, The Gold Coin* "makes an important point" about the nature of true wealth and the consequences of greed. A critic for

The author shares eleven true stories about her childhood in Cuba in this poignant and humorous work. (Cover illustration by Antonio Martorell.)

Publishers Weekly described the story as "unusual" and "rewarding" and concluded that it is "worthy of repeated readings."

Where the Flame Trees Bloom, as Ada explains in the book's introduction, is based on her own childhood memories of Cuba. At night, members of the family told tales similar to the eleven short stories she presents. There is the story about how Ada's grandfather was forced to deal with his wife's death and the economy's collapse at the same time. Another story recounts how Ada's blind great-grandmother crafted dolls for poor children. Ada also recalls the time when her schoolteacher uncle feared that his pupils had been struck by lightning, an experience that helped him realize the significance of his job as a teacher. According to a critic in the *Bulletin of the Center for Children's Books,* Ada's "writing evokes the warmth and character of her family," and *School Library Journal* contributor Marilyn Long Graham described Ada's writing as "elegant."

In *Me llamo Maria Isabel* (*My Name Is Maria Isabel*), Maria Isabel's family moves, and she must attend a new school. There are already two Marias in her class, so the teacher decides to call her Mary Lopez instead of Maria Isabel. Maria Isabel is bothered by this because she is named for her two grandmothers. In addition, she cannot think of herself as "Mary," and she forgets that

the teacher is referring to her with that name. When Maria Isabel writes about her feelings in an essay, her teacher realizes her mistake and calls Maria Isabel by the name she prefers. As Irvy Gilbertson wrote in *Five Owls,* the "link of Maria Isabel's name with her heritage is an important theme in this story," and various Spanish words are used to "expose the reader to a different culture."

Ada wrote *Dear Peter Rabbit* in English, and her daughter translated it into Spanish. In this book, which received a Parent's Choice Honor Award, Ada weaves the tales of various storybook characters together. The three little pigs, the Big Bad Wolf, Little Red Riding Hood, Peter Rabbit, Baby Bear, along with Goldilocks (recast as the daughter of Mr. McGregor, who almost catches Peter Rabbit in the beloved Beatrix Potter stories), send letters to one another. After Pig One invites Peter Rabbit to his straw house for a housewarming party, the characters come closer and closer to meeting one another. "Children will be enchanted by this opportunity to meet familiar faces in new settings," commented *School Library Journal* reviewer Joy Fleishhacker. Pointing out that Ada's book belongs to the genre of fairy tale parodies, Roger Sutton asserted in *Bulletin of the Center for Children's Books* that *Dear Peter Rabbit* "is as clever as most in the genre."

The pride Maria Isabel has in her family and heritage is taken to task when her new teacher insists on calling her Mary in *My Name Is Maria Isabel.* (Illustration by K. Dyble Thompson.)

Find out what happens when Peter Rabbit, Goldilocks, the Three Little Pigs, and other storybook characters cross paths in this collection of letters. (Cover illustration by Leslie Tryon.)

Due to Ada's persistence and talent, fewer children learning either Spanish or English will have to suffer through the boring textbooks or second-rate stories she knew as a child. The author spoke of the benefits of this bilingual approach in her publicity release: "Nothing can surpass the inherent musicality of the [Spanish] language, the deep cultural values incorporated in it," she noted. "Yet [Spanish-speaking] children also need to read the literature that their peers are reading in English, so that their introduction to American culture occurs through the best medium the culture has to offer."

■ **Works Cited**

Ada, Alma Flor, "Alma Flor Ada" (publicity release), Atheneum, 1994.

Fleishhacker, Joy, review of *Dear Peter Rabbit, School Library Journal,* July, 1994, p. 73.

Gilbertson, Irvy, review of *My Name Is Maria Isabel, Five Owls,* September-October, 1993, p. 14.

Review of *The Gold Coin, Publishers Weekly,* January 11, 1991, p. 103.

Graham, Marilyn Long, review of *Where the Flame Trees Bloom, School Library Journal,* February, 1995, p. 96.

Persson, Lauralyn, review of *The Rooster Who Went to His Uncle's Wedding, School Library Journal,* May, 1993, p. 92.

Review of *The Rooster Who Went to His Uncle's Wedding, Kirkus Reviews,* May 1, 1993, p. 591.

Sutton, Roger, review of *Dear Peter Rabbit, Bulletin of the Center for Children's Books,* April, 1994, p. 249.

Welton, Ann, review of *The Gold Coin, School Library Journal,* April, 1991, p. 88.

Review of *Where the Flame Trees Bloom, Bulletin of the Center for Children's Books,* February, 1995, p. 190.

■ **For More Information See**

PERIODICALS

Booklist, June 1, 1993, p. 1828.
Publishers Weekly, April 26, 1993, p. 76.
School Library Journal, February, 1988, p. 92; September, 1992, p. 196; April, 1993, p. 117.

* * *

ADAMS, Debra
See SPEREGEN, Devra Newberger

* * *

ALEXANDER, Sally Hobart 1943-

■ **Personal**

Born October 17, 1943, in Owensboro, KY; daughter of Robert (in sales) and Kathryn (a nurse; maiden name, Borup) Hobart; married Robert Alexander (a professor), June 29, 1974; children: Joel, Leslie. *Education:* Bucknell University, B.S.; University of Pittsburgh, M.S.W. *Politics:* Democrat. *Religion:* Protestant. *Hobbies and other interests:* Running, piano.

■ **Addresses**

Home—5648 Marlborough Rd., Pittsburgh, PA 15217. *Agent*—Kendra Marcus, 617 Meadowview, Orinda, CA.

■ **Career**

Elementary school teacher in Long Beach, CA, 1965-69; Guild for the Blind, Pittsburgh, PA, teacher, 1969-70; St. Francis Hospital, Pittsburgh, child therapist, 1973-76. Western Pennsylvania School for Blind Children, consultant, 1976-77. Vice president of Stanton Heights Civic Association. *Member:* Society of Children's Book Writers and Illustrators.

■ **Awards, Honors**

Booklist Editor's Choice for Outstanding Nonfiction, 1990.

■ **Writings**

Mom Can't See Me, photographs by George Ancona, Macmillan, 1990.
Sarah's Surprise, illustrated by Jill Kastner, Macmillan, 1990.

Sally Hobart Alexander with her daughter, Leslie, in *Mom's Best Friend.*

Mom's Best Friend (sequel to *Mom Can't See Me*),
     photographs by Ancona, Macmillan, 1992.
Maggie's Whopper, illustrated by Deborah Kogan Ray,
     Macmillan, 1992.
Taking Hold: My Journey into Blindness (nonfiction),
     Macmillan, 1994.

■ Sidelights

Sally Hobart Alexander has received praise from critics
for her books *Mom Can't See Me* and *Mom's Best
Friend,* two stories based on the author's personal
experience with her own blindness. Using her daughter
Leslie's point of view, Alexander depicts a loving family
that has learned to cope with having a blind parent. In a
Horn Book review of *Mom Can't See Me,* Martha V.
Parravano remarked, "Though the book does not gloss
over some of the difficulties of blindness, on the whole it
is overwhelmingly positive." *Mom's Best Friend* tells
about Alexander's seeing-eye dog and informs the
reader what must be done for a blind person and her dog
to work well together.

Alexander was born in Owensboro, Kentucky. But as
she told *SATA,* "I didn't stay long enough to acquire the
southern accent. My family moved to eastern Pennsylvania, where I lived until college. A small rural town,
Conyngham had fields, woods, and streams, where my

friends and I hiked, swam, and acted out *Robin Hood,
Treasure Island,* and many stories of our own making.

"Although TVs were plentiful, there weren't the numerous channels to entice my friends and me. We took
nature and our imaginations and held circuses, haunted
houses, and plays for the neighborhood. From writing
stories, we turned to composing songs. Soon we learned
that they showed neither talent nor taste, so we returned
to writing and acting out our creations on a tape
recorder."

After graduating from college, Alexander taught third-
grade students in southern California, a job she enjoyed
immensely until a rare disease caused her to lose her
eyesight. "I was unhappy to leave that last year, when
my visual difficulties began," she told *SATA.* "I entered
an excellent training program in Pittsburgh for newly
blinded adults. For a year afterward, I taught at the
Greater Pittsburgh Guild for the Blind. Then I entered
graduate school at the University of Pittsburgh and
obtained a master's degree in social work. For three
years I was a child therapist at St. Francis hospital. But
when my son Joel was born I resigned.

"Soon I entertained him with tales of *Robin Hood* and
Treasure Island, and when my daughter Leslie arrived
three years later, I was experienced and could concoct a
story within seconds about any characters they supplied,
even a grape and an apple. Within a year I joined a
writing workshop and typed my stories on paper. My
message to anyone interested in writing is simple: If I
can do it, you can, too!"

■ Works Cited

Parravano, Martha V., review of *Mom Can't See Me,
Horn Book,* March, 1991, pp. 212-13.

■ For More Information See

PERIODICALS

Bulletin of the Center for Children's Books, November,
     1990, p. 52; December, 1990, p. 77; March, 1992, p.
     173; February, 1993, p. 168.
Horn Book Guide, July, 1990, pp. 35, 121; fall, 1992, p.
     221; spring, 1993, p. 91.
Kirkus Reviews, July 15, 1990, p. 1001; February 15,
     1992, p. 249; September 1, 1992, p. 1125.
School Library Journal, November, 1990, p. 101; Janu-
     ary, 1991, p. 68; August, 1992, p. 132; December,
     1992, p. 95; April, 1995, p. 138.

                              *   *   *

ALMON, Russell
See CLEVENGER, William R(ussell)
and DOWNING, David A(lmon)

ANDERSON, Peggy Perry 1953-

■ Personal

Born December 2, 1953, in Tulsa, OK; daughter of Albert (a commercial artist) and Mary (a nurse; maiden name, Land) Perry; married Kurt Anderson (in sales), August 6, 1977; children: Brandon, Ariel, Haley. *Education:* Attended Oklahoma Christian College, 1972-74; Tulsa University, B.F.A. (commercial art), 1976. *Religion:* Church of Christ. *Hobbies and other interests:* Writing music, painting, playing the guitar.

■ Addresses

Home and office—Broken Arrow, OK.

■ Career

Mobley Art and Design, graphic artist, 1976-91; writer and illustrator. *Member:* Society of Children's Book Writers and Illustrators.

■ Writings

SELF-ILLUSTRATED

Time for Bed, the Babysitter Said, Houghton, 1987.
Wendle, What Have You Done?, Houghton, 1994.

PEGGY PERRY ANDERSON

ILLUSTRATOR

Virginia Poulet, *Blue Bug Goes to the Library,* Children's Press, 1979.
Poulet, *Blue Bug's Book of Colors,* Children's Press, 1981.
Poulet, *Blue Bug Goes to School,* Children's Press, 1985.
The Ugly Little Duck, Children's Press, 1986.
Poulet, *Blue Bug Goes to Paris,* Children's Press, 1986.
Poulet, *Blue Bug's Christmas,* Children's Press, 1987.
Poulet, *Blue Bug Goes to Mexico,* Children's Press, 1990.
Bessie Holland Heck, *Danger on the Homestead,* Dinosaur Press, 1991.
Heck, *Taming the Homestead,* Dinosaur Press, 1994.

■ Work in Progress

An ABC poetry book, a book about a rollerskating alligator, a color book for toddlers, a dinosaur book, and a "Joe the Frog" book.

■ Sidelights

Peggy Perry Anderson told *SATA* that she has been drawing ever since she "could hold a crayon. It just seemed natural that one day I would be an artist. I loved to read and that led me to an interest in illustration. I enjoy creating characters and making them come alive with action. I try to entertain when I make up stories and, of course, my greatest reward is watching children laugh and enjoy the books I've done.

"If I could share something I've learned from becoming a writer and illustrator it would be—DON'T GIVE UP! Lots of rejection slips and lots of changes in the stories made me learn patience. Last, but not least, PRAC-TICE, PRACTICE, PRACTICE! It really is worth the effort when a goal is reached or a dream comes true!"

■ For More Information See

PERIODICALS

School Library Journal, April, 1994, p. 95.

* * *

ANTHONY, Piers 1934-
(Robert Piers, a joint pseudonym)

■ Personal

Full name Piers Anthony Dillingham Jacob; born August 6, 1934, in Oxford, England; came to United States, 1940, naturalized U.S. citizen, 1958; son of Alfred Bennis and Norma (Sherlock) Jacob; married Carol Marble, June 23, 1956; children: Penelope Carolyn, Cheryl. *Education:* Goddard College, B.A., 1956; University of South Florida, teaching certificate, 1964. *Politics:* Independent. *Religion:* "No preference." *Hobbies and other interests:* Tree farming.

PIERS ANTHONY

■ Addresses

Office—c/o Tor Books, 175 Fifth Ave., New York, NY 10010.

■ Career

Novelist. Electronic Communications, Inc., St. Petersburg, FL, technical writer, 1959-62; freelance writer, 1962-63, 1966—; Admiral Farragut Academy, St. Petersburg, FL, teacher of English, 1965-66. *Military service:* U.S. Army, 1957-59. *Member:* Authors Guild, Authors League of America, National Writers Union.

■ Awards, Honors

British Fantasy Award, 1977, and Hugo Award nomination, 1978, both for *A Spell for Chameleon.*

■ Writings

SCIENCE FICTION

Chthon, Ballantine, 1967.
(With Robert E. Margroff) *The Ring,* Ace Books, 1968.
Macroscope, Avon, 1969.
(With Margroff) *The E.S.P. Worm,* Paperback Library, 1970.
Prostho Plus, Berkley, 1973.
Race against Time, Hawthorne, 1973.
Rings of Ice, Avon, 1974.

Triple Detente, DAW Books, 1974.
Phthor (sequel to *Chthon*), Berkley Publishing, 1975.
(With Robert Coulson) *But What of Earth?,* Laser (Toronto), 1976, corrected edition, Tor Books, 1989.
(With Frances T. Hall) *The Pretender,* Borgo Press, 1979.
Mute, Avon, 1981.
Ghost, Tor Books, 1986.
Shade of the Tree, Tor Books, 1986.
(Editor with Barry Malzberg, Martin Greenberg, and Charles G. Waugh) *Uncollected Stars* (short stories), Avon, 1986.
Total Recall, Morrow, 1989.
Balook, illustrated by Patrick Woodroffe, Underwood-Miller, 1990.
Hard Sell, Tafford, 1990.
(With Roberto Fuentes) *Dead Morn,* Tafford, 1990.
MerCycle, illustrated by Ron Lindahn, Tafford, 1991.
(With Philip Jose Farmer) *Caterpillar's Question,* Ace Books, 1992.
Killobyte, Putnam, 1993.

"OMNIVORE" SERIES; SCIENCE FICTION NOVELS

Omnivore, Ballantine, 1968.
Orn, Avon, 1971.
Ox, Avon, 1976.

"BATTLE CIRCLE" SERIES; SCIENCE FICTION NOVELS

Sos the Rope, Pyramid, 1968.
Var the Stick, Faber, 1972.
Neq the Sword, Corgi, 1975.
Battle Circle (omnibus volume; contains *Sos the Rope, Var the Stick,* and *Neq the Sword*), Avon, 1978.

"CLUSTER" SERIES; SCIENCE FICTION NOVELS

Cluster, Avon, 1977, published in England as *Vicinity Cluster,* Panther, 1979.
Chaining the Lady, Avon, 1978.
Kirlian Quest, Avon, 1978.
Thousandstar, Avon, 1980.
Viscous Circle, Avon, 1982.

"TAROT"; SCIENCE FICTION NOVEL PUBLISHED IN THREE PARTS

God of Tarot, Jove, 1979.
Vision of Tarot, Berkley Publishing, 1980.
Faith of Tarot, Berkley Publishing, 1980.
Tarot (contains *God of Tarot, Vision of Tarot,* and *Faith of Tarot*), Ace Books, 1988.

"BIO OF A SPACE TYRANT" SERIES; SCIENCE FICTION NOVELS

Refugee, Avon, 1983.
Mercenary, Avon, 1984.
Politician, Avon, 1985.
Executive, Avon, 1985.
Statesman, Avon, 1986.

FANTASY

Hasan, Borgo Press, 1977.
(With Robert Kornwise) *Through the Ice,* illustrated by D. Horne, Underwood-Miller, 1989.

(With Mercedes Lackey) *If I Pay Thee Not in Gold*, Baen, 1993.

"MAGIC OF XANTH" SERIES; FANTASY NOVELS

A Spell for Chameleon, Del Rey, 1977.
The Source of Magic, Del Rey, 1979.
Castle Roogna, Del Rey, 1979.
The Magic of Xanth (omnibus volume; contains *A Spell for Chameleon, The Source of Magic,* and *Castle Roogna*), Doubleday, 1981, published as *Piers Anthony: Three Complete Xanth Novels*, Wings Books, 1994.
Centaur Aisle, Del Rey, 1982.
Ogre, Ogre, Del Rey, 1982.
Night Mare, Del Rey, 1983.
Dragon on a Pedestal, Del Rey, 1983.
Crewel Lye: A Caustic Yarn, Del Rey, 1985.
Golem in the Gears, Del Rey, 1986.
Vale of the Vole, Avon, 1987.
Heaven Cent, Avon, 1988.
Man from Mundania, Avon, 1989.
(With Jody Lynn Nye) *Piers Anthony's Visual Guide to Xanth*, illustrated by Todd Cameron Hamilton and James Clouse, Avon, 1989.
Isle of View, Morrow, 1990.
Question Quest, Morrow, 1991.
The Color of Her Panties, Avon, 1992.
Demons Don't Dream, Tor Books, 1993.
Harpy Thyme, Tor Books, 1994.
Geis of the Gargoyle, Tor Books, 1995.
Roc and a Hard Place, Tor Books, 1995.

"INCARNATIONS OF IMMORTALITY" SERIES; FANTASY NOVELS

On a Pale Horse, Del Rey, 1983.
Bearing an Hourglass, Del Rey, 1984.
With a Tangled Skein, Del Rey, 1985.
Wielding a Red Sword, Del Rey, 1986.
Being a Green Mother, Del Rey, 1987.
For Love of Evil, Morrow, 1988.
And Eternity, Morrow, 1990.

"DRAGON'S GOLD" SERIES; FANTASY NOVELS; WITH ROBERT E. MARGROFF

Dragon's Gold, Tor Books, 1987.
Serpent's Silver, Tor Books, 1988.
Chimaera's Copper, Tor Books, 1990.
Orc's Opal, Tor Books, 1990.
Mouvar's Magic, Tor Books, 1992.
Three Complete Novels (contains *Dragon's Gold, Serpent's Silver,* and *Chimaera's Copper*), Wings Books, 1993.

"APPRENTICE ADEPT" SERIES; SCIENCE FICTION/ FANTASY NOVELS

Split Infinity, Del Rey, 1980.
Blue Adept, Del Rey, 1981.
Juxtaposition, Del Rey, 1982.
Double Exposure (omnibus volume; contains *Split Infinity, Blue Adept,* and *Juxtaposition*), Doubleday, 1982.
Out of Phaze, Ace Books, 1987.
Robot Adept, Ace Books, 1988.

Unicorn Point, Ace Books, 1989.
Phaze Doubt, Ace Books, 1990.

"MODE" SERIES; SCIENCE FICTION/FANTASY NOVELS

Virtual Mode, Putnam, 1991.
Fractal Mode, Putnam, 1992.
Chaos Mode, Putnam, 1993.

"JASON STRIKER" SERIES; WITH ROBERTO FUENTES; MARTIAL ARTS NOVELS

Kiai!, Berkley Publishing, 1974.
Mistress of Death, Berkley Publishing, 1974.
The Bamboo Bloodbath, Berkley Publishing, 1974.
Ninja's Revenge, Berkley Publishing, 1975.
Amazon Slaughter, Berkley Publishing, 1976.

"GEODYSSEY" SERIES; HISTORICAL SCIENCE FICTION

Isle of Woman, Tor Books, 1993.
Shame of Man, Tor Books, 1994.

OTHER

Steppe (science fiction/history), Millington, 1976, Tor Books, 1985.
Anthonology (short stories), Tor Books, 1985.
Bio of an Ogre: The Autobiography of Piers Anthony to Age 50, Ace Books, 1988.
Pornucopia (erotic fantasy), Tafford, 1989.
Firefly (novel), Morrow, 1990, Avon, 1992.
Tatham Mound (historical fiction), Morrow, 1991.
Alien Plot (short stories), Tor Books, 1992.
Letters to Jenny (nonfiction), Tor Books, 1993.
(Editor with Richard Gilliam) *Tales from the Great Turtle*, Tor Books, 1994.

Contributor to *Science against Man*, edited by Anthony Cheetham, Avon 1970; *Nova One: An Anthology of Original Science Fiction*, edited by Harry Harrison, Delacorte Press, 1970; *Again, Dangerous Visions*, edited by Harlan Ellison, Doubleday, 1972; *Generation*, edited by David Gerrold, Dell, 1972; and *The Berkley Showcase*, edited by Victoria Schochet and John Silbersack, Berkley Publishing, 1981. Also contributor, with Robert Margroff under joint pseudonym Robert Piers, of a short story to *Adam Bedside Reader*. Contributor of short stories to periodicals, including *Analog, Fantastic, Worlds of If, Worlds of Tomorrow, Amazing, Magazine of Fantasy and Science Fiction, SF Age, Vegetarian Times, Twilight Zone, Books and Bookmen, The Writer, Gauntlet, Chic, Far Point, Starburst, Vertex,* and *Pandora*.

■ Adaptations

Macroscope, A Spell for Chameleon, The Source of Magic, Castle Roogna, Through the Ice, Virtual Mode, and *Fractal Mode* have been adapted to audio cassette.

■ Work in Progress

Spider Legs, a science fiction novel.

■ Sidelights

Within a childhood scarred by illness, death, and isolation, prolific science fiction and fantasy author Piers Anthony escaped by immersing himself in books. "From the time I was 13, I had been hooked on science fiction," Anthony recalled in an interview with the *Science Fiction Radio Show* (*SFRS*) published in *The Sound of Wonder.* "It's what I did for entertainment. It was a whole different world, multiple worlds, each one of them better than the one I knew. And so when I thought about writing [science fiction], I thought I could be original because I had read everything in the field." He began to write at age twenty, deciding in college to make writing his career. As an adult, Anthony's therapy became his livelihood. His many popular series—including the "Magic of Xanth," with eighteen volumes published and more in progress—and his various novels and collections add up to more than one hundred books since 1967. "I am an SF writer today," he told Cliff Biggers in a *Science Fiction* interview, "because without SF and writing I would be nothing at all today."

In Anthony's first science fiction work, a mine worker imprisoned on the planet Chthon attempts a daring escape. (Cover illustration by John Jude Palencar.)

Among the traumatic events of Anthony's youth were his family's moves to Spain when he was five and to the United States the next year, the loss of his cousin to cancer at fifteen, and his parents' divorce at eighteen. The effects of these occurrences are detectable throughout his writings. In *Piers Anthony,* Michael R. Collings points out several instances where Anthony's stories mirror his early life: the psychological turmoil suffered by many of his characters, including Brother Paul in *Tarot,* which often parallels his own as a child; the vegetarianism he advocates in *Omnivore,* a result of his overwhelming aversion to death; the strength and health of his heroes, as in the illness-free world of *Chthon,* representing Anthony's personal ideal.

After eight years of submitting stories to magazines, Anthony sold his first piece, "Possible to Rue," to *Fantastic* in 1962. In the next several years, he worked variously as a freelance writer and English teacher, but finally decided to devote all of his time to writing. *Chthon,* Anthony's first novel, was published in 1967, received numerous award nominations, and caught the attention of both critics and readers in the science fiction genre. The next year brought a prize from a contest jointly sponsored by Pyramid Books, Kent Productions, and the *Magazine of Fantasy and Science Fiction* for *Sos the Rope,* the first entry in the "Battle Circle" series.

Chthon traces the escape efforts of Aton Five, imprisoned on the planet Chthon and forced to work in its garnet mines. A *Publishers Weekly* reviewer commented on the many elements of the book, including language, myth, suspense, and symbolism, "a bursting package, almost too much for one book, but literate, original and entertaining." Those elements and Anthony's liberal use of them would become his trademark. In a detailed analysis of *Chthon* and its sequel, *Phthor,* Collings noted Anthony's liberal references to mythological symbols. Literary references are present as well, exemplified by the resemblance of the prison caverns of Chthon to Dante's depiction of Hell in *The Inferno.* In *Chthon,* "Anthony has created a whole new world, a dream universe which you find yourself living in and, after a while, understanding," Leo Harris declared in *Books and Bookmen.* "Very poetic and tough and allegorical it all is, and it will rapidly have thee in thrall." While *Chthon* focuses on Aton's life, *Phthor* follows Aton's son, Arlo, who symbolizes Thor of Norse mythology. "The mythologies embedded in *Chthon* and *Phthor* go far beyond mere ornamentation or surface symbolism," Collings noted. "They define the thematic content of the novels. Initially, there is a clear demarcation between myth and reality.... Yet early in *Chthon* Anthony throws that clear demarcation into question."

Anthony's first trilogy begins with *Sos the Rope,* based on a chapter of his 1956 B.A. thesis novel entitled "The Unstilled World." The first installment of the "Battle Circle" books, *Sos the Rope* explores the efforts of a group of radiation survivors led by Sos as they attempt to rebuild their society after the Blast. Yet the resulting Empire soon becomes a destructive force and Sos sets out to destroy it. The novel speaks against the dangers of centralized civilization and overpopulation: millions of shrews, like the Biblical plague of locusts, invade the area and consume every living creature within their reach. Eventually the horde destroys itself with its enormity and its wholesale pillaging. The shrews' rampage and ultimate demise serve as a metaphor for man's overcrowding and abuse of the environment. Humankind, like the shrews, will be decimated when it outgrows the Earth's ability to sustain it. In *Var the Stick* and *Neq the Sword,* the "Battle Circle" story is completed. The books' titles are actually characters' names; the trilogy's warriors are named after their weapons. Collings observed similarities to the epic works of Homer, Virgil, and John Milton in "Battle Circle," which "investigates the viability of three fundamental forms of epic: the Achilean epic of martial prowess; the Odyssean epic of wandering; and the Virgillian/Miltonic epic of self-sacrifice and restoration."

The "Omnivore" trilogy provided a forum for Anthony to further his exploration of the dangers humankind continues to inflict upon itself, and introduced his support of vegetarianism. "Like *Battle Circle, Chthon,* and *Phthor,*" Collings observed, "*Omnivore* deals with control—specifically, with controlling the most dangerous omnivore of all, man." Three interplanetary explorers, the herbivorous Veg, carnivorous Cal, and omnivorous Aquilon, play out Anthony's views. The three journey to the planet Nacre, reporting back to investigator Subble and subsequently revealing to readers their adventures and clues to the secret threatening to destroy Earth. in the sequel, *Orn,* the three explorers venture to the planet Paleo, which resembles the Earth of sixty five million years past, and encounter Orn, a creature whose racial memory endows it with the knowledge of its ancestors and enables it to survive the changes bombarding its planet. In *Ox,* the final volume of the trilogy, Veg, Cal, and Aquilon gradually uncover the existence of a sentient super-computer while exploring alternate worlds. As with other Anthony books, reviewers noted that the "Omnivore" volumes contain substantial discussions of technical and scientific issues. A *Publishers Weekly* reviewer described *Ox* as "a book for readers willing to put a lot of concentration into reading it." The similarly complex *Macroscope,* described by Collings as "one of Anthony's most ambitious and complex novels," seeks to place man in his proper context within the galaxy. The book increased Anthony's reputation but, due to a publisher's error, was not submitted for consideration for the important Nebula Award and lost one crucial source of publicity. Nevertheless, *Macroscope* was a milestone in Anthony's career. In a *Luna Monthly* review, Samuel Mines declared, "*Macroscope* recaptures the tremendous glamour and excitement of science fiction, pounding the reader into submission with the sheer weight of its ideas which seem to pour out in an inexhaustible flood."

Beginning with the "Cluster" series, Anthony began writing "trilogies" that expanded past the usual three books. "Cluster" became a series of five, and the still-active "Magic of Xanth" stands at eighteen novels plus

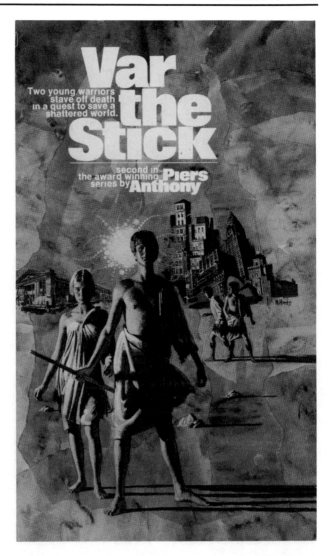

An exiled warrior wanders the earth in the second installment in Anthony's "Battle Circle" series.

the companion book *Piers Anthony's Visual Guide to Xanth.* The "Apprentice Adept" series, with seven entries published between 1980 and 1990, was also originally planned as a trilogy. In the case of the "Xanth" books, Anthony attributed his decision to continue the series to reader response. "We did a third [Xanth novel], and said, 'Let's wrap it up as a trilogy and not do any more,'" Anthony remarked to *SFRS.* "Then the readers started demanding more, and more, and more, and finally both the publisher and the author were convinced. It's hard to say 'No' when the readers are begging for more."

Anthony branched out from science fiction into fantasy writing with *A Spell for Chameleon,* the first of the "Xanth" books, published in 1977. Although one early work, *Hasan,* was fantasy, it was his second fantasy novel, *Chameleon,* that established Anthony in the genre. The switch to fantasy came as a result of Anthony's much-publicized split with his first publisher, Ballantine Books. As the author related to *SFRS,* Ballantine "was sending me statements-of-account that were simply not true. . . . I sent a letter demanding a

An accidental mind switch sends a wizard from Phaze to the scientific land of Proton in Anthony's 1987 work. (Cover illustration by Darrell Sweet.)

correct statement and correct payments. Rather than do that, they blacklisted me for six years." Anthony moved to Avon Books; six years later, with a new administration at Ballantine, the author found himself invited back and wanted to give Ballantine another chance. His contract at Avon, however, prohibited him from writing science fiction for another publisher, so he decided to try fantasy. Luckily, Anthony knew and liked the fantasy editor at Ballantine, Lester del Rey; Ballantine's Del Rey imprint went on to publish the first nine "Xanth" novels as well as the early "Apprentice Adept" and "Incarnations of Immortality" entries. Anthony differentiates between his science fiction and fantasy works in their content as well as their popularity. "For the challenge and sheer joy of getting in and tackling a difficult problem and surmounting it, science fiction is better," Anthony remarked to *SFRS*. "But if I need money, fantasy is better." He later added, "I talk about writing fantasy in the sense of doing it for the money, but I also enjoy it. If I didn't enjoy it, I wouldn't do it for the money."

Anthony is best known for the "Xanth" books, the series that continues almost two decades after its first book. The "Xanth" stories are generally less complex and easier to read than Anthony's earlier works, appealing to younger readers as well as adults. *A Spell for Chameleon,* a 1978 Hugo Award nominee, introduced Bink, who tackles another recurring topic in Anthony's novels: maturity and control. The first "Xanth" installment chronicles Bink's growing-up; later volumes feature his son, Dor. The land of Xanth, which closely resembles the state of Florida, is a place where everyone and everything—even a rock or tree—has a magical talent, except Bink. *Chameleon* follows Bink on his quest to discover his talent or face exile to the boring, powerless land of Mundania. In the process, Bink gains not only knowledge of his talent but emotional maturity as well. Bink sets out on another adventure in *The Source of Magic,* assigned to discover the source of all magic in Xanth. In *Castle Roogna,* Bink's son Dor travels eight hundred years back in time to rescue his nurse's

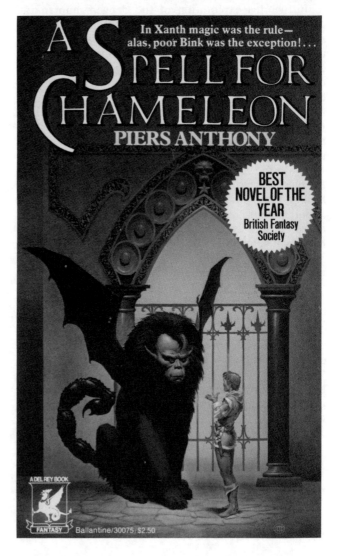

The first of Anthony's highly praised "Xanth" fantasy novels introduces young Bink, the only inhabitant of Xanth who does not possess magical powers. (Cover art by Michael Whelan.)

boyfriend. Throughout each book, Bink and Dor encounter innumerable illusions and feats of magic. "Piers Anthony . . . apparently decided to invest his magical land of Xanth with every fantastical conception ever invented," a reviewer for *Isaac Asimov's Science Fiction Magazine* remarked. "It has quests, enchanted castles, riddles, unicorns, griffins, mermaids, giants (not to mention invisible giants), zombies, ghosts, elves, magicians, man-eating trees, enchantresses, and a host of inventions from Anthony's own fertile mind."

"The Magic of Xanth" continued with *Centaur Aisle, Ogre, Ogre,* and *Night Mare,* the next "trilogy" of "Xanth" books. The first of these finds Dor filling in for Xanth's King Trent while he and Queen Iris take a trip to Mundania, good experience for Dor since he will one day become king. When the King and Queen fail to return, Dor sets out on another adventure. Anthony once again explores the process of maturing, as Dor leads a search party through Xanth and into Mundania, and falls in love with Princess Irene. In *Ogre, Ogre,* the half-human, half-ogre Smash must protect the half-human, half-nymph Tandy. A stupid, insensitive creature at the beginning of the tale, Smash gradually acquires more human traits until he finally realizes that he is in love with Tandy.

Nickelpede

Written with Jody Lynn Nye, *Piers Anthony's Visual Guide to Xanth* offers fans of the series a closer look at the magical creatures that populate Xanth, including this Nickelpede. (Illustration by Todd Cameron Hamilton and James Clouse.)

Later entries in the series added to Anthony's portrait of the fantastic land of Xanth, with storylines including the rescue of the kingdom by a creature responsible for delivering bad dreams (*Night Mare*), the adventures of three-year-old Princess Ivy, lost and wandering in the forest with newfound friends Hugo and the Gap Dragon (*Dragon on a Pedestal*), the diminutive Golem's quest to rescue a lost baby dragon and prove himself worthy of attention (*Golem in the Gears*), Prince Dolph's protest against the Adult Conspiracy that keeps children ignorant of adult matters (*Heaven Cent*), Princess Ivy's trip to Mundania in search of Good Magician Humfrey (*Man from Mundania*), and the search of Gloha, Xanth's only half-harpy/half-goblin, for advice from Magician Trent to further a quest for her true love (*Harpy Thyme*). Richard Mathews applauded the "Xanth" series in *Fantasy Review,* asserting that it "ranks with the best of American and classic fantasy literature."

Anthony's use of puns and other language tricks is a hallmark of the "Xanth" novels. "In Xanth," Collings noted, Anthony "incorporates much of this interest in language in furthering the plot and in establishing the essence of his fantasy universe. In Xanth, language is literal, especially what in Mundania would be called metaphors." As a result, the critic continued, "breadfruit bears loaves of bread; shoetrees bear shoes in varying sizes and styles; nickelpedes are like centipedes, only five times larger and more vicious; and sunflowers are flowers whose blossoms are tiny suns blazing at the top of the stalk—a potent weapon if an enemy looks directly at them." In a *Voice of Youth Advocates* review of *Ogre, Ogre,* Peggy Murray found that Anthony's stories, "full of sophomoric humor and bad puns, have tremendous appeal with YA fantasy readers." In fact, some of the puns in *Harpy Thyme* were sent to Anthony by his readers.

Cluster, the first novel in the series of the same name, was published in the same year as the first "Xanth" book. Intergalactic travel and adventure are again the subjects in the "Cluster" books, in which Anthony introduces the concept of Kirlian transfer, a type of out-of-body travel that requires much less energy than the outmoded "mattermission." The Kirlian transfer and other innovations are fundamental to the outcomes of the First and Second Wars of Energy, described in the first two volumes, and to the battle of an intergalactic force against the space amoeba in *Kirlian Quest.* "More than anything, the Cluster series is an exercise in enjoyment" for Anthony, Collings remarked. The author relishes the opportunity to create bizarre beings and situations unlike any the reader has experienced. The original "Cluster" trilogy led to *Tarot,* published in three volumes as *God of Tarot, Vision of Tarot,* and *Faith of Tarot.*

From the ending of *Kirlian Quest,* Anthony created *Tarot,* which he had intended for publication as one volume. Anthony emphasized in his interview with *SFRS* that *Tarot* is not a trilogy, but "a quarter-million-word novel." The novel was published not only in three parts, but in two different years. "It bothered me because I feel that this is the major novel of my career," Anthony remarked in the *SFRS* interview published in 1985. "Split into three parts and published in two years—it washed me out totally. I had no chance to make a run for any awards or anything like that. It was simply gone." He resents referrals to the book as a trilogy because they imply that each volume is a full novel, when in fact they are each one-third of a novel. Brother Paul, a character introduced in the "Cluster" trilogy and featured in *But What of Earth?*, is the central figure in *Tarot*, in which Anthony attempts to develop a definition of God. Collings acknowledged that the "brutality, horror, and disgust" present in the book were not unlike those of many other Anthony novels, but combined with religious references proved controversial and offensive to many readers. *Tarot* "is certainly not for the squeamish, nor is it altogether for those who enjoyed the first installment of Tarot civilization in the Cluster novels. Anthony himself admits this," Collings noted.

The Incarnation of Good is showcased in this final volume of Anthony's "Incarnations of Immortality" fantasy series. (Cover illustration by Rowena Morrill.)

Anthony returns to pure fantasy in the "Incarnations of Immortality" series, which begins with *On a Pale Horse* and is set in "a world very much like ours, except that magic has been systematized and is as influential as science," a *Publishers Weekly* reviewer commented. The abstract concepts of Time, War, Nature, Fate, and Death are all real people—the Incarnations—and all are involved in the battle of Satan against God. In *Bearing an Hourglass,* a grief-stricken man agrees to take on the role of Chronos, the Incarnation of Time, and soon finds himself locked in a battle with Satan. *Booklist* reviewer Roland Green noted the religious and ethical content of the series that "even people who may disagree with [Anthony's] ideas will recognize as intelligently rendered." Subsequent volumes feature the Incarnations of Fate (*With a Tangled Skein*), War (*Wielding a Red Sword*), Nature (*Being a Green Mother*), Evil (*For Love of Evil*), and finally, Good (*And Eternity*). "This grand finale ... showcases Anthony's multiple strengths" including his humor, characterizations, and themes, a *Library Journal* reviewer declared.

Virtual Mode is a novel "to which teens relate well," Anthony remarked to *Authors and Artists for Young Adults* (*AAYA*). Published in 1991, *Virtual Mode* introduced the "Mode" series, in which characters traverse the universe through the use of "skew paths" anchored by other people. As the anchors change, the paths and destinies of the travelers are affected and new stories are presented. In *Virtual Mode,* Darius of Hlahtar ventures to Earth to bring the girl he loves, the suicidal Colene, back to his universe. Together Darius and Colene discover that they must build a skew path to complete the journey. *Publishers Weekly* writer Sybil Steinberg described Colene as "a clearly defined character, virtues, flaws and all" who is "brought fully to life in this skillful, enjoyable book."

Similarly, YA readers will enjoy *MerCycle,* Anthony's story about five people recruited to pedal bicycles under the waters of the Gulf of Mexico on a secret mission to save the Earth from collision with a meteor. The novel was originally written in 1971 but then shelved after it was unable to find a publisher. After establishing his reputation as a best-selling author, Anthony returned to the manuscript, revised it extensively, and added it to his oeuvre. The story deals heavily with themes of human nature and survival: the bicyclists experience being "out of phase" and "phased in" to other Earth life, are kept unaware of their mission, and meet up with Chinese mermaids. "The result," wrote a critic in *New York Times Book Review,* "is an engaging tall tale, spun out of the most unpromising raw material."

Anthony told *AAYA* that, like *Virtual Mode, Tatham Mound* is another of his works most likely to appeal to young adults. The story of fifteen-year-old Throat Shot, a sixteenth-century Florida Indian, *Tatham Mound* is based on an actual Indian burial mound discovered in North Florida and features historically accurate reconstructions of Spanish explorer Hernando de Soto's march across Florida and his battles with the Indian tribes of the area. A *Library Journal* reviewer described

This 1991 story of underwater adventurers recruited for a secret mission explores themes of human nature and survival. (Cover art by Ron and Val Lindahn.)

Tatham Mound as a "heartfelt tribute to a lost culture" and a "labor of both love and talent."

Also based on history, but spanning eight million years, are the works in the "Geodyssey" series—*Isle of Woman* and *Shame of Man. Isle of Woman* is comprised of a series of vignettes that center on the lives of two prehistoric families who are reborn into succeeding centuries up to twenty-first century America. According to Jackie Cassada in a *Library Journal* review, *Isle of Woman* is Anthony's "most ambitious project to date." *Shame of Man* explores evolution one generation at a time, beginning with families of gorillas and chimpanzees on through the Homo Sapiens of 2050 A.D. Called "speculative fiction" by *Voice of Youth Advocates* reviewer Kim Carter, *Shame of Man* encompasses more than twenty-five years of Anthony's research in "history, archaeology, anthropology, and human nature," as well as showcasing some of the author's own theories on these subjects.

Virtual Mode, Tatham Mound, and *Shame of Man* exemplify Anthony's desire to produce works of lasting value along with those written simply for entertainment. While he wants readers to enjoy his work, the author hopes also to provoke contemplation of the serious issues he presents. "I'd like to think I'm on Earth for some purpose other than just to feed my face," Anthony remarked to *SFRS.* "I want to do something and try to leave the universe a better place than it was when I came into it."

■ Works Cited

Review of *And Eternity, Library Journal,* December, 1989, p. 176.

Anthony, Piers, remarks in *Authors and Artists for Young Adults,* Volume 11, Gale, 1993, pp. 9-19.

Biggers, Cliff, "An Interview with Piers Anthony," *Science Fiction,* November, 1977, p. 60.

Carter, Kim, review of *Shame of Man, Voice of Youth Advocates,* February, 1995, p. 343.

Cassada, Jackie, review of *Isle of Woman, Library Journal,* September 15, 1993, p. 108.

Review of *Chthon, Publishers Weekly,* June 5, 1967, p. 180.

Collings, Michael R., *Piers Anthony,* Starmont House, 1983.

Green, Roland, review of *Bearing an Hourglass, Booklist,* July, 1984, p. 1497.

Harris, Leo, review of *Chthon, Books and Bookmen,* April, 1970, pp. 26-27.

Lane, Daryl, William Vernon, and David Carson, *The Sound of Wonder: Interviews from "The Science Fiction Radio Show,"* Volume 2, Oryx, 1985.

Mathews, Richard, "Xanth Series Extolled," *Fantasy Review,* March, 1984, pp. 24-25.

Review of *MerCycle, New York Times Book Review,* September 13, 1992, p. 28.

Mines, Samuel, review of *Macroscope, Luna Monthly,* September, 1970, p. 22.

Murray, Peggy, review of *Ogre, Ogre, Voice of Youth Advocates,* April, 1983, p. 44.

Review of *On a Pale Horse, Publishers Weekly,* September 2, 1983, p. 72.

Review of *Ox, Publishers Weekly,* July 26, 1976, p. 78.

Review of *A Spell for Chameleon, Isaac Asimov's Science Fiction Magazine,* September, 1979, p. 18.

Steinberg, Sybil, review of *Virtual Mode, Publishers Weekly,* January 4, 1991, p. 61.

Review of *Tatham Mound, Library Journal,* August, 1991, p. 150.

■ For More Information See

BOOKS

Contemporary Literary Criticism, Volume 35, Gale, 1985, pp. 34-41.

PERIODICALS

Analog, January, 1989, p. 182; August, 1992, pp. 165-166.
Fantasy and Science Fiction, August, 1986, pp. 37-40.
Horn Book, October 6, 1989, p. 84.
Kirkus Reviews, August 15, 1993, p. 1034.
Kliatt, November, 1992, p. 13.
New York Times Book Review, April 20, 1986, p. 27.

Publishers Weekly, July 25, 1986, p. 174; August 29, 1986, p. 388; May 29, 1987, p. 73; February 10, 1989, p. 58; August 11, 1989, p. 444; August 25, 1989, p. 58; April 20, 1990, p. 61; May 11, 1990, p. 251; August 10, 1990, p. 431; November 2, 1990, p. 58; December 21, 1990, p. 57; October 18, 1991, p. 55; July 20, 1992, p. 237; November 29, 1993, pp. 57-58; September 5, 1994, p. 96.
Voice of Youth Advocates, December, 1992, p. 290; August, 1994, p. 152.
The Writer, August, 1989, pp. 11-13, 35.
Writer's Digest, January, 1991, p. 32.

*   *   *

APPIAH, Peggy 1921-

■ Personal

Born May 21, 1921, in England; daughter of Stafford (a British cabinet minister) and Isobel (Swithenbank) Cripps; married Joe E. Appiah (a barrister and Ghanaian government official), July 18, 1953 (died, 1990); children: Anthony, Isobel, Adwoa, Abena. *Education:* Attended Maltman's Green School and Whitehall Secretarial College. *Religion:* Christian. *Hobbies and other interests:* Arts, crafts, handwork, history, social welfare, studying Ashanti culture and history, collecting Ashanti gold weights, gardening.

■ Addresses

Home—P.O. Box 829, Kumasi, Ashanti, Ghana.
Agent—David Higham Associates, 5-8 Lower John St., London W1R 4HA, England.

■ Career

Novelist and freelance writer, 1965—. British Ministry of Information, London, England, research assistant, 1943-45; Racial Unity, London, secretary, 1951-53. Kumasi Children's Home, Kumasi, Ashanti, Ghana, chair of advisory committee, 1968-93. *Member:* Society for the Aid of Mentally Retarded Children.

■ Writings

CHILDREN'S BOOKS

Ananse the Spider: Tales from an Ashanti Village, illustrated by Peggy Wilson, Pantheon, 1966.
Tales of an Ashanti Father, illustrated by Mora Dickson, Deutsch, 1967, Beacon, 1989.
The Children of Ananse, illustrated by Dickson, Evans, 1968.
The Pineapple Child and Other Tales from Ashanti, illustrated by Dickson, Evans, 1969, Beacon, 1989.
The Lost Earring (reader), illustrated by J. Jarvis, Evans, 1971.
Yao and the Python (reader), illustrated by Jarvis, Evans, 1971.
Gift of the Mmoatia, illustrated by Nii O. Quao, Ghana Publishing, 1972.

PEGGY APPIAH

Why There Are So Many Roads (folktales), illustrated by A. A. Teye, African University Press, 1972.
Ring of Gold, illustrated by Laszlo Acs, Deutsch, 1976.
Why the Hyena Does Not Care for Fish and Other Tales from the Ashanti Gold Weights, illustrated by Joanna Stubbs, Deutsch, 1977, Ghana Publishing, 1996.
Abena and the Python, Quick Service Books, 1991.
Afua and the Mouse, Quick Service Books, 1991.
Kofi and the Crow, Quick Service Books, 1991.
The Twins, Quick Service Books, 1991.
Kyekyekulee, Grandmother's Tales, Quick Service Books, 1993.
Busybody, Asempa, 1995.
The Rubbish Heap, Asempa, 1995.

ADULT BOOKS

A Smell of Onions (novel), Longman, 1971.
A Dirge Too Soon (novel), Ghana Publishing, 1976.
Poems of Three Generations, University of Science and Technology, 1978.

■ Work in Progress

Translating Ashanti proverbs and providing explanations, for a book to be edited by her son, Anthony Appiah; *Ratteltat,* a children's book to be published in Namibia in 1996; a book on the history of Asante place names; three books to be published in Nigeria.

■ Sidelights

English-born Peggy Appiah had always wanted to write children's books, and raising a family in Ghana—where children's books and even toys were relatively scarce—

encouraged her to do so. Blending a love of Ashanti myth and fable with memories of her own favorite children's tales, she began to collect tales from the west coast of Africa that would teach many of the same lessons learned in Aesop. The result was a first volume of folktales, *Ananse the Spider: Tales from an Ashanti Village,* which *Kirkus Reviews* lauded for its authentic rendering: "Her versions sound as good as they read." Appiah had hit on a motif and theme that resonated for her and her readers. "All the books I have so far published have been about Ashanti, where I live," she once reported in *Twentieth-Century Children's Writers.* "The country is full of stories," she wrote. The same could be said about Appiah's own life.

Born in 1921 on the edge of the Cotswolds in England, the daughter of a Labor politician with a 'Sir' in front of his name, Appiah had no idea that her life and travels would ultimately lead her to Africa. She grew up in Goodfellows, a rambling country home. The house and grounds provided a world within the harsher outside world, where she and her sisters Theresa and Diana and brother John could grow to love nature and to find sustenance in it, learning the names of all the wildflowers and setting up their own garden plots. There were nannies and dogs and a name with history to it: Ancestors on her father's side extended back to William the Conqueror. Sir Stafford Cripps, however, was anything but a typical lord of the manor. A socialist, Cripps was reviled by his own class for, as Appiah put it in *Something about the Author Autobiography Series* (*SAAS*), "letting down the side." As a young girl at Goodfellows, Appiah was introduced to the likes of Jawarlal Nehru and other fighters for freedom, for her father was a staunch supporter of colonial independence. Even though she lived amidst the trappings of upper class ease, Appiah's life did not at all resemble a typical English childhood.

Appiah began writing poetry at an early age, encouraged by both parents, although for them such an activity was all but expected. Appiah went to various schools, but as she stated in *SAAS,* she disliked school, especially as she approached puberty: "I hated my own school at that age, not per se, but because I never felt at home there and thought of myself as not popular, unattractive, unsuccessful, greasy, and spotty!" There was also a fair amount of travel; in 1938 she accompanied her father on a trip to Jamaica. Graduating from the equivalent of high school, Appiah first thought she would attend university in Edinburgh instead of Oxford, which was the expected thing, but settled instead for a time on an art history course in Florence. With the coming of World War II in 1939, Appiah returned to England and enrolled in a secretarial college, intent on learning something of practical use. She finished the course just in time to travel with her mother and sister Theresa to Moscow, where her father had been posted as ambassador.

The family travelled west across the Atlantic and Canada with stopovers in the Rocky Mountains. Then came the Pacific crossing and travels through Japan and Korea before boarding the trans-Siberian railway for the week-long train journey to Moscow. Appiah remained in Moscow, learning the language and becoming familiar with the culture, until the German attack on the Soviet Union. She then spent time in Iran working for the British Army, which was running the railways. Eventually she ended up back in England, working for the Ministry of Information as a research assistant. Her experiences in Moscow as well as her secretarial training came in handy in this new posting.

Her hard work and long hours during the war took their toll. With the peace, Appiah had a breakdown and entered a clinic in Zurich, then spent a summer studying art in Lugano. Back in England, she attended art school and set up in a studio. In 1948, Appiah accompanied her mother on a trip to China. The journey was quasi-official, for during the war Appiah's mother had organized the Aid to China Fund, and now that government invited her to see how the aid had been put to use. The result was a thirty thousand mile voyage from the Gobi Desert to Moukden, Peking, and Shanghai. The author met not only Chiang Kai-shek, but also Mao Tse Tung. At the end of the journey, Appiah and her mother went to India, where they stayed with their friend Nehru and his daughter Indira Ghandi. It was a journey that would stay with Appiah and inform the rest of her life.

Once back in England, Appiah took up her painting again, but with less fervor than before, for she was beginning to feel a new calling. Joining a church council, she became involved with youth matters of the World Council of Churches and soon went to work for an organization known as Racial Unity, whose purpose was to create harmony between the races. By 1952 she had become secretary of Racial Unity and it was also that year that she met her future husband, Joe E. Appiah, a law student from Ghana. One year later the couple married, causing shock in some corners. At the time, interracial marriage—especially one involving the daughter of Sir Stafford Cripps—was not a commonplace event. Her family, however, was supportive: By this time Appiah's father had died, but her mother was there to give her away at the ceremony at St. John's Wood Church in London.

Once Joe Appiah had finished his studies in England, the couple set up home in Kumasi, Ghana, in the ancient west coast region of Ashanti, rich in culture and tradition. There were two children within three years, and Appiah was a busy mother while her husband got on with his legal profession. But these were also turbulent times for Ghana, and Appiah's husband was caught between the power of an old friend, Kwame Nkrumah, and that of an Ashanti nationalist movement. The author, however, had little time for politics then, busy with her children and with learning about life in Kumasi, its customs and costumes. Soon the family had grown to three children, and by 1961 to four. It was during these years that Appiah began collecting Ashanti stories, both fables and those that were associated with antique gold weights which she collected. The weights were made of brass, "in every possible shape from animals to guns, birds to insects, peanuts to people, sieves to spades," she once told *SATA*. "[They] were used for weighing the gold which was the main form of currency until the introduction of money. I started going to the villages to ask questions about them." The villagers obliged her by telling her the stories and fables that the figures represented.

Soon Appiah started to put these tales together into stories for her own children. She noticed the similarity of many of them to the fables of Aesop with which she had grown up. The stories talk about village and forest life, both themes close to her heart, as she had grown up in the country with a real love and appreciation for nature. Some of the characters were reminiscent of those of Appiah's childhood; for example the trickster spider, Kwaku Ananse, committed antics similar to those of Brer Rabbit. From telling the stories to her own children, Appiah soon started writing them down. She had been writing poetry all through the years, but now began to concentrate on these Ashanti tales. "It was undoubtedly the [lack of] children's books and reading aloud that started me on my own career as a writer of books for children," she recalled in her *SAAS* essay. "I

Appiah, who has lived in Ghana for many years, combined local folklore with stories from her own childhood to create this 1966 collection. (Cover illustration by Peggy Wilson.)

realised early that there were few books for children with a local background, and not many children were lucky enough in town to have elders in the family who told them the folktales."

Meanwhile the political turmoil in Ghana continued. Appiah's husband went to prison for the first time in 1961, and was released a year later. Over the next eighteen years, he would be in and out of custody as well as in and out of governmental positions several times as new power brokers took over the government. Appiah's children were educated mainly in England, and she spent large blocks of time at a house they had purchased in Brighton. Appiah's mother helped to raise the children as they came to boarding schools in England. Appiah, meanwhile, continued to write.

Appiah's first published book was *Ananse the Spider: Tales from an Ashanti Village.* Appiah incorporated many of the tales the local villagers had told her about the spider being successful in his tricks or outwitted by other, more clever animals. In the work, the main character was "caught in a home-spun web" by Appiah, *Kirkus Reviews* concluded. Appiah continued her folktales with *Tales of an Ashanti Father,* a compilation of twenty-two stories of mostly animal doings. She again uses Kwaku Ananse, but also incorporates lizards and tortoises. Several of the tales are reminiscent of Western stories: "The Tortoise and the Hare" is similar to the Aesop tale of the same name and "Why the Lizard Stretches His Neck" reminded a reviewer in *Publishers Weekly* of a Rudyard Kipling story. "The tales move quickly in this sparkling, varied collection," the reviewer commented. The story is "admirably spare in the telling yet also colorful," *Horn Book* concluded.

Appiah continued her series of Ashanti folktales with *The Children of Ananse* and *The Pineapple Child and Other Tales from Ashanti,* the latter of which is "justifiably labelled a 'Children's Classic,'" according to a reviewer in *Growing Point.* In this collection, Appiah again focusses on animal fables which give explanations for a multitude of natural phenomena, and on simple stories of village folk which illuminate the complexity of human beings. Greed, death, the reason for rain—these and a myriad more motifs are incorporated into Appiah's folktales "richly suggesting the atmosphere of community life in Ghana," according to *Growing Point.*

"To write stories for children," Appiah explained in *SAAS,* "one has to be very conscious of one's surroundings. The folktales really bring the animals alive and you learn the different characteristics and what they stand for. The little royal antelope is king of the beasts. The tortoise is the wise man, the dog rather a fool. The cat is unlucky to some areas as is the owl. The elephant is a big fool."

The next several books were something of a departure for Appiah. She wrote two school readers based on Ashanti fables with comprehension questions included, and then with *Gift of the Mmoatia* she developed a full novel in which two little girls, one British and the other

Ghanaian, make friends and share adventures. The Mmoatia of the title are the magical little people of Ghana, similar to elves in other cultures. With *Why There Are So Many Roads,* Appiah returned to the more traditional rendering of folktales and the book was again intended as a student reader.

Appiah's *Ring of Gold* is another departure from the folktale theme. "A good, old-fashioned children's book," Rosemary Stones, writing in *Times Literary Supplement,* called the work. The story of two town cousins, Abena and Kwame, visiting their country cousins, Adwoa and Kabwena, *Ring of Gold* tells about the difficult task of setting up a library in a small town. The discovery of a gold ring helps the children in their money-making schemes, as do the efforts of a couple in England, and in the end the little village gets not only a library, but also a museum. Appiah contrasts city and country throughout her book and interweaves local lore in the story. "Much background knowledge about the country can be acquired" from the work, noted a *Junior Bookshelf* writer. A *Growing Point* contributor found it to be "a leisurely, good-hearted story of an Ashanti village."

"I find writing stories something like life in a village," Appiah explained to *SATA.* "There are not too many people at a time and one can keep track of their movements. I usually start my story with some incident which strikes me; then the people take over, as they do in real life. Sometimes they don't do at all what I expect. I find it difficult to cut down on the incidents and in deciding which to keep. Just as in real life one's characters are doing things all the time and you have to pick out the relevant actions. I'm always being told 'keep to the story.' But stories in life don't have a beginning and an end!" Appiah wrote two novels for adults in the 1970s, as well as compiling her own poetry with that of her son, Anthony. A further installment in her Ashanti tales is *Why the Hyena Does Not Care for Fish and Other Tales from the Ashanti Gold Weights.* With these stories, Appiah uses the figures represented in her collection of brass gold weights to tell traditional fables. "This is a book to intrigue scholars and the general reader alike," noted *Growing Point.* "Her style is simple and uncluttered, always lively and reads well aloud," commented a reviewer in *Times Literary Supplement.*

More recently, Appiah has been writing short children's books with African settings in simple English for publication in Africa. With the death of her husband in 1990, Appiah has spent more time traveling in England and in Africa, but has continued her studies of Ashanti lore and her love of story-telling. "Ghana is good for writing because one never knows what is going to happen from day to day," she once told *SATA.* "The unexpected is always turning up and life sometimes takes on the quality of a grown-up fairy story. I have always loved fairy stories and folk tales, so I'm never surprised by events. One learns to laugh with people over all sorts of things, even if one should not, and to enjoy even what is sad because it is shared with other

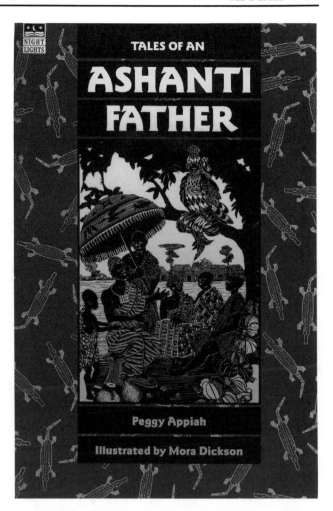

Readers can learn about animal characters ranging from lizards to leopards in these ancient West African tales. (Cover illustration by Mora Dickson.)

people. The main pleasure in life is sharing things with people and that is why I enjoy writing."

■ Works Cited

Review of *Ananse the Spider: Tales from an Ashanti Village, Kirkus Reviews,* October, 1, 1966, p. 1050.

Appiah, Peggy, essay in *Something about the Author Autobiography Series,* Volume 19, Gale, 1995, pp. 53-112.

Mitchison, Naomi, "Appiah, Peggy," *Twentieth-Century Children's Writers,* 4th ed., St. James Press, 1995.

Review of *The Pineapple Child and Other Tales from Ashanti, Growing Point,* July, 1989, pp. 5178-5182.

Review of *Ring of Gold, Growing Point,* March, 1977, p. 3059.

Review of *Ring of Gold, Junior Bookshelf,* October, 1977, p. 295.

Stones, Rosemary, review of *Ring of Gold, Times Literary Supplement,* December 10, 1976, p. 1554.

Review of *Tales of an Ashanti Father, Horn Book,* August, 1981, p. 441.

Review of *Tales of an Ashanti Father, Publishers Weekly,* January 13, 1989, p. 91.

Review of *Why the Hyena Does Not Care for Fish and Other Tales from the Ashanti Gold Weights, Growing Point,* November, 1977, p. 3204.
Review of *Why the Hyena Does Not Care for Fish and Other Tales from the Ashanti Gold Weights, Times Literary Supplement,* December 2, 1977, p. 1410.

■ **For More Information See**

PERIODICALS

Booklist, June 1, 1981, p. 1296.
Books, April, 1989, p. 12.
Junior Bookshelf, April, 1978, p. 84.

New York Times Book Review, November 6, 1966, p. 48.
School Library Journal, January, 1982, p. 58.
Times Educational Supplement, November 18, 1977, p. 31; July 15, 1983, p. 18; March 27, 1987, p. 26; July 24, 1987, p. 23.
Times Literary Supplement, October 16, 1969, p. 1193.

—*Sketch by J. Sydney Jones*

*   *   *

AUSTIN, R. G.
See GELMAN, Rita Golden

B

BACON, R(onald) L(eonard) 1924-

■ Personal

Born in 1924 in Melbourne, Australia.

■ Addresses

Home—3/5a McIntyre Rd., Mangere Bridge, Auckland, New Zealand.

■ Career

Teacher and writer. Favona Primary School, Auckland, New Zealand, principal.

■ Awards, Honors

Russell Clark Award, New Zealand Library Association, 1978, for *The House of the People;* New Zealand Picture Story Book of the Year Award, for *The Fish of Our Fathers.*

■ Writings

FICTION AND FOLKTALES FOR CHILDREN

The Boy and the Taniwha, illustrated by Para Matchitt, Collins, 1966, International Publications Service, 1976.
Rua and the Sea People, illustrated by Matchitt, Collins, 1968, International Publications Service, 1976.
Again the Bugles Blow, illustrated by V. J. Livingston, Collins, 1973, International Publications Service, 1973.
The House of the People (Maori legend), illustrated by Robert Jahnke, Collins, 1977.
Hatupatu and the Bird Woman (Maori legend), illustrated by Stanley J. Woods, Collins, 1979.
The Fish of Our Fathers (Maori legend), illustrated by Jahnke, Waiatarua, 1984.
Creation Stories, illustrated by Jahnke, Shortland, 1984.
Maui Stories, illustrated by Cliff Whiting, Shortland, 1984.

Maori Legends: Seven Stories, illustrated by Philippa Stitchbury, Shortland, 1984.
The Home of the Winds (Maori legend), illustrated by Jahnke, Waiatarua, 1985.
Hemi Dances, illustrated by Sandra O'Callaghan, Waiatarua, 1985.
Hotu-Puku, illustrated by Frank Bates, Waiatarua, 1985.
Little Pukeko and the Tiki, illustrated by Bates, Waiatarua, 1985.
Maui and Kuri, illustrated by Bates, Waiatarua, 1985.
Ruru and the Green Fairies, illustrated by Bates, Waiatarua, 1985.
A Legend of Kiwi, illustrated by Steven Dickinson, Waiatarua, 1987.
Hemi and the Whale, illustrated by O'Callaghan, Waiatarua, 1988.
The Bone Tree, illustrated by Mark Wilson, SRA, 1994.

Also author of the children's books, *The Green Fish of Ngahui,* 1989; *The Banjo Man,* illustrated by Kelvin Hawley, 1990; *The Clay Boy,* illustrated by Chris Gaskin, 1990; *A Mouse Singing in the Reeds,* 1990; and *Three Surprises for Hemi,* 1990.

READERS FOR CHILDREN

Wind, illustrated by Philippa Stitchbury, Ashton, 1984.
The Bay, illustrated by Sandra Morris, Ashton, 1986.
Jessie's Flower, illustrated by Liz Dodson, Shortland, 1986.
The Greatest, illustrated by Bryan Pollard and Margaret McGrath, Shortland, 1987.
Let's Make Music, illustrated by Deirdre Gardiner, Shortland, 1987.
In My Bed, illustrated by Morris, Shortland, 1988.
In My Room, illustrated by Glenda Jones, Shortland, 1988.
Just Me, illustrated by Kelvin Hawley, Shortland, 1988.
Off to Work, illustrated by Hawley, Shortland, 1988.
Our Dog Sam, illustrated by Helen Funnell, Shortland, 1988.
Save Our Earth, illustrated by Rodney McRae, Shortland, 1988.

The House of the People

BACON & JAHNKE

R. L. Bacon received the Russell Clark Award for this Maori tale about the building of a new meeting house. (Cover illustration by Robert Jahnke.)

The Scarecrow, illustrated by Isabel Lowe, Shortland, 1988.

Weaving, illustrated by Heidi Fegan, Shortland, 1988.

Grandma's Bicycle, illustrated by Philip Webb, Shortland, 1988.

NONFICTION FOR CHILDREN

Codes and Messages, Shortland, 1987.

Games and Their Past, illustrated by Ian McNee and Rachel Jones, Shortland, 1987.

(With Carol Hosking) *Rainy Day Ideas!,* illustrated by Jones, Shortland, 1987.

Weaving, illustrated by Fegan, Shortland, 1988.

FOR ADULTS

In the Sticks (novel), illustrated by David More, Collins, 1963.

Along the Road (novel), illustrated by More, Collins, 1964.

Auckland: Gateway to New Zealand, photographs by Gregory Riethmaier, Collins, 1968.

Auckland: Town and Around, photographs by Riethmaier, Collins, 1973.

Publishing a Book, photographs by Richard Redgrove, Shortland, 1987.*

BARBASH, Shepard 1957-

■ Personal

Born December 6, 1957, in New York, NY; son of Maurice (a developer) and Lillian (an arts administrator; maiden name, Like) Barbash; married Vicki Ragan (a photographer), May 25, 1986; children: Edwin. *Education:* Harvard University, B.A., 1981; attended Indiana University of Music. *Politics:* Independent. *Religion:* Jewish.

■ Addresses

Home—1732 Meadowdale Ave., Atlanta, GA 30306.

■ Career

Patriot Ledger, Quincy, MA, correspondent for music and film reviews, 1981-82; Associated Press, New York City, statistical worker-newsman, 1982-83; the *Hudson Dispatch,* Union City, NJ, court and county politics reporter, 1983-84; the *Advocate,* Stamford, CT, business reporter and real estate columnist; *Houston Chronicle,* Houston, TX, bureau chief for Mexico and Central America, 1987-88. Stringer, freelance writer for *Barron's,* AP-Dow Jones, *Newsday, American Banker, Euromoney's Latin Finance* magazine, 1986-89; stringer for the *New York Times,* covering real estate, 1992—.

■ Awards, Honors

National Journalism Award, American Newspaper Publishers Association, First Prize for Best Sports Story, 1975; First Prize for architecture writing, American Institute of Architects, Connecticut Chapter, 1984.

■ Writings

Oaxacan Woodcarving: The Magic in the Trees, photographs by wife, Vicki Ragan, Chronicle Books, 1993.

■ Work in Progress

A book of limericks A to Z for his wife's project, *The Eatable Alphabet Album;* a book on the Atlanta Project, Jimmy Carter's anti-poverty crusade.

■ Sidelights

Shepard Barbash told *SATA:* "I became a writer because my sisters scared me away from the sciences as a boy and because I knew I would never make it as a classical pianist. Following a happy and conventional childhood on the south shore of Long Island, I attended Harvard University and graduated in 1981 with a B.A. in history and science. After my sophomore year, I took a year off to study piano at the Indiana University of Music. Music remains my first love to this day: I still play piano, and over the years have sung in choruses and small a capella groups wherever I've lived.

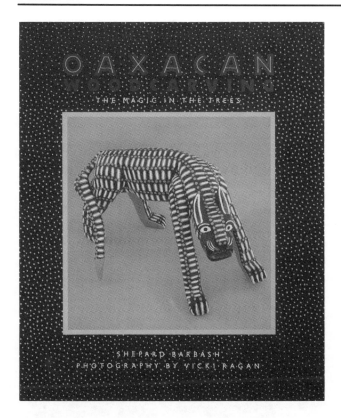

Shepard Barbash spent two years in the Oaxaca valley in Mexico chronicling the lives and works of its celebrated folk artists.

"I write nonfiction exclusively, and have never tried so much as a short story. I was in journalism for seven years until 1989, when my wife and I began work full-time on our book about the wood-carvers of Oaxaca (pronounced 'wa-*hah*-ka')."

"Nothing beats newspaper work for variety. My first job was as a dictationist taking down baseball stories over the phone for the Associated Press in New York City. My last job was as a correspondent in Mexico City for *Euromoney's Latin Finance* magazine. In between, I covered the county courts and Hackensack Meadowlands for the *Hudson Dispatch* in Union City, New Jersey. I wrote real estate columns and analyses of Fortune 500 Companies as a business reporter for the *Stamford Advocate* in Connecticut. I went to Mexico and worked for Pete Hamill at the *Mexico City News,* then freelanced for *Barron's,* the *Wall Street Journal, American Banker,* and *Newsday.* I covered Mexico and Central America as bureau chief for the *Houston Chronicle* in Mexico City.

"In New Jersey, I wrote about billion-dollar cocaine busts and giveaways of elephant manure. In Stamford, I deciphered quarterly earnings reports by day and covered the National Hockey League playoffs by night. In Mexico, I wrote about fraudulent elections and folk art, bus crashes and hurricanes, presidential summit meetings and multilateral debt renegotiations, con artists and kidnapped babies. I sneaked an interview in prison with the wife of a wanted Klansman. I met shrimp farmers

and cowboys in Panama; learned Spanish from peasants and economists; caught German measles in Veracruz and chicken pox in Honduras. I had the time of my life.

"Ultimately, though, I tired of the daily grind of journalism—what Russell Baker has called 'the eight-hundred-word mind'—and of living in Mexico City, the most polluted place on earth, and of putting up with the insensate demands of well-meaning editors (I never did last longer than fifteen months at any one newspaper). Hence our decision to move to Oaxaca and do the book. (We also feared for the health of our newborn son.)

"My wife, Vicki Ragan, did the photos for the book—more than one hundred of them. Without her, it would not have been published." The book includes brief biographies of some of the carvers, facts about their way of life and about the Mexican countryside. Jane Van Wiemokly, reviewing for *Voice of Youth Advocates,* called it a "fascinating look at a little discussed folk art."

Barash reported to *SATA:* "I have won only one award, barely worth mentioning: a piece for the *Advocate* on an innovative greenhouse won first prize for architecture reporting. The competition was sponsored by the Connecticut chapter of the American Institute of Architects, and I doubt there were more than a handful of entries. I don't put much stock in awards. The two accomplishments of which I am most proud never won me anything. The first was a series of investigative stories I wrote which helped send a small-fry Mafioso cop to prison for burning down his go-go bar in New Jersey. (I was a cub reporter at the time, while my subject, Carmine Balzano, had been indicted and acquitted seven times previously on other charges, including murder.) The second was my reporting as a foreign correspondent in Mexico. Among other things, I predicted—more accurately than any of my peers—the economic and political consequences of that country's presidential elections.

"By far the most interesting thing I have done professionally is the two years of research living among the peasant carvers of the Oaxaca valley. The experience has made it impossible for me to return to daily journalism. Indeed I have lasted more than twice as long with this one project as I ever did at any newspaper. At this point, I intend to spend the rest of my professional life writing books."

■ Works Cited

Van Wiemokly, Jane, review of *Oaxacan Woodcarving: The Magic in the Trees, Voice of Youth Advocates,* October, 1993, p. 238.

■ For More Information See

PERIODICALS

Bloomsbury Review, November, 1993, p. 18.
Bookwatch, July, 1993, p. 10.
Los Angeles Times Book Review, May 9, 1993, p. 13.
Publishers Weekly, May 24, 1993, p. 83.

Wilson Library Bulletin, June, 1994, p. 34.*

* * *

BARNET, Nancy 1954-

■ Personal

Born October 7, 1954, in Santa Monica, CA; daughter of Ronald P. (a financial manager) and Wanda (an artist; maiden name, Blakeley) Stolee; married Brian James Barnet (a law enforcement officer), May 5, 1973; children: Kathlene, Kristen. *Education:* California State University at Sacramento, B.A., 1985. *Politics:* Republican. *Religion:* Christian. *Hobbies and other interests:* Reading, computers.

■ Addresses

Home and office—Elk Grove, CA.

■ Career

Illustrator, 1986—. Member of Elk Grove Chamber of Commerce, 1987-90. *Member:* Society of Children's Books Writers and Illustrators, Colored Pencil Society of America (charter member), Graphic Artists' Guild, Sacramento Illustrators Guild (president, 1991).

■ Awards, Honors

Artist's Magazine art competition, honors, 1991, 1993.

■ Illustrator

Helen V. Griffith, *Dream Meadow*, Greenwillow, 1994.
Caron Lee Cohen, *Where's the Fly?*, Greenwillow, 1996.
Sarah Tatler, *The Beach*, ScottForesman, 1996.

Illustrations have appeared in *California Journal, Calliope Magazine, Healing Journal, Home Life Magazine, Los Angeles Times, Prevention Magazine, Signs of the Times Magazine*, and others.

■ Sidelights

Nancy Barnet told *SATA:* "Being the daughter of an artist can be inspiring. I remember being fascinated by the colors and textures of oil paints on a palette. When I was five years old, I got up *very* early one morning to add a few of my own touches to one of my mother's works-in-progress. I couldn't understand why she was so upset. My subsequent punishment didn't deter me from my next masterpiece—a large whale done in indelible red lipstick on my bedroom carpet.

"I must say the most enduring parts of my education *to this day* were the weekly trips to the school library my classes made during my elementary school years. Mrs. Orbach, our school librarian, tantalized us by reading short books in whole or longer works in part and opened doors to so many avenues of exploration I could hardly read fast enough. I became a voracious reader, a

NANCY BARNET

wonderful habit that remains with me. All of those early years reading the stories, pouring over the illustrations prepared me for future possibilities. The dream of writing and drawing for young people stayed in my heart even when I thought I wanted to be an astronaut, fashion merchandiser, or journalist.

"And now I am a professional illustrator. It's a challenging job full of deadlines, surprises, and satisfaction. I wouldn't trade these possibilities for anything."

* * *

BARRETT, Jennifer
See PLECAS, Jennifer

* * *

BARRETT, Tracy 1955-

■ Personal

Born March 1, 1955, in Cleveland, OH; daughter of Richard Sears (a psychologist) and Shirley Irene (a teacher; maiden name, Peters) Barrett; married Gregory Giles (a telephone interconnect owner), November, 1983; children: Laura Beth, Patrick. *Education:* Attended Intercollegiate Center for Classical Studies, Rome, Italy, 1974-75; Brown University, A.B. (in Classics), 1976; University of California, Berkeley, Ph.D. (Italian and French), 1988. *Politics:* Democrat.

TRACY BARRETT

■ Addresses

Home and office—2802 Acklen Ave., Nashville, TN 37212.

■ Career

Vanderbilt University, Nashville, TN, lecturer in Italian, 1984—. *Member:* National Women's Book Association, Society of Children's Book Writers and Illustrators, Tennessee Writer's Alliance.

■ Writings

NONFICTION FOR CHILDREN

Nat Turner and the Slave Revolt, Millbrook Press, 1993.
Harpers Ferry: The Story of John Brown's Raid, Millbrook Press, 1994.
Growing Up in Colonial America, Millbrook Press, in press.

OTHER

(Translator and author of introduction) *Cecco, as I Am and Was: The Poems of Cecco Angiolieri,* International Pocket Library, 1994.

Also author of five children's stories for the educational series "Reading Works," 1975. Editorial assistant, *Ro-*

mance Philology, 1978-79, and *Kidney International,* 1984.

■ Work in Progress

First Day, a book for children.

■ Sidelights

Tracy Barrett told *SATA:* "I teach Italian language at a university and am the author of several scholarly articles on Italian literature as well as a forthcoming book of translations into English of a medieval Italian poet. I started writing for children in 1992 when I began feeling that my teaching was getting repetitious and I needed to branch out into different areas. As a child, I had always said I would be a writer when I grew up, but this ambition got lost in the shuffle of graduate school, marriage, and family. Perhaps because of my academic background, I am more drawn to nonfiction than to fiction when writing for children. I enjoy researching complicated and sometimes confusing events and organizing them into coherent and exciting narratives."

Barrett's efforts have resulted in two books about important events in American history. *Nat Turner and the Slave Revolt,* published as part of the "Gateway Civil Rights" series, tells the story of an African American slave and preacher who came to believe that God wanted him to free the slaves. Based on his visions, Turner led a group of slaves in a bloody revolt that took the lives of over 260 people. The book begins with

Barrett stresses accuracy and a balanced perspective when covering historical topics such as Nat Turner, the preacher and slave who led a famous revolt in 1831.

Turner's court conviction in 1831, traces his upbringing and education, and concludes with the famous revolt. In a review for *Booklist,* Janice Del Negro praised Barrett's objectivity, stating that she "attempts to place the event in its historical context in a concise, noninflammatory text." Betsy Hearne, writing in the *Bulletin of the Center for Children's Books,* however, claimed that the book could have benefitted from more background on the history of slavery. Hearne noted that Barrett's emphasis on the details of the slave revolt—compared to her generalizations about slave owners' cruelty—"makes Turner seem less a leader than a madman."

Barrett's next book was *Harpers Ferry: The Story of John Brown's Raid,* published as part of the "Spotlight on American History" series. The book profiles John Brown, an abolitionist who took weapons during a raid on the United States arsenal at Harpers Ferry, West Virginia, in 1859. Reviewing several books in the series for *School Library Journal,* George Gleason noted that they "cover their subjects well and occasionally include unusual tidbits of information."

Barrett shared her thoughts on writing nonfiction for children with *SATA:* "When writing nonfiction, an author must pay scrupulous attention to accuracy and must present a balanced view. Children are interested in the truth and are willing to think about quite 'adult' issues if they are presented in a way accessible to them. This does not mean talking down to children; it means keeping in mind their more limited exposure to ideas and helping them learn how to formulate their own ideas and opinions."

■ Works Cited

Del Negro, Janice, review of *Nat Turner and the Slave Revolt, Booklist,* August, 1993, pp. 2051-52.
Gleason, George, review of *Harpers Ferry: The Story of John Brown's Raid, School Library Journal,* January, 1994, p. 118.
Hearne, Betsy, review of *Nat Turner and the Slave Revolt, Bulletin of the Center for Children's Books,* April, 1993, p. 240.

■ For More Information See

PERIODICALS
Horn Book Guide, spring 1994, pp. 156, 169.

*   *   *

BARRON, Rex 1951-

■ Personal

Born December 11, 1951, in New Brunswick, NJ; son of Lloyd Eugene (a chemist and sales manager) and Lillian (a homemaker; maiden name, Benestad) Barron. *Education:* University of California at Los Angeles, B.A. (cum laude), 1975; attended Art Center College of Design, 1976-78. *Hobbies and other interests:* Folk guitar and classical music, attending figure drawing workshops.

REX BARRON

■ Addresses

Home and office—6349 Admiral Rickover NE, Albuquerque, NM 87111. *Agent*—Alice Martell, 555 Fifth Ave., Suite 1900, New York, NY 10017.

■ Career

Illustrator. Animator and background/layout artist for animation studios including Hanna-Barbera, Ralph Bakshi Productions, and Filmation Studio, Los Angeles, CA, for film and television productions including *The Lord of the Rings, Starchaser, Fat Albert and the Cosby Kids,* and *The Pink Panther,* 1979-89.

■ Illustrator

Tom Ross, *Eggbert, the Slightly Cracked Egg,* Putnam, 1994.
Dee Lillegard, *The Day the Daisies Danced,* Putnam, 1996.

■ Work in Progress

Illustrating Tom Ross's *Irma, the Flying Bowling Ball,* for Putnam.

■ Sidelights

Rex Barron told *SATA:* "An active fantasy world has always seemed essential to me. As an artist, the ability to create a fictional plane of existence compelling and consistent enough to encourage a complete suspension of disbelief is for me the ultimate goal, whether it be in painting, writing, film, or music. My childhood sensibilities were definitely shaped by pop media, including comic books, while my awareness of 'highbrow' art came from classical music, to which I fortunately had an early introduction as a boy soprano. This included bit parts in opera productions in New York.

"My inclination toward drawing was encouraged by my parents, and I remember my mother giving me a Dover book of old master drawings when I was about eleven. To this day, I attend life drawing workshops every week, a practice I recommend to all aspiring artists and illustrators. It was in just such a group that I received a tip that led to my first job in animation."

Barron also revealed that the "things that continue to give me fulfillment and inspiration are: twentieth-century symphonies, well-crafted and deeply felt figurative paintings (from the Renaissance to the present), and cheapo sci-fi and epic films from the fifties and sixties. The writings of Carl Jung and Joseph Campbell also hover in the margins of my thought."

*   *   *

BELLER, Susan Provost 1949-

■ Personal

Born April 7, 1949, in Burlington, VT; daughter of Edward Roland (a machinist) and Lauretta (a nurse; maiden name, Lamothe) Provost; married W. Michael Beller (a program manager), December 18, 1970; children: Michael, Jennifer, Sean. *Education:* Catholic University of America, B.A., 1970; attended University of Maryland School of Library and Information Sciences, 1973-74; University of Vermont, M.Ed., 1990. *Politics:*

SUSAN PROVOST BELLER

Independent. *Religion:* Catholic. *Hobbies and other interests:* Reading, travel to historic places.

■ Addresses

Home and office—R.R. 1, Box 1128A, Charlotte, VT 05445. *E-mail*—Kidsbks@aol.com.

■ Career

Fairfax City Adult Education, Fairfax, VA, genealogy instructor, 1980-82; Christ the King School, Burlington, VT, librarian, 1982-86; Bristol Elementary School, Bristol, VT, librarian, 1986-93; full-time writer, 1993—. Has also worked as an instructor at the University of Vermont; created and conducts a hands-on history program for schools; member of teachers' advisory board, Shelburne Museum and Vermont Folklife Center. *Member:* Society of Children's Book Writers and Illustrators.

■ Writings

Roots for Kids: A Genealogy Guide for Young People, Betterway, 1989.
Cadets at War: The True Story of Teenage Heroism at the Battle of New Market, Shoe Tree Press/Betterway, 1991.
Woman of Independence: The Life of Abigail Adams, Shoe Tree Press/Betterway, 1992.
Mosby and His Rangers: Adventures of the Gray Ghost, Shoe Tree Press/Betterway, 1992.
Medical Practices in the Civil War, Shoe Tree Press/ Betterway, 1992.
To Hold This Ground: A Desperate Battle at Gettysburg, Margaret K. McElderry Books, 1995.

■ Work in Progress

Confederate Ladies: Life in Richmond during the Civil War; Hannah's Story, a fictional account of medicine during the Civil War.

■ Sidelights

"I consider myself to be mostly a 'teller of stories,'" Susan Provost Beller told *SATA,* "and I find the true stories from the adventure of history to be the ones I most enjoy telling. I have always been a reader of history. I especially loved to read biographies during my childhood. As an adult, I began reading more of the primary source material of history—diaries and letters and reminiscences by people who were actually involved in a historical event. The stories I found in this reading, especially the ones from the Civil War, were fascinating and much too interesting to be left to just adult readers. So I became a writer of history, in addition to being a reader of it. All I try to do is to take my favorite stories from history and share them with younger readers, using the words of the people who were really there as much as possible.

"I began as a genealogist, finding my own stories from history and helping others find theirs. I started doing genealogical research when my son Michael was born. By the time Jennie was born three years later, everyone in both families knew that I was interested in 'old stuff,' and I was offered a ninety-five-year-old christening dress for her to wear that had been worn by my great-grandmother. After my son Sean was born, we moved to Maryland and all three of the kids became used to picnics in cemeteries as we traced my husband's roots in the West Virginia panhandle area.

"By 1980 I was teaching an advanced genealogy course in Virginia, where we lived at the time. My son Michael 'volunteered' me to come to a career day at his school to explain what a genealogist does. That led to an invitation to help his class work on their family trees. I found myself adapting material that I used with adults into a format suitable for younger researchers. Over the next several years, now working as a school librarian in Vermont, I was offering a twelve-week enrichment course in genealogy for middle-school students.

"While working on my master's degree, I took a children's literature course which required me to complete an original project. I contracted to organize and develop my genealogy materials into a book for children. The book begun in that class became *Roots for Kids: A Genealogy Guide for Young People,* my first book. Being an author led to invitations to speak at schools and public libraries around Vermont.

"When I gave talks, there was a story I always told to convince kids that history was not boring (as they would often tell me). It was the story of the Virginia Military Institute cadets who fought in a Civil War battle in 1864. Nearly every time I told the story, someone would want to know where they could read more about this battle. But there were no books for young readers that ever mentioned this story. In fact, the books on history for young readers that I was seeing as a school librarian generally left out most of the great stories, and almost never included quotes from the people who were there at the time. I finally decided to write the story of the cadets and to write it as a real history, based on actual letters, reminiscences, and school files. That story served as the basis for my second book, *Cadets at War: The True Story of Teenage Heroism at the Battle of New Market.*"

About 250 young cadets were recruited to help bolster the numbers of the Confederate troops at New Market. Although nearly one-quarter of them were wounded and ten died, they played an important role in the battle and turned back the Union forces. The book also describes events that occurred before and after the battle, and includes a number of maps and photographs. In a review for *School Library Journal,* David A. Lindsey called *Cadets at War* "a fascinating, readable account," and said that Beller's use of historical letters "helps readers understand the feelings, motivations, and experiences" of the cadets.

As Beller told *SATA,* "The next story I wanted to tell had nothing to do with the Civil War. I had always been fascinated with the life of Abigail Adams, and over the years I had collected every book that was written about her. I wanted to tell her story, using her own wonderful letters to speak for her." The result was *Woman of Independence: The Life of Abigail Adams,* published in 1992. The book includes eighteen chapters, each of which profiles Adams in one of her many roles, including wife, mother, patriot, historian, and first lady. In addition to providing a vivid picture of Adams, Beller also "paints the hardships and joys of an emerging nation," according to Valerie Childress in *School Library Journal.* "This was a fun project for me," Beller commented, "and the best moment came when I was given a special tour of her home by the curator of the Adams Historic Site. She let me go beyond the ropes into the places usually closed to the public. For me to walk where Abigail had walked and to see her cherished belongings up close was a magical moment.

Based on first-hand accounts, Beller's study of the teenage cadets who fought in the Civil War is among the few books for young people on this subject.

"Civil War stories kept calling me back," Beller continued, "and my next two books were about that fascinating period in our history. Talking about medicine during the Civil War always intrigued my listeners, so I just had to tell that story! Using the photographs and memoirs of Union and Confederate doctors and nurses, I wrote *Medical Practices in the Civil War,* which seems to be the book that audiences most want to talk about when I visit schools. They love all the gory details and are fascinated by the lack of medical knowledge at the time." In a review for *Kliatt,* Sherri Forgash Ginsberg said the book is "packed with fascinating information" about wounds and diseases, surgery and anesthesia, the first female doctors, and the deplorable conditions found in army camps at the time. Beller also explains how improvements in medical treatment and the design of military hospitals made during the Civil War influenced the future of medicine in the United States. The book was selected as recommended reading by A&E's *Civil War Journal* and by the National Museum of Civil War Medicine.

"My next book, *Mosby and His Rangers: Adventures of the Gray Ghost*—the story of the famous Confederate guerrilla fighter and his men—captivates listeners and readers who want to know about the adventurous side of the Civil War," Beller told *SATA.* "The memoirs of these irregulars make great reading, so it was easy to tell their story from their own perspective." John S. Mosby was an unassuming man with a brilliant tactical mind who led a group of soldiers through two years of relentless assaults on Union targets. "All in all, the book is an interesting glimpse into this historic period," Cecilia P. Swanson concluded in a *Kliatt* review.

"My newest book, *To Hold This Ground: A Desperate Battle at Gettysburg,* gives me the chance to tell what I think is one of the most exciting stories of the entire Civil War," Beller continued. "Two colonels, Joshua Lawrence Chamberlain of Maine and William Calvin Oates of Alabama, fought against each other on the far end of the Union line on Little Round Top on July 2, 1863. In the middle of a much larger battle, their fight on this one hill gave each of them the chance to change the course of the Civil War. The two men went on to become governors of their states and to lead lives that paralleled each other in many respects.

"There are so many great stories from our history that have fascinated me, and I hope to be able to continue to share them with young readers. History, the real stories of real people, is the most fascinating adventure of them all!"

■ Works Cited

Childress, Valerie, review of *Woman of Independence: The Life of Abigail Adams, School Library Journal,* September, 1992.

Ginsberg, Sherri Forgash, review of *Medical Practices in the Civil War, Kliatt,* May, 1993, p. 31.

Lindsey, David A., review of *Cadets at War: The True Story of Teenage Heroism at the Battle of New Market, School Library Journal,* June, 1991.

Swanson, Cecilia P., review of *Mosby and His Rangers: Adventures of the Gray Ghost, Kliatt,* July, 1993, p. 34.

■ For More Information See

PERIODICALS

Booklist, May 15, 1992, p. 1671.
Bulletin of the Center for Children's Books, July 1991, p. 259.
Kliatt, September 1992, pp. 27-28.*

* * *

BENSON, Linda M(aria) 1959-

■ Personal

Born August 6, 1959, in Orange, NJ; married Ron Logan (a teacher and artist), June 18, 1989. *Education:* Pratt Institute, B.F.A (cum laude), 1981; attended Columbia University, 1985, and the School of Visual Arts, 1991.

■ Addresses

Home—218 Lincoln Place, Brooklyn, NY 11217.

■ Career

Freelance illustrator, 1981—. School of Visual Arts, New York City, teacher of illustration, 1987—; Fashion Institute of Technology, New York City, teacher of illustration, 1993. Guest lecturer on illustration at Parsons School of Design, School of Visual Arts, Suffolk Community College, and Society of Illustrators. *Exhibitions:* Exhibitor in group shows at galleries in New York City, Japan, Greenwich, CT, and elsewhere; one-woman show in Brick, NJ, 1979.

■ Awards, Honors

Two Girls in Sister Dresses has been selected for the Children's Books of the Year List, Child Study Children's Book Committee, 1995.

■ Illustrator

Jean Van Leeuwen, *Two Girls in Sister Dresses,* Dial, 1994.

* * *

BENTLEY, Bill
See BENTLEY, William (George)

WILLIAM BENTLEY

BENTLEY, William (George) 1916-
(Bill Bentley)

■ Personal

Born September 17, 1916, in St. Louis, MO; son of George (a theatrical agent) and Genevieve (a home-maker) Bentley; married Lois Anita (died, 1993); children: Linda Jean Emilson, Elizabeth. *Education:* Central Washington University, M.Ed.; attended St. Louis University.

■ Addresses

Home—4724 Northwest Fourth St., Plantation, FL 33317.

■ Career

Teacher in Washington, Illinois, and Florida; served on the visiting faculty of universities in Florida, Alabama, Delaware, Georgia, and Tennessee, as well as the University National and the University of Costa Rica. Education consultant to countries in the Caribbean and Central America, the Peace Corps, and the Alabama State Department of Education. *Military service:* Participated in the invasion of Iwo Jima.

■ Awards, Honors

Four certificates of recognition, Broward County Schools, Florida, for outstanding teacher and meritorious service.

■ Writings

Learning to Move and Moving to Learn, Citation Press, 1970.
The Alligator Book: Sixty Questions and Answers, illustrated by Barbara Wolff, Walker, 1972.
(Under name Bill Bentley) *Ulysses S. Grant,* F. Watts, 1993.

Also author of *Indoor and Outdoor Games,* Fearon Publishing, and *Physical Education for Young Children,* Teaching Press; editor of *Action,* Spice Series. Contributor of articles to periodicals, including *Instructor, Early Years, Grade Teacher, My Weekly Reader, Ford Times, Athletic Journal,* and *Civil War Times.*

■ Work in Progress

A math book for teachers; Civil War vignettes.

■ Sidelights

William Bentley spent much of his career as a physical education teacher in several regions of the United States, and this experience led to his first few books of activities and games for children. He also taught at the college level and acted as an education consultant for Central American and Caribbean countries. Of his life outside of teaching, Bentley told *SATA:* "My father being a theatrical agent enabled me to meet many interesting people in my early years. While I became a career educator, I also had some interesting part-time pursuits along the way: sports publicity at St. Louis University, and at a racetrack one summer. I have also been a part-time scout for two major-league baseball teams. My military experience, including the invasion of Iwo Jima, gave me valuable equity in writing *Ulysses S. Grant.*"

Bentley's biography of Civil War General Ulysses S. Grant, published in 1993, covers his childhood, his education at West Point, and his family life. The book also details his impressive leadership on the battlefield during the Civil War, as well as some of the controversy that arose during his terms as president of the United States. Elizabeth M. Reardon, in a review for *School Library Journal,* said that *Ulysses S. Grant* includes "good anecdotes" and "fine-quality archival and full-color photographs, maps, and reproductions."

Reviews were somewhat less favorable for Bentley's 1972 work, *The Alligator Book: Sixty Questions and Answers.* Intended for beginning readers, it provides simple information about alligators in a question-and-answer format. The questions range from "How do the eggs hatch?" to "What should a person do if he sees an alligator?" In the *New York Times Book Review,* Georgess McHargue claimed that the book "suffers from serious errors and oversimplifications, perhaps partly as a result of its format." Julie Cummins, writing in *Library Journal,* however, stated that the format was "attractive" and made the book "more appealing" than comparable texts.

■ Works Cited

Cummins, Julie, review of *The Alligator Book: Sixty Questions and Answers, Library Journal,* July, 1973, p. 2190.

McHargue, Georgess, review of *The Alligator Book: Sixty Questions and Answers, New York Times Book Review,* May 27, 1973.

Reardon, Elizabeth M., review of *Ulysses S., Grant, School Library Journal,* February, 1994, p. 106.*

*   *   *

BONSALL, Crosby Barbara (Newell) 1921-1995
(Crosby Newell)

OBITUARY NOTICE—See index for *SATA* sketch: Born January 2, 1921, in Queens, NY; died following a stroke, January 10, 1995, in Boston, MA. Author and illustrator of children's books. During her writing career, Bonsall penned more than forty stories for youngsters. She began writing and illustrating for juvenile readers after working for advertising firms, sometimes writing under the name Crosby Newell. Among her early works are *The Surprise Party, Captain Kangaroo's Book,* and *Tell Me Some More.* Her later works include *The Goodbye Summer, Who's Afraid of the Dark?, The Case of the Double Cross,* and *The Amazing, the Incredible Super Dog.* She also collaborated with photographer Ylla on *I'll Show You Cats,* which was named a best illustrated children's book for 1964 by the *New York Times.*

OBITUARIES AND OTHER SOURCES:

BOOKS

The Writers Directory: 1994-1996, St. James Press, 1994, p. 125.

PERIODICALS

New York Times, January 20, 1995, p. B8.

*   *   *

BOSSE, Malcolm J(oseph) 1933-

■ Personal

Born May 6, 1933, in Detroit, MI; son of Malcolm Clifford (a stockbroker) and Thelma (Malone) Bosse; married Marie-Claude Aullas (a translator), July 4, 1969; children: Malcolm-Scott. *Education:* Yale University, B.A., 1950; University of Michigan, M.A., 1956; New York University, Ph.D., 1969. *Hobbies and other interests:* Tai-Chi Chuan, yoga, Oriental mythology, archaeology, myrmecology (the study of ants), Asian history, art (especially sculpture), music (especially jazz), watching football on television, classical ballet, Chinese cooking, jogging, swimming.

MALCOLM J. BOSSE

■ Addresses

Office—Department of English, City College of the City University of New York, New York, NY 10031.

■ Career

Barron's Financial Weekly, New York City, editorial writer, 1950-52; free-lance writer, 1957-66; novelist, 1959—; City College of the City University of New York, New York City, professor of English, 1969—. Lecturer in India, Bangladesh, Burma, Thailand, Malaysia, Singapore, Taiwan, China, Hong Kong, Japan, and Fiji Islands. *Military service:* U.S. Navy, 1950-54; received two Bronze Stars. Also served in U.S. Army and U.S. Merchant Marines. *Member:* PEN, Authors Guild, Authors League of America, Society of Eighteenth Century Studies and Scholars (England), Modern Language Association of America, Yale Club, Andiron Club, Fulbright-Hays Alumni Association, Henry James Associates, Phi Gamma Delta, Phi Beta Kappa.

■ Awards, Honors

Masefield Award, Yale University, 1949, for poetry and fiction; Avery and Jule Hopwood Awards, University of Michigan, 1956, for poetry and fiction; best novels of the year citation, *Saturday Review of Literature,* 1960, for *The Journey of Tao Kim Nam;* University Scholar Award, New York University, 1969; Newberry Library Fellowship, 1970; Edgar Allan Poe nominations, for best first mystery, 1974, for *The Incident at Naha,* and for best mystery of the year, 1975, for *The Man Who Loved Zoos;* certificate of merit, Society of the Dictionary of International Biography, 1976, for distinguished service to the community; National Endowment for the Arts creative writing fellowship, 1977-78; Fulbright-Hays lectureship grants for India, 1978 and 1979, and for Indonesia, 1987; Notable Book citation, American Library Association (ALA), 1979, best books of the year citation, Library of Congress, 1980, Dorothy Canfield Fisher Award nomination, 1981, Preis der Leseratten for best children's book of the year, German Television ZDF Schulerexpress, 1984, Dutch Children's Book Prize, 1984, Prix du livre pour la jeunesse de la fondation de France, 1986, and Prix Lecture-Jeunesse, 1987, all for *The Seventy-nine Squares;* special commendation from International Communication Agency, 1980, for work in India; Notable Book citation, ALA, 1981, notable book in the field of social studies citation, National Council of Social Studies Teachers, 1981, and Deutscher Jugendliteraturpreis nomination, 1984, all for *Cave beyond Time;* Notable Book citation, ALA, 1982, Honor List of Book Awards, Austrian Ministry of Education and Arts, 1982, Deutscher Jugendliteraturpreis, 1983, American Book Award nomination, Parent's Choice Award, Omar Award, and notable children's trade book in the field of social studies citation, all for *Ganesh;* Parent's Choice Award, 1994, for *The Examination.*

■ Writings

NOVELS FOR CHILDREN

The Seventy-nine Squares, Crowell, 1979.
Cave beyond Time, Crowell, 1980.
Ganesh, Crowell, 1981, published as *Ordinary Magic,* Farrar, Straus, 1993.
The Barracuda Gang, Dutton, 1982.
Captives of Time, Delacorte, 1987.
Deep Dream of the Rain Forest, Farrar, Straus, 1993.
The Examination, Farrar, Straus, 1994.

NOVELS FOR ADULTS

The Journey of Tao Kim Nam, Doubleday, 1959.
The Incident at Naha (mystery), Simon & Schuster, 1972.
The Man Who Loved Zoos (mystery), Putnam, 1974.
The Warlord, Simon & Schuster, 1983.
Fire in Heaven (sequel to *The Warlord*), Simon & Schuster, 1986.
Stranger at the Gate, Simon & Schuster, 1989.
Mister Touch, Ticknor & Fields, 1991.
The Vast Memory of Love, Ticknor & Fields, 1992.

OTHER

(Coeditor) *Foundations of the Novel,* Garland, 1974.
(Coeditor) *The Flowering of the Novel,* Garland, 1975.
(Coeditor) *The Novel in England: 1700-1775* (contains *Foundations of the Novel* and *The Flowering of the Novel*), Garland, 1977.

Coeditor of "Representative English Mid-Eighteenth Century Fiction, 1740-1775" series for Garland, 1975. Contributor of major critical essay to *Charles Johnstone's Chrysal: 1760-1765,* Garland Publishing. Member of advisory board, *Pequod* magazine. Also contribu-

tor of articles, short stories, and poems to periodicals, including *Literary Criterion, Remington Review, Voyages, California Quarterly, North American Review, Michigan Quarterly, Artesian, Massachusetts Review,* and *New York Times.* Work included in *Mississippi Valley Writers Collection.*

■ Adaptations

The Man Who Loved Zoos was made into a French film titled *Agent Trouble,* 1987.

■ Sidelights

Novelist Malcolm J. Bosse, perhaps best known for his adult bestseller *The Warlord,* "remains one of the most intriguingly versatile and skillful storytellers around," a *Publishers Weekly* reviewer states. Critics of children's literature have also noted this versatility, for Bosse has written young adult novels whose protagonists range from a modern gang member to a fourteenth-century female clockmaker to a tribesman in Borneo to a pair of brothers in sixteenth-century China. Whatever their subjects, however, Bosse's books benefit from his ability to make his settings and characters come alive, as well as his firsthand experience with many of the places he writes about.

Bosse was interested in writing from an early age and published his first poetry at age fifteen. He received little encouragement from his "decidedly nonliterary" family, however, as he told *Publishers Weekly* interviewer Robert Dahlin: "My father was a stockbroker, and my mother was a housewife," Bosse recalled. "They wanted me to become a doctor, but in a rebellious frame of mind, I dropped pre-med and went into American studies—sociology, economics, history." Bosse wrote his first novel, 1959's *The Journey of Tao Kim Nam,* while he was completing his master's degree at the University of Michigan; told from the viewpoint of a Vietnamese refugee, the book drew on the author's experiences in Asia while serving in the armed forces. His travels there inspired a lifelong interest in the Orient, one supplemented by frequent trips to lecture in places like India, China, Thailand, and Japan.

Bosse published just two novels—both acclaimed mysteries—in the twenty years following his first book, focusing instead on getting his doctorate and establishing his academic career. With the 1979 young adult novel *The Seventy-nine Squares,* however, the author began a period of prolific creativity, producing two novels every three years. In this award-winning book, fourteen-year-old Eric Fisher, a gang member on probation for vandalism, learns about life through his relationship with a dying ex-convict. Years earlier, Mr. Beck was convicted of killing his wife, and served forty years in prison. Because he is dying of cancer, the eighty-two-year-old Beck is released from prison to live out his few remaining months in his garden. Eric is unsure why he finds Mr. Beck fascinating, but he keeps returning to the old man's garden, visiting and studying each of the garden's seventy-nine squares according to the old

DEEP DREAM OF THE RAIN FOREST

MALCOLM BOSSE

A war orphan and two young tribespeople use their dreams to help them survive the rain forest in Bosse's 1993 adventure story. (Cover illustration by Tim Tanner.)

man's Zen-like instructions. In this way, Eric learns to "see."

Conflict arises when Eric's family and local townspeople learn of Beck's background and try to run him out of town, at the same time that Eric's old gang decides to reassert their hold on the boy. "The story is so compelling and the imagery so visual that the reader seems to see it all happening," Anne G. Toensmeier remarks in the *Interracial Books for Children Bulletin.* "This is only appropriate because the story is about learning to see." Other critics have similarly praised Bosse's portrait of friendship; *New York Times Book Review* contributor Jack Forman, for instance, calls the novel "a very moving, very private story." While *Bulletin of the Center for Children's Books* reviewer Zena Sutherland faults some passages as overlong, she nonetheless observes that "Bosse has some impressive things to say about understanding, forgiveness, and loyalty." *The Seventy-nine Squares,* concludes a *Publishers Weekly* critic, "is vivid, carefully plotted and a strong lesson in values."

For his second young-adult novel, Bosse wrote the coming of age story *Cave beyond Time.* With a "fascinating blend of fact and legend," observes Patricia Anne Reilly of *Best Sellers,* the author has created "a real winner." Ben, a disillusioned and bored fifteen-year-old orphan, is bitten by rattlesnakes during an archaeological dig in Arizona. While unconscious, he dreams he is a nomad and a hunter in a prehistoric tribe, where he battles wild animals and learns from various father figures. "The extraordinarily vivid re-creation of primitive life," comments Ann A. Flowers in *Horn Book,* makes "a strong, often touching novel filled with absorbing detail, head-long action, and echoes of the past."

Ganesh, another novel for young adults which was later published as *Ordinary Magic,* uses some of the insights Bosse gained as a lecturer in India for two years. "Ganesh," the name of the elephant-headed Hindu god of strength and wisdom, is the nickname of Jeffrey Moore, an American born and raised in India. His first fourteen years there are a happy and pleasant time, with such diversions as studying yoga and playing ball. Orphaned, he is sent to live with his understanding Aunt Betty in the American Midwest, where, because of his foreign mannerisms, he is not easily accepted by his peers. Jeffrey's place in the community, however, is secured when he uses the peaceful resistance theories of the *Satyagraha* to fight the government over a planned highway that would destroy Aunt Betty's home. "*Ganesh* is not a book to be read by children looking only for light entertainment," maintains Bryna J. Fireside of the *New York Times Book Review.* "It is, rather, a shining little jewel to be savored and treasured by those who already know the merits of fine literature." Praising Bosse's portrayal of a different culture, *Times Literary Supplement* writer Dominic Hibberd calls *Ganesh* "an absorbing book, written without frills," while Martha Cruse of the *Voice of Youth Advocates* applauds: "What a refreshing book!"

Bosse turned to historical fiction with *Captives of Time,* a novel for young adults set in medieval Europe. Anne and Niklas Valens are children who must travel across plague-ridden Europe to find their uncle after their parents are murdered. Together, Anne and her uncle create a design for a clock tower, a revolutionary invention. It is Anne's mission, after her uncle's death, to carry the plan to the city and help build the new clock. Everyone from the aristocracy to the working class has some stake in seeing the project fail, and Anne's unusual ability to read and figure lead some to believe she is a witch. Despite encountering danger and tragedy, Anne perseveres with her vision of the future.

In the *Los Angeles Times,* Carol Meyer praises Bosse's accurate portrayal of the brutality and cruelty of the Middle Ages as one that "never condescends, never simplifies for his young adult readers. Bosse's characters are emotionally contemporary but historically anchored in a detailed panorama of Medieval Europe." *New York Times Book Review* contributor Maureen Quilligan, however, finds that Anne's forward-looking attitude makes the book "so wildly anachronistic as to negate history." In contrast, Ruth M. McConnell of *School Library Journal* believes "readers will be grateful" for the historical detail Bosse provides, especially since "the crafting is so good and the writing so vivid." "Told with compelling conviction," Sutherland concludes in *Bulletin of the Center for Children's Books,* Bosse's novel "brings the past to life in a remarkably effective story."

Set on the Indonesian island of Borneo in the 1920s, *Deep Dream of the Rain Forest* is a similarly "ambitious adventure story," Betsy Hearne remarks in the *Bulletin of the Center for Children's Books.* The orphaned son of British colonials, Harry Windsor seeks adventure by accompanying his uncle on a trip inland; there he is kidnapped by Bayang, a young Iban tribesman who is searching for the meaning of a powerful dream with the assistance of the outcast woman Duck Foot. As the three learn they must cooperate to survive and discover the meaning of Bayang's dream, "the action is nonstop and compelling," Hearne observes. "For me the excitement lay as much in the setting" as in Bosse's plot, Sue Krumbein reveals in *Voice of Youth Advocates.* With the novel's description of survival in the rain forest, the critic continues, "the place comes alive, and it is interesting the way the author has developed both the setting and the plot to create a very satisfying story." This well-developed setting, along with Bosse's insight into his characters, "leave the reader feeling a bit breathless, and amazed," a *Parents' Choice* writer states. With its portrayal of people of a different time and culture, concludes Ellen Fader in *School Library Journal,* "this is a multilayered story that has many rewards."

Another historical work with a similarly vivid backdrop is *The Examination,* which takes place in China of the sixteenth century. Lao Chen is a young scholar who wishes to enter the civil service of the Ming Dynasty, and must travel across the country to Beijing in order to take the required tests. His younger brother, Lao Hong, decides to accompany his brother for the long and treacherous journey. The two brothers encounter many obstacles during their travels—including capture and torture by pirates—before reaching their destination. There Chen faces the final hurdle of taking his examination, the result of which will affect both brothers' lives. The novel "excels as both fiction and history," a *Publishers Weekly* reviewer writes, for "Bosse memorably conveys the workings of a culture ... and his detailed descriptions ... have a visceral impact." As a *Kirkus Reviews* critic similarly concludes: "Bosse renders a graphic picture of 16th-century China—its violence, ceremony, scholarship, and strict class order—in this stimulating and timeless story."

"To write a good book for teenagers, you [are] required to write with clarity and honesty and economy," Bosse told Dahlin of *Publishers Weekly.* He further explained to *SATA:* "I consider any reader above ten or twelve years old (depending on the rate of maturation) to be an adult. I write for a young person as I would for someone my own age, leaving out perhaps the worst of my

This 1994 novel concerns two sixteenth-century Chinese brothers who journey to Beijing, where each faces a difficult test. (Cover illustration by Richard Jordan.)

philosophical reflections or distortions, which, of course, is all for the best."

■ Works Cited

Cruse, Martha, review of *Ganesh, Voice of Youth Advocates,* June, 1981, p. 27.

Dahlin, Robert, "PW Interviews: Malcolm Bosse," *Publishers Weekly,* May 20, 1983, pp. 238-39.

Review of *Deep Dream of the Rain Forest, Parents' Choice,* Volume 18, number 4, 1994, p. 28.

Review of *The Examination, Kirkus Reviews,* August 15, 1994, p. 1121.

Review of *The Examination, Publishers Weekly,* September 12, 1994, pp. 92-93.

Fader, Ellen, review of *Deep Dream of the Rain Forest, School Library Journal,* October, 1993, p. 148.

Fireside, Bryna J., review of *Ganesh, New York Times Book Review,* August 9, 1981, p. 24.

Flowers, Ann A., review of *Cave beyond Time, Horn Book,* February, 1981, p. 57.

Forman, Jack, review of *The Seventy-nine Squares, New York Times Book Review,* December 9, 1979, p. 35.

Hearne, Betsy, review of *Deep Dream of the Rain Forest, Bulletin of the Center for Children's Books,* October, 1993, p. 39.

Hibberd, Dominic, "Cultures on Other Terms," *Times Literary Supplement,* July 23, 1982, p. 790.

Krumbein, Sue, review of *Deep Dream of the Rain Forest, Voice of Youth Advocates,* December, 1993, p. 288.

McConnell, Ruth M., review of *Captives of Time, School Library Journal,* November, 1987, pp. 112-13.

Meyer, Carol, review of *Captives of Time, Los Angeles Times,* January 23, 1988.

Quilligan, Maureen, review of *Captives of Time, New York Times Book Review,* January 31, 1988, p. 36.

Reilly, Patricia Anne, review of *Cave Beyond Time, Best Sellers,* January, 1981, p. 349.

Review of *The Seventy-nine Squares, Publishers Weekly,* July 2, 1979, p. 106.

Sutherland, Zena, review of *The Seventy-nine Squares, Bulletin of the Center for Children's Books,* January, 1980, p. 88.

Sutherland, Zena, review of *Captives of Time, Bulletin of the Center for Children's Books,* January, 1988, p. 82.

Toensmeier, Anne G., review of *The Seventy-nine Squares, Interracial Books for Children Bulletin,* Volume 11, Numbers 3 and 4, 1980, p. 22.

Review of *The Vast Memory of Love, Publishers Weekly,* July 6, 1992, p. 38.

■ For More Information See

PERIODICALS

Best Sellers, February, 1980.

Booklist, May 1, 1959; October 1, 1974; October 1, 1979; November 1, 1980; April 15, 1981.

Bulletin of the Center for Children's Books, December, 1980, p. 66; July/August, 1981, p. 207.

Chicago Sunday Tribune, April 5, 1959.

Childhood Education, April, 1980.

China News, August 7, 1980.

Christian Century, April 8, 1959.

English Journal, May, 1980.

Language Arts, September, 1981.

Ms., August, 1980.

New Yorker, September 9, 1974.

New York Herald Tribune, April 12, 1959.

New York Times, May 12, 1983; January 23, 1986.

New York Times Book Review, March 22, 1959; August 25, 1974; June 5, 1983; February 9, 1986; May 19, 1991.

Observer, October 15, 1972; February 2, 1975.

Publishers Weekly, February 28, 1972; February 22, 1991; July 6, 1992.

School Library Journal, September, 1979, pp. 152-53; November, 1980, p. 83; May, 1981, p. 70.

Times Literary Supplement, February 2, 1973.

Voice of Youth Advocates, June, 1980; December, 1980; December, 1989, p. 231.

Washington Post Book World, August 18, 1974.*

BRISLEY, Joyce Lankester 1896-1978

OBITUARY NOTICE—See index for *SATA* sketch: Born January 6, 1896, in Bexhill, Sussex, England; died September 20, 1978. Illustrator and author of children's books. The author of bestselling short stories for young readers, Brisley often wrote about Milly-Molly-Mandy, a girl who embodied the perfect child in both her behaviors and adventures. Brisley, who also illustrated her own books, published her first book, *Milly-Molly-Mandy Stories,* in 1928. Other works in the series include *Further Doings of Milly-Molly-Mandy* and *Milly-Molly-Mandy and Billy Blunt.* She also wrote several books about a boy named Bunchy, such as *Another Bunchy Book,* and issued works about biblical characters and stories like *Children of Bible Days.* A contributor to various periodicals, she illustrated books for other authors, including *Pretenders' Island* by Ursula Moray Williams, published in 1940. Some of Brisley's earlier works, written in the 1920s and 1930s, were reissued in the 1970s and 1980s.

OBITUARIES AND OTHER SOURCES:

BOOKS

Twentieth-Century Children's Writers, 4th edition, St. James Press, 1995, pp. 147-48.

* * *

BROOKS, Caryl 1924-

■ Personal

Born July 3, 1924, in New York, NY; daughter of Herbert (an umbrella manufacturer) and Adeline (an interior decorator; maiden name, Gray) Henryson; married C. Robert Brooks (vice president of Totes),

CARYL BROOKS

May 21, 1944 (deceased); children: Liza, Chris, Jody. *Education:* Attended Skidmore College. *Hobbies and other interests:* Collector of early Americana.

■ Addresses

Home—1385 York Ave., New York, NY 10021. *Agent*—Theron Raines, 71 Park Ave., New York, NY 10016.

■ Career

Writer.

■ Writings

The Empty Summer, Scholastic, 1993.

■ Work in Progress

Recipe for Love, a sequel to *The Empty Summer.*

■ Sidelights

Caryl Brooks is a native New Yorker who says she has been writing "forever," although her first published work did not appear until she was in her sixties. "Life, somehow, seemed to get in the way," she explained to *SATA.* "Marriage, children, car pools, vaporizers, dogs and cats took up all of my time. It wasn't until an illness—an inner ear virus disabling me for three years—that I promised myself to write in a different way, a commitment beyond any I'd ever made. Thus, my first published work—*The Empty Summer.*"

Writing in *School Library Journal,* reviewer Marilyn Makowski commented that *The Empty Summer* "wisely offers no pat solutions." The book tells the story of fifteen-year-old Maggie who, summering in Martha's Vineyard, idolizes the beautiful and popular high-schooler Kimberly Porter. Kimberly seems to have it all—intelligence, good looks, a budding modeling career, and a devoted boyfriend. As Maggie soon learns, however, appearances can be deceiving. Kimberly is an emotionally troubled teen who takes pills, is obsessed with her father's death, and eventually commits suicide.

Calling the book "a first novel by a promising author," Evie Wilson-Lingbloom stated in a *Voice of Youth Advocates* review that it was "grounded in the pain of adolescent growth experiences." This pain is clearly evident in the guilt Maggie feels at not having recognized Kimberly's cries for help. "This novel is undeniably memorable," Sybil S. Steinberg concluded in her *Publishers Weekly* review, "and may serve to enlighten [teenagers and adults] about signs of instability that should be taken seriously."

■ Works Cited

Makowski, Marilyn, review of *The Empty Summer,* *School Library Journal,* August, 1993, p. 186.

Steinberg, Sybil S., review of *The Empty Summer,* *Publishers Weekly,* July 19, 1993, p. 156.
Wilson-Lingbloom, Evie, review of *The Empty Summer,* *Voice of Youth Advocates,* December, 1993, p. 288.

■ For More Information See

PERIODICALS

Children's Book Review Service, September, 1993, p. 9.
Horn Book Guide, spring, 1994, p. 85.
Kirkus Reviews, August 1, 1993, p. 998.

* * *

BRUTSCHY, Jennifer 1960-

■ Personal

Surname pronounced "*broo*-chee"; born February 28, 1960, in Kansas City, MO; daughter of Glen Aaron (an accountant) and Eva Lee (a homemaker; maiden name, Foster) Olson; married Marc Warren Brutschy (an analytical chemist), August 1, 1982. *Education:* University of California at Berkeley, B.A. (geography), 1981, teaching certificate (Ryan Multiple Subject elementary credential and supplementary English credential), 1982. *Politics:* "Registered Democrat." *Religion:* "Not a member of organized religion." *Hobbies and other interests:* Weaving, quilting, dollmaking, weather watching, studying wildlife, flying stunt kites, reading.

JENNIFER BRUTSCHY

■ Addresses

Home—8467 Beverly Ct., Dublin, CA 94568.
Agent—Kendra Marcus, BookStop Literary Agency, 67
Meadow View Rd., Orinda, CA 94563.

■ Career

Dublin Public Library, Dublin, CA, library assistant,
1988—. Former preschool and kindergarten teacher.
Member: Society of Children's Book Writers and Illustrators.

■ Awards, Honors

Celeste and Crabapple Sam was a Junior Library Guild
Selection, 1993; Marion Vannett Ridgway Memorial
Award, presented for an outstanding first published
picture book, 1994, for *Winter Fox.*

■ Writings

Winter Fox (picture book), illustrated by Allen Garns,
    Knopf, 1993.
Celeste and Crabapple Sam (picture book), illustrated by
    Eileen Christelow, Lodestar, 1994.

Contributor of haiku poetry to periodicals, including
Modern Haiku, Haiku Quarterly, Woodnotes, and *Frog
Pond.*

■ Work in Progress

Two picture books: *Just One More Story,* for Orchard
Books, and *Blarney, Bread, and Mulligan Stew.*

■ Sidelights

"I have always wished for more than one life," Jennifer
Brutschy told *SATA.* "This is one of the reasons I write.
When I was a kid, I wanted to grow up to be many
things: a truck driver, a teacher, an artist, a forest
ranger. I wanted to be a writer, too, but it was different
with writing. I didn't need to *be* a writer; I felt I already
was a writer. I spent Saturday mornings with a nickel
tablet and a Sharpie pen, writing poetry and stories. I
discovered somewhere along the way that a writer really
does live many lives and has the power to create all
kinds of people and situations.

"I write children's books because I've always been in
love with children's literature. As a child, some of my
best friends were characters in books: Elizabeth Enright's Melendy family, Beverly Cleary's Ramona, and
many, many others. They lived lives just close enough to
mine to be familiar, and just exotic enough to spark my
imagination. Even in high school, I continued to read
children's books. The long, dark rows of adult books in
the library seemed alien; I even believed for awhile that
they were dirty books. And the required classics in
school were full of war and death and long, boring
descriptions. So I spent my spare time with my old
childhood favorites.

"My early writing was mostly poetry. I was captivated
by words and imagery. I wanted to find the exact word
for what I saw or felt. Happenings, feelings, and ideas
seemed to float and drift away unless they were solidly
anchored by the written word. I still feel this need to pin
down experiences with precise words. I found that in my
early adult years, haiku was a form that satisfied this
need. I wrote lots of haiku and was published in several
magazines.

"Then, one day, I had an experience that was too big for
a haiku. I saw a fox loping across the field beyond the
school I taught at. I had never before seen a fox in the
wild, and I felt transformed by the experience. I was sure
the magic would disappear if I spoke out loud about my
experience, so I carried it around like a secret. I tried
writing my feelings as a poem, but it didn't quite work.
So, I set my attempts aside for awhile. But the experience still haunted me and demanded to be written
about. So, one day, I tried again and discovered with
great pleasure that what I was writing was a picture
book."

Brutschy's *Winter Fox* starts off as an innocent story
about a little girl named Rosemary and her pet rabbit,
but it becomes more serious toward the end. Rosemary
loves the pet that her father gave her and takes good care
of it until one night it is carried off by a fox. Brokenhearted, she begs to go with her father when he decides
to hunt the fox down. But when Rosemary sees the
fox—who, in the middle of winter, has become emaciat-

**After a fox steals her pet rabbit, Rosemary learns the
truth about life in the wild in Brutschy's award-winning
picture book. (Cover illustration by Allen Garns.)**

ed with hunger—she comes to understand that the fox only did what it had to in order to survive. Reviewers were impressed by Brutschy's honest treatment of her subject. Hazel Rochman noted in *Booklist* that the story "could easily have been sentimental," but Brutschy instead manages to be "understated." "What gives this story power," wrote *New York Times Book Review* contributor Sara Stein, "is Rosemary's response when actually faced with the 'winter-thin, butterscotch-pale' fox . . . . Rosemary's tears, shed both for her rabbit and for its hungry predator, are utterly believable."

In another emotionally sensitive tale, Brutschy's *Celeste and Crabapple Sam* relates how one insistent, loveable girl manages to touch the heart of a crabby old man. When Celeste is able to convince Crabapple Sam to come to her family's fish fry, she ends a twenty-year-old quarrel between him and her grandfather and enables them to become friends again. Reviewers had as much praise for this tale as they did for *Winter Fox*. Noting that Brutschy's text is strong enough not to need illustrations, Martha Gordon stated in *School Library Journal* that *Celeste and Crabapple Sam* is a "delightful tale of intergenerational friendship," perfect for story-telling. A *Kirkus Reviews* critic called it an "energetic and entertaining tale, deftly pointing out that a gruff manner may be overcome with persistence, and may mask real affection."

Although her career as a picture book author is just beginning, Brutschy indicated to *SATA* that she knew from the start that she had made the right choice in writing *Winter Fox*. "I had stumbled into a format that I loved," she said. "Picture books satisfied my need for poetry *and* my love of stories. Besides, as a writer, I'm more of a sprinter than a long-distance runner. I work best in spurts, and picture books lend themselves to this type of writing. Lots of my writing is done in my head and on little scraps of paper. When I feel ready, I sit down at the computer with my scraps of notes and ideas. It's not as scary for me to face a blank computer screen as it is to face a blank piece of paper. When I'm done with a draft, however, I get away from the computer and revise with a pen. When it sounds right, I go back to the computer to type my revisions.

"All of my books have grown, in part, out of real experiences, and they are like souvenirs to me. They mark a place or a time I want to hold onto. They are far more personal and meaningful to me than another souvenir, such as a photograph or a seashell. And, when my stories are published along with someone's beautiful illustrations, they are like moments locked in time that I can share with other people. But I'm always on the lookout for that idea or character that will lead me into creating new people, new lives, and new books."

■ Works Cited

Review of *Celeste and Crabapple Sam, Kirkus Reviews,* December 15, 1993, p. 1587.

Gordon, Martha, review of *Celeste and Crabapple Sam, School Library Journal,* March, 1994, p. 190.

Rochman, Hazel, review of *Winter Fox, Booklist,* November 15, 1993, p. 632.

Stein, Sara, review of *Winter Fox, New York Times Book Review,* November 14, 1993, p. 24.

■ For More Information See

PERIODICALS

Booklist, December 15, 1993, p. 762.
Horn Book Guide, spring, 1994, p. 27.
Kirkus Reviews, October 1, 1993, p. 1270.
Publishers Weekly, November 1, 1993, p. 78.
School Library Journal, February, 1994, p. 78.

*   *   *

BUCHIGNANI, Walter 1965-

■ Personal

Born July 27, 1965, in Montreal, Quebec, Canada; son of Giancarlo (a welder) and Giovanna (a nurse's aide; maiden name, Michelucci) Buchignani. *Education:* Vanier College, D.E.C. Arts (with honors), 1984; Concordia University, B.A. (with distinction), 1988. *Hobbies and other interests:* Reading, writing, playing hockey, guitar.

■ Addresses

Home—2-320 Laird Blvd., Town of Mount Royal, Quebec, Canada H3R 1Y2. *Office—The Gazette,* 250 St. Antoine W., Montreal, Quebec, Canada H2Y 3R7.

■ Career

Journalist. *The Gazette,* Montreal, Canada, feature writer and copy editor, 1987—.

■ Writings

Tell No One Who You Are: The Hidden Childhood of Regine Miller (juvenile nonfiction), Tundra Books, 1994.

Contributor to *Caribbean News.*

■ For More Information See

PERIODICALS

Booklist, November 1, 1994.
Publishers Weekly, November 14, 1994.
Quill and Quire (Toronto), October, 1994.

*   *   *

BURNS, Theresa 1961-

■ Personal

Born January 14, 1961, in Chicago, IL; daughter of Robert (a computer programmer) and Audrey (a potter; maiden name, Vetter) Burns. *Education:* California

THERESA BURNS

College of Arts and Crafts, B.F.A. (illustration) and Art Therapy certificate, 1983; attended the Art Students League, New York City, and McFatter Vocational Technical Center.

■ Addresses

Home—129 South Almar Dr., Wilton Manors, FL 33334.

■ Career

Freelance illustrator for newspapers, magazines, clothing companies, toy companies, and architectural firms; also painter of portraits and murals. *Exhibitions:* Paintings have appeared in one-woman shows in Florida, New York, and Arkansas. *Member:* Society of Children's Book Writers and Illustrators, Graphic Artists Guild, Society of Business Women, South Florida Book Group.

■ Writings

SELF-ILLUSTRATED

You're Not My Cat, Lippincott, 1989.

ILLUSTRATOR

Frog Frolics, Discovery Toys, 1991.
Bernard Wiseman, *Little New Kangaroo,* Clarion, 1993.
Deborah Dennard, *Travis and the Better Mousetrap,* Cobblehill Books/Dutton, 1996.

Provided illustrations for educational books for Silver, Burdett & Ginn, 1994.

■ Work in Progress

Author and illustrator of *Dandelions, Paul's Bad Dream, Dear Aunt Lou, The Tree That Bloomed All Year, Toby Takes a Bath,* and *The Night the Moon Ran Away.*

■ Sidelights

Theresa Burns told *SATA,* "When I was five years old, I told my best friend that I was going to grow up and write books for 'us.' I feel lucky in that I've always known what I wanted to do with my life and lucky to be able to make a living at it.

"My parents have always been very supportive of me. They always took my brother and me to art museums, and they collected art books of many different painters. I first taught myself to draw by copying some of the cartoon characters in my father's collection of cartoon books. My mother is a potter, and my father had dabbled in metal sculpture. My older brother is a filmmaker. I was taught at a young age to find work that makes me happy.

"I have learned many different skills within the arts so that I am able to do several different things, from computer graphics to showing fine art pieces in galleries. This has helped me immensely in my freelance career. Writing and illustrating books, however, is my primary passion.

"I often do work for free—to get my name out and to lend my talent to a good cause. I think it's important to do this, particularly when first starting out—it gives an artist/writer good practice and helps them to make a name for themselves. I also *always* talk to children at art shows and when I'm visiting schools. I read my new manuscripts to them. They are always very truthful, insightful, and *blunt,* which is very helpful to me.

"I try to write as much as I can. I almost always carry a notebook with me and jot down ideas, which I then work on later. If I've been having a hard time with a manuscript, I simply put it in the back of my filing cabinet and leave it for a few months if I can—this helps. My favorite 'benefits' from writing and illustrating books are the pictures and letters sent to me from children who like my books. These are precious gifts."

■ For More Information See

PERIODICALS

Publishers Weekly, May 12, 1989, p. 291.

School Library Journal, September, 1989, p. 222; February, 1994.

* * *

BUTLER, Octavia E(stelle) 1947-

■ Personal

Born June 22, 1947, in Pasadena, CA; daughter of Laurice (a shoe-shiner) and Octavia Margaret (a maid; maiden name, Guy) Butler. *Education:* Pasadena City College, A.A., 1968; attended California State University at Los Angeles, 1969; attended University of California at Los Angeles.

■ Addresses

Home—P.O. Box 40671, Pasadena, CA 91114.

■ Career

Freelance writer, 1970—. Has worked variously as a dish washer, floor sweeper, inventory taker, and telephone solicitor. *Member:* Science Fiction Writers of America.

■ Awards, Honors

YWCA Achievement Award for the Creative Arts, 1980; Hugo Award, World Science Fiction Society, 1984, for short story "Speech Sounds"; Hugo Award, Nebula Award, Science Fiction Writers of America, Locus Award, *Locus* magazine, and Best Novelette award,

OCTAVIA E. BUTLER

Science Fiction Chronicle Reader, all 1985, all for novelette "Bloodchild"; Nebula Award nomination, 1987, for novelette "The Evening and the Morning and the Night."

■ Writings

Patternmaster, Doubleday, 1976.
Mind of My Mind, Doubleday, 1977.
Survivor, Doubleday, 1978.
Kindred, Doubleday, 1979, 2nd edition, Beacon Press, 1988.
Wild Seed, Doubleday, 1980.
Clay's Ark, St. Martin's, 1984.
Dawn: Xenogenesis, Warner Books, 1987.
Adulthood Rites, Warner Books, 1988.
Imago, Warner Books, 1989.
Parable of the Sower, Four Walls Eight Windows, 1993.
Bloodchild, TGW, 1995.

Also author of the novelette "The Evening and the Morning and the Night." Contributor to anthologies, including *Clarion,* 1970, and *Chrysalis 4,* 1979. Contributor to periodicals, including *American Visions, Essence, Future Life, Isaac Asimov's Science Fiction Magazine, Omni, Transmission,* and *Writers of the Future.*

■ Sidelights

A winner of the coveted Nebula and Hugo awards, Octavia E. Butler is one of the leading science fiction authors writing today. Butler's talent was already evident by the time she had finished her first three novels, *Patternmaster, Mind of My Mind,* and *Survivor.* As *Extrapolation* contributor Frances Smith Foster argued in a 1982 article, "There should exist no doubt that in [Butler's] contribution [to science fiction] this writer has already given us 'something really first rate.'"

Butler stands out among science fiction writers for another reason: she is one of the few black writers of science fiction, and is among the first black women to venture into the genre. By 1994, as Thomas Wiloch noted in the *Bloomsbury Review,* Butler enjoyed "a solid reputation among both science fiction aficionados and feminists for her novels featuring strong African American women characters." Yet while Butler's identity as a black woman enriches her work and often generates it, she told Lisa See in a *Publishers Weekly* interview that the fact that her leading female characters are black "is not the most important thing on my mind. I'm just interested in telling a story, hopefully a good one.... I write about the things that interest me."

Butler has loved science fiction since she was a child. Her father died when she was a baby, and she was raised by her mother, grandmother, and other relatives with strict Baptist discipline in Pasadena, California. Butler felt alienated from children her own age; she preferred the company of adults and books. It was not long before she outgrew children's books, and she attempted to read books from the adult section at the public library. As the library didn't allow children in the adult section, Butler moved to the magazine section and discovered science fiction. By the time she was twelve, she began to write her own science fiction stories, and within a year she started submitting them to magazines.

At Pasadena City College, where she won a short story contest, Butler attended courses in English, history, social studies, and anthropology. When she left school, she began to take evening classes at UCLA and informed her work with discussions at the Writers Guild of America West Open Door program. However, it was not until she participated in the Clarion Science Fiction Writers' Workshop, where she learned a great deal about her craft and other science fiction writers, that she sold two stories. Butler supported her writing career by working as a dish washer, floor sweeper, inventory taker, and telephone solicitor.

Finally, in 1975, Butler began to concentrate full-time on her writing and made progress almost instantly. *Patternmaster,* which is based on the first stories she had written as a child, was accepted by Doubleday, along with two other books, *Mind of My Mind* and *Survivor.* In these first books of the "Patternist" series, according to Foster, Butler demonstrates that she is "not just another woman science fiction writer. Her major characters are black women, and through her characters and the structure of her imagined social order, Butler consciously explores the impact of race and sex upon future society."

The "Patternist series," in the words of Hoda M. Zaki in *Women's Review of Books,* "imagines the future evolution of the human race into three warring groups." The first of these groups is led by Doro, the Patternmaster, whose story is thoroughly explained in *Mind of My Mind.* Originally a Nubian, he has survived for over four thousand years by taking over healthy bodies—of all races and ages, but preferably black male like his original Nubian body—and relinquishing them before they fail. By carefully selecting his mates, Doro creates a line of mentally and physically superior descendants. His daughter, Mary, links these patternists together telepathically and organizes them.

The second two groups are created when an American spaceship returns to Earth carrying a disease which forces its victims to deliberately spread it. The Clayark disease kills half of the Earth's people, and those who survive it bear mutated yet superior beings called the Clayarks. The Patternists emerge to create a rule enabling humanity to survive the Clayark crisis. They allow the Missionaries of Humanity—a religious group of mutes that believes the only correct human form is an unmutated one—to seek a new home planet.

As Foster emphasized, black female characters stand out in the Patternist series. In *Patternmaster,* Amber is "a significant and complex individual who functions as a symbol, a catalyst, and a mentor" and tips the scales in a struggle between brothers to inherit the Pattern by teaching Teray "humane tendencies." In *Mind of My Mind,* Mary unseats her father as the Patternmaster and

Combining history and science fiction, *Wild Seed* sets the stage for Butler's earlier "Patternist" books by depicting African culture from 1690 to 1840. (Cover illustration by Wayne Barlowe.)

"defines the limits of and represents an alternative to Doro's power." Finally, in *Survivor,* Alanna Verrick, a human raised by Missionaries, decides to marry a Hao (a fur-covered, blue alien). Rather than focusing on "racial conflict or even racial tension," Foster wrote, "Butler explores the future implications of racism and sexism by focusing upon relationships between powerful persons who are various types of Other."

Set on Earth during the years 1690 to 1840, *Wild Seed* is the prequel to the first three "Patternist" books. Blending historical fact with science fiction, it describes Doro's more distant past and the lives of Africans from the time before Europeans began to sell them as slaves to just before the Civil War in the United States. As in the first "Patternist" books, a black woman emerges as an important character. Anyanwu, characterized by Elizabeth A. Lynn in the *Washington Post Book World* as "intelligent, resolute," and "powerful," challenges Doro's attempts to control her. Tom Easton praised this book in *Analog Science Fiction/Science Fact* and recom-

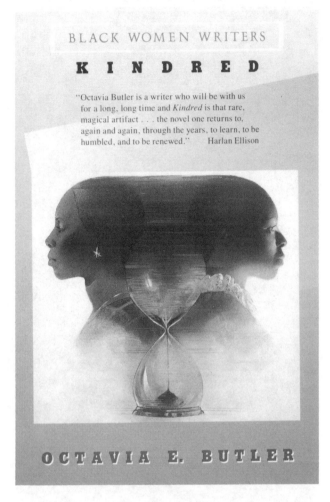

A black woman is transported back in time to save a white ancestor and ensure her own birth in Butler's powerful 1979 novel. (Cover illustration by Laurence Schwinger.)

mended it as a candidate for a Nebula award, adding, "It's that good."

Like *Wild Seed, Clay's Ark* explains the details taken for granted in the earlier "Patternist" novels. *Clay's Ark* relates the story of Asa Elias ("Eli") Doyle, the American space traveler who carried Clayark disease to earth. Together with some survivors of the disease he has spread and their superior, mutant children, Eli goes into hiding. Nevertheless, the disease spreads beyond their enclave. In the words of Algis Budrys in *Magazine of Fantasy and Science Fiction,* the "race of *homo sapiens* is doomed; what has been brought back from the stars is the end of human history." While *Fantasy Review* critic John R. Pfeiffer felt that *Clay's Ark* doesn't measure up to some of her earlier works, he concluded that "Butler's craft is now so strong that even one of her works of intermission is a delicious confection."

As Butler was writing the books in the "Patternist" series, she began a new, non-science fiction project that was published in 1979 as *Kindred.* Butler explained to See in her interview why she decided to write this book: "I had this generation gap with my mother. She was a maid and I wished she wasn't. I didn't like seeing her go through back doors.... If my mother hadn't put up with all those humiliations, I wouldn't have eaten very well or lived very comfortably. So I wanted to write a novel that would make others feel the history: the pain and fear that black people have had to live through in order to endure."

Kindred does just that—its protagonist, Dana, a young, struggling black writer, experiences life as a slave when she is transported from contemporary times to the early nineteenth century (for minutes in contemporary time but months and years in the past) to save a white ancestor. As Beverly Friend relates in *Extrapolation,* Dana makes "six trips into the past, called each time by Rufus's [the ancestor] near encounter with death. Each return Dana makes to the present is triggered by the possibility of her own death. Once she returns during a hideous beating; another time she causes the return by desperately slitting her own wrists."

Once, Dana is transported back in time while in her husband Kevin's embrace, and he is pulled into the past with her. As Kevin is white, they cannot live together in this past world. Dana is transported home without him, and when she returns to the past again, her ancestor prevents her from contacting Kevin. Although Dana escapes to find her husband, as Friend writes, "she is caught. Nothing in her twentieth-century education or experience had prepared her to succeed."

Finally, Rufus rapes Dana's great-grandmother and ensures Dana's birth in the future. As Dana kills Rufus, she is transported back to the future, losing her left arm in the process. According to Friend, the message of *Kindred* is that "contemporary woman is not educated to survive ... she is as helpless, perhaps even more helpless, than her predecessors." In addition to bearing a solemn message, *Kindred* is an entertaining read. *Magazine of Fantasy and Science Fiction* contributor Joanna Russ described the story as "exciting and fast-moving and the past occurs without a break in style—a technique that makes it more real—even down to characters' speech."

Butler returned to more traditional science fiction with the books in the Xenogenesis series. The story begins with *Dawn: Xenogenesis,* which takes place after the Earth's atmosphere has been destroyed by nuclear war. A group of survivors is captured by the Oankali, aliens who offer to save them (including the protagonist, Lilith) if they will cooperate in creation of a race of humanoids, or "constructs." The Oankali combine their genetic material with that of the humans and begin to repair the Earth's biosphere.

In *Adulthood Rites* Lilith's son, Akin, a young construct with the mental powers of an adult, is kidnapped by the humans who have refused to cooperate and cannot bear children of their own. *Imago* tells the story of the first construct who is an olloi, the neuter Oankali sex which mediates between the male and female. This humanoid is rejected by the Oankali and finds human mates who are fertile yet defective. Once again, Butler's science fiction carries a message traditional books in the genre have ignored. According to a critic in *Publishers Weekly,* "Moving bitter truths emerge about the obligations and constraints of family and people" in *Adulthood Rites.*

Like the Earth in the Xenogenesis series, the world in the *Parable of the Sower* has been devastated. Yet this time economic collapse and environmental depletion have led to the decline of civilization in the early twenty-first century. Lauren, the black, teenage daughter of a minister, narrates her story in diary entries and poems. Lauren suffers from "hyperempathy," a condition that causes her to feel the pain of others around her. This affliction, along with her religious upbringing, leads her to develop a new religion she calls "Earthseed." Based on the motto "God is Change," Earthseed promotes adaptability and faith in the dream of space colonization. After her own deteriorating neighborhood in Southern California is destroyed and her father is killed, Lauren travels throughout California with a band

After her community is destroyed, a hyperempathic teenager becomes the leader of a new religious group in this novel set in the twenty-first century. (Cover illustration by John Jude Palencar.)

of survivors who gradually come to regard her as a prophet.

Parable of the Sower, which has been marketed as a mainstream novel rather than science fiction, received praise from such critics as Gary K. Wolfe. Wolfe wrote in a *Locus* review: "Butler makes us empaths, too: we feel the fear and pain of all the little catastrophes." Another *Locus* contributor, Faren Miller, described Earthseed as "simply the most emotionally *and* intellectually appealing religion I've encountered in nearly four decades of reading sf." Gerald Jonas concluded in the *New York Times Book Review* that *Parable of the Sower* is a "gripping tale of survival and a poignant account of growing up sane in a disintegrating world" that "succeeds on multiple levels."

Butler has offered science fiction readers a fresh perspective and has taken up issues traditional writers have neglected. Yet while Butler's contribution to science fiction is unmistakable, novels like *Kindred* and *Parable*

The second novel in the "Xenogenesis" series deals with the resisters, who kidnap Lilith's son Akin to raise as their own.

of the Sower have brought her voice a wider audience than just fans of that particular genre. As Margaret Anne O'Connor asserted in the *Dictionary of Literary Biography,* "Feminists and critics of Afro-American literature write admiringly of her handling of issues of gender and race," while "general readers find that these novels ... present compelling stories of all-too-human beings."

■ Works Cited

Review of *Adulthood Rites, Publishers Weekly,* May 6, 1988, p. 98.

Budrys, Algis, review of *Clay's Ark, Magazine of Fantasy and Science Fiction,* August, 1984, pp. 34-35.

Easton, Tom, review of *Wild Seed, Analog Science Fiction/Science Fact,* January 5, 1981, p. 168.

Foster, Frances Smith, "Octavia Butler's Black Female Fiction," *Extrapolation,* spring, 1982, pp. 37-49.

Friend, Beverly, "Time Travel as a Feminist Didactic in Works by Phyllis Eisenstein, Marlys Millhiser, and Octavia Butler," *Extrapolation,* spring, 1982, pp. 50-55.

Jonas, Gerald, review of *Parable of the Sower, New York Times Book Review,* January 2, 1994, p. 22.

Lynn, Elizabeth A., "Vampires, Aliens, and Dodos," *Washington Post Book World,* September 28, 1980, p. 7.

Miller, Faren, review of *Parable of the Sower, Locus,* December, 1993, pp. 17, 19, 60.

O'Connor, Margaret Anne, "Octavia E. Butler," *Dictionary of Literary Biography,* Volume 33: *Afro-American Fiction Writers after 1955,* Gale, 1984, pp. 35-41.

Pfeiffer, John R., "Latest Butler a Delicious Confection," *Fantasy Review,* July, 1984, p. 44.

Russ, Joanna, review of *Kindred, Magazine of Fantasy and Science Fiction,* February, 1980, pp. 96-97.

See, Lisa, "Octavia E. Butler," *Publishers Weekly,* December 13, 1993, pp. 50-51.

Wiloch, Thomas, review of *Parable of the Sower, Bloomsbury Review,* May/June, 1994, p. 24.

Wolfe, Gary K., review of *Parable of the Sower, Locus,* April, 1994, pp. 19, 52.

Zaki, Hoda M., "Fantasies of Difference," *Women's Review of Books,* January 1, 1988, pp. 13-14.

■ For More Information See

BOOKS

Black Writers, 2nd edition, Gale, 1994, pp. 103-5.

Contemporary Literary Criticism, Volume 38, Gale, 1986, pp. 61-66.

Smith, Jessie Carney, editor, *Notable Black American Women,* Gale, 1992, pp. 144-47.

PERIODICALS

Black American Literature Forum, summer, 1984, pp. 78-87.

Booklist, May 1, 1989, p. 1511.

Essence, April, 1979.

Janus 4, winter, 1978-79, pp. 28-29.

Kirkus Reviews, May 15, 1976, p. 612; April 15, 1977, p. 453.

Los Angeles Times, January 30, 1981.

Ms., March, 1986; June, 1987.

Thrust: SF in Review, summer, 1979, pp. 19-22.

Voice of Youth Advocates, October, 1987, p. 174.*

C

CALDER, Lyn
See CALMENSON, Stephanie

* * *

CALHOUN, Mary
See WILKINS, Mary Huiskamp

* * *

CALMENSON, Stephanie 1952-
(Lyn Calder)

■ Personal

Born November 28, 1952, in Brooklyn, NY; daughter of
Kermit (a podiatrist and educator) and Edith (a medical
secretary; maiden name, Goldberg) Calmenson. *Education:* Brooklyn College of the City University of New
York, B.A. (magna cum laude), 1973; New York University, M.A., 1976.

■ Addresses

Office—c/o Morrow Junior Books, 1350 Avenue of the
Americas, New York, NY 10019.

■ Career

Teacher of early childhood grades at public schools in
Brooklyn, NY, 1974-75; Doubleday & Co., New York
City, editor of children's books, 1976-80; Parents Maga-
zine Press, New York City, editorial director of Read-
Aloud Book Club, 1980-84; author of children's books,
1984—. *Member:* Society of Children's Book Writers
and Illustrators, Mystery Writers of America, Authors
Guild, Authors League of America, PEN.

STEPHANIE CALMENSON

■ Writings

JUVENILE

(Editor) *Never Take a Pig to Lunch and Other Funny
Poems about Animals,* illustrated by Hilary Knight,
Doubleday, 1982.
My Book of the Seasons, Western Publishing, 1982.

One Little Monkey, illustrated by Ellen Appleby, Parents Magazine Press, 1982.

Barney's Sand Castle, illustrated by Sheila Becker, Western Publishing, 1983.

That's Not Fair!, Grosset & Dunlap, 1983.

The Kindergarten Book, illustrated by Beth L. Weiner, Grosset & Dunlap, 1983.

Where Will the Animals Stay?, illustrated by Appleby, Parents Magazine Press, 1983.

The Birthday Hat: A Grandma Potamus Story, illustrated by Susan Gantner, Grosset & Dunlap, 1983.

Where Is Grandma Potamus?, illustrated by Gantner, Grosset & Dunlap, 1983.

The After School Book, illustrated by Weiner, Grosset & Dunlap, 1984.

Ten Furry Monsters, illustrated by Maxie Chambliss, Parents Magazine Press, 1984.

All Aboard the Goodnight Train, illustrated by Normand Chartier, Grosset & Dunlap, 1984.

Waggleby of Fraggle Rock, illustrated by Barbara McClintock, Holt/Muppet Press, 1985.

Ten Items or Less, Western Publishing, 1985.

(Compiler with Joanna Cole) *The Laugh Book: A New Treasury of Humor for Children,* illustrated by Marylin Hafner, Doubleday, 1986.

The Toy Book, Western Publishing, 1986.

What Babies Do, Western Publishing, 1986.

The Little Bunny, illustrated by Chambliss, Simon & Schuster, 1986.

The Shaggy Little Monster, illustrated by Chambliss, Simon & Schuster, 1986.

The Little Chick, illustrated by Chambliss, Simon & Schuster, 1986.

Little Duck's Moving Day, Western Publishing, 1986.

Fido, illustrated by Chambliss, Scholastic Inc., 1987.

Tiger's Bedtime, Western Publishing, 1987.

The Giggle Book, illustrated by Chambliss, Parents Magazine Press, 1987.

One Red Shoe (The Other One's Blue!), Western Publishing, 1987; also published as *Bunny's New Shoes.*

Arthur's Good Manners, Western Publishing, 1987; also published as *Spaghetti Manners.*

Who Said Moo?, Parachute Press, 1987.

A Visit to the Firehouse, Parachute Press, 1987.

Where's Rufus?, illustrated by Chambliss, Parents Magazine Press, 1988.

(Compiler with Cole) *The Read-Aloud Treasury for Young Children,* illustrated by Ann Schweninger, Doubleday, 1988.

The Children's Aesop: Selected Fables, illustrated by Robert Byrd, Doubleday, 1988.

Little Duck and the New Baby, Western Publishing, 1988.

No Stage Fright for Me!, Western Publishing, 1988.

The Little Witch Sisters, illustrated by R. W. Alley, Parents Magazine Press, 1989.

What Am I? Very First Riddles, illustrated by Karen Gundersheimer, Harper, 1989.

The Principal's New Clothes, illustrated by Denise Brunkus, Scholastic Inc., 1989.

(With Cole) *Safe from the Start: Your Child's Safety from Birth to Age Five,* illustrated by Lauren Jarrett, Doubleday, 1989.

One Hundred One Silly Summer Jokes, Scholastic, Inc., 1989.

One Hundred One Funny Bunny Jokes, Scholastic, Inc., 1990.

(Compiler with Cole) *Miss Mary Mack and Other Children's Street Rhymes,* illustrated by Alan Tiegreen, Morrow Junior Books, 1990.

(Compiler with Cole) *Ready, Set, Read!: The Beginning Reader's Treasury,* illustrated by Anne Burgess, Doubleday, 1990.

Wanted: Warm, Furry Friend, illustrated by Amy Schwartz, Macmillan, 1990.

Come to My Party, illustrated by Beth Weiner Lipson, Parents Magazine Press, 1991.

Dinner at the Panda Palace, illustrated by Nadine Bernard Westcott, HarperCollins, 1991.

Hopscotch, the Tiny Bunny, illustrated by Barbara Lanza, Western Publishing, 1991.

Zip, Whiz, Zoom!, illustrated by Dorothy Stott, Little, Brown, 1991.

(Compiler with Cole) *The Eentsy, Weentsy Spider: Fingerplays and Action Rhymes,* illustrated by Tiegreen, Morrow Junior Books, 1991.

(Compiler with Cole) *The Scary Book,* illustrated by Chris Demarest and others, Morrow Junior Books, 1991.

The Addams Family (novelization), Scholastic, Inc., 1991.

Roller Skates, illustrated by True Kelley, Scholastic Inc., 1992.

(Compiler with Cole) *Pat-a-cake and Other Play Rhymes,* illustrated by Tiegreen, Morrow Junior Books, 1992.

It Begins with an A, illustrated by Marisabina Russo, Hyperion Books for Children, 1993.

(Adapter) George Lucas, *Race to Danger,* directed by Joe Johnston, Random House, 1993.

(Compiler with Cole) *Pin the Tail on the Donkey and Other Party Games,* illustrated by Tiegreen, Morrow Junior Books, 1993.

(Compiler with Cole) *Six Sick Sheep: 101 Tongue Twisters,* illustrated by Tiegreen, Morrow Junior Books, 1993.

Tom and Jerry: The Movie, Scholastic Inc., 1993.

Hotter Than a Hot Dog!, illustrated by Elivia Savadier, Little, Brown, 1994.

Kinderkittens Show and Tell, illustrated by Diane De Groat, Scholastic Inc., 1994.

Marigold and Grandma on the Town, illustrated by Mary Chalmers, HarperCollins, 1994.

Rosie, A Visiting Dog's Story, illustrated by Justin Sutcliffe, Clarion Books, 1994.

(Editor) *Walt Disney's Winnie the Pooh and Tigger Too,* Disney Press, 1994.

Where is Eeyore's Tail, Disney Press, 1994.

(With Cole) *Crazy Eights and Other Card Games,* illustrated by Tiegreen, Morrow Junior Books, 1994.

(Compiler with Cole) *Give a Dog a Bone: Stories, Poems, Jokes, and Riddles about Dogs,* illustrated by John Speirs, Scholastic Inc., 1994.

(With Cole) *Why Did the Chicken Cross the Road?: And Other Riddles, Old and New,* illustrated by Tiegreen, Morrow Junior Books, 1994.

(With Cole) *The Gator Girls,* illustrated by Lynn Munsinger, Morrow Junior Books, 1995.

(With Cole) *Yours 'Til Banana Splits: 201 Autograph Rhymes,* illustrated by Tiegreen, Morrow Junior Books, 1995.

Also author of *Beginning Sounds: A Little People Workbook,* published by Parachute Press. Calmenson's book *Ten Items or Less* has been translated into French.

JUVENILE; UNDER PSEUDONYM LYN CALDER

Bambi and the Butterfly, Western Publishing, 1983.

The Three Bears, Western Publishing, 1983.

Happy Birthday, Buddy Blue: A Rainbow Brite Story, Western Publishing, 1984.

Blast Off, Barefoot Bear!, Cloverdale Press, 1985.

Waggleby of Fraggle Rock, Holt, 1985.

Gobo and the Prize from Outer Space, Holt/Muppet Press, 1986.

The Sesame Street ABC Book, Western Publishing, 1986.

The Sesame Street Book of First Times, Western Publishing, 1986.

Gobo and the Prize from Outer Space, illustrated by Frederic Marvin, Holt, 1986.

The Bambi Book, Western Publishing, 1987.

The Little Red Hen, Western Publishing, 1987.

Little Red Riding Hood, Western Publishing, 1987.

If You Were a Cat; If You Were a Fish; If You Were a Bird; If You Were an Ant, Prentice-Hall, 1989.

Mickey Visits the Fair: A Book about Numbers, Western Publishing, 1990.

Magellan's Hats, illustrated by Jim Mahon and David Prebenna, Western Publishing, 1991.

Blue-Ribbon Friends, Disney Press, 1991.

Gold-Star Homework, Disney Press, 1991.

Good Night, Magellan, illustrated by Tom Brannon, Western Publishing, 1991.

The Perfect Bow, illustrated by Sue Shakespeare, Golden Books, 1991.

Walt Disney Presents The Little Mermaid, Ariel above the Sea, illustrated by Franc Mateu, Western Publishing, 1991.

What Will I Wear?, illustrated by Mateu, Western Publishing, 1991.

Sebastian's Story, Western Publishing, 1992.

Lemonade for Sale, Golden Books, 1992.

Walt Disney's Alice's Tea Party, illustrated by Jesse Clay, Disney Press, 1992.

Where's Fifi?, Western Publishing, 1992.

Also author of *Minnie 'n Me Stories,* four stories under the pseudonym Lyn Calder, 1992.

■ Adaptations

One Little Monkey was given a BBC television reading, 1984; *Dinner at the Panda Palace* was a PBS "Storytime" Book.

An elephant, two lions, three pigs, and many other animals make for a dining experience—and a counting book—young readers won't soon forget. (Cover illustration by Nadine Bernard Westcott.)

■ Sidelights

Stephanie Calmenson told *SATA:* "To have become a children's book writer is a happy surprise for me. I have always loved books, language, and working with children. Growing up, though, I had little confidence in my writing abilities. All the way through college, if given the choice between writing and another course, I would choose the other, thinking I had a better chance at succeeding.

"All that changed when I was studying for my master's degree in Elementary Education. Two courses were required: Introduction to Children's Literature and Writing for Children. In the first, I discovered how much I loved children's picture books; I devoured them. My enthusiasm spilled over to the second class, Writing for Children. My very first story was published in a children's magazine. I was off and running.

"I have been an elementary school teacher, a children's book editor, and am now a full-time writer. While I am no longer in a classroom, I continue to think of myself as a teacher, speaking to children through my books. How do I begin a book? I get an idea that appeals to me. Then, before beginning to write, I always ask myself the same question: What will this book give to a child? The first answer has to be pleasure. If a book is not pleasing, it will not be read. I go on from there.

"I will use *Dinner at the Panda Palace* as an example. I remember exactly when I got the idea for that book. I overheard a young boy as he was walking into a restaurant say to his mother, 'Mommy, I am going to ask for a table for two.' Right then and there, I decided to write a counting book in which diners, from one to a group of ten, ask for tables at a restaurant. I love animals and know that most children do, too. So the diners became an assortment of animals: 'An elephant came first with a trunk that was gray. He'd been out on the road selling peanuts all day. "I'm enormously hungry. My bag weighs a ton. I would like to sit down. Have you a table for one?"' There are monkeys swinging across the chandeliers, peacocks showing off their plumage, and so on. Now I had a book that was a counting book and an animal identification book. If I were a teacher of young children, I thought, I might welcome a book like this. Still, I wanted to give children something more.

"So as soon as the restaurant is filled, a tiny mouse comes knocking at the door. Will she get to sit down, or will she be turned away? In the end, Mr. Panda says what I would like to say to all the children who read the book: 'No matter how many, no matter how few, there will always be room at the Palace for you!' With that ending, I was satisfied. I felt there was a chance that the book could give a child something important: the feeling of having a special place in the world.

"Where do my ideas come from? An idea can emerge from an observation, a dream, a memory, a feeling, a wish. What are my subjects? As long as I am having fun with the language, I can write about anything. I have written books about numbers, letters, everyday objects. I have written about being brave enough to tell the truth;

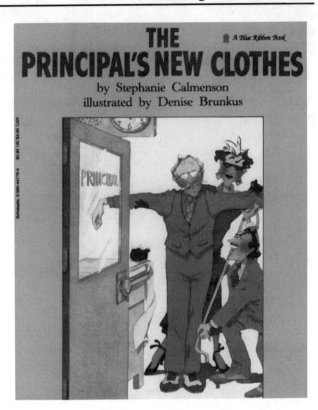

Kids will especially enjoy the principal's embarrassment at the conclusion of this modern adaptation of "The Emperor's New Clothes." (Cover illustration by Denise Brunkus.)

about not having to be perfect; about not judging others too quickly. I have written about friends, families, and most recently, about my own dog, Rosie, who is a working dog."

In *Rosie, A Visiting Dog's Story,* Calmenson explains how she trained her Tibetan terrier, Rosie, to visit hospital rooms, nursing homes, and other such places to bring laughter and companionship into the lives of those who are sick or lonely. Calmenson describes how to choose a dog for this purpose and how to prepare for the visits. The text is simple in keeping with the author's audience. She concludes her book with the addresses of various associations that can supply readers with more information. Margaret A. Bush in *Horn Book* called *Rosie* an "appealing photo-documentary."

Calmenson confided to *SATA* that she does get writer's block. "I have times when I think there is nothing left in the world to write about. Or, I get an idea and cannot figure out how to bring it to life on the page. But I have been writing long enough to know that, truly, the possibilities are endless. It's just a matter of waiting out the dry periods before getting excited with writing all over again."

Calmenson retold twenty-eight fables in *The Children's Aesop.* She chose a greater number of stories that contain human characters than most anthologies of Aesop's works have included, and supplied her characters' motivations; for example, she gave both the hare

The loving relationship between a girl and her grandmother is simply expressed in this story of a trip to the beach. (Cover illustration by Elivia Savadier.)

It Begins with an A

Stephanie Calmenson

Illustrated by Marisabina Russo

Riddle enthusiasts will have fun using rhymes and pictures to guess the letter described on each page of this book. (Cover illustration by Marisabina Russo.)

and the tortoise's point of view. The morals are printed at the bottom of each page. Calmenson preserves the "informal, colloquial tone of the writing," Carolyn Phelan remarked in *Booklist*.

The Principal's New Clothes is an adaptation of Hans Christian Andersen's story. The vain, clothes-conscious elementary school principal is the equivalent of the emperor, the two untrustworthy tailors work on the outfit in the gymnasium, and the unveiling takes place at a school assembly. A kindergartner points out that the principal is only wearing underwear, and the children throw articles of clothing at him in an attempt to help. The principal reappears wearing the odd assortment and presents the child with a gold star for her honesty. "These modern-day trappings invite readers to set their favorite folktales in their own neighborhoods," concluded Susan Hepler in *School Library Journal*.

Calmenson's *Hotter Than a Hot Dog!* is about the special relationship between a girl and her grandmother

as they escape the city heat by spending the afternoon on the beach. "The delightful slice of city life is made real by the author's use of concrete details," according to Maeve Visser Knoth in *Horn Book*. Jan Shepherd Ross in *School Library Journal* described the text as "lyrical" and lauded the description of the beach through the girl's sense of sight, smell, touch, and taste. Diane Roback and Elizabeth Deveraux in *Publishers Weekly* said, "Calmenson's bubbly narrative voice convincingly mimics a child's own storytelling."

Marigold and Grandma on the Town is very similar in theme to *Hotter Than a Hot Dog!*, although the girl and her grandmother here are bunnies. With thoughtful detail, Calmenson tells the story of little bunny Marigold feeding ducks in a park and acting up in a coffee shop. Marigold's temper tantrums and worries are realistically portrayed. Marigold's grandmother buys her a hat, and, on the way home, they get their picture taken in a photo booth. "Lively characters, childlike dilemmas, and cheerful artwork make this newest 'I Can

Read' just right for the intended audience," declared Maeve Visser Knoth in *Horn Book*. Deborah Stevenson said in the *Bulletin of the Center for Children's Books* that "events are individually mild but collectively important."

Wanted: Warm, Furry Friend is another story about bunnies. When gray rabbit Ralph first sets eyes on white rabbit Alice, he feels instant dislike, which she reciprocates. Ralph answers a personal ad and believes the writer is his soul mate, not realizing that it is Alice with whom he is corresponding. While sparks fly between the two whenever they meet, they are tender to one another in their letters. "The telling is delicious," Richard Donahue and Diane Roback remarked in *Publishers Weekly*.

Calmenson has also created several beginner books. *It Begins with an A* is an alphabet book with two-line, rhyming riddles on each page. Calmenson uses small words and short sentences, mindful of her young readers. The answers to the riddles and a review of the alphabet are on the last two pages of the book. This book is "full of things relevant to a child's life," noted Kathryn Broderick in *Booklist*. *What Am I? Very First Riddles* is another book of rhyming riddles aimed at young listeners. The answers are revealed in the text and in the pictures, making it easy for young children to answer them. The riddles are based on everyday objects and on items that are special to children, such as ice cream, a birthday cake, and a rainbow. The rhymes are kept brief, just four lines long. There are fifteen riddles in all. Ellen Fader in *Horn Book* declared that "children will be reading this book to themselves in no time at all."

"I no longer work in a classroom with children," Calmenson explained to *SATA*. "I work alone in front of a computer. I do not speak aloud; I speak on paper. But through my words, I still get to explore the world with children. And that is pure joy."

■ Works Cited

Broderick, Kathryn, review of *It Begins with an A, Booklist*, June 1 and 15, 1993, p. 1842.

Bush, Margaret A., review of *Rosie, Horn Book*, July, 1994, p. 470.

Donahue, Richard, and Diane Roback, review of *Wanted: Warm, Furry Friend, Publishers Weekly*, October 26, 1990, p. 68.

Fader, Ellen, review of *What Am I? Very First Riddles, Horn Book*, May/June, 1989, p. 353.

Hepler, Susan, review of *The Principal's New Clothes, School Library Journal*, March, 1990, p. 154.

Knoth, Maeve Visser, review of *Marigold and Grandma on the Town, Horn Book*, March/April, 1994, p. 194.

Knoth, Maeve Visser, review of *Hotter Than a Hot Dog!, Horn Book*, May/June, 1994, pp. 309-10.

Phelan, Carolyn, review of *The Children's Aesop: Selected Fables, Booklist*, April 1, 1992, pp. 1452-53.

Roback, Diane, and Elizabeth Deveraux, review of *Hotter Than a Hot Dog!, Publishers Weekly*, February 28, 1994, p. 87.

Ross, Jan Shepherd, review of *Hotter Than a Hot Dog!, School Library Journal*, May, 1994, p. 89.

Stevenson, Deborah, review of *Marigold and Grandma on the Town, Bulletin of the Center for Children's Books*, March, 1994, p. 217.

■ For More Information See

PERIODICALS

Books for Keeps, November, 1992, p. 77.
Books for Your Children, spring, 1993, p. 8.
Bulletin of the Center for Children's Books, May, 1989, p. 218; June, 1994, p. 315.
Horn Book, May/June, 1991, p. 351.
Kirkus Reviews, July 15, 1989, p. 1072; July 15, 1992, p. 929; April 1, 1993, p. 452; January 1, 1994, p. 64.
Publishers Weekly, May 30, 1986, p. 61; April 26, 1993, p. 77.
School Library Journal, May, 1985, p. 106; August, 1985, p. 53; December, 1989, p. 77; September, 1991, p. 230; February, 1992, p. 41; June, 1992, p. 106; January, 1993, pp. 90-91; April, 1994, p. 117; April, 1995, p. 100.

*   *   *

CAMERON, Scott 1962-

■ Personal

Born July 3, 1962, in Mississauga, Ontario, Canada; son of James Angus and Theresa Elizabeth (Compeau) Cameron. *Education:* Ontario College of Art, 1980-84. *Hobbies and other interests:* Wildlife and the environment.

■ Addresses

Home and office—1510 Spring Rd., Mississauga, Ontario, Canada L5J 1N1.

■ Career

Freelance illustrator, 1986—. *Member:* World Wildlife Fund, Endangered Animal Sanctuary, Canadian Society of Children's Authors, Illustrators and Performers.

■ Awards, Honors

Governor General's Award for illustration, finalist, and the Mr. Christie Prize for Best Children's Book, both for *Beethoven Lives Upstairs*.

■ Illustrator

Pierre Berton, *The Capture of Detroit*, McClelland & Stewart, 1991.

Berton, *The Death of Isaac Brock*, McClelland & Stewart, 1991.

SCOTT CAMERON

Barbara Nichol, *Beethoven Lives Upstairs,* Lester, 1993, Orchard Books, 1994.
Janet Lunn, *The Root Cellar,* Lester, 1994.

■ Work in Progress

Illustrations for Beatrice Schenk de Regniers's *David and Goliath,* William McKibben's *The Token Gift,* and Lunn's *Shadow in Hawthorn Bay,* all due in 1996.

■ Sidelights

Scott Cameron told *SATA:* "I have been influenced by American painters and illustrators all my life. But since I work in Canada, little of what I've done has appeared in the U.S. Another great influence on me is where I live. My section of Mississauga, even with its streets and houses, is still basically a forest. Growing up not only with dogs and cats (I have six cats at the moment) but with the trees, squirrels, raccoons, rabbits, birds, and foxes has shaped and coloured how I feel about the world and my work. It shapes my work because when I look around I see bushes and vines, tall grass and tangled branches, everything has a shaggy roughness to it. I've never liked paintings that were too slick and photographic. To me they seem stiff and lifeless. I respond better to work where the looser application of paint and suggestions of detail come closer to what I see and to me feel more alive. People who have influenced me in this way are painters such as Claude Monet, John Singer Sargent, Carl Rungius, Bob Kuhn, and most recently Tom Browning, and illustrators like Frank

Frazetta, Frederic Remington and, most importantly of all, N. C. Wyeth.

"The natural world is incredibly important to me. And I hope I can express this even more in the future by writing my own stories to illustrate."

*   *   *

CAPONIGRO, John Paul 1965-

■ Personal

Born June 23, 1965, in Boston, MA; son of Paul and Eleanor (Morris) Caponigro; married Alexandra. *Education:* Yale University, B.A.; University of California at Santa Cruz, B.A.

■ Addresses

Home and office—R.R. 1, Box 1055, Cushing, ME 04563.

■ Career

Self-employed artist (fine art and illustration) and writer; Infinity Studios, Cushing, ME, owner, 1989—.

■ Awards, Honors

Winner, Illustrators of the Future Contest, 1991.

■ Illustrator

Daniel Cohen, *A Ghost in the House,* Cobblehill Books, 1993.

■ Work in Progress

The Elemental Series and *Hymns to Gaia* (fine art and digital images); *The North American Tradition* (in five volumes: *Creation, Hero, Trickster, Nature, Supernature);* research on Irish fairy tales and mythological collections.

■ Sidelights

John Paul Caponigro told *SATA* about his work as an artist and writer: "I'm often asked, 'Where did you get that idea?' I reply, 'Where do ideas come from?' But I secretly wonder if I should ask, 'How did that image find me?'

"Inspiration comes from a variety of sources. Influence is incessant. Amid the myriad impressions and experiences I am subject to, I try to find the eye of the storm, that special place where inspiration rings clearly and purely. It is in these transcendent moments that I feel we are able to access our fullest potential and are able to come in contact with the greater mysteries of life.

"It would seem natural that those images which reach their fullest expression through me would be images I am particularly oriented to. And to that I can say I find

JOHN PAUL CAPONIGRO

no greater inspiration than nature herself and the stories of man coming in contact with her.

"I see style as language, not so much something I am personally attached to but a vocabulary that enables expression. Rather than be preoccupied with a personal style, I prefer to concentrate on how style can bring content to a given work.

"That is not to say I am not concerned with a personal style, but rather I feel that it is inevitable and that many times it is as much a mystery as the images that appear before me.

"I am primarily concerned with making images, but whether those images take shape in graphite, silver or the printed word I prefer to leave up to the images themselves. As with style so with media; each provides a vessel for communication with unique properties.

"I simply strive for fluency in the vocabularies of style and material so that when inspiration strikes I will be ready and able to give it its fullest expression.

"I find the interrelation of words and pictures infinitely fascinating. Each in itself has proved to be an incredible tool for expression, communication and discovery. I strive to find points at which their union can bring a synergistic effect—where the limits of each can be transcended through the other.

"My recent efforts represent a new beginning for me. In my internal world they represent for me the step between acolyte and initiate. It is only now that I feel equal to the task of bringing the images before my mind's eye into focus."

*   *   *

CHANIN, Michael 1952-

■ Personal

Born May 13, 1952, in Newark, NJ; son of William Chanin (a salesman) and Beatrice Chanin-Kaplan (an office manager; maiden name, Pickar); married Kim Juneau (a self-employed artisan), August 10, 1986. *Education:* University without Walls, degree (counseling), 1985; University of San Francisco, M.A. (counseling), 1988. *Hobbies and other interests:* Meditation, exploring ways for a peaceful coexistence, computers.

■ Addresses

Office—c/o H. J. Kramer, Inc., P.O. Box 1082, Tiburon, CA 94920.

■ Career

Writer. Palomares Residential Treatment Facility, Santa Cruz, CA, social worker, 1992-95. Counselor, 1987—. *Member:* Center for World Networking.

■ Writings

Grandfather Four Winds and Rising Moon, illustrated by Sally Smith, H. J. Kramer, 1993.

■ Work in Progress

The Chief's Blanket, a picture book, for H. J. Kramer.

■ Sidelights

Michael Chanin's first published book for children, *Grandfather Four Winds and the Rising Moon,* tells how Grandfather Four Winds and a sacred apple tree help a young boy understand some important values. Chanin explained such values, which "transcend culture," to *SATA:* "Salutary values, intrinsic to human nature, like gratitude, courage, faith and humility, can contribute to establishing individual and world peace. The inspiration for my stories comes from two very different places. I am a social worker for an adolescent residential treatment facility where I come in contact with many troubled, conflict-oriented families. Families that are sorely lacking in wholesome values. I am also interested in spiritual traditions that embrace qualities that offer peaceful solutions to life's challenges. In the face of these two disparate realities, I write stories to offer myself and others hope at a time when hopelessness is so prevalent, and to inspire readers to create a world where people truly care and respect each other, the planet and all of life."

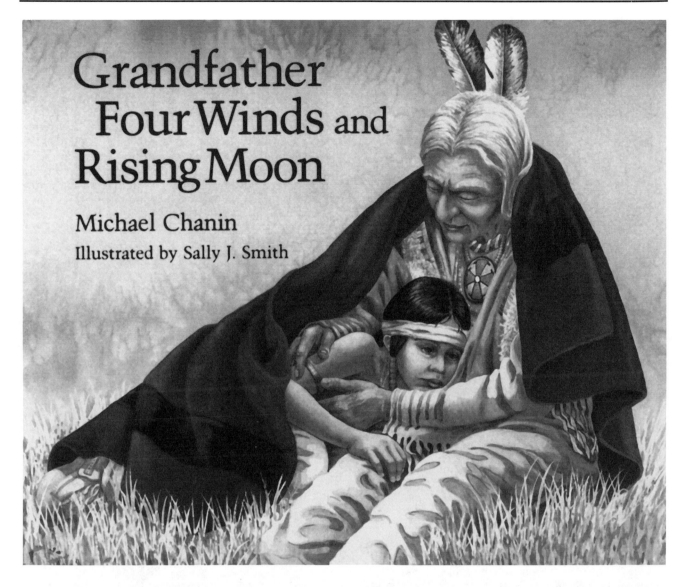

Grandfather Four Winds and Rising Moon

Michael Chanin

Illustrated by Sally J. Smith

Grandfather Four Winds' story about a sacred apple tree helps calm Rising Moon's fears about the drought, in Michael Chanin's poignant picture book. (Cover illustration by Sally J. Smith.)

■ For More Information See

PERIODICALS

Children's Book Watch, May, 1994, p. 60.

* * *

CHARBONNEAU, Eileen 1951-

■ Personal

Born April 11, 1951, in Long Island, NY; daughter of Vincent (a business owner) and Katherine (Zorovich) Charbonneau; married Edward Gullo (a news correspondent), August 19, 1972; children: Abigail, Mariah, Susannah. *Education:* State University of New York at Fredonia, B.A.; attended River Arts Film School. *Hobbies and other interests:* Genealogy, contra-dancing, shape-note singing.

■ Addresses

Home—P.O. Box 155, Philomont, VA 22131-0155. *Agent*—Susan Yven, Susan Herner Rights Agency, P.O. Box 303, Scarsdale, NY 10583.

■ Career

Free-lance writer, 1974—. Worked variously as a teacher, waitress, and department store receiver. Community theater director and actress. La Leche League leader and district advisor; Girl Scouts leader. *Member:* Society of Children's Book Writers and Illustrators, Young Adult Writers Network.

■ Awards, Honors

Golden Medallion Award, Romance Writers of America, 1989, for *The Ghosts of Stony Clove;* Phyllis A. Whitney Award; Christopher Columbus Discovery Award in Screenwriting; first place, Philadelphia Writ-

EILEEN CHARBONNEAU

ers' Conference, Juvenile Writing Category, MARA Award, Fiction from the Heartland Competition, Best Books citation, American Library Association, and Holt Medallion Award, all for *In the Time of the Wolves.*

■ Writings

The Ghosts of Stony Clove, Orchard Books, 1988.
In the Time of the Wolves, Tor Books, 1994.
The Mound Builders' Secret (Z-Fave "You-Solve-It Mystery" series), Zebra Books, 1994.
Disappearance at Harmony Festival (Z-Fave "You-Solve-It Mystery" series), Zebra Books, 1994.
Blood River (Z-Fave "You-Solve-It Mystery" series), Zebra Books, 1996.
Honor to the Hills, Tor Books, 1996.

Contributor to periodicals, including *New York Times, Newsday, Mothering, Lady's Circle,* and *Midwifery Today;* fiction editor for a literary magazine and a state newsletter.

■ Work in Progress

Waltzing in Ragtime and *The Randolph Legacy,* historical novels under contract with Tor Books.

■ Sidelights

Eileen Charbonneau's reputation for writing evocative historical fiction has grown since the publication of her award-winning books, *The Ghosts of Stony Clove* and *In the Time of the Wolves.* As Charbonneau explained to *SATA,* her ethnicity and childhood experience have

motivated her to write fiction that emphasizes the importance of tolerance and understanding. "Growing up, I remember feeling stuck in the middle of my parents' ten children. I 'unstuck' myself by figuring out that I was the only one of us who could say, 'I have older brothers and sisters *and* younger brothers and sisters.' That position made me unique and gave me a place. My family's story was the first I wanted to tell. I'm a multi-ethnic product of Irish, Slovene, French, Canadian, and Native American roots that somehow came together on the sidewalks of New York City when this century was young. Striving to understand another person's viewpoint comes naturally—chances are that view is part of me."

Charbonneau's first book, *The Ghosts of Stony Clove,* is set in the Catskill Mountains in the early nineteenth century and allows readers to appreciate the perspective of Asher, a half-Native American, half-French adolescent boy. While Asher is ostracized by most of the townspeople because of his ancestry and because he is an indentured servant, he develops a friendship with Ginny Rockwell, whose father has died and left her and her mother penniless. Wandering around the woods

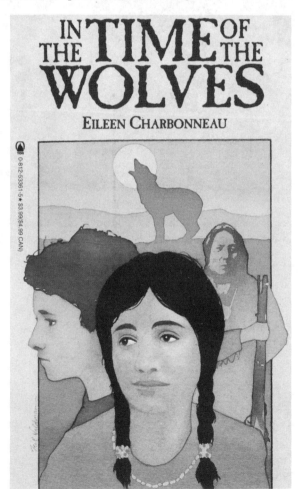

The award-winning sequel to *The Ghosts of Stony Clove* finds Asher and Ginny's fourteen-year-old son Joshua feeling torn between his father's beliefs and his desire for acceptance. (Cover illustration by Neil Waldman.)

near the old Sutherland house, which is rumored to be haunted by the ghost of a man who committed a crime long ago, Asher and Ginny find that Sutherland is alive. When Asher sets out to find the family that abandoned him when he was just five years old to go out West, Ginny goes to work for Squire Sutherland and cares for him. Squire Sutherland leaves the house and land to Ginny when he dies. Years later, Asher returns and the couple fall in love.

According to Elizabeth Mellett in *School Library Journal, The Ghosts of Stony Clove* is "fast-paced" as well as "entertaining," and Asher and Ginny's feelings for each other are "touching and convincing." A *Horn Book* critic recommended *The Ghosts of Stony Clove* as a "good introduction to historical fiction." A *Booklist* critic concluded that while the book offers adventure and romance, some readers may "find deeper themes of prejudice and revenge to ponder." Readers who enjoyed *The Ghosts of Stony Clove* may also appreciate its sequel, *In the Time of the Wolves,* which tells the story of Asher and Ginny's son, Joshua.

Three of Charbonneau's books are "You-Solve-It Mysteries." Readers of *The Mound Builders' Secret, Disappearance at Harmony Festival,* and *Blood River* are challenged to solve each story's mystery by following the text and searching for clues on the book's cover. The story's conclusion can only be reached after the seal on the final chapter is broken. In *The Mound Builders' Secret,* Tad visits an archaeological dig and meets Linda, the half-Cherokee teenager who supervises it. When the site is desecrated, Tad and Linda work together to find out who is sabotaging the site. *Disappearance at Harmony Festival* also features Tad and Linda. This time, they must find Linda's friend, Rising Fawn, after she disappears.

Charbonneau told *SATA* that her writing career does more than satisfy her creative urge. "I revel in writing because I can sing the beauty of my father's hands, my mother's song. I forge from words a perception of time and place. And people. People past, present, and never were take on lives of their own to challenge and stimulate my perceptions. They allow me to experience both the real world and the worlds under my pen.

"An actress needs a stage, a plumber needs a broken sink. I need paper, a writing tool, and perseverance. It gets disheartening when a phrase will not turn itself right, when a character balks at the plot I've set her in, when a cherished work is not catching a publisher's interest. But I've learned to find my chief joy in the process of creation, not the degree of success. Because all the rejections in the world can't keep me from my desk. Only my own despair can do that. I have stories to tell. My hope is that they will reach further than myself and touch other hearts."

■ Works Cited

Review of *The Ghosts of Stony Clove, Booklist,* May 15, 1988, p. 1606.

Review of *The Ghosts of Stony Clove, Horn Book,* July, 1988, p. 501.
Mellett, Elizabeth, review of *The Ghosts of Stony Clove, School Library Journal,* June, 1988, p. 115.

■ For More Information See

PERIODICALS

Chicago Sun-Times, August 14, 1988, p. 19.
Kirkus Reviews, May 1, 1988, p. 689.
Voice of Youth Advocates, October, 1988, p. 180.

*   *   *

CLARK, Clara Gillow 1951-

■ Personal

Born May 22, 1951, in Lookout, PA; daughter of Lee (a farmer) and Naomi Inez (Keesler) Gillow; married Gerald R. Houck (divorced), married H. W. "Dutch" Varrichio, January 13, 1995; children: J. Jay. *Education:* Attended New School for Social Research, 1984-88, Luzerne County Community College, and University of Scranton; presently enrolled at University of Wisconsin. *Politics:* Republican. *Religion:* Methodist/Protestant. *Hobbies and other interests:* Reading, writing, walking, and regional history.

■ Addresses

Office—P.O. Box 566, Honesdale, PA 18431.

■ Career

Writer. Wayne County Historical Society, Pennsylvania, member of board of trustees; member of Friends of the Wayne County Library. *Member:* Society of Chil-

CLARA GILLOW CLARK

dren's Book Writers and Illustrators, Teachers and Writers Collaborative, Authors Guild, Authors League of America, Children's Literature Association, International Reading Association.

■ Awards, Honors

Kansas State Reading Circle selection and "Lamplighter" award nomination, both for *Annie's Choice.*

■ Writings

Annie's Choice, Boyds Mills, 1993.
Nellie Bishop, Boyds Mills, 1996.

Also author of the short story "The Clock," which appeared in *Sing Heavenly Muse!,* 1994.

■ Work in Progress

Willie and the Rattlesnake King, nineteenth-century historical fiction; research on rafting on the Delaware and orphans on canal in the nineteenth century; a sequel to *Annie's Choice.*

■ Sidelights

Clara Gillow Clark found the inspiration to write *Annie's Choice* from an experience her mother had in her youth—being denied the opportunity to attend high school. As Clark pondered this situation, "understanding began to form like a pearl, and I began to see how choices made in the past had caused an intergenerational ripple," she wrote in the Boyds Mills publicity newsletter "The Bridge." "I began to understand who I was, by learning who I was not. I was not middle class, I was a peasant . . . .

"As I wrote about Annie's life, I began to better understand my own, and to understand how I had ended up on the road leading to unfulfilled dreams—being married at eighteen, not going to college until I was in my thirties—and why it had taken me so long to acquire a skill for writing. And as I wrote, again insight flashed—Annie's story was not only my mother's story, it was my own."

Set in rural New York in 1928, *Annie's Choice* takes place on a farm where Annie lives with her parents, an older brother, and younger siblings. An older sister has left the farm to live in town. When Annie's eighth grade teacher, Miss Osborne, encourages her to attend high school, Annie is left with having to choose whether she should convince her hard-working parents that furthering her education is worthwhile or just continue helping her mother out on the farm. Annie's decision is then put to the test when her mother becomes pregnant and she is needed at home. In a review of *Annie's Choice* for *Publishers Weekly,* Sybil S. Steinberg wrote that "Clark depicts a time, place and way of life with notable style and charm." "The book offers some interesting insights into women's options," added reviewer Sally Bates Goodroe for *School Library Journal.*

Clark addressed where she gets her ideas in "The Bridge": "I think that I wrote for many years without much success because I didn't have any real ideas. That is, I had no idea which stories were important for me as an individual to write. So, in getting workable ideas for my novels, I first had to learn some hard lessons about ideas before I could tap into my inner wellspring of creativity.

"Now, an idea can be about anything—a person, a place, or a thing—but in order to take on any real shape or life of its own, an idea must come to intersect with and embody some emotion within the writer. Otherwise the idea, no matter how ingenious or imaginative or unusual, will ultimately fail as literature. This seems obvious to me now, but when I first began to write I didn't know this.

" . . . I believe that in order to know who you are, you must first come to understand who you are not. Once you determine who you are not, you will have already begun the process of getting to ideas—the ideas that have power, the ideas that are seedpods of emotional truth.

"So, finally, to answer the question, where *do* my ideas come from? They come from my heart, the place where ideas and emotional truth meet."

■ Works Cited

Clark, Clara Gillow, "The Bridge" (Boyds Mills publicity newsletter), 1994.
Goodroe, Sally Bates, review of *Annie's Choice, School Library Journal,* November, 1993, pp. 104, 106.
Steinberg, Sybil S., review of *Annie's Choice, Publishers Weekly,* August 23, 1993, p. 73.

■ For More Information See

PERIODICALS

Voice of Youth Advocates, December, 1993, p. 288.

*   *   *

CLEVENGER, William R(ussell) 1954-
(Russell Almon, a joint pseudonym)

■ Personal

Born July 3, 1954, in Marion, IN; children: William, Joseph, Peter. *Education:* Brigham Young University, B.S. (zoology), 1978, M.S. (cell biology), 1980.

■ Addresses

Home—1510 South Melrose Dr., Vista, CA 92083.

■ Career

Neurocrine Biosciences, molecular biologist, 1985—.

William R. Clevenger (right), with coauthor David Downing and a cardboard Magic Johnson.

◼ Writings

(With David A. Downing, under joint pseudonym Russell Almon) *The Kid Can't Miss!*, Avon Books, 1992.

Why the Sky Is Blue, Michael Freidman, 1993.

The Human Body, Michael Freidman, in press.

◼ Work in Progress

Collaborating with Downing on a young adult novel.

◼ Sidelights

William R. Clevenger, coauthor of a young adult novel with David A. Downing under the joint pseudonym Russell Almon (a combination of their middle names), told *SATA:* "Basketball has always been my favorite sport. The fast pace, frequent scoring, team-oriented play—in every way it is an exciting and fun activity. But though I played the game at every opportunity since childhood, I never developed a reliable outside shot. Often I found myself wondering, 'If there was just *some* way to make that three-pointer go in every time....' That kind of daydreaming, along with my natural tendency to cheat, led to the story David and I wrote together. David's masterful character development and storytelling skills turned this initial idea about a 'loaded' basketball into a published novel."

That novel was *The Kid Can't Miss!,* which follows the activities of a hapless ninth-grade boys' basketball team, the Sheffield Marauders. After they suffer an embarrassing defeat at the hands of eighth graders on the playground, a science-whiz classmate named Heidi offers them a sure-fire method of winning. She has invented a Spacial Position Indicator Device, or SPIDER, which can be placed inside a basketball to ensure

that it goes through the hoop every time. With the help of the device, Phang Wu becomes an ace three-point shooter and the Marauders defeat their arch rivals. Before long, however, the players begin to value individual performance over teamwork, and their close friendships start to fall apart. Finally, the team decides that "often when you take shortcuts, you end up cheating yourself," as Barbara J. McKee put it in a *Kliatt* review. And when the Marauders first play without using SPIDER, they discover that all of their skills have improved. Although Raymond E. Houser, writing in *Voice of Youth Advocates,* found some of the technology in the book farfetched, he stated that "the values it tries to teach are real. Life requires honesty, team play, and hard work." In a review for *Booklist,* Sheilamae O'Hara called *The Kid Can't Miss!* "an unusual sports story in which the characters are as important as the action."

Speaking of his partnership with Downing, Clevenger told *SATA:* "Working with him is an excellent way to learn how to write, and I can hardly wait to see how our next story turns out!"

◼ Works Cited

Houser, Raymond E., review of *The Kid Can't Miss!,* *Voice of Youth Advocates,* December 1992, p. 273.

McKee, Barbara J., review of *The Kid Can't Miss!,* *Kliatt,* April 1992, p. 4.

O'Hara, Sheilamae, review of *The Kid Can't Miss!,* *Booklist,* June 15, 1992, p. 1825.

◼ For More Information See

PERIODICALS

Children's Book Watch, April, 1992, p. 6.
Publishers Weekly, January 27, 1992, p. 98.

*   *   *

COLLARD, Sneed B. III 1959-

◼ Personal

Born November 7, 1959, in Phoenix, AZ; son of Sneed B. Collard Jr. (a professor of biology) and Patricia Anne Huffine Case (a high school biology teacher); married, 1987 (divorced, 1989). *Education:* Attended University of California, Davis, 1978-79; attended University of Washington, Friday Harbor Marine Laboratories, 1982; University of California, Berkeley, B.A. (biology with marine emphasis; with honors), 1983; University of California, Santa Barbara, M.S. (scientific instrumentation), 1986. *Politics:* "I don't belong to any particular party, but consider myself progressive." *Hobbies and other interests:* Swimming, bicycling, hiking, travelling, scuba diving, reading, going to movies, and planting oak trees.

■ Addresses

Office—c/o Charlesbridge Publishing, 85 Main St., Watertown, MA; or c/o Boyds Mills Press, 815 Church St., Honesdale, PA 18431.

■ Career

Freelance writer, 1984—. University of California, Berkeley, zoology department research assistant and research diving program assistant instructor, 1982-83; California Department of Fish and Game, wild trout program, seasonal aide, 1983; Woodward-Clyde Consultants, environmental consultant, 1984; University of California, Santa Barbara, Neuroscience Research Institute, director of computer laboratory, 1986-92. California Department of Agriculture, dutch elm disease project, agricultural aide, 1980; University of California, Santa Barbara, lab assistant, 1981. *Member:* Society of Children's Book Writers and Illustrators, Association of Booksellers for Children, Planned Parenthood, Common Cause, and "about fifteen environmental groups."

■ Awards, Honors

Third prize, 1987, and second prize, 1989, *The Humanist* North American Essay Contest; honorable mention, *Writer's Digest* article writing competition, 1990; District Tall Tales Speech Contest winner, Toastmasters International, 1991; Competent Toastmaster Award, 1992.

■ Writings

NONFICTION; FOR CHILDREN

Sea Snakes, illustrated by John Rice, Boyds Mills, 1993.
Do They Scare You? Creepy Creatures, illustrated by Kristin Kest, Charlesbridge Publishing, 1993.
Where Do We Live?, Charlesbridge Publishing, 1996.
Where Do They Live?, Charlesbridge Publishing, 1996.
Alien Invaders: The Ongoing Problem of Exotic Species Invasions, F. Watts, 1996.

"WORLD OF DISCOVERY" SERIES

Green Giants—Twelve of the Earth's Tallest Trees, illustrated by Doug Talalla, NorthWord Press, 1994.
Tough Terminators—Twelve of the Earth's Most Fascinating Predators, illustrated by Talalla, NorthWord Press, 1994.
Smart Survivors—Twelve of the Earth's Most Remarkable Living Things, illustrated by Talalla, NorthWord Press, 1994.

OTHER

Contributor of articles and stories to periodicals, including *Highlights for Children, Cricket, Christian Science Monitor, Images—Health Literacy '95, Pennywhistle Press, Clubhouse, Children's Digest, Misha, Outdoor California, Western Outdoors, Islands, EarthSteward Journal, Environmental Action,* and *The Humanist.*

SNEED B. COLLARD III

■ Work in Progress

A humorous middle-grade fiction series; *Forest in the Clouds,* for F. Watts, expected 1997.

■ Sidelights

Sneed B. Collard III told *SATA:* "I feel very lucky to be a published writer. When I was growing up, I didn't say to myself 'I am going to be an author,' but somehow I just *knew* it would happen. This is not as mysterious as it sounds. The way things turned out in my young life, I got to travel a lot. My parents were divorced when I was about eight and this made me very sad. The good thing about it, though, was that my dad moved to Florida and I got to go see him twice a year. I also travelled a lot with my mom and stepfather. With all of these experiences, I felt a growing need to share with other people the things I had seen, heard, tasted, and smelled (even if they didn't smell too good!)." Since both his parents were biologists, Collard acquired a love of nature during his early years.

After graduating from high school in 1977, Collard decided to travel and "learn more about the real world" before going to college. "I got a summer job working as a cook at Mount Rushmore in South Dakota. With the money I earned, I flew to Israel and spent four and a half months living with a family and working on a kibbutz. From Israel I took a ferry to Europe and hitchhiked through Greece." In retrospect, he stated, "taking a year off from school was one of the best decisions I ever made," despite the fact that his parents disapproved of the idea. "By the time I had travelled for a year, I was eager to plunge into college," he recalled. In addition, his travels helped him to expand his knowledge of the earth's ecosystems, which would prove useful in his studies and later in his writing.

Collard majored in biology at the University of California at Berkeley, as he explained: "I had always loved biology and I still do. In fact, I don't understand why *everyone* does not study biology. If you know about biology, your life will never be dull. Every animal and plant that you see will be an entire world waiting to be explored." Upon graduation, he got a job counting trout in mountain streams for the California Department of Fish and Game. Working in the outdoors and living in a van provided him with plenty of opportunities to contemplate his future: "I was lying in my sleeping bag, thinking about my life—and trout, of course—and I suddenly said to myself, 'Sneed, if you are going to do something with your life, now is the time.' Right then, I decided to become a writer."

Although he published several articles in magazines such as *Outdoor California* and *Children's Digest,* Collard found that writing was a difficult way to make a living. As a result, he returned to graduate school at the University of California at Santa Barbara and learned to design instruments using computers. He then worked at

the university for the next six years as manager of a computer laboratory. He continued to devote his off hours and weekends to writing, however. His break came in 1990, when the children's book publisher Boyds Mills Press asked if he would be interested in submitting a book about reptiles. After consulting with his father to select an appropriate subject, Collard began researching his first book, *Sea Snakes.*

"I rushed off to the library to read everything I could find on sea snakes," he told *SATA.* "This was easy, because almost *nothing* had been published on these unusual marine reptiles. I devoured what little information I could find, but I still didn't know enough, so I tracked down all of the sea snake scientists (say that real fast five times!) listed in the books I'd read and called them up one by one. Most of the scientists were very helpful. Once I had all of the information together, I sat down and wrote the first draft of the book in a single day. Of course, the first draft is not the hardest part of writing a book. The ten *other* drafts are what really take time! After a month, however, I was ready to submit the manuscript." Collard quit his job to write full-time in 1992, and to his great joy, Boyds Mills Press published his first book in 1993.

Published in 1993, Collard's first book describes a unique reptile and how it adapts to its environment.

Sea Snakes, which a *Kirkus Reviews* critic called "an intriguing first look at an unusual reptile," describes the appearance and behavior of the snakes that are found in tropical seas around the world. The book is intended to help children understand the complex adaptations snakes make to their environment, and it includes numerous photographs and drawings. Karey Wehner wrote in *School Library Journal* that "this title will help fill a gap," but also pointed out that it could have benefitted from captions to accompany the photographs. Captions were added in its second printing and *Sea Snakes* appeared on the final nomination list for the American Library Association Recommended Books for Reluctant YA Readers.

Collard's next project was *Do They Scare You? Creepy Creatures,* which he completed in a month with the help of many of the scientists he worked with at the University of California at Santa Barbara. The book includes information on twenty-two animals with scary reputations, such as vampire bats, sharks, scorpions, tarantulas, and piranhas. Collard told *SATA* that his intention was to "show people how wonderful creepy creatures are and how our fears of animals are blown all out of proportion." The last creature Collard profiles in the book is the imaginary "razor-toothed, slime-encrusted bone muncher," which he invented as a way to "poke fun at our fears."

In 1994 Collard wrote three books for the "World of Discovery" series, each describing twelve plants or animals that are unique in some way. For example, *Green Giants* presents twelve of the tallest species of trees from around the world, and shows how animals and people depend upon trees for survival. Similarly, *Tough Terminators* profiles twelve of the world's most efficient and interesting predators—from the ladybug and the pitcher plant to the giant octopus and the tiger—and relates their importance in the food web. Finally, *Smart Survivors* details the adaptation techniques used by species like the firefly, the strangler fig, and the polar bear to survive in challenging environments.

Collard explained to *SATA* that he came to write these sorts of books "because I care about this planet and the future of all species on it. People have a lot of good in them, but we've also done a lot of damage because we don't understand how *all* living things are important to each other. I write about creepy creatures and other things because I want people to learn about things they don't know about. To me, getting to learn something new is the greatest gift in life. I also hope that when people read my books, they will care more about the plants and animals I care about, and make better decisions about how to live on Earth."

When he is not writing, Collard spends his time travelling and speaking to groups about writing, science, and the environment. Despite the fact that being a writer has been difficult for him, particularly financially, Collard has enjoyed the support of his family and remained pleased with his career choice. He offered this advice for young people: "If you want something in life, don't be afraid to go after it. Different people will always tell you how you *should* live your life. Many of these people mean well, but they cannot see inside you, so what they tell you may not be right for you. However, just because you decide to do or be something does not mean it will be easy. To achieve something important and valuable takes a lot of hard work and you have to stick to it, even when it is hard and painful."

■ Works Cited

Review of *Sea Snakes, Kirkus Reviews,* February 15, 1993, pp. 224-25.
Wehner, Karey, review of *Sea Snakes, School Library Journal,* March 1993, p. 205.

■ For More Information See

PERIODICALS

Booklist, March 15, 1993.
Horn Book Guide, fall, 1993, pp. 339, 346.

* * *

COPLANS, Peta 1951-

■ Personal

Born August 30, 1951, in Cape Town, South Africa; daughter of Carl (a physician) and Ruth (a librarian; maiden name, Newman) Coplans; married Stanley Becker (an artist); children: Cleo, Adam. *Education:* University of Cape Town, South Africa, B.F.A., 1971; postgraduate studies at Central School of Art and Design, London. *Religion:* Jewish.

■ Addresses

Office—c/o Andersen Press, 20 Vauxhall Bridge Rd., London SW1V 2SA England.

■ Career

Writer/illustrator, 1980—. Creator with Stanley Becker of "Chic Pix," satirical art. Art teacher, 1974-75. *Exhibitions:* Best of British Illustration, 1979, 1980; European Illustration, 1980; First International Exhibition Avant-Garde Postcards, Musee de Art Moderne, Paris World Tour (French Cultural Ministry); works in permanent collections of Victoria and Albert Museum, British Museum Library, and University of Valencia, Spain.

■ Writings

SELF-ILLUSTRATED

Spaghetti for Suzy, Andersen, 1992, Houghton, 1993.
Dottie, Andersen, 1993, Houghton, 1994.
Frightened Fred, Andersen, 1994.
Cat and Dog, Andersen, 1995, Viking, 1996.

PETA COPLANS

ILLUSTRATOR

Francesca Simon, *Spider School,* Orion, 1996, Dial, 1996.

Contributor, with Stanley Becker, of "Chic Pix" art to the *Guardian.*

■ Adaptations

Spaghetti for Suzy was adapted for the BBC-TV children's educational program *Words & Pictures,* 1993; *Dottie* was adapted for the BBC-TV program *Harum-Scarum,* 1993.

■ Work in Progress

A new picture book.

■ Sidelights

Peta Coplans was born in Cape Town, South Africa, in 1951. She completed her fine art undergraduate work at the University of Cape Town in 1971 and then post-graduate studies in London, but she told *SATA* that she did not have an opportunity to write and illustrate children's picture books until her children were born.

Called "a simple, funny book" with an "offbeat charm," by *School Library Journal* contributor Beth Tegart, Coplans's first book, *Spaghetti for Suzy,* was published in 1992. It is the story of a girl who will eat only spaghetti until she meets up with some animal friends in a park one day. The animals take Suzy's noodles and illustrate the many unique and functional uses of pasta, before sharing with her the wonders of fresh fruit. Tegart also noted that the illustrations are "vividly colored stylized cartoons."

Coplans related to *SATA* the influence of horticulture in her designs and illustrations. "Growing and studying plants takes up much of my leisure time—it stimulates my interest in form, colour, and atmosphere." Her second book, *Dottie,* is the story of a dog who celebrates her individuality by planting and tending a garden. Because gardening is considered unusual behavior for a dog, Dottie's parents tell her to stick to burying bones and chasing postmen. Persistence and a local survey of other animals proves fruitful, however, as Dottie finds a number of her animal friends in unconventional activities, from a rollerskating duck to a painting rabbit.

Coplans told *SATA:* "My favorite childhood stories were Ludwig Bemelman's 'Madeline' series and Jean de Brunhoff's 'Babar' books, all of which I still read and love. I had always wanted to create my own picture books, and the fact that I'm now busy on my fourth book gives me great pleasure. I enjoy book signings, school visits, library readings, and meeting lots of kids!"

■ Works Cited

Tegart, Beth, review of *Spaghetti for Suzy, School Library Journal,* May, 1993, p. 82.

■ For More Information See

PERIODICALS

Independent on Sunday, November 22, 1992, p. 44; November 20, 1994, p. 44.
Junior Bookshelf, February, 1993, p. 12; June, 1995, p. 93.
Kirkus Reviews, March 15, 1994, p. 394.
Mail on Sunday, November 20, 1994.
Observer, July 4, 1993.
School Library Journal, April, 1994, p. 101.
Washington Post Book World, May 8, 1994, p. 18.

D

PATRICIA BRENNAN DEMUTH

DEMUTH, Patricia Brennan 1948-

■ Personal

Surname is pronounced "*dee*-muth"; born March 16, 1948, in Sioux City, IA; daughter of William Robert (a plant manager) and Anastasia (a homemaker; maiden name, Hermes) Brennan; married Jack Demuth (a photographer), August 31, 1974; children: Daniel, Luke. *Education:* University of Wisconsin, Madison, B.A., 1970; University of Illinois at Chicago, M.A., 1992. *Religion:* Roman Catholic. *Hobbies and other interests:* Playing blues piano.

■ Addresses

Agent—Jane Jordan Browne, Multimedia Product Management, 410 South Michigan Ave., Ste. 724, Chicago, IL 60625.

■ Career

Freelance educational writer and editor, 1973—. Served as senior consultant to develop English as a Second Language and reading curriculum for Motorola. *Member:* Society of Children's Book Writers and Illustrators, Children's Reading Round Table.

■ Awards, Honors

Junior Literary Guild selection, 1979, for *City Horse;* best books of the year citation, *School Library Journal,* first annual book award, Massachusetts Farm Bureau, and Notable Children's Trade Book in the Field of Social Studies citation, all 1982, and Society of Midland Authors Award, 1983, all for *Joel: Growing Up a Farm Man;* children's choices for 1987 citation, International Reading Association and American Library Association, *Weekly Reader* selection, 1987, and Georgia Children's Picture Storybook Award, University of Georgia College of Education, 1989, all for *Max, the Bad-Talking Parrot;* Bank Street selection, and best book for children recommendation, CBS *This Morning,* both 1991, both for *The Ornery Morning.*

■ Writings

FICTION

Max, the Bad-Talking Parrot, illustrated by Bo Zaunders, Dodd, Mead, 1986.
The Ornery Morning, illustrated by Craig McFarland Brown, Dutton, 1991.
Pick up Your Ears, Henry, illustrated by Bob Barner, Macmillan, 1992.
In Trouble with Teacher, Dutton, 1995.

NONFICTION

(With husband, Jack Demuth) *City Horse,* Dodd, Mead, 1979.

Joel: Growing Up a Farm Man, photographs by J. Demuth, Dodd, Mead, 1982.

Snakes, illustrated by Judith Moffatt, Grosset & Dunlap, 1993.

Inside Your Busy Body, illustrated by Paige Billin-Frye, Grosset & Dunlap, 1993.

Gorillas, illustrated by Paul Lopez, Grosset & Dunlap, 1994.

Cradles in the Trees: The Story of Bird Nests, illustrated by Suzanne Barnes, Macmillan, 1994.

Those Amazing Ants, illustrated by S. D. Schindler, Macmillan, 1994.

OTHER

Also author of more than thirty reading, language arts, writing, science, and social studies textbooks for various publishers, including Macmillan, HarperCollins, Houghton, Addison-Wesley, and Harcourt. Author and editor of other educational products, including teacher's guides, journals, stories for basal readers, workbooks, and tests.

■ Work in Progress

(With husband, J. Demuth) *Busy at Day Care: Head to Toe,* a photodocumentary about day care; *Montgomery on His Own,* a sequel to *In Trouble with Teacher.*

■ Sidelights

Patricia Brennan Demuth told *SATA:* "I grew up in a small town in a big family. There were nine of us Brennan children—four girls in a row, followed by five boys. The safety of a rural Iowa town in the fifties and the warm hold of a big loving family provided a precious childhood commodity: time to explore. Mom, busy with infants, had neither time nor inclination to program our play." So Demuth's days were filled with a variety of diversions, including the game "I Dare," green apple fights, bike riding, and singing.

"And reading," Demuth continued. "Books transported my siblings and me to distant worlds—to Heidi's mountain home, down the Mississippi with Huck, into the family rooms of the Little Women. The children in these books were universal characters, and they reached out from their worlds to carry us far and away from our dusty town. Today no pleasure is greater for me than to imagine (or meet) the real children who, during their own private moments and in their own private spaces, are moved by something I've written. It's a delight when they let me know one of my characters has said something special to them."

In addition to the house she grew up in, Demuth also spent a great deal of time at a farm outside of town that her father bought to earn extra money for the family by raising sheep. "The farm, only eighty acres, was our vast prairie, a setting where natural forces delivered daily challenges and surprises," Demuth explained. "These

sensate experiences imbedded themselves into my psyche more deeply than I could have imagined at the time and they often surface as I write. Three of my first four books had farm settings."

Demuth's husband, Jack, who is also her business partner, has been a part of her life since these early days of childhood. The two met in second grade and grew up together in Jesup, Iowa. Five years after Jack's return from the Vietnam War, the couple was married and living in New York City. "New York was the setting for our first book—*City Horse,* the life of a horse who worked for the New York mounted police," related Demuth. "By the time we did our second book, *Joel: Growing Up a Farm Man,* we had two children, Daniel and Luke, and they moved with us to a farm for one year while we documented the life of Joel, an Illinois lad who helped his family tend the land that was first tilled by his great-great-grandfather. Jack, a photojournalist, took the pictures for both books. Doing photodocumentaries has been a wonderful experience for me. In addition to the opportunity of working with my husband, I appreciate the thrill of stepping into the thick of a new world."

Since these first photodocumentaries, Demuth has gone on to write several picture books and children's textbooks. "I am one of those authors who cannot seem to restrict herself to one genre," she maintained. "Much to my own surprise, my last five books have been natural science books. The research stage for all my science books has been great fun—an 'ooh' and 'ahh' experience at every turn. In my science books, I try to present the world in all its lavish—but factual—detail, to instill in children a wonder for the world they inhabit. My hope is that knowledge itself will inspire children to cherish and

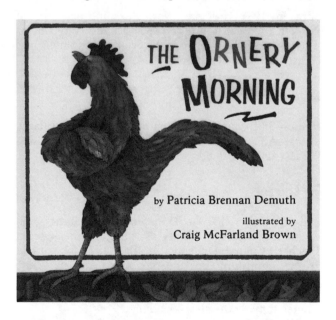

When rooster refuses to crow one morning, Farmer Bill is at his wit's end trying to coax the other animals to do their jobs, until his daughter suggests a solution. (Cover illustration by Craig McFarland Brown.)

tend the earth and its creatures. Science is, after all, extraordinary truth.

"Our children are not growing up in an easy world today, and we parents seem to have a grim task indeed. The dismal and dreary headlines portend a bleak future—until I put down the newspaper and look around for a real living kid. I visit the schools often and what I find there are children still full of boundless energy, still curious, exuberant, funny, eager to live and love, given half a chance." As a children's book author, Demuth sees herself as able to nourish these parts of the child—"their imaginations, their senses of humor, their awe. Ours is a fine and fortunate task—because the children give back in abundance."

■ For More Information See

PERIODICALS

Booklist, July, 1993, p. 1980.
Bulletin of the Center for Children's Books, June, 1979; May, 1982; May, 1995, p. 304.
Junior Literary Guild, March, 1979.
Publishers Weekly, February 19, 1982, p. 65; April 25, 1986, pp. 73-74.
School Library Journal, October, 1986, pp. 158-59; December, 1991, p. 89; March, 1993, p. 174.
Wilson Library Bulletin, April, 1992, p. 94.

*   *   *

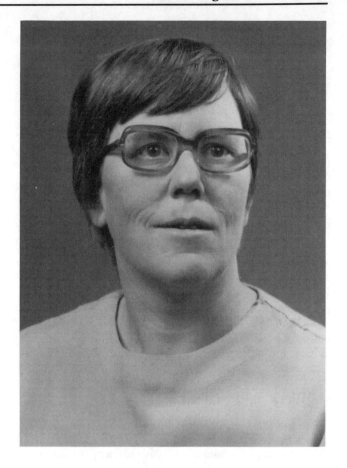

ANNE LOUISE de ROO

de ROO, Anne Louise 1931-

■ Personal

Born in 1931 in Gore, New Zealand; daughter of William Fredrick (a health inspector) and Amy Louisa (Hayton) de Roo. *Education:* University of Canterbury, Christchurch, New Zealand, B.A., 1952.

■ Addresses

Home—38 Joseph St., Palmerston North, New Zealand.
Agent—A.P. Watt & Son, 26-28 Bedford Row, London WC1R 4HL, England.

■ Career

Full-time writer, 1978—. Dunedin Public Library, Dunedin, New Zealand, library assistant, 1956; Dunedin Teacher's College, Dunedin, librarian, 1957-59; Church Preen, Shropshire, England, governess and part-time gardener, 1962-68; part-time secretary in Barkway, Hertfordshire, England, 1969-73; medical typist in Palmerston North, New Zealand, 1974-78.

■ Awards, Honors

ICI Bursary, 1981.

■ Writings

FOR CHILDREN

The Gold Dog, Hart-Davis (London), 1969.
Moa Valley, Hart-Davis, 1969.
Boy and the Sea Beast, illustrated by Judith Anson, Hart-Davis, 1971, Scholastic, 1974.
Cinnamon and Nutmeg, Macmillan (London), 1972, Nelson (Nashville), 1974.
Mick's Country Cousins, Macmillan, 1974.
Scrub Fire, Heinemann, 1977, Atheneum, 1980.
Traveller, Heinemann, 1979.
Because of Rosie, Heinemann, 1980.
Jacky Nobody, Methuen (Auckland, New Zealand), 1983, Methuen (London), 1984.
The Bats' Nest, Hodder & Stoughton (Auckland and London), 1986.
Friend Troll, Friend Taniwha, illustrated by R. H. G. Jahnke, Hodder & Stoughton, 1986.
Mouse Talk, Church Mouse Press (Palmerston North, New Zealand), 1990.
The Good Cat, Church Mouse Press, 1990.
Hepzibah Mouse's ABC, Church Mouse Press, 1991.
Sergeant Sal, Random Century (Auckland), 1991.
Hepzibah's Book of Famous Mice, Church Mouse Press, 1993.

PLAYS

The Dragon Master, music by John Schwabe, first produced in Palmerston North, New Zealand, 1978.

The Silver Blunderbuss, music by Schwabe, first produced in Palmerston North, 1984.

FOR ADULTS

Hope Our Daughter, Church Mouse Press, 1990.
Becoming Fully Human, Church Mouse Press, 1991.
And We Beheld His Glory, Church Mouse Press, 1994.

■ Sidelights

Anne Louise de Roo's novels for young people demonstrate how the rugged terrain of her native land has shaped New Zealand history and culture. Nature is a profound, beautiful, and often dangerous force in her works of historical fiction as well as in her contemporary dramas. At the same time, de Roo's stories emphasize the strength and adaptability of New Zealand's indigenous people, European immigrants, and their descendants as they cope with the wilderness and learn to live with each other. While de Roo once told *SATA* that she is delighted by the idea that her novels introduce New Zealand to children in other parts of the world, she asserted that she is "a New Zealand writer, principally concerned with the building up in a young country of a children's literature through which children can identify themselves and their roots, whether European or Maori."

De Roo wrote her first five books during the twelve years she lived in England. *The Gold Dog* and *Moa Valley* are both set on South Island in New Zealand. *The Gold Dog* is set in the mountains of Central Otago, where Gabriel Read discovered gold in 1861, and traces an exciting hunt for lost treasure. *Moa Valley* describes the ordeal of young people lost in an unexplored wilderness. *Boy and the Sea Beast* is set on North Island and was inspired by the true story of two famous dolphins in New Zealand: Pelorous Jack and Opo. According to Tom Fitzgibbon, a contributor to *Twentieth-Century Children's Writers,* "*Boy and the Sea Beast* marks a stage when a new direction enters [de Roo's] work. Up to this point, it is clear that de Roo is technically very effective but, while the quality of suspense is strong, the solution to the action comes too easily and character is subordinated to the need for a happy ending. This is much less so in *Boy and the Sea Beast.*" In this tale, a boy forms a strong friendship with a dolphin named Thunder, whom he saves from exploitation, but by the end of the story Thunder must leave the boy to live free in the wild.

Tessa, who lives on a dairy farm in the hot bushland near the side of a mountain in New Zealand, is not very pleased with her life as *Cinnamon and Nutmeg* begins. She is regarded as a tomboy, and she doesn't get along well with her older sister, who insists on staying inside the house to sew and bake. Tessa's father, who used to dote on her, adores the family's new baby boy, Daniel, and Tessa feels neglected. To add to her troubles, Tessa is teased by her schoolteacher. Tessa occupies herself by reading the books her witty Aunt Helen left at the farm. When Tessa finds Nutmeg, a wild baby goat whose mother has been killed by a gun shot, and Cinnamon, a Jersey purebred, orphaned calf, she finds solace in secretly nurturing the animals. As the goat and calf grow older, she is forced to reveal them to her family, and she begins to search for Cinnamon's owner. While no one claims the cow at first, some dishonest neighbors provide false papers of ownership, and it takes the arrival of Tessa's Aunt Helen to help unravel the mystery and save Cinnamon. Although, according to a *Bulletin of the Center for Children's Books* reviewer, *Cinnamon and Nutmeg* contains an "all-threads-tied" conclusion, the story is "satisfying and logical."

The characters from *Cinnamon and Nutmeg* reappear in *Mick's Country Cousins.* This book begins as Mick, who is half-Maori, is sent to live with his cousins on the farm. Mick has led a troubled life; his father has abandoned the family, his mother has not been able to control her sons, and his brother, Kevin, has been sent to a detention center for delinquent boys. Mick's arrival at the farm does not solve his problems. He is convinced that his cousins have agreed to his presence as a farm hand rather than as a member of their family. Mick keeps company with the family that wrongly claimed the calf Cinnamon in *Cinnamon and Nutmeg* and deliberately does his chores incorrectly. Nevertheless, Mick

When Tessa's brother is born, she feels neglected and decides to run away—but instead discovers a special secret about an abandoned calf. (Cover illustration by Unada.)

gradually begins to understand that he is accepted by his cousins. By the time his brother escapes from the detention center and attacks their aunt, Mick is ready to defend her and his new life in the bush country. A critic for *Junior Bookshelf* commented that the "portrait of Mick ... is quite something," and Barbara Britton argued in the *Times Literary Supplement* that *Mick's Country Cousins* is "an extremely good novel, full of comprehension of difficult feelings."

As she once told *SATA*, de Roo's years abroad allowed her to return to New Zealand "with a new perspective and a new and deeper appreciation of the natural beauty of New Zealand's forests, mountains and sea." This "deeper appreciation" is reflected in *Scrub Fire*. According to Patricia Manning in *School Library Journal*, de Roo evocatively describes the "flora and fauna" in the New Zealand wilderness in great detail in this novel, "lend[ing] credence to her tale." It begins when thirteen-year-old Michelle reluctantly accompanies her younger brothers on a camping trip in New Zealand led by her aunt and uncle. She is horrified when her Uncle Don's attempt at wilderness cooking sets the scrub on fire, and the group of campers scatters as the fire spreads. Although Michelle spends some time in the wilderness alone, she is soon reunited with her two brothers, who use survival tactics during the twelve days they are lost to reach safety. By the time the children are rescued, as a critic for *Kirkus Reviews* remarked, Michelle is "a bigger and better person."

Traveller, Because of Rosie, Jacky Nobody, and *The Bats' Nest* are historical novels. *Traveller* introduces Tom Farrell, who travels from New England in the 1850s expecting a job as a cadet on a sheep farm, and Harriet Wills, who is betrothed to Tom's new boss and accompanies Tom on the journey across the sea. When Tom and Harriet arrive in New Zealand, they learn that Tom's boss (Harriet's betrothed) has drowned. Tom sets out to find the sheep farm on his own, and Harriet boldly sets up her own shop. A clever, courageous sheepdog, Traveller, saves Tom's life, journeys with him, and leads him to a notorious convict. As a reviewer for *Junior Bookshelf* wrote, de Roo makes it clear that "folly or carelessness are quickly repaid by nature" in the rugged New Zealand wilderness.

Jacky Nobody exemplifies de Roo's talent for blending historical fact with fiction. This work tells the story of a half-Maori boy living during an uprising in New Zealand in the 1840s. When the orphaned boy, who lives with missionaries, realizes that he is the son of an elite Maori woman and an English sailor, he returns to live with Maori people and even becomes a Maori warrior. Jacky describes the haka, or war dance, that the Maori warriors perform, and the series of events leading to violent conflict. Readers learn how the Maori chief brings down the British flag and how the Red Coats arrive to stop the rebellion. At the end of the book, Jacky watches the settlement he grew up in burning.

De Roo once told *SATA* that, in addition to writing dramatic novels and historical fiction, she sometimes

In this 1977 work, a family camping in New Zealand accidentally sets the scrub on fire, and the three children end up lost in the bush for twelve days. (Cover illustration by Pamela Carroll.)

needs to "branch out ... into the realms of fantasy and fairy tale." This aspect of her writing career manifests itself in *Friend Troll, Friend Taniwha*—which features a Scandinavian giant as well as a Maori sea monster—and in de Roo's musical plays for children. "The theatre is a lifelong love and much of my spare time is devoted to amateur theatre, which is particularly strong in a small country with little scope for professional theatre." De Roo continued, "The spoken word, its sounds and possibilities, has always fascinated me, from youthful poetry writing onwards, and even in books, the dialogue is the part in which I always feel most at home."

■ Works Cited

Britton, Barbara, review of *Mick's Country Cousins*, *Times Literary Supplement*, December 6, 1974, p. 1376.

Review of *Cinnamon and Nutmeg, Bulletin of the Center for Children's Books,* December, 1974, p. 60.

Fitzgibbon, Tom, "Anne de Roo," *Twentieth-Century Children's Writers,* 4th edition, St. James Press, 1994, pp. 295-96.

Manning, Patricia, review of *Scrub Fire, School Library Journal,* November, 1980, p. 72.

Review of *Mick's Country Cousins, Junior Bookshelf,* February, 1975, p. 60.

Review of *Scrub Fire, Kirkus Reviews,* November 1, 1980, p. 1394.

Review of *Traveller, Junior Bookshelf,* August, 1979, p. 216.

■ For More Information See

PERIODICALS

Bulletin of the Center for Children's Books, January, 1981, p. 91.

Kirkus Reviews, January 15, 1974, p. 55.

Times Educational Supplement, September 27, 1985, p. 28.

Times Literary Supplement, December 4, 1969, p. 1394; July 18, 1980, p. 806.*

*   *   *

DOMANSKA, Janina 1913(?)-1995

OBITUARY NOTICE—See index for *SATA* sketch: Born c. 1913 in Warsaw, Poland; emigrated to the United States, 1952; naturalized citizen, 1964; died following a stroke, February 2, 1995, in Naples, FL. Educator, artist, and author/illustrator of children's books. During Domanska's prolific career in juvenile fiction, she illustrated some forty-five books, writing, adapting, and translating more than twenty of them herself. In the late 1940s and early 1950s, she taught at the Academy of Fine Arts in Rome, Italy. She also had her art featured in various solo and group shows. Domanska worked as a textile designer in the mid-1950s before venturing into children's books in 1960. Her work as an illustrator has included pictures for books such stories as *Clocks Tell the Time* by Alma R. Reck; *The Bremen Town Musicians* by Elizabeth Shub; and *The Art of Polish Cooking* by Alina Zeranska. Among her own self-illustrated writings are *King Krakus and the Dragon, Marek, the Little Fool, What Happens Next?, Busy Monday Morning,* and *A Was an Angler.* Domanska was the recipient of numerous awards, including a notable children's book of the year citation from the American Library Association for *The Coconut Thieves* and a Caldecott Honor Book Medal for *If All the Seas Were One Sea.*

OBITUARIES AND OTHER SOURCES:

BOOKS

Who's Who in America, 40th edition, Marquis, 1978, p. 863.

PERIODICALS

New York Times, February 15, 1995, p. D21.

DOMM, Jeffrey C. 1958-

■ Personal

Born June 22, 1958, in Detroit, MI; son of Robert A. (a teacher) and Mary Lou (a secretary; maiden name, Oversby) Domm; married Kristin Bieber (a teacher and writer), July 14, 1984; children: Lukas Nathanial, Jakob Mathias. *Education:* Detroit Center for Creative Studies, B.F.A.; Columbia College, M.A. *Religion:* Lutheran.

■ Addresses

Home—14 Green Bay Dr., R.R. 4, Eastern Passage, Nova Scotia, Canada B3G 1L1.

■ Career

Freelance creative director for advertising, 1981—. Nova Scotia College of Art and Design, part-time professor, 1991—; independent documentary filmmaker. *Member:* Graphic Designers Association (Canada); Illustrators Guild.

■ Illustrator

Doe Boyle, *Gray Wolf Pup,* TMC Soundprints, 1993.
Animals Don't Talk, Aegina Press, 1994.
Rebecca Rupp, *Everything You Never Learned About Birds,* Storey Communications, 1994.

■ Sidelights

Jeffrey C. Domm told *SATA:* "My love for the natural world has been a prominent element in my art since I began to draw. I find it extremely gratifying to begin a

Jeffrey C. Domm's love of wildlife shows in his charming illustrations of wolves for Doe Boyle's 1993 book, *Gray Wolf Pup.*

project with a white canvas in front of me and to watch that image come to life a little at a time. When I paint wildlife I find myself concentrating first on the eye of that animal. Once I have achieved the character of the eye I can proceed with the painting, knowing that I have the character and life of that particular species captured.

"With a B.F.A. in design and illustration and an M.A. in film and video production, I have been blessed with the opportunity to travel to many parts of the world. A few years back I produced a film for a large corporation which took me around the world. My fondest memory of the trip was sitting for hours in the middle of a penguin colony in South America. I have recently returned from Hawaii where I was a camera operator and a creative director for a film which explores the environmental destruction of the last remaining North American rain forest.

"My art is an expression of my desire to preserve the precious world we live in."*

* * *

DOWNING, David A(lmon) 1958-
(Russell Almon, a joint pseudonym)

■ Personal

Born October 26, 1958, in Boise, ID; son of Allen L. (a farmer) and Virginia S. (a homemaker; maiden name, Norton) Downing; married Paula S. Wittmann (a teacher), April 18, 1992. *Education:* University of Oregon, B.A. (English), 1980; University of Washington, M.F.A. (creative writing), 1988.

■ Addresses

Home—143 Northwest 79th St., Seattle, WA 98117.

■ Career

University of Washington Extension, Seattle, instructor in fiction writing, 1990—; CNA Companies (an architectural and engineering firm), Kirkland, WA, marketing writer, 1992—.

■ Awards, Honors

Kidd Fiction Award, University of Oregon, and Oregon Magazine Fiction Contest award, both 1980, both for "Through Summer Mud"; Louisa Kern award, 1987, for "The Rocks"; Young Writer's Fiction Contest award, *NW Magazine, Portland Oregonian,* 1988, for "Madonna."

■ Writings

(With William R. Clevenger, under joint pseudonym Russell Almon) *The Kid Can't Miss!,* Avon Books, 1992.

■ Work in Progress

Collaborating with Clevenger on a young adult novel; working independently on a short story collection.

■ Sidelights

David A. Downing, coauthor of a young adult novel with William Clevenger under the joint pseudonym Russell Almon (a combination of their middle names), told *SATA:* "I met Bill through a mutual friend about a year before we started writing *The Kid Can't Miss!* I read a short story Bill had written centered around kids playing basketball. It was Bill's first effort, and I thought it was great. I told him so the next time we met and mentioned that I'd always wanted to write a book for junior high-aged kids—in particular, a sports story, since I recalled whipping through the available sports fiction all too quickly as a kid. Our conversation picked up momentum, and we ended up tossing around the possibility of trying to collaborate on a story 'someday.'

"Two weeks later, Bill had sketched out his idea for *The Kid Can't Miss!* and delivered it to me. I was impressed by his enthusiasm and drive and liked his idea, so we went to work. We worked out the story's outline together, divided its chapters up among the three characters whose points of view we'd decided to use, and then met each week to critique and revise our efforts. I wrote the first draft of the chapters from Bean's point of view; Bill wrote Phang Wu's chapters; and we alternated drafting Bradley's sections. Each week, each of us would write a first draft of a chapter and rewrite the other person's chapter from the previous week. During our sessions—usually early in the morning before work, sometimes on weekends—we'd sit down together in front of the computer and haggle over final changes to our rewrites. It was a great time, a lot of laughs. We finished the book on schedule.

"Bill has since moved from Seattle to San Diego, and it's taken us a while to gear up for another collaboration. We finally began the process during the summer of 1994, though, and expect to finish our next book in 1995."

* * *

DUNLAP, Julie 1958-

■ Personal

Born July 2, 1958, in Kansas City, MO; daughter of John Carl Dunlap (an architectural draftsman) and Jean Nash (an elementary teacher; maiden name, Rennick); married Michael W. Vogel (a professor), June 6, 1981; children: Nathan, Hannah, Sarah. *Education:* Attended Woods Hole Marine Biology Laboratory summer course, 1978; University of Missouri—Kansas City, B.S. (with highest honors), 1979; Yale University, M.Phil., 1984, Ph.D., 1987. *Politics:* Democrat. *Hobbies and other interests:* Bird watching, hiking, studying

JULIE DUNLAP

environmental history, exploring nature with her children.

■ Addresses

Home—7315 Kerry Hill Ct., Columbia, MD 21045.

■ Career

University of Missouri, Kansas City, MO, Biology Department teaching assistant, 1978-79; Yale University, New Haven, CT, Biology Department teaching fellow, 1980; Yale University Forestry School, postdoctoral researcher, 1987-88; Humane Society of the United States, Washington, DC, associate director of higher education, 1989-90; Environmental education consultant, 1990—. *Member:* Society of Children's Book Writers and Illustrators, National Audubon Society, Sierra Club, Howard County Bird Club.

■ Awards, Honors

University of Missouri Curators' Scholarship, 1977-79; Phi Beta Kappa Scholarship, 1978-79; Geraldine Dodge Fellowship for study in human-animal ecology, Yale University, 1981-84.

■ Writings

Aldo Leopold: Living with the Land (biography), illustrated by Antonio Castro, Twenty-First Century Books, 1993.

Parks for the People: A Story about Frederick Law Olmstead (biography), illustrated by Susan Fair Lieber, Carolrhoda Books, 1994.

Contributor of articles to *Audubon Naturalist News, Baltimore's Child, Cobblestone, Society for Children's Book Writers and Illustrators Bulletin,* and the *Washington Post.* Also author of numerous academic publications, including (with S. Kellert) "Animal Welfare and Rights in Zoos and Zoological Parks," *Encyclopedia of Bioethics,* Macmillan; articles in *Sharing Is Caring Newsletter, Humane Innovations and Alternatives in Animal Experimentation, Between the Species, Anthrozoos;* book reviews in *Animals Agenda* and *Anthrozoos.*

■ Work in Progress

Eye on the Wild: A Story about Ansel Adams, for Carolrhoda Books; *Birds in the Bushes: A Story about Margaret Morse Nice,* for Carolrhoda Books; researching a biography of botanist Carolus Linnaeus; planning books about scientists, environmentalists, and wildlife.

■ Sidelights

With the publication of *Aldo Leopold: Living with the Land,* Julie Dunlap began to share her understanding of ecology with a wide audience of grade-school and middle-school children. In this work, Dunlap explains the myriad ways in which Aldo Leopold, a seminal figure in the conservation movement, contributed to the study and philosophy of ecology. At the same time, as

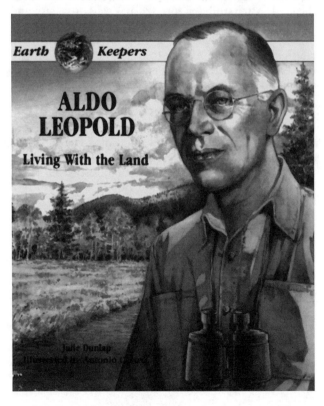

Part of the "Earth Keepers" series, Dunlap's 1993 work discusses the life and ideas of ecologist and author Aldo Leopold. (Cover illustration by Antonio Castro.)

Kay Weisman writes in *Booklist*, Dunlap provides an "important historical perspective" that describes the changes in perspectives of ecology and conservation "over the last 100 years."

Dunlap told *SATA* how *Aldo Leopold* emerged from her childhood interests and adult education: "Writing was my favorite pastime as a child. In elementary school, I wrote poems, short stories, a play, and a novel about my other love—horses. But science classes began to capture my attention. I grew fascinated with all aspects of nature, especially wildlife, and developed a deep concern for protecting endangered species. I didn't know anyone who was both a writer and a scientist, so I chose to study biology and tried to forget about writing.

"While studying wildlife conservation in graduate school, I discovered a book by Aldo Leopold called *A Sand County Almanac*. It tells the story of how—and why—Leopold worked to restore the ecological health of a run-down old farm. The author of those moving essays was an ecologist and realized that writing as well as science is a critical tool in conservation. The most important books in my life had been children's books, such as [Scott O'Dell's] *The Island of the Blue Dolphins*, and I decided to write a biography of Aldo Leopold in the hope of inspiring children to share his (and my) concern for the earth."

In *Aldo Leopold*, Dunlap explains how Leopold grew up in the late nineteenth century on a farm in Iowa, where his parents taught him to appreciate nature and care for the land. After studying forestry at Yale University and working as a forest ranger in the Apache National Forest, Leopold began to develop the idea that would later help shape the American conservation movement: that the land and the people and animals that inhabit it are interdependent.

As a professor at the University of Wisconsin, Leopold conducted experiments and studies that demonstrated his path-breaking ideas about what came to be known as ecology. He also began to restore the health of a depleted farm in Sand County. The collection of essays he wrote about the farm's transformation from a wasteland to a thriving, green haven for living things, *A Sand County Almanac*, continues to inspire the environmental movement. In addition, as a game management chair in Wisconsin, Leopold promoted critical conservation legislation.

Dunlap works as an environmental education consultant and continues to write books about leaders who have changed our perspective on the natural world—or the way human beings should live with it. She expressed enthusiasm about her career as a writer to *SATA:* "Now my work combines my fascination with science and my joy in writing—a beautiful compromise."

■ Works Cited

Weisman, Kay, review of *Aldo Leopold*, *Booklist*, February 15, 1994, p. 1078.

■ For More Information See

PERIODICALS

Authors of Books for Young People, Winter, 1994, p. 13.
School Library Journal, February, 1994, p. 108.

* * *

DURRELL, Gerald (Malcolm) 1925-1995

OBITUARY NOTICE—See index for *SATA* sketch: Surname accented on the first syllable; born January 7, 1925, in Jamshedpur, India; died January 30, 1995, on the Channel Island of Jersey, off the coast of England. Zoologist, naturalist, and author. Durrell is remembered for his study of the animal kingdom, which included researching various creatures and their natural habitats, the collection of wildlife for zoos, the preservation of endangered species, and the authorship of humorous tales about his adventures in the wild. Durrell was born in India but returned with his family to England in 1928. Beginning his career as a student animal keeper at the Whipsnade Zoological Park in England, Durrell began leading zoological expeditions in the late 1940s to places such as Cameroon, Nigeria, and Guyana. In 1958 he founded the Jersey Wildlife Preservation Trust on the Channel Island of Jersey, and he later founded the Wildlife Preservation Trust International in Pennsylvania and the Wildlife Preservation Trust Canada in Toronto. Durrell's work with animals also led him into the world of television and a collaboration with the British Broadcasting Corporation on television series such as *Two in the Bush* and *The Stationary Ark*. The brother of noted poet and author Lawrence Durrell, he also penned more than thirty-five works of memoirs, fiction, nonfiction, and the children's book, *The New Noah*. A number of his writings reached bestseller status, such as *A Zoo in My Luggage*, *The Aye-Aye and I*, and *The Bafut Beagles*. Noted for their lighthearted and humorous presentation, Durrell's memoirs include *My Family and Other Animals* and *Birds, Beasts, and Relatives*. His interest in the animal world is also evident in his fiction such as *The Donkey Rustlers*. Durrell was named an Officer of the Order of the British Empire in 1982.

OBITUARIES AND OTHER SOURCES:

PERIODICALS

Los Angeles Times, February 2, 1995, p. A20.
Times (London), January 31, 1995, pp. 1, 23.

E–F

ANN E. ESKRIDGE

ESKRIDGE, Ann E. 1949-

■ Personal

Born July 17, 1949, in Chicago, IL; daughter of Arnett E. V. and Marguerite (Hinds) Eskridge. *Education:* University of Oklahoma, B.A., 1971; Michigan State University, M.A., 1981; attended Ferris State College and Recording Institute of Detroit.

■ Addresses

Home and office—17217 Fairfield, Detroit, MI 48221. *Agent*—Marie Dutton Brown, 625 Broadway, No. 902, New York, NY 10012.

■ Career

WXYZ-TV, Detroit, MI, reporter, 1972-76; free-lance public relations agent, Detroit, 1976-78; Lt. Governor of Michigan, executive assistant, 1978-79; Michigan State Treasurer, administrator, 1979-81; Statewide Nutrition Commission, administrator, 1982-83; Detroit Council President Erma Henderson, administrative assistant, 1983; Golightly Vocational Technical Center, Detroit, instructor in mass media, 1983-90; free-lance writer and teaching consultant, Detroit, 1990-92; Michigan Consolidated Gas Company, speechwriter, 1992-95; free-lance writer, 1995—. *Chicago Daily Defender,* reporter, summers, 1968-69; *Oklahoma Daily,* reporter, 1970; *Oklahoma Journal,* reporter, 1970; KWTV (Oklahoma City), reporter, 1970-71; WBEN-TV (Buffalo, NY), reporter, 1971-72. Has conducted various workshops, including a creative scriptwriting workshop for Henry Ford High School, 1991, and playwriting for the theater, for a youth training program for Urban Arts Corporation, 1992; has given numerous lectures and demonstrations on scriptwriting at local colleges; has also served on a variety of boards including the Michigan Film and Video Production Industry Council (president), Detroit Producers Association, Black Professionals in Film and Video (vice president), and WTVS-TV, as well as being appointed vice president of the Public Benefit Corporation by Detroit Mayor Dennis Archer. *Member:* Detroit Women Writers.

■ Awards, Honors

Distinguished Service Award, Detroit City Council, 1974; Mayor's Award of Merit, Detroit, 1975; Alpha Kappa Alpha Award, 1975; grants from Detroit Public Education Fund and New Detroit, 1984-85, Michigan Council of the Arts, 1986 and 1988, Wayne County Intermediate School District, 1987-88, Women's Scriptwriting Project Funding Exchange, 1991, Center for New Television, 1992, and Arts Foundation of Michigan, 1992; award from National Black Programming Consortium, teen category, Ohio State University

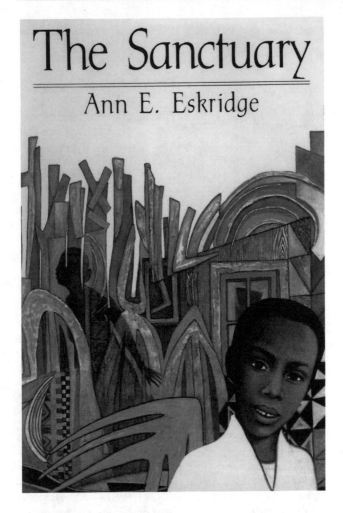

Although the neighbors call Lucy's backyard sanctuary an eyesore, Little Man is determined to stop them from tearing it down. (Cover illustration by Nubia Owens.)

award, and Communications Excellence to Black Audiences (CEBA) Award of Distinction, all 1991, for "Brother Future."

■ Writings

The Sanctuary, Cobblehill Books, 1994.
The Sanctuary (play; based in part on the author's book of the same title), Child's Play, 1995.

Contributor of numerous articles to periodicals, including *Michigan Chronicle, Detroit Free Press, Detroit News,* and *Monthly Detroit Magazine.*

SCREENPLAYS

"Brother Future," *Wonderworks,* PBS, 1991.

Also author of *Echoes Across the Prairie* (miniseries), optioned by Longbow Productions. Has also created various commercial and industrial video tapes for companies, including Ford, Wayne County Foster Care, and Adult Well Being Services.

■ Work in Progress

A Black historical saga.

■ Sidelights

Ann E. Eskridge told *SATA:* "I have worked as a television reporter, public relations consultant, political appointee, and teacher. Writing was an integral part of all the jobs I had. However, I didn't take my writing seriously until I began teaching high school students how to write for the media. I started writing about my students.

"One work produced in this period was 'Brother Future,' a *Wonderworks* family movie airing on PBS in 1991. I have won numerous writing grants and was chosen to participate in various writing workshops. My first children's book, *The Sanctuary,* published by Cobblehill Books, an imprint of Penguin, has received critical acclaim. Currently, it is being optioned for a TV movie, and a miniseries I wrote is also being developed for television.

"Although I was born and raised in Chicago, I have made Detroit my home for many years. I hope to continue writing for television and for children."

■ For More Information See

PERIODICALS

Kirkus Reviews, June 1, 1994, p. 773.
Publishers Weekly, May 2, 1994, p. 310.
Quill & Quire, May, 1994, p. 38.
School Library Journal, May, 1994, p. 112.

*   *   *

FARNSWORTH, Bill 1958-

■ Personal

Born October 11, 1958, in Norwalk, CT; son of John M. and Gloria (Mulcahy) Farnsworth; married Deborah M. Jajer (in retail), October 6, 1984; children: Allison Marie, Caitlin Elizabeth. *Education:* Ringling School of Art, graduated with honors, 1980.

■ Addresses

Home—99 Merryall Rd., New Milford, CT, 06776.
Office—30 Elm St., New Milford, CT 06776.

■ Career

Illustrator, 1980—.

■ Illustrator

The Illustrated Children's Bible, Harcourt, 1993.
Dorothy and Thomas Hoobler, *French Portraits,* Raintree Steck-Vaughn, 1994.
Sanna Baker, *Grandpa Is a Flier,* A. Whitman, 1995.

BILL FARNSWORTH

Cheryl Ryan, *Sally Arnold,* Cobblehill Books/Dutton, 1995.
Christmas Menorah, A. Whitman, 1995.
Anica's Days, Lothrop, 1996.

■ Sidelights

Bill Farnsworth told *SATA:* "Real people and events that have in some way influenced our lives are the core of what I paint. From book jackets, children's books and magazine illustration to private portrait commissions and limited edition prints and plates, the research involved with a particular painting can be quite extensive, especially if it is some kind of historical matter. Whatever the wide variety of subject matter might be, my personal goal is to give the client more than what they asked for and aim for the very best painting I've ever done. The whole process of reading a manuscript, doing the research, and producing the finished art is very exciting and fun. An artist must continually grow with every project in order to improve and sharpen his skills as a draftsman. And what will ultimately make your personal view unique is what you have to say from your heart."

*   *   *

FATCHEN, Max 1920-

■ Personal

Born August 3, 1920, in Adelaide, South Australia, Australia; son of Cecil William (a farmer) and Isabel

(Ridgway) Fatchen; married Jean Wohlers (a teacher), May 15, 1942; children: Winsome, Michael, Timothy. *Education:* Attended high school in South Australia. *Religion:* Methodist. *Hobbies and other interests:* Fishing, travel.

■ Addresses

Home—15 Jane St., Smithfield, South Australia 5114, Australia. *Agent*—John Johnson Ltd., 45-47 Clerkenwell Green, London EC1R 0HT, England.

■ Career

Adelaide News and *Sunday Mail,* Adelaide, South Australia, journalist and special writer, 1946-55; *Advertiser,* Adelaide, journalist, 1955-84, literary editor, 1971-81, special writer, 1981-84. *Military service:* Royal Australian Air Force, 1940-45. *Member:* Order of Australia.

■ Awards, Honors

Book of the Year Younger Honor, Children's Book Council of Australia, 1988, for *A Paddock of Poems;* commendation, Children's Book Council of Australia, for *The River Kings;* Runner-up, Book of the Year Award, Children's Book Council of Australia, for *The Spirit Wind;* Advance Australia Award for literature, South Australia section, 1991.

■ Writings

FICTION FOR CHILDREN

The River Kings, illustrated by Clyde Pearson, Hicks Smith (Sydney, Australia), 1966, Methuen (London), 1966, St. Martin's, 1968.
Conquest of the River, illustrated by Pearson, Hicks Smith, 1970, Methuen, 1970.
The Spirit Wind, illustrated by Trevor Stubley, Hicks Smith, 1973, Methuen, 1973.
Chase through the Night, illustrated by Graham Humphreys, Methuen (Sydney and London), 1977.
The Time Wave, illustrated by Edward Mortelmans, Methuen, 1978.
Closer to the Stars, Methuen, 1981.
Had Yer Jabs?, Methuen, 1987.

POETRY

Songs for My Dog and Other People, illustrated by Michael Atchison, Kestrel, 1980.
Wry Rhymes for Troublesome Times, illustrated by Atchison, Kestrel, 1983.
A Paddock of Poems, illustrated by Kerry Argent, Omnibus, Puffin, 1987.
A Pocketful of Rhymes, illustrated by Argent, Omnibus, 1989.
A Country Christmas, illustrated by Timothy Ide, Omnibus, 1990.
The Country Mail Is Coming: Poems from Down Under, illustrated by Catherine O'Neill, Joy Street Books, 1990.
(With Colin Thiele) *Tea for Three,* illustrated by Craig Smith, Moondrake, 1994.

Peculiar Rhymes and Lunatic Lines, illustrated by Lesley Bisseker, Orchard Books, 1995.

Contributor of light verse to the *Denver Post.*

VERSE; ILLUSTRATED BY IRIS MILLINGTON; PUBLISHED BY LONGMAN

Drivers and Trains, 1963.
Keepers and Lighthouses, 1963.
The Plumber, 1963.
The Electrician, 1963.
The Transport Driver, 1965.
The Carpenter, 1965.

FOR ADULTS

Peculia Australia: Verses, privately printed, 1965.
Just Fancy, Mr. Fatchen! A Collection of Verse, Prose and Fate's Cruel Blows, Rigby (Adelaide), 1967.
Forever Fatchen, Advertiser (Adelaide), 1983.
Mostly Max, Wakefield Press, 1995.

■ Adaptations

Chase through the Night was adapted as a television series by Independent Productions, 1983; *The River Kings* was adapted as a television mini-series by Prospect Productions and broadcast by Australian Broadcasting Corporation, 1991.

■ Sidelights

As a native Australian and journalist, Max Fatchen has traveled and lived throughout Australia. In his fiction and poetry for children, Fatchen shares his experiences and celebrates the Australian people and landscape. While Fatchen has been popular in Australia, the charm of his works will not be lost on readers from other lands. His adventure novels for teens, including *The River Kings* and *Chase through the Night,* and his poetry collections for younger readers, such as *Songs for My Dog and Other People* and *The Country Mail Is Coming,* provide readers with an understanding of the land and language of Australia and the lives of young people there, while addressing universal concerns and themes as well.

Fatchen appreciates the thrill of travel and adventure and hopes to pass it along to his readers. As he once explained to *SATA,* he wants his readers "to be standing beside me or running beside me, breathless with interest as we clamber up some old riverbank or hang onto a rail in the wild sea. A book is a voyage and I don't just want my readers to be passengers anxious to get off because they feel seasick with all the words, but eager members of the crew shouting, 'land ho' when we sight the islands of imagination.... Stories must be honest, and honest stories are not always happy, but they can be moving, vivid, arresting, so that you never want to put them down.... That's what I want my stories to be."

Fatchen was born and raised on a hay farm in Angle Vale, in rural Australia. "My early life revolved around the farm; I was an only child and I daydreamed a good

Max Fatchen with poodle, Butterfly, who inspired *Songs for My Dog.*

deal as I learned to drive a team of eight Clydesdale horses. I liked ploughing best; the singing sound as the furrows turned, the warm Australian day, the hawks hovering as if pinned to the sky." Fatchen remembered spending time with the members of his small church: "There were tea meetings, where the tables groaned with cakes and pastries, where big men expounded their faith, and tea came from large coppers fired by logs of wood. It was this beginning that made me aware of the feeling and mood of landscape."

Fatchen's work as a journalist took him far from Angle Vale. On his travels he discovered remote parts of his native land that fascinated him with their beauty. He recalled how he flew with "surveyors among the islands of the Gulf of Carpenteria" and "with helicopter pilots across swamps where the geese rose in living carpets or past muddy estuaries, where the seagoing crocodiles, drawn up like small canoes, lifted their heads as we came down low to buzz them as we passed.

"When I traveled along the Australian river, the Murray, with old riverboat men, again the feeling of the landscape, the movement of the river, the birds that congregated in small families on the long sandspit, and the river towns tucked around the bends all found their

Petra and her mother are kidnapped by a band of thieves in this 1983 screen adaptation of Max Fatchen's novel, *Chase through the Night*.

way into my books. When I was at sea with the trawler men, getting more stories for my paper, I watched the conflict between men and the sea, enjoyed the yarns in the fo'castle, wedged myself in the corner of the wheelhouse as the great grey-bearded waves went roaring past in the Australian bight."

Fatchen enjoyed meeting people he encountered on his journeys and listening to their stories. These people included "the railway men on the slow outback trains, where the heat can buckle the rails; the cattle men along the Birdsville track in Australia's interior, where, at night, while your campfire flickers, you are aware of the immense, brooding land out there in the darkness under its lonely stars and its remote moon." The stories of "the songmen of the Aboriginal tribes" especially intrigued him. According to Fatchen, these "old men who knew the legends and who talked about them to me as we sat at night by the moonlit rivers of Arnhem Land ... taught me about the way landscape has its poetry and meaning."

While Fatchen's adventure novels for teens exemplify his enthusiasm for settings, they are animated with local color and lively plots. According to *Library Journal* contributor Joseph L. Buelna, Fatchen combines humor

and "suspense" in an "entertaining mixture" in *The River Kings*. Set in nineteenth-century Australia, *The River Kings* begins when Shawn runs away from his home. The thirteen-year-old boy finds work on the boats that trade goods up and down the Murray River despite the fact that the railroad industry is taking business from the boats. *Conquest of the River*, which a *Times Literary Supplement* critic described as a "tough racy book," continues Shawn's adventures on the Murray.

The Spirit Wind, also set in the nineteenth century, follows Jarl Hansen as he serves as a deckhand on a ship named the *Hootzen*. The ship, which leaves Norway for Australia, is menaced by a mate whose maliciousness forces Jarl to flee the ship in South Australia. There, he meets Nunganee, a character who is based on the Aboriginal men Fatchen met during his travels. Nunganee and Jarl learn much from each other before *The Spirit Wind* reaches its conclusion.

In *The Time Wave*, Josef, the son of a millionaire, takes a vacation on a Pacific island that is periodically flooded by a gigantic wave. He is forced to begin an adventure when he and his new friend Gina are kidnapped. Gina's great-grandmother was stranded on the island when one of the gigantic waves wrecked her ship years ago, and now Gina can't stop dreaming of the wave. As the children attempt to escape their captors, the threat of the wave looms over them. *The Time Wave* contains some suspenseful moments. As one critic wrote in *Junior Bookshelf,* the scene in which a professional killer seeking revenge on Josef's father chases the children is "nerve-shattering" and "really quite something."

Chase through the Night also involves a kidnapping. This time, Petra and her mother become the hostages of the thieves they have recognized. When they are taken to the small town where Petra's friend Ray lives, Ray tricks the thieves and foils their plans. Although *Times Literary Supplement* contributor David Bartlett complained about the story's "stereotyped characters," Margery Fisher, writing in *Growing Point,* admired the author's skillful use of setting and the "unity of atmosphere and plot."

Like his fiction, Fatchen's poetry presents universal themes as well as information about life in Australia. Yet in his poems Fatchen's hallmark is his insightful, childlike perspective. In the collection *Wry Rhymes for Troublesome Times,* for example, nonsense poems voice complaints about parents, aunts, and authority figures and describe the poet's pet peeves. Others toy with traditional nursery rhymes. According to *School Librarian* reviewer Colin Mills, Fatchen is "at his best with word play and mild satire" in this work. Similarly, *Songs for My Dog and Other People,* as *School Librarian*

critic Marcus Crouch asserted, maintains the perspective of an Australian child but is "quite complex" technically, and Fatchen "handles rhymes and rhythms with professional ease."

The forty-one poems in *The Country Mail Is Coming: Poems from Down Under* explore life in rural Australia as well as new babies, dinosaurs, haunted shipwrecks, and the letters in the mailman's bag. Although, as Ellen Fader related in *Horn Book,* the poems include Australian words like "takeaway," "heeler," and "bathers" that non-Australians might not understand, the meanings of the poems "are never obscured." Kathleen Whalin concluded in *School Library Journal* that *The Country Mail Is Coming* is "energetic" and "illuminating."

While Fatchen's books allow Australian children to take pride in their country's natural beauty and diverse cultures, they also inform children not native to that land of Australia's delights. A child of any nationality may find Fatchen's love of travel and adventure infectious. Those children who cannot leave home right away for an exciting journey across the land, over the sea, around an island, or on a river may take comfort in the idea that reading a book like one of Fatchen's is an adventure. Fatchen once invited *SATA*'s readers to begin an adventure with him: "Come aboard my book. We're sailing in five minutes!"

■ Works Cited

Bartlett, David, review of *Chase through the Night,* *Times Literary Supplement,* December 2, 1977, p. 1412.

Buelna, Joseph L., review of *The River Kings, Library Journal,* November 15, 1968, pp. 4412-13.

Review of *Conquest of the River, Times Literary Supplement,* December 11, 1970, p. 1457.

Crouch, Marcus, review of *Songs for My Dog and Other People, School Librarian,* June, 1981, p. 143.

Fader, Ellen, review of *The Country Mail Is Coming, Horn Book,* May/June, 1990, pp. 342-43.

Fisher, Margery, review of *Chase through the Night, Growing Point,* October, 1977, pp. 3185-86.

Mills, Colin, review of *Wry Rhymes for Troublesome Times, School Librarian,* March, 1984, p. 61.

Review of *The Time Wave, Junior Bookshelf,* February, 1979, p. 50.

Whalin, Kathleen, review of *The Country Mail Is Coming, School Library Journal,* August, 1990, p. 153.

■ For More Information See

BOOKS

Something about the Author Autobiography Series, Volume 20, Gale, 1995.

PERIODICALS

Booklist, April 1, 1990, p. 1548.
Kirkus Reviews, September 1, 1968, p. 978.
School Librarian, March, 1979, p. 54.

The poems in this collection capture the author's childhood in the Australian countryside. (Cover illustration by Catherine O'Neill)

FERRIS, Jeri Chase 1937-

▪ Personal

Born May 24, 1937, in Lincoln, NE; daughter of Harry Dean Liebers (a dairyman) and Eleanor Chase Doolittle; married Thomas J. Ferris (a teacher), August 25, 1956; children: Thomas Allan, Mark Dean. *Education:* California State College, B.A., 1967; Pepperdine University, M.Ed., 1975. *Politics:* "Realistic." *Religion:* Presbyterian/Episcopalian. *Hobbies and other interests:* Horses and riding, reading, classical and choral music, woodworking, handcrafts, gardening, the Internet, "and, of course, my four perfect grandchildren."

▪ Addresses

Office—c/o Lerner Publications, 241 First Ave. N., Minneapolis, MN 55401.

▪ Career

Los Angeles Unified School District, Los Angeles, CA, teacher, 1967-93; children's book author. *Member:* Society of Children's Book Writers and Illustrators, Authors Guild, Authors League of America, Women's National Book Association, PEN Center West, California Reading Association, FOCAL, Southern California Council on Literature for Children and Young People, Santa Monica Bay Area Reading Association.

▪ Awards, Honors

Outstanding Science Trade Book for Children citation, 1988, for *What Are You Figuring Now?: A Story about Benjamin Banneker;* Carter G. Woodson Award, National Council for the Social Studies, 1989, for *Walking the Road to Freedom: A Story about Sojourner Truth;* Notable Children's Trade Book in the Field of Social Studies citation, Outstanding Science Trade Book for Children citation, and Society of School Librarians International Award-winning Title, all 1989, Carter G. Woodson Outstanding Merit Book, 1990, and Sequoyah Children's Book Award Masterlist, 1991, all for *Arctic Explorer: The Story of Matthew Henson;* Notable Children's Trade Book in the Field of Social Studies citation, 1991, Carter G. Woodson Award, and Southern California Council on Literature for Children and Young People Award for significant contribution to the field of biography, both 1992, and New York Public Library Book for the Teen Age citation, all for *Native American Doctor: The Story of Susan LaFlesche Picotte;* Notable Children's Trade Book in the Field of Social Studies, and Carter G. Woodson Award, both 1995, for *What I Had Was Singing: The Story of Marian Anderson;* National Education Association's Author-Illustrator Human and Civil Rights Award, 1995, to the author "whose books promote an understanding and appreciation of human and civil rights."

Jeri Chase Ferris uses a narrative style to tell the story of a slave who spoke out against slavery in this 1988 book. (Cover illustration by Peter E. Hanson.)

▪ Writings

Go Free or Die: A Story about Harriet Tubman, illustrated by Karen Ritz, Carolrhoda Books, 1988.

Walking the Road to Freedom: A Story about Sojourner Truth, illustrated by Peter E. Hanson, Carolrhoda Books, 1988.

What Are You Figuring Now?: A Story about Benjamin Banneker, illustrated by Amy Johnson, Carolrhoda Books, 1988.

What Do You Mean?: A Story about Noah Webster, illustrated by Steve Michaels, Carolrhoda Books, 1988.

Arctic Explorer: The Story of Matthew Henson, Carolrhoda Books, 1989.

Native American Doctor: The Story of Susan LaFlesche Picotte, Carolrhoda Books, 1991.

What I Had Was Singing: The Story of Marian Anderson, Carolrhoda Books, 1994.

▪ Work in Progress

A biography of Thomas Jefferson, fall, 1995/spring, 1996; historical young adult fiction on the Siege of Leningrad.

■ Sidelights

Such historical figures as Harriet Tubman, Matthew Henson, and Marian Anderson are made accessible to children through the lively and thorough biographies of Jeri Chase Ferris. "My goal is to make these determined men and women inescapably alive, to make their deeds inescapably real, and to plant seeds of similar determination and self-confidence in the children who read about them," Ferris told *SATA*. "My goal is that children, no matter their ethnic and social backgrounds and despite the obstacles, will say to themselves, 'I, too, can make a difference.'"

Recalling her childhood as "the ideal writer's childhood," Ferris grew up in Nebraska on a small farm with her own horse and an unending supply of books from the local Andrew Carnegie library. "Add a considerable amount of isolation and imagination, helped along by massive doses of 'Let's Pretend' every Saturday morning, the freedom to gallop with the wind, and shelves of books from that Carnegie library. It is impossible *not* to be a writer," Ferris told *SATA*.

At the time, however, the thought of being an author never entered Ferris's mind; "in fact when I was young it somehow escaped me that all those books on the library shelves were *written* by someone," she recalled for *SATA*. "So although books were my inseparable companions, it didn't occur to me to write one myself. Creating stories such as those in the library, which took me into another world, were done by some magical process completely outside my experience. Or so I thought, then."

Instead, Ferris planned to be a librarian, a veterinarian, or an archaeologist; in reality she became first a secretary and a mother, and finally a teacher. And each of these occupations made valuable contributions to Ferris's later writing career. It was only after putting her husband through two degrees with the income from her secretarial job that Ferris returned to school to earn her own master's degree. Her teaching career which followed lasted for over twenty-five years, during the course of which she primarily taught first, second, and/or third grade in a large school near downtown Los Angeles.

The students Ferris taught and their needs set her to writing her first biography. "In searching for books for my students, books in which they would find people they could emulate, I found (or rather didn't find) great and brave men and women who had been overlooked," Ferris explained to *SATA*. "These heroes had changed the world around them for the better, but had not been recognized, often because of their race. In some cases, if not completely overlooked, at least they had not been written about in a lively and accessible way for young students."

The first two figures Ferris brought to life for children were Harriet Tubman and Sojourner Truth. Both were born into slavery in the late 1700s and early 1800s, but

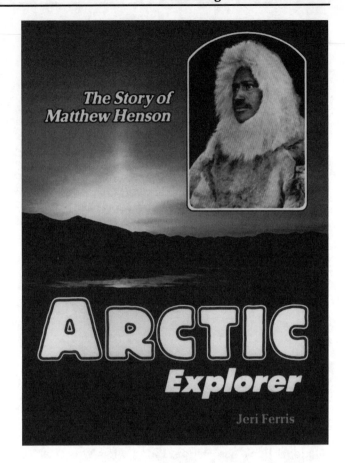

The author garnered numerous awards for this work on the African American explorer who discovered the North Pole along with Robert Peary.

were able to secure their freedom. And having done this, they helped other slaves reach for and capture this same freedom. Tubman did so through her work with the Underground Railroad, and Truth spent the majority of her life singing and speaking out against slavery and in support of women's rights. Ferris presents all the necessary facts in *Go Free or Die: A Story about Harriet Tubman* and *Walking the Road to Freedom: A Story about Sojourner Truth,* but does so in a narrative style that focuses on selected events and includes fictional dialogue and emotions. Frances Bradburn, writing in *Wilson Library Bulletin,* finds these biographies to be "spellbinding stories of two courageous black women." And Phillis Wilson asserts in *Booklist* that "these two women's stories come alive through Ferris' sensitive interpretations."

Noah Webster, a teacher like Ferris herself, is the focus of her 1988 biography *What Do You Mean?: A Story about Noah Webster.* It was after Webster became a teacher that he first noticed the scarcity of textbooks, so he wrote a grammar, a speller, and a reader. The success of these books managed to only increase the wealth of the printers, while Webster lived in debt for most of his life. He continued writing, though, and eventually produced his *American Dictionary of the English Language,* published in 1828. "This beginning biography, in sharing intimate details about Webster, has fine poetic imagery, humor, and flow," observes Reva Pitch Margolis in *School Library Journal.* Writing in *Booklist,* Wilson points out: "Ferris' word portrait of this feisty, contentious man ... provides fascinating reading."

The lesser known half of the team to discover the North Pole receives Ferris's attention in *Arctic Explorer: The Story of Matthew Henson.* Although he accompanied Robert Peary on the five expeditions that spanned eighteen years and finally brought the two men to the North Pole, Matthew Henson was ignored because of his race. It was not until 1988 that he was recognized as the co-discoverer of the North Pole and was buried next to Peary in Arlington National Cemetery. Using Henson's own accounts and the accounts of others present during the polar expeditions, Ferris proves that Henson was necessary to Peary's success. *School Library Journal* contributor Pamela K. Bomboy maintains that *Arctic Explorer* is "accurately written and filled with precise details," adding that it "is a jewel of an adventure story."

The story of Marian Anderson, the African-American singer whose career accelerated several important events of the civil rights movement, is told in *What I Had Was Singing: The Story of Marian Anderson.* The singer's famous Lincoln Memorial Easter Sunday concert is accurately described in Ferris's biography, as is Anderson's childhood and her church training and early career. "With a dignity well suited to the subject, this simply written biography presents the basic facts and humanizing details of Marian Anderson's life," describes Julie Corsaro in *Booklist.* And a *Kirkus Reviews* contributor states that Ferris's use of "anecdotes from the singer's own recollections, meticulously researched," are "told in moving but unsentimental prose."

■ Works Cited

Bomboy, Pamela K., review of *Arctic Explorer: The Story of Matthew Henson, School Library Journal,* June, 1989, p. 118.

Bradburn, Frances, review of *Go Free or Die: A Story about Harriet Tubman* and *Walking the Road to Freedom: A Story about Sojourner Truth, Wilson Library Bulletin,* September, 1988, p. 63.

Corsaro, Julie, review of *What I Had Was Singing: The Story of Marian Anderson, Booklist,* July, 1994, pp. 1938-39.

Margolis, Reva Pitch, review of *What Do You Mean?: A Story about Noah Webster, School Library Journal,* May, 1989, pp. 117-18.

Review of *What I Had Was Singing, Kirkus Reviews,* June 15, 1994, p. 844.

Wilson, Phillis, review of *Go Free or Die* and *Walking the Road to Freedom, Booklist,* March 1, 1988, p. 1179.

Wilson, Phillis, review of *What Do You Mean?, Booklist,* February 1, 1989, p. 938.

■ For More Information See

PERIODICALS

Booklist, January 1, 1989, p. 787; June 1, 1989, p. 1722.
Bulletin of the Center for Children's Books, December, 1991, pp. 87-88.
Horn Book, July, 1989, p. 498; January, 1992, p. 91.
Kirkus Reviews, November 1, 1988, p. 1603.
School Library Journal, March, 1988, pp. 206-7; February, 1989, p. 78; December, 1991, p. 140.

*   *   *

FLEMING, Virginia (Edwards) 1923-

■ Personal

Born May 31, 1923, in Highlands, NC; daughter of Grover David (owner of a dairy business and a painter) and Helen (a homemaker; maiden name, Heacock) Edwards; married Frank Fleming, July 17, 1942 (deceased); married Henry Urbanek (a research engineer), September 29, 1984; children: (first marriage) Rosemary Louise, Clifford Frank, Michael. *Education:* Brevard College, A.A., 1942; attended Glassboro State College. *Religion:* Presbyterian. *Hobbies and other interests:* Reading, word games, square dancing, piano, theatre, mountain hiking.

■ Addresses

Home—516 McKinley Ave., Pitman, NJ 08071.

VIRGINIA FLEMING

■ Career

First Presbyterian Church, Pitman, NJ, nursery school teacher, 1973-83, deacon, 1976-80. *Member:* Penn Laurel Poets, New Jersey Poetry Society, North Carolina Poetry Society, Society for Poets of Southern New Jersey, Philadelphia Writers Organization.

■ Awards, Honors

Children's Book of the Year, Child Study Children's Book Committee at Bank Street College, 1994, for *Be Good to Eddie Lee;* has received over seventy poetry and fiction awards.

■ Writings

So Tender the Spirit (poetry), New Jersey Council of the Arts, 1985.
Wellspring (poetry), New Jersey Council of the Arts, 1986.
Be Good to Eddie Lee, illustrated by Floyd Cooper, Philomel, 1993.

Contributor of stories and poems to *Wayah Review,* sponsored by the North Carolina Arts Council; contributor of poems to *North Carolina's 400 Years,* North Carolina Poetry Society, and *Here's to the Land,* North Carolina Poetry Society; has also published poems in two regional North Carolina history books, and anthologies published by the North Carolina Poetry Society and the New Jersey Poetry Society.

■ Work in Progress

Red Wolf Howling, a children's book; *Summer Visitors,* a novel; researching early North Georgia and western North Carolina history, 1776-1800, and Cherokee Indians in that period for a novel.

■ Sidelights

"As long as I can remember, reading and writing have been as much a part of my life as eating and sleeping—in fact, they often take preference," Virginia Fleming told *SATA.* "I could read before I started school and I began writing poetry at the age of eight. My first published work was a poem sent by my fifth grade teacher to the county newspaper, not as an assignment, but just because she felt it was good work and, probably, to encourage me. Literature always took a prominent place in my home in the Blue Ridge mountains of North Carolina and in the public school there, where the teachers were underpaid, but truly dedicated to seeing that the mountain children left school with a knowledge of the outside world and credits necessary for entering college.

"I can't remember when I did not want to write. Although some were carried off in a cedar chest during a burglary of our homeplace, I still find remnants of a book, poems and stories, and journal writings among

Eddie Lee, who has Down's Syndrome, follows Christy and JimBud into the woods, where he teaches Christy an important lesson about understanding and compassion. (Cover illustration by Floyd Cooper.)

closets and bookcases that were written during my growing-up years.

"Because it bothers me when I hear people say that they can not understand poetry, I endeavor to write poems that I feel anyone can understand. I want everyone to relate to my writing. The true desire of my heart is to express in writing the beautiful experiences that outweigh the hardships of growing up in the unique atmosphere of a small town in the Blue Ridge during the depression years.

"My work day begins right after breakfast when I retreat to my room for writing and stay until noon. My husband, who is retired, cooperates by disappearing during these hours to pursue his own interests. I really need quiet with no distractions in order to do my best writing. Sometimes I write in bed late at night or early in the morning when I am working on an intense or time-limited piece."

Fleming's first fictional effort is *Be Good to Eddie Lee,* a story for ages four to eight that tells the story of Christy, her friend JimBud, and the neighbor boy, Eddie Lee. Christy's mother has told her to "be good to Eddie Lee," as Eddie Lee has Down's Syndrome and is different from the other kids. Christy wants to spend the afternoon with JimBud, but Eddie Lee follows them. Christy allows Eddie Lee to join them, and is pleased when she actually enjoys her afternoon with the sweet-natured Eddie Lee as she begins to see things through his eyes. A

Publishers Weekly reviewer noted that Fleming's "characters ring true without being stereotypes and her message about acceptance and friendship is poignant, not heavy-handed."

"*Be Good to Eddie Lee* was not an intended 'moral' lesson," Fleming told *SATA*. "Rather than plotting the story and outcome, I just develop the characters and setting and the story unfolds as I write. I had three children of my own, taught nursery school for ten years, was a Den Mother for several years, and now have five grandchildren, so my experience with children allows me the freedom of expressing the feelings that children have."

■ Works Cited

Review of *Be Good to Eddie Lee, Publishers Weekly,* October 11, 1993, p. 86.

■ For More Information See

PERIODICALS

Horn Book Guide, spring, 1994, p. 65.
Kirkus Reviews, November 1, 1993, p. 1389.
School Library Journal, February, 1994, p. 84.

* * *

FRAUSTINO, Lisa Rowe 1961-
(S. L. Robel, a joint pseudonym)

■ Personal

Born May 26, 1961, in Dover-Foxcroft, ME; daughter of Franklin (a foreman) and Carole Linda (a postal clerk; maiden name, Reardon) Rowe; married Daniel V. Fraustino (an English professor), October 30, 1982; children: Julia, Dan, Olivia. *Education:* University of Maine at Orono, B.A. (English; with honors), 1984; University of Scranton, M.A. (English), 1988; Binghamton University (formerly State University of New York), Ph.D. (English), 1993. *Politics:* "Independent-minded Democrat." *Hobbies and other interests:* "Reading; watching my kids dance, swim, and make music; boating; camping; working out; cooking and eating; movies."

■ Addresses

Home—303 Main Ave., Clarks Summit, PA 18411.

■ Career

Author. National Education Corporation, Scranton, PA, editor, 1985-86; University of Scranton, Scranton, PA, instructor, 1987-90, 1994; Dick Jones Communications, Dalton, PA, associate editor, 1989-91; Institute of Children's Literature, Redding Ridge, CT, instructor, 1989-94; Hollins College, Roanoke, VA, instructor, 1995. Speaker and workshop presenter. *Member:* Society of Children's Book Writers and Illustrators (regional advisor, 1987—), Modern Language Association of

LISA ROWE FRAUSTINO

America, Authors Guild, Authors League of America, Children's Literature Association, La Plume Workshop for Children's Writers (originator), Maine Publishers and Writers Alliance, PennWriters.

■ Awards, Honors

Highlights for Children fiction contest winner, 1992, for "Back to the River."

■ Writings

Grass and Sky, Orchard Books, 1994.
Ash, Orchard Books, 1995.
Junkyard Purple, Orchard Books, in press.

Also author of screenplays: *The Olden Days,* 1988, and *Empty Words.* Contributor of short stories to *Wee Wisdom, Pennywhistle Press, With, Clubhouse, Pegasus Anthology,* and *Highlights for Children;* contributor of articles to periodicals, including *Best Sellers, Babytalk, Children's Writer, Once Upon a Time,* and under pseudonym S. L. Robel, with Susan Campbell Bartoletti, to *Pegasus Anthology.* Copy editor, *The Legal Studies Forum,* 1985-87.

■ Work in Progress

Land of the Adri, a middle-grade fantasy about the spirit of rocks and the power of dreams; *Blind Sight,* a picture book; *Lazybones,* a picture book; *House of Faces,* a middle grade novel; *The Last Man,* a young adult novel; a book about pixies in Celtic lore.

When Ash starts exhibiting strange behavior in this 1995 novel, his younger brother Wes struggles to understand what's causing it. (Cover illustration by Julie Granahan.)

■ Sidelights

"The only thing I hope to achieve in my books is the best storytelling I can possibly wring out of myself," Lisa Rowe Fraustino told *SATA*. "I dream that my best will be enough to carry a young reader through my book and straight to the library for another by someone else.

"I write every day in a very cluttered office in my home. My office is cluttered because I have more books than I have bookshelves, because I have many more interesting things to do than clean, and because I have many interesting things doing all at once. My desk holds piles of manuscripts in various stages of completion. I write many, many drafts of each story. Rather than work straight through on one project until it's publishable, I'll set aside draft three of one story to work on draft six of another or perhaps finish the first draft of something new. When I have a new idea that keeps me awake at night, I'll get up and write it down.

"If I start listing the authors who have influenced me and my work, I will definitely leave important people out because I read so much and try to be someone on whom nothing is lost. But perhaps I've learned the most from studying the works of Katherine Paterson. Also, in no particular order, I love Natalie Babbitt, J. M. Barrie, Beverly Cleary, A. A. Milne, E. L. Konigsburg, Sid Fleischman, Robert Cormier, Paul Zindel, and J. D. Salinger. My view of these and many other contemporary writers and their work is jealous and admiring. There are other writers and works I don't envy and admire, but my mother taught me early on, 'If you don't have something good to say, don't say anything at all.'

"My advice to aspiring writers is to read every book you can; books hold the best writing lessons. Live the fullest life you can; experiences hold the best writing details—provided that you notice details. And write every minute you can; you have to write hundreds of pages, and learn from hundreds of mistakes, before you can be in control of your craft. It takes years of study and practice to write well, but don't be discouraged. Consider the time an enjoyable apprenticeship."

■ For More Information See

PERIODICALS

Booklist, March 15, 1994, p. 1347.
Kirkus Reviews, April 15, 1994.
Publishers Weekly, February 28, 1994, p. 88.*

G

MARIE GARAFANO

GARAFANO, Marie 1942-

■ Personal

Born December 8, 1942, in Philadelphia, PA; daughter of Joseph (a clothing manufacturer) and Rose (a homemaker; maiden name, Longo) Garafano; married Richard A. Melaragni (divorced, 1978); children: Claudia Fitzgerald, Jessica. *Education:* Philadelphia College of Art (now University of the Arts), B.F.A. *Politics:* Liberal Democrat. *Hobbies and other interests:* Reading, tennis.

■ Addresses

Home—641 North 65th St., Philadelphia, PA 19151.

■ Career

Free-lance illustrator. *Member:* Graphic Artists Guild.

■ Illustrator

Sook Nyul Choi, *The Year of Impossible Goodbyes,* Houghton, 1991.
S. P. Williams, *Ginger Goes on a Diet,* Houghton, 1993.
Sook Nyul Choi, *Echoes of the White Giraffe,* Houghton, 1993.
Sook Nyul Choi, *A Gathering of Pearls,* Houghton, 1994.

Also illustrator of five journals for Running Press: *The Gardener's Notebook, Cat Notebook II, Flower Notebook, Love Notebook,* and *Fatherhood Notebook.*

■ Sidelights

Marie Garafano has been influenced by such painters and illustrators as Degas, Ingres, Corot, and Arthur Rackham. She told *SATA,* "I consider myself a late bloomer. Although I always wanted to be an artist, I didn't really pursue a professional career until I was approximately thirty-five. And now, I have as much enthusiasm and love of my ork as any twenty-year-old.

"The things I respond to in my work are a wash, a line, a particular turn of a wrist in a drawing. I love drawing. I love mood. And I work toward that in my work."*

* * *

GARDNER, Theodore Roosevelt II 1934-

■ Personal

Born July 20, 1934, in Allentown, PA; son of Theodore Roosevelt (a judge) and Margaret Schaffer (a homemaker) Gardner; married Virginia Louis Twining (a bookseller); children: Melora Eden, Julia Susan, Abigail. *Education:* University of Southern California, B.A., 1956.

■ Addresses

Office—c/o Allen A. Knoll, Publishers, 200 West Victoria, Santa Barbara, CA 93101.

THEODORE ROOSEVELT GARDNER II

■ **Career**

Writer.

■ **Writings**

The Paper Dynasty (adult fiction), Knoll, 1990.
Off the Wall (compilation of humorous newspaper columns), Knoll, 1993.
Something Nice to See (children's book), illustrated by Peter J. Hamlin, Knoll, 1994.

■ **Sidelights**

Theodore Roosevelt Gardner II told *SATA:* "Having read more than four thousand children's books to my three daughters as they were growing up, I thought it might be fun to write one. I have always had a sensitivity to cruelty and its prevalence even among children. As a character in my book *Something Nice to See* says: 'People being nasty to people is wrong and this has gone on much too long.' That becomes the theme of *Something Nice to See,* my children's book that takes place during the building of Watts Towers, the country's most endearing and enduring folk art. Set in captivating rhyme, the story is about a young lad who learns to read before his classmates, causing resentment because he is different. The lad befriends Sam Rodia, the creator of the Watts Towers, who teaches him about tolerance and loving and respecting people in spite of their differences.

I worship the Watts Towers, and often visited them as a student in South Central Los Angeles. The Watts Towers of Sabato (Sam, Simon) Rodia were built single-handedly over the course of thirty-three years, from 1921 to 1954, without the benefits of machine equipment, scaffolding, welding, bolts, or drawing boards. The tallest tower is one hundred feet high. The Watts Towers are a unique monument to the human spirit and to the persistence of one man's undaunted vision."

* * *

GELMAN, Rita Golden 1937-
(R. G. Austin, a joint pseudonym)

■ **Personal**

Born July 2, 1937, in Bridgeport, CT; daughter of Albert (a pharmacist) and Frances (an artist and community activist; maiden name, Friedman) Golden; married Steve Gelman (an editor and writer), December 11, 1960 (divorced, 1987); children: Mitchell, Jan. *Education:* Brandeis University, B.A., 1958; University of California, Los Angeles, M.A., 1984; Ph.D. candidate; additional study at Northeastern University, Yeshiva University, and New York University.

■ **Addresses**

Home—c/o 2 Tudor City Place, New York, NY 10017.

■ **Career**

Young Americans magazine, New York City, staff writer, 1958-60; Crowell-Collier Publishing Co., New York City, editor, 1961-62; Book-of-the-Month Club, New York City, juvenile consultant, 1972-76; Macmillan Publishing Co., New York City, editor, 1973-74; freelance writer, 1974—. Guest lecturer, University of California, Los Angeles, 1976-78; faculty member, Sixth Annual Writers' Conference in Children's Literature, 1977; faculty member in extension program, California State University, Northridge, 1978-79; lecturer, ASEAN (Association of Southeast Asian Nations) Publisher's Conference, Singapore, 1993. *Member:* PEN, Society of Children's Book Writers and Illustrators.

■ **Awards, Honors**

Best Science Book for Children Award, American Institute of Physics, 1987, and Science-Writing Award, 1988, both for *Splash! All About Baths;* American Library Association award, 1988, for *Inside Nicaragua: Young People's Dreams and Fears;* John Burroughs Association commendation, for Outstanding Nature Book for children, for *Dawn to Dusk in the Galapagos: Flightless Birds, Swimming Lizards, and Other Fascinating Creatures,* 1991.

■ **Writings**

FOR CHILDREN

Dumb Joey, illustrated by Cheryl Pelavin, Holt, 1973.

The Can, illustrated by John Trotta, Macmillan, 1975.

Comits: A Book of Comic Skits, illustrated by Robert Dennis, Macmillan, 1975.

The Me I Am, photographs by Michal Heron, Macmillan, 1975.

Fun City, illustrated by Tom Herbert, Macmillan, 1975.

(With Steve Gelman) *Great Quarterbacks of Pro Football,* Scholastic, 1975.

Why Can't I Fly?, illustrated by Jack Kent, Scholastic, 1976.

Hey, Kid!, illustrated by Carol Nicklaus, F. Watts, 1977.

More Spaghetti, I Say!, illustrated by Kent, Scholastic, 1977, new version illustrated by Mort Gerberg, 1992.

(With Susan Kovacs Buxbaum) *OUCH!: All About Cuts and Other Hurts,* illustrated by Jan Pyk, medical consulting by Joel Buxbaum, Harcourt, 1977.

(With Joan Richter) *Professor Coconut and the Thief,* illustrated by Emily McCully, Holt, 1977.

(With S. Gelman), *America's Favorite Sports Stars,* Scholastic, 1978.

Cats and Mice, illustrated by Eric Gurney, Scholastic, 1978.

(With Marcia Seligson) *UFO Encounters,* Scholastic, 1978.

(With Warner Friedman) *Uncle Hugh: A Fishing Story,* illustrated by Eros Keith, Harcourt, 1978.

Hello, Cat. You Need a Hat, illustrated by Gurney, Scholastic, 1979.

The Biggest Sandwich Ever, illustrated by Gerberg, Scholastic, 1980.

The Incredible Dinosaurs, illustrated by Christopher Santoro, Random House, 1980.

Favorite Riddles, Knock Knocks, and Nonsense, illustrated by Gerberg, Scholastic, 1980.

Great Moments in Sports, Scholastic, 1980.

Benji at Work, Scholastic, 1980.

(With S. K. Buxbaum) *Boats That Float,* illustrated by Marilyn MacGregor, F. Watts, 1981.

Fabulous Animal Facts That Hardly Anybody Knows, illustrated by Margaret Hartelius, Scholastic, 1981.

Mount St. Helens, the Big Blast, Scholastic, 1981.

ESP and Other Strange Happenings, Scholastic, 1981.

Mortimer K Saves the Day, illustrated by Bernie Gruver, Scholastic, 1982.

Benji Takes a Dive, Scholastic, 1982.

(With S. K. Buxbaum) *Body Noises,* illustrated by Angie Lloyd, Knopf, 1983.

Wet Cats, illustrated by Gurney, Scholastic, 1985.

Listen and Look: A Safety Book, illustrated by Cathy Beylon, Marvel Books, 1986.

Care and Share: A Book about Manners, illustrated by Beylon, Marvel Books, 1986.

A Koala Grows Up, illustrated by Gioia Fiammenghi, Scholastic, 1986.

Pets for Sale, illustrated by Fredrick Winkowski, 1986.

(With S. K. Buxbaum) *Splash! All About Baths,* illustrated by Maryann Cocca-Leffler, Little, Brown, 1987.

Leave It to Minnie, illustrated by Gerberg, Scholastic, 1987.

Inside Nicaragua: Young People's Dreams and Fears, F. Watts, 1988.

RITA GOLDEN GELMAN

Stop Those Painters, illustrated by Gerberg, Scholastic, 1989.

Monkeys and Apes of the World, F. Watts, 1990.

Monsters of the Sea, illustrated by Jean Day Zallinger, Little, Brown, 1990.

Dawn to Dusk in the Galapagos: Flightless Birds, Swimming Lizards, and Other Fascinating Creatures, photographs by Tui De Roy, Little, Brown, 1991.

A Monkey Grows Up, illustrated by Fiammenghi, Scholastic, 1991.

What Are Scientists? What Do They Do? Let's Find Out, illustrated by Mark Teague, Scholastic, 1991.

Vampires and Other Creatures of the Night, illustrated by C. B. Mordan, Scholastic, 1991.

Body Battles, illustrated by Elroy Freem, Scholastic, 1992.

I Went to the Zoo, illustrated by Maryann Kovalski, Scholastic, 1993.

A Panda Grows Up, illustrated by Mary Morgan, Scholastic, 1993.

Body Detectives, A Book about the Senses, illustrated by Freem, Scholastic, 1994.

Queen Esther, Scholastic, in press.

Body Builders, You Are What You Eat, Scholastic, in press.

The Biggest Sandwich Ever was published in Dutch and Spanish; *Body Battles* and *What Are Scientists? What Do They Do? Let's Find Out* were published in Spanish; *Body Noises* was published in Japanese, Danish, and Swedish; *Fabulous Animal Facts That Hardly Anybody Knows* was published in German; *A Koala Grows Up* was published in French; *Splash! All About Baths* was published in Danish.

"WHICH WAY" SERIES; WITH NANCY AUSTIN; UNDER JOINT PSEUDONYM R. G. AUSTIN

The Castle of No Return, illustrated by Mike Eagle, Archway, 1982.

Vampires, Spies, and Alien Beings, illustrated by Anthony Kramer, Archway, 1982.

The Spell of the Black Raven, illustrated by Kramer, Archway, 1982.

Famous and Rich, illustrated by Eagle, Archway, 1982.

Lost in a Strange Land, illustrated by Lorna Tomei, Archway, 1982.

Curse of the Sunken Treasure, illustrated by L. Tomei, Archway, 1982.

Cosmic Encounters, illustrated by Doug Jamieson, Archway, 1982.

Creatures of the Dark, illustrated by Gordon Tomei, Archway, 1982.

Invasion of the Black Slime, illustrated by Joseph A. Smith, Archway, 1983.

Trapped in the Black Box, illustrated by Jamieson, Archway, 1983.

Poltergeists, Ghosts, and Psychic Encounters, illustrated by Smith, 1984.

Islands of Terror, illustrated by G. Tomei, Archway, 1984.

Several of the books in the "Which Way" series were published in Portuguese.

"SECRET DOOR" SERIES; WITH NANCY AUSTIN; UNDER JOINT PSEUDONYM R. G. AUSTIN

Wow! You Can Fly!, illustrated by Smith, Archway, 1983.

Giants, Elves and Scary Monsters, illustrated by Ed Parker, Archway, 1983.

The Haunted Castle, illustrated by Winslow Pels, Archway, 1983.

The Secret Life of Toys, illustrated by Sal Murdocca, Archway, 1983.

The Visitors from Outer Space, illustrated by Blanche Sims, Archway, 1983.

The Inch-High Kid, illustrated by Dennis Hockerman, Archway, 1983.

The Magic Carpet, illustrated by Pels, Archway, 1983.

Happy Birthday to You, illustrated by Smith, Archway, 1983.

The Monster Family, illustrated by Sims, Archway, 1984.

Brontosaurus Moves In, illustrated by Smith, Archway, 1984.

The Enchanted Forest, illustrated by Pels, Archway, 1984.

Crazy Computers, illustrated by Smith, Archway, 1984.

■ Work in Progress

Rice Is Life, a book about life in the rice fields of Bali, focusing on the way rice grows, the animals that live among the plants, and the farmers' relationship to the goddess of rice, Dewi Sri; *Bali Tales,* a long saga that tells of a hawk and a mouse who live in Bali and the friendship that develops between them.

■ Sidelights

"I never would have become a writer if I hadn't had Miss Curnias in the eighth grade," Rita Golden Gelman told *SATA.* "Our class put out a school newspaper called the Beardsley Press. We collected stories and poems and news items from all the other classes in the school. Miss Curnias typed them onto mimeograph stencils, and we decorated the stencils with a pin-pointed thing called a stylus. (That was before computers.) I wasn't very good at the decorating, but Miss Curnias said I wrote good stories and poems. So, whenever we needed to fill up a page, I wrote something. That was the year I became a writer.

"When I talk to other writers, they often tell me that when they were children, they wrote a lot and read all the time. I wish I had. But the truth is that I played a lot. I lived in a two-family house, just down the street from Beardsley Park. That park was a major character in my childhood. In the summer in the park, we swam in the lake and waded in the brook; we caught grasshoppers to feed to the praying mantises we had caught the day before; we rolled down the grassy hills and we trapped lightning bugs in bottles at night. There was a zoo in the park, and I collected peacock feathers by putting chewing gum on the end of a long stick, sliding the stick though the square holes in the wire fence, and then

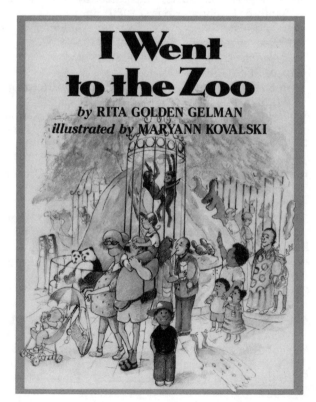

While visiting the zoo, a young boy decides to take all the animals home with him—with hilarious results. (Cover illustration by Maryann Kovalski.)

pressing the gummed tip onto the molted feathers. That was the summer.

"In the fall we piled up the leaves into giant mounds and dived into them until we were buried. In the winter we sledded, built snowmen and forts, and had spectacular snowball fights in the park. And in the spring, we roller-skated, played hide-and-seek, and climbed trees. Today, when I'm writing books for children, the girl who leaped into piles of leaves, scared her parents by presenting them with frogs, and stomped in puddles just because they were there, is still very much a part of me. I'm over fifty now, and I'm still quite capable of leaping into leaf piles. I love the smell, the crackle, and all the memories that come to me when I'm over my head in autumn leaves.

"The characters that I write about have a lot of me in them. *I Went to the Zoo* is about a boy who takes all the zoo animals home with him, elephants, lions, koalas, pandas, and peacocks, among others. As a child, I got to know the animals in the Beardsley Park Zoo, and I often wished that I could take them home with me. I once put an injured squirrel on my mother's bed when she was sick; she was not interested in sharing her bed with a rodent. I frequently smuggled frogs into the house and spent hours searching for them under couches and radiators. *I Went to the Zoo* carries those experiences into the absurd.

"My favorite book, *Why Can't I Fly?,* comes from the part of me that used to lie in the grass as a child and watch the birds. I still dream about flying, soaring, riding the wind. The main character in *Why Can't I Fly?* is a monkey named Minnie who wants more than anything to fly. She keeps trying and trying, until finally, with the help of her friends, she does the impossible.

"'The impossible' is a pretty relative thing. What is impossible for one person, may be quite possible for someone else. A lot depends on how hard you try and how capable you are of listening to the voice inside your head instead of the voices outside. Much of the time, a little flexibility and a lot of will, can make the impossible happen. But not always.

"The book, *Why Can't I Fly?* inspired the most touching letter I ever received. It was from a woman in Florida. She wrote that a six-year-old friend of hers named Jessica had just died of a terrible genetic disease. When Jessica was four, someone had given her a copy of *Why Can't I Fly?* Jessica learned how to read from that book, and she carried it with her wherever she went. Every day she read it to her family, her friends, her nurses. Every time she read it, she would laugh, and everyone would laugh with her.

"When Jessica died, a friend of the family read the book at Jessica's funeral. The last scene in *Why Can't I Fly?* shows Minnie sitting on a sheet and being carried off into the sky by her friends. There's a big grin on her face as she waves goodbye. Minnie's story had become Jessica's story as well, trying and trying and finally

The author's favorite book concerns a monkey who tries so hard to fly that she does the impossible. (Cover illustration by Jack Kent.)

flying away. Two years later I wrote another book about Minnie (*Leave It to Minnie*) and dedicated it to Jessica's family, 'so others may laugh because Jessica did.'

"When I'm not writing, what I like most to do is to learn about other people's lives, people I meet on buses, on trains and in planes, people in line with me at the supermarket, old people, children, people in wheel chairs, people on the street. I have always been interested in learning about how people live their lives. And I have always had a fascination with other cultures. This passion for learning about other people's experiences lured me into studying anthropology in graduate school at UCLA (in 1980), where I spent endless hours reading about how people live and thinking about how they become what they become.

"After I received my master's degree, but before I finished the work for a Ph.D., I realized something else about myself: I needed to see and touch and smell and hear the sounds of other cultures, to live with the people, to eat in their homes, to talk to them in their languages. Reading about them was too far away from the real thing.

"So I sold or gave away all my possessions and set off to discover what it was like to live in other worlds. For three and a half years I lived in Mexico, Guatemala,

Nicaragua, and the Galapagos Islands of Ecuador. I learned to speak Spanish and to cook Mexican food, and I learned how to weave from the Indian population of Guatemala. In Nicaragua I discovered what it was like to live in a country under siege. And in the Galapagos, I lived on a boat and visited islands populated by sea lions, iguanas, frigate birds, and blue-footed boobies.

"In 1989, I went to Indonesia. I lived with the Dayak people in the Indonesian province of Kalimantan on the island of Borneo, and I studied orangutans in the rain forest there. I stayed for three years with a royal family on the island of Bali. I have climbed the mountains of Irian Jaya (the Indonesian half of the island of New Guinea) and sat around the cooking fires with the tribal families who live there; I have traveled in a dugout boat through the rivers of the Asmat area in the south, learning from the natives about their woodcarving skills and attending their ancestral ceremonies.

"Since 1989, I have been living primarily on the Indonesian island of Bali, where I stay with families, join them in their special ceremonies, and learn (in both English and Indonesian) about their lives and how they think and feel about the world. Wherever I live, I continue to write books for young people, sometimes about the countries I visit and sometimes about universal subjects. I also try to contribute something to the people I live with, by teaching English, by sharing my own culture with them, by reading them my books, and even by cooking western foods now and then for my friends to try. Sometimes I ask questions, but mostly I learn about people by making friends, living with families, and sharing their lives. My travels have taught me something very important: there is no right or wrong way to 'do' life. The options are infinite.

"I never know when I'm going to meet an idea that will become a book. One day I received a call from a friend who owned a Swensen's ice cream store. She was in a panic because all her workers had called in sick. Could I help? Absolutely. I was very excited. When I was a teenager, I had worked at the soda fountain in my father's drugstore—making sundaes and ice cream sodas, serving up milkshakes and banana splits. I couldn't wait to once again scoop and squirt and dribble syrups over ice cream. But it turned out that my friend wanted me in the kitchen.

"She stood me at a long counter that was covered with stacks of turkey and chicken and tomatoes and lettuce and tuna fish salad. The stacks were divided by pieces of waxed paper so that the sandwich maker, me, would give just the right amount of filling. On the wall above the counter were the lists of sandwiches and their ingredients. I spent the next five hours staring at the piles and letting my imagination wander. The next day I began writing *The Biggest Sandwich Ever,* about a sandwich the size of a house. I wanted to get more and more ridiculous as the sandwich got higher and higher. I remember sitting one day with my editor and seriously discussing which was more ridiculous: squirting catsup out of a fire hose, or dropping pickles from an airplane. I

love the discussions I get to have when I write silly books.

"I've written a number of books about food … I like to cook and I love to eat. In one book Minnie can't stop eating spaghetti (*More Spaghetti, I Say!*). 'I love it, I love, I love it, I do,' she says. So do I. My most recent food-book is about nutrition ('What they say is really true. What you eat turns into you.') I also think there's a book in me about pizza, but I haven't written it yet.

"I wrote another book called *Hey, Kid!* after taking a five-hour bus trip with my six-year-old daughter. For the entire trip she sang and talked, talked and sang. It was as though she was running on one of those never-ending batteries; there wasn't a silent moment. By the end of the trip, I was ready to give her away. Instead, I wrote about Sam, a lovable, friendly, wispy character who is probably still dropping in on unsuspecting people who adore him until they discover that he can't stop talking and singing. Then they give him away.

"I've written a lot of nonfiction books, usually about things I want to study. Writing a nonfiction book about a subject is a lot like taking a minicourse. You have to read tons of books, talk to experts, and develop your own opinions. I have written about UFO's and ESP, about the country of Nicaragua, and the islands and animals of the Galapagos. I've written a lot of other books about animals: pandas, koalas, monkeys, sea creatures, and dinosaurs.

"I wrote one book called, *Fabulous Animal Facts That Hardly Anybody Knows.* What a lot of fun I had doing that one. I just sat in the library on the floor in front of the animal shelves and read. Every time I found myself saying, 'I didn't know that!,' I wrote it down. I filled several notebooks. When I was ready to do a thirty-two-page picture book, I chose the facts that were the most fun.

"When I visit classrooms, I'm always asked what it's like being an author. Obviously, it's different for different people. I like the fact that I don't have to go into an office and work regular hours, and that I can sit around barefoot, in sweat pants and a T-shirt while I work. And I like saying that I'm a writer when people ask me what I do.

"A lot of people think being a writer is something extraordinary. 'Oh, my God,' said one fourth-grade girl when I visited her class, 'she touched my shoulder!' But anyone who knows writers will tell you that we're the same as everyone else. Anyone can be a writer. It does help if there's a Miss Curnias around to give you encouragement. Who knows? If I'd been assigned to the other eighth-grade class, I might have become a teacher or a social worker or even a zookeeper!

"Because most people don't know that writers are ordinary people, being one gets you 'Oh, really!,' which is a lot better than 'Oh, how nice.' The main problem with being a writer is that you have to write. That

TEXT BY RITA GOLDEN GELMAN · PHOTOGRAPHS BY TUI DE ROY

DAWN TO DUSK IN THE
GALÁPAGOS
Flightless Birds, Swimming Lizards, and Other Fascinating Creatures

Gelman offers a scientific portrait of the many creatures who call the Galapagos Islands home in this visually stunning volume.

means, most of the time, sitting in a room by yourself and putting words into a computer or onto paper. Every once in a while, when I'm writing, I feel as though I'm flying or dancing or skiing down a mountain. The words just keep flowing out, and I fill with music and joy and passion.

"But most of the time, writing is just hard work. I go over everything I write hundreds of times. I want every word to be perfect. I try to say things as simply and as clearly as possible, and I make thousands of changes before I send it off to an editor. I read every line out loud dozens of times to hear if it has an easy rhythm, to see if the sounds go well together, to hear if the sentences are the right length. Sometimes, after I have been writing for several hours, I'm exhausted, even

though I haven't moved out of my chair. (That's a little bit misleading. The fact is that I usually get up every fifteen or twenty minutes and walk around.)

"Now for someone like me, who loves talking and being with people, writing is a strange profession. But if you look at my list of books, you'll see that I have collaborated on lots of them. I like what happens when two heads work together. I worked on most of my science books with my friend, Susan Buxbaum (*OUCH!: All About Cuts and Other Hurts; Body Noises; Splash! All About Baths; What are Scientists? What Do They Do? Let's Find Out*). We have fun doing it. Susan does the research and explains everything to me. Then, I do the writing. I wrote the 'Which Way' series with another friend, Nancy Lamb Austin. And I've worked with others as well. I like collaborating. When Nancy and I wrote together, we laughed a lot; and we always began our working sessions with about a half hour of talking, discussing world events, family problems, and friends. Only then were we ready to work.

"There are books, though, that I can't write with someone else. They can only come from me. It's in writing those books that the 'flying' sometimes occurs. Every once in a while, I sit for hours (but it feels like minutes) without getting up, without even being aware that time is passing. And later, when I read over what I've written, I'm surprised. Sometimes I feel as though I'm reading someone else's words. It's as though the words came from some inner place and skipped right over my awareness. At times like that, being a writer is fantastic. It's magical. At times like that, I can't imagine being anything else."

■ For More Information See

PERIODICALS

Booklist, December 15, 1981, p. 553.
Bulletin of the Center for Children's Books, February, 1974, p. 94.
Horn Book, July/August, 1991, pp. 477-78.
Kirkus Reviews, August 15, 1973, p. 882; April 1, 1977, p. 355; May 1, 1991, p. 612.
New York Times Book Review, November 13, 1983.
Publishers Weekly, October 8, 1973, p. 97.
School Library Journal, May, 1977, p. 76; October, 1977, p. 102; February, 1979, p. 42; December, 1981, pp. 79-80; December, 1981, p. 85; July, 1991, pp. 79-80; November, 1993, p. 79.

*   *   *

GOLDENTYER, Debra 1960-

■ Personal

Born February 2, 1960, in Philadelphia, PA; daughter of Bernard (a civil engineer) and Nancy (a school psychologist; maiden name, Gross) Goldentyer; married Mark Schaeffer (a video producer), October 10, 1987. *Education:* Brandeis University, B.A., 1981; Boston University School of Law, J.D., 1984.

■ Addresses

Home and office—933 Rose Ave., Oakland, CA 94611. *Electronic mail*—71044.2743@compuserve.com.

■ Career

Schaeffer & Goldentyer, Oakland, CA, partner in the production of videos and multimedia materials for education and training, 1989—. Assistant sysop, work-at-home forum, and section leader, video and multimedia section of Public Relations and Marketing Forum, both for Compuserve. *Member:* International Association of Business Communications (co-chair, indepen-

DEBRA GOLDENTYER

dents roundtable, 1994, and electronic communications, 1995).

■ Writings

"TEEN HOT LINE" SERIES

Dropping out of School, Raintree Steck-Vaughn, 1994.
Gangs, Raintree Steck-Vaughn, 1994.
Family Violence, Raintree Steck-Vaughn, 1995.
Parental Divorce, Raintree Steck-Vaughn, 1995.

OTHER

You and the Law, Southwestern, 1992.

*   *   *

GOODE, Diane (Capuozzo) 1949-

■ Personal

Born September 14, 1949, in Brooklyn, NY; daughter of Armand R. (a dentist) and Paule (Guerrini) Capuozzo; married David A. Goode (an author and professor), May 26, 1973; children: Peter. *Education:* Attended the Ecole des Beaux Arts, Aix-en-Provence, France, 1971-72; Queens College of the City University of New York, B.F.A., 1972.

■ Addresses

Home and office—33 Prospect Ave., Watchung, NJ 07060.

DIANE GOODE

■ Career

Children's book illustrator and writer, 1975—. Substitute teacher at New York City public schools, 1972-73; teacher of a studio workshop on children's book illustration, University of California, Los Angeles, 1976-79. *Exhibitions:* Metropolitan Museum of Art, 1982.

■ Awards, Honors

Southern California Council on Literature for Children and Young People award for illustration, 1976, for *The Selchie's Seed* and *Little Pieces of the West Wind,* and 1978, for *Dream Eater;* Caldecott honor book award, 1983, for *When I Was Young in the Mountains* by Cynthia Rylant; Parents' Choice Award, 1985, for *Watch the Stars Come Out* by Riki Levinson, and 1986, for *I Go with My Family to Grandma's* by Levinson; *Redbook* Top Ten Children's Picture Books citation, 1985, and Reading Rainbow Feature Selection, both for *Watch the Stars Come Out;* Child Study Children's Book Committee Best Children's Books of the Year, 1987, for *I Go with My Family to Grandma's,* and 1989, for *I Hear a Noise; American Bookseller* Picks of the List citations, for *Where's Our Mama?, Diane Goode's American Christmas, The Diane Goode Book of American Folk Tales & Songs, Watch the Stars Come Out,* and *I Go with My Family to Grandma's;* Notable Children's Trade Books in the Field of Social Studies citations, National Council of Social Studies-Children's Book Council, for *The Diane Goode Book of American Folk Tales & Songs, Watch the Stars Come Out, I Go with My Family to Grandma's,* and *When I Was Young in the Mountains;* American Library Association Notable Book citation, for *Tattercoats: An Old English Tale, Watch the Stars Come Out,* and *When I Was Young in the Mountains;* Teachers' Choice awards, National Council of Teachers of English, for *Watch the Stars Come Out* and *When I Was Young in the Mountains;* Library of Congress Children's Book of the Year citation, for *When I Was Young in the Mountains;* Children's Choice citation, International Reading Association-Children's Book Council, for *The Unicorn and the Plow.*

■ Writings

SELF-ILLUSTRATED

(Reteller) Julian Hawthorne, *Rumpty Dudget's Tower,* Knopf, 1987.
I Hear a Noise, Dutton, 1988.
The Diane Goode Book of American Folk Tales and Songs, collected by Ann Durell, Dutton, 1989.
Diane Goode's American Christmas, Dutton, 1990.
Where's Our Mama?, Dutton, 1991.
Diane Goode's Silly Stories and Songs, Dutton, 1992.
The Little Book of Cats, Dutton, 1993.
The Little Book of Farm Friends, Dutton, 1993.
The Little Book of Mice, Dutton, 1993.
The Little Book of Pigs, Dutton, 1993.
Diane Goode's Book of Scary Stories and Songs, Dutton, 1994.
Diane Goode's Christmas Magic: Poems and Carols, Random House, 1994.
Zaza, Dutton, in press.

ILLUSTRATOR

Christian Garrison, *Little Pieces of the West Wind,* Bradbury, 1975.
Shulamith Oppenheim, *The Selchie's Seed,* Bradbury, 1975.
Garrison, *Flim and Flam and the Big Cheese,* Bradbury, 1976.
Flora Annie Steele, *Tattercoats: An Old English Tale,* Bradbury, 1976.
(And translator) Madame de Beaumont, *Beauty and the Beast,* Bradbury, 1978.
Garrison, *The Dream Eater,* Bradbury, 1978.
Emoeke de Papp Severo, translator, *The Good-Hearted Youngest Brother* (translation of the Hungarian folk tale, "A joszivu legenyke"), Bradbury, 1981.
Louise Moeri, *The Unicorn and the Plow,* Dutton, 1982.
Cynthia Rylant, *When I Was Young in the Mountains,* Dutton, 1982.
Hans Christian Andersen, *The Fir Tree,* Random House, 1983.
J. M. Barrie, *Peter Pan,* edited by Josette Frank, Random House, 1983.
Christmas Carols ("My Little Library of Christmas Classics" series), Random House, 1983.
Carlo Collodi, *The Adventures of Pinnochio,* Random House, 1983.
Clement Clarke Moore, *The Night before Christmas,* Random House, 1983.
Amy Ehrlich, adapter, *The Random House Book of Fairy Tales,* Random House, 1985.

Riki Levinson, *Watch the Stars Come Out,* Dutton, 1985.

Deborah Hautzig, *The Story of the Nutcracker Ballet,* Random House, 1986.

Levinson, *I Go with My Family to Grandma's,* Dutton, 1986.

(And translator) Charles Perrault, *Cinderella,* Knopf, 1988.

Noel Streatfield, *Ballet Shoes,* Random House, 1991.

Lloyd Alexander, *The House Gobbaleen,* Dutton, 1995.

Also illustrator of record album covers. *Watch the Stars Come Out* was translated into Spanish as *Mira como salen las estrellas,* Dutton, 1992.

■ Sidelights

"When I was a child I loved books and art," Diane Goode told *SATA.* "Reading allowed me to escape into the reality of others and drawing let me create my own. My father was of Italian descent, and my mother was French. My brother and I enjoyed the richness of both cultures. We traveled to Europe every summer from the time we were infants, visiting family and the great cathedrals and museums of the world. These early impressions helped shape my appreciation for life and art. I was bedazzled by Michelangelo's 'Descent from the Cross.' Could marble be warm and luminous? Could monumental forms be at once tender and powerful? Man's creative ability seemed staggering. I saw the works of Da Vinci, Rembrandt, Botticelli, Lautrec, Monet, Manet, Cezanne, and all the great artists. I was awestruck. I was in love with art!

"I have been drawing ever since I can remember, but my formal education began at Queens College in art history. I soon switched to fine arts, where I tried my hand at everything: drawing, painting, sculpture, etching, and color theory. I took a year off to study at Les Beaux Arts in Aix-en-Provence. It was an artist's dream.

"After graduating, I taught high school for a year, putting together a portfolio at night. In my blissful ignorance of publishing, I had decided to illustrate children's books. It was just as well that I was so naive or else I would have been too afraid to try. As luck would have it, I was contracted to illustrate my first picture book in 1973. I was twenty-four then and knew nothing at all about commercial art. Since I was living in California, my New York publisher taught me color separation over the phone!

"All of my work is done on opaline parchment. I sketch lightly in pencil and use watercolors applied with very fine sable brushes. Sometimes I use color pencil with the paint to soften the atmosphere. I always begin with several rough dummies and then work on the individual pages, sketching very loosely and fast to establish movement and composition. I do these dozens of times, repositioning, enlarging, reducing, adding, and omitting. There are always hundreds of sketches for each book. It sounds tedious, but it is the most exciting part of creating the book.

Goode's cheerful illustrations for Cynthia Rylant's ***When I Was Young in the Mountains*** **received a Caldecott Honor Award in 1983.**

"I've been married since 1973. Our son Peter was born in 1978 and is a fine artist already. I often rely on him to read manuscripts for an opinion and critique of my work. He has helped me see the world through a child's eyes.

"We have lived in four states and have had many small pets along the way: parrots, love birds, hamsters, cats, and mice. We've settled in Watchung, New Jersey, and each day we are visited by wild deer, raccoons, rabbits, hedgehogs, a pheasant, and an owl. We now have a Welsh Corgi named Katie. We love to travel in France and we love to cook. I still read as much as I can. I listen to books on tape as I paint.

"Working in the field of children's literature has been a great joy. How lucky to be able to do the work I love and also contribute in some small way to the lives of our children. How lucky to find in my work the two things I've cherished since childhood: art and books."

■ For More Information See

PERIODICALS

Bulletin of the Center for Children's Books, September, 1991, p. 10.

Horn Book, March, 1988, p. 199; September, 1988, p. 615; September, 1992, p. 592.

Horn Book Guide, spring, 1994, p. 113.

Junior Bookshelf, June, 1992, p. 102.

New York Times Book Review, December 4, 1983, p. 79.

Publishers Weekly, July 29, 1988, p. 230; June 29, 1992, p. 61; September 7, 1992, p. 67; July 4, 1994, p. 60.
School Library Journal, January, 1988, p. 66; February, 1989, p. 69; September, 1992, p. 215; September, 1994, p. 207.
Washington Post Book World, February 9, 1992, p. 11.

* * *

GORDON, John (William) 1925-

■ Personal

Born November 19, 1925, in Jarrow, County Durham, England; son of Norman (a teacher) and Margaret (Revely) Gordon; married Sylvia Ellen Young, January 9, 1954; children: Sally, Robert. *Education:* Educated in Jarrow and Wisbech, England.

■ Addresses

Home—99 George Borrow Rd., Norwich, Norfolk NR4 7HU, England.

■ Career

Isle of Ely and Wisbech Advertiser, Wisbech, England, reporter, 1947-49, sub-editor, 1949-51; *Bury Free Press,* Bury St. Edmunds, Suffolk, England, chief reporter, then sub-editor, 1951-58; *Western Evening Herald,* Plymouth, England, sub-editor, 1958-62; *Eastern Evening News,* Norwich, Norfolk, England, columnist and sub-editor, 1962-73; *Eastern Daily Press,* Norwich, sub-editor, 1973-85; writer. *Military service:* Royal Navy, 1943-47.

■ Writings

JUVENILE FICTION

The Giant under the Snow, Hutchinson, 1968, Harper, 1970.
The House on the Brink, Hutchinson, 1970, Harper, 1971.
The Ghost on the Hill, Kestrel, 1976, Viking, 1977.
The Waterfall Box, Kestrel, 1978.
The Spitfire Grave and Other Stories, Kestrel, 1979.
The Edge of the World, Atheneum, 1983.
Catch Your Death and Other Ghost Stories, illustrated by Jeremy Ford, Hardy, 1984.
The Quelling Eye, Bodley Head, 1986.
The Grasshopper, Bodley Head, 1987.
Ride the Wind, Bodley Head, 1989.
Blood Brothers, Signpost, 1989.
Secret Corridor, Blackie, 1990.
The Burning Baby and Other Ghosts, Walker, 1992, Candlewick, 1993.
Gilray's Ghost, Walker, 1995.

OTHER

Ordinary Seaman (memoir), Walker, 1992.

Contributor to anthologies, including *Young Winter's Tales 2,* Macmillan, 1971, and to periodicals.

JOHN GORDON

■ Work in Progress

A young adult novel.

■ Sidelights

John Gordon shortens the gap between fantasy and reality in his novels and short stories for children and young adults. The "other" worlds his characters stumble into exist simultaneously with the real world they live in on a daily basis. Drawing from the history of the Fen Country in England, where he grew up, Gordon populates his tales with ghosts and creatures from the past, leading readers through several suspenseful twists and turns before revealing all. "Gordon has confidently mastered the art of holding his reader in suspense, often delaying a climax until the byways of a carefully engineered plot have been explored," maintains *Junior Bookshelf* reviewer G. Bott.

Spending his days as a sub-editor for a newspaper, Gordon constructed his first tales in the mornings before the rest of his family arose. The first of these stories to be published, *The Giant under the Snow,* follows a group of children, including Jonk, as they cross over from their modern world to a co-existing one. In this "other" world of ancient magic, there are witches and invading Leathermen, and the children learn the power of flying. In the end, the evil forces must deal with a prehistoric giant that rises from under the snow. Dennis Hamley, writing in *Twentieth-Century Children's Writers,* observes that *The Giant under the Snow* "formed a stunning debut for a writing career which flourishes and constantly surprises."

This first children's book was followed with a young adult novel set in a house which Gordon actually visited before—and after—writing *The House on the Brink*. Peckover House exists in Wisbech, England, by the River Nene, and the story Gordon sets there concerns the house's owner, Mrs. Knowles, and a teenage boy, Dick Dodds. Both observe and are affected differently by what appears to be a blackened log which rises out of the fen, seeming to move closer and closer to the house with each sighting. "Few authors have a more convincing way of suggesting the cohesions and moods of the young 'teens than John Gordon," writes *Growing Point*'s Margery Fisher. "His dialogue is brilliantly elliptical, comic and perceptive, and he moves so confidently from real to surreal that the reader makes the transition without realizing it." Hamley asserts that *The House on the Brink* "is a riddling, difficult, memorable book close to the status of classic."

Returning to the theme of parallel worlds, Gordon published *The Edge of the World* in 1983. Claiming to have seen a ghost in the form of a flying horsehead, young Tekker Begdale and his friend Kit soon discover that they possess mental powers which enable them to enter another world. This second world is filled with

These five chilling tales involve unnatural death intruding upon everyday events. (Cover illustration by Robert Mason.)

ghosts and looks like a surreal red desert. Through their travels, Tekker and Kit become involved in an old love triangle between some of the town's elderly residents. While they are trying to tie up loose ends in this lost romance, Tekker and Kit must also fight to save Kit's brother Dan, who accompanied them to this "other" world and was attacked by the horsehead ghosts. "Gordon has created two teen heroes as earnest, wide-eyed and persistent as the heroes of Nancy Drew and the Hardy Boys stories," describes Jack Forman in *School Library Journal*, adding that Gordon's "breathlessly fast pace" will capture readers. Paul Heins points out in his *Horn Book* review of *The Edge of the World* that "horror as well as tension gives the narrative a driving force, and touches of humor help to humanize the marvelous and the grotesque elements of the story."

Having created the fantasy world in *The Edge of the World* and several others since writing his first novel, Gordon returned to the setting of *The Giant under the Snow* for its sequel, *Ride the Wind*. Although twenty years passed between the writing of these two novels, only two years have passed in the lives of their protagonists. Jonk and his friends once again find themselves struggling with forces of evil from the "other" world. The leading evil character is the Warlord, who is trying to recover an ancient gold dish that the children found in their first adventure. The Warlord has the help of the spidery Leathermen, and the only ally of the children is Elizabeth Goodenough, a white witch with fading magical powers. She is, however, able to give the children a magical mist stone that enables them to become weightless and ride the wind. Although he believes that children may have a hard time suspending their disbelief for *Ride the Wind*, Geoffrey Trease states in the *Times Literary Supplement* that "Gordon writes with undeniable vigour and is a master of poetic phrasing." Patricia Peacock, however, hails the author's lifelike characters and declares the story a success, maintaining in *School Librarian*: "Some fairy godmother gave John Gordon the gift of gluing his books to the hands of his readers, and this sequel ... is riveting."

Also spellbinding are Gordon's short stories of the supernatural, which have been collected in several volumes, including *The Spitfire Grave and Other Stories, Catch Your Death and Other Ghost Stories*, and *The Burning Baby and Other Ghosts*. "Like most novelists who are masters of construction, Gordon is equally at home in the short story," observes Hamley, adding that Gordon's collections "contain narratives which, in their uncompromising spareness, are disturbing, even shocking." One story concerns a young boy who plans his own suicide following the suicide of his father. Another has the spirit of a drowned boy luring another boy into the same icy pool of water. And the stories in *The Burning Baby and Other Ghosts* include everything from an unborn baby coming back to haunt its murderer to a ten-year-old being smothered and fed to eels.

Robert Protherough, in his *School Librarian* review of *The Burning Baby and Other Ghosts*, explains that "the stories grip from the beginning and raise the reader's curiosity." In addition, the critic notes, "Gordon writes vividly, the characters and settings are firmly realised, and the dialogue is convincing." Deborah Stevenson similarly points out in the *Bulletin of the Center for Children's Books* that "Gordon is skilled at spare but meaningful characterization as well as the occasional doomsday sentence." As Hamley concludes: "These stories push to the very edge the power of imagination to work in real, tangible settings."

All of Gordon's stories are set in such an imaginative reality, a reality that is based on the author's own dreams. He once told *SATA:* "Stories are dreams in disguise. There are dreams hidden in all my stories. They are necessary, but they must remain hidden because they are mine and mean nothing to anybody else. The stories that surround them are meant to make you have similar dreams, your *own* dreams, which will again be secret. Stories are a way of sharing secrets too deep to mention."

■ Works Cited

Bott, G., review of *The Spitfire Grave and Other Stories,* Junior Bookshelf, June, 1980, p. 142.

Forman, Jack, review of *The Edge of the World,* School Library Journal, January, 1984, pp. 75-76.

Hamley, Dennis, "John Gordon," *Twentieth-Century Children's Writers,* 4th edition, St. James Press, 1995, pp. 392-94.

Heins, Paul, review of *The Edge of the World,* Horn Book, October, 1983, p. 581.

Fisher, Margery, review of *The House on the Brink,* Growing Point, May, 1982, p. 3893.

Peacock, Patricia, review of *Ride the Wind,* School Librarian, August, 1989, p. 114.

Protherough, Robert, review of *The Burning Baby and Other Ghosts,* School Librarian, November, 1992, p. 158.

Stevenson, Deborah, review of *The Burning Baby and Other Ghosts,* Bulletin of the Center for Children's Books, October, 1993, p. 44.

Trease, Geoffrey, "Dream Cottage," *Times Literary Supplement,* April 7, 1989, p. 379.

■ For More Information See

PERIODICALS

Bulletin of the Center for Children's Books, September, 1977.

Growing Point, January, 1988, pp. 4906-7.

Junior Bookshelf, June, 1984, p. 138; February, 1988, p. 57; April, 1989, pp. 80-81.

School Librarian, March, 1980, pp. 55, 58.

Signal, May, 1972.

Times Literary Supplement, March 30, 1984, p. 335.

Voice of Youth Advocates, February, 1984, p. 343.

Wilson Library Bulletin, May, 1994, p. 98.

GROHMANN, Susan 1948-

■ Personal

Born October 26, 1948, in Boston, MA; daughter of Jacob and Myra Elizabeth (Burke) Broudy; married Mark Grohmann (a day care center owner), May 23, 1970; children: Kyle, Russell. *Education:* Attended Barnard College. *Politics:* Democrat.

■ Addresses

Home—Palm Beach County, Florida.

■ Career

Children's book author and illustrator. Classroom volunteer, Palm Beach County Public Schools; secretary, Acreage Pines Community Elementary School Parent-Teacher Association, 1991-93; Acreage Pines Community Elementary School Advisory Council, secretary, 1993-94, chairperson, 1994-95.

■ Writings

(Self-illustrated) *The Dust under Mrs. Merriweather's Bed,* Whispering Coyote Press, 1994.

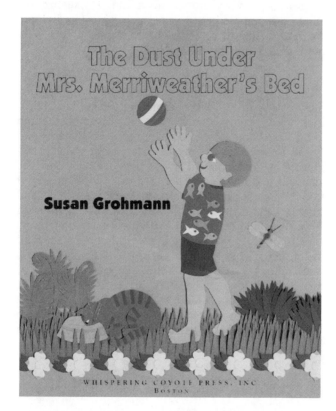

Illustrated with her own collages, Susan Grohmann's first book was inspired by her son's comment that the sky looked as though it had been vacuumed.

■ Work in Progress

"Little Book Boy," a 2,290-word work of fiction for children, set in Japan in the 1800s, is currently making the rounds in search of a publisher. "The story was inspired by a *netsuke* carving, and draws on the 11th century Japanese literary classic, *Tale of Genji*. I would like to illustrate the story with the same cut-paper technique I used in *Mrs. Merriweather*. The kimonos, buildings and gardens should translate beautifully to the collage medium."

■ Sidelights

Susan Grohmann told *SATA:* "The idea for the story of *Mrs. Merriweather* came to me while I was outside in the yard with my two sons looking up at the sky. My oldest son commented that the completely clear sky looked as though it had been vacuumed. The image of someone up there with a big vacuum cleaner stuck with me and continued to develop. Since then I always keep my ears open to the imaginings of children. Bringing up my boys and reading many stories to them definitely played a large part in getting me started.

"Making the collages for *Mrs. Merriweather* was so much fun that whenever an idea which has the potential to become a story crosses my mind, I visualize the characters and settings in cut paper. I imagine I would be just as happy being an illustrator as I was both writing and illustrating the story.

"I had been volunteering in elementary school classes before *Mrs. Merriweather* came out. Since its publication, teachers have been very kind in welcoming me into their classrooms to read the story to their students and speak to them about my experiences in writing and illustrating the book. The teachers feel it helps the children to know that writers are real people. Many of the children at the school already knew me as Kyle and Russell's mom, who washes and cooks and helps with homework and scolds just like any other mom. Many children think that writing is something WAY beyond them, but if they discover that writers are 'just plain folks,' they might begin to think, 'Hey, I could do that too!' Schools are now beginning to teach the process of writing, above and beyond the rules of grammar. This should help the students tremendously, and I hope whatever insights I can offer will help encourage them in their efforts."

■ For More Information See

PERIODICALS

Publishers Weekly, January 17, 1994.

PHILIP GROSS

GROSS, Philip (John) 1952-

■ Personal

Born February 27, 1952, in Delabole, Cornwall, England; son of Juhan Karl (a teacher) and Mary Jessie (a teacher; maiden name, Holmes) Gross; married Helen Gamsa (a clinical psychologist), August 28, 1976; children: Rosemary, Jonathan. *Education:* University of Sussex, B.A. (with honors), 1973; Polytechnic of North London, diploma in librarianship, 1977.

■ Addresses

Home—87 Berkeley Rd., Bishopston, Bristol BS7 8HQ, England.

■ Career

Collier Macmillan Ltd., London, England, editorial assistant, 1973-76; Croydon Public Libraries, Croydon, England, librarian, 1976-84; freelance writer and tutor of creative writing, 1984—.

■ Awards, Honors

Eric Gregory Award, Society of Authors, 1981; National Poetry Competition first prize, 1982, for "The Ice Factory"; West of England Playwriting Competition joint first prize, British Broadcasting Corporation, 1986, for radio play "Internal Affairs"; Poetry Book Society choice, 1988, for *The Air Mines of Mistila;* bursary from Arts Council, 1989, for work for young people; Signal Poetry Award, 1994, for *The All-Nite Cafe.*

■ Writings

Familiars (poems), Harry Chambers, 1983.
The Ice Factory (poems), Faber, 1984.
Cat's Whisker (poems), Faber, 1987.
(With Sylvia Kantaris) *The Air Mines of Mistila* (verse fable), Bloodaxe, 1989.
Manifold Manor (poems for young people), illustrated by Chris Riddell, Faber, 1989.
The Song of Gail and Fludd (novel for young people), Faber, 1991.
The Son of the Duke of Nowhere (poems), Faber, 1991.
The All-Nite Cafe (poems for young people), Faber, 1993.
Plex (novel for young people), Scholastic, 1994.
I.D. (poems), Faber, 1994.
The Wind Gate (novel for young people), Scholastic, 1995.
Scratch City (poems for young people), Fable, 1995.

■ Sidelights

Philip Gross had already established himself as a poet of note by the time he penned his first children's book. Derek Stanford, writing in *Books & Bookmen,* called Gross "a fluent, laconic poet who has a strength on the surface of his verse, and below." Mark Ford, in a review of *Cat's Whisker* in *Times Literary Supplement,* noted the smooth manner in which Gross pulled together strange images, and concluded by calling him "A careful, highly accomplished poet." Other critics have remarked on Gross's use of anecdote and the accessibility of his poems, which often deal with events of common concern.

Gross later applied all of his tools and craftsmanship to create two books of poems for children, *Manifold Manor* and *The All-Nite Cafe.* Like his works for adults, these books feature a strong narrative line, clever word play, and an eye for detail. But most importantly, the critics agree, Gross does not write down to his younger readers. Instead, he creates books of poetry that can be shared by readers of all ages, that bridge the gap between young and old.

Gross's life seemed to bridge gaps as well. "I am an east-west hybrid," he once commented. "My father is a refugee from Estonia, and my mother was born and bred in Cornwall. Origins and a sense of where home is matter to me, but seem complicated and not to be taken for granted." In one of his volumes of poetry for adults, *The Son of the Duke of Nowhere,* Gross examines this hybrid nature and looks back to his youth in Cornwall, where one of his great escapes was listening to the short-wave radio. Gross went on to attend the University of Sussex and graduated with honors in 1973, then took a job as an editorial assistant in London. In 1976, he was married and also changed his profession to librarian. All the while he was writing poetry, and his work was finally recognized in 1981 with a prestigious Gregory Award

from the Society of Authors. His 1982 poem, "The Ice Factory," earned first prize in the National Poetry Competition of that year and was later collected in his second book of poetry. But increasingly, after he had children of his own, Gross began to think back upon his youth in Cornwall.

He admitted that he had a "mixed feeling" about these "memories of childhood, a mix of strangeness and affection. Responsibility for the everyday care of a small son and daughter brought back a great deal that I'd half forgotten." His own children seem to have spurred Gross toward his writings for children. "Having the care of two small 'soft targets' also makes me very aware of threats to our lives, both individual and collective, and challenges me to try to think and write about them with as much clarity and craft as possible," Gross explained.

The result of such efforts was *Manifold Manor,* Gross's first book of poems for young readers. Dennis Hamley described the book in *School Librarian* as "a truly Gothic journey through a deserted house with a Dantesque jackdaw as guide." Hamley further commented that the book, with its author's afterword (or "Tailpiece," as Gross called it), provided a rich source of writing technique and word games. Likewise, John Mole called the book "crafty and mysterious" in a review for *Times Educational Supplement,* and commended Gross for not talking down to young readers.

The collection of poems ranges from the mysterious to the humorous, telling the episodic story of the various legends and inhabitants of Manifold Manor. It begins with the tantalizing first lines: "The sign says PRIVATE / Tall scrolled-iron gates / are rusted shut / Nobody comes here, but . . . ." *Junior Bookshelf* declared it to be "one of the most unusual and technically accomplished collections . . . to have appeared for some time." The fact that Gross did not make concessions for younger readers in terms of ideas or vocabulary was a plus for reviewers.

Two years later, Gross came out with a prose book for children, *The Song of Gail and Fludd.* While *Manifold Manor* takes children on a tour of the dark, interior world of post-adolescent experience, *The Song of Gail and Fludd,* conversely, is an evocation of the outside journey, or "a brilliantly inventive variation on the Rites of Passage novel," according to Mole in another *Times Educational Supplement* review.

The names of the two protagonists provide the first clue that the book concerns something elemental and forceful. Gail, short for Abigail, is a poor little rich girl ensconced in a large old house and protected from the outside world by her distant mother. A war is going on in this mythical land, and one day it breaks into Gail's life quite literally and she is left on her own in the hostile country. She becomes partners with a strange little boy named Frankie Ludd, shortened to Fludd, and the duo meander about the countryside gathering picaresque adventures and knowledge about life. A pair of clowns, Dumbgast and Flabberfound, provide a sort of cynical

Greek chorus for the pair's adventures. The whole concoction provides a metaphor for the pains of growing up. A *Junior Bookshelf* reviewer called it "a most remarkable novel," while Mole praised Gross as "a skilled artificer."

With the 1993 publication of *The All-Nite Cafe,* Gross returned to creating poetry for younger readers. A compilation of poems in both rhyming couplets and free verse, *The All-Nite Cafe* contains themes which range from fear and anxiety to humor and wit, and uses ghosts, dreams, and twilight as subject matter. Once again, Gross created first and foremost a book of poems, according to reviewers. The fact that the poems are accessible and include themes that might especially appeal to younger readers is almost incidental. Nicholas Bielby, writing in *Times Educational Supplement,* noted that by honestly exploring his own disquiets, Gross was able to "genuinely speak to other people, including teenagers." The poems in the collection display "the sort of off-beat vision of the world and quirky humor which children find so appealing," Cathryn Crowe commented in *Magpies.*

Part of the title poem demonstrates Gross's rhythm and word choice: "It's not a tavern but a cavern, not a cafe but a cave. / There's nothing on the menu but *Whatever You Crave.*" Gross explores inner landscapes with many of these poems, but he does not shy away from social issues, as seen in "History Lesson": " . . . they want to scratch. You are the itch. / A thousand years stand by, hissing *Witch! / Nigger! Yid! /* With surrounding onlookers 'learning not to see'." Several reviewers commented on Gross's rhythmic use of language—some of it giving almost the feel of rap music—and the immediacy of his imagery. Andy Sawyer, writing in *School Librarian,* called the poems in *The All-Nite Cafe* "haunting," and concluded that they are for "older children in search of something creepy but not horrific." *The All-Nite Cafe* garnered the Signal Poetry Award for 1994.

■ Works Cited

Bielby, Nicholas, review of *The All-Nite Cafe, Times Educational Supplement,* March 26, 1993, sec. 2, p. 12.

Crowe, Cathryn, review of *The All-Nite Cafe, Magpies,* July, 1994, p. 39.

Ford, Mark, "Careful Incisions," *Times Literary Supplement,* January 8-14, 1988, p. 39.

Gross, Philip, *Manifold Manor,* Faber, 1989.

Gross, Philip, *The All-Nite Cafe,* Faber, 1993.

Hamley, Dennis, review of *Manifold Manor, School Librarian,* November, 1989, p. 157.

Review of *Manifold Manor, Junior Bookshelf,* October, 1989, p. 238.

Mole, John, review of *Manifold Manor, Times Educational Supplement,* July 28, 1989, p. 21.

Mole, John, review of *The Song of Gail and Fludd, Times Educational Supplement,* July 19, 1991, p. 23.

Sawyer, Andy, review of *The All-Nite Cafe, School Librarian,* May, 1993, p. 70.

Review of *The Song of Gail and Fludd, Junior Bookshelf,* June, 1991, pp. 125-126.

Stanford, Derek, review of *The Ice Factory, Books & Bookmen,* August, 1984.

■ For More Information See

PERIODICALS

British Book News, November, 1983, pp. 705-706; July, 1987, p. 446.

London Review of Books, October 13, 1988, pp. 15-17; January 9, 1992, pp. 22-23.

New Statesman, November 6, 1987, p. 31.

Observer (London), October 23, 1988, p. 42.

Times Literary Supplement, December 16-22, 1988; August 30, 1991, p. 22.

*   *   *

GUNN, Robin Jones 1955-

■ Personal

Born April 18, 1955, in Baraboo, WI; daughter of Travis Garland (a teacher) and Barbara (a teacher; maiden name, Clawson) Jones; married Ross Gunn III (a pastor), August 13, 1977; children: Ross IV, Rachel Elizabeth. *Education:* Attended Biola University, La Mirada, CA. *Politics:* Republican. *Religion:* Protestant.

ROBIN JONES GUNN

A young woman struggles with concerns about her future and relationships as she travels through Europe in this 1994 novel. (Cover illustration by David R. Darrow.)

■ Addresses

Home—8002 Northeast Hwy 99, Suite 52, Vancouver, WA 98665. *Electronic mail*—74477, 2447 (CompU-Serve).

■ Career

Writer. Weekend announcer, interviewer on "His People Radio Magazine," and host of "Kids Korner" weekly program, KNIS Radio, Carson City, NV, and KCSP Radio, Casper, WY; speaker at women's group meetings, public and private schools, retreats, and writer's conferences.

■ Awards, Honors

First place in article writing contest, 1988, and Sherwood E. Wirt Award, 1989, both from Biola University Writer's Institute; Lucille Gardner Poetry Award, Mount Hermon Writer's Conference, 1993; second place for first-person article, Evangelical Press Association, 1994.

■ Writings

"CHRISTY MILLER" SERIES

Summer Promise, Focus on the Family, 1988.
A Whisper and a Wish, Focus on the Family, 1989.
Yours Forever, Focus on the Family, 1990.
Surprise Endings, Focus on the Family, 1991.
Island Dreamer, Focus on the Family, 1992.
A Heart Full of Hope, Focus on the Family, 1992.
True Friends, Focus on the Family, 1993.
Starry Night, Focus on the Family, 1993.
Seventeen Wishes, Focus on the Family, 1993.
Sweet Dreams, Focus on the Family, 1994.
A Promise Is Forever, Focus on the Family, 1994.

"MRS. ROSEY-POSEY" SERIES

Mrs. Rosey-Posey and the Chocolate Cherry Treat, illustrated by Bill Duca, Chariot Books, 1991.
Mrs. Rosey-Posey and the Treasure Hunt, illustrated by Duca, Chariot Books, 1991.
Mrs. Rosey-Posey and the Empty Nest, illustrated by Duca, Chariot Books, 1993.

"JESUS IS WITH ME" SERIES

Jesus Is with Me When I Celebrate His Birthday, illustrated by N. C. Gary and David Acquistapace, David C. Cook, 1988.
Jesus Is with Me When I Go to the Park, illustrated by Gary and Acquistapace, David C. Cook, 1988.
Jesus Is with Me When I Have a Babysitter, illustrated by Gary and Acquistapace, David C. Cook, 1988.
Jesus Is with Me When I Help My Mommy, illustrated by Gary and Acquistapace, David C. Cook, 1988.

"PALISADES PURE ROMANCES" SERIES

Secrets, Questar Publishers, 1995.
Whispers, Questar Publishers, 1995.

OTHER

God's Mountains, Meadows, and More: A Book about Places God Has Made, illustrated by Dawn Lauck, Chariot Books, 1994.
Only You, Sierra ("Sierra Jensen" series), Focus on the Family, 1995.

Also author of the "Billy 'n' Bear" series, six books for toddlers, published by Concordia; contributor of articles to periodicals, including *Virtue, Christian Parenting Today, Christian Herald, Decision, Focus on the Family, Worldwide Challenge,* and *Brio.* Three books in the "Christy Miller" series have been translated into Finnish.

■ Work in Progress

A series of three contemporary adult romance novels for Questar Publishers.

■ Sidelights

Robin Jones Gunn—author of the popular "Christy Miller" series for young adults as well as several series of picture books for children—was a storyteller from an early age. "My mom recently found my grade school report cards," Gunn told *SATA*. "At the end of first grade my teacher wrote, 'Robin does not yet have a grasp of basic math skills. However, she has kept the entire class entertained all year with her endless stories.'" Still, she was not certain whether she had what it took to become a published author.

Overcoming an initial lack of self-confidence, Gunn started her first young adult novel after helping her husband, a pastor, in his work with a youth group. She became concerned about some of the books she saw the teenage girls reading, but she couldn't find many books she liked better at the local Christian bookstore. So Gunn began writing stories she felt teenagers would enjoy, and then she tested her ideas on her junior high Sunday school classes. The students often made helpful suggestions and even came up with new ideas. The result of their input was the "Christy Miller" series, which combines adventure and romance with Christian values.

In each book in the series, teenaged Christy faces a moral dilemma involving peer pressure, her desire to be popular, or her interest in boys. However, she is able to count on her Christian values and her relationship with God to help her make good decisions. The "Christy Miller" series also offers young adults an opportunity to share in adventures, such as when Christy visits Hawaii in *Island Dreamer* and goes on a missionary trip to Europe in *A Promise Is Forever*. "An overall factor in all my writing," Gunn concluded for *SATA*, "is my deep commitment to Jesus Christ."

■ For More Information See

PERIODICALS

School Library Journal, November, 1993, p. 125.
Voice of Youth Advocates, April, 1994, p. 26.

H

PETER J. HAMLIN

HAMLIN, Peter J. 1970-

■ Personal

Born March 12, 1970, in Spokane, WA; son of Frederick J. Hamlin (a pilot) and Joyce J. Barner. *Education:* Attended Washington State University, 1989-90, Western Washington University, 1990-92, and Art Center College of Design, Pasadena, CA.

■ Addresses

Office—P.O. Box 94053, Pasadena, CA 91109.

■ Career

Illustrator. *Member:* Society of Children's Book Writers and Illustrators.

■ Awards, Honors

Selected from a nationwide contest to be the illustrator for *Something Nice to See.*

■ Illustrator

Theodore Roosevelt Gardner II, *Something Nice to See,* Knoll, 1994.

■ Work in Progress

Kinetic art; researching historical children's book illustrators.

■ Sidelights

Peter J. Hamlin told *SATA,* "Illustrating *Something Nice to See,* by Theodore Roosevelt Gardner II, put things in high gear—especially for style, development, and output. It substantiated the fact that, from an illustrator's point of view, there are opportunities out there; and childhood memories like catching fireflies, the Christmas-day countdown, or being chased by big, furry dogs (it was scary at the time, now it's somewhat funny) can indeed hearten the illustration process.

"Though those memories didn't necessarily relate directly to the book's content, they have in common a sense of freshness for me—enchantment, you might say—that was a handy tool that helped keep things alive. Anyway, I want to continue illustrating children's books and have a medium-sized furry dog someday."

CHERYL HANNA

HANNA, Cheryl 1951-

■ Personal

Born January 7, 1951, in Ann Arbor, MI; daughter of Leonard Morton (a dentist) and Irene (a homemaker; maiden name, Dix) Hanna; stepdaughter of Gwili Ford Hanna. *Education:* Attended Pratt Institute, 1969-74. *Politics:* Democrat. *Religion:* Protestant. *Hobbies and other interests:* Portraiture, fine arts.

■ Addresses

Office—c/o HarperCollins Children's Books, 10 East 53rd St., New York, NY 10022. *Agent*—(books) Marie Brown, Marie Brown Associates, 625 Broadway, New York, NY 10012; (art) Carol Bancroft, Carol Bancroft and Friends, P.O. Box 959, Ridgeway, CT 06877.

■ Career

Freelance illustrator, designer, and fine artist, 1985—. Previously a graphic designer at Crowley, Milner & Co., The Design Source, and Curriculum Concepts; Al Hutt Associates, Detroit, staff illustrator, 1974; Children's Museum, Detroit, educator and designer, 1975-76. Arts and crafts instructor at New York Urban Coalition and Alexander Crummell Center. *Exhibitions:* (book art) Design Masters, New York City, 1989; National Museum of Women in the Arts, Washington, DC, 1991-92,

1995; Newark Museum, Newark, NJ, 1993; Cinque Gallery, New York City, 1993, 1995; Lorraine Kessler Gallery, Poughkeepsie, NY, 1994. (Fine art) Brooklyn Museum, Brooklyn, NY, 1980; Gallery 62 of the National Urban League, New York City, 1985; Detroit Repertory Theatre Gallery, Detroit, MI, 1993.

■ Awards, Honors

American Library Association (ALA) Notable Book, 1987; Notable Children's Trade Book in the Field of Social Studies, National Council for the Social Studies, 1987; *An Enchanted Hair Tale* was a Reading Rainbow Review Book; Children's Book of the Year, Child Study Association, 1991, for *Hard to Be Six.*

■ Illustrator

Alexis De Veaux, *An Enchanted Hair Tale,* Harper & Row, 1987.
Arnold Adoff, *Hard to Be Six,* Lothrop, 1991.
Dorothy and Thomas Hoobler, *Next Stop, Freedom: The Story of a Slave Girl,* Silver Burdett, 1991.
Garnet Nelson Jackson, *Phillis Wheatley, Poet,* Modern Curriculum Press, 1993.
Jackson, *Selma Burke, Artist,* Modern Curriculum Press, 1994.
Monalisa DeGross, *Donavan's Word Jar,* HarperCollins, 1994.
Robert H. Miller, *The Story of "Stagecoach" Mary Fields,* Silver Burdett, 1995.
Ramona R. Hanna, *My Name Is Jasmine but They Call Me Jaz,* Stage Two Press, 1996.

Contributor of illustrations to periodicals, including *New York Times* and *Essence.*

■ Work in Progress

Writing and illustrating *My Sister's Wedding, In My Grandmother's House, Somewho,* and *Nightlight;* researching Negro League baseball players, Harriet Tubman, Louis Armstrong, 1930s carnivals, griffins and other fantastic animals.

■ Sidelights

Cheryl Hanna told *SATA:* "Some critical influences include Maurice Sendak, Tom Feelings, Roger Hane, and Leo and Diane Dillon, among others. These are the illustrators I loved most when I was a student. At heart, I'm a fantasist, and even in a straightforward domestic tale I will look for the fantasy, magic, mystery, and romance that lie hidden in everyday life.

"As far as children's book illustration goes, I believe that we're living in a golden age and that a lot of important work is being done. The alchemy that makes a book a 'keeper' is mysterious. Hard work and talent—even genius—don't necessarily guarantee success. There's a special magic in a successful book, sometimes in a very humble guise.

"The most important thing an aspiring illustrator can do is to soak him or herself in the field, past and present. Look at, read, touch, browse through, handle as many children's books as possible. Don't neglect the wonderful work that has been done internationally.

"A real love and respect for children's literature, and a sincere desire to communicate something wonderful and real to the succeeding generation—these are the most important things an illustrator can bring to the table. Talent and technical ability are secondary.

"It is also important that the aspiring illustrator understand that the art of the picture book is a very specific, demanding, and engaging discipline of its own.

"Speaking for myself, I may say that there is no greater privilege for an artist than to help to shape the imaginative world of a child's inner being, and to have one's work become a vehicle for a parent to convey love to a child."

■ For More Information See

PERIODICALS

American Visions, December, 1987, p. 40; December, 1991, p. 36.
Booklist, November 15, 1987; March 1, 1991; June 16, 1994; April 1, 1995.
Bulletin of the Center for Children's Books, July, 1991.
Kirkus Reviews, February 15, 1991; June 15, 1994.
Publishers Weekly, November 13, 1987, p. 69.
Quarterly Black Review of Books, summer, 1994, p. 36; April, 1995, p. 2.
School Library Journal, August 14, 1994; April 1, 1995.

*   *   *

HARRIS, Mark Jonathan 1941-

■ Personal

Born October 28, 1941, in Scranton, PA; son of Norman (a lawyer) and Ruth (Bialosky) Harris; married Susan Popky (a clinical psychologist), June 9, 1963; children: Laura, Jordan. *Education:* Harvard University, B.A. (magna cum laude), 1963.

■ Addresses

Office—School Cinema TV, University of Southern California, Los Angeles, CA 90089-2211. *Electronic mail*—markharris@cntv.usc.edu.

■ Career

Associated Press, Chicago, IL, reporter, 1963-64; documentary and educational filmmaker, 1964-75; California Institute of the Arts, Valencia, faculty member, school of film-video, 1976-83; University of Southern California, Los Angeles, assistant professor of cinema-television, 1983-1987, associate professor, 1987-94, professor, 1994—, co-director of documentary produc-

MARK JONATHAN HARRIS

tion, 1985-91, Division of Film and Television Production Chair, 1991—. Film consultant, 1989—; lecturer on writing, 1989—. Associate producer of documentary film, *As They Like It,* 1965; executive producer of documentary film, *How Will I Survive?,* 1992. University committee memberships include Neighborhood Academic Initiative Advisory Board; Faculty Research and Innovation Fund Selection Committee; Graduate Curriculum Committee; USC Publications Advisory Committee; Tenure and Promotions Committee. *Member:* International Documentary Association, Academy of Motion Picture Arts and Sciences (documentary executive committee member), Writers Guild of America, PEN, Society of Children's Book Writers and Illustrators, Southern California Council on Literature for Children and Young People, University Film/Video Association.

■ Awards, Honors

Regional Emmy Awards, Academy of Television Arts and Sciences, both 1965, for *The Golden Calf* and *As They Like It;* First Prize, International Film and Television Festival for Public Service Spots, 1967, for two sixty-second spots commemorating the 450th anniversary of Protestant Reformation; Academy Award for short documentary film, Academy of Motion Picture Arts and Sciences, and Golden Eagle, Council on International

Non-Theatrical Events, both 1968, for *The Redwoods;*
Award of Merit, Vancouver International Film Festival,
and Special Award, Leipzig International Film Festival,
both 1968, for *Huelga!;* Gold Medal, New York Interna-
tional Film and Television Festival, 1969, for *The Day
Grandpa Died;* Merit Award, Athens International
Scriptwriting Competition, 1975, for *The Mustangers;*
Selection Children's Choice, International Reading As-
sociation, 1980, for *With a Wave of the Wand;* Andrew
Mellon Grant, California Institute of the Arts, 1981;
Golden Spur Award for Best Western Juvenile Fiction,
Western Writers of America, 1981, Dorothy Canfield
Fisher Book Award nomination, 1982-83, and Mark
Twain Award nomination, 1983-84, all for *The Last
Run;* Fellowship in Writing for Children, Mary Louise
Kennedy—*Weekly Reader,* Bread Loaf Writers' Confer-
ence, 1982; Blue Ribbon, American Film Festival,
Special Jury Award, Houston Film Festival, Golden
Eagle, Council on International Non-Theatrical Events,
and Best of Festival, National Educational Film Festi-
val, 1985, all for *The Homefront;* Selection, Weekly
Reader Book Club, 1985, for *Confessions of a Prime-
Time Kid;* Award for Best California Children's Book,
Friends of Children and Literature, 1990, Dorothy
Canfield Fisher Children's Book Award nomination,
1990-91, and Sequoyah Young Adult Award, 1991-92,
all for *Come the Morning;* Best Health and Medical
Film, Silver State Film Festival, 1994, for *How Will I
Survive?*

■ Writings

BOOKS FOR YOUNG PEOPLE

With a Wave of the Wand, Lothrop, 1980.
The Last Run, Lothrop, 1981.
Confessions of a Prime-Time Kid, Lothrop, 1985.
Come the Morning, Bradbury, 1989.
Solay, Bradbury, 1993.

NONFICTION

(With Franklin D. Mitchell and Steven J. Schechter)
The Homefront: America During World War II,
introduction by Studs Turkel, Putnam, 1984.

SCREENPLAYS

The Rainbow Boys, Potterton Productions, 1971.
The Magician, Canadian Broadcasting Corporation,
1972.
Raging Waters, Pat Wells Productions, 1989.
Come the Morning, World Wide Pictures, Inc., 1993.

DOCUMENTARY FILMS

(Coauthor) *Wild Horses, Brave Men,* BFA Educational
Media, 1964.
The Golden Calf, KGW-TV, Portland, OR, 1965.
(And producer) *Huelga!,* King Screen Productions,
1967.
(And coproducer) *The Redwoods,* King Screen Produc-
tions, 1967.
(And producer) *The Foreigners,* King Screen Produc-
tions, 1968.
(And coproducer) *The Homefront,* University of South-
ern California, 1984.

EDUCATIONAL FILMS AND FILMSTRIPS

(And director) *The Day Grandpa Died,* King Screen
Productions, 1969.
(And director) *Wheels, Wheels, Wheels,* King Screen
Productions, 1969.
(And director) *Almost Anyone Can Build a House,*
Learning Corporation of America, 1970.
(And director) *The Story of a Pair of Blue Jeans,*
Learning Corporation of America, 1970.
(And director) *The Story of a Peanut Butter Sandwich,*
Learning Corporation of America, 1970.
(Coauthor and codirector) *Two Grasslands: Texas and
Iran,* Learning Corporation of America, 1971.
(Coauthor) *History of Technology* (twelve filmstrips),
Learning Corporation of America, 1972.
(And producer and director) *How Many Ways Do I
Grow,* BFA Educational Media, 1974.
Communications Panorama (twelve filmstrips), Double-
day Multimedia, 1975.

OTHER

Contributor of short stories to periodicals, including
Neworld, February/March, 1979; *Writers Forum X,*
September, 1984; *New Mexico Humanities Review,*
Summer, 1985; *Buffalo Magazine,* March 20, 1988
(syndicated by *Fiction Network*); and *Sqraffito,* 1995.

After Ben's father disappears, the rest of the struggling
family moves to Los Angeles, where they soon become
homeless. (Cover illustration by Neil Waldman.)

Also author of screenplay *Birds of a Feather,* 1974; co-author with Trevor Greenwood of screenplays *The Mustangers,* 1975, and *Black Tide,* 1976. Author of *Speak for Myself* (a documentary film), 1966; author and director of *Toward 2,000* (a video for the Toyota Company), 1990. Author and producer of two sixty-second public-service television spots for National Lutheran Council of the United States to commemorate the 450th anniversary of the Protestant Reformation, 1967.

Author of "Modulate Your Voice, Please" (essay), in *Infant Tongues: The Voice of the Child in Literature,* edited by Liz Goodenough, Mark Heberle, and Naomi Sokoloff, foreword by Robert Coles, Wayne State University Press, 1994. Contributor of numerous profiles, commentaries, and book reviews to magazines and newspapers, including *Chicago Tribune, International Herald Tribune, Los Angeles Herald Examiner, Los Angeles Times, Newsday, New York Times, Prime Time, TV Guide,* and *Washington Post.* Past contributing editor of *New West.*

■ Sidelights

Award-winning writer, film director, and teacher Mark Jonathan Harris has devoted much of his career to the entertainment and education of young people. He has written and directed several documentary films and filmstrips for school use, contributed reviews of children's books to various newspapers and journals, and penned five books for children. "If there has been a common concern in all my work," Harris once told *SATA,* "it is how people respond to the critical social problems of our society. Whether it is an impoverished farm worker striking for the right to unionize, or a confused twelve-year-old trying to cope with the turmoil of middle-class divorce, I have tried to explore the struggle that occurs when individuals confront the crucial social forces that shape their lives."

One of the critical social problems Harris confronts in his work for children is poverty. As he wrote in a *New York Times Book Review* article, "Of all industrial countries, the United States has the highest proportion of children living in poverty. Approximately 13 million children—one out of every five—in this country are poor. Yet recent children's books have largely ignored the subject." He continued, "Books are still one of the most important ways that children extend the range of their experience.... In our increasingly divided society, it is critical that we not disdain or ignore the experience of one-fifth of our children."

Harris allows readers insight into the lives of poor and homeless children in *Come the Morning.* In this novel, thirteen-year-old Ben, his younger brother and sister, and his mother have been abandoned by Ben's father. Ben believes that his father is living in Los Angeles and convinces his mother that they must leave El Paso to search for him. When the family reaches Los Angeles, they live among the homeless, and Ben must help them survive.

Melissa, a fifth grader whose recent move from New York to California has left her unhappy, encounters a space alien who challenges her to do something about her problems. (Cover illustration by Doron Ben-Ami.)

Two of Harris's other books for young people, *Confessions of a Prime-Time Kid* and *Solay,* explore the ways children cope with situations they cannot completely control. *Confessions of a Prime-Time Kid* presents the memoirs of Meg Muldaur, a thirteen-year-old television star. While Meg reports that her life as a star is sometimes fun, she explains the difficulties of living in an adult world as a child. She cannot attend school regularly, is pressured to give interviews, and must attend party after party. Meg's relationship with her brother has soured because his own acting career has come to a halt. According to a reviewer for *Bulletin of the Center for Children's Books,* the "details of show business," including publicity, agents, and rehearsals, are balanced with Meg's problems in the book.

In *Solay,* Melissa's parents relocate and she is forced to adjust to her new life in California. The ten-year-old girl hates California and the school she attends. A proper and scholarly New Yorker, she especially loathes the group of popular girls who scoff at and play jokes on her because she is smart. Melissa's parents are too busy to help her deal with her problems. It is Solay, an alien girl and an expert trickster, who befriends and supports her.

Though Solay has been sent to Earth to revise her behavior, she shows Melissa how to respond to the "Fashion Critics" with taunts and tricks of her own. Melissa's strategy of vengeance gets her into trouble, and her parents are finally forced to give her the attention she needs. By the time Solay returns to her planet, Melissa's problems are resolved. *Publishers Weekly* applauded the humor in *Solay,* and found the book to be "both sensitive and gloriously entertaining."

Harris once explained to *SATA* how he began his career as a writer and filmmaker: "I began my career as a wire service reporter, then switched to making educational and documentary films during the politically turbulent 1960s. *Huelga!* was documented the first year of the Delano grape strike. *The Redwoods* was made to help the Sierra Club establish a Redwood National Park. *The Foreigners* examined a group of Peace Corps volunteers battling poverty and powerlessness in Colombia. In the 1970s, when the money for political films began running out, I turned to teaching and journalism," Harris continued.

"As I've grown older I've found I'm much more interested in creating my own characters than in report-

ing about real ones," Harris explained to *SATA.* "I began with a twelve-year-old protagonist in *With a Wave of the Wand* and moved up to a fourteen-year-old hero in *The Last Run,* reliving my own childhood and gradually working my way up to adulthood. Soon I expect to be able to write about thirty-year-olds.

"I am particularly interested in writing for children because children value feelings, honesty, and hope in the books they read and so do I. As long as children continue to seek these values in their reading, I will continue writing novels with youthful heroes and heroines."

■ Works Cited

Review of *Confessions of a Prime-Time Kid, Bulletin of the Center for Children's Books,* July-August, 1985.
Harris, Mark Jonathan, "It's So Much Easier to Write About the Rich," *New York Times Book Review,* November 12, 1989, p. 46.
Review of *Solay, Publishers Weekly,* May 24, 1992, p. 88.

■ For More Information See

PERIODICALS

Booklist, October 1, 1992, p. 340.
Locus, May, 1993, p. 33.
Los Angeles Times Book Review, September 5, 1993, p. 9.
New York Times Book Review, February 26, 1984.
Washington Post, February 29, 1984.

*   *   *

HAYS, Thomas Anthony 1957-
(Tony Hays)

■ Personal

Born August 22, 1957, in Madison, TN; son of Robert Douglas and Charlyne Welch Hays; married Holly Lynn Lentz, December 30, 1989 (divorced, June 2, 1994). *Education:* Tennessee Technological University, B.S. (history), 1980, M.A. (educational psychology and counselor education), 1982; East Texas State University, M.A. (English and creative writing), 1991. *Politics:* Democrat. *Religion:* Baptist. *Hobbies and other interests:* Cats.

■ Addresses

Home—c/o Whitfield, P.O. Box 7420, Salmah, Kuwait 22085. *Agent*—Joan Brandt, 788 Wesley D. NW, Atlanta, GA 30305.

■ Career

YMCA of Sendai, Sendai, Japan, English instructor, 1992; Motlow State Community College, Tullahoma, TN, English instructor, 1992-94; freelance writer, 1994—. Part-time English instructor; lecturer at confer-

In Harris's 1980 story, a girl tries to work out her parents' problems, with little success. (Cover illustration by Stan Skardinski.)

ences and festivals. Member, Masonic Lodge. *Member:* Mystery Writers of America, American Literature Association, Robert Penn Warren Circle, Appalachian Writers Association, Sigma Tau Delta, Pi Delta Phi, Alpha Mu Gamma.

■ Writings

FICTION; UNDER NAME TONY HAYS

Murder on the Twelfth Night, Iris Press, 1993.
Murder in the Latin Quarter, Iris Press, 1993.

OTHER

Hardin County, Tennessee, Records, 1820-1860, Southern Historical Press, 1985.

Founder and editor in chief, *The Distillery: Artistic Spirits of the South,* 1993-94. Contributor of articles and short fiction to periodicals, including *Ancestry Newsletter, Civil War Times Illustrated, Southern Magazine, Heritage Quest, Cats Magazine, Mountain Laurel, Carolina Literary Companion, Appalachian Heritage, Unknowns, Innisfree, Skylark,* and *Buffalo Spree.*

■ Work in Progress

Is Murder Necessary?

■ Sidelights

Tony Hays told *SATA:* "*Murder on the Twelfth Night* began as comic relief from a graduate seminar I was taking in Shakespeare. We were reading eight plays in sixteen weeks, required to be able to cite play, speaker, scene, act, and the significance of lines pointed out by the instructor. Such intensity sent me hurtling towards some kind of survival technique to ward off insanity. It appeared in the form of a murder mystery with William Shakespeare as the detective.

"But what began as a short story soon evolved into a novel, and then my creative writing instructor informed me that I'd found my thesis. And, so, the earliest version of the novel was borne out of the sake of academic necessity. Even then, however, she saw its marketability. Occasionally, she'd stop editing and say, 'Now, before you get ready to publish this, we'll need to do this.'

"Would I change anything now if I had it to do over again? Sure, there are things I could do better now, but as with Faulkner, there are too many other stories to tell to worry any longer about this one."

■ For More Information See

PERIODICALS

Voice of Youth Advocates, February, 1994, p. 368; June, 1994, p. 83.

*   *   *

HAYS, Tony
See HAYS, Thomas Anthony

JAY HEALE

HEALE, Jay (Jeremy Peter Wingfield) 1937-

■ Personal

Born June 28, 1937, in Burnham-on-Sea, Somerset, England; son of T. Wingfield (an Anglican priest) and Florence Berys Pym Heale. *Education:* Attended Bradfield College, 1950-55; Brasenose College, Oxford, M.A., 1963; University of Cape Town, higher diploma in education (with distinction), 1980. *Politics:* Moderate. *Religion:* Anglican.

■ Addresses

Home and office—P.O. Box 541, Grabouw, 7160 South Africa.

■ Career

Author, educator, and publisher. Bramcote School, Scarborough, Yorkshire, England, assistant master, 1955-56; Holmewood House, Langton Green, Kent, England, housemaster and senior English, 1959-68, 1974-75; Monterey School, Cape Town, South Africa, housemaster in charge of English and library, second master, 1969-72; Fenrose Publishers, Tunbridge Wells, managing director, 1973-75; Somerset House School, Somerset West, South Africa, deputy head in charge of English, history, and library, 1975-87; Boy Scouts of South Africa, *Scouting About,* national editor, 1992—. Hans Christian Andersen Award committee, jury-elect, 1996. *Member:* International PEN.

■ Awards, Honors

Carl Lohann Award, 1992, for "outstanding contribution to the promotion of the children's book in South Africa."

■ Writings

(Compiler) *The Teacher's Relief Book,* illustrated by Richard Ayres, Fenrose, 1973.

(Editor and arranger) *School Quad: Being a Word-Picture of the English Public School in 1974, Created from the Writings of Pupils from Bradfield College, Cranleigh School, Radley College and Sutton Valence School,* Fenrose, 1974.

(Compiler) *They Made This Land* (nonfiction), illustrated by Bill Ashton, Donker, 1981.

The Tokoloshe Stone, Tafelberg, 1986.

The Devil of Bain's Kloof, De Jager-HAUM, 1987.

(Author and collator) *Storytime* (short stories), Tafelberg, 1987.

The Scout Target (nonfiction), Boy Scouts of South Africa, 1989.

The Scout Trail (nonfiction), Boy Scouts of South Africa, 1989.

Scowler's Luck: An Adventure in the Fish River Canyon, De Jager-HAUM, 1990.

Listen and Speak (adult nonfiction), Shuter and Shooter, 1991.

South African Animal Adventures (nonfiction), Struik, 1991.

(Author and collator) *Storyland* (short stories), Tafelberg, 1991.

Ice Trap, De Jager-HAUM, 1993.

Getting Your Children Hooked on Books (nonfiction), Bookchat, 1994.

Meet Shakespeare! (adult nonfiction), Maskew Miller Longman, 1994.

Poland (nonfiction), Marshall Cavendish, 1994.

South African Authors and Illustrators (nonfiction), Bookchat, 1994.

South African Sea Adventures (nonfiction), Struik, 1994.

Wild Verse and Worse (poetry), Bookchat, 1994.

Portugal (nonfiction), Marshall Cavendish, 1995.

South African Myths and Legends (nonfiction), Struik, 1995.

True South African Animal Tales (nonfiction), Struik, 1995.

Also compiler of *SACBIP-South African Children's Books in Print,* Bookchat, 1988, 1991, 1992, 1993, 1994, 1995. Contributor to *Doer-Land-Y/Far Far Away,* South African illustrated children's books, South African National Museum, 1986; *Towards Understanding/Op Weg na Begrip,* Children's Literature for Southern Africa, Maskew Miller Longman, 1988; *Encyclopedia of PostColonial Literatures in English,* Routledge, 1994. Founding editor, *Bookchat* magazine, 1976—; editor, *Scouting About* magazine, 1993—.

■ Work in Progress

"From the Bushveld to Biko," a cross-section of South African children's literature, due in 1995-96; contributions to *Encyclopedia of Children's Literature,* from Routledge, and *The Oxford Companion to African Literatures,* from Oxford. Always ongoing: research in South African children's literature.

■ Sidelights

Jay Heale told *SATA:* "I fell in love with books as a child (in England) and spent the 26 years of my teaching career trying to pass on a similar love of books to children. When I moved to South Africa in 1968, I found a dearth of locally written children's books, so eventually I tried to write some.

"Having now stopped teaching, I divide my energies between factual and fictional writing, knowing that both are needed. Since 1976 I have also edited *Bookchat,* which remains the only magazine in South Africa dedicated to children's books.

"The book I am most proud of creating is *Scowler's Luck,* the story of a non-achiever in school who finds his own success on a rugged camping trip. I have known so many children like that. But I also enjoy the various sets of true South African adventures I have researched and written (e.g., *South African Animal Adventures, South African Sea Adventures*) as the detective work involved is most exciting.

"I can also be proud of having introduced South Africa to IBBY, the International Board on Books for Young People. As a service, I research and publish an annual annotated list of *South African Children's Books in Print,* known as SACBIP. I have lectured on children's literature throughout South Africa (and in the USA), to parental, school, and university audiences.

"Reading and book love are not yet established firmly enough in South Africa for authors to make a living from their work. So I also edit a quarterly magazine, *Scouting About,* for the Boy Scouts of South Africa; and I have occasional engagements as a professional actor. When I can, I relax (with a book) in my cottage in the peace of the Cape mountains."

■ For More Information See

PERIODICALS

School Library Journal, August, 1994, p. 162.

*   *   *

HEISEL, Sharon E(laine) 1941-

■ Personal

Born September 20, 1941, in Tower, MN; daughter of Douglas Eugene (a mechanic) and Florence Celina (a homemaker; maiden name, Hall) Johnson; married

SHARON E. HEISEL

Manville Marion Heisel (an attorney), May 31, 1974. *Education:* Attended Southern Oregon State College and Reed College; George Washington University, B.S.; Portland State University, M.S., 1975. *Hobbies and other interests:* Transformation of wood, fiber, and clay into objects of functional and aesthetic value.

■ Addresses

Home—3775 Roads End Blvd., Central Point, OR 97502. *Electronic mail*—MANVILLE@Delphi.com. *Agent*—Jean V. Naggar Literary Agency, 216 East 75th St., New York, NY 10021.

■ Career

Sacred Heart Junior High School, Medford, OR, science teacher, 1978-87; Providence Hospital, Medford, OR, health educator, 1988-93. Also active in children's advocacy and literacy (Laubach teacher). *Member:* PEN, Society of Children's Book Writers and Illustrators, Mensa.

■ Writings

A Little Magic, Houghton, 1991.
Wrapped in a Riddle, Houghton, 1993.
The Romance Side, Bantam, 1996.

■ Work in Progress

Juvenile mysteries; *Mythology and Physics of Color in Light;* research on daily life in ancient Egypt, and the history of Chinese miners in the California and Oregon gold rush.

■ Sidelights

When Sharon E. Heisel went back to college at the age of twenty-six, she explained to *SATA,* "I decided to study something about which I was truly ignorant. I majored in biology. A new and wonder-filled world opened to me." After earning a master's degree in invertebrate zoology, Heisel "formed a personal mission. I would reveal the unexpectedly beautiful world of science to young people in order to enrich their lives. Writing was the vehicle for that mission. Being childless, I quickly encountered my own ignorance about the language and customs of American youth. That led me to become a junior high science teacher." Heisel continued writing as she taught, and in the early 1990s she began accomplishing her mission with the publication of two mysteries for young adults that feature "many concepts from history and science," *A Little Magic* and *Wrapped in a Riddle.*

Heisel explained to *SATA* that a "second constant in my books is the essential goodness of ordinary people. This comes directly from my experience as a teacher. My books may have evil or misguided characters since those people are common in the world and they add the element of tension which is essential in a story, but most of the characters are simple, decent human beings, doing the best they can every day."

"The theme of *A Little Magic* is a concept from the philosophy of science: our first step in explaining the universe is the creation of myth and magic," Heisel related to *SATA.* "Eventually, the rational processes develop, but both views are part of a single continuum." *A Little Magic* begins when Jessica and her cousin Corky begin to worry about the strange figures and noises they notice in the forest. While Corky, whose father has just died, is sure that the activity is supernatural, Jessica is skeptical. She is busy with a science project and preoccupied with her social life. When one of Jessica's guests disappears from her carefully planned thirteenth birthday party, however, she and Corky are forced to confront their fears in order to find the girl. According to Patricia Gosda of *Voice of Youth Advocates, A Little Magic* is "an engaging and well-paced mystery." Tatiana Castleton of *School Library Journal* stated that Heisel "strikes a good balance between Jessica's concerns with school, friends, and a first romance" and solving the mystery.

Like *A Little Magic, Wrapped in a Riddle* also includes facts about science and history. In this book, Jessica and other characters from *A Little Magic* join eleven-year-old Miranda as she investigates some strange happenings at her grandmother's Jumping Frog Inn. Although her grandmother, GrandAnn, is not very concerned when the housekeeper is hit on the head or when things

Wishing for magic to help her plan the perfect birthday party, Jessica instead becomes embroiled in a dangerous mystery. (Cover illustration by Pat Grant Porter.)

disappear from the fruit shed, she is upset when she finds that someone has stolen a packet of letters written to her great-grandmother by Mark Twain. Miranda begins to watch the inn's boarders for clues and is ultimately trapped by a criminal in an underground gold mine adjoining the fruit shed. Miranda not only solves the mystery and escapes but, as Kathryn Jennings of *Bulletin of the Center for Children's Books* noted, she "turns out to be a real hero in the tradition of Nancy Drew." Heisel told *SATA* that she included "a lot of information about the writings of Mark Twain" in *Wrapped in a Riddle,* and that "riddles and puns permeate the book." A critic for *Kirkus Reviews* predicted that readers "will enjoy the riddles throughout; they may also find themselves suddenly interested in reading Mark Twain."

While Heisel continues to further her goal of educating and entertaining young adult readers, she told *SATA* that "writing is the hardest work I have ever done. I write five days a week, usually from six o'clock in the morning until two in the afternoon. Each book develops differently, but always the fun comes when the story starts to flow. The writing reaches a point where it is like a whirlpool. It sucks you in and drags you along and,

although you may struggle so that the perturbations show in the water, the overall effect is a kind of inevitable drowning. Apparent inevitability is my goal in writing fiction. Like anything that seems effortless, it requires hard work."

■ Works Cited

Castleton, Tatiana, review of *A Little Magic, School Library Journal,* April, 1991, p. 119.
Gosda, Patricia, review of *A Little Magic, Voice of Youth Advocates,* June, 1991, pp. 96-97.
Jennings, Kathryn, review of *Wrapped in a Riddle, Bulletin of the Center for Children's Books,* November, 1993, p. 84.
Review of *Wrapped in a Riddle, Kirkus Reviews,* September 15, 1993, p. 1202.

■ For More Information See

PERIODICALS

Booklist, May 15, 1991, p. 1798; October 1, 1993, p. 344.
Horn Book Guide, spring, 1994, p. 77.
School Library Journal, February, 1994, p. 102.

* * *

HEWITT, Margaret 1961-

■ Personal

Born April 30, 1961, in Long Island, NY; daughter of Thomas J. and Joan E. Hewitt; married William Low (an artist), October 18, 1986. *Education:* Attended State University of New York at Purchase, 1979-81; Parsons

Hewitt's lively illustrations lend a colorful flair to *Green Earrings and a Felt Hat,* Jerry Newman's exploration of the ups and downs of friendship.

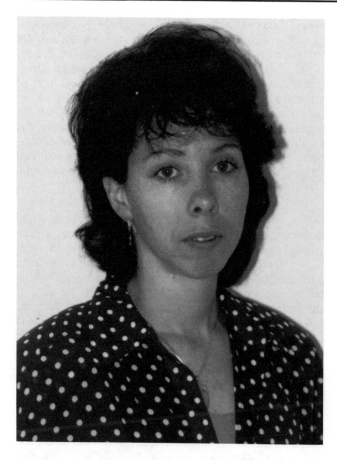

MARGARET HEWITT

School of Design, Manhattan, B.F.A., 1984; attended School of Visual Arts, New York City, 1991-92.

■ Addresses

Home and office—144 Soundview Rd., Huntington, NY 11743.

■ Career

Free-lance commercial artist, 1987—. *Exhibitions:* New York Public Library.

■ Illustrator

Rosemary Stones, editor, *More to Life than Mr. Right,* Holt, 1989.

J. Clarke, *Teddy B. Zoot,* Holt, 1990.

Alice Feinstein, editor, *Visual Encyclopedia of Natural Healing,* Rodale Press, 1991.

Glenyse Ward, *Wandering Girl,* Holt, 1991.

Jerry Newman, *Green Earrings and a Felt Hat,* Holt, 1993.

Abigail Thomas, *Pearl Paints,* Holt, 1994.

Contributor of illustrations to *Ladies' Home Journal, Working Mother,* and *Parenting Digest;* designer of textiles for Baby Gap; creator of advertising art for companies including American Express, Master Card, and Revlon.

■ Sidelights

Margaret Hewitt has provided illustrations for a variety of books, ranging from children's picture books and young adult novels to adult book covers. In addition, she has created advertising art and textile designs as a free-lance commercial artist. Hewitt counts Matisse, Picasso, Schiele, and modern illustrators of the 1960s and 1970s among her artistic influences. She has typically worked in a mixed media of pastel, ink, and gouache on a variety of papers, but she views her style as frequently changing to match her interests. "I'm looking forward to the future, to seeing what my art will look like in ten or twenty years," Hewitt told *SATA.* "I'm certain that my work won't look the way it looks now, but it will continue to be fun, colorful, simple, and sophisticated."*

*   *   *

HILLENBRAND, Will 1960-

■ Personal

Born May 31, 1960, in Cincinnati, OH; son of Earl and Alice (Zins) Hillenbrand; married Jane Barnick (a teacher), June 28, 1986; children: one. *Education:* The Art Academy of Cincinnati, 1982, B.F.A.; also attended Ohio State University.

■ Addresses

c/o Diane Foote, Holiday House, 425 Madison Ave., New York, NY 10017.

■ Career

Illustrator and art director.

■ Awards, Honors

Gold medal, Society of Illustrators, 1990.

■ Illustrator

Elvira Woodruff, *Awfully Short for the Fourth Grade,* Holiday House, 1990.

Verna Aardema, reteller, *Traveling to Tondo: A Tale of the Nkundo of Zaire,* Knopf, 1991.

Marjorie Weinman Sharmat, *I'm the Best!,* Holiday House, 1991.

Woodruff, *Back in Action,* Holiday House, 1991.

Steven Kroll, *The Magic Rocket,* Holiday House, 1992.

Patricia Wittmann, *Go Ask Giorgio!,* Macmillan, 1992.

Natalia M. Belting, *Moon Was Tired of Walking on Air: Origin Myths of South American Indians,* Houghton, 1992.

Eric A. Kimmel, *Asher and the Capmakers: A Hanukkah Story,* Holiday House, 1993.

Mirra Ginsburg, *The King Who Tried to Fry an Egg on His Head: A Russian Tale,* Macmillan, 1994.

Roxanne Dyer Powell, *Cat, Mouse, and Moon,* Houghton, 1994.

Rosalind C. Wang, *The Treasure Chest: A Chinese Tale*, Holiday House, 1995.

Judy Sierra, *The House that Drac Built*, Harcourt, 1995.

Connie Nordhielm Wooldridge, adaptor, *Wicked Jack*, Holiday House, 1995.

Barbara Diamond Goldin, reteller, *Coyote and the Firestick: A Northwest Coast Indian Legend*, Harcourt, 1996.

■ Work in Progress

Another collaborative book with Eric Kimmel and Judy Sierra.

■ Sidelights

Will Hillenbrand has lived almost all of his life in Cincinnati, Ohio, where he grew up in a family whose everyday routines centered on the neighborhood. Much of his childhood revolved around his parents' barber shop and the local baseball diamond. The youngest of four boys with diverse personalities and talents, Hillenbrand found himself in drawing. His curiosity was piqued by the cartoon sketches of an older brother and he discovered in drawing a satisfying pastime. He exercised his art wherever he could; his crayon pictures were as likely to appear on the stairwell wall to the basement as on paper at the kitchen table, not always to his mother's delight.

There were few books in the Hillenbrand household, among them an encyclopedia from which his father read Clement Moore's "The Night before Christmas" each holiday season. Lacking pictures, the memory for Hillenbrand is of the sound of his father's voice with a timbre and a sense of mystery that were an early introduction to the pleasures of storytelling. His grandmother, who lived nearby, was another storyteller. She offered her grandchildren a repertoire of memorable stories from her earlier life on a farm. The Hillenbrand boys were regular visitors to her house, especially during thunderstorms, when she dreaded being alone. The youngest Hillenbrand was also a weekly regular at the local library, strategically located near the baseball diamond, where he found in books another medium for the telling of tales.

Among Hillenbrand's favorite authors then and now are Maurice Sendak, Arnold Lobel, and E. H. Shepard. He finds himself caught up in the spirit of Sendak, whose characters are costumed, animated, and orchestrated across richly drawn stages. In the work of Shepard and Lobel, Hillenbrand admires the ability to create animal characters who are fully individual, yet who remain true to their animal nature and environment.

Although Hillenbrand was drawing from early childhood, the limited resources of the local parochial school offered no opportunity to develop his talent or interest in art. When his older brother switched to the public high school, Hillenbrand followed and, as a second semester sophomore, enrolled in his first art class. The experience was daunting to a young man convinced that his late start would prove an insurmountable disadvantage. But he soon realized that he had a good eye for composition and was comfortable with graphic design. Hillenbrand decided that art was the vocational direction he wanted to take. His father, however, was leery of art as a bread-winning occupation and had to be convinced to let his son try the program at a local art academy on a trial basis. By the completion of his studies, Hillenbrand was sure of his choice of profession. During the summers, he produced commercial artwork at a local television station and later accepted a job at an advertising agency.

During a class in picture book art at Ohio State University taught by Ken Marantz, Hillenbrand the graphic designer and Hillenbrand the storyteller merged. His projects from this class comprised his first picture book portfolio and later he travelled to New York to submit his work to potential publishers. If he needed any further encouragement, he found it in Jane Barnick, a teacher whom he had first known as a young girl sitting on the steps of the house next to his family home. Now she kindled his interest in the illustrated book through her use of children's literature in her classroom. Their shared enthusiasm for children's picture books began a relationship that brought marriage in 1986. Even now they both admit that during a blue mood they are most likely to find solace in a children's bookstore.

Hillenbrand works in a small bright room in the upstairs of his home. The shelves are lined with small objects of childhood, each seeming itself to embody a small story. There sit, for example, several Chinese marionettes,

WILL HILLENBRAND

Hillenbrand's haunting illustrations for Roxanne Dyer Powell's *Cat, Mouse and Moon* evoke the nightly ritual of a cat hunting a mouse.

nesting eggs, stuffed toys, a miniature ball bat, a clay turtle. On the walls are small drawings and varied photographs, mostly of children who bear resemblance to some of the characters in Hillenbrand books. And, of course, there are the large white binders that make up a library of his work-to-date. In producing the artwork for a story, Hillenbrand begins with the sketches from his current binder. He decides which sketches he will develop, then scans them into his computer. From his experience in graphic art, he is very at ease with technologies that help him edit his work. His computer software allows him to play with size, line, position and shading for each drawing. He also composes his pages on the computer screen, deciding, for example, where each page will break and which type font best suits the story. The software has the capability for adding color to

the finished sketches, but Hillenbrand still prefers to complete this stage by hand. "I enjoy working with brush and color, usually oil pastels," he told *SATA*. "Maybe sometime a particular project may give me a reason to use the computer for color, but not yet."

When Hillenbrand reads a story for the first time, he does not try to analyze it. He tries to enter and accept the story's wonder. Believing that wonder and mystery are part of a child's natural world, Hillenbrand reads and rereads the text to enter into that world. Immersed there he finds the mythology that deepens and stretches the wonder. Hillenbrand believes that the experience of myth is accessible to the child; it is "mystery at a natural level." Especially in illustrating folktales, Hillenbrand uses his art to establish a strong link between the imagined life of his characters and the physical world.

For a young illustrator, Hillenbrand has taken on a diverse selection of stories to tell. With each picture book, Hillenbrand has added a new facet to his craft. He has said that a story is like a jewel to be turned in different lights to discover all of its subtle beauties.

*   *   *

HOBSON, Sally 1967-

■ Personal

Born January 15, 1967, in Chiswick, London, England; daughter of Peter Jesse (a university lecturer), and Patricia (a child welfare worker; maiden name, Powell) Hobson; companion of Anthony George Bonning (a writer); children: Thorfinn Peter Hobson-Bonning, Lochlunn Padraic and Sorley McQuater Hobson-Bonning (twins); stepchildren: Jaye Heather Bonning, Merlin Charles Bonning. *Education:* Attended Esher College, and Kingston University, 1985-86; Falmouth School of Art, B.A. (with honors), 1990. *Politics:* Apolitical. *Religion:* Agnostic.

■ Addresses

Home and office—Glenroan Cottage, Glenroan Farm, Barwhillanty, Knockvennie, Castle Douglas, Galloway DG7 3NU, Scotland.

■ Career

Children's book illustrator. Animation painter for Universal Pictures/Amblimation, for *An American Tail: Fievel Goes West,* London, England, 1990-91.

■ Awards, Honors

Mother Goose Award runner-up, 1994, "for the most exciting newcomer to British children's illustration."

■ Illustrator

Ragnhild Scamell, *Three Bags Full,* Orchard Books, 1993.
Chicken Little, Simon & Schuster, 1994.
Vivian French, *The Little Red Hen and the Sly Fox,* All Books for Children, 1995, published as *Red Hen and Sly Fox,* Simon & Schuster, 1995.

■ Work in Progress

The Big Prints, by Ragnhild Scamell, for All Books for Children.

■ Sidelights

Sally Hobson told *SATA:* "Ever since I can remember I have been drawing; the primary influence being my father, who is a talented amateur artist. On completion

of my secondary education I attended Esher College near London, which has an outstanding art department. That is where I gained my artistic confidence. This was followed by a foundation course at the nearby Kingston University, another great influence.

"My next step was a B.A. degree at Falmouth School of Art, one of Britain's top art schools. Cornwall has an extraordinary landscape and atmosphere—a place of legend. I was as influenced by the countryside as by the course and spent a lot of time away from the school drawing and painting the hills, the land, and the sea. It was this experience that developed in me the desire to do book illustration.

"Between my degree and the publication of *Three Bags Full* I have lived a varied and hectic life which has included working on the animated film *An American Tail: Fievel Goes West,* and spending two months travelling across South America, which included walking the Inca Trail. I have (perhaps) finally settled in the hills of Galloway in the southwest of Scotland. Here the landscape has a stunning beauty; we live, quite literally, on top of a hill with panoramic views in all directions.

"I think art is about observation. There is nothing in *Three Bags Full,* or the books I have done since, that cannot be seen outside my window, everything being based on real people, scenes, animals and objects."

SALLY HOBSON

■ For More Information See

PERIODICALS

Publishers Weekly, April 12, 1993, p. 60; October 10, 1994, p. 69.

* * *

HODGSON, Harriet 1935-

■ Personal

Born September 27, 1935, in Flushing, NY; daughter of Alfred (a salesman) and Mabel C. (a homemaker) Weil; married C. John Hodgson (a physician), August 10, 1957; children: Helen, Amy. *Education:* Wheelock College, B.S. (with honors), 1957; University of Minnesota, M.A., 1960; American Management Association in conjunction with Winona State University, Certificate in Management.

■ Addresses

Home and office—1107 FoxCroft Ln. S.W., Rochester, MN 55902.

■ Career

Freelance writer and editor; teacher. KSMQ, Austin, MN, producer and host of "Parenting Today"; writer and narrator of "Parent Talk," a weekly commentary program aired on Minnesota Public Radio; radio appearances on more than ninety talk shows, including "Night Talk" and others broadcast by CBS and WCCO; television appearances on "Good Company," WOR New York, CNN, and other East Coast Stations. Represented the Minnesota Medical Association Alliance as a delegate to the White House Conference for a Drug-Free America. Member of Adolescent Health Committee, Zumbro Valley Medical Society and Auxiliary; chair, Substance Abuse Committee, Minnesota Medical Association Auxiliary. *Member:* Minnesota Medical Association Alliance (communications chair).

■ Writings

Artworks, Monday Morning Books, 1986.
Gameworks, Monday Morning Books, 1986.
A Parent's Survival Guide: How to Cope When Your Kid Is Using Drugs, HarperCollins/Hazelden, 1986.
My First Fourth of July Book (poetry), illustrated by Linda Hohag, Children's Press, 1987.
Parents Recover Too: When Your Child Comes Home from Treatment, Hazelden Foundation, 1988.
Rochester: City of the Prairie, Windsor Publications, 1989.
When You Love a Child: For the Times When Caring for Kids Is Difficult, Deaconess Press, 1992.
Powerplays: How Teens Can Pull the Plug on Sexual Harassment, Deaconess Press, 1993.
Alzheimer's: Finding the Words, A Communication Guide for Those Who Care, Chronimed Publishing, 1995.

HARRIET HODGSON

Also author of *Leader's Guide to Powerplays* (a sexual harassment curriculum and workbook); *Contraptions,* Monday Morning Books; *Toyworks,* Monday Morning Books; *I Made It Myself!,* Warner Books; *E Is for Energy, M Is for Me,* Minnesota State Department of Education; and a poem, "First Steps, First Snow," included in the *American Anthology of Poetry.*

Contributor of "Sisters and Brothers" chapter published in the *Mayo Clinic Complete Book of Pregnancy and Baby's First Year.* Contributor of articles to periodicals, including special features for the *Rochester Post Bulletin;* consultant for the manuscript revision of *My Weight Control Handbook,* Mayo Foundation for Education and Research; writer of monthly column for *Aviation, Space & Environmental Medicine.*

■ Sidelights

Harriet Hodgson's extensive nonfiction writing career, her expertise as a teacher, and her years of experience on radio talk shows about parenting have contributed to the success of two of her many books, *A Parent's Survival Guide: How to Cope When Your Kid Is Using Drugs* and *Powerplays: How Teens Can Pull the Plug on Sexual Harassment.* According to Diane Weddington of the *Contra Costa Times,* Hodgson wrote *A Parent's Survival Guide* after giving lectures on the subject and then "being overwhelmed by church members and friends" to share her knowledge with them. In what Beth E. Andersen in *Voice of Youth Advocates* called a "brief, power-packed manual," Hodgson provides parents who suspect that their children may be using drugs with reassurance and a reliable source of information. *A Parent's Survival Guide* includes a list of drug abuse symptoms which allows parents to identify the effects of various drugs, a description of types of therapy, and guidelines for taking action. Andersen declared that parents coping with a drug-using child and "confused about where to start can find no better first choice" of books than *A Parent's Survival Guide.*

Hodgson told *SATA,* "I started writing when my daughters were in grade school and have been a nonfiction writer for nineteen years. My first sale, *I Made It Myself!,* focuses on recycling and reusing throwaways. Writing allows me to examine a broad range of topics, such as recycling/reuse, energy conservation, drug addiction, history, parenting, sexual harassment, aging, and sibling rivalry.

"Although I write in Minnesota, my work reaches beyond the boundaries of the state. Recently I received a letter from a teenager in Ohio. She said she was preparing a speech and thanked me for writing *Powerplays: How Teens Can Pull the Plug on Sexual Harassment.* Her letter made me feel good inside and suddenly the countless hours I spent on thirty-two revisions seemed worthwhile."

Powerplays may help teens avoid the confusion surrounding sexual harassment by learning to recognize it and defend themselves from it. In the book, Hodgson explains that sexual harassment is nothing new, discusses why teenagers are especially vulnerable when adults "prime" them, and demonstrates that harassers are more interested in their power relationship with the victim than sex. Hodgson's book provides a clear format, with a question to head each chapter and the main points of each chapter summarized in boxes. A list of sources victims can turn to for help and forms for victims to use to record incidents are included. Noting Hodgson's "good teaching procedure" in *Powerplays,* Aldyth Graham in *Voice of Youth Advocates* asserted that the book is "for parents and teachers as well as teens."

Hodgson's own experience, along with her hope to put an end to sexual harassment, motivated her to write *Powerplays.* When Hodgson was in the eighth grade, a teacher made some inappropriate suggestions to her. She soon found out that the teacher had harassed other students as well. "I was lucky," she told Pauline Walle of the *Rochester Post-Bulletin.* "My principal believed me," and the teacher was fired. "When all is said and done," Hodgson told Walle, "I want my twin grandchildren to live in a harassment-free world." For the present, she advised teens "to develop street smarts and use them constantly."

She also told *SATA:* "My writing stems from my early childhood and art education degrees and life experience. In the past I was inspired by my children. Today, I am inspired by other family members and my twin grandchildren. Writing for young children and teens is especially challenging due to the spare language that is

required. Every word must count. Hard work counts, too, and I have often started my writing day at 5:00 a.m. While I am working on one book, another is perking in my mind. Sometimes I have surprised myself with the topics I have chosen. I think of writing as an exciting journey, filled with twists and turns and endless surprises."

■ Works Cited

Andersen, Beth E., review of *A Parent's Survival Guide: How to Cope When Your Kid Is Using Drugs, Voice of Youth Advocates,* October, 1987, p. 191.

Graham, Aldyth, review of *Powerplays: How Teens Can Pull the Plug on Sexual Harassment, Voice of Youth Advocates,* December, 1993, pp. 320-21.

Walle, Pauline, "Flirting or Harassment?," *Rochester Post-Bulletin* (Minnesota), September 7, 1993, p. 1D.

Weddington, Diane, "Survival Guide for Parents of Drug Users," *Contra Costa Times,* January 10, 1987, p. 13A.

■ For More Information See

PERIODICALS

Children's Book Watch, October, 1993, p. 1.
Detroit Free Press, May 4, 1993, p. 4C.
Library Journal, May 1, 1992, p. 102.

* * *

HOPKINSON, Amanda 1948-

■ Personal

Born October 25, 1948, in London, England; daughter of Tom Hopkinson (a writer) and Gerti Deutsch (a photographer); married a professor, 1970 (marriage ended); children: Rebecca, Luke, Jake, Joel. *Education:* University of Warwick, B.A. (with honors), 1970; Oxford University, Ph.D. *Politics:* Socialist. *Religion:* "Jewish by birth, Roman Catholic by conversion."

■ Addresses

Home—13 Connaught Rd., London N4 4NT, England. *Agent*—Curtis Brown, Regent St., London W1, England.

■ Career

Writer.

■ Writings

FOR CHILDREN

Mexico, Raintree Steck-Vaughn, 1992.

OTHER

Julia Margaret Cameron, Virago, 1986.
(Translator) Claribel Alegria, *They Won't Take Me Alive,* Women's Press, 1987.

AMANDA HOPKINSON

(Editor and translator) *Lovers and Comrades: Women's Resistance Poetry from Central America,* Women's Press, 1988.

(Translator) Claribel Alegria, *Family Album,* Women's Press, 1989.

Desires and Disguises: 5 Latin American Photographers, Serpent's Tail, 1992.

The Forbidden Rainbow, photographs by Julio Etchart, Serpent's Tail, 1992.

(Translator) Carmen Boullosa, *The Miracle Worker,* Jonathan Cape, 1994.

A Hidden View: Photography from Bahia, Brazil, Frontline States, 1994.

(Editor) *Contemporary Photographers,* Gale, 1995.

(Translator) Diamela Eltir, *Sacred Cow,* Serpent's Tail, 1995.

History through Photography: Images from the Hulton Deutsch Collection, Koenemann, 1995.

Chicano/Latino Writings, Bloomsbury, 1996.

■ **For More Information See**

PERIODICALS

Horn Book Guide, fall, 1993, p. 388.
School Library Journal, August, 1993, p. 175.
Times Educational Supplement, February 14, 1992, p. 36.

HORGAN, Paul (George Vincent O'Shaughnessy) 1903-1995

OBITUARY NOTICE—See index for *SATA* sketch: Born August 1, 1903, in Buffalo, NY; died following a cardiac arrest, March 8, 1995, in Middletown, CT. Historian, librarian, illustrator, educator, and author. Horgan was best known for his award-winning histories of the American southwest, receiving two Pulitzer Prizes in history for his writings on the Rio Grande and nineteenth-century Santa Fe bishop, Jean Baptiste Lamy. While serving as a librarian at the New Mexico Military Institute from 1926 to 1942, Horgan began his writing career, which was to include a number of genres and a wide variety of subjects. Horgan, who moved to New Mexico when he was twelve, came to know the diverse influences that shaped the region. His two-volume 1954 epic, *Great River: The Rio Grande in North American History,* looks at the four cultures that inhabit the river valley—Native American, Spanish, Mexican, and Anglo-American. Taking ten years to research and write, the book showed the solid crafting and attention to detail that earned Horgan acclaim; for his second Pulitzer-winning work, the 1975 biography *Lamy of Santa Fe: His Life and Times,* he combed the archives of the Catholic Church in the Vatican. The American west and southwest were also favorite subjects of Horgan's. Among his novels are *A Distant Trumpet,* which was adapted for the screen, *Mexico Bay,* and *A Lamp on the Plains.* In a writing career that spanned more than six decades, Horgan saw the publication of seventeen novels, four volumes of short stories, poems, plays, two children's books (the nonfiction, self-illustrated 1931 work, *Men at Arms,* and the 1963 fictional story, *Toby and the Nighttime*), and additional works of history and biography (including an homage to composer Igor Stravinsky). He also illustrated some of his books and many of their dust jackets. In addition, the author taught at Wesleyan University for parts of the 1960s and 1970s, where he was director of the Center for Advanced Studies and became an author in residence.

OBITUARIES AND OTHER SOURCES:

PERIODICALS

New York Times, March 9, 1995, p. B13.

*   *   *

HUNT, Jonathan 1966-

■ **Personal**

Born July 30, 1966, in New Haven, CT; son of Herbert A. III (an ironworker) and Norrene (a secretary; maiden name, Oakley) Hunt; married Lisa Behnke (an illustrator and author), October 8, 1988. *Education:* Paier College of Art, B.F.A., 1988. *Hobbies and other interests:* Book collecting, hiking.

■ Addresses

Home—Florida. *Office*—c/o Simon & Schuster Children's Books, 15 Columbus Circle, New York, NY 10023.

■ Career

Freelance illustrator and author of children's books and fantasy, 1989—; Moon-Shine Studios, Claremont, NH, co-owner, 1991-95. Instructor of illustration, Lebanon College, Lebanon, NH, 1990-95; conducts workshops and makes school and library visits. *Exhibitions:* An illustration from *The Mapmaker's Daughter* was exhibited at a Society of Illustrators show in New York City. *Member:* Society of Children's Book Writers and Illustrators, Association of Science Fiction and Fantasy Artists.

■ Writings

SELF-ILLUSTRATED

Illuminations, Bradbury Press, 1989.
(With wife, Lisa Hunt) *One Is a Mouse: A Counting Book,* Macmillan, 1995.
Leif's Saga, Simon & Schuster, 1996.

ILLUSTRATOR

M. C. Helldorfer, *The Mapmaker's Daughter,* Bradbury Press, 1991.
David Francis Birchman, *Victorious Paints the Great Balloon,* Bradbury Press, 1991.
Rhoda Blumberg, *Jumbo,* Bradbury Press, 1992.
Birchman, *A Tale of Tulips, a Tale of Onions,* Four Winds Press, 1994.
Helldorfer, *Moon Trouble,* Bradbury Press, 1994.

Also contributor of illustrations, with Lisa Hunt, to *Asimov's, Analog, Cricket, Haunts, Marion Zimmer Bradley's Fantasy Magazine,* and *Offworld.*

■ Sidelights

Jonathan Hunt told *SATA* that "as far back as I can remember, I have been drawing and making up stories." At that time, he recalled for *Publishers Weekly* interviewer Molly McQuade, he specialized in drawing superheroes who saved the world: "Everyone had fists, because I couldn't draw fingers. I did a lot of world-shattering catastrophes, enormous evil by incredible villains, things that could never happen in real life." His favorite heroic figure was that of King Arthur, and as he grew older, the artist told *SATA,* he maintained a "fascination for history and how it relates to and influences the literary and art genres of fantasy." Hunt developed his artistic talent and imagination throughout high school and college, and as he began his career as a writer and illustrator his interest in history, legend, and fantasy emerged as a critical factor in his success.

Illuminations, which Hunt began to write and illustrate as a college project, presents an object, concept, symbol, or legendary figure from medieval history for each letter

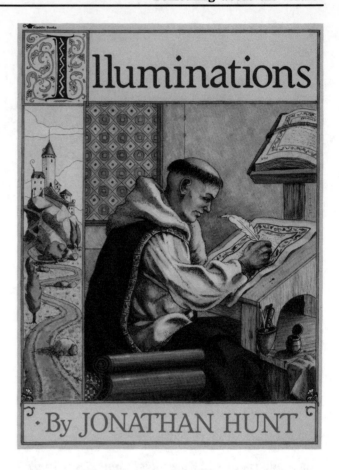

Hunt's self-illustrated alphabet book uses dramatically stylized lettering to describe popular characters and concepts from the Middle Ages.

of the alphabet. Hunt studied each subject—including Alchemy, the Black Death, Coat of Arms, Dragon, Excalibur, and Merlin—thoroughly before writing about it and rendering it in the style of an illuminated manuscript. The project was discovered at a writer's conference, and, after Hunt worked with editors and sent the text to historians to check it for accuracy, *Illuminations* was published. A *Publishers Weekly* critic concluded that *Illuminations* "will pique the interest of readers" and Betsy Hearne of the *Bulletin of the Center for Children's Books* wrote that it will "please students hooked on knights, dragons," and other medieval lore. In assessing the "eye-catching" artwork, Denise Wilms of *Booklist* commented that *Illuminations* is "rich with detailed, often dramatic illustrations."

Hunt's enthusiasm for history and meticulous research have contributed to the books he illustrates for texts crafted by other writers. When he began to work on Rhoda Blumberg's *Jumbo,* a book about a celebrity elephant brought to nineteenth-century America from England, for example, "I spent many weeks visiting libraries and museums to research the lifestyle, clothing and settings" of that era, the artist told *SATA.* Hunt's careful study of the era is reflected in his illustrations. As a *Kirkus Reviews* critic noted, the "larger scenes" in *Jumbo* are expressive, "effectively capturing the mood and times." Hazel Rochman of *Booklist* likewise observed that Hunt's watercolor illustrations "exhibit extraordinary depth and detail."

When Hunt illustrated David Francis Birchman's *A Tale of Tulips, a Tale of Onions,* which is set during the seventeenth-century tulip craze in Holland, he "consulted historical texts describing both the ludicrous and sometimes tragic consequences of 'tulipomania.'" Hunt told *SATA* that he also studied gardening catalogs that friends had given him for "technical advice regarding 'bizarres' (multi-colored, or speckled tulips)." The illustrations for *A Tale of Tulips, a Tale of Onions* present a stage with performers acting out the text in front of an audience on each page. Hunt's other artwork includes M. C. Helldorfer's fantasy *The Mapmaker's Daughter,* as well as her tall tale about Paul Bunyan, *Moon Trouble.*

Although Hunt journeyed to "an ancient Norse house site in northern Newfoundland" to illustrate *Leif's Saga,* his own book about Leif Eriksson's discovery of America, he and his wife, Lisa Hunt, found inspiration for *One Is a Mouse* on a New York train. *One Is a Mouse,* a counting book for young readers written and illustrated by the Hunts, did not require the intense research of Jonathan Hunt's other books. As he explained to *SATA:* "Commuters scrambling and piling into the passenger car somehow translated into the animals that pile recklessly on top of each other in the book."

In addition to collaborating on projects for children's and fantasy magazines and books, the Hunts run their own art company, Moon-Shine Studios, teach illustration at a local college, and visit schools and libraries to share their talent and enthusiasm for illustration with children. In 1995 they moved to Florida, where, according to the artists, they "are supervised" by their five cats.

Jonathan Hunt with wife Lisa.

■ Works Cited

Hearne, Betsy, review of *Illuminations, Bulletin of the Center for Children's Books,* October, 1989, p. 35.

Review of *Illuminations, Publishers Weekly,* July 28, 1989, p. 217.

Review of *Jumbo, Kirkus Reviews,* November 1, 1992.

McQuade, Molly, "Flying Starts: New Faces of 1989," *Publishers Weekly,* December 22, 1989, pp. 27-28.

Rochman, Hazel, review of *Jumbo, Booklist,* November 1, 1992.

Wilms, Denise, review of *Illuminations, Booklist,* September 15, 1989, p. 183.

■ For More Information See

PERIODICALS

Los Angeles Times Book Review, November 26, 1989, p. 27.

New York Times Book Review, November 26, 1989, p. 23.

School Library Journal, September, 1989, p. 241.

*   *   *

HUNT, Lisa B(ehnke) 1967-

■ Personal

Born January 13, 1967, in Spokane, WA; daughter of David W. (an attorney) and Annelies (an executive secretary; maiden name, Koloska) Behnke; married Jonathan D. Hunt (an author and illustrator), October 8, 1988. *Education:* Attended Paier College of Art. *Politics:* Moderate. *Religion:* Agnostic.

■ Addresses

Home—Florida. *Office*—c/o Simon & Schuster Children's Books, 15 Columbus Circle, New York, NY 10023.

■ Career

Freelance illustrator and writer. Art instructor, Lebanon College, Lebanon, NH; frequent speaker and demonstrator at schools throughout New England. *Exhibitions:* Has exhibited solo work and work with husband Jon at art shows and conventions, winning several ribbons. *Member:* Society of Children's Book Writers and Illustrators, Association of Science Fiction and Fantasy Artists.

■ Writings

(Self-illustrated; with husband, Jonathan Hunt) *One Is a Mouse: A Counting Book,* Macmillan, 1995.

Contributing writer to *ASFA Bulletin.*

ILLUSTRATOR

D. J. Conway, *Maiden, Mother, Crone* (adult), Llewellyn, 1994.

Sirona Knight, *Greenfire* (adult), Llewellyn, 1995.

Illustrator, with Jonathan Hunt, of 1992 New Hampshire "Discover-Read" poster; illustrator for several trade paperbacks. Contributor of illustrations to periodicals, including *Asimov's, Analog, Cricket, Creation Spirituality, Haunts,* and *Marion Zimmer Bradley's Fantasy Magazine.*

■ Work in Progress

A series of Moon Goddess paintings and interior illustrations for Llewellyn Publications; several untitled sequels to *One Is a Mouse;* research into world mythology with an emphasis on goddesses.

■ Sidelights

Lisa Hunt told *SATA:* "The process of taking an idea and developing it into a finished piece of art or story is an all-consuming passion that has been an important part of my life for as long as I can remember.

"When I was a child, I was often caught daydreaming in class. My sixth-grade teacher told my parents during a conference that I was 'in the clouds.' In actuality, I was writing stories in my mind. I would often come up with an image in school and then rush home to put it down on paper. I was a shy child, and fantasizing was the perfect means for me to express myself.

"Even now when I am not in my studio working, I am contemplating and sifting through the images and ideas that are constantly floating about in my head. I am never short of ideas! As a matter of fact, I have a notebook filled with potential projects that would take several lifetimes to fully execute.

"I believe that my interest in books has been the impetus and the continuing inspiration for my art. I have shelves of books that occupy every available wall in my home. I am particularly fascinated in world mythology and have great respect for the late Joseph Campbell. I have done numerous interior illustrations for Llewellyn Publications. Llewellyn specializes in 'new age/spirituality.' These assignments have enabled me to express my great love for mythological themes and the archetypes that they celebrate.

"For the book *One Is a Mouse,* my husband Jonathan and I took a real-life situation and developed it into a story that exemplifies the humor inherent in most human behavior. While riding a rush-hour train from New York City, we amused ourselves by watching commuters scramble into the train cars in quest of a place to sit. In *One Is a Mouse* we use anthropomorphic animals to play out this scene in a ridiculous manner. Collaborating with Jonathan was pure joy! While working on *One Is a Mouse,* we listened to tapes of Benny Goodman and literally danced in between painting!

"The inspiration for my writing and art comes from many sources; some, but not all of which are positive.

Probably the most satisfying aspect of what I do is when I try to take a potentially negative situation and transform it into something that celebrates the human spirit."

* * *

HUNTER, Norman (George Lorimer) 1899-1995

OBITUARY NOTICE—See index for *SATA* sketch: Born November 23, 1899, in Sydenham, Kent, England; died February 23, 1995. Magician, advertising copywriter, and author. For nearly fifty years Hunter wrote numerous lighthearted, nonsensical children's books. His most popular character was Professor Branestawm, an absent-minded but clever inventor whose gadgetry sometimes backfired on him. Branestawm originally starred in several children's magazine stories, which Hunter later published in a 1933 collection, *The Incredible Adventures of Professor Branestawm.* An instant hit, it was serialized on the BBC radio show, "Children's Hour," and decades later, in 1992, Penguin Books added the story collection to their series of beloved Puffin Classics. The character would appear in subsequent writings, including *Professor Branestawm's Compendium of Conundrums, Riddles, Puzzles, Brain Twiddlers, and Dotty Descriptions* and *Professor Branestawm's Pocket Motor Car.* An avid magician, Hunter also wrote several books on the craft for adults and children. He performed regularly at London's Little Theatre and Maskelyne's Theatre of Magic, even though he earned his living as an advertising copywriter. In later years Hunter did children's magic shows at schools, libraries, and bookstores, connecting some of his tricks with the fictional inventions and adventures of Professor Branestawm.

OBITUARIES AND OTHER SOURCES:

BOOKS

Who's Who of Children's Literature, Schocken, 1968.
Twentieth-Century Children's Writers, St. Martin's, 1978.

PERIODICALS

Cricket, January, 1975.
Junior Bookshelf, February, 1975; April, 1977.
Times (London), February 27, 1995, p. 21.

* * *

HURT-NEWTON, Tania 1968-

■ Personal

Born February 12, 1968, in Nairobi, Kenya; daughter of Robin Hurt (a safari operator) and Madelaine (a care assistant; maiden name, Ferrar) Newton. *Education:* Attended West Sussex College of Design, 1986-88; Camberwell College of Arts, B.A. (with honors), 1992. *Politics:* "Left." *Hobbies and other interests:* "My favorite pastime is doodling, but I do lots of other things around this—cycling, jogging, travelling, reading, ceramics, old cars with lots of chrome."

■ Addresses

Home—Flat 1, 81 Lorna Rd., Howe, East Sussex BN3 3FL, England.

■ Career

Illustrator.

■ Illustrator

Blaise Douglas, *What I Want to Do When I Grow Up,* Walker Books, 1994.
Stella Maidment, *Great Games for Globe Trotters,* Walker Books, 1994.
Dyan Sheldon, *Love, Your Bear, Pete,* Candlewick Press, 1994.
Elephantastic, Kingfisher, 1995.

Polly Pirate's Puzzle Pun, Walker Books, 1995.
Patricia Sechi-Johnson, *Bloomsbury Book of Everything,* Bloomsbury, 1995.

■ Sidelights

Tania Hurt-Newton told *SATA,* "I realized my ability to draw when I got my first pair of specs, aged ten, when I noted you could actually *see* the grass you walked on and telephone wires above! Since then I've enjoyed drawing and now illustrate full time—packaging, books, editorial work, exhibition design—you name it! I've been out of college for three years now and it looks like a good career ahead as an illustrator. Influences: my old-time favorite has to be Edward Lear, but I love the works of Richard Scarry, Dr. Seuss, and more recently Martin Chatterton, Nick Sharrat, Lucy Cousins. Advice: the only thing I could say is to just 'go for it!' See as many people as you can, but don't expect to get work from everyone. Enjoy what you do and everyone will be able to tell. The main thing is to be positive."

J

GAIL JARROW

JARROW, Gail 1952-

■ Personal

Born November 29, 1952, in Dallas, TX; married Robert Jarrow (a college professor), May, 1974; children: Kyle, Tate, Heather. *Education:* Duke University, B.A., 1974; Dartmouth College, M.A., 1980. *Hobbies and other interests:* Gardening, cross country skiing, reading, travel.

■ Addresses

Agent—Virginia Knowlton, Curtis Brown Ltd., 10 Astor Pl., New York, NY 10003.

■ Career

Children's book author and teacher. Taught elementary and middle school math and science in Cambridge, MA, and Hanover, NH, 1974-79; freelance writer, 1983—; Institute of Children's Literature, Redding Ridge, CT, instructor, 1991—. *Member:* Authors Guild, Society of Children's Book Writers and Illustrators.

■ Writings

FICTION

That Special Someone, Berkley, 1985.
If Phyllis Were Here, Houghton, 1987.
The Two-Ton Secret, Avon, 1989.
Beyond the Magic Sphere, Harcourt, 1994.

NONFICTION

(With Dr. Paul Sherman) *The Naked Mole-Rat: Solving the Mystery,* Lerner, 1996.

Also author of stories and articles in periodicals, including *3-2-1 Contact, Highlights, Child Life, Spider,* and *Pennywhistle Press.*

■ Sidelights

Gail Jarrow told *SATA:* "I grew up in a small Pennsylvania town near Philadelphia, surrounded by extended family and by the same classmates from kindergarten through high school. Despite these close ties, as an only child I spent many hours alone, using my imagination to create triumphs and tragedies for my dolls and stuffed animals. When I learned to write down my thoughts, these pretend games were transformed into stories. I 'published' the first one, 'The King's Lesson,' at age seven. The same spark that inspired me then keeps my creative fires burning today.

"During my school years, I wrote stories and poetry and was the editor of the high school newspaper. A strong interest in animals and plants, however, led me to study biology at Duke University and later to teach elementary and middle school science and math for five years in New England. But I didn't abandon the love of writing. And while working on my master's degree at Dartmouth College, I took a course in children's literature that fanned those creative fires again.

"Soon after finishing my graduate degree, I left full-time teaching to start my family and to begin my writing career. Combining my science background with my writing skills, I became a freelance writer of science articles for *3-2-1 Contact* magazine. Later I began writing short stories and novels for both middle-grade children and young adults.

"My strong childhood memories, my teaching experience, and my enjoyment of children's literature first led me to write for young people. I continue to create for them because I believe it is important for children to discover the joy and satisfaction of reading. I hope that my books will provide pleasure and entertainment, while broadening the young reader's view of the world.

"Ideas for stories come from my past experiences, from my daily life, and from the activities of my children and their friends. For example, I developed the fantasy game in *Beyond the Magic Sphere* after observing my children as they created adventures in their secret land called 'The Green Realm.'

"I can usually pinpoint the day when I begin to think about a story idea. I witness an action that becomes the basis of the plot. I overhear a comment that suggests a conflict. Or I spot an interesting person in the grocery store, and I wonder about her life story. The details of the novel gradually come to me as a steady accumulation of characters, bits of dialogue, and scenes which are later seasoned and combined in my imagination.

"My themes are often influenced by my concern that today's over-programmed children lack the free time to develop *their* imaginations. The ability to think creatively comes from practice and nurturing. This skill plays an essential role in a child's success no matter what path his life takes. Creativity leads to better ideas whether one is a writer, artist, scientist, mechanic, teacher, or businessman. My books celebrate this power of imagination."

■ For More Information See

PERIODICALS

Booklist, October 15, 1987, p. 396; October 15, 1994.
Kirkus Reviews, August 15, 1987, p. 1241.
School Library Journal, September, 1987, p. 180; November, 1994.

JOHNSON, Patricia Polin 1956-

■ Personal

Born February 23, 1956, in Long Beach, CA; daughter of Ramon G. (a title insurance representative) and Rosaura C. (a bank teller; maiden name, Carrillo) Polin; married Allan H. Johnson (an actuary), August 18, 1979. *Education:* University of Southern California, B.A., 1978. *Hobbies and other interests:* Bicycling, reading, jogging, quilting, traveling.

■ Career

Writer. *Member:* Society of Children's Book Writers and Illustrators.

■ Writings

(With Donna Reilly Williams) *Morgan's Baby Sister: A Read-Aloud Book for Families Who Have Experienced the Death of a Newborn,* Resource Publications, 1993.

■ Work in Progress

Three other books in the "Helping Children Who Hurt" series: *Our Family Is Divorcing,* a book about a mother with cancer, and a book about a step-family.

■ Sidelights

Patricia Polin Johnson told *SATA,* "Since childhood, I've always enjoyed being creative, especially writing everything from letters to manuscripts. I 'fell' into writing for children after a few years of exploring different genres. Writing for children is where I feel most comfortable—it's my niche! The child in me comes out when I write for children; I'm happiest when I am at my computer, lost in my childlike world.

"*Morgan's Baby Sister* reveals many of the feelings I experienced during my own miscarriage. The loss I had then helped develop my compassion, which I believe comes out in my writing. In fact, *Morgan's Baby Sister* was one of the ways I healed personally from our miscarriage. I look forward to publishing more books in our 'Helping Children Who Hurt' series and helping more families."*

*   *   *

JOHNSON, Stephen T. 1964-

■ Personal

Born in 1964 in Madison, WI. *Education:* University of Kansas, B.F.A., 1987; attended Universite de Bordeaux and the Conservatoire des Beaux-Arts, Bordeaux, France, 1984-85.

STEPHEN T. JOHNSON

■ Career

Illustrator; guest lecturer and instructor. Illustrator of cover art for magazines, including *Forbes* and *Time;* illustrator of CD covers for record companies; creator of artwork for State Ballet of Missouri, Association of Kansas Theatre, and Georgia Department of Industry, Trade, and Tourism. *Exhibitions:* Works were exhibited in a one-man show at the Center for the Arts Gallery, Moorhead State University, Moorhead, MN, 1991; works have also appeared in several group exhibitions, including the Society of Illustrators Museum and the Norman Rockwell Museum, and in public collections, including the National Portrait Gallery.

■ Awards, Honors

Best of Show Award, Lawrence Art Center, 1987; Philip Isenberg Memorial Award, Pastel Society of America, 1992; David Humphrey's Memorial Award, Allied Artists of America, 1992; Alice Melrose Memorial Award, Audubon Artists, 1993; Knickerbocker Artists Award, Salmagundi Club, 1993; H. K. Holbein Award, Pastel Society of America, 1993; Yarka Art Materials Award, Audubon Artists, 1994; Washington Square Outdoor Award, Salmagundi Club, 1995.

■ Writings

(Self-illustrated) *Alphabet City,* Viking Penguin, 1995.

ILLUSTRATOR

Robert D. San Souci, *The Samurai's Daughter,* Dial Books, 1992.

Melissa Hayden, *The Nutcracker Ballet,* Andrews & McMeel, 1992.

San Souci, *The Snow Wife,* Dial Books, 1993.

Charles Dickens, *A Christmas Carol,* adapted by Donna Martin, Andrews & McMeel, 1993.

Sheila MacGill-Callahan, *When Solomon Was King,* Dial Books, 1995.

Steven Schnur, *Tie Man's Miracle,* Morrow, 1995.

Steve Sanfield, *The Girl Who Wanted a Song,* Harcourt, in press.

* * *

JORDAN, Martin George 1944-

■ Personal

Born August 16, 1944, in Lytham, St. Annes, Blackpool, England; son of George (a civil servant) and Hannah Louise (Gadston) Jordan; married Tanis Blamey (a writer), December 17, 1967. *Education:* Self-taught artist. *Hobbies and other interests:* Body-building, reading, travel, wildlife, running, and cycling.

■ Addresses

Agent—Gina Pollinger, 222 Old Brompton Rd., London SW5 0B2, England.

■ Career

Painter, 1984—. Creator of posters for The Body Shop and Friends of the Earth; designer of limited edition t-shirts, 1989; contributor of six paintings to an environmental package sponsored by Shell Oil Company and the Royal Geographical Society for distribution to schools throughout England. *Exhibitions:* Exhibitor in three one-man shows at Covent Garden, London, 1984; exhibitor in numerous mixed shows in London, including the Barbican, the British Museum of Natural History, the Royal Geographical Society, Kensington Church Street, Addison Ross, the Alpine Gallery, Witeleys of Bayswater, Nomadic Zone at North Audley Street, the Grosvenor House Hotel, and the Venezuelan Cultural Centre; exhibitor at Oxford University, and in galleries in New York, Chicago, and Berlin. Works are held in the Oppenheim Collection, and in the collections of Edward Goldsmith, James Sharkey, and John Aspinall. *Member:* Royal Geographical Society (fellow).

■ Awards, Honors

Sir Peter Kent Conservation Book Prize, and recommendation from the John Burroughs List of Nature Books for Young Children, both 1993, for *Jungle Days, Jungle Nights.*

The Jordans' expeditions in South America resulted in this rich study of life in the Amazon rain forest. (Illustration by Martin George Jordan from Tanis Jordan's *Jungle Days, Jungle Nights.*)

■ Illustrator

Tanis Jordan, *Journey of the Red-Eyed Tree Frog,* Green Tiger, 1991 (published in England as *Ronnie the Red-Eyed Tree Frog,* Kingfisher, 1991).
T. Jordan, *Jungle Days, Jungle Nights,* Kingfisher Books, 1993.
T. Jordan, *Angel Falls,* Kingfisher Books, 1995.

Also coauthor with wife, Tanis Jordan, of *South American River Trips* and *Out of Chingford: Round the North Circular and Up the Orinoco.*

■ Adaptations

Out of Chingford has been optioned for film.

■ Work in Progress

Another book about the Venezuelan jungle.

■ Sidelights

The husband-and-wife team of Martin George Jordan and Tanis Jordan have collaborated to produce several books based on their expeditions into the remote tropical forests of South America. Three of the books—*Journey of the Red-Eyed Tree Frog, Jungle Days, Jungle Nights,* and *Angel Falls*—are intended for children and serve to raise young people's awareness of conservation issues. The remaining two books, written for adults, describe the couple's experiences in the jungle and have become "cult books for travellers" to the region, as the duo explained to *SATA*. Martin Jordan—an accomplished artist whose paintings have appeared in numerous shows and galleries—typically illustrates their books, while Tanis Jordan writes the text.

The couple met in 1961, when Martin was seventeen and Tanis was fifteen years old, and it was "love at first sight" for both young people. The Jordans were married six years later, spending their honeymoon driving across the Sahara Desert in a tiny Morris Minor car. Since then, the duo have continued their adventurous ways, travelling to South America every two to three years to make solitary expeditions into the rain forest for several months. On each of their eight excursions to date, they have spent time "exploring the rivers and the jungles" together in their own boat. The couple has also travelled in West Africa, where Martin contracted malaria and "almost died alone in the jungle," as he admitted to *SATA*. In 1993 the Jordans bicycled across Spain, where Martin Jordan had lived for several months prior to their marriage.

Martin Jordan informed *SATA* that their travels, particularly to remote areas of South America, provided the "inspiration for many paintings" and led directly to their first book for children, *Journey of the Red-Eyed Tree Frog*. This book, which a reviewer for the *Reading Teacher* called "a talking animal fantasy about endangered plants and animals," follows tiny Hops-a-Bit as he wanders deep into the Amazon jungle in search of the Great Wise Toad. Hops-a-Bit has learned that his island home is about to be destroyed by humans, so he decides to ask the Great Wise Toad for help and advice. Along the way, he encounters a number of interesting species that reside in the region. The story has a happy ending, as a group of concerned people step in at the last minute to protect the young toad's habitat. In a review of several books in the children's nature genre for *School Library Journal*, Kathy Piehl appreciated the strong conservationist message in *Journey of the Red-Eyed Tree Frog,* though she claimed that "reading such books produces a painless, 'feel-good' response, as though simply identifying and voicing the problem will result in solutions." The large-format book is illustrated with twenty-one of Martin Jordan's oil paintings.

The Jordans' next book for children, *Jungle Days, Jungle Nights,* has enjoyed even greater success, winning the Sir Peter Kent Conservation Book Prize and receiving a recommendation on the John Burroughs List of Nature Books for Young Children. Like their previous book, it became a best-seller in England, the United States, and the Far East. *Jungle Days, Jungle Nights* traces the cyclical changes that take place in plant and animal life during a year in the tropical rain forest. The

MARTIN GEORGE and TANIS JORDAN

book begins by describing the dry season, later contrasting this against the rainy season. The book also includes information about many fascinating native creatures, including leafcutter ants, which cultivate their own little gardens, and Orinoco crocodiles, which must swallow rocks in order to submerge themselves in the water. Eva Elisabeth Von Ancken, writing in *School Library Journal,* called *Jungle Days, Jungle Nights* "A spectacular combination of luminous, glowing illustrations and poetic text," and praised the gentle manner in which it introduces readers to the complex environment of a tropical rain forest. In a review for *School Librarian,* Angela Redfern stated that "Everything has been painstakingly observed and thoroughly researched" to produce an "extraordinary book." Redfern also commented on the Jordans' ability to let their focus on ecological issues "grow naturally from the text." A *Publishers Weekly* reviewer praised Martin Jordan's paintings for combining "dramatic composition and brilliant colors with accurate detail," and also complimented Tanis Jordan's "graceful, informative narrative."

One "extra bonus" of the books' vast popularity, as Martin Jordan told *SATA,* has been that his original oil paintings "are fast being bought up by collectors." The Jordans also extend their interest in protecting the environment beyond their books. Martin Jordan often donates art work to environmental groups for auction, for example, and he contributed six pictures to an environmental package that was intended for distribution in schools across England. The couple are both fellows of the Royal Geographical Society and have presented lectures there. In addition, Tanis Jordan is chair of the Globetrotters Club, a London-based international travel organization that was established fifty years ago. She has published several travel articles in periodicals, and she also recorded a pilot for a proposed radio travel series.

The Jordans live "in organized chaos" near Epping Forest on the outskirts of London, they explained to *SATA*, "with an assortment of wildlife including five guinea pigs and two hand-reared hedgehogs." In addition to writing and travelling, Tanis Jordan—who has been a hairdresser since she was fourteen years old—owns and operates a salon.

■ Works Cited

Review of *Journey of the Red-Eyed Tree Frog, Reading Teacher,* April, 1994, p. 588.
Review of *Jungle Days, Jungle Nights, Publishers Weekly,* October 25, 1993, p. 61.
Piehl, Kathy, "The Rain Forest You Save May Be Your Own," *School Library Journal,* September, 1994, p. 144.
Redfern, Angela, review of *Jungle Days, Jungle Nights, School Librarian,* February, 1994, p. 25.
Von Ancken, Eva Elisabeth, review of *Jungle Days, Jungle Nights, School Library Journal,* December, 1993, p. 106.

*   *   *

JORDAN, Tanis 1946-

■ Personal

Born August 17, 1946; daughter of Claude Reginald and Emily Louise (maiden name, Buck) Blamey; married Martin George Jordan (an artist), December 17, 1967. *Hobbies and other interests:* Cycling, body-building, wildlife, and travel.

■ Addresses

Agent—Gina Pollinger, 222 Old Brompton Road, London SW5 0B2, England.

■ Career

Writer. Hairdresser, 1960—, and owner of salon. *Member:* Royal Geographical Society (fellow), Globetrotters Club (chair).

■ Awards, Honors

Sir Peter Kent Conservation Book Prize, and recommendation from the John Burroughs List of Nature Books for Young Children, both 1993, both for *Jungle Days, Jungle Nights.*

■ Writings

Journey of the Red-Eyed Tree Frog, illustrated by M. G. Jordan, Green Tiger, 1991 (published in England as *Ronnie the Red-Eyed Tree Frog,* Kingfisher, 1991).
Jungle Days, Jungle Nights, illustrated by M. G. Jordan, Kingfisher Books, 1993.
Angel Falls, illustrated by M. G. Jordan, Kingfisher Books, 1995.

Also co-author with husband, Martin George Jordan, of *South American River Trips* and *Out of Chingford: Round the North Circular and Up the Orinoco.* Contributor of travel articles to periodicals.

■ Adaptations

Out of Chingford has been optioned for film.

■ Work in Progress

Another book about the Venezuelan jungle; a series of stories for younger children.

■ Sidelights

See entry on husband, Martin George Jordan, for joint sidelights covering Tanis Jordan.

■ For More Information See

PERIODICALS

Publishers Weekly, October 25, 1993, p. 61.
Reading Teacher, April 1994, pp. 588-89.
School Librarian, February 1994, p. 25.
School Library Journal, December 1993, p. 106, September 1994, p. 144.

K

JEFF KAUFMAN

KAUFMAN, Jeff 1955-

■ Personal

Born July 6, 1955, in St. Paul, MN; son of Fred and Janet Kaufman; married Julie Kirgo (a writer), March 22, 1980; children: Anna, Daniel.

■ Addresses

Agent—Gina Maccoby Literary Agency, 1123 Broadway, #1009, New York, NY 10010.

■ Career

Los Angeles Times Book Review, Los Angeles, CA, artist, 1989—; freelance illustrator. Mary Hogan Elementary School, school board member.

■ Writings

(Self-illustrated) *Milk Rock,* Holt, 1994.

ILLUSTRATOR

Is Somewhere Always Far Away?, Holt, 1993.
Just around the Corner, Holt, 1993.

* * *

KENT, David
See LAMBERT, David (Compton)

* * *

KING, Christopher (L.) 1945-

■ Personal

Born June 29, 1945; son of Lowell and Phyllis Wright King; married Chitra Yang (a physician), September 7, 1969; children: Matthew. *Education:* Attended the Gunnery, 1964; Swarthmore College, B.A., 1968; Columbia University, M.A., 1974. *Politics:* Independent. *Religion:* Society of Friends. *Hobbies and other interests:* Drawing, sculpture, swimming, boating, poetry, drama.

■ Addresses

Agent—Wendy Schmalz, Harold Ober Associates, 425 Madison Ave., New York, NY 10017.

In this humorous approach to gardening, Christopher King uses rhyme and metaphor to describe the way carrots, peas, cornstalks, and other vegetables prepare for sleep. (Cover illustration by Mary GrandPre.)

■ Career

Writer; creator of educational programs for children. Educational Dimensions, Stamford, CT, educational documentary filmmaker; vice-president and executive producer, Spoken Arts Multimedia, 1976-88; producer, King Productions, 1988—. Producer of *Peacewatch,* a cable television program dealing with peace issues.

■ Awards, Honors

Award for audio-visual productions, *Learning* magazine; CBS fellow, Columbia University.

■ Writings

The Boy Who Ate the Moon, illustrated by John Wallner, Philomel, 1988.
The Vegetables Go to Bed, illustrated by Mary GrandPre, Crown, 1994.

Also author of plays, *Our Appointed Rounds,* 1992, and *A Mother in My Head,* 1993, both produced by the Mark Twain Masquers.

■ Work in Progress

Jasper the Dragon, Momster, and *Go to Sleep, Count Your Sheep,* all children's books; *A Moving Day* and *The Man Upstairs,* both plays; and *Waiters,* a musical.

■ Sidelights

Christopher King shared his inspiration for writing with *SATA:* "My grandfather Clarence King once penned a few lines on 'unpublished works.' The gist of the little essay, printed up by a family member after his death, was that anyone and everyone can say that they are working on their unpublished manuscript. The insight I received from this is that our lives are our works. Some aspects of them we get to share broadly, perhaps with several thousand people. Other aspects are for a much smaller audience, perhaps whispered softly only to our pillows as we fall asleep." King has managed to combine the "broad" aspects of his life with those "whispered softly" in his published bedtime stories, *The Boy Who Ate the Moon* and *The Vegetables Go to Bed.*

The Boy Who Ate the Moon tells the story of a boy who decides to grab the moon, a silver cookie, out of a tree despite the advice of animals. When the boy realizes that the sugar dust which covers the moon is delicious, he eats the entire thing. Full of moon magic, he then begins a fantastic journey, floating over mountains and cities. The "boymoon" finally finds his way home at sunrise, and he wakes up in his father's arms. Ellen Brooks, Jr., in *Children's Book Review Service,* described *The Boy Who Ate the Moon* as "whimsical" and "enjoyable."

According to Janet M. Bair in *School Library Journal, The Vegetables Go to Bed* is a "delightful selection" for bedtime, and its tone resembles that of Margaret Wise Brown's popular favorite *Goodnight Moon.* In the rhyming verse text of *The Vegetables Go to Bed,* corncobs "snuggle up in corn silk," potatoes close their eyes, and onions cry themselves to sleep as night falls. Carrots, tomatoes, peas, cabbages, beans, brussels sprouts, and even spinach dreaming of "green wonderlands" all get ready for bed in their own special ways. Although Diane Roback and Elizabeth Devereaux in *Publishers Weekly* commented that King's verse seemed "forced," they noted that the text of *The Vegetables Go to Bed* contains some "clever wordplay."

As King expressed to *SATA,* "In my years of creating educational programs for children I have developed stronger and stronger convictions that we must dedicate ourselves to the ability of each child to develop his or her unique abilities to the fullest extent. There is no universal standard of excellence or intelligence, only each one's singular mix of talents; and no career is innately more prestigious than another. We must nurture both the tap dancer and the middle manager."

He explained to *SATA* that books were an important part of his own childhood. "I developed my love of literature and respect for my own imagination in listening to books being read to me when I was very young. I befriended Peter Rabbit, Winnie the Pooh, Mowgli, the Sammayad, the Joy Streets, and all the hues of Lang's fairy tales. My mother recited Lear and my father recited Cyrano. I grew up with the understanding that words were the most endlessly fascinating toys and they almost never broke. Now, in all my works I strive for that ability of Thurber's Golux in *The Thirteen Clocks,* to see everything as though I were seeing it for the very first time."

■ Works Cited

Bair, Janet M., review of *The Vegetables Go to Bed, School Library Journal,* July, 1994, p. 79.
Brooks, Ellen Jr., review of *The Boy Who Ate the Moon, Children's Book Review Service,* November, 1988, p. 27.
Roback, Diane, and Elizabeth Devereaux, review of *The Vegetables Go to Bed, Publishers Weekly,* April 11, 1994, p. 63.

■ For More Information See

PERIODICALS

Publishers Weekly, October 14, 1988, p. 71.

School Library Journal, December, 1988, p. 88.

*   *   *

KORNBLATT, Marc 1954-

■ Personal

Born September 13, 1954, in Edison, NJ; son of Lloyd (a veterinarian) and Dolores (a homemaker and business manager; maiden name, Nelson) Kornblatt; married Judith Deutsch (a college professor), November 24, 1985; children: Jacob, Louisa. *Education:* Brandeis University, B.A., 1976; New York University, M.A., 1985; studied playwriting with Donald Peterson and acting with Ted Kazanoff, Stephen Strimpell, Austin Pendleton, Alice Spivak, and Stella Adler.

■ Addresses

Home—1108 Garfield St., Madison, WI 53711.

■ Career

Freelance writer; storyteller in libraries and schools; public information officer, Wisconsin Department of Natural Resources. Actor in films, including *Special Effects, The Important Thing, Acts of a Young Man, Nighthawks, The Warriors,* and *Altered States;* appeared on television series *Another World;* appeared in regional

MARC KORNBLATT

theater productions and Off-Off Broadway; appeared as Spiderman for Marvel Comics. Worked variously as a bartender, waiter, doorman, furniture mover, typist, and staff reporter for *The Westsider* and *Chelsea Clinton News*. *Member:* Society of Children's Book Writers and Illustrators, Dramatists Guild, Council for Wisconsin Writers.

■ Awards, Honors

Finalist, Drama League New Play Contest, Ann White Theater New Play Contest, and Shipping Dock Theater New Play Contest, all for *Last Days of a Translator;* finalist, West Coast Ensemble New Play Contest and Siena College New Play Contest, both for *Clifford's Voices;* second prize, short fiction, Council for Wisconsin Writers, for "Wind and Rain."

■ Writings

"TIME MACHINE" SERIES

(With Susan Nanus) *Mission to World War II,* Bantam, 1986.
Flame of the Inquisition, Bantam, 1986.

PICTURE BOOKS

The Search for Sidney's Smile, illustrated by John Steven Gurney, Simon & Schuster, 1993.
Eli and the Dimplemeyers, illustrated by Jack Ziegler, Macmillan, 1994.

PLAYS

The Great Soul, Macmillan, 1991.
Plain Jane, Macmillan, 1991.
Bar Talk (one-act; for adults), first produced at Nat Horne Theater, New York, 1992.
Clifford's Voices (for adults), first public reading at Mint Theater, New York, 1993.
Last Days of a Translator, staged reading at John Houseman Theater, New York, 1995.

Contributor of plays to the periodical *Search,* including *Cold War Casualties,* 1989; *Biblical Warfare,* 1990; *Bloodbath at Cuyahoga,* 1990; and *The War at Home,* 1990.

OTHER

Paul Revere and the Boston Tea Party ("Time Traveler" series), illustrated by Ernie Colon, Bantam, 1987.

Also contributor of short stories to periodicals, *Jewish Spectator, Wisconsin,* and *Cricket,* and contributor of articles to periodicals, including *Child, Parents, Update, Milwaukee Journal,* and *New York Daily News.* Author of guest columns for the *Capital Times.*

■ Sidelights

Marc Kornblatt, an author of books in the Bantam "Time Machine" and "Time Traveler" series for young adults as well as the picture books *The Search for Sidney's Smile* and *Eli and the Dimplemeyers,* told *SATA:* "I think I wanted to be a writer early on—at least

as far back as elementary school—but wasn't sure I was cut out for the job until I was nearly thirty. After college, I thought I had more to say as an actor than as a playwright." During his years as an actor, Kornblatt appeared in regional theater productions, in plays Off-Off Broadway, and in television shows, films, and commercials. He also worked as a bartender, waiter, doorman, furniture mover, and typist in order to support himself.

"I probably would have remained a full-time performer if I had landed more consistent stage and screen work," Kornblatt recalled to *SATA.* "It was during one long period of unemployment that I took up writing again and decided that maybe I had something to say after all. Moreover, as a writer I discovered that I always would have my manuscripts to work on, as opposed to being a performer where I didn't really exist unless I was in a show or film.

"My career as a children's book author began as a fluke," Kornblatt continued. "My friend (Susan Nanus, coauthor of *Mission to World War II*), needed help finishing a young adult novel she had been asked to write. She came to me, knowing that I, as a newspaper reporter, was pretty good with deadlines, and because she knew (better than I) that I was a lot younger at heart than I let on. Since then I have found that I enjoy writing for children, and performing as a storyteller, as much as anything I have ever done."

After writing *Mission to World War II* with Nanus, Kornblatt wrote two other books for the Bantam "Time Machine" and "Time Traveler" series on his own. Notable among these is *Flame of the Inquisition,* which presents a quest to gain information in Spain during the years of the infamous Inquisition. Kornblatt provides a cast of characters, information about the Inquisition, and a story plot, but readers must choose various plot options themselves. John Naud, a critic for *Voice of Youth Advocates,* appreciated the "originality" of the plot and character development, and called *Flame of the Inquisition* "a unique work." Elaine E. Knight in *School Library Journal* found the book to be "unusually chilling" with some "bloodcurdling scenes."

Kornblatt's first picture book for younger children, *The Search for Sidney's Smile,* begins when Sidney wakes up frowning. His father attempts to make Sidney smile by buying him an ice cream cone and by taking him to the movies, playground, and zoo, but nothing makes Sidney's smile return until his father gives him a big hug. Kathy Piehl in *School Library Journal* observed that Sidney's father "spends an extended period of time with his son, and genuinely tries to have fun with him."

Eli and the Dimplemeyers, Kornblatt's second picture book, is based on an anecdote a friend told him about her son's imaginary friends. In the book, which according to Nancy Seiner in *School Library Journal* possesses "a streak of happy insanity," Eli discovers that an entire family—Donald Dimplemeyer, his wife Doris, their daughter Drusilla, and their son Trip—live in his house,

Eli Finkel has a hard time convincing his parents that their home is occupied by the invisible Dimplemeyer family in the outrageously funny *Eli and the Dimplemeyers*. (Illustration by Jack Ziegler.)

but only he can see them. Eli has a difficult time keeping the Dimplemeyers safe from his family members, who unknowingly sit on or run into his invisible friends. In an effort to protect the Dimplemeyers from further dangers, Eli tells his parents about them. But they don't believe their son and even suggest that he might need to see a psychiatrist. Finally, Eli's grandmother suggests that the Dimplemeyers find a new home in the backyard; Eli builds them a tree house and the situation is resolved. As Diane Roback and Elizabeth Devereaux in *Publishers Weekly* noted, Kornblatt "leaves the final say" about whether or not the Dimplemeyers are imaginary "up to readers." According to Hazel Rochman in *Booklist,* children who read *Eli and the Dimplemeyers* "will recognize how imagination can be a powerful force against authority."

In addition to novels and picture books for young people, Kornblatt has published short stories and plays and contributed articles to magazines and newspapers. He writes at home and cares for his son Jacob and daughter Louisa while his wife works as a college professor. Kornblatt also works as a storyteller in libraries and schools and serves as a public information officer for the Wisconsin Department of Natural Resources.

■ Works Cited

Knight, Elaine E., review of *Flame of the Inquisition, School Library Journal,* April, 1987, p. 116.
Naud, John, review of *Flame of the Inquisition, Voice of Youth Advocates,* June, 1987, p. 95.
Piehl, Kathy, review of *The Search for Sidney's Smile, School Library Journal,* December, 1993, p. 90.
Roback, Diane, and Elizabeth Devereaux, review of *Eli and the Dimplemeyers, Publishers Weekly,* March 14, 1994, p. 73.
Rochman, Hazel, review of *Eli and the Dimplemeyers, Booklist,* January 15, 1994, p. 937.
Seiner, Nancy, review of *Eli and the Dimplemeyers, School Library Journal,* May, 1994, p. 97.

■ For More Information See

PERIODICALS

Horn Book Guide, fall, 1993, p. 263.
School Library Journal, January, 1988, p. 96.

* * *

KOSSMAN, Nina 1959-

■ Personal

Born December 17, 1959, in Moscow, Russia; daughter of Leonid (a linguist) and Maya (a biologist; maiden name, Sternberg) Kossman; married Andy Newcomb (a computer scientist), May, 1990. *Education:* Bennington College, B.A., 1980; Hunter College, M.A. (teaching English as a second language), 1987; University of Pittsburgh, M.A. (Russian literature), 1990. *Politics:* Democrat. *Religion:* Jewish.

■ Addresses

Home—25-22 14th St., Long Island City, NY 11102.

■ Career

Writer and translator. Defense Language Institute, Monterey, CA, instructor of Russian, 1980-82; Williams College, Williamstown, MA, teaching assistant of Russian, 1982-83; Vassar College, New York City, teaching assistant of Russian, 1983-84; Department of Justice, New York City, translator, 1985-86; Talented Handicapped Artists' Workshop, art therapist, 1986-87; Board of Education, New York City, instructor of English as a second language, 1986-87; Hostos Community College, Bronx, NY, English as a second language adjunct instructor, 1987-88; Board of Education, New York City, teacher of English as a second language (grades K-8), 1991-94. Fellowship Panelist, National Endowment for the Arts, 1994. *Exhibitions:* Oil paintings have appeared in group exhibitions in New York City, including St. John's University Gallery, 1984; Pleiades Gallery, 1985; Cork Gallery, Avery Fisher Hall, Lincoln Center, 1985; Rockefeller Center, 1985; Circlework Visions Gallery, 1988; Ward-Nasse Gallery, 1991. *Member:* Society of Children's Book Writers and Illus-

NINA KOSSMAN

trators, American Literary Translators Association, Poetry Society of America, PEN Club/Centre for Writers in Exile.

■ Awards, Honors

Award of Excellence, Chung-Cheng Gallery, 1984; Award of Excellence, St. John's University Gallery, 1984; Winner of Juried Show, Pleiades Gallery, 1985; UNESCO/PEN Short Story Award, 1995.

■ Writings

(Translator) Marina Tsvetaeva, *In the Inmost Hour of the Soul: Poems of Marina Tsvetaeva*, Humana, 1989.
(Self-illustrated) *Pereboii* (poetry; title means "Syncopated Rhythms"), Khudozhestvennaya Literatura (Moscow), 1990.
Behind the Border: Memories of a Russian Childhood (for children), Lothrop/Morrow, 1994.
(Translator) Tsvetaeva, *Poem of the End: Selected Lyrical & Narrative Poetry*, Ardis, 1995.

Five chapters from *Behind the Border* are scheduled to appear in *Cricket*—one chapter each monthly issue beginning September, 1996.

Contributor of short fiction to periodicals such as *Mundus Artium, Sepia* (England), and *New Southern Literary Messenger.* Contributor of poetry to Russian periodicals. Contributor of poetry to anthologies, including *Twentieth Century Poems on the Gospels,* Harcourt, 1995; and to periodicals such as *Connecticut*

Poetry Review, International Poetry Review, International Women Poets, Orbis (England), *Prairie Schooner, Quarterly West,* and *Voices International.*

Translator of poetry appearing in anthologies: *20th Century Russian Poetry,* Doubleday, 1993; *Contemporary Russian Poetry Anthology,* Zephyr Press, 1995; *Twentieth Century Poems on the Gospels,* Harcourt, 1995. Translator of poetry appearing in periodicals, including *City Lights, Poet Lore, Vassar Review,* and *Modern Poetry in Translation.*

Behind the Border: Memories of a Russian Childhood has been translated into Japanese.

■ Sidelights

Nina Kossman told *SATA* that *Behind the Border: Memories of a Russian Childhood* "is an autobiography written from a child's point of view. It portrays not only events in my own personal history, but also gives a portrait in miniature of the society where I grew up. Since the breakup of the Soviet Union, the society I once knew has stopped existing. This makes it all the more important to record and to explain the past, in order to understand the future not only of Russia, but of the other countries that sprang up in place of the huge Soviet empire. I believe that the themes touched upon in this book will personalize children's lessons in social studies by showing them that each one of us is a bearer of a particular culture and that it is through ourselves that our heritage is realized and transmitted. Hopefully, it will encourage youngsters to question their parents or grandparents about their own heritage and immigrant beginnings, and so help to bridge 'culture gaps' that develop as children grow up in an environment so unlike that of their immigrant elders."

■ For More Information See

PERIODICALS

Booklist, August, 1994, p. 2040.
Kirkus Reviews, July 15, 1994, p. 988.
Publishers Weekly, August 8, 1994, p. 440.
School Library Journal, October, 1994, p. 134.

*   *   *

KROHN, Katherine E(lizabeth) 1961-

■ Personal

Born February 5, 1961, in Bitburg, Germany; daughter of Don Ray (a physician) and Betty Jo (a homemaker; maiden name, Stevens) Krohn. *Education:* University of Michigan, B.A., 1983. *Hobbies and other interests:* Traveling, hiking, camping, photography, painting, cooking gourmet vegetarian dinners, baking cookies.

KATHERINE E. KROHN

■ **Addresses**

Home and office—Eugene, OR. *Agent*—c/o Lerner Publications, 241 First Ave. N., Minneapolis, MN 55401.

■ **Career**

Freelance writer, 1991—.

■ **Awards, Honors**

International Reading Association (IRA) Young Adult Choice Award, 1994, for *Lucille Ball: Pioneer of Comedy;* IRA Children's Choice Award, 1994, for *Roseanne Arnold: Comedy's Queen Bee.*

■ **Writings**

Lucille Ball: Pioneer of Comedy, Lerner, 1992.
Roseanne Arnold: Comedy's Queen Bee, Lerner, 1993.
Elvis Presley: The King, Lerner, 1994.
Marilyn Monroe, Lerner, 1996.

■ **Work in Progress**

A biography for children of Opal Whiteley, "the child-diarist and naturalist who lived in the Eugene area of Oregon in the early part of the century."

■ **Sidelights**

Katherine E. Krohn told *SATA:* "When I was in grade school in the 1960s, I liked to read biographies of famous people. I enjoyed peering inside someone else's world—nosing around a bit. More than anything, my reading a biography gave me a sense of *possibility.* So much could be accomplished if a person set their mind to it. I saw how someone could overcome difficulties to achieve their goals in life. I saw how life, for everyone, has its ups and downs, and that nothing great is accomplished without faith and perseverance.

"I grew up to be a biographer for young readers. I have written books on artists of all kinds—movie stars, singers, writers, a television personality, and a comedian. I enjoy my work very much. I research each subject thoroughly, and by the time the biography is written I feel like I know my subject personally. Sometimes I am so engrossed in a book project that I even dream about a subject. During the writing of *Roseanne Arnold: Comedy's Queen Bee,* I dreamed I was a guest on TV's *Roseanne,* and she even invited me over to her house for a big homemade dinner after the show! I guess you could say I really get into my work!

"I believe that much can be learned from the story of an exceptional individual. Fortunately, children today have the opportunity to choose from a vast and diverse selection of biography titles."

L

LAMBERT, David (Compton) 1932-
(David Kent)

■ Personal

Born December 27, 1932, in Southborough, Kent, England; son of Cecil Compton (a businessman) and Hilda Mildred (a homemaker; maiden name, Shepherd) Lambert; married Wendy Patricia Holmes (a doctor), September 26, 1960; children: Sally Joanna. *Education:* Cambridge University, B.A., 1955. *Hobbies and other interests:* Walking, cycling, table tennis, reading, natural history.

■ Career

Rathbone Books, London, England, editor, 1957-62; Educational Research Publications, London, editorial director of textbooks, 1962-67; free-lance writer, 1967—

■ Awards, Honors

Outstanding Science Books for Children award, National Science Teachers Association, 1978, for *Seashore;* Special Award to Field Guides—Older, New York Academy of Sciences, 1989, for *The Field Guide to Geology;* Junior Prize (co-winner), Rhone-Ponlenc Prizes for Science Books, 1994, for *The Ultimate Dinosaur Book.*

■ Writings

(With Laurie Lee) *The Wonderful World of Transportation,* Garden City Books, 1960, published in England as *Man Must Move: The Story of Transport,* Rathbone Books, 1960, revised edition published as *The Wonderful World of Transport,* Macdonald & Co., 1969.

(Contributing editor) *History: Civilization from Its Beginnings,* Macdonald & Co., 1962.

In Search of Science, Hamlyn, 1966.

The Colour Encyclopedia of Knowledge, Collins, 1973.

Horses and Ponies, Purnell, 1977.

Seashore (juvenile), Sampson Low, 1977, Warwick, 1978.

Dinosaurs, edited by Jennifer Justice, Crown, 1978.

Exploring the Age of Dinosaurs, Ward Lock, 1978.

(With Maurice Chandler and Bernard Moore) *The Book of Key Facts,* Paddington Press, 1978.

The World of Animals (juvenile), Warwick, 1978.

The Earth and Space (juvenile), Warwick, 1979.

(With Jeremy Kingston) *Catastrophe and Crisis,* Facts on File, 1979.

(With Stuart Holroyd) *Mysteries of the Past,* Aldus, 1979.

The Oceans, Ward Lock, 1979, Warwick, 1980.

The Seashore, Concertina, 1979.

Wild Mammals of the Countryside, Concertina, 1979.

(Contributor) John Paton, editor, *Finding Out* (children's encyclopedia), Silver Burdett, 1980.

The Active Earth (juvenile), Lothrop, 1981.

Animal Life (juvenile), edited by Jacqui Bailey, Kingfisher, 1981, Warwick, 1982.

Birds, Kingfisher, 1981, Warwick, 1982.

Dinosaur World (juvenile), Kingfisher, 1981, Rand McNally, 1982.

Dinosaurs (juvenile), illustrated by Ross Wardle, Granada, 1981, Rourke, 1981.

Dogs (juvenile), illustrated by Bernard Robinson and Wardle, Rourke, 1981.

First Picture Book of Animals (juvenile), illustrated by Mike Atkinson and others, Kingfisher, 1981, Warwick, 1982.

Ghosts (juvenile), Rourke, 1981.

(And editor, with Martyn Bramwell and Gail Lawther) *The Brain,* Perigee, 1982.

Dinosaurs (juvenile), Kingfisher, 1982.

Dinosaurs (juvenile), illustrated by Christopher Forsey and others, F. Watts, 1982.

Earthquakes (juvenile), F. Watts, 1982.

Planet Earth (juvenile), edited by Bailey, Kingfisher, 1982, Warwick, 1983, second edition published as *The Superbook of Our Planet,* Kingfisher, 1986.

(With the Diagram Group) *A Field Guide to Dinosaurs,* Avon, 1983, published in England as *Collins Guide to Dinosaurs,* Collins, 1983.

Reptiles (juvenile), Gloucester Press, 1983.

The Seasons (juvenile), F. Watts, 1983.

Weather (juvenile), F. Watts, 1983.

The Work of the Wind (juvenile), Wayland, 1983, Bookwright Press, 1984.

The Oceans, Wayland, 1983.

The Solar System (juvenile), Bookwright Press, 1984.

Vegetation (juvenile), Bookwright Press, 1984.

(With Ralph Hardy) *Weather and Its Work,* Orbis, 1984.

(With Mark Lambert, Brian Williams, and Jill Wright) *Where Is It* (question-and-answer encyclopedia), Kingfisher, 1984.

Planet Earth, Facts on File, 1985.

Volcanoes (juvenile), illustrated by Michael Roffe and others, F. Watts, 1985.

Earthquakes and Volcanoes, Wayland, 1985.

(With Jane Insley) *Great Discoveries and Inventions,* Orbis, 1985.

Pollution and Conservation (for schools), Wayland, 1985.

(With Anita McConnell) *Seas and Oceans,* Orbis, 1985.

(With Edward Ashpole and Susan Jones) *Rainbow Biology Encyclopedia,* W.H. Smith, 1985.

Trees of the World (for schools), Wayland, 1985.

(With the Diagram Group) *The Field Guide to Prehistoric Life,* Facts on File, 1985, published in England as

The Cambridge Field Guide to Prehistoric Life, Cambridge University Press, 1985.

Ancient Peoples, Wayland, 1986.

Maps and Globes (for schools), Wayland, 1986.

Rocks and Minerals, F. Watts, 1986.

Snakes, F. Watts, 1986.

The World before Man, Facts on File, 1986.

The Age of Dinosaurs, illustrated by John Francis, Random House, 1987.

(With the Diagram Group) *Field Guide to Early Man,* Facts on File, 1987.

Grasslands, Wayland, 1987.

Polar Regions, Wayland, 1987.

Seas and Oceans, Wayland, 1987.

Action Dinosaurs, illustrated by David Woodruffe, Purnell/Macdonald, 1988.

(With the Diagram Group) *The Field Guide to Geology,* Facts on File, 1988, published in England as *The Cambridge Guide to the Earth,* Cambridge University Press, 1988.

Earth Science on File, Facts on File, 1988.

(With the Diagram Group) *The Dinosaur Data Book: The Definitive, Fully Illustrated Encyclopedia of Dinosaurs,* Avon Books, 1990.

Dinosaurs, Warwick Press, 1990.

Forests, illustrated by Martin Camm, Troll, 1990.

(With Rachel Wright) *Dinosaurs: Facts, Things to Make, Activities,* F. Watts, 1991.

Fires and Floods, New Discovery Books, 1992.

The Golden Concise Encyclopedia of Mammals, illustrated by Jim Channel, John Francis, and George Fryer, Western Publishing Company, 1992.

The Children's Animal Atlas: How Animals Have Evolved, Where They Live Today, Why So Many Are in Danger, Millbrook Press, 1993.

The World's Population, Thomson Learning, 1993.

The Ultimate Dinosaur Book, Dorling Kindersley, 1993.

Seas and Oceans, illustrated by Carolyn Scrace and Mark Bergin, Raintree Steck-Vaughn, 1994.

Stars and Planets, illustrated by Bill Donohoe and Tony Townsend, Raintree Steck-Vaughn, 1994.

BIBLE STORIES; UNDER PSEUDONYM DAVID KENT

The Desert People, Kingfisher, 1981.

Escape From Egypt, Kingfisher, 1981.

Kings of Israel, Kingfisher, 1981.

The Last Journey, Kingfisher, 1981.

Miracles and Parables, Kingfisher, 1981.

The Time of the Prophets, Kingfisher, 1981.

Bible Stories, Galley Press, 1985.

■ Sidelights

For more than thirty years, David Lambert has been writing books for young people covering a wide variety of scientific topics. "I write popular educational books for children and anyone else intrigued by the way the natural world works," he once mentioned. "I studied English language in college but learned to write readable text as an editor with now-long-defunct Rathbone Books. In the 1950s and early 1960s this British firm produced full-color educational books for teenagers,

"An excellent basic reference."
—*Booklist*

THE FIELD GUIDE TO GEOLOGY

David Lambert and the Diagram Group

David Lambert gives young amateurs a thorough introduction of the Earth's 4.6 billion years' of evolution in this 1988 publication, which won an award from the New York Academy of Sciences.

using illustrations closely integrated with texts aimed at an international (largely American) market.

"Rathbone's editors rewrote for laymen much indigestible text provided by academics. Clear exposition was in; purple prose out. The firm favored the drill sergeant's formula: 'First you tell them what you're going to tell them. Then you tell them. Then you tell them what you've told them.' Editing involved sniffing out muddled and gappy thinking and delving into unfamiliar technical subjects to clarify particular points. The end products were chapters broken down into double-page spreads containing closely linked paragraphs, launched by lead sentences. Rewrites stressed short sentences with lively, active-voiced verbs. Editors avoided technical jargon and explained each unfamiliar term the first time it appeared. They were less creative writers than craftsmen like plumbers or carpenters—or newspaper journalists. Indeed, liaison with designers and artists taught Rathbone wordsmiths that a well-captioned diagram could often express complex facts more clearly than an acre of text.

"Covering an encyclopedic range of material, some editors eventually turn popularizers, planning and writing texts and working with designers for a number of publishers and packagers. That's how I got into the business." The two-page per chapter format was one that Lambert used in many of his early books, including the *First Picture Book of Animals*—which prompted a *Junior Bookshelf* reviewer to declare that "every page has its quota of the strange and wonderful"—as well as *Birds, Reptiles,* and *Earthquakes.*

A longer, more in-depth work, *Collins Guide to Dinosaurs,* published in 1983, covers its subject thoroughly, including information on dinosaur anatomy, behavior, and evolution, along with detailed descriptions of individual dinosaurs. Reviewing the book in *Growing Point,* C. T. Fisher called it "most useful" and found one chapter in particular to "surpass in detail any other book on dinosaurs." Likewise, a critic in *Junior Bookshelf* review stated that "dinosaur enthusiasts of any age will revel in this comprehensive reference book."

Lambert has written numerous books on the subject of dinosaurs during his career. One, *Action Dinosaurs,* published in 1988, provides what Margery Fisher in *Growing Point* called "educational play" and a "pleasant exercise in learning." It includes detailed instructions for making a Pteranodon, a Tyrannosaurus Rex, a Brontosaurus, and a Triceratops. Another Lambert book, *The Dinosaur Data Book,* was described by Hans O. Anderson in *Science Books and Films* as "well written, superbly illustrated, and thoroughly comprehensive." Hugh M. Flick, Jr., in his review in *Kliatt,* said that this book "contains more details about the lives of dinosaurs than most people have ever considered." In 1993, *The Ultimate Dinosaur Book* was published and met with great praise for its depth of information. Peter Dodson, writing in *Science Books and Films,* called it an "all-around terrific offering."

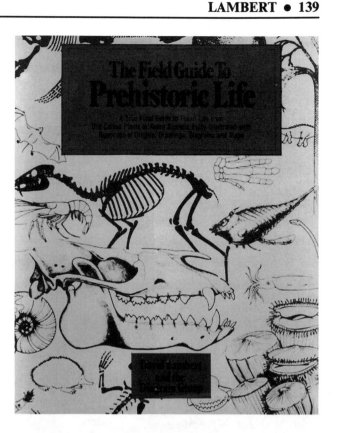

In another one of his informative field guide books, Lambert provides a clearly written and authoritative look into the complex study of fossils and the evolution of life.

Booklist reviewer Ray Olson described another of Lambert's works on the topic, *The Field Guide to Prehistoric Life,* as a "very useful guide" which "provides an excellent introduction to paleontology for a popular audience." *The Field Guide to Prehistoric Life* is part of a series that also includes *The Field Guide to Early Man* and *The Field Guide to Geology,* which received a Special Award to Field Guides—Older from the New York Academy of Sciences in 1989. The book was "highly recommended" by Judith A. Douville in *Science Books and Films* as being "fun to use and quite difficult to put down."

Lambert also authored a number of books focusing on earth science, including *Planet Earth, Weather, Seas and Oceans, Rocks and Minerals, Maps and Globes,* and *Volcanoes.* According to Lavinia C. Demos in *Appraisal: Science Books for Young People,* the latter book is "an inviting research tool." In addition to his science titles, Lambert, under the pseudonym David Kent, has written a series of children's books which explore the Bible from creation through the conversion of the Apostle Paul.

■ Works Cited

Anderson, Hans O., review of *The Dinosaur Data Book, Science Books and Films,* November, 1990, p. 127.
Review of *Collins Guide to Dinosaurs, Junior Bookshelf,* December, 1983, p. 260.

Demos, Lavinia C., review of *Volcanoes, Appraisal: Science Books for Young People,* fall, 1986, p. 62.

Dodson, Peter, review of *The Ultimate Dinosaur Book, Science Books and Films,* March, 1994, p. 41.

Douville, Judith A., review of *The Field Guide to Geology, Science Books and Films,* November/December, 1989, p. 71.

Review of *First Picture Book of Animals, Junior Bookshelf,* June, 1982, p. 98.

Fisher, C. T., review of *Collins Guide to Dinosaurs, Growing Point,* September, 1983, p. 4136.

Fisher, Margery, review of *Action Dinosaurs, Growing Point,* November, 1988, p. 5055.

Flick, Hugh M. Jr., review of *The Dinosaur Data Book, Kliatt,* September, 1990, p. 47.

Olson, Ray, review of *The Field Guide to Prehistoric Life, Booklist,* June, 1985, p. 1423.

■ For More Information See

PERIODICALS

Appraisal: Science Books for Young People, winter, 1983, p. 37; spring, 1987, p. 38.

Booklist, May 1, 1986, p. 1308; October 15, 1993, p. 402.

Children's Book Review Service, August, 1982, p. 137.

Growing Point, November, 1981, p. 3978.

Horn Book Guide, fall, 1993, p. 349.

Junior Bookshelf, February, 1993, p. 32.

Publishers Weekly, November 8, 1993, p. 80.

Science Books and Films, August, 1994, p. 175.

School Librarian, May, 1994, p. 77.

School Library Journal, May, 1987, p. 102; March, 1994, p. 243.

Times Educational Supplement, January 28, 1994, p. 14; April 1, 1994, p. R13.

*   *   *

LARRABEE, Lisa 1947-

■ Personal

Born November 10, 1947; daughter of Fred Henry, Jr. (a businessman) and Gloria (Goff) Larrabee, and stepmother, Willa Jean (a homemaker; maiden name, Manning) Larrabee; married Donnie Fay Jackson (a draftsman), January 7, 1994; children: Robert Michael Berry. *Education:* Attended University of Kansas, 1965-67, and 1979-82. *Religion:* Episcopalian. *Hobbies and other interests:* Painting—outsider art.

■ Addresses

Home—P.O. Box 179, Perdido, AL 36562.

■ Career

University of Kansas, Lawrence, KS, Department of Political Science, office manager, 1976-83; City of Lawrence, Lawrence, word processor, 1983-84; AAA Typing Service, Lawrence, owner and operator, 1983-87; University of Kansas, Department of Music, secre-

LISA LARRABEE

tary, 1984-85; Rubins, Kase, Rubins & Cambiano, PC, Kansas City, MO, legal secretary, 1985-87; University of Kansas, KU Psychological Clinic, office manager and bookkeeper, 1987-89; Poarch Creek Indians, Atmore, AL, office manager of WASG/WYDH radio stations, economic development assistant in the Tribal Chairman's office, and administrative assistant in the Planning Department, 1989-93; Bender Shipbuilding & Repair Co., Inc., Mobile, AL, secretary, 1993-94; G5B Graphics, Perdido, AL, owner, writer, and artist, 1993—; ALTO Products Corp. AL, Atmore, office manager, 1994. Volunteer, officer, member of board of directors, vice-president, secretary, and treasurer of Headquarters, telephone crisis/suicide prevention center, 1983-89; member of board of directors, secretary, and vice-president of Atmore Arts Council, 1990-92.

■ Awards, Honors

Notable Children's Trade Book in the Area of Social Studies citation, Children's Book Council, 1994, for *Grandmother Five Baskets.*

■ Writings

Grandmother Five Baskets, Harbinger House, 1993.

■ Work in Progress

A children's book and a young adult book.

■ Sidelights

Lisa Larrabee told *SATA:* "For me, a successful story will share a basic emotional and/or spiritual element of myself. In *Grandmother Five Baskets,* the character of Sarah McGhee (Grandmother Five Baskets) uses basket-making to illustrate spiritual philosophies of life which I believe are fundamental.

"With all my stories, there must be an emotional connection between myself and the story. Long before I am really aware that there is a story to tell, bits and pieces of it have been appearing and reappearing in my mind.

"Finally, and most importantly, the characters in a story must be people important to me. Their eccentricities, and ways of seeing and being with the world must spark my imagination. When that happens, I know these are characters who will hold a reader's attention. "When I am able to combine all these elements, emotional and spiritual with a strong character, then I feel a story is a success."

*   *   *

LEEDY, Loreen (Janelle) 1959-

■ Personal

Born June 15, 1959, in Wilmington, DE; daughter of James Allwyn (an auditor) and Grace Anne (a registered nurse; maiden name, Williams) Leedy. *Education:* Attended Indiana University—Bloomington, 1978-79; University of Delaware, B.A. (cum laude), 1981.

■ Addresses

Home—P.O. Box 3362, Winter Park, FL 32790.

LOREEN LEEDY

■ Career

Craftsperson, specializing in jewelry, 1982-84; writer and illustrator, 1984—. Lecturer at writing workshops. Speaker for schools and conventions. *Exhibitions: Fraction Action* included in the Society of Illustrators' Original Art show, New York City, 1994; art depicting sea turtles, from *Tracks in the Sand,* shown at the Greensburgh Nature Center in Scarsdale, NY. *Member:* Authors Guild, Authors League of America, Society of Children's Book Writers and Illustrators.

■ Awards, Honors

Parents' Choice Award for Illustration, 1987, for *Big, Small, Short, Tall;* Parents' Choice Award in Learning and Doing, 1989, for *The Dragon Halloween Party;* Ezra Jack Keats Award for excellence in the arts, 1989; Best Books citation, *Parents Magazine,* 1990, for *The Furry News,* and 1992, for *The Monster Money Book;* Outstanding Science Trade Book citation, National Science Teachers Association and Children's Book Council, 1994, for *Tracks in the Sand.*

■ Writings

SELF-ILLUSTRATED

A Number of Dragons, Holiday House, 1985.
The Dragon ABC Hunt, Holiday House, 1986.
The Dragon Halloween Party, Holiday House, 1986.
Big, Small, Short, Tall, Holiday House, 1987.
The Bunny Play, Holiday House, 1988.
A Dragon Christmas: Things to Make and Do, Holiday House, 1988.
Pingo, the Plaid Panda, Holiday House, 1988.
The Potato Party and Other Troll Tales, Holiday House, 1989.
The Dragon Thanksgiving Feast: Things to Make and Do, Holiday House, 1990.
The Furry News: How to Make a Newspaper, Holiday House, 1990.
The Great Trash Bash, Holiday House, 1991.
Messages in the Mailbox: How to Write a Letter, Holiday House, 1991.
Blast off to Earth!: A Look at Geography, Holiday House, 1992.
The Monster Money Book, Holiday House, 1992.
Postcards from Pluto: A Tour of the Solar System, Holiday House, 1993.
The Race, Scott Foresman, 1993.
Tracks in the Sand, Doubleday, 1993.
The Edible Pyramid: Good Eating Every Day, Holiday House, 1994.
Fraction Action, Holiday House, 1994.
Who's Who in My Family?, Holiday House, 1995.

ILLUSTRATOR

David A. Adler, *The Dinosaur Princess and Other Prehistoric Riddles,* Holiday House, 1988.
Tom Birdseye, *Waiting for Baby,* Holiday House, 1991.

The Furry News **teaches children some of the basics of journalism, as readers follow Big Bear and his friends' plans to start a local newspaper.** (Illustration by the author.)

■ Work in Progress

2 X 2=BOO!, a set of multiplication tables (with a Halloween theme), of which the author says, "When I was struggling to learn the multiplication tables in fourth grade, I never dreamed they could be the inspiration for writing!"

■ Sidelights

Loreen Leedy once commented: "Reading, writing, and making art have been important to me throughout my lifetime. The picture book is a unique art form in which the words and artwork work together to tell the story or convey information. When developing a book, I work back and forth between the text and the illustrations to create a unified whole. Most of my books incorporate humor to engage the young reader, and many are informational."

Leedy's picture books are generally regarded as simple yet entertaining and instructive introductions to a variety of subjects. *The Bunny Play* pictures the efforts of a group of rabbits to mount a staging of "Little Red Riding Hood." A *Publishers Weekly* reviewer notes that Leedy "delves into the behind-the-scenes information with exuberance," while the story is described by *Booklist* contributor Barbara Elleman as "a delightful entree into the theater world for the youngest first-nighters." *The Furry News: How to Make a Newspaper* centers on Big Bear's decision to publish a newspaper of

his own that would cover neighborhood events not found in the city paper. As in many of her informational picturebooks, Leedy appends a glossary of key terms to this work, which a *Publishers Weekly* contributor describes as a "clever, irresistible introduction to the many particulars of newspaper writing and production." *Messages in the Mailbox: How to Write a Letter* introduces young readers to many forms of correspondence, both formal (invitations, thank you notes, letters to the editor) and informal (love letters). A *Kirkus Reviews* critic notes that Leedy's "expressive characters and sample messages enliven tips on appropriate topics to write about" and other helpful information. *School Library Journal* contributor Sharron McElmeel adds that *Messages in the Mailbox* is "a superb book that shouldn't be missed."

Other Leedy picture books have addressed ecological concerns, geography, biology, and mathematics. In *The Great Trash Bash,* the animals of Beaston and Mayor Hippo must confront a rapidly growing problem: "Beaston has too much trash." Leedy's story explores the pros and cons of each proposed solution, and appends a list of ideas for cutting down on solid waste; *School Library Journal* contributor Ruth Smith considers the book "timely, appealing, and funny." *Blast off to Earth! A Look at Geography* is also considered an appealing introduction to its subject. The book pictures alien teacher Quark and his students as they journey to earth on a class trip. Quark's instructive comments highlight

A group of bunnies puts on a production of "Little Red Riding Hood," teaching youngsters all about what it takes to produce a play, in Leedy's self-illustrated 1988 story.

the distinguishing aspects of each continent and of the globe as a whole. *Postcards from Pluto: A Tour of the Solar System* conversely explores space as the robot guide Dr. Quasar conducts a group of multicultural children on a spaceship field trip. Information is imaginatively conveyed to the reader in postcards that the young people send to earth, relating their experiences and impressions. Mathematics is the subject of Leedy's *Fraction Action,* which *Kirkus Reviews* has deemed "a lucid introduction to an often vexing topic." The book features a lively cast of animal characters, plenty of humor, and a large variety of everyday things that can be understood in terms of halves, thirds, and fourths.

"I choose a subject such as writing letters, then devise a set of characters and a setting for the action to take place," Leedy explains. "In *Messages in the Mailbox,* Mrs. Gator and her students write busily in a swampy Florida classroom. In *The Edible Pyramid,* a suave feline waiter shows his customers the variety of foods available in the restaurant, thereby exploring the U.S.D.A.'s newly developed Food Guide Pyramid. Other interesting subjects that may inspire future books include computers, cats, fashion, cars, exercise, and the food chain."

■ Works Cited

Review of *The Bunny Play, Publishers Weekly,* March 18, 1988, p. 86.

Elleman, Barbara, review of *The Bunny Play, Booklist,* March 15, 1988, p. 1264.

Review of *Fraction Action, Kirkus Reviews,* February 15, 1994, p. 229.

Review of *The Furry News: How to Make a Newspaper, Publishers Weekly,* March 30, 1990, p. 62.

Leedy, Loreen, *The Great Trash Bash,* Holiday House, 1991.

McElmeel, Sharon, review of *Messages in the Mailbox: How to Write a Letter, School Library Journal,* September, 1991, p. 246.

Review of *Messages in the Mailbox: How to Write a Letter, Kirkus Reviews,* October 15, 1991, p. 1345.

Smith, Ruth, review of *The Great Trash Bash, School Library Journal,* May, 1991, p. 80-81.

■ For More Information See

PERIODICALS

Appraisal, autumn, 1991, pp. 37-8; fall, 1993, pp. 33-4.

Booklist, September 15, 1986, p. 133; November 1, 1988, p. 485; October 1, 1990, pp. 339-40; March 15, 1992, pp. 1388-89; October 15, 1993, p. 437; March 15, 1994, p. 1368.

Bulletin of the Center for Children's Books, May, 1990, p. 218; December, 1991, p. 97; March, 1992, pp. 184-85; March, 1994, pp. 224-25; February, 1995, p. 206.

Delaware Today, October, 1986.

Publishers Weekly, August 9, 1985, p. 74; August 22, 1986, p. 97; March 20, 1987; October 14, 1988, p. 73; March 24, 1989, p. 67; November 10, 1989, p. 60; November 2, 1992, p. 70.

School Library Journal, August, 1986, p. 84; December, 1986, p. 91; September, 1987, p. 166; October, 1988, p. 35; July, 1989, p. 68; December, 1989, p. 84; May, 1990, pp. 98-99; January, 1993, p. 92; May, 1993, p. 88; October, 1993, p. 119.

*   *   *

LEVIN, Betty 1927-

■ Personal

Born September 10, 1927, in New York, NY; daughter of Max (a lawyer) and Eleanor (a musician; maiden name, Mack) Lowenthal; married Alvin Levin (a lawyer), August 3, 1947; children: Katherine, Bara, Jennifer. *Education:* University of Rochester, A.B. (high honors), 1949; Radcliffe College, M.A., 1951; Harvard University, A.M.T., 1951.

■ Addresses

Home—Old Winter St., Lincoln, MA 01773.

■ Career

Museum of Fine Arts, Boston, MA, assistant in research, 1951-52; part-time teaching fellow, Harvard Graduate School of Education, 1953; creative writing fellow, Radcliffe Institute, 1968-70; Massachusetts coordinator, McCarthy Historical Archive, 1969; Pine Manor Open College, Chestnut Hill, MT, instructor in literature, 1970-75; Minute Man Publications, Lexington, MA, feature writer, 1972; Center for the Study of

BETTY LEVIN

Children's Literature, Simmons College, Boston, special instructor in children's literature, 1975-77, adjunct professor of children's literature, 1977-87; instructor at Emmanuel College, Boston, 1975, and at Radcliffe College, Cambridge, MA, 1976—. Member of the steering committee, Children's Literature New England. Sheep farmer. *Member:* Authors Guild, Authors League of America, Masterworks Chorale, Children's Books Authors (Boston), Middlesex Sheep Breeders Association.

■ Awards, Honors

Judy Lopez Memorial Award, 1989, for *The Trouble with Gramary;* Best Book for Young Adults citation, American Library Association, 1990, for *Brother Moose;* New York Public Library Books for the Teen Age list, 1993, for *Mercy's Mill; Parents' Choice* Story Book Award, 1994, for *Away to Me, Moss!*

■ Writings

JUVENILE NOVELS

The Zoo Conspiracy, illustrated by Marian Parry, Hastings House, 1973.
The Sword of Culann, Macmillan, 1973.
A Griffon's Nest (sequel to *The Sword of Culann*), Macmillan, 1975.
The Forespoken (sequel to *A Griffon's Nest*), Macmillan, 1976.
Landfall, Atheneum, 1979.
The Beast on the Brink, illustrated by Parry, Avon, 1980.
The Keeping-Room, Greenwillow, 1981.
A Binding Spell, Lodestar/Dutton, 1984.
Put on My Crown, Lodestar/Dutton, 1985.
The Ice Bear, Greenwillow, 1986, MacRae (London), 1987.
The Trouble with Gramary, Greenwillow, 1988.
Brother Moose, Greenwillow, 1990.
Mercy's Mill, Greenwillow, 1992.
Starshine and Sunglow, illustrated by Joseph A. Smith, Greenwillow, 1994.
Away to Me, Moss!, Greenwillow, 1994.
Fire in the Wind, Greenwillow, 1995.

OTHER

Contributor to books, including *Innocence and Experience: Essays and Conversations on Children's Literature,* compiled and edited by Barbara Harrison and Gregory Maguire, Lothrop, 1987; and *Proceedings for Travelers in Time,* Green Bay Press, 1990. Also contributor of articles to periodicals, including *Harvard Educational Review, Horn Book,* and *Children's Literature in Education.* Levin's manuscripts are housed in the Kerlan Collection, University of Minnesota, Minneapolis.

■ Work in Progress

Gift Horse.

■ Sidelights

Betty Levin builds her young adult characters in either realistic or fantastic settings, sometimes overlapping the two. Ancient myths and real historical events are also important elements of these novels, as is magic. Among the real settings Levin uses in her stories are modern-day Maine in *The Trouble with Gramary,* ancient Ireland in *The Sword of Culann,* and the Orkney Islands in *The Forespoken.* And as her characters move through these settings, they often unravel mysteries and reach a higher level of maturity by the end of their adventures. "Levin is not an easy writer," stated Adele M. Fasick in *Twentieth-Century Children's Writers,* but she added that "readers who are willing to immerse themselves in the strange settings and to struggle to understand the significance of mysterious events will find themselves embarking on an enriching experience. Levin's work grows in strength and scope with each book published."

And so it is with the author's memories of the past; as described in her essay in *Something about the Author Autobiography Series* (*SAAS*), they grow in strength with each one remembered. Pieces of Levin's childhood come to her on a regular basis in the form of memory fragments. Among these pieces of memories are the day when her best friend's older sister knocked her down and sat on her, and the day she went skating with her older brothers but never actually got to skate—it took her too long to catch up and to put her skates on properly. "Early memories are like scraps of trash set loose by a space capsule," observed Levin in *SAAS.* "Detached fragments continue to orbit, but outside the scheme that spawned them. They are so unfixed that it is often impossible to date them. Yet they float across our consciousness. When we recognize the truth of them, we suspect that in some way they are still a part of us."

Levin grew up with her two older brothers in a total of three different places—a farm in Bridgewater, Connecticut; in New York City; and in Washington, D.C. Other family members included Levin's parents, Kitty Healy, who came from Ireland to live with the family, and Robby, who had grown up on a farm in Virginia. Kitty served as a sort of second mother to Levin, at least until she married Walter Beck and had her first child, Katherine. The early stories that left lasting impressions on Levin were told to her by both her mother and Kitty; among her favorites were those dealing with animals. And this love of animals became a reality for Levin as she acquired a puppy, to be joined by a rabbit, a cat, and a pony. "Looking back, it seems to me that I spent a large part of my childhood with real and pretend animals," Levin said in *SAAS.*

The majority of Levin's childhood summers were spent on the family farm, a place that nourished her affinity for animals. It was here that she first learned of the partnership possible between a human and a dog; and this partnership has helped Levin numerous times throughout her life, especially in her adult career as a sheep farmer. One summer did differ from the rest,

When her seaside hometown becomes a tourist attraction and her house and business are subsequently threated, Merkka Weir's grandmother, Gramary, begins to act strangely in Levin's mystery-filled 1988 novel. (Cover illustration by David Montiel.)

though—the summer of 1936 when the Levin family took a train trip across the country. One of the longest stops the family made was near Santa Fe, New Mexico, where Levin passed bliss-filled days in this new-found paradise of desert and horses. "That trip instilled in me a love of trains," Levin related in *SAAS*. "It also gave me an idea of paradise.... I never wanted to go back there. I wanted to keep the place as it had been for me in the summer of 1936."

Other changes gradually came about in Levin's childhood, the largest being a result of World War II. Her mother began working with an organization that helped Hitler refugees, and her father began spending more and more time in Washington, D.C. until the family moved there in the fall of 1940. Leaving all her friends behind during her transition from childhood to adolescence was hard for Levin, but she maintained ties with these friends through the books they all read. Among these were those considered to be "real" literature, like *Caddie Woodlawn* and *Oliver Twist,* and those that offered the pleasures of "junk" reading, such as *Gone with the Wind.* "It didn't entirely replace good litera-

ture," asserted Levin in *SAAS,* "but it had a strong grip on me, along with movies and movie magazines.... Romanticism saved me from absolute degradation. When I discovered Emily Bronte's *Wuthering Heights,* I found even more to satisfy than the sudsy romance of books like *Gone with the Wind.*"

The real world of these years was far removed from the romances that Levin read, and she was very aware of what Hitler was doing and the effects it had in the community around her; racism became a part of daily life. "I had grown up with friends of all backgrounds," Levin revealed in *SAAS.* "I had hardly been aware of racial differences. That first year in Washington was a shock.... I was struggling, and not very well, with the realization that people really can systematically hurt other people." Levin's mother helped during this period of adjustment, taking her daughter to a concert of the great black contralto Marian Anderson, and enrolling her in the National Cathedral School. In this place of serious academia, Levin learned with a multicultural student body and was encouraged to pursue her interest in writing.

The restoration of property to war victims sent Levin's father overseas to Europe before the end of the war, and her mother continued her work for the War Department. Thus, it took time for them to actually move back to New York, but Levin was sent ahead to start her senior year at the Lincoln School with her friend Andy Wolf. "Lincoln was academically undemanding and socially fantastic," Levin pointed out in *SAAS.* "I lived for the weekends, for parties and dates." In the midst of her social activities, Levin was accepted into the University of Rochester and, joined by her parents, moved into a new apartment. The summer between high school and college was filled with a variety of advertising jobs on Madison Avenue. At the end of the summer, Levin was offered a full-time job at an agency, but instead set off for college.

Originally planning to major in voice, Levin quickly decided that she was out of her league and changed her studies to history and literature. The majority of her friends were into books, poetry, and politics; and it was through this circle of friends that Levin met her future husband, Alvin Levin. Having been in the army, Alvin wanted to get married more quickly than Levin, but she decided he was more important than her freedom; the couple was married the summer before their junior year of college. Living in a one-room apartment, the Levins finished college in Rochester and spent the summer working before joining Levin's family at the farm.

Eventually deciding to attend law school, Levin's husband received a scholarship from Harvard Law School and the couple moved to Boston in the summer of 1949. Halfway through this first year in Boston, Levin too started graduate school. "It was for a seminar on the American city that I wrote a 250-page paper on literature about New York City," recalled Levin in *SAAS.* "I discovered and included children's books in that study. It was the beginning of my interest in the history of children's literature, which I have taught now for so many years."

Living in a variety of apartments, Levin held numerous jobs while her husband completed law school. Among these were a job at the Museum of Fine Arts, a part-time teaching fellowship, and a research job for a historian. Inheriting a bit of money at the same time that her husband was between his clerkship and his new job, Levin was able to finance a trip for the two of them to Scotland and England. Travelling with their young daughter Kathy, the Levins were welcomed into several homes and visited both legendary estates and places that would only be of interest to sheep dog enthusiasts. And by the time they returned home, the couple was determined to build their own small farm next to some friends in Lincoln.

During her second summer here, and after the birth of her second child, Bara, Levin was diagnosed with polio during an epidemic of the disease in Boston; her husband contracted the disease two weeks later. Levin was lucky enough to suffer no lasting effects from the disease, but Alvin suffered with it for two years before he was able to return home. Things began to return to normal, and Levin had her third child, Jennifer. "But we had to learn new ways of living and being parents, because Alvin never did recover the use of his legs and arms and much of his upper torso," explained Levin in *SAAS*. "And the children grew up learning how to help him with his daily needs in countless ways." And as the children grew, so did the Levin household as more sheep, puppies, stray cats, and a pony joined the family.

This happy home was eventually lost, though, when the Minute Man National Historical Park was established and the Levins were forced to sell their home. Around the same time, the family began spending part of each of their summers in Maine. Staying mostly in coastal towns, the Levin family spent many days on their small sailboat and explored the islands of the bay. In addition, summers were also passed on the family farm, where everyone congregated, including Levin's brothers and their families.

By the 1960s and early 1970s, Levin had become increasingly active in civil rights and the movement to end the Vietnam War. These interests eventually led to her husband serving as a delegate at the Democratic Convention. And just as this activity brought new friends into Levin's life, so did the sheep and sheep dogs she raised. All of these activities and influences finally led Levin to the writing of juvenile novels. A fellowship in creative writing at the Bunting Institute from 1968 to 1970 was followed by a teaching career and the writing of a fantasy trilogy containing elements of Celtic and Norse mythology. And from there, a number of other worlds and historical periods emerged to fill Levin's novels.

These worlds first appeared in Levin's early trilogy—*The Sword of Culann, A Griffon's Nest,* and *The Forespoken.* In all three novels, Claudia, who lives on an island off the coast of Maine, travels back in time through the use of an ancient sword hilt. In the first two stories she is accompanied by her stepbrother Evan, and they visit both ancient Ireland during the historical struggle between Queen Medb and Cuchulain (the House of Culann) and the Orkney Islands during medieval times. But in the final story, *The Forespoken,* Claudia alone returns to the Orkney Islands during the nineteenth-century in search of the crow belonging to the old man who originally gave her the sword hilt.

"Levin is skillful in writing of the physical realities of both worlds, especially the cold, dampness, dirt, and hard physical labour," observed Fasick of the trilogy. A *Kirkus Reviews* contributor wrote of *The Sword of Culann:* "The characters are stirring creations, . . . and although the plot is labyrinthian it's well worth staying on for the surprises and layered revelations at every turn." Finding the use of symbols, magic, and historical events to be implausible in *A Griffon's Nest,* another *Kirkus Reviews* contributor concluded that "for the agile mind" the story is "an unusual adventure in time travel." In a *School Library Journal* review of the final novel of the trilogy, *The Forespoken,* Andrew K. Stevenson found the numerous subplots confusing, but asserted that "characterization is good, and the mystery and brutality of the islands is powerfully conveyed."

Maine is again the setting in Levin's 1984 mystery/fantasy *A Binding Spell.* Very unhappy about her family's move to a farm in Maine, Wren seems to be the only one able to see glimpses of a ghost horse in the mist around the farm. Her two brothers are already too busy with their new friend Larry to notice anything, so Wren must investigate on her own. These inquiries lead Wren to Larry's reclusive Uncle Axel, the original owner of the ghost horse. Through her efforts to bring Axel back into reality, Wren is able to rid him of his haunted past, and the ghost horse disappears. "Levin's characters are meticulous, and intermittent scenes are quite vivid," described Denise M. Wilms in *Booklist.* And a *School Library Journal* reviewer maintained that in *A Binding Spell* "Levin writes in an evocative prose which turns even the commonplace into something magical."

Nearly all the elements in *The Ice Bear,* published in 1986, are magical ones. This is one of the first fantasy books in which Levin constructs her story in only one world. Set in the primitive Kingdom of Thyrne, *The Ice Bear* focuses on Wat, a bakeshop boy, and Kaila, a silent girl from the north, as they flee to the Forest of Lythe to defend a white Ice Bear. Wat hopes to gain a reward from the king for protecting the precious animal, but Kaila wants only to return to her home in the north with the bear. During the course of their journey, both Wat and Kaila face many dangers, learning the consequences of their actions and the true meaning of freedom. "As always in Levin's work a poignant tone underlies the action," pointed out Ruth S. Vose in *School Library Journal.* Zena Sutherland asserted in the *Bulletin of the Center for Children's Books* that *The Ice Bear* "has a good pace and sweep; the characters change and grow; the setting is roundly conceived."

Continuing to set her books in just one genre and time period, Levin crafts the stories in *The Trouble with Gramary* and *Starshine and Sunglow* against a realistic backdrop. Fourteen-year-old Merkka lives in a Maine seaside village with her mother, father, younger brother, and grandmother in *The Trouble with Gramary.* As the town becomes a tourist attraction, they try to force Merkka's family from their home because of the welding business her grandmother, Gramary, runs out of the backyard. Struggling to understand her grandmother's ways, Merkka eventually learns to appreciate her non-conformity. "Although Merkka doesn't always understand her grandmother, the natural affinity between the two is unmistakable," noted Nancy Vasilakis in *Horn Book.* Eleanor K. MacDonald mentioned in her *School Library Journal* review that *The Trouble with Gramary* is "a novel in which place, character, and circumstance mesh into a believable and satisfying whole."

Starshine and Sunglow also has a realistic fusing of character and setting. Young Ben, Kate, and Foster come to the rescue in this story when their neighbors the Flints decide not to grow sweet corn for the first time in many years. Having supplied this corn to the neighborhood for as long as Ben, Kate, and Foster can remember, the Flints are tired of dealing with the numerous animals who raid their fields. So, the children organize the growing of the corn, setting up two scarecrows (Starshine and Sunglow) made out of an old mop and an old broom at opposite ends of the field. As the crops grow, though, the scarecrows mysteriously move to different locations in the field and are dressed in different clothes. In the meantime, the children and the rest of the community bond together to grow the corn and stop the critters from stealing it. "Accurate information about the challenges of farming are woven into the plot," observed Lee Bock in *School Library Journal.* A *Kirkus Reviews* contributor pointed out that the focus in *Starshine and Sunglow* "is on the nurturing of community spirit," concluding that "Levin has honed her easily read story with a grace and subtle humor."

Although Levin has been writing since the early 1970s, it is only in recent years that awards have been given to her works, including *Mercy's Mill,* which was listed on the New York Public Library Books for the Teen Age, and *Away to Me, Moss!,* which received a *Parents' Choice* Story Book Award in 1994. *Mercy's Mill* is a time-travel story in which three characters—Mercy, who lives in colonial America; Jonah, who is from the nineteenth century; and Sarah, who is a modern-age teenager—find that they are able to interact with each other at an old mill and house in Massachusetts. Jonah and Mercy were both slaves who managed to escape their unhappy lives by travelling through time: Mercy travelled through time to meet Jonah, and Jonah moved forward in time to cross paths with Sarah. Sarah, who is unhappy with her own life, including a new stepfather and a home that she dislikes, finds the prospect of escaping through time appealing, but as she learns more about the mill and its history she becomes troubled by Jethro's secrets. Sarah tells her family's social worker about Jethro, who tells her in turn that "in her opinion

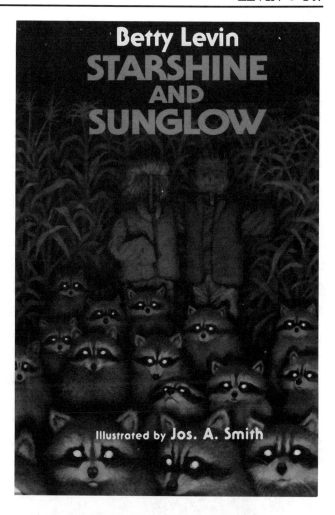

In this 1994 story, strange things start to happen after Kate, Ben, and Foster begin putting up scarecrows to keep the animals away from the cornfields. (Cover illustration by Jos. A. Smith.)

Jethro has not really traveled from another time period; that he is an abused boy who has created another history for himself as a way of escaping reality," according to Maeve Visser Knoth in *Horn Book.* In this way, Levin's readers have to decide for themselves whether or not Jethro's tale is true; but what is really important in the story is how Sarah grows to become less self-involved and more caring about her family through her experiences at the mill.

In the same way that *Mercy's Mill* is not merely a time-travel story, *Away to Me, Moss!* is not just another dog story. Using her own extensive knowledge of sheep dogs and herding, Levin creates a "heartfelt and satisfying portrayal" of the understanding bond between dogs and people in this novel, as Wendy E. Betts put it in her *Five Owls* review. The novel tells of how the desire of a young girl named Zanna to help a Border collie develops into a caring relationship with the dog's owner, Rob Catherwood, as well. Rob, who has suffered a stroke, can no longer give the commands Moss needs to herd sheep, and Moss has become unmanageable because of his frustration in not being able to do the work that is so much a part of him. In trying to help Moss and Rob,

Zanna learns all about sheep herding, and discovers to her surprise that she loves the work. Levin complicates the tale further when she tells of Zanna's parents' trial separation, and how Rob might have to give up Moss to help pay for his rehabilitation. Toward the end of the novel, Zanna must leave Moss and Rob when her parents decide to reconcile and move out west, but, happily, Rob is able to keep Moss, and Zanna promises herself that she will visit them again one day. Critics praised Levin's adept handling of such a complicated plot: "the stress of both Zanna's and Rob's families is skillfully paralleled," according to Betsy Hearne in the *Bulletin of the Center for Children's Books.* "Levin sketches adult problems adroitly," remarked a *Kirkus Reviews* contributor, "... while never losing focus on Zanna and Moss."

Although Levin's work presents a variety of settings and messages, the author sees a connection between all her works. She explained in *SAAS,* "The themes I'm drawn to and the situations I explore through fiction reflect not only the places and people and ways of life I love, but also the baffling aspects of the human condition—human traits that sadden and trouble me. I see connec-

Sarah has an uneasy feeling about the old mill her parents are restoring, and her forebodings prove true when she meets a mysterious boy there who has an incredible story to tell. (Cover illustration by Jos. A. Smith.)

tions between some of the tiny experiences in my early childhood and unavoidable truths about callousness and cruelty."

■ Works Cited

Review of *Away to Me, Moss!, Kirkus Reviews,* October 15, 1994, pp. 1410-11.

Betts, Wendy E., review of *Away to Me, Moss!, Five Owls,* February, 1995, pp. 63-64.

Review of *A Binding Spell, School Library Journal,* December, 1984, p. 101.

Bock, Lee, review of *Starshine and Sunglow, School Library Journal,* June, 1994, p. 132.

Fasick, Adele M., "Betty Levin," *Twentieth Century Children's Writers,* 4th edition, St. James Press, 1995.

Review of *A Griffon's Nest, Kirkus Reviews,* April 15, 1975, p. 465.

Hearne, Betsy, review of *Away to Me, Moss!, Bulletin of the Center for Children's Books,* December, 1994, pp. 135-36.

A *Parents' Choice* Story Book Award winner, Levin's 1994 novel tells how Zanna learns about love and trust from a Collie named Moss and the dog's paralyzed owner.

Knoth, Maeve Visser, review of *Mercy's Mill, Horn Book,* January/February, 1993, p. 92.

Levin, Betty, essay in *Something about the Author Autobiography Series,* Volume 11, Gale, 1991.

MacDonald, Eleanor K., review of *The Trouble with Gramary, School Library Journal,* April, 1988, p. 102.

Review of *Starshine and Sunglow, Kirkus Reviews,* May 15, 1994, p. 702.

Stevenson, Andrew K., review of *The Forespoken, School Library Journal,* October, 1976, p. 118.

Sutherland, Zena, review of *The Ice Bear, Bulletin of the Center for Children's Books,* January, 1987, pp. 91-92.

Review of *The Sword of Culann, Kirkus Reviews,* November 1, 1973, pp. 1212-13.

Vasilakis, Nancy, review of *The Trouble with Gramary, Horn Book,* May/June, 1988, pp. 353-54.

Vose, Ruth S., review of *The Ice Bear, School Library Journal,* October, 1986, p. 192.

Wilms, Denise M., review of *A Binding Spell, Booklist,* November 15, 1984, p. 449.

■ For More Information See

PERIODICALS

Booklist, May 1, 1990, p. 1598; December 1, 1992, p. 670.

Bulletin of the Center for Children's Books, January, 1976, p. 81; April, 1981, p. 155; July/August, 1985; May, 1990, p. 219.

Fantasy Review, January, 1987, p. 45.

Horn Book, February, 1977; December, 1979, pp. 669-70; September/October, 1994, pp. 587-88.

Kirkus Reviews, July 15, 1976, p. 799; August 15, 1992, p. 1064.

Learning Teacher, May, 1993, p. 33.

Publishers Weekly, June 18, 1973, p. 70; September 21, 1992, p. 95.

Quill & Quire, February, 1991, p. 25.

School Library Journal, September, 1973, p. 71; October, 1973, p. 126; November, 1979, pp. 89-90; July, 1990, p. 77; September, 1992, p. 278.

Times Educational Supplement, June 5, 1987, p. 64.

Times Literary Supplement, July 24, 1987, p. 804.

Voice of Youth Advocates, August, 1981, pp. 29-30; August, 1988, p. 132.

Wilson Library Bulletin, October, 1988, p. 78.

*   *   *

LEWIS, Kim 1951-

■ Personal

Born May 26, 1951, in Montreal, Canada; married (husband is a farm manager); children: Sara, James. *Education:* Sir George Williams University, B.F.A. (with distinction), 1972; Hornsey College of Art, certificate, 1973.

KIM LEWIS

■ Addresses

Home—The Riding, Bellingham, Hexham, Northumberland, NE48 2DU, England.

■ Career

Camden Arts Centre, London, England, assistant to the gallery administrator, 1973-75; Middlesex Polytechnic Fine Art Department, London, fine art printmaking technician, 1975-78; Charlotte Press Printmaking Workshop, Newcastle upon Tyne, England, resident lithographer, 1978-80; self-employed artist and print-maker, 1980—. *Exhibitions:* Works have appeared in one-woman shows in a variety of English cities, including Newcastle, Cambo, Stamfordham, Alston, Hexham, and Carlisle.

■ Writings

SELF-ILLUSTRATED

The Shepherd Boy, Walker Books, 1990.
Emma's Lamb, Walker Books, 1991.
Floss, Walker Books, 1992.
First Snow, Walker Books, 1993.
The Last Train, Walker Books, 1994.
My Friend Harry, Walker Books, 1995.

ILLUSTRATOR

Berlie Doherty, *Willa and Old Miss Annie,* Walker Books, 1994.

Also illustrator of several book covers for Bloodaxe Books.

■ Sidelights

After finishing her bachelor's degree, Kim Lewis moved to rural Northumberland, which provides the setting for her children's tales about farm life in England. Lewis was inspired to write her first children's book, *The Shepherd Boy,* when her husband landed a job as manager at a sheep farm in the North Tyne Valley. She quickly fell in love with life in the English countryside, enchanted by the landscape that was so similar to the area outside her native Montreal. Her two children also became involved with the daily routines of working on the farm, and so it was a natural progression for Lewis to base the characters in her stories on her own children and their adventures, sometimes even naming her characters after them.

Lewis's simple stories are distinguished by their lack of sentimentality and realistic portrayal of English farm life, while still effectively conveying the author's personal affection for the land. As one *Publishers Weekly* contributor observed in a review of *Floss,* "While fully aware of the pastoral charm of this existence, she is never sentimental for she knows that farm life can be difficult."

The Shepherd Boy tells of James's longing to be just like his father, who is a shepherd. By the end of the story, he receives a shepherd's crook and a sheepdog to raise as his own. Farm animals often play an important role in Lewis's stories. In *Emma's Lamb,* for example, little Emma wants to raise a small lamb but comes to realize that it is best for the lamb's mother to raise it. In *First Snow,* Sara loses her Teddy in the snow, but it is rescued by one of the family's dogs. And a sheepdog is featured even more prominently in *Floss,* in which the title character, a border collie, has to learn the difference between work and play.

With a background in art, Lewis also illustrates her books, sometimes using lithography and sometimes colored pencil on paper. Critics have praised the soft lines and accurate details of her artwork. Barbara Chatton, writing in a *School Library Journal* review of *Emma's Lamb,* remarked that her choice of colors captures "realistic details of the old kitchen, stone buildings, and fences of an English farm."

■ Works Cited

Chatton, Barbara, review of *Emma's Lamb, School Library Journal,* July, 1991, p. 60.
Review of *Floss, Publishers Weekly,* March 9, 1992, p. 55.

■ For More Information See

PERIODICALS

Horn Book Guide, July, 1990, p. 39; fall, 1991, p. 236; fall, 1992, p. 238; spring, 1994, p. 42.
Kirkus Reviews, January 15, 1992, p. 122; July 15, 1994, p. 989.

School Library Journal, December, 1990, p. 82; April, 1992, p. 96; November, 1993, p. 86.
Times Educational Supplement, March 29, 1991, p. 23.

* * *

LISS, Howard 1922-1995

OBITUARY NOTICE—See index for *SATA* sketch: Born July 22, 1922, in Brooklyn, NY; died January 15, 1995, in Manhattan, NY. Author. Liss wrote numerous books about sports for adults and children. He served in the U.S. Army from 1943 to 1946 and worked as a factory hand and a shipping clerk before turning his attention to writing. First crafting comedy materials for radio and television shows, Liss later started writing books in the early 1960s. His published works cover a broad range of sports, including auto racing, baseball, boxing, soccer, lacrosse, fishing, skiing, hockey, and football. Liss also wrote a number of volumes with or about sports stars. Among his books are *Playoff,* which recreates ten outstanding football championship games, *The Big Book of Strange but True Sports Stories, The Giant Book of More Strange Sport Stories,* and the non-sports titles *Heat, Unidentified Flying Objects,* and *Friction.* In addition, Liss authored the syndicated comic strips *Johnny Hazard, Buck Rogers, Ben Casey,* and *Dark Shadows,* and edited *The Green Berets.* He won the Cartoonists Society Award for best adventure strip of the year in 1970 for *Johnny Hazard.*

OBITUARIES AND OTHER SOURCES:

PERIODICALS

New York Times, February 3, 1995, p. D19.

* * *

LoTURCO, Laura 1963-

■ Personal

Born December 28, 1963, in New York; daughter of Robert Charles (a maintenance engineer) and Marie Antoinette (a bus driver; maiden name, Pirone) LoTurco. *Education:* School of Visual Arts, B.F.A., 1986; attended Parsons School of Design and Art Students League. *Hobbies and other interests:* Traveling, classical and choral music, English castles, ancient history.

■ Addresses

Home—6 Pierrepont St., #1B, Brooklyn, NY 11201.

■ Career

Illustrator. Prepared illustrative and creative work for advertising prepress industry, 1983-94. *Member:* Society of Children's Book Writers and Illustrators.

■ Illustrator

Victoria Sherrow, *Huskings, Quiltings, and Barn Raisings,* Walker, 1992.
Nancy O'Keefe Bolick and Sallie G. Randolph, *Shaker Villages,* Walker, 1993.

■ Work in Progress

Writing and illustrating a picture book.

■ Sidelights

Laura LoTurco told *SATA,* "After I graduated from the School of Visual Arts, I continued to study at Parsons School of Design and the Art Students League in New York. I took workshops for art therapy in child development.

"My first illustrated book, *Huskings, Quiltings and Barn Raisings,* was published in 1992 by Walker and Company. I met the art director through the Graphic Artists Guild. He liked my style, so a few months later he called with an assignment. This led to a second commission from the same publisher in 1993 to produce the illustrations for *Shaker Villages,* a historic study of the origin of the Shaker movement in America. For research material I went to a Shaker village-turned-museum in Hancock, Massachusetts. It makes a difference being able to get involved in the subject I'm illustrating.

"I enjoy traveling and have done a considerable amount, highlighting cultural, artistic, and architectural treasures throughout Europe, as well as gathering visual reference for my work. For now, I'm working on a picture book of my own. I would like to continue to produce work that appeals to children."

M

WENHAI MA

MA, Wenhai 1954-

■ Personal

Born August 17, 1954, in Heilongjiang, China; son of Longchi and Min (Qu) Ma; married Shu-Ching Z. Ma (an artist), 1981; children: Dorothy B. *Education:* Central Academy of Drama, B.F.A.; Carnegie-Mellon University, M.F.A. *Religion:* Christian.

■ Addresses

Home—709 Pineburr Pl., Durham, NC 27703. *Office*—210 Branson Theatre, Drama Program, Duke University, Durham, NC 27708.

■ Career

Freelance illustrator. Lecturer at the Central Academy of Drama, China, 1984-87; Duke University, Durham, NC, assistant professor, 1987—. *Member:* Society of Children's Book Writers and Illustrators.

■ Awards, Honors

The Painted Fan was selected for the original art exhibit by the Society of American Illustrators, 1994.

■ Illustrator

Marilyn Singer, *The Painted Fan* (picture book), Morrow, 1994.
Barbara Diamond Goldin, *Red Means Good Fortune: A Story Set in San Francisco Chinatown,* Viking, 1994.
Nina Jaffe, reteller, *Older Brother, Younger Brother: A Korean Folktale,* Viking, 1995.
Brenda Seabrooke, *The Swan's Gift,* Candlewick Press, 1995.

■ Work in Progress

The Suncatcher, a picture book, for Candlewick Press.

*   *   *

MacMILLAN, Dianne M(arie) 1943-

■ Personal

Born August 26, 1943, in St. Louis, MO; daughter of Luckie Stradtman (a used car salesman) and Dee (a homemaker and real estate salesperson; maiden name, Maniscalco) Webb; married James Robert MacMillan (a

DIANNE M. MacMILLAN

general contractor), August 14, 1965; children: Jennifer Dorand, Kathy, Shannon. *Education:* Miami University, Oxford, OH, B.S. (education). *Politics:* Independent. *Religion:* Catholic. *Hobbies and other interests:* Reading, hiking, golf, bowling, traveling.

■ Addresses

Home—1127 North Ridgeline Rd., Orange, CA 92669.

■ Career

Teacher of elementary school in St. Louis, MO, 1965-71; tutor for children with reading and learning problems, 1972-78; free-lance writer, 1977—. Homeless Ministry Coordinator, 1987-91. *Member:* Society of Children's Book Writers and Illustrators (regional advisor of Orange, Riverside, and San Bernardino counties), Authors Guild, Pen Center USA West, Southern California Council on Literature for Children and Young People.

■ Awards, Honors

Highlights for Children Patriotic Feature of the Year, 1992.

■ Writings

(With Dorothy Freeman) *My Best Friend Martha Rodriguez,* illustrated by Warren Fricke, Julian Messner, 1986.

(With Freeman) *My Best Friend Duc Tran: Meeting a Vietnamese-American Family,* illustrated by Mary Jane Begin, Julian Messner, 1987.
(With Freeman) *My Best Friend Mee-Yung Kim: Meeting a Korean-American Family,* illustrated by Bob Marstall, Julian Messner, 1989.
Martin Luther King, Jr. Day, Enslow, 1992.
(With Freeman) *Kwanzaa,* Enslow, 1992.
Easter, Enslow, 1993.
Jewish Fall Holidays, Enslow, 1993.
Elephants: Our Last Land Giants, Carolrhoda, 1993.
Chinese New Year, Enslow, 1994.
Jewish Holidays in the Spring, Enslow, 1994.
Ramadan and Id al-Fitr, Enslow, 1994.
Tet: Vietnamese New Year, Enslow, 1994.

Contributor of articles and stories to periodicals, including *Jack & Jill, Christian Science Monitor, Christian Adventure, Cobblestone, The Vine, The Beehive, Highlights for Children, Alive for Young Teens, Children's Playmate, Parish Family Digest, The Friend,* and *On the Line.*

■ Work in Progress

Los Angeles Area Missions, Lerner; *Cheetahs,* Carolrhoda.

A young girl learns about Korean traditions when her friend introduces her to her family in *My Best Friend Mee-Yung Kim.* (Illustration by Bob Marstall.)

■ Sidelights

Dianne MacMillan's books are designed to teach young readers about the cultures of people from all over the world. In her collaborative books with Dorothy Freeman, such as *My Best Friend Duc Tran: Meeting a Vietnamese-American Family* and *My Best Friend Mee-Yung Kim: Meeting a Korean-American Family,* MacMillan tells simple fictional stories about Anglo-American children who meet and make friends with children who teach them new and interesting things about their families' traditions. Most of MacMillan's more recent efforts are straightforward, nonfiction books that teach about the holidays celebrated in different cultures.

MacMillan told *SATA,* "I live in a wonderful world of books. I began writing for children officially in 1977, but deep inside I've always been a writer. I've always been able to express my feelings and emotions better on paper. (Everyone in my family knows to watch out for one of my 'letters.') In grade school, I looked forward to the monthly visits of the bookmobile. I was happiest when I was lost in a Nancy Drew mystery or a historical pioneer adventure.

"When I grew up, I became a teacher and mother. The world of children's books was still a big part of my life. When I stopped teaching, I missed the daily interaction with children and children's books. So I began to write. I choose to write for children because children are open to life, honest, and filled with enthusiasm. Their curiosity and sense of wonder give new meaning and hope to each generation. When writing, I try to tap into that honesty and curiosity. I love research and I'm fascinated by discoveries of little-known facts and trivia. I think kids share that fascination. Libraries and bookstores are pieces of 'heaven' for me and there never is enough time to spend as long as I'd like.

"The initial writing of a story or nonfiction book is difficult because I'm trying to sort in my mind the details, words, and scenes to put down. Which will be most interesting? Most clear? Entertaining? There are as many choices as words. Once my first draft is complete, I attack rewriting with zeal and gusto. This is the fun part. If I can give my readers new information, or a sense of belonging, perhaps a chuckle, or a bit of entertainment, then I have succeeded. The best part of living constantly in a world of books is that I keep learning, exploring, growing, and asking 'Why?'"

■ For More Information See

PERIODICALS

Bulletin of the Center for Children's Books, January, 1990, p. 115.
Horn Book, July, 1989, p. 75.
Kirkus Reviews, July 1, 1987, p. 995.
School Library Journal, April, 1987, p. 99; September, 1987, p. 180; January, 1993, p. 92; February, 1994, p. 113.

GREGORY MAGUIRE

MAGUIRE, Gregory 1954-

■ Personal

Born June 9, 1954, in Albany, NY; son of John (a journalist) and Helen (McAuliff) Maguire. *Education:* State University of New York at Albany, B.A., 1976; Simmons College, M.A., 1978; Tufts University, Ph.D., 1990. *Politics:* Democrat. *Religion:* Roman Catholic. *Hobbies and other interests:* Painting in oils or water colors, song writing, traveling.

■ Addresses

Agent—William Reiss, John Hawkins and Associates, 71 West 23rd St., Suite 1600, New York, NY 10010.

■ Career

Freelance writer, 1977—. Vincentian Grade School, Albany, NY, teacher of English, 1976-77; Simmons College Center for the Study of Children's Literature, Boston, MA, faculty member and associate director, 1979-87; Children's Literature New England, Cambridge, MA, co-director and consultant, 1987—. Fellow at Bread Loaf Writers' Conference, 1978; residencies at Blue Mountain Center, 1986-90 and 1995; artist in residence, Isabella Stewart Gardner Museum, 1994.

■ Awards, Honors

100 Best Books of the Year citation, New York Public Library, 1980, for *The Daughter of the Moon;* Children's

Books of the Year citation, Child Study Children's Books Committee, 1983, and Teachers' Choice Award, National Council of Teachers of English, 1984, both for *The Dream Stealer;* Best Book for Young Adults citation, American Library Association (ALA), and Choices award, Cooperative Children's Book Center, 1989, both for *I Feel Like the Morning Star;* Parents' Choice Award, and Children's Books of the Year citation, Child Study Committee, both 1994, for *Missing Sisters;* Notable Children's Book citation, ALA, 1994, for *Seven Spiders Spinning.*

■ Writings

FOR CHILDREN AND YOUNG ADULTS

The Lightning Time, Farrar, Straus, 1978.
The Daughter of the Moon, Farrar, Straus, 1980.
Lights on the Lake, Farrar, Straus, 1981.
The Dream Stealer, Harper, 1983.
The Peace and Quiet Diner (picture book), illustrated by David Perry, Parents' Magazine, 1988.
I Feel Like the Morning Star, Harper, 1989.
Lucas Fishbone (picture book for young adults), illustrated by Frank Gargiulo, Harper, 1990.
Missing Sisters, McElderry, 1994.
Seven Spiders Spinning, Clarion, 1994.
The Good Liar, O'Brien Press, 1995.
Oasis, Clarion, 1996.

OTHER

(Editor with Barbara Harrison) *Innocence and Experience: Essays and Conversations on Children's Literature,* Lothrop, 1987.
Wicked: The Life and Times of the Wicked Witch of the West (adult fiction), HarperCollins, 1995.

Reviewer for *Horn Book, School Library Journal,* and *Christian Science Monitor;* contributor of story "The Honorary Shepherds" to collection *Am I Blue,* about growing up gay and lesbian, 1994.

■ Work in Progress

Six Haunted Hairdos, a sequel to *Seven Spiders Spinning.*

■ Sidelights

Gregory Maguire writes about people on the edge of crisis, about people who come through, who survive. In forms as various as science fiction and fantasy, realistic problem novels, and rhyming picture books, Maguire has explored the themes of loss, freedom, spirituality, the power of love, memory and desire. Not one to shy away from complex plot development in his young adult titles, Maguire also has a lighter side: his production might best be demonstrated by two 1994 titles: *Missing Sisters* and *Seven Spiders Spinning.* The former is a realistic portrait of growing up Catholic and handicapped; the latter is a broad farce about seven Ice Age spiders who have some fun in a small Vermont town.

"Maguire's talents now look unpredictable," Jill Paton Walsh wrote in *Twentieth-Century Children's Writers* in 1989. "Formidable and still developing." Paton Walsh was a prescient critic: since that time Maguire has authored several more children's books as well as adult fiction and has edited writings on children's literature. While living in London for five years, he became a sought-after speaker on children's literature and creative writing in the United States. If fantasy was his first inspiration, he has since expanded his genres to include realism and humor. Yet through all of his stories, both light and serious, one motif recurs: the loss of a mother.

In fact, it was Maguire's own mother who was lost, dying as she gave birth to him. With his writer father sick at the same time, Maguire and his three other siblings were sent to stay with relatives for a time, and finally Maguire ended up in an orphanage until he was reunited with his newly remarried father. "It's right out of Dickens," Maguire conceded in an interview for *Something about the Author* (*SATA*). "But given the potential tragedy of those first couple of years, my childhood continued very warm and rewarding and free of any significant trauma." Three more children were born in the second marriage, so that Maguire grew up in a family of seven children whose father and breadwinner wrote a humor column for the Albany *Times-Union* and worked for the New York Health Department as a science writer. "It wasn't exactly an affluent upbringing," Maguire said. "There were library books, paper and crayons, and that was it for the entertainment center. We did have a television, but that was really my father's hobby. We kids got to watch a few programs, but only ones we voted on and chose together. My parents were very strict about that. And it paid off. Talking with adult audiences now, I always tell them that one of the greatest stimulants to their kids' creativity is boredom. But children rarely have a chance to be bored anymore. We're always being entertained, by the t.v., the radio, computers."

Maguire grew up in a family that cared deeply about words. In addition to writing professionally, Maguire's father was also well known around Albany, New York as a great storyteller. Maguire's stepmother wrote poetry. A dictionary was kept with the cookbooks in the kitchen in case anybody needed to look up a word during dinner when the whole family was gathered together. "We were all very interested in word derivation, spurred on by my father and mother. Our favorite family story revolves around that passion. One night at dinner someone asked to have the butter passed, and my three-year-old brother, seated in his high chair, cocked his head. 'Butter,' he said reflectively. 'Is that from the Latin or the Greek?' So I guess we all had a love for words instilled in us from the beginning." Maguire wrote his first story at age five and continued writing them—some as long as a hundred pages—throughout high school and college. In fact, he was only a junior in college when he wrote what would be his first published book, *The Lightning Time.* He began writing songs and painting at an early age, as well, two other creative outlets he has continued to develop. Life at the Irish-Catholic Maguire household was strict and regimented: "I had to pass the New York state drivers' test before I was allowed to ride a two-wheeled bicycle," Maguire recounted. "Now that's not just a Catholic upbringing; that's *strict*."

Maguire attended Catholic school until he was eighteen. "In general," Maguire recalled for *SATA*, "I liked school. Although I was not at the top of the class, the nuns encouraged the creativity they saw in me. I have few of the horror stories that others do when they talk of their Catholic education. I thought that most of my teachers were intelligent and perceptive." A highlight of Maguire's early career in school was the authoring of a school play for Thanksgiving, a play with Catholic Pilgrims. "I didn't learn until I was in college that the Pilgrims weren't Catholic." But the play was a rousing success, so much so that when Maguire returned to the same school twelve years later as a teacher fresh out of college, he discovered the play was still being produced each Thanksgiving.

Maguire was also reading heavily in these years, and his interests tended toward fantasy writers such as Jane Langton, Madeleine L'Engle, and T. H. White. "I loved Langton's *The Diamond in the Window* when I read it at nine, and I even got the transcendental mysticism in it," Maguire said in his interview. "It was the first book I understood on several levels, and that was an eye-opener for me to see how powerful a book could be. White's *The Once and Future King* was another favorite. All of these book took you out of yourself and put you in another place and time. I thought that was wonderful magic and tried to do it with my own stories."

Maguire's stories led to the writing of *The Lightning Time* when he was 20. "I went to SUNY in Albany," Maguire recalled, "and it was a very unmemorable experience. I was living at home and the courses were not very demanding. It just wasn't what my idea of college should be. When I was a junior majoring in English and art, I wrote a book for independent study, throwing in lots of the places and characters from my own youth. I went away to study in Dublin for a year, and when I came back I re-read the book and only then did I see it was probably a young adult title—the protagonist is 12." Maguire had one copy of the manuscript and sent it out four times over the next two years, choosing houses that published his favorite authors. The fourth bought it. "I was very lucky," Maguire told *SATA*. *The Lightning Time* tells the story of young Daniel Rider, whose mother is in the hospital (the first of the missing mothers). The boy is staying with his grandmother in the Adirondacks. He meets a mysterious female cousin and together the two struggle to keep Saltbrook Mountain free from development. There is magic lightning that allows animals to talk, a villainous developer, and plenty of eerie effects. *Publishers Weekly* thought that Maguire handled this first novel "with professional aplomb," and Ethel L. Heins concluded in *Horn Book* that Maguire "creates tension successfully, and writes with conviction and style."

Maguire followed up the success of this first fantasy with a related title, *The Daughter of the Moon*, featuring another cousin of Daniel Rider's, twelve-year-old Erikka. Again the missing mother theme is explored, this time with the real mother dead and Erikka being brought up by a stepmother in Chicago. Searching for more refinement in life, Erikka is drawn to a local bookshop as well as to a painting that an aunt has left with her. The painting is magic and Erikka can actually escape into the scene painted there, ultimately retrieving a long-lost lover of the Chicago bookshop owner. There are further sub-plots and with so much going on in the story, Marjorie Lewis, writing in *School Library Journal*, commented that the sidelights "clog the arteries" of Maguire's novel. *Horn Book*, while noting that some elements of the ambitious novel did not work, nevertheless concluded that Maguire "has created a fascinatingly complex heroine and a rich collection of adult and child characters."

Lights on the Lake was the third of Maguire's early fantasy novels which were meant to form a trilogy of sorts. Again the protagonist is Daniel Rider and he is once again in upstate New York, at Canaan Lake. This is favorite Maguire country, a love for the region having

An aunt gives twelve-year-old Erikka a magical painting that she can use to transport herself to another world in this 1980 story.

been developed in his youth. The one friend Daniel makes, an Episcopalian priest, leaves on a vacation, and Daniel finds himself living in two different dimensions, influenced by the strange mists on the lake. A poet devastated by the death of his friend occupies Daniel's attention, and he sees a way to help the poet, by bridging space and time, the living with the dead. "The provocative theme incorporates philosophical and spiritual concepts," noted Mary M. Burns in *Horn Book.* And though the *Bulletin of the Center for Children's Books* thought that the elements of fantasy and realism did not work together, the reviewer did concede that Maguire "has a strong potential for polished and substantive writing."

"I basically look at those first three novels as novice work," Maguire told *SATA* in his interview. "I was writing books as I thought books should be written. I wasn't really in touch with my own sense of what makes a book. They were imitative in form, but drew very heavily from my own past and preoccupations. When I look back at those three books, I see that I was working on the theme of accepting responsibility. But with my next book, I created my own form. I wasn't imitating anything else I'd read." That next book was *The Dream Stealer,* set in Russia and blending several age-old motifs from Russian folktales: the Firebird, Vasilissa the Beautiful, and Baba Yaga. The story of how two children set out to save their village from the terrible wolf, the Blood Prince, *The Dream Stealer* blends magic and realism to create a "fantasy full of tension and narrative strength," according to Heins of *Horn Book.* "A first rate fantasy with blood chilling villainy countered with high humor and heroism," concluded Helen Gregory, reviewing the book in *School Library Journal.* And Paton Walsh, writing in *Twentieth-Century Children's Writers,* noted that the book was the work "of a writer finding his voice, and putting not a foot wrong."

"I'm still proud of that book," Maguire said. "I fictionalized a handful of different folk and fairy tales and blended them in a plot with its own trajectory and characterization. I was writing a book that connected more to my inner child, and not simply a story developed from the books I read."

Meanwhile, Maguire had taken a position at Simmons College in their fledgling program in children's literature and was earning his doctorate in that field. "I'm not sure there is a lot of carryover from being an academic in children's literature to the writing of it," Maguire explained to *SATA.* "You surely do not have to study literature or creative writing to be able to write. Reading helps, of course, and to that extent, a study of children's literature can help in the writing of it. You keep up with what is being published and you're exposed to many more books than you would be otherwise. But teaching children's literature doesn't automatically make somebody a children's book writer, just as all English literature professors are not necessarily fiction writers." Busy with studies and teaching as well as with the compilation of a book of essays in children's literature, Maguire did not publish his next fiction title for five

Drawing on Russian folklore, Maguire spins a tale about how two children named Pasha and Lisette save their village from an evil demon wolf who wants to steal people's dreams. (Cover illustration by Trinka Hakes Noble.)

years. The 1989 *I Feel Like the Morning Star* was a bit of a departure in that the fantasy element was played down. Set in a post-atomic underworld, the book has a science fiction form, but is at heart an adventure novel about three rebellious teenagers who want to break out of their prison-like underworld colony. Again, some critics, such as Roger Sutton in *Bulletin of the Center for Children's Books,* called attention to Maguire's penchant for figurative language and detail which "mired" an otherwise suspenseful escape novel. Others however, as with Jane Beasley in *Voice of Youth Advocates,* thought that the "suspense builds to a 'can't-put-it-down' threshold." And Pam Spencer, writing in *School Library Journal,* called the book a "top choice for young adults."

"Ultimately, *Morning Star* is about bucking authority," Maguire said. "It was during this time that I was involved with anti-nuclear demonstrations. The book grew out of those concerns." A for-hire picture book, *The Peace and Quiet Diner,* followed and then came *Lucas Fishbone,* an attempt at a sophisticated picture book for young adults. "Actually," Maguire told *SATA,* "the writing in *Lucas* is some that I'm the most proud of. The story is a poetic meditation on death and the cycle of life, but somehow it never found its audience." Critics, like *School Library Journal* contributor Heide Piehler, found the work "overwhelming and confusing," and *Publishers Weekly* called the book "overwritten."

There followed another hiatus in Maguire's publishing career. He continued to write his usual five pages a day, but was discouraged after the poor reception of *Lucas Fishbone*. While living in London he did the writing on what would become *Missing Sisters*. "I saw something on television while on a speaking tour in the U.S.," Maguire explained. "It was the story of how two brothers who were separated at birth later re-discovered each other, and the story made a real impression on me." Maguire took that germ of an idea with him when he returned to England. Shorter than his other books, *Missing Sisters* is also Maguire's first realistic story, employing none of the fantasy and science fiction elements of his earlier books. It is set in the 1960s and tells the story of a hearing and speech-impaired girl who loses the one person close to her—a Catholic nun—but also finds her own missing sister. "The storytelling is sure and steady," wrote Sutton of *Bulletin of the Center for Children's Books*. "An unusual and compelling picture of life in a Catholic home," commented *Horn Book*. The book won a Parents' Choice Award and

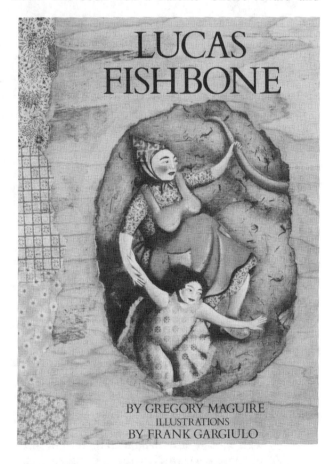

LUCAS FISHBONE

BY GREGORY MAGUIRE
ILLUSTRATIONS
BY FRANK GARGIULO

The deep love between a grandmother and her grandchild is movingly expressed in this sophisticated picture book for teens. (Cover illustration by Frank Gargiulo.)

Maguire's vision was once again redeemed. "What I really wanted to accomplish with the book was pretty simple," Maguire explained in his interview. "To portray the positive effects of a religious childhood. I'm not trying to proselytize with this book, but I did have good experiences with the nuns when I was a kid, and I think it's important that people acknowledge the way religion can create a social context, can form community."

Maguire's next title was inspired by reactions of the kids to his speaking engagements. "Over the years," Maguire explained to *SATA,* "I've developed a very funny presentation. The kids usually howl at my speech, but when they learn that I don't have any humorous books, they're disappointed." Maguire set out to cure that disappointment with *Seven Spiders Spinning,* which has been compared to Roald Dahl meeting Mother Goose. Seven spiders from Siberia escape en route to a lab for study and make their way to Vermont where they discover seven girls who they focus on as their mothers. The problem is, the spiders literally have the kiss of death, and the girls dispatch several of them. There are humorous subplots galore in this "high-camp fantasy-mystery," according to *Publishers Weekly.* Hazel Rochman in *Booklist* commended Maguire on the "comic brew" and noted that the book would be "the stuff of many a grade-school skit." "A lighthearted fantasy," concluded *Kirkus Reviews,* "that, while easily read, is as intricately structured as a spider's web." Readers have agreed with the critics, and Maguire is at work on the sequel, *Six Haunted Hairdos.* "Who knows what works?" Maguire said in his interview. "Actually, I write for myself. I think all literary writers have to. For better or worse, I don't pay much attention to criticism because I know the effect I am looking for, nor do I obsess about the effects my books might have on those who read them other than to hope they might make readers think, might make them look at life and the world in different ways."

The Good Liar, published in Ireland, was another stylistic departure for Maguire. Set in occupied France in 1942 and written in epistolary style, it tells the story of three brothers who have a fibbing contest that ultimately becomes a matter of life and death. *Oasis,* another young adult title, explores the effects of the loss of his father on the thirteen-year-old boy, Hand. "I was looking at the idea of crisis with the character Hand," Maguire explained. "At the idea that the rest of the world doesn't slow down when you're in crisis. You just have to keep functioning." Maguire's largest departure in writing, however, has been a leap into adult fiction with his *Wicked: The Life and Times of the Witch of the West.* "It was an amazing amount of fun working on that novel," Maguire said. "I could indulge myself in the complexity of an adult book. It spans 38 years in a person's life and has over forty characters."

But Maguire has no intention of leaving children's books behind. "Ideally," he concluded, "I'd like to continue writing for both children and adults. It's all writing. I still remember the writers I read as a child and the wonderful worlds they introduced me to. Children

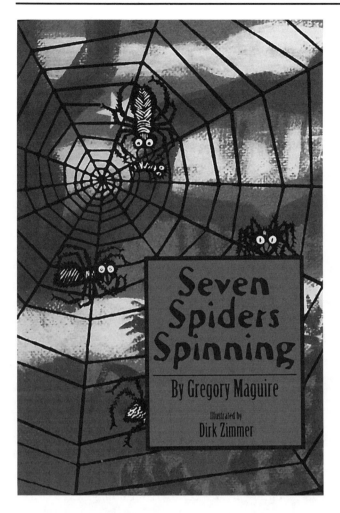

In this unusual Halloween tale, seven spiders defrosted from an Ice Age glacier grow meaner and meaner as they grow bigger and bigger. (Cover illustration by Dirk Zimmer.)

deserve the best that can be served up to them, and as a child I certainly profited from reading fantastic writers. I'd like someday to be a good enough writer to enrich a child's life as mine was enriched."

■ Works Cited

Beasley, Jane, review of *I Feel Like the Morning Star, Voice of Youth Advocates,* June, 1989, p. 117.
Burns, Mary M., review of *Lights on the Lake, Horn Book,* April, 1982, pp. 167-168.
Review of *The Daughter of the Moon, Horn Book,* June, 1980.
Gregory, Helen, review of *The Dream Stealer, School Library Journal,* February, 1984, p. 75.
Heins, Ethel L., review of *The Lightning Time, Horn Book,* October, 1978, pp. 517-518.
Heins, Ethel L., review of *The Dream Stealer, Horn Book,* October, 1983, pp. 576-577.
Lewis, Marjorie, review of *The Daughter of the Moon, School Library Journal,* May, 1980, p. 69.
Review of *The Lightning Time, Publishers Weekly,* June 5, 1978, p. 89.

Review of *Lights on the Lake, Bulletin of the Center for Children's Literature,* February, 1982.
Review of *Lucas Fishbone, Publishers Weekly,* September 28, 1990, pp. 101-102.
Maguire, Gregory, interview with J. Sydney Jones for *Something about the Author,* conducted March, 1995.
Review of *Missing Sisters, Horn Book,* July-August, 1994, pp. 454-455.
Paton Walsh, Jill, "Maguire, Gregory," *Twentieth-Century Children's Writers,* 3rd edition, St. James Press, 1989, pp. 626-627.
Piehler, Heide, review of *Lucas Fishbone, School Library Journal,* December, 1990, p. 84.
Rochman, Hazel, review of *Seven Spiders Spinning, Booklist,* September 15, 1994, p. 136.
Review of *Seven Spiders Spinning, Kirkus Reviews,* July 15, 1994, p. 989.
Review of *Seven Spiders Spinning, Publishers Weekly,* August 1, 1994, p. 80.
Spencer, Pam, review of *I Feel Like the Morning Star, School Library Journal,* May, 1989, p. 127.
Sutton, Roger, review of *I Feel Like the Morning Star, Bulletin of the Center for Children's Books,* May, 1989, p. 230.
Sutton, Roger, review of *Missing Sisters, Bulletin of the Center for Children's Literature,* June, 1994, pp. 327-328.

■ For More Information See

PERIODICALS

Booklist, June 1, 1994, p. 1798.
Bulletin of the Center for Children's Books, July-August, 1980, p. 219.
Kirkus Reviews, July 15, 1978, p. 750; May 1, 1980, p. 585; February 1, 1982, p. 136; March 1, 1989, p. 380; February 15, 1994, p. 229.
School Library Journal, September, 1978, p. 143; May, 1994, p. 116.
Wilson Library Bulletin, December 1989, p. 113; September, 190, p. 12.

—Sketch by J. Sydney Jones

* * *

MALONE, James Hiram 1930-

■ Personal

Born March 24, 1930, in Winterville, GA; son of Ralph (a laborer) and Sarah Lena (a homemaker; maiden name, Echols) Malone; married Mary Louise Liebaert (a school teacher), 1972 (divorced, 1982); children: Andrew Ralph, Matthew Martin. *Education:* Morehouse College, A.A., 1951; Center for Creative Studies College of Art and Design, A.A., 1962. *Politics:* Democrat. *Religion:* Unitarian. *Hobbies and other interests:* Poetry, photography, tennis, woodworking, reading.

JAMES HIRAM MALONE

■ **Addresses**

Home and office—1796 North Ave. N.W., Atlanta, GA 30318-6441.

■ **Career**

K-mart International Headquarters, Troy, MI, senior graphics designer, 1980-83; *Atlanta Journal & Constitution,* Atlanta, GA, ad promotions creative director, 1983-90; Bianco Art Collections of Atlanta, fine art producer/painter, 1990-92; *Atlanta News Leader,* author of "Street Beat" column and artist, 1992—; free-lance cartoonist for periodicals; author and illustrator. Guest author, reader, lecturer, and storyteller at schools, festivals, conferences, and coffee houses. Active in many civic, public, and community organizations, including Neighborhood Planning, Black Artists Network and Advocacy, Literacy Action of Atlanta, and Atlanta Arts Council. Volunteer at Atlanta's Homeless Association, Inc., and for Christmas in July (for homeless children). *Exhibitions:* Has exhibited fine art paintings at art galleries, museums, art festivals, malls, and parks. *Military service:* U.S. Army, 1950-59; became Sergeant First Class. *Member:* International Black Writers Association (vice-president, 1994), First World Writers Association (vice-president, 1993-94), Visual Vanguard Art Group (board member), High Museum of Art, Writers Resource Center (consultant), Nexus Art Association, Center for Creative Studies College of Art and Design Alumni Association.

■ **Awards, Honors**

Scholastic Magazine National Scholastic Art Award, 1949; Atlanta University Art Award, 1949; Famous Artists Art Award, National Cartoonists Society, 1956; National Newspaper Publishers Association Award, 1973; Michigan's Artists Book Award, Willis Gallery, 1980, for *Brother; Atlanta Journal & Constitution* Creative Ad Awards, 1984-87; Atlanta Symphony Poster Contest Award, 1985; United Way Human Support Awards and Helping Hand Awards, 1985, 1986, 1988; Atlanta newspapers publishing grant, 1986; Center for Creative Studies Alumni Art Award, 1986; Bronze Jubilee Community Art Award, 1986; Atlanta Employer's Voluntary Employment Association Task Force on Youth Motivation Awards, 1987, 1988, 1989; Southern Drawl Exhibition Award, Mobile College, 1993; International Black Writers Association Merit Award, 1994; Nexus Family History Artbook Project Youth Motivation Award, 1994.

■ **Writings**

SELF-ILLUSTRATED

Here and There Poetry, Hilltop Press, 1954.
Blues Poetry, Hilltop Press, 1954.
Grandma Sarah's Closet, Funtime Books, 1960.
Brother, Jamlou Publishers, 1970.
Say Literacy Guide, Writeway, 1986.
No-Job Dad, Victory Press, 1992.

Also author and illustrator of *Y'All Come Back,* 1988, and *Atlanta, the Democrats Are Coming,* 1988.

OTHER

Contributor to *Word Up Anthology,* 1990. Contributor of writings and illustrations to periodicals, including *Atlanta Pictorial Reporter, Jackson Journal, Army Times, Soul, Detroit Free Press, Illustrator, Ebony, Liberator, Michigan Chronicle, Atlanta Journal & Constitution, Intown Extra, Catalyst,* and *Atlanta News Leader.*

■ **Work in Progress**

The Cart, a self-illustrated picture book about an Asian-American grocery vendor and his family; *Malone: Art Journal,* a self-illustrated autobiography; research for a book on storefront churches, illustrated with photographs.

■ **Sidelights**

James Hiram Malone told *SATA:* "I remember when I was a barefoot toddler living in Atlanta's Fourth Ward District being a busy-bee little wall scribbler. As high as my arms could reach I decorated walls, woodwork, furniture, and any place that boy and crayons got together. At that age I was an artist and I had a story to tell. And I told it.

"In the first grade, my free-hand drawing of the three bears eating was at a very slanted table. Even the chair rungs wouldn't meet in the right places. But what I remember best is Miss Barnette, my teacher, saying to me, 'My, my, young man, that is very good!'" This encouragement helped build Malone's image of himself, as did the stories his mother told and the drawings she created as she told them.

"Along with my mother's natural talent of building my self-esteem, I also relied on the neighborhood movie house," Malone explained to *SATA*. "I lived for the Saturday afternoon matinees, because at this young age I lived in fantasy land and fairytale land to escape from poverty realization. My first creative writings were all just daydreams of being like a hero on the movie screen. It was sometime later before anything was put on paper. I borrowed my friend's shoeshine box and learned early to shine shoes for movie fare.

"During my youthful years of movie-going, all of what most of my friends cared about were full-of-action, fast-motion, and sometimes funny happenings. However, what I wondered about was, 'Where were the colored heroes?' Even the cowboy hats were white. Being aware of this trend, later I reflected on this policy in my writings and artwork. *Here and There Poetry* and *Blues Poetry* (both 1954) are bittersweet efforts to really understand society. And I found out that keeping up with news headlines is a challenge to any writer and especially a writer of color."

While he spent his weekends at the movie theater, Malone became active in various school activities during the week, including the high school newspaper and the yearbook. Proud to be a part of these projects, Malone still found himself bothered by the disparity between his school supplies (including textbooks) and the supplies at the suburban schools. "I kept my sanity by tuning out this mundane situation by dreaming up stories I wanted to write about as I sat there in the classroom," he remembered for *SATA*. "I had an amazing memory, didn't have to make notes because my resources were constant, plus I always 'wrote' in my head before applying it to paper. I was daydream writing; 'writing' about my cousin who lived around the corner from me, my aunt, down the street from my other cousin and across the street from my uncle. These memory pieces were later freelanced to periodicals. Slices of life that started at adolescence and were my survival kit all through high school; living in the same neighborhood, family ties. Modern family ties dissolved after desegregation and families moved to the suburbs. Closer living was closer togetherness."

More schooling and the army set Malone on his freelance writing and illustrating career, during the course of which he has published in numerous magazines and newspapers. And all of this writing and illustrating eventually led to his self-illustrated children's books. "*Grandma Sarah's Closet,* my juvenile picture book effort of 1960, was inspired by my Grandmother Sarah and how she related to her grandchildren," Malone told *SATA*. "This was a very limited edition experiment to get the feel of the marketplace and

Story and Art by James Hiram Malone

In this self-illustrated book, Malone addresses the issue of a child's embarrassment over his father's unemployment.

to challenge my production capabilities. Working on this book paved the way for better understanding and smoother sailing for my later efforts."

Malone's latest effort in this genre is *No-Job Dad,* which relates the story of a young boy, Joey, who is afraid to ask his father to school on career day. Despite the fact that he is unemployed at the moment, the father comes to school and puts his son's fears to rest. "How I got my concept of *No-Job Dad* was thinking about what kind of book I wanted to do, a juvenile picture book. After this, how many characters. It had to be mainstream and simple, something kids would like.

"At that time, the economy wasn't anything to brag about, either, so *No-Job Dad* could relate to society as a whole. Deciding on three characters, Joey, the son and student, and his mother and father, I then thought of a conflict. I always wondered what would happen if a parent of a student was invited to career day at school and the parent didn't have a job at that time. So, now I had my plot, theme, and conflict all rolled into one. And this has to be, because juvenile picture books are based on simplicity, simplicity, simplicity. My youth and childhood came out in the production of *No-Job Dad;* I had to think young to write young. Yep, I had to smile all the while like a juvenile! Yeah."

■ For More Information See

PERIODICALS

Atlanta Journal & Constitution, May, 1994; June, 1994.
Impresario Magazine, November/December, 1972.

*   *   *

MARTIN, Jane Read 1957-

■ Personal

Born September 17, 1957, in Princeton, NJ; daughter of
Henry Read (a cartoonist) and Edith Aiken (a homemaker; maiden name, Matthews) Martin; married
Douglas McGrath (a writer). *Education:* Denison University, B.A., 1979. *Politics:* Democrat. *Hobbies and
other interests:* Movies, theatre, musicals, volunteering
with cancer-related hospitals and charities.

■ Addresses

Home—New York, NY. *Agent*—Sarah Winer, William
Morris Agency, 1325 Avenue of the Americas, 16th
floor, New York, NY 10025.

■ Career

Saturday Night Live, NBC-TV, secretary to Jane Curtin,
1979-80, assistant to the producers, 1980-81; *Good
Morning New York,* WABC-TV, associate producer and
talent coordinator, 1982; assistant to Woody Allen on
several films, including *Broadway Danny Rose, Hannah*

JANE READ MARTIN

and Her Sisters, New York Stories, and *Scenes from a
Mall,* 1983-90; associate producer of *Alice* (a film
written and directed by Woody Allen), Orion, 1990; *The
Joan Rivers Show,* Tribune Entertainment, senior associate producer and associate producer, 1991-93; *The
Male Cross-Dresser Support Group* (a forty-seven-second
film written and directed by Tama Janowitz), coproducer, 1992; *Can We Shop Starring Joan Rivers,* QRT
Enterprises, producer, 1993-94; free-lance writer,
1994—.

■ Writings

(With Patricia Marx) *Now Everybody Really Hates Me,*
  illustrated by Roz Chast, HarperCollins, 1993.
(Coauthor and co-creator with Marx and Charlie
  Hauck) *Now Everybody Really Hates Me* (television
  pilot; based on book of the same title), CBS-TV,
  1993.
(With Marx) *Now I Will Never Leave the Dinner Table,*
  illustrated by Chast, HarperCollins, 1996.

Also author of *Rosebud,* a short film selected for the
Edinburgh Film Festival, 1992.

■ Work in Progress

Red Ribbons, a book about AIDS.

■ Sidelights

Jane Read Martin told *SATA:* "I fell into children's
book writing quite by accident. My first book, *Now
Everybody Really Hates Me* (coauthored with Patricia
Marx), was actually based on something that I had
written as a child and my father had the good sense to
save. According to my parents, when I was nine years
old I was sent to my room (unfairly, I thought), where I
wrote the original *Now Everybody Really Hates Me.* The
entire book was only half a page long, but my parents
thought it was funny so they saved it for me. Eventually
I showed it to Patty Marx who suggested we turn it into
a children's book. We decided to expand on the original
by writing a book that would appeal to adults as well as
children, because adults are the ones who not only buy
the books, but read them over and over and over to
children."

Martin and Marx accomplished this goal; Deborah
Stevenson writes in her *Bulletin of the Center for
Children's Books* review of *Now Everybody Really Hates
Me:* "Children and adults will both find this funny, if
not always in quite the same way." The main character
of the book, Patty Jane Pepper, is sent to her room in
much the same way Martin was as a child. Feeling that
she is being unjustly punished, Patty Jane devises
numerous plans to get back at her parents—she could
stay in her room forever, or dig an escape tunnel with
her pointy dress-up shoes. "The deadpan humor of the
authors ... is perfectly suited to Roz Chast's wonder-
fully waggish illustrations," maintains Andrea Barnet in
the *New York Times Book Review,* adding that "the
marriage of text and pictures is ... seamless." Patty

Jane's further adventures in *Now I Will Never Leave the Dinner Table* find this sassy young girl stuck at the dinner table until she eats *ALL* of her spinach.

■ Works Cited

Barnet, Andrea, review of *Now Everybody Really Hates Me, New York Times Book Review,* April 24, 1994, p. 24.

Stevenson, Deborah, review of *Now Everybody Really Hates Me, Bulletin of the Center for Children's Books,* December, 1993, pp. 129-30.

■ For More Information See

PERIODICALS

Booklist, October 15, 1993, p. 453.
Horn Book Guide, spring, 1994, p. 44.
Publishers Weekly, July 12, 1993, p. 78.
School Library Journal, March, 1994, p. 205.
Time, December 20, 1993, p. 64.

*   *   *

MARVIN, Isabel R(idout) 1924-

■ Personal

Born June 10, 1924, in Port Arthur, TX; daughter of a minister and a nurse; married David H. Marvin (a school administrator), February 19, 1946; children: Kathleen, David H. Jr., Mary J. Hager. *Education:* University of Minnesota, B.S. (secondary education). *Politics:* Independent. *Religion:* Protestant. *Hobbies and other interests:* Reading, biking, swimming.

■ Addresses

Home—655 Lincoln St. N., Northfield, MN 55057 (summer); and #89, 100 East Hackberry, McAllen, TX 78501 (winter).

■ Career

English/Spanish teacher, St. Louis County Schools, 1964-65; Rosemont Schools, Rosemont, MN, English/journalism teacher, 1965-66; English/journalism teacher, Farmington Schools, 1966-86; instructor, Writer's Digest School, 1987—. *Military service:* U.S. Army Women's Auxiliary Corps, 1945-46; became sergeant. *Member:* Society of Children's Book Writers and Illustrators, Rio Grande Writers' Guild, Northfield Writers Group.

■ Awards, Honors

Minnesota Town and Country Art Show award, 1967; Milkweed Editions juvenile literature prize, 1993.

■ Writings

Bridge to Freedom, Jewish Publishers Society, 1991.

ISABEL R. MARVIN

Josefina and the Hanging Tree, Texas Christian University Press, 1992.
Saving Joe Louis, Kingston Publishers Limited, 1992.
Shipwrecked on Padre Island, illustrated by Lyle Miller, Hendrich-Long, 1993.
A Bride for Anna's Papa, illustrated by Kay Sather, Milkweed Editions, 1994.
Green Fire, Windswept House, 1994.
Mystery of the Ice Cream House, Windswept House, 1994.
Mystery of the Puerto Rican Penny, Windswept House, 1995.

Has also published over one hundred short stories and articles.

■ Work in Progress

The Windreapers, a historical novel for young adults; *The Junkyard Caper,* a juvenile novel; a historical novel on the "La Bahia" massacre.

■ Sidelights

A former English and journalism teacher, Isabel R. Marvin switched careers late in life to write historical fiction for children. "When I was forty with a husband and three children, I went back to college full time for two years, graduated, and taught for twenty-two years," Marvin told *SATA.* "I became so interested in writing—

mostly for children—that I ... quit [teaching] to freelance full time. I sold my first short story at age fifty-nine, and went on to sell over one hundred stories and articles and seven juvenile novels, two not yet released. It's never too late, and that's what I tell my ... students.

"My motivation for writing children's books was that in trying to find juvenile novels that kids liked and their parents *approved*, I decided I could walk that middle line and write historical novels for classroom use." Marvin's novels have received praise from critics, who appreciate the author's accurate historical details and careful characterizations. Not limited to a single area or time period, Marvin has written stories set in such diverse places as nineteenth-century Texas and turn-of-the-century Minnesota.

Josefina and the Hanging Tree, for example, describes the struggles of two Mexican families during the Cart Wars of 1857. "Marvin's fast-paced, historical yarn has strong subplots and is rich in both Texas flavor and Mexican culture," observed Deborah Abbott in *Booklist*. A *Publishers Weekly* critic also noted Marvin's skill with historical facts in a review of *A Bride for Anna's Papa*, which follows the adventures of a twelve-year-old girl living in Minnesota in the early 1900s. "Of special interest," remarked the reviewer of this book, "is Marvin's exploration of the [family's] Finnish heritage."

■ **Works Cited**

Abbott, Deborah, review of *Josefina and the Hanging Tree, Booklist,* October 15, 1992, p. 419.
Review of *A Bride for Anna's Papa, Publishers Weekly,* May 23, 1994, p. 89.

■ **For More Information See**

PERIODICALS

Horn Book Guide, fall, 1991, p. 278; fall, 1993, p. 301.
School Library Journal, June, 1993, p. 108; July, 1994, p. 103.

*   *   *

MAYO, Gretchen Will 1936-

■ **Personal**

Born April 13, 1936, in Dayton, OH; daughter of John F. (a sales promotion executive) and Julia Dolan (an English teacher; maiden name, Schumacher) Will; married Thomas J. Mayo (a marketing director), 1963; children: Megan, Molly, Ann. *Education:* Marquette University, B.S. (journalism), 1958; University of Dayton, teaching certificate (elementary education), 1959; attended Milwaukee Institute of Art and Design, 1982-83, 1984. *Religion:* Episcopalian. *Hobbies and other interests:* Traveling, hiking, reading, wildlife, movies, plays, winter in the north.

GRETCHEN WILL MAYO

■ **Addresses**

Home and office—5213 Lakefield Rd., Cedarburg, WI 53012.

■ **Career**

Teacher, 1958-63; Community Newspapers, Milwaukee, WI, reporter, 1966-70; artist, 1970-88. Teacher of college-level workshops on developing children's books and of elementary and secondary school workshops and programs on writing and illustrating; speaker/consultant for Chase/Pheifer/Puerling, Milwaukee, educational consultants. *Member:* Society of Children's Book Writers and Illustrators, Authors Guild, Authors League of America, Friends of the Cooperative Children's Book Center, Chicago Children's Reading Round Table.

■ **Awards, Honors**

Outstanding Science Trade Book citation, and Chicago Book Clinic Award for Outstanding Art in a Children's Book, both 1979, for *The Kangaroo;* New Jersey Author's Award, New Jersey Institute of Technology, 1981, for *I Hate My Name;* Notable Children's Trade Book in the Field of Social Studies citation, Original Children's Book Art Award, New York Master Eagel Gallery, and CCBC Choices, all 1987, for *Star Tales: North American Indian Stories;* Notable Children's Trade Book in the Field of Social Studies citation, Original Children's

Book Art Award, New York Society of Illustrators exhibit, and CCBC Choices, all 1989, for *Earthmaker's Tales: North American Indian Stories about Earth Happenings;* Outstanding Citizen award, Pi Lambda Theta, 1993; CCBC Choices, 1993, International Reading Association/CBC Children's Choice Award, 25 Best in Multicultural Books citation, *Boston Globe,* and Outstanding Achievement in Children's Literature by a Wisconsin author/illustrator citation, Wisconsin Library Association, 1994, all for *Meet Tricky Coyote!* and *That Tricky Coyote!*

■ Writings

RETELLER; SELF-ILLUSTRATED

Star Tales: North American Indian Stories, Walker, 1987, paperback edition published in two volumes as *Star Tales* and *More Star Tales,* 1990.

Earthmaker's Tales: North American Indian Stories about Earth Happenings, Walker, 1989, paperback edition published in two volumes as *Earthmaker's Tales* and *More Earthmaker's Tales,* 1990.

Meet Tricky Coyote!, Walker, 1993.

That Tricky Coyote!, Walker, 1993.

Here Comes Tricky Rabbit!, Walker, 1994, published as one volume with *Big Trouble for Tricky Rabbit!,* 1996.

Big Trouble for Tricky Rabbit!, Walker, 1994, published as one volume with *Here Comes Tricky Rabbit!,* 1996.

ILLUSTRATOR

Paula Hogan, *The Kangaroo* (part of the "Life Cycle" series), Raintree, 1979.

Eva Grant, *I Hate My Name,* Raintree, 1980.

Barbara Steiner, *Whale Brother,* Walker, 1988.

Cary Siter, *Moon of Falling Leaves,* F. Watts, 1988.

Barbara Joosse, *Anna, the One and Only,* HarperCollins, 1988.

Susan Rowen Masters, *The Secret Life of Hubie Hartzel,* HarperCollins, 1990.

Joosse, *Anna and the Cat Lady* (sequel to *Anna, the One and Only*), HarperCollins, 1992.

Also illustrator of Laura Greene's *Help: Getting to Know about Needing and Giving,* Human Sciences; has illustrated textbooks for Silver Burdette and Ginn, Scott Foresman, and Scholastic.

■ Adaptations

Star Tales was read on National Public Radio; *Earthmaker's Tales* was read on National Public Radio and Canada Broadcasting, and recorded for Talking Books for the Blind, 1992.

■ Work in Progress

Coauthoring a picture book with an Oneida tribal leader; several short stories and early readers. Researching wolves, wild geese, hawks, bigotry, and unconscious stereotyping.

■ Sidelights

After spending her early career as an elementary school teacher and journalist, Gretchen Will Mayo turned her attentions to writing and illustrating books for the students she once taught. As an illustrator for stories by other authors, Mayo has created artwork for a variety of tales, but as an author herself she began by focusing her attention on retelling the myths and legends of American Indians.

"The stories in many of my books originated with dozens of American Indian nations, but every one of them relates to experiences I have had as well," the author told *SATA.* "This timeless connection to universal experiences and feelings has always drawn me to culture stories and myths. I especially love those belonging to the American Indians, rooted in a land which I, too, call 'home,' springing from an oral storytelling tradition which I greatly admire."

Mayo's own background is Midwestern. "I grew up in southern Ohio," she related, "where I swam in the streams, made mud slides, and searched for arrowheads and fossils along with dozens of cousins, my three brothers and our 'little' sister. Among my happiest early memories are the stories I read or listened to ... especially the ones my mother read about Babar, the elephant. When I was in the second grade, I invented a comic strip about the wild adventures of 'Harold and Wanda.' I sat on the school steps each morning with my friends and drew pictures of those two rascals. They broke all the rules that I wished I could break. While I drew, I pretended that I was right there with Harold and Wanda. That's how I learned what fun it could be to fit words together with pictures.

"Now, whenever I write I am like an actor, still pretending I'm someone else. But instead of working on a stage, I do my acting on paper. The story may be about Rabbit, Coyote, or an old man shaping a horse out of mud. No matter! For a while, that's me there on the page. I become Rabbit so I can speak Rabbit's words. I have a good time when I let my imagination fly.

"The same thing happens when I illustrate a story. I imagine myself within the setting of the story along with the characters. I imagine what they must see or feel. Those thoughts, running through my mind like a movie, influence the colors I choose and the style of my art. For this reason, my illustrations for one book may look quite different from another one. Since I began illustrating the hard way—without any real training—I'm always learning new techniques as I work. The excitement of finding a color or shape or medium that is just right usually follows a time of risk-taking and trial. Truly, creativity is a process, not an event.

"The best storytelling and my best illustrations seem to spring from reentering emotionally charged moments that I remember from my past. I connect these feelings to the events that my characters experience in the story. So, when Rabbit plays a trick on Fox, I think of the fun I

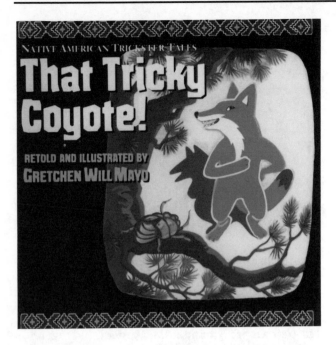

Mayo adapts several of the Native American coyote fables in this amusing collection for young readers. (Cover illustration by the author.)

had playing a trick on one of my brothers ... or all three of them.''

Mayo's interest in American Indian legends has a very specific origin, she revealed to *SATA*. "I wrote my first collection of traditional American Indian stories because of something that was missing. When my children were quite young, I wanted to tell them stories about the stars, as my father had done for me. I searched unsuccessfully for respectfully told American Indian star stories to read to them, stories which had risen out of this land rather than places which were oceans away. It astounded me that in this country children could look at the night sky and recite stories about the constellations from other nations all over the globe. But in libraries and bookstores we found no collections of American Indian stories about the stars for them to read—none written specifically for children. So I began the long process of researching, writing, and illustrating *Star Tales*, which eventually led to my other collections of American Indian stories: *Earthmaker's Tales, More Earthmaker's Tales, Meet Tricky Coyote!, That Tricky Coyote!, Here Comes Tricky Rabbit!*, and *Big Trouble for Tricky Rabbit!*''

Mayo further commented, "I hope that when a child or an adult opens my finished book, the visual and verbal components will speak to them as a unit—all parts working together to communicate successfully on several levels. Then the reader will become participant. They'll live for a while in another place and the story circle will be complete.

"It's risky business to write stories belonging to cultures other than your own. The writer (as well as the illustrator) needs to be sensitive and painstakingly responsible. If you are working outside of your own culture and living in a different frame of reference, you can be misled by the wording of old narrations or translations of stories. These translations usually don't illuminate the rich texture of detail and tradition underlying the story. In the case of traditional American Indian stories, many of them were recorded for the first time by non-Indians. I spent years gathering stories and researching the stories behind the stories of each of my books. I avoided retelling stories that I saw to be sacred, those held to be holy in the same manner as I regard my Bible stories. I surrounded the stories I wrote with introductions and afterwords—any information I could gather about the history of each story or about those who had narrated and recorded them. This information was often very hard to find.

"Recently I had the great honor of being asked by an Oneida tribal leader to coauthor a traditional story from her culture. It's been exciting and enlightening to experience working with her on this old story. She adds layer after layer of traditional detail, and the piece is enriched by a texture which only she could bring to it.

"The writing and illustrating which I do in the future will be greatly influenced by these experiences. I belong to a culture which has a history of colonizing other peoples. I've learned to ask myself how this fact of my life has shaped my attitudes. I've often stopped myself and wondered, 'What is being said that I have not wished to hear?' The wonderful thing is, when I have been attentive to questions such as these, I have been led to a deepening of friendships with intelligent, creative people of many cultures. I think those questions will generate some of my new books."

■ For More Information See

PERIODICALS

Booklist, September 1, 1993, p. 66; August, 1994, p. 2046.
Bulletin of the Center for Children's Books, May, 1993, p. 290.
Kirkus Reviews, May 15, 1994, p. 703.
Publishers Weekly, May 31, 1993, p. 55.
School Library Journal, September, 1993, p. 225; July, 1994, p. 96.

*   *   *

McCAFFERTY, Jim 1954-

■ Personal

Full name, James T. McCafferty III; born March 12, 1954, in Tupelo, MS; son of James T. (a Methodist preacher) and Miriam (a librarian; maiden name, Stamps) McCafferty; married Malinda Hamilton, January 1, 1983; children: Bess, Jack, Sadie. *Education:* Milsaps College, B.A. (cum laude), 1976; University of Mississippi School of Law, J.D., 1978. *Religion:* Methodist. *Hobbies and other interests:* Canoeing, hunting, fishing, walking.

JIM McCAFFERTY

■ Addresses

Home—767 Sherwood Dr., Jackson, MS 39216. *Office*—Box 5092, Jackson, MS 39296.

■ Career

Lawyer in Jackson, MS; self-syndicated newspaper columnist (outdoor topics), appearing in 14 newspapers, 1986-93; freelance writer and photographer for magazines and newspapers, including *Outdoor Life, Field & Stream, Southern,* and *Ford Times;* children's book writer. Chairman of board of directors, University of Mississippi Wesley Foundation, 1986-89; member of board of directors, Friends of the Jackson Zoo, 1991—, and secretary, 1993—; member of board of directors, Books for the World, 1992—. *Member:* Outdoor Writers Association of America, Southeastern Outdoor Press Association (member of board of directors, and chairman of ethics committee, 1990-92; legal advisor to board of directors, 1992—).

■ Awards, Honors

Third place, Magazine Feature Article Division, 1987, and first place, Weekly Newspaper Column Division, 1987 and 1989, Southeast Outdoor Press Association Excellence in Craft Competition; third place, Archery Category, 1988, and second place, Environment/Conservation Category, 1989, Magazine Division, Outdoor

Writers Association of America Writing Contest; Children's Crown Collection citations, National Christian Schools Association, 1993, for *Holt and the Teddy Bear,* and 1994, for *Holt and the Cowboys.*

■ Writings

Holt and the Teddy Bear, Pelican Publishing, 1991.
Holt and the Cowboys, illustrated by Florence S. Davis, Pelican Publishing, 1993.

■ Work in Progress

Holt and the Outlaws, third in a series.

■ Sidelights

Jim McCafferty told *SATA:* "The unwritten history and the unsung hero have always been my passions. In my magazine writing days, those were the stories I sought out. I wrote my first children's book, *Holt and the Teddy Bear,* not because I wanted to write a children's book, but because I believed a children's book was the best way to present an interesting episode from the life of a fascinating, yet virtually forgotten, figure from American history: Holt Collier. The book recounts Holt's indispensable role in Theodore Roosevelt's 1902 hunting trip that resulted in the naming of the Teddy Bear.

"As I researched the historical Holt Collier, I discovered that the Teddy Roosevelt hunt was just one of many exciting events in Holt's life. I resolved to tell at least a couple more Holt stories. My second book was *Holt and the Cowboys,* the true story of how Holt overcame the prejudices of some cowboys to win their friendship and a job on a Texas ranch. My third book, tentatively entitled *Holt and the Outlaws,* will be the story of how Holt infiltrated a gang of robbers and cutthroats on a Mississippi River island during the Civil War and helped bring the criminals to justice.

"I loved the character of Holt Collier, not only because he was an unrecognized American folk hero, but because he was an African-American folk hero. My only school-aged child attends school in a district where 85 percent of the children are African-American. Many of them are from disadvantaged backgrounds. From my visits to my daughter's school and my associations with her classmates, I am all too aware of the need for books about historical, African-American heroes like Holt Collier.

"Although I fell into writing children's books by accident, it is among the most enjoyable things I have ever done. It's not the writing I love so much as the research and, especially, the frequent visits I'm privileged to enjoy with children at schools and young authors' programs."

MARY ANN McDONALD

McDONALD, Mary Ann 1956-

■ Personal

Born November 29, 1956, in Roaring Spring, PA; daughter of Walter Clifford and Annamary (a homemaker; maiden name, Long) Biddle; married Douglas Wood (divorced, 1989); married Joe McDonald (an author and wildlife photographer), June 29, 1991. *Education:* Elizabethtown College, B.S. (magna cum laude), 1978. *Politics:* Independent. *Religion:* Church of the Brethren.

■ Addresses

Home and office—R.R. #2, Box 1095, McClure, PA 17841-9340.

■ Career

M. S. Hershey Medical Center, Hershey, PA, junior researcher, 1978-80, researcher, 1980-83, senior researcher, 1983-87, research support assistant, 1987-90; free-lance wildlife photographer, 1990—.

■ Awards, Honors

Two first place awards, 1994 BBC Wildlife Photographer of the Year Competition.

■ Writings

AND PHOTOGRAPHER

Jupiter, Child's World, 1993.
Flying Squirrels, Child's World, 1993.
The Amish, Todtri Productions, 1995.
Rattlesnakes, Capstone Press, 1995.
Pythons, Capstone Press, 1995.
Garter Snakes, Capstone Press, 1995.
Leopards, Child's World, 1995.
Grizzly Bears, Child's World, 1996.
Woodpeckers, Child's World, 1996.
Boa Constrictors, Child's World, 1996.
Pythons, Child's World, 1996.

Also contributor of photographs to children's books, coffee table books, calendars, and magazines.

■ Sidelights

Mary Ann McDonald told *SATA:* "I have always enjoyed writing, starting in the sixth grade with a play I wrote about Juliet Lowe and the founding of the Girl Scouts. I not only wrote the script, but directed and starred in the play, also. Since then, I have written everything from variety show skits to medical research papers.

"My present career and passion of wildlife photography takes me all over this country and the world. Sharing the experiences with my husband, Joe, we capture the natural world with our cameras, and thus teach many people about animals and places they may have never seen or heard of. During our travels we also get to meet and work with children, and whether that child lives in India, Kenya, or Pennsylvania, they have a common fascination with the natural world around them. By writing children's books and illustrating them with photographs, I hope to reach out to the next generation of conservationists and environmentalists, because the saving of endangered species or wilderness areas will inevitably be in their hands."

*   *   *

McNULTY, Faith 1918-

■ Personal

Born November 28, 1918, in New York, NY; daughter of Joseph Eugene (a judge) and Faith (Robinson) Corrigan; married Charles M. Fair, 1938 (divorced); married John McNulty, 1945 (died, 1956); married Richard H. Martin, 1957 (died, 1984); children: John Joseph McNulty. *Education:* Attended Barnard College, 1937-38.

■ Addresses

Home—P.O. Box 370, Wakefield, RI 02880. *Office*—*New Yorker,* 20 West 43rd St., New York, NY 10036.

FAITH McNULTY

■ Career

New Yorker Magazine, New York City, staff writer, 1953-94, author of annual review of the year's children's books, 1979-91. Previously employed as a newspaper reporter and magazine editor.

■ Awards, Honors

Dutton Animal Book Award, 1966, for *The Whooping Crane: The Bird That Defies Extinction;* A Book Can Develop Empathy Award, New York State Humane Association and the Fund for Animals, 1990, for *The Lady and the Spider;* D.H.L. from University of Rhode Island and Milwaukee School of Engineering.

■ Writings

CHILDREN'S BOOKS

The Funny Mixed-up Story, Wonder Books, 1959.
Arty the Smarty, Wonder Books, 1962.
When a Boy Gets up in the Morning, Knopf, 1962.
When a Boy Goes to Bed at Night, Knopf, 1963.
Prairie Dog Summer, Coward, 1972.
Woodchuck, illustrated by Joan Sandin, Harper, 1974.
Whales: Their Life in the Sea, illustrated by John Schoenherr, Harper, 1975.
Mouse and Tim, illustrated by Marc Simont, Harper, 1978.
How to Dig a Hole to the Other Side of the World, Harper, 1979.
The Elephant Who Couldn't Forget, illustrated by Simont, Harper, 1980.

Hurricane, illustrated by Gail Owens, Harper, 1983.
The Lady and the Spider, illustrated by Bob Marstall, Harper, 1986.
Peeping in the Shell: A Whooping Crane Is Hatched, illustrated by Irene Brady, Harper, 1986.
With Love from Koko, illustrated by Annie Cannon, Scholastic, 1990.
Orphan: The Story of a Baby Woodchuck, illustrated by Darby Morrell, Scholastic, 1992.
A Snake in the House, illustrated by Ted Rand, Scholastic, 1994.
Dancing with Manatees, illustrated by Lena Shiffman, Scholastic, 1994.
If You Go to the Moon, Scholastic, 1996.
A Flea and His Dog, Scholastic, 1996.
How to Fly Around the World on Your Own Wings, Scholastic, 1996.

ADULT BOOKS

(With Elisabeth Keiffer) *Wholly Cats,* Bobbs-Merrill, 1962.
The Whooping Crane: The Bird That Defies Extinction, introduction by Stewart L. Udall, Dutton, 1966.
Must They Die?: The Strange Case of the Prairie Dog and the Black-Footed Ferret, Doubleday, 1971.
The Great Whales, Doubleday, 1974.
The Burning Bed, Harcourt, 1980.
The Wildlife Stories of Faith McNulty, illustrated by Robin Brickman, Doubleday, 1980.

■ Adaptations

The Burning Bed was adapted as a television movie by NBC-TV, 1984; *The Lady and the Spider* was performed on *Reading Rainbow,* 1987.

■ Sidelights

The nature and science oriented books of Faith McNulty introduce children and adults to a wide variety of animals while making a strong case for preserving endangered species and conserving nature. Most of her stories appeared first in the *New Yorker,* where she has been a staff writer since 1953. Carol Van Strum maintains in the *Washington Post Book World* that McNulty's "observations ... gently remind us that for all our knowledge, technology and power, we are animals, no more or less worthy in the scheme of life than hawk or mouse. We eat, sleep, reproduce, play, work, love and die subject to the same natural laws that govern all living things, and if our ingenuity has given us dominion over other creatures, it has burdened us also with responsibility for them."

McNulty's interest in nature and its creatures stems back to her own childhood. Growing up in New York City, she explains in *Junior Library Guild,* "I hated the city and loved the country, where I spent my summers at my grandmother's house.... My playmates were animals."

Despite her dislike for the city, though, McNulty pursued her career in New York City, first as a

A spider makes a home in a head of lettuce in a woman's garden in *The Lady and the Spider,* which demonstrates a healthy respect for all life. (Illustration by Bob Marstall.)

newspaper reporter, then in various editorial positions, and finally as a staff writer for the *New Yorker.* Her escape is her farm in Rhode Island, where she has lived since 1960, and where she can write about anything she wants; the subject is most often animals. In such early adult works as *The Whooping Crane: The Bird That Defies Extinction* and *Must They Die?: The Strange Case of the Prairie Dog and the Black-Footed Ferret,* McNulty relates the history of these animals, with information on how the government is either hindering or helping their survival.

Similar stories of other animals, as well as conservation concerns, make up the majority of McNulty's books for children. Among these are *Woodchuck,* in which the life-cycle of woodchucks is related through the fictional story of a female waking up from hibernation in the spring, mating, breeding, and then returning to her hole in the fall. *Whales: Their Life in the Sea,* published in 1975, is a nonfiction account of the evolution of whales, describing the various families, their life cycles, and physical features. Beryl Robinson, writing in *Horn Book,* maintains that in *Woodchuck* McNulty presents the life of this small creature "with clarity, simplicity, and effectiveness." And an *Appraisal* reviewer observes that *Whales* is "generally interesting, straightforward, and factual."

In addition to animals, McNulty also often includes human characters in her children's books. These people

interact with the animals, sometimes caring for them until they are old enough or well enough to be released back into their natural habitats. Such is the case with *Mouse and Tim.* Finding a baby deer mouse, which is as small as a bumblebee, Tim takes her home to raise until she is old enough to make it on her own. The mouse and Tim take turns narrating the story, discussing such topics as the food being fed to the mouse and their growing friendship. *Mouse and Tim* is "a beguiling story of a little boy and a wild mouse," describes Virginia Haviland in *Horn Book.*

The wildness of nature and its natural forces is the focus of McNulty's 1983 work, *Hurricane.* Although he is helping his parents prepare their New England home for an upcoming storm, John is distracted by worries about his tree house being destroyed. As the day progresses, John notices the many changes occurring, and his parents explain what goes into the formation of a hurricane. In the end, after the fury of the storm has passed, John's tree house, along with everything else, is still intact. "Demonstrating that nature is at once terrible and beautiful, McNulty's scientific explanations are simple and direct," concludes Daniel P. Woolsey in *School Library Journal.*

More personal experiences with nature are the subject of McNulty's *Orphan: The Story of a Baby Woodchuck* and *With Love from Koko.* The first is the author's account of the baby woodchuck she found at the end of her driveway one day. Remembering how she nursed animals as a child, McNulty took the woodchuck inside, using her bathroom as a home until he was ready to be released back into the wilderness. *With Love from Koko* introduces basic information about gorillas as it relates the events surrounding McNulty's first visit to this famous animal (Koko) that is so similar to humans. *Orphan* "will appeal to any children who have ever

McNulty uses the snake's point of view to tell the story of a reptile's escape after a boy captures him in a jar in *A Snake in the House.* (Illustration by Ted Rand.)

rescued, or dreamed of rescuing, a wild animal," writes Cynthia Zarin in the *New Yorker,* who concludes: "This graceful book, in addition to being a good story, can serve as a practical guide." Ellen Fader, in her *School Library Journal* review of *With Love from Koko,* also praises McNulty, pointing out that she "does an exceptionally fine job of capturing the anticipation, fear, and excitement of her first visit with Koko."

The Lady and the Spider, published in 1986, and McNulty's 1994 work *A Snake in the House* bring people back into the picture, but also add a new element—how the actions of these people affect the creatures around them. The lady of *The Lady and the Spider* is unaware of the spider living in her garden until she picks his home (a head of lettuce) one day and brings it in to eat. Finding the spider, she stops herself from throwing it away as she notices just how perfectly it is made, and its will to survive. *A Snake in the House* holds a stronger message about capturing animals and holding them captive. Having been captured by a young boy, the snake of the title spends a few dangerous days in the house looking for a way out. Eventually making it outside, the snake finds itself at the boy's mercy, and is finally set free. Karey Wehner, reviewing *The Lady and the Spider* in the *School Library Journal,* concludes: "The book's message, that all life has value, is powerful, all the more so for being understated." Jenna Roberts similarly observes in the *New York Times Book Review* that in *A Snake in the House* "the message about enjoying nature without possessing it is worth hearing, and the little snake's trials demonstrate it ably."

Although McNulty's messages reach both children and adults through her many writings, it is her works for children that offer the author more of a challenge. McNulty reveals in *Junior Library Guild:* "The possibilities in style and subject are virtually endless, limited only by the writer's ingenuity in finding ways to express ideas in their most basic form. To strip an idea down to its essentials is a real test of skill."

■ Works Cited

Fader, Ellen, review of *With Love from Koko, School Library Journal,* March, 1990, p. 210.

Haviland, Virginia, review of *Mouse and Tim, Horn Book,* June, 1978, p. 266.

McNulty, Faith, comments in *Junior Library Guild,* April-September, 1986.

Roberts, Jenna, review of *A Snake in the House, New York Times Book Review,* June 5, 1994, p. 30.

Robinson, Beryl, review of *Woodchuck, Horn Book,* April, 1975, p. 143.

Van Strum, Carol, *Washington Post Book World,* November 2, 1980.

Wehner, Karey, review of *The Lady and the Spider, School Library Journal,* September, 1986, p. 124.

Review of *Whales: Their Life in the Sea, Appraisal,* winter, 1976.

Woolsey, Daniel P., review of *Hurricane, School Library Journal,* September, 1983, p. 109.

Zarin, Cynthia, review of *Orphan: The Story of a Baby Woodchuck, New Yorker,* November 23, 1992, p. 80.

■ For More Information See

PERIODICALS

Booklist, November 1, 1966, p. 293; December 1, 1980, p. 499; January 1, 1987, p. 710.

Bulletin of the Center for Children's Books, May, 1975, p. 151; June, 1978; September, 1983; October, 1986; February, 1994, pp. 194-95.

Five Owls, May/June, 1992, pp. 60-61.

Horn Book, June, 1980.

Library Journal, May 1, 1971, pp. 1623-24; November 15, 1980, p. 2424.

New Yorker, December 11, 1971, p. 164.

Publishers Weekly, June 27, 1966, p. 97; March 16, 1990, p. 68.

School Library Journal, March, 1975, p. 88; September, 1975, p. 108; April, 1978, p. 73; December, 1986, p. 106.

* * *

MEDDAUGH, Susan 1944-

■ Personal

Surname is pronounced *med-*aw; born October 4, 1944, in Montclair, NJ; daughter of John Stuart (a naval captain and insurance executive) and Justine (Leach) Meddaugh; married Harry L. Foster (an editor), November, 1982; children: Niko (son). *Education:* Wheaton College, Norton, MA, B.A., 1966. *Politics:* "Unaffiliated and opinionated." *Hobbies and other interests:* Reading mysteries, parenting.

■ Addresses

Home and office—56 Maple St., Sherborn, MA 01770.

■ Career

Houghton Mifflin, Co., Boston, MA, trade division of the children's book department, designer, and art director, 1968-78; writer and illustrator of children's books, 1978—.

■ Awards, Honors

Parents' Choice Literature Award (with Verna Aardema), 1985, for *Bimwili and the Zimwi: A Tale from Zanzibar; New York Times* Best Illustrated Books citation, 1992, Charlotte Award, New York State Reading Association, and Keystone State Reading Association award, both 1994, Pennsylvania Young Reader's Award and Nebraska Golden Sower Award, both 1995, and Parent's Choice Award, all for *Martha Speaks;* Parents' Choice Illustration Award, 1994, and Oppenheim Toy Portfolio Platinum Award Best Book, all for *Martha Calling.*

■ Writings

SELF-ILLUSTRATED

Too Short Fred, Houghton, 1978.
Maude and Claude Go Abroad, Houghton, 1980.
Beast, Houghton, 1981.
Too Many Monsters, Houghton, 1982.
Tree of Birds, Houghton, 1990.
The Witches' Supermarket, Houghton, 1991.
Surprise! (wordless picture book), Houghton, 1991.
Martha Speaks, Houghton, 1992.
Martha Calling, Houghton, 1994.
Hog-Eye, Houghton, 1995.

ILLUSTRATOR

Anne Epstein, *Good Stones,* Houghton, 1977.
Carol-Lynn Waugh, *My Friend Bear,* Atlantic/Little, 1982.
Jean and Claudio Marzollo, *Red Sun Girl,* Dial, 1983.
J. and C. Marzollo, *Blue Sun Ben,* Dial, 1984.
J. and C. Marzollo, *Ruthie's Rude Friends,* Dial, 1984.
Verna Aardema, *Bimwili and the Zimwi: A Tale from Zanzibar,* Dial, 1985.
J. and C. Marzollo, *The Silver Bear,* Dial, 1987.
Ruby Dee, *Two Ways to Count to Ten: A Liberian Folktale,* Holt, 1988.
Beatrice Schenk de Regniers, *The Way I Feel—Sometimes,* Clarion Books, 1988.
John Ciardi, *The Hopeful Trout and Other Limericks,* Houghton, 1989.
Eve Bunting, *No Nap,* Clarion Books, 1989.
Bunting, *In the Haunted House,* Clarion Books, 1990.
Bunting, *A Perfect Father's Day,* Clarion Books, 1991.
Susan Wojciechowski, *The Best Halloween of All,* Crown, 1992.
Linda Breiner Milstein, *Amanda's Perfect Hair,* Tambourine Books, 1993.
Jennifer Armstrong, *That Terrible Baby,* Tambourine Books, 1994.
Sarah Wilson, *Good Zap, Little Grog,* Candlewick, 1995.

■ Work in Progress

Another "Martha" book, for Houghton; illustrator of *The Most Beautiful Kid in the World.*

■ Sidelights

Susan Meddaugh writes and illustrates children's books with the eye of someone who knows the trade inside and out. This is no coincidence, for Meddaugh worked a decade as a designer and art director for children's books at Houghton Mifflin before setting out on her own as a writer and illustrator. "For years I had been advising illustrators to do their own books," Meddaugh said in an interview with *Something about the Author* (*SATA*). "Finally I took my own advice." Ten books and nearly a score of illustrated works later, Meddaugh's readers are happy for it. "Susan Meddaugh has a gift for building a picture book out of one funny scene after another," wrote Mary Lou Burket in *Five Owls.* Her quirky and humorous picture books have won awards as well as a large audience, and her canine character

Martha, a hound with an attitude, has escaped the pages of fiction to become a cover story "Face to Watch" in *Boston Magazine.* For Meddaugh it is all a matter of serendipity. "I know it sounds trite," Meddaugh told *SATA,* "but I never planned on being a children's book writer. Now, though, it really feels right. It was an incredibly lucky accident."

"Growing up in my family was a little like being in an extended George Burns and Gracie Allen routine," the author related in her interview. "My younger brother, John, and I were the audience for our parents' performance. There was also a fine supporting cast of characters (relatives) contributing to the plot. Housework was not high on my mother's list of priorities. She was dramatic and whimsical." Meddaugh's father, a retired Navy captain, was a general manager at the home office of the Prudential. But it was his World War II experience during his African landings and in the South Pacific that truly informed his life. "My father has been cracking us up with wry comments and a sort of humorous view of the world for eighty-plus years," Meddaugh added.

"I was a very shy child," Meddaugh told *SATA.* "As a result, I enjoyed fantasy games and drawing. It's funny when I think of it, but now I'm really only doing what I did when I was ten. Except that now I get paid for it." Meddaugh grew up in suburban New Jersey, in a neighborhood with plenty of children. Books were an

SUSAN MEDDAUGH

important ingredient of her childhood, but not all-consuming. "I don't remember having tremendous amounts of books, but the ones there were, such as Dr. Seuss and *Curious George* by H. A. Rey, made an impression." Meddaugh's father was a fine storyteller, making up his own tales, and her mother read to her regularly. But it was drawing and painting that attracted Meddaugh the most. In high school words and images came together in an innovative class. "We had a combined art and English section," Meddaugh explained. "And it was a revelation for me. It was very new for its day, and the instructors were enthusiastic. They said, 'Just be original. Have one original thought and you'll get an A.'" Otherwise, school was more or less mundane for Meddaugh. "I was expected to do well, and I did. I had a few excellent teachers along the way, particularly in art and French. But it was an awkward time for me."

Upon graduation from high school, Meddaugh—or her mother—chose a small, liberal arts, all-female school—Wheaton College. "It was completely away from everything happening in the world at the time," Meddaugh told *SATA*. "I majored in French because I had enjoyed a high school French class, but I wanted to do art. By the time I was a junior the college had employed a couple of wonderful art teachers, but there were only three of us who wanted to take studio art classes. So we had two years of private lessons. We were so naive then. I remember when we were going to have our first nude model and we just looked at each other. 'When they say nude, do they mean really nude?' But Wheaton was a good experience for me. Those were my days of serious painting. Oils. Pictures of sad girls who all looked liked they stepped out of Degas. I loved drawing people. Even when I wanted to go abstract, there was always something you could read in my pictures."

Out of college, Meddaugh realized that her French degree was not going to be her ticket. "I knew I didn't want to teach, and short of translation, what else is there to do with a foreign language degree?" So she followed her instincts and drew on her artistic background. She went to New York, portfolio in hand, and landed a job as a "Girl Friday" at an advertising agency, which lasted only a few months. She was then offered a job as an assistant editor of cookbooks at a large New York publisher. "Can you imagine! Home-ec was at the bottom of the list on my aptitude tests; cooking was not really my thing." From New York, Meddaugh moved on to Boston, where she took a temporary job at Houghton Mifflin that eventually turned into a ten-year stint in children's books. "Publishing was different then," Meddaugh recalled. "Houghton was in its old brick building. I even applied for the job wearing white gloves. The pace was leisurely, and I basically learned on the job."

As a designer of children's books she learned the basics of the thirty-two page format and the technique of pre-separated art in which illustrators did the work that computer scanners now do, drawing separate black and white sketches for the addition of yellow, red, and blue in each illustration. She was also responsible for hiring

illustrators for book projects, and increasingly began to wonder if her own illustration skills could be put to use some day. "I learned to develop a feeling for the books and how they should look, and I internalized the notion that a good picture book is a very specific form," Meddaugh explained to *SATA*. "Both art and text move the story. Together they tell the story, and there can be no superfluous parts, not in such a short format. Also, expression and originality are essential, and theme—if there is one—comes out of the story. You cannot start with theme and create a story around it. So I learned the trade, but it really wasn't my chosen area. I wanted to use my art more directly. And also, genetically, I'm just not made to get up early. I like to work late at night and get up late in the morning. So finally I left to go freelance."

Meddaugh's first book, *Too Short Fred,* was a transitional work for her. "I needed to move away from fine art, which I had been doing, to a more expressive and exaggerated form for children's books, so I chose to portray animals at first." In *Too Short Fred,* the title character, an undersized cat, faces five trials in which he must overcome his height disadvantage. A school bully who steals Fred's lunch gets worm sandwiches for his troubles; at a school dance Fred is partnered with a girl much taller than himself but who turns out to be a great dancer; a race down a snowy hill turns into victory for Fred when he falls and rolls to the bottom first. Working in colored pencils, Meddaugh drew her cats to easily bring to mind humans. "It was well received," Meddaugh said in her interview, "but with those early books I really had no confidence in line yet." The trademark whimsy and humor of her books was, however, already detectable. A reviewer in *Publishers Weekly* noted that

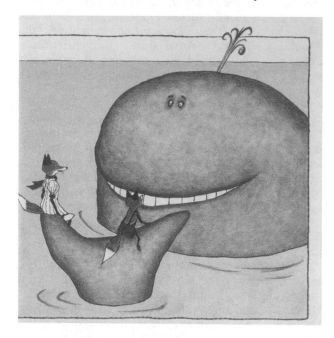

Two young foxes cause trouble on a ship crossing the Atlantic Ocean and end up making friends with a whale in *Maude and Claude Go Abroad.* (Illustration by the author.)

the book would be "fun and reassuring for boys and girls who are different, in any way" and also called attention to the illustrations which were "rich in texture."

Meddaugh's second book, *Maude and Claude Go Abroad,* was inspired by a brother-sister relationship like her own, in which the older sister looks out for the younger sibling. The Foxes put their two children, Maude and Claude, aboard an ocean liner to sail for France. En route, Claude falls overboard, and Maude—who has been instructed by her parents to watch out for him—does the only sensible thing: she jumps in after him. Told in punning and humorous rhyme, the story follows the adventures of the two as they hitch a ride with a whale who, before delivering them safely in France, must first outwit the harpooners following him. Maude solves this problem, sitting on the whale's spout so that it looks like they are riding a floating island. A "gem of a story," a contributor in *Publishers Weekly* called the book, but not all the critics liked it. "It got one very crucial bad review," Meddaugh told *SATA,* "and it just sank."

But Meddaugh was undaunted; her third book, *Beast,* introduced human characters in the form of a little girl and her family. It also included a big, furry beast that comes out of the forest to terrorize the girl's family. But the young child does not think the beast is as bad as her family believes; perhaps it is only hungry? She is more curious than scared, and soon learns that the beast has need for more than food: it is lonely and needs a friend, too. Employing cartoon-like drawings and a rhythmic pattern of text, *Beast* relates a simple message: that you should find out things for yourself and not rely just on what others tell you. By combining a very appealing and realistic narrative to a parable, Meddaugh created an "exceptional blend," noted Donnarae MacCann and Olga Richard in *Wilson Library Bulletin,* adding, "this is nothing less than a perfect book." A contributor in *Publishers Weekly* agreed, concluding that children would be "thrilled to discover this story and its singularly imaginative color paintings."

"I start with the visual image," Meddaugh explained. "My books are more image-oriented than word. And during the writing of these early books I was still learning the basics of being able to tell a story, be it in words or pictures. You can not write from an adult standpoint. It's an intuitive process, and you have to wait for that internal 'ah' that lets you know you've got it right. Writing for children is definitely not an exact science." Meddaugh employed this instinctual talent in her fourth children's book, *Too Many Monsters,* an "entrancing tale," according to a critic in *Publishers Weekly.* Howard the monster lives with ninety-nine other monsters—the difference between them being that Howard is kind and wants no part of their dirty tricks. He desires only to get away from them and be on his own, a wish that is fulfilled when they chase him up a tree and it comes crashing down, letting in light to the forest and scaring the meanies away. The *Publishers Weekly* critic called attention to the "meticulously colored" illustrations: green monsters except for laven-

The birds were not fooled.

Harry's pet bird has some very staunch and stubborn friends who won't leave Harry's tree despite all his tricks in *Tree of Birds*. (Illustration by the author.)

der Howard, and the change from blue-green forest depths to warm and bright colors at the end when the tree comes down. "I was still working in pencil," Meddaugh recalled for *SATA,* "and those drawings took forever. It was the last of my books I would do in pre-separated art."

In fact, it was the last book of her own Meddaugh would write for eight years, too busy with being a wife and full-time mother to create new characters. She did, however, continue to illustrate others' books, and in 1985 teamed up with Verna Aardema on the award-winning *Bimwili and the Zimwi: A Tale from Zanzibar.* She has also illustrated several books for the prolific Eve Bunting, as well as many others. "It's clearly not as rewarding doing illustrations for somebody else's book as for your own. But it is still enjoyable. Still a challenge. It's the kind of work that gives me both freedom and structure. I need that mix. I love taking classes, but after they're over, and the teacher stops pushing, I start asking myself what I'm supposed to be doing now. So the structure of children's books is good for me. And really, there is a freedom in doing children's books that you don't find in any other commercial art. Once you prove yourself, you're free to set your own limits, to perceive the story the way *you* want to."

The birth of Meddaugh's son had unexpected advantages. "With the arrival of Niko," Meddaugh said in her interview with *SATA,* "I just had no time anymore, no time to work my art over and over. From then on my art became more spontaneous and looser." An art class in 1990 also helped the process, giving Meddaugh more confidence in her line. The result was *Tree of Birds,* the story of Harry, a boy who brings an injured bird home with him one day, only to be inundated by an enormous flock of birds—all Green Tufted Tropicals according to Harry's bird book—in search of their lost member. The flock, nesting in a tree outside his house, won't leave, even when Harry tries dressing up in a cat costume or when the temperature drops and snow is on the way. Harry has grown attached to his bird and does not want to lose her, but when the birds outside turn blue in the cold, his guilt overcomes him and he sets his bird free.

At least that was the idea. Instead, the entire flock comes *inside* his house.

"I absolutely hate sad endings," Meddaugh said. "I knew all along that the book would have to end with Harry releasing his friend. But then one day it dawned on me that I could do anything I wanted with the book. It was my book. Suddenly the ending came to me. It was a surprise for me, as well. That's why *Tree of Birds* is my favorite book: I was finally free to be myself." The critics agreed with Meddaugh. Mary M. Burns, writing in *Horn Book,* noted that the book had "expressive watercolors" and "tongue-in-cheek text." Burns con-

"There, there," Anna soothed.

Then she said, "A beast this nice must be protected."

A frightening sound coming from the night turns out to have a not-so-frightening source in *Beast,* which tells of a young girl's courage to make an unusual friend. (Illustration by the author.)

In *The Witches' Supermarket* Helen accidentally stumbles upon a supermarket for witches who need brooms and potion ingredients, and who definitely do not appreciate Helen's dog, Martha.

cluded that *Tree of Birds* was "funny without being forced" and that picture-book audiences would be "delighted by this lighthearted variant on the stray pet theme." "Children will reach for it again and again," commented a *Publishers Weekly* reviewer, and Zena Sutherland in *Bulletin of the Center for Children's Books* called the story "wildly anthropomorphic."

Son Niko provided further inspiration in addition to forcing Meddaugh to loosen up her art. His comments have also literally inspired two of Meddaugh's books, *The Witches' Supermarket* and *Martha Speaks*. "It was at Halloween," Meddaugh explained to *SATA,* "and

Niko asked me where the witches got all their stuff—the dried spiders and all that. And then he wondered if they didn't have a witches' supermarket. Well, I just couldn't let that one go." The result was the story of Helen and her dog Martha (the first incarnation of the Meddaugh family pet in print) who end up in a very strange supermarket indeed. All the customers are dressed in witches' garb, and too late Helen realizes these are not just Halloween costumes. The witches themselves realize at about the same time that the little girl witch is only in costume for Halloween. Martha the dog, in a cat costume, saves the day when she wreaks a bit of havoc with the witches' real cats. "Imaginative Halloween

fun," stated a contributor in *Kirkus Reviews,* and Liza Bliss, writing in *School Library Journal,* called *The Witches' Supermarket* "a book that's as much fun as Halloween itself."

Meddaugh was then inspired to write a new Martha tale after hearing another comment by Niko: If Martha ate alphabet soup, would she be able to talk? He was joking, but this question supplied Meddaugh with a mental image of their dog swallowing the noodle alphabets, and instead of going to her stomach, they go directly to the brain. The resulting book, *Martha Speaks,* not only has Martha talking, but at such length that she bores the family to the point that they finally censure her. But

Martha redeems herself, saving the family from burglars with her newfound speech. Mary Lou Burket in *Five Owls* noted the contrast between controlled elements like the timing of jokes, and the looser art and lettering, which led her to conclude that Meddaugh "makes it seem easy to do."

The popularity of the first Martha book led Meddaugh to use the crafty canine again in *Martha Calling,* in which the talking dog enters a radio call-in contest and wins the family a vacation weekend. Martha soon learns, however, that there are no dogs allowed in the hotel where the family is booked. Not to worry: Martha disguises herself as an invalid grandmother in a wheel-

She made embarrassing comments.

Mom said that fruitcake you sent wasn't fit for a dog. But I thought it was delicious.

A talking dog might seem like a really cool pet to have, but in *Martha Speaks* Martha's owners soon discover that it's no blessing at all when their dog won't shut up. (Illustration by the author.)

chair and enjoys one adventure after another. Again the art work is loose and cartoon-like, and done in simple colored pencil. A reviewer in *Parents' Choice* applauded the sequel, adding a caution that adult readers might suffer "hoarseness from constant requests to 'Read it again!'" A *Publishers Weekly* contributor praised the illustrations, noting that young readers would be sure to be "drawn in once again by Meddaugh's witty and unaffected cartooning," and Deborah Stevenson in *Bulletin of the Center for Children's Books* concluded that *Martha Calling* was a "rollicking followup." The critics were not the only ones to approve: both the Martha books won numerous awards.

"I am frankly amazed and puzzled at the success of the Martha books," Meddaugh told *SATA*. "You just never know what is going to work with the readers. I know what works for me, what makes me laugh. But it's not always what makes others laugh. Ultimately what I am striving for is to have kids get involved with the images I create, to find some meaning and, yes, humor in them. And that's a pretty tall order in today's world with all the competing images we have around us all the time. Doing picture books is a sort of funny field. In one way it's hard to take it seriously, but on the other hand it *is* serious. It's important to get kids reading. If they laugh at Martha and it helps them to read, fine. I've done my job. But my work is also a great self-indulgence. Here I am drawing pictures of dogs and making up stories just like I did when I was a kid."

Meddaugh took a departure from dogs with her 1995 work *Hog-Eye,* a picture book with pigs as the main characters, getting on the wrong bus and having myriad adventures, Meddaugh-style. "Ideas are everywhere," Meddaugh concluded in her *SATA* interview. "You relax and wait for them; they can't be forced. I guess I think of myself as a visual story-teller. It takes me a long time. It doesn't come quickly for me except at the end of a project. I like to work best in pen and ink and watercolor wash. Color for me has been a big challenge throughout my career, but I feel now that I'm getting less muddy, more vibrant. Overall, I'm getting more confident as I go along. It's just something I love to do. And that's important. With all the commercialization of children's books that is happening now—the blockbuster bestseller mentality that is taking over children's publishing just as it has the adult market—it's important to remember that the best children's books are the ones that are timeless. They are the ones created by people who are in it not so much for the money, but because they just love doing picture books."

■ Works Cited

Review of *Beast, Publishers Weekly,* February 20, 1981, p. 94.

Bliss, Liza, review of *The Witches' Supermarket, School Library Journal,* November, 1991, p. 103.

Burket, Mary Lou, review of *Martha Speaks, Five Owls,* November/December, 1992, p. 33.

Burns, Mary M., review of *Tree of Birds, Horn Book,* September/October, 1990, p. 595.

MacCann, Donnarae, and Olga Richard, review of *Beast, Wilson Library Bulletin,* March, 1982, p. 530.

Review of *Martha Calling, Parents' Choice,* volume 18, number 4, 1994.

Review of *Martha Calling, Publishers Weekly,* August 15, 1994, p. 95.

Review of *Maude and Claude Go Abroad, Publishers Weekly,* February 22, 1980, p. 108.

Meddaugh, Susan, interview with J. Sydney Jones for *Something about the Author,* March, 1995.

Stevenson, Deborah, review of *Martha Calling, Bulletin of the Center for Children's Books,* September, 1994, p. 19.

Sutherland, Zena, review of *Tree of Birds, Bulletin of the Center for Children's Books,* March, 1990, p. 170.

Review of *Too Many Monsters, Publishers Weekly,* March 5, 1982, p. 70.

Review of *Too Short Fred, Publishers Weekly,* July 31, 1978, p. 98.

Review of *Tree of Birds, Publishers Weekly,* March 16, 1990, p. 69.

Review of *The Witches' Supermarket, Kirkus Reviews,* August 15, 1991, p. 1091.

■ For More Information See

PERIODICALS

Bulletin of the Center for Children's Books, June, 1982, p. 192; September, 1991, p. 16.

Kirkus Reviews, October 1, 1978, p. 1070; March 15, 1980, p. 361.

New York Times Book Review, November 8, 1992, p. 32.

School Library Journal, May, 1981, p. 58; April, 1982, pp. 59-60.

—*Sketch by J. Sydney Jones*

* * *

MILNE, Terry
See MILNE, Theresa Ann

* * *

MILNE, Theresa Ann 1964-
(Terry Milne)

■ Personal

Born August 23, 1964, in Cape Town, South Africa; daughter of Bruce (an architect) and Margaret (a botanical guide; maiden name, Esser) Milne; married Paul Devilliers (an architect), April 11, 1992. *Education:* University of Cape Town, B.A.F.A, 1986; University of Stellenbosch, B.A. (with honors), 1989. *Hobbies and other interests:* Contemporary dance, walking in the mountains with husband Paul and bull terrier Hans, poetry, reading.

■ Addresses

Home—10 Parkvilla Rd., Observatory, Cape Town, South Africa 7925. *Agent*—Laura Cecil, 17 Alwyne Villas, London N1 2HG, England.

■ Career

Freelance book illustrator, dancer. Has danced professionally with "Jazzart" dance company, Cape Town, South Africa.

■ Illustrator

UNDER NAME TERRY MILNE

Rosemary Kahn, *Grandma's Hat* (picture book), David Philip, 1989.

Martin Waddell, *The Toymaker: A Story in Two Parts,* Candlewick Press, 1992.

Elizabeth Thiel, *The Polka Dot Horse,* Simon & Schuster, 1993.

Penelope Lively, *The Cat, the Crow, and the Banyan Tree,* Candlewick Press, 1994.

Vivian French, *The Apple Trees* (nonfiction picture book), Walker Books, 1994.

■ Work in Progress

Writing and illustrating a picture book story of her own; illustrating a collection of children's stories by South African writers; illustrating a full-color picture book

THERESA ANN MILNE

called *The Terrible Graakwa,* written by a group of South African writers.

■ Sidelights

Terry Milne told *SATA:* "I completed a B.A.F.A. degree majoring in painting at the University of Cape Town Michaelis Art School. I always enjoyed painting in a figurative and representational style and felt more comfortable with a smaller format than the larger canvasses preferred by my lecturers and contemporaries. I also love poetry and literature and have often looked in that sphere for inspiration and a stucture within which to work. Throughout the Fine Art course I often had the feeling that I was really a frustrated illustrator.

"I was very fortunate to meet the well-known and internationally admired South African illustrator, Niki Daly, who was at the time lecturing in art and illustration at the University of Stellenbosch. I was very much inspired by his enthusiasm and his work to become an illustrator of children's books.

"I studied under Niki Daly at the University of Stellenbosch and obtained a B.A. Honours degree with distinction in 1989. Niki's continued support, his enthusiasm and prolific output remains a source of inspiration for my own work.

"I moved to London in 1989 to establish contacts with overseas publishers and to be nearer the source of my childhood picture books. I stayed in London for two and a half years and illustrated three picture books while living there.

"Since early childhood I have been a daydreamer—I think this is partly why I enjoy the comfort of the other-worldliness that picture books offer. I derive great pleasure from enveloping myself in the particular atmostphere of the story I am illustrating.

"About *The Cat, the Crow, and the Banyan Tree* by Penelope Lively: I have always been intrigued by the bizarre and whimsical images found in the stories of Lewis Carroll and the magical illustrations of these stories by Sir John Tenniel. I looked at these as well as Grandville's illustrations of *Un Autre Monde* and *Les Animaux* for inspiration while I was working on *The Cat, the Crow, and the Banyan Tree.*

"When starting a new book, I usually experiment with different materials and techniques while developing the characters and the atmosphere of the story. Through this process I find the materials that best evoke the particular spirit of the story. For *The Cat, the Crow, and the Banyan Tree,* I worked with thin washes of oil paint on magazine paper from which the original image had been removed with thinners. I used an etching needle to engrave into the paper a dense hatched linework to build up a dark, mysterious environment.

"Three other well known illustrators I particularly admire are Ernest Shephard, Edward Ardizzone and Harold Jones.

"I live in Cape Town in an old neighbourhood close to the City. I share a Victorian house with my architect husband Paul, our bull terrier dog Hans and our two Ginger cats, Molly and Kerneels."

*   *   *

MITCHELL, Margaree King 1953-

■ Personal

Born July 23, 1953, in Holly Springs, MS; daughter of Joe Jr. (a farmer) and Susie Mae (a homemaker; maiden name, Bowen) King; married Kevin Lee Mitchell (an account executive), October 9, 1982; children: Nelson. *Education:* Brandeis University, B.S., 1975. *Politics:* Democrat. *Religion:* Baptist.

■ Addresses

Home—3706 Straightfork Dr., Houston, TX 77082. *Office*—6763 Highway 6 S., Suite 1100-335, Houston, TX 77083.

■ Career

Monumental Baptist Church, Memphis, TN, drama department director, 1987-1990. Member, Little Rock School District Bi-racial Committee; vice-president,

MARGAREE KING MITCHELL

Fulbright Elementary School PTA Board; parliamentarian, Rees Elementary PTO Board.

■ Awards, Honors

Finalist, Writers Guild of America, East Foundation Fellowship Program, 1991, for "Corporate Lies"; finalist, Theatre Memphis New Play Competition, 1991, for *The Hi-Rise;* International "Best of 1993" citation (English/language arts), Society of School Librarians, 1993, Coretta Scott King Honor Award (illustration), Notable Children's Trade Book citation, National Council for the Social Studies, Notable Children's Book citation, American Library Association, and "Pick of the List" citation, *American Bookseller,* all 1994, and "Living the Dream" Award, 1995, all for *Uncle Jed's Barbershop.*

■ Writings

Uncle Jed's Barbershop, illustrated by James Ransome, Simon & Schuster, 1993.
Grandaddy's Gift, Bridgewater Books, 1996.

Also author of "Once Upon a Dream" (a script), presented in an Arkansas Screen Writers Association workshop, 1992; "Corporate Lies" (a script); "School's Out" (a television script), 1994; *The Hi-Rise* (a play); "Overflowing Waters" (a short story), *Purpose,* 1986;

and "Moment of Decision" (a short story), *Teens Today,* 1986, *Youth!,* 1987.

■ Work in Progress

Research on the Buffalo Soldiers.

■ Sidelights

Margaree King Mitchell's first book, *Uncle Jed's Barbershop,* provides children with a valuable lesson: with hard work and persistence, dreams can come true. According to Mary Luins Small, writing in the *Austin American-Statesman, Uncle Jed's Barbershop* is important in "these times when the demand for instant gratification causes many people to go dreamless." In addition, Small noted, the book helps children "understand the background of the civil rights movement."

"One of the deciding factors that caused me to write *Uncle Jed's Barbershop* occurred while I was volunteering in my son's first grade class," Mitchell explained to *SATA.* "There were some students in the class who had no support from home. This was the first time some of the students had even seen a book. They had no concept of why they were even in school. They constantly told me what they could not do. I knew that it was important that the children view themselves positively. I thought if I could somehow write a book that would inspire children to achieve their dreams, then maybe children

Uncle Jed endures many setbacks in the segregated South of the 1920s before he realizes his dream of opening his own barber shop in Mitchell's acclaimed book *Uncle Jed's Barbershop.*(Illustration by James Ransome.)

would be motivated to stay in school and look to the future for a better life for themselves."

Uncle Jed's niece, Sarah Jean, narrates the story in *Uncle Jed's Barbershop.* She recalls that Uncle Jed was a traveling barber, and the only black barber in the entire county. His clients, mostly sharecroppers, paid him money when they could, but they usually offered him chickens, eggs, vegetables, and butter instead. When Uncle Jed visited Sarah Jean's childhood home, he gave her pretend haircuts and shared his dream: to open a barbershop of his own. Although no one really believed that Jed would get his barbershop, he saved his money diligently.

When Sarah Jean fell ill, she had to wait in the "colored" waiting room at the hospital and the doctors would not treat her without receiving payment first. Uncle Jed, who was the only member of the family with enough money to make the payment, spent the money he had been saving for his shop in order to save her. Sarah Jean recovered, but Uncle Jed's dream continued to elude him. The $3,000 he managed to save at the bank was lost with the onset of the Great Depression, and he had to start saving all over again. Finally, at the age of seventy-nine, Uncle Jed opened his dream shop, and the family was present to celebrate. Even though Uncle Jed died soon afterward, Sarah Jean knew that he died happy. In addition, as the grown-up Sarah Jean relates, "He taught me to dream, too."

Reviewers have praised *Uncle Jed's Barbershop.* Roger Sutton of the *Bulletin of the Center for Children's Books,* for example, wrote that while the book is "honest about how difficult life was for black sharecroppers ... in the segregated South," it "isn't grim." Louise L. Sherman of *School Library Journal* observed that "Mitchell's text is eloquent in its simplicity" and concluded that the book is "touching and inspirational." Despite the positive reviews, however, Mitchell has relied on the opinions of children to determine whether or not her first book is a success.

She told *SATA,* "Shortly after *Uncle Jed's Barbershop* was published, I was invited to read the book to seven- and eight-year-olds during story hour at the public library. As I was leaving, a little girl was waiting for me by the door. She said to me, 'I liked your story about Uncle Jed. I want to be a doctor when I grow up. But my grandma keeps telling me that I never will be one. Now I know I can be a doctor.' I knew then that I had achieved my goal in writing *Uncle Jed's Barbershop.*"

■ **Works Cited**

Sherman, Louise L., review of *Uncle Jed's Barbershop, School Library Journal,* October, 1993, pp. 105-106.

Small, Mary Luins, review of *Uncle Jed's Barbershop, Austin American-Statesman,* January 16, 1994, p. F7.

Sutton, Roger, review of *Uncle Jed's Barbershop, Bulletin of the Center for Children's Books,* September, 1993, p. 19.

■ For More Information See

PERIODICALS

Booklist, September 1, 1993, p. 69.
Kirkus Reviews, July 15, 1993, p. 938.
Publishers Weekly, August 2, 1993, pp. 78-79.

* * *

MOFFETT, Jami 1952-

■ Personal

Born December 22, 1952, in Rochester, NY; daughter of Rupert (a teacher) and Judy (a writer) Rhinehart; married Jesse Seales (divorced); married Robert G. Moffett; children: Alexandra, Cale, Markell. *Education:* Attended Roberts Wesleyan College, 1971-73. *Politics:* "Neither party in particular, vote for the best candidate." *Religion:* "Bible-believing Christian, non-denominational." *Hobbies and other interests:* "Refinishing furniture, reading, drawing, volleyball, antiquing, and garage sale hunting for anything from the 1940s and back."

■ Addresses

Home—3719 Southwest 100th, Seattle, WA 98146. *Electronic mail*—ALCAMA@A.O.L.

■ Career

Illustrator. Worked previously as a waitress and in the music retail industry, including ten years as a sign and display artist for Tower Records. *Member:* Colored Pencil Society of America.

■ Illustrator

Mary Marecek, *Breaking Free from Partner Abuse: Voices of Battered Women Caught in the Cycle of Domestic Violence,* Morning Glory Press, 1993.
Kathryn Ann Miller, *Did My First Mother Love Me?: A Story for an Adopted Child,* Morning Glory Press, 1994.
Christine L. Schmitt, *It Takes a Lot of Courage,* Paulist Press, 1995.

Also illustrator of the cover for *Too Soon for Jeff,* Morning Glory Press; illustrator of Spring Quarter Bible pictures, and of an instruction booklet for *Jubilee!* Contributor of illustrations to magazines, including *Aglow, Creator, Reader, Mission Media, Mother's at Home, Parents with Teenagers,* and *Vista.*

■ Sidelights

Jami Moffett explained to *SATA* her desire to illustrate: "I love starting with a blank piece of paper and seeing a piece unfold before my eyes. The drawing begins to unfold and emotions flow out of my head into my hand and onto the paper. It is a form of stress relief, I get a sense of self-esteem from it all and I thoroughly enjoy

JAMI MOFFETT

both the process and the end result. There is no question in my mind that the gift of drawing was given to me from God and therefore I try to use that gift accordingly. I work with Christian publications as much as possible, or for something with a message."

In addition to the satisfaction she gains from the actual illustrating process itself, Moffett had other reasons for choosing this field of employment. "I enjoy it so much, and it was a 'job' that allowed me to create my own hours around the children," she related to *SATA.* "While we would be able to buy more *things* if I had a regular job, with benefits and all, a steady paycheck ... still I would barely see the children and someone else would be raising them. That's an important factor to me. I love to draw and illustration was a natural choice. I love to draw children, so illustrating children's books and magazines fit the bill."*

* * *

MOLAN, Christine 1943-

■ Personal

Born July 3, 1943, in Bristol, England; married Barrie Morgan (a musician), March 18, 1977; children: Will, Jenny. *Education:* University of the West of England, B.A. (first class honors). *Politics:* Socialist. *Religion:* Church of England. *Hobbies and other interests:* Social history, archeology, folk music.

■ Addresses

Office—27 Cotham Rd., Cotham, Bristol BS6 6DJ, England.

■ Career

Illustrator and writer. University of the West of England, Bristol, England, part-time and visiting lecturer on illustration. Bristol City Museum, Departments of Archaeology and Education Services, Bristol, England, Bristol Castle Project liaison, 1992-93. *Member:* Association of Illustrators.

■ Writings

SELF-ILLUSTRATED

The Vikings in Vinland, Belitha Press (London), 1985, published as *The Story of the Vikings,* Torstar, 1986.
The Viking Saga (based on translations of the Groenlendinga saga and Eirik's saga by Magnus Magnusson and Herman Palsson, originally published as *The Vinland Sagas,* 1965), Raintree, 1985.

ILLUSTRATOR; FOLKLORE AND FICTION FOR CHILDREN

Henry Wadsworth Longfellow, *Hiawatha,* Raintree, 1984.
Felicity Trotman and Shirley Greenway, retellers, *Davy Crockett,* Raintree, Torstar, 1986.
Michael Morpurgo, *Jo-Jo the Melon Donkey,* Prentice-Hall, 1987.
Trotman, *William Tell,* Raintree, 1988.
Anne De Graaf, reteller, *Heidi,* Crossway, 1989.
Tim Vicary, *Mrs. Pankhurst,* Oxford University Press, 1990.
Anthony Masters, compiler, *Heroic Stories,* Kingfisher Books, 1994.

ILLUSTRATOR; "PEOPLE OF THE BIBLE" SERIES; RETOLD BY CATHERINE STORR

Jesus Begins His Work, Raintree, 1982.
Joseph and His Brothers, Raintree, 1982.
Miracles by the Sea, Raintree, 1983.
The First Easter, Raintree, 1984.
Joseph the Dream Teller, Raintree, 1984.
David and Goliath, Raintree, 1985.
Jesus and John the Baptist, Raintree, 1985.
Joseph and the Famine, Raintree, 1985.
Jesus the Healer, Raintree, 1986.

ILLUSTRATOR; NONFICTION

Fiona Macdonald, *Drake and the Armada,* Hampstead Press, 1988.
Peter Ryan, *Explorers and Mapmakers,* Hamish Hamilton, 1989, Lodestar, 1990.
Margaret Berrill, *Mummies, Masks and Mourners,* Hamish Hamilton, 1989, Lodestar, 1990.
Geoffrey Trease, *Hidden Treasure,* Dutton, 1989.
Chris Chelepi, *Growing Up in Ancient Greece,* Eagle, 1990, Troll, 1993.
Mike Corbishley, *Growing Up in Ancient Rome,* Eagle, 1990, Troll, 1993.

Christine Molan has illustrated many books about history, including this illustration for *Growing Up in Ancient Greece* by Chris Chelepi.

Michael Poulton, *Life in the Time of Augustus,* Cherry-tree, 1991, Mirabel Books, 1992, published as *Augustus and the Ancient Romans,* Raintree Steck-Vaughn, 1993.
Bible World, Volumes 1-6, Lion Publishing, 1993-94.

OTHER

Also Illustrator of *Flora MacDonald,* by Mollie Hunter; *A Gift for Hans* and *She Was Good For Nothing,* both by Hans Christian Andersen, Scandinavia Publishing House; *The Adventures of Tom Sawyer* and *Huckleberry Finn,* both by Mark Twain, Longman; *Columbus,* by Ronald Latham, Macdonald Educational. Contributor to educational and historical series, including *Oxford Junior History,* Volumes 1 and 2, 1983-86; contributor to English course and foreign language course material published by Oxford University Press, Longman Group, and Mary Glasgow Books. Illustrator of black and white line drawings and over two hundred book covers for authors including Jill Paton Walsh, William Armstrong, K. M. Peyton, Meryl Doney, Leon Garfield, Betsy Byars, Pete Johnson, John Rowe Townsend, and Michelle Magorian, and published by Collins, C.U.P., Penguin, Simon & Schuster, Transworld, and Walker Books.

■ Work in Progress

Exploration of oil mediums in a fine art painting course.

■ Sidelights

Christine Molan explained to *SATA* how her childhood shaped her career as a writer and illustrator. "I was often confined to bed as a child with chronic asthma. I read and drew avidly. When I read, pictures came to mind (and it was a great escape from worry about missing the academic side of school!) Later, in my teen years, I loved Shakespeare and social history, and after some years as a graphic designer, I returned, at the age of twenty-nine, to study an illustration course at Bristol—where all my earlier interests fell into place. I have never looked back."

Although, as she revealed to *SATA*, Molan works "in chaos," she is well aware of the messages and feelings she wants to send her readers. "I am deeply interested in social history, how people lived and, more recently, in archaeology too. I can't bear to hear anyone (especially a child) say that 'history is BORING' because history is about us, ordinary people, generation after generation, dealing within the communications, technology, and ethics of each period in time. I wish I could convey that—it's always my aim. I collect historical artifacts and ephemera to keep this in mind. My earlier love of drama and classic literature makes me want the reader/ viewer to get into the scene—I love the dramatic effects of weather, interesting lighting, and real locations."

■ For More Information See

PERIODICALS

Junior Bookshelf, October, 1986, p. 187.*

*   *   *

MULLINS, Hilary 1962-

■ Personal

Born June 19, 1962, in Stamford, CT; daughter of Ronald Richard Mullins (a marketing consultant) and Janet Hayward Burnham (a writer and artist); companion of April Evans (a nonprofit administrator). *Education:* Wesleyan University, B.A., 1984. *Politics:* "Ecofeminist." *Religion:* "Pagan."

■ Addresses

Office—c/o Publicity Director, Naiad Press, Inc., P.O. Box 10543, Tallahassee, FL 32302.

■ Career

Onion River Co-op, Burlington, VT, shift worker, 1987-91; Pacific Research and Training Alliance, Oakland, CA, administrative assistant, 1991-93; freelance writer, 1993—.

■ Awards, Honors

Lambda Gay and Lesbian Literary Award in Young Adult Fiction, 1993, for *The Cat Came Back.*

■ Writings

YOUNG ADULT

The Cat Came Back, Naiad Press, 1993.

HILARY MULLINS

OTHER

Cats (and Their Dykes), Her Books, 1991.
The Romantic Naiad, Naiad Press, 1993.
Women on Women III, Plume, 1993.
Sleeping with Dionysus, Women, Ecstasy and Addition, Crossing Press, 1994.
The Mysterious Naiad, Naiad Press, 1994.
Tomboys!, Alyson Publications, 1995.

■ Work in Progress

Bringing Small Things in from the Dark, a novel; *Wild Blue,* a screenplay.

■ Sidelights

Hilary Mullins's first novel, *The Cat Came Back,* is written in the form of the diary of seventeen-year-old Stephanie Roughgarden, who goes by the name Stevie. The journal entries begin in January of 1980, when Stevie is a senior at a preppy Connecticut private school and captain of the varsity girls' ice hockey team, and end on graduation day, June 7, 1980. Stevie is involved in several troubling relationships. The ice hockey coach is so verbally and physically abusive that several of the team members quit, and Stevie must decide whether to follow suit or bow to the headmaster's pressure to stay. Stevie is also in the midst of a three-year sexual affair with Rik, an English teacher who seduced her when she was fourteen, and she has failed to live up to her father's expectations about getting into Harvard.

Throughout all this angst and chaos, Stevie find herself increasingly attracted to and eventually falling in love

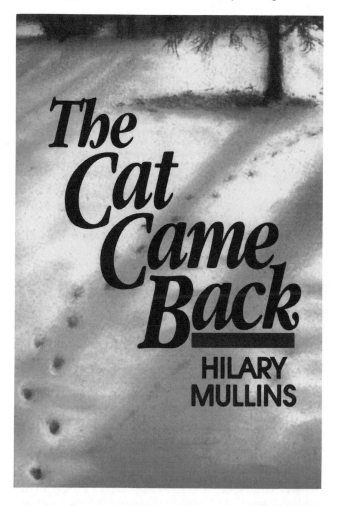

Mullins sensitively explores the issue of lesbianism in this novel about seventeen-year-old Stevie Roughgarden's sexual awakening.

with the vivacious Andrea Snyder, an ice hockey teammate. The two develop a strong friendship which eventually grows into a tender and passionate romance. A reviewer in *Publishers Weekly* noted that Mullins creates a "sympathetic portrayal of Stevie coming to terms with her lesbianism." The diary entries continue on as Stevie goes through what Hazel Rochman, writing in *Booklist,* calls her "initial attraction and excitement, then her doubt and denial." Rochman concluded that "many teenagers will recognize their conflicts here."

Mullins told *SATA:* "Ever since I went into therapy about ten years ago and saw how I began to open and change for the better, I have had an ongoing fascination with (and respect for) the possibility of transformation in every human being. Consequently, most of my writing since that point has been about transformation, about people who feel stuck and hopeless but who then find some part of themselves they were not aware of, some part, often a bit mysterious, leading them willynilly toward the light and what they need to begin actualizing their potential.

"I wrote my first novel, *The Cat Came Back,* to chart one girl's progress out of a situation of harm toward a relationship of mutual respect and affection. I wrote this book in the hope that other people, both younger and older, could see through it their own potential for selfempowerment and change."

■ Works Cited

Review of *The Cat Came Back, Publishers Weekly,* August 2, 1993, p. 77.
Rochman, Hazel, review of *The Cat Came Back, Booklist,* October 1, 1993, p. 331.

■ For More Information See

PERIODICALS

Booklist, March 15, 1994, p. 1361.
Voice of Youth Advocates, December, 1993, p. 296.

N–O

NEWBERGER, Devra
   See SPEREGEN, Devra Newberger

* * *

NEWELL, Crosby
   See BONSALL, Crosby Barbara
   (Newell)

* * *

NIVOLA, Claire A. 1947-

■ Personal

Born October 10, 1947, in New York, NY; daughter of Costantino (a sculptor) and Ruth (a housewife and jewelry maker; maiden name, Guggenheim) Nivola; married Timothy Gus Kiley (in publishing), September 18, 1982; children: Anther N. Kiley, Alycia A. Kiley. *Education:* Radcliffe College, B.A. (magna cum laude), 1969.

■ Addresses

Home—6 Columbus St., Newton Highlands, MA 02161.

■ Career

Freelance illustrator, painter, sculptor, graphic designer. Urban Systems Research and Engineering (consulting firm), Cambridge, MA, graphic designer, 1975-80; *Newsweek,* New York City, graphic designer, 1980-83. Freelance children's book illustrator, 1970-78, 1994; has done commissioned work, including paintings, sculptures, and bas-reliefs in Tennessee and Boston, MA, throughout the 1970s, and 1992; freelance designer for Shady Hill School, Routledge and Kegan Paul, and Sigo Press, 1984-86.

■ Illustrator

Maria Cimino, *The Disobedient Eels and Other Italian Tales,* Pantheon, 1970.
Henry Horenstein, *Black and White Photography,* Little, Brown, 1974.
Betty Miles, *Save the Earth! An Ecology Handbook for Kids,* Knopf, 1974.
Ruth Nivola, *The Messy Rabbit,* Pantheon Books, 1978, published in England as *The Unready Rabbit.*
Betty Jean Lifton, *Tell Me a Real Adoption Story,* Knopf, 1994.

Also illustrator of books by Fabio Coen.

■ Sidelights

Claire A. Nivola told *SATA:* "As I consult my resume ... I realize just what a piecemeal process my 'career' has been. The daughter of an artist father and a mother equally gifted with her hands, I drew and sculpted from earliest childhood, often by my father's side in his studio. School—the very fine education I received and which I do not regret—is what probably broke the spell. Being a conscientious student meant that, over the years, I increasingly spent more time at my school work and less time drawing. Having grown up surrounded by art, I took art somewhat for granted, like breathing and walking, and once out of college, found that I did not approach my trade with drive or ambition, and certainly not with the savvy of self-promotion. Because of this my course was uncertain: I tried illustration, mural painting, exhibiting works done on my own, and graphic design—all attempts to find an application of my skills to something that might become a profession.

"My first 'break' was in children's book illustration. My father had been asked to illustrate a collection of Italian fables by the then head of Pantheon children's books, a fellow Italian named Fabio Coen. My father gave the job to me, and over the next eight years Fabio Coen gave me two more books to illustrate and a good deal of encouragement.

CLAIRE A. NIVOLA

"At 35 I married and had, over the next three years, two children. I was tempted to fill in 'motherhood' under the category of 'Primary Career,' because motherhood has been the most true and fulfilling time of my life. Swimming against the contemporary tide, I stayed home with my children, and continue to do so, eleven years later. What work I have taken on was only what could be done at home, without sacrificing my time as a mother. Even the large commission of 53 bas-relief panels for the Aquarium in Chatanooga, Tennessee in 1992, was done in the playroom by the kitchen, with my son and daughter commenting on each panel before it was shipped off for casting. That project, although in sculpture form, was closely related to book illustration. The panels, which are set into the Aquarium's external walls at intervals, tell the story of man's changing relationship to the Tennessee river from early times through to the present day. Two years later, I was asked to illustrate Betty Jean Lifton's *Tell Me a Real Adoption Story*. The editor at Knopf was someone I had known some twenty years before in the offices of Fabio Coen!

"It seems I am coming full circle. Having passed many years reading to my own children—often more than once—the books I loved as a child, as well as discovering new ones, my appreciation for the best of children's literature has only grown stronger. Writing for children,

I feel, is a serious business. The words *and* the images become a vivid part of a child's childhood and that is a responsiblity I would never take lightly."

* * *

OAKLEY, Graham 1929-

■ Personal

Born August 27, 1929, in Shrewsbury, Shropshire, England; son of Thomas (a shop manager) and Flora (Madeley) Oakley. *Education:* Attended Warrington Art School, 1950. *Politics:* Labour Party. *Religion:* Church of England. *Hobbies and other interests:* Music.

■ Addresses

Home and office—1 Upper Camden Pl., Bath, England. *Agent*—c/o Macmillan Children's Books, 4 Little Essex St., London WC2R 3LF, England.

■ Career

Freelance artist and book illustrator, 1957-60, 1977—. Scenic artist for English repertory companies, 1950-55; Royal Opera House, Covent Garden, London, England,

GRAHAM OAKLEY

designer's assistant, 1955-57; worked for Crawford's Advertisting Agency, 1960-62; British Broadcasting Corporation, London, television set designer for motion pictures and series, including *How Green Was My Valley, Nicholas Nickleby, Treasure Island,* and *Softly, Softly,* 1962-77. *Military service:* British Army, 1945-47.

■ Awards, Honors

Kate Greenaway Medal high commendation, 1976, and *New York Times* Best Illustrated Children's Books of the Year citation, 1977, both for *The Church Mice Adrift;* Illustration Special Citation, *Boston Globe-Horn Book,* 1980, for *Graham Oakley's Magical Changes;* Kate Greenaway Medal commendation, and Kurt Maschler Award runner-up, Book Trust, both 1982, for *The Church Mice in Action.*

■ Writings

AND ILLUSTRATOR

The Church Mouse, Atheneum, 1972.
The Church Cat Abroad, Atheneum, 1973.
The Church Mice and the Moon, Atheneum, 1974.
The Church Mice Spread Their Wings, Macmillan (London), 1975, Atheneum, 1976.
The Church Mice Adrift, Macmillan, 1976, Atheneum, 1977.
The Church Mice at Christmas, Atheneum, 1980.
Graham Oakley's Magical Changes, Atheneum, 1980.
Hetty and Harriet, Atheneum, 1981.
The Church Mice in Action, Macmillan, 1982, Atheneum, 1983.

Henry's Quest, Atheneum, 1986.
The Diary of a Church Mouse, Macmillan, 1986, Atheneum, 1987.
The Church Mice Chronicles (contains *The Church Mouse, The Church Cat Abroad,* and *The Church Mice and the Moon*), Macmillan, 1986.
Once Upon a Time: A Prince's Fantastic Journey, Macmillan, 1990.
More Church Mice Chronicles, Macmillan, 1990.
The Church Mice and the Ring, Atheneum, 1992.
The Foxbury Force, Macmillan, 1994.

ILLUSTRATOR

John Ruskin, *The King of the Golden River,* Hutchinson, 1958.
Robert Louis Stevenson, *Kidnapped,* Dent, 1959.
Hugh Popham, *Fabulous Voyage of the Pegasus,* S. G. Phillips & Co., 1959.
Charles Kervern, *White Horizons,* University of London Press, 1962.

Arthur, Humphrey, and Sampson the cat are forced out of the Wortlethorpe Church Vestry by errant rats, until Sampson devises a unique plan to get their home back in *The Church Mice Adrift.* (Illustration by the author.)

Mollie Clarke, adaptor, *The Three Feathers: A German Folk Tale Retold,* Hart-Davis, 1963, Follett, 1968.

Richard Garnett, *The White Dragon,* Hart-Davis, 1963, Vanguard, 1964.

Garnett, *Jack of Dover,* Vanguard, 1966.

Brian Read, *The Water Wheel,* World's Work, 1970.

Tanith Lee, *Dragon Hoard,* Farrar, Straus, 1971.

Elizabeth MacDonald, *The Two Sisters,* World's Work, 1975.

Also illustrator of *Monsters and Marlinspikes* by Hugh Popham, 1958; *Discovering the Bible* by David Scott Daniell, 1961; *Skillywidden,* by Mollie Clarke, 1965; *The Bird-Catcher and the Crow-Peri,* by Clarke, 1968; *Grandmother's Footsteps,* by Patricia Ledward, 1966; *Stories Told around the World,* by Taya Zinkin, 1968; and *The Ancient World,* by Robert Ogilvie, 1969. Oakley's work has been published in Germany and Japan.

■ Sidelights

As he told *Publishers Weekly,* Graham Oakley thinks that "the picture book for young children should be the work of the same person as author of the plot and illustrator." In Oakley's own picture books, especially those of the popular "Church Mice" series, the text complements, rather than dominates, the illustrations: the subdued text provides an understated or even contradictory summary of the action in the highly detailed, often hilariously chaotic illustrations that fill each page. While some critics complain that the illustrations in the Church Mice series are busy and confusing, other critics, and many children, are delighted by them.

With so much emphasis on the pictures rather than the prose, Oakley's books succeed because, as critics have noted, his illustrations are thoughtful, well drafted, and invested with emotion. As Jane Langton commented in a *New York Times Book Review* article on *The Church Mice Adrift,* the "brilliant author-artist ... draws like an angel." According to Langton, Oakley provides "an Olympian view" as well as every "small detail" at once in his illustrations. In the words of *New York Times Book Review* contributor Elaine Edelman in a review of *Hetty and Harriet,* Oakley approaches his stories like a "film director," viewing the action from various perspectives.

Oakley, who has worked as a designer at the Royal Opera House and for the British Broadcasting Corporation, conceived of the "Church Mice" books when he

Santa brings the church mice some delectable treats in the happy conclusion to *The Church Mice at Christmas.* (Illustration by the author.)

was animating the stories of other writers as a freelance illustrator. He planned on writing and illustrating a series of stories about the buildings in a fictional, small English town. After Oakley created the town of Wortle-thorpe and its church and gave literary life to the cat and mice which inhabit the church in *The Church Mouse,* he abandoned his former plan and continued to invent new church mice stories.

The Church Mouse introduces Arthur, a mouse, and Sampson, a large orange tabby cat. Living in the church has reformed Sampson; he refuses to harm the meek mice and treats Arthur like a brother. He helps Arthur get board and a job for himself and the town's mice at the church. The mice come to rely on Sampson, especially when there's heavy physical work to do. A scene in which the mice allow Sampson to babysit their children exemplifies Oakley's use of understated text and flamboyant illustrations: the text assures readers that the mice "didn't mind a bit about hurting his [Sampson's] feelings, or any other part of him for that matter," while the illustrations show the little mice getting ready to pour ink on Sampson, binding him with string, swinging from his whiskers, tying his whiskers, dipping his tail in glue, and swimming in his milk bowl.

When Sampson falls asleep during a sermon, he unconsciously chases the mice throughout the church: the ensuing uproar disturbs the congregation. Although the mice are fired from their job, they decide to take action when a burglar attempts to rob the church. Foiling the crook's plan when they pile up pyramid-style on top of Sampson and ring the church bell to wake the townspeople, the mice are forgiven because of their brave deed. Margery Fisher praised the story in *Growing Point,* as well as the illustrations, saying that the "story goes with a swing and the slapstick and circumstantial detail are livened with a measure of wit." She later remarked that the illustrations "must be studied with care, for there is a great deal to be seen and admired." *New York Times Book Review* critic Judy Noyes wrote that children "should find" the book's "lively touch of nonsense" irresistible.

The Church Cat Abroad continues the adventures of Sampson and his mice friends. In order to earn money to fix the church roof, Sampson sees a television agent who finds him a job starring in a cat food commercial. Sampson and two other mice travel to a South Sea island for the shoot. This second church mice book also received favorable reviews. While *School Library Journal* contributor M. K. Pace worried that some children would not be familiar with some of Oakley's British colloquialisms, the critic thought they would appreciate the "delightful double entendres" of the illustrations. Edward Hudson commented in *Children's Book Review* that the illustrations of characters are "drawn and painted with the eye of a talented analytical artist."

Arthur and Humphrey leave home on their own in *The Church Mice Spread Their Wings,* an owl carries them to the belfry of the church, and they glide away in a paper airplane. After a few complicated adventures, they

In *The Church Mice in Action* the mice enter Sampson in a cat show, but when he is catnapped they must come to his rescue. (Illustration by the author.)

return home to discover that their friends thought they were dead and enjoy the funeral they have lovingly prepared for them. According to Langton in another *New York Times Book Review,* this book "fairly bulges with extravagant detail" and the illustrations are "made with joy and loving care and passion."

By the time *The Church Mice Adrift* was published in 1976, according to Elaine Moss in the *Times Literary Supplement,* the church mice stories had become "established favourites in the eight to ten age group." The fourth book in the series features a battle between the mice and rats, whose homes are being destroyed by developers. *The Church Mice at Bay* in the words of *Horn Book* reviewer Ann A. Flowers, is a "witty commentary" on life in a town like Wortlethorpe. A critic for *Babbling Bookworm Newsletter* described it as "a comic masterpiece."

The "Church Mice" series continues with *The Church Mice at Christmas* and *The Church Mice in Action.* In the first of these books, the church mice once again thwart the intentions of a robber. This time, however, the robber is disguised as Santa Claus. In *The Church Mice in Action,* Sampson enters a cat show to earn money for the church roof. When Sampson is kidnapped, the mice rescue him with a clever plan. This book, like the others in the church mice series, provides a dismal view of humanity and celebrates mouse society; as Donnarae MacCann and Olga Richard wrote in *Wilson Library Bulletin,* tastelessly dressed people are crowded and living in "urban congestion" in the illustrations while an "appealing population of animals" inhabits "peaceful landscapes."

The Diary of a Church Mouse begins with Humphrey's New Year's resolution to write his life story. When Arthur tells him that he is still too young to write his memoirs, Humphrey starts to keep a diary. He relates a year's worth of memorable events and ends the diary at Christmas, when 57 mice, all intending to surprise the mouse children, dress up as Santa. *The Church Mice and the Ring* begins when a dog named Percy wanders into the churchyard. The church mice and Samson care for

him as best they can, but they can't feed him enough to keep him satisfied. The cat and mice think sending Percy home with a little girl who falls in love with him will make everyone happy, but first they must convince the girl's parents to love the puppy too. In the process, they break into a jewelry store and are sent to jail.

As Oakley worked on the books in his Church Mice series, he began some new projects. Two of these, *Hetty and Harriet* and *The Foxbury Force,* present the same wild plots and chaotic illustrations of the "Church Mice" series but feature new characters and settings. Hetty and Harriet are hens who leave the farm in search of a "perfect place" and almost wind up in an "Egg Production Plant," among other inappropriate places for sentient chickens. In the end, Hetty and Harriet find

Two silly hens discover that leaving their farmyard to search for a perfect place to live might not be such a bright idea in this 1981 story. (Cover illustration by the author.)

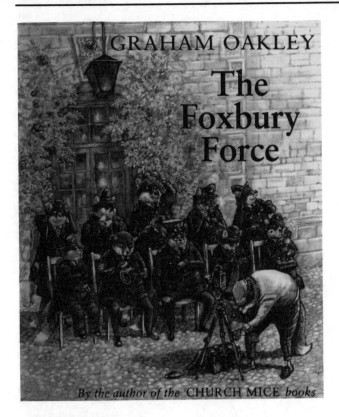

GRAHAM OAKLEY

The Foxbury Force

By the author of the CHURCH MICE books

The police of the Foxbury Constabulary have a neat little arrangement with the Town Burglars, until one day when the Foreman Burglar decides to spoil it all—with hilarious results. (Cover illustration by the author.)

that their old farm is the "perfect place" for them. According to Linda Yeatman in *British Book News,* the hens are "portrayed with ... affection, humour and realism." *Junior Bookshelf* critic Marcus Crouch concluded that the work is "as sound in its social implications as it is excellent fun."

Oakley creates a humorous fictional world—populated by foxes—in *The Foxbury Force,* where police and crooks have created a comfortable relationship in which the robbers will steal their booty but then allow themselves to be caught each time. Trouble comes when the crooks decide to have a real robbery, and the Foxbury Force must rely on their long-unused resourcefulness to catch them after they burglarize a castle. *The Foxbury Force,* in the words of a critic for *Junior Bookshelf,* is "relentlessly funny."

Henry's Quest and *Once Upon a Time* both involve quests. The first book is set in a dismal future in which punk-rock kings inhabit "castles" (the shells of abandoned department stores). Although the king of Henry's land does not know what gasoline is, he thinks that it will make the king's collection of old cars work again and sends Henry to find it. *Once Upon a Time* is the story of a prince and his page who set out to find a bride for the prince. When the prince recklessly drives the pair into Storyland, they find themselves in the middle of several familiar fairy tales. While the prince does not

recognize the cues he needs to play his role in the fairy tales, his page gives him wise advise and their quest is a success.

While many of his books have been praised for their illustrations, Oakley stretched his artistic skills to their experimental limits in the award-winning *Graham Oakley's Magical Changes.* Unlike his other books *Magical Changes* has no text. In this "brilliant and bizarre" book, as Leigh Dean described it in *Children's Book Review Service,* Oakley presents a painting containing vertical bars on each of thirty-two horizontally-split pages. By turning either the top or bottom of the pages, the reader may discover over 4,000 new illustrations linked by continuous bars. For example, as Elaine Moss, writing in *Signal,* explained, a picture of six men carrying six umbrellas (their handles are the bars) becomes a picture of men holding six lollipops (the bars are the lollipop sticks), or six spaghetti strands. The result, as a reviewer for *Publishers Weekly* observed, is either "comic or fearful surrealism." After noting that the "basic," unflipped pictures are "in themselves, satiric," *World of Children's Books* reviewer Jon C. Stott concluded that *Magical Changes* "offers a often humorous, often ironic commentary on life." Moss asserted in *Signal* that this "experiment in picture-book making ... is likely to become a landmark in the history of the genre."

■ Works Cited

Review of *The Church Mouse at Bay, Babbling Bookworm Newsletter,* November, 1979, p. 3.

"A Conversation with Graham Oakley," *Publishers Weekly,* February 26, 1979, pp. 74-5.

Crouch, Marcus, review of *Hetty and Harriet, Junior Bookshelf,* February, 1982, p.19.

Dean, Leigh, review of *Graham Oakley's Magical Changes, Children's Book Review Service,* June, 1980, p. 103.

Edelman, Elaine, review of *Hetty and Harriet, New York Times Book Review,* May 30, 1982, p. 14.

Hudson, Edward, review of *The Church Cat Abroad, Children's Book Review,* spring, 1974, p. 12.

Fisher, Margery, review of *The Church Mouse, Growing Point,* November, 1972, pp. 2027-28.

Flowers, Ann A., review of *The Church Mice at Bay, Horn Book,* June, 1979, p. 294.

Review of *The Foxbury Force, Junior Bookshelf,* June, 1994, p. 97.

Review of *Graham Oakley's Magical Changes, Publishers Weekly,* February 15, 1980, p. 110.

Langton, Jane, review of *The Church Mice Adrift, New York Times Book Review,* May 8, 1977, p. 41.

Langton, Jane, review of *The Church Mice Spread Their Wings, New York Times Book Review,* May 2, 1976, p. 46.

MacCann, Donnarae, and Olga Richard, review of *The Church Mice in Action, Wilson Library Bulletin,* October, 1983, p. 131.

Moss, Elaine, "A Delicate Balance," *Times Literary Supplement,* December 10, 1976, p. 1551.

Moss, Elaine, "W[h]ither Picture Books? Some Tricks of the Trade," *Signal,* January, 1980, pp. 3-7.

Noyes, Judy, review of *The Church Mouse, New York Times Book Review,* December 10, 1972, p. 8.

Oakley, Graham, *The Church Mouse,* Atheneum, 1972.

Pace, M. K., review of *The Church Cat Abroad, School Library Journal,* December, 1973, p. 44.

Stott, Jon C., review of *Magical Changes, The World of Children's Books,* 1981, p. 26.

Yeatman, Linda, review of *Hetty and Harriet, British Book News,* spring, 1982, p. 3.

■ For More Information See

BOOKS

Children's Literature Review, Volume 7, Gale, 1984, pp. 212-23.

PERIODICALS

Booklist, November 15, 1992, p. 610.
Bulletin of the Center for Children's Books, March, 1987, p. 133.
Junior Bookshelf, August, 1990, p. 165.
New York Times Book Review, May 4, 1975, p. 42.
Punch, January 16, 1980.
School Librarian, November, 1990, pp. 143-44.
School Library Journal, April, 1975, p. 42; December, 1986, p. 107.
Spectator, November 11, 1972, pp. 759-60.

*   *   *

OLIVIERO, Jamie 1950-

■ Personal

Born February 9, 1950, in New York, NY; son of Vincent James (in industrial management) and Beth (a teacher; maiden name, Fabricant) Oliviero; married Dianne Movoz (a teacher), August 27, 1988; children: Luke, Ben. *Education:* South Hampton College, B.F.A., 1972; studied at H.B. Studio, New York; studied with Tony Montanarro, Master Mime and Storyteller, Portland, ME; studied with performers from the Big Apple Circus, New York.

■ Addresses

Home—1003 Warsaw Ave., Winnipeg, Manitoba R3M ICI, Canada.

■ Career

Performing Arts Foundation of Long Island, Long Island, NY, performer and musician, teacher of mime, clowning, and improvisation, and Arts-in-Education specialist (school visitor), 1972-78; Manitoba Theatre Workshop, Manitoba, Canada, director of theatre school, 1978-80; independent artist working in schools through the Manitoba Arts Council Artist-in-Schools program, and independently in Fukoka School, Ninohe,

JAMIE OLIVIERO

Japan (1989), Kunai College, Morwell, Australia (1990), and Bangkok, Thailand (1990), Kenya, and New York, 1981—; affiliated with productions for the Manitoba Theatre for Young People, Prairie Theatre Exchange, Fort Whyte Nature Centre, Winnipeg International Children's Festival, Winnipeg Folk Festival, and CBC Radio and Television.

■ Writings

The Fish Skin, illustrated by Brent Morriseau, Hyperion, 1993.

Som See and the Magic Elephant, illustrated by Jo'Anne Kelly, Hyperion, 1995.

The Day Sun Was Stolen, illustrated by Sharon Hitchcock, Hyperion, 1995.

■ Sidelights

Jamie Oliviero told *SATA,* "I am first and foremost a storyteller; part of an ancient and honorable profession. It's something that I've grown into and continue to grow with. I spend most of my time working in schools, performing and teaching workshops. Each day reveals to me more and more the power of stories to teach, explain, entertain, and most of all to touch people and make them aware of their own thoughts and feelings."

■ For More Information See

PERIODICALS

School Library Journal, May, 1995, pp. 93-94.*

P

ROBERT PATEMAN

PATEMAN, Robert 1954-

■ Personal

Born April 7, 1954, in London, England; son of William Ernest (a builder) and Ivy (a dressmaker; maiden name, Hawks) Pateman; married Anne Margaret Braseby. *Education:* Southampton University, England, B.Ed. (with honors). *Politics:* "No strong feelings. I have been out of England too long to closely follow British politics." *Religion:* Church of England. *Hobbies and other interests:* Stamp collecting, travel, photography, jogging, amateur dramatics.

■ Addresses

Office—17 Hawthorn Close, Langley Green, Crawley, Sussex, England.

■ Career

International School of Tanganyika, fourth-grade teacher, 1982-85; El Alsson School, Cairo, Egypt, kindergarten teacher, 1985-87; International School of Beijing, China, sixth-grade and physical education teacher, 1987-90; Jakarta International School, computer teacher, 1990-94; full-time writer, 1994—. *Member:* Jakarta Players (drama group), Jakarta Hash House Harriers.

■ Writings

AND PHOTOGRAPHER

Cultures of the World: Egypt, Times Editions, 1992.
Cultures of the World: Kenya, Times Editions, 1993.
Cultures of the World: Denmark, Times Editions, 1995.
Cultures of the World: Belgium, Times Editions, 1996.
Cultures of the World: Bolivia, Times Editions, 1996.

Also provided 37 photographs for *Travel Bug Guide to China,* Sun Tree, 1994. Photographs have also appeared in *Women in Society—Kenya, Women in Society— Egypt, Cultures of the World: Burma, Travel Bug Guide to Britain,* and the first Tanzanian Wildlife Calendar.

OTHER

Co-author with Gary Gentry of a play, *Heart of Hope,* first amateur production, 1995. Also contributor of over 200 articles to magazines, including *New African, The Middle East, Newslinks, Junior Education, Stamp Monthly, South China Morning Post, Cairo Today, VISIT ASEAN, Railways News, World Soccer, Basketball News, Trailfinder,* and *Athletic Weekly.*

■ Work in Progress

Two more books for the "Cultures of the World" series, on Iceland and Costa Rica; a children's book retelling traditional puppet stories from around the world.

■ Sidelights

Robert Pateman told *SATA:* "I suppose I have always wanted to write. It is not something that has grown or developed, it's just something that has always been there. I don't think a day has gone by since I left college that I have not written or at least thought about writing. Yet strangely I am not sure I actually enjoy the process of writing. I love the search for the original idea: traveling in a new city and finding a subject to write about; hearing a conversation at dinner and writing it down on a napkin; hunting through old brown newspapers and stumbling across some forgotten news item. I love, at the other end of the process, seeing my work in print. Placing an article in a new magazine is always a great feeling. When my first book was published I must have picked it up and glanced through it every single day for more than a year. Yet the actual writing often feels like hard work, and I hate the proofreading and frustration of reading something for a fourth or fifth time and still finding mistakes."

"After college I started teaching, and that was when I also started writing magazine articles regularly. I mainly write about collecting, sport, and travel—but I suppose I am quite versatile. I have written articles on subjects such as Islam in China or conservation in African game parks. After four years of teaching in England, my wife and I accepted jobs at the International School in Tanzania, where we taught the children of the diplomat and business community. At the time we thought we would only be overseas for a couple of years, but that was twelve years ago, and we still have no plans to return to England. After Tanzania, we went to Cairo, to Beijing, and then to Jakarta, which is still our home. The experiences have been incredible. We have camped in the middle of the Egyptian desert, hiked to remote hill tribes in Flores, walked out of our tent in Africa and come face to face with elephants. We were in China at the time of the Tien-an Men Square massacre, something else I plan to write about one day."

"My first book was *Egypt* in the *Cultures of the World* series. I had six months set aside to write the book when I received an urgent phone call. Times Editions were going to postpone their *Russia* title and they wanted to bring *Egypt* forward. Could I have it written and finished in eight weeks? To be honest I didn't know, but when you are trying to establish yourself I feel you take whatever is going, so I agreed. To make matters worse the eight weeks fell across the Christmas holidays and I was traveling in India. I wrote the book on planes, buses, trains, and rickshaws. One golden moment saw me sitting in front of the Taj Mahal while I wrote about the Great Pyramids of Giza!"

■ For More Information See

PERIODICALS

Horn Book Guide, spring, 1993, p. 148; fall, 1993, p. 386.
School Library Journal, March, 1993, pp. 206, 208; July, 1993, p. 108.

* * *

PETERS, Patricia 1953-

■ Personal

Born September 16, 1953, in East Chicago, IN; daughter of Peter Silaghi and Stella (Suchanuk) Waite. *Education:* Indiana University, B.F.A., 1976, M.F.A., 1981; attended Art Institute of Chicago and Central School of Art and Design, London, England. *Hobbies and other interests:* "Travel, gardening, strong interest in comparative religion and the use of symbols within each religion, working with ideas of spirituality in art, particularly in my own paintings."

■ Addresses

Home—2706 Farmington Dr., Alexandria, VA 22303.

■ Career

Muralist, 1982—. *Member:* Society of Children's Book Writers and Illustrators.

■ Illustrator

Mother Goose Nursery Rhymes (signed English), Gallaudet University Press, 1992.

PATRICIA PETERS

The Prophets of God, Episcopal Seminary of Alexandria, 1994.

■ Work in Progress

Researching *Angels (the Dark/the Light).*

*   *   *

PETERSON, Cris 1952-

■ Personal

Born October 25, 1952, in Minneapolis, MN; daughter of Willard C. (an engineer) and Carmen (a political consultant; maiden name, Fossom) Hoeppner; married Gary Peterson (a dairy farmer), February 10, 1973; children: Ben, Matt, Caroline. *Education:* University of Minnesota, B.S. (education and history), 1972. *Politics:* Republican. *Religion:* Lutheran. *Hobbies and other interests:* Flower gardening, quilting, knitting, collecting antiques, participating in a variety of sports.

■ Addresses

Home and office—23250 South Williams Rd., Grantsburg, WI 54840.

■ Career

Dairy farmer and substitute teacher in Grantsburg, WI, 1973—; insurance agent, Grantsburg, 1986—; Universal Press Syndicate, Kansas City, nationally syndicated columnist, 1992—. Local historical society, president, 1974-86; 4-H Club, general leader, 1986-94; Sunday school superintendent, 1993—; new children's literature consultant for regional elementary schools. *Member:* International Reading Association, Society of Children's Book Writers and Illustrators.

■ Awards, Honors

Author of the Month citation, *Highlights for Children,* October, 1989; Science Feature of the Year citation, *Highlights for Children,* 1992, for article "New Dining for Dairy Cows."

■ Writings

Extra Cheese, Please!: Mozzarella's Journey from Cow to Pizza, photographs by Alvis Upitis, Boyds Mills, 1994.

Also author of "Huckleberry Bookshelf," a weekly children's book column appearing in twenty newspapers nationwide, for Universal Press Syndicate. Contributor of stories and articles to periodicals, including *Highlights for Children* and *Cricket.*

CRIS PETERSON

■ Work in Progress

Harvest Year for Boyds Mills, publication expected in 1996; *Family Literacy Book* for Universal Press, 1995; research on agricultural history.

■ Sidelights

Besides helping her husband run a 300-acre Wisconsin dairy farm—which entails milking 45 Holstein cows twice each day—Cris Peterson writes a weekly column about children's books that is syndicated to twenty newspapers nationally, speaks frequently on reading, writing, history, and farming, and participates in many activities with her three children. She combined her varied interests to produce *Extra Cheese, Please!: Mozzarella's Journey from Cow to Pizza,* a book that provides children with an inside view of every step in the cheese production process.

"My writing career began when I gave mouth-to-mouth resuscitation to a newborn calf and I knew I had a good story," Peterson explained in *The Bridge.* "The calf lived. The story sold. In the eight years since that fateful farmyard rescue, I've learned that nothing in farming or publishing is usually that easy." She got the idea for *Extra Cheese, Please!* after attending a writers workshop in 1988. "I knew I wanted to help kids understand where their food comes from," she stated in *The Bridge.* However, self doubts and her busy daily life on the farm

Extra Cheese, Please!

MOZZARELLA'S JOURNEY FROM COW TO PIZZA

BY *Cris Peterson* ▲ PHOTOGRAPHS BY *Alvis Upitis*

Peterson traces the cheese-making process from its source—in this case, Annabelle the cow—to the plant, to the store, and finally as a pizza topping in this informative and engaging book.

prevented her from developing the story for over two years.

Finally, her friend Alvis Upitis, who would eventually provide the photographs for *Extra Cheese, Please!*, convinced her to give it a try. "Already a self-proclaimed dairy cow expert, I spent a day at our local cheese factory learning the cheese-making process," Peterson noted in *The Bridge.* "I formed the resulting information into a tightly written, somewhat boring text." Boyds Mills accepted the idea for publication, but it took another two years of working closely with editor Karen Klockner for Peterson to complete the final version.

First, Peterson had to rewrite the story in her own voice, making it "more personalized" so "a kid in the city" could understand it. Following Klockner's suggestion, she wrote the next version as a letter to a child "who had never seen a cow," according to *The Bridge.* Then came the time-consuming task of filling in all the necessary photos with Upitis. In order to create the photo of kids eating pizza for the cover of the book, Peterson cooked a total of twelve pizzas and gave her family indigestion. Despite all the hard work, however, she felt the final product was worth it.

Extra Cheese, Please! begins on the author's dairy farm—where Annabelle the cow has a calf and produces milk—and follows each step of the process, including

THE FOG'S NET   PAT PFLIEGER
Illustrated by RUTH GAMPER

When the Fog reneges on its promise not to harm Devorah's brother if she weaves it a net, Devorah must rescue him in Pat Pflieger's haunting tale. (Cover illustration by Ruth Gamper.)

milking the cows, pasteurizing the milk, converting milk into curds and whey, processing these byproducts at the cheese mill, packaging the resulting cheese, and selling it at a retail store for its final destination as part of a pizza. The book also includes a glossary and Peterson's own pizza recipe. In a review for *School Library Journal,* Carolyn Jenks called the book "attractive and informative," while Kay Weisman commented in *Booklist* that the "clear, simple text" makes it "an appealing addition to primary farm and nutrition units."

■ Works Cited

Jenks, Carolyn, review of *Extra Cheese, Please!, School Library Journal,* April, 1994, pp. 121-22.
Peterson, Cris, "Kissing Calves and Birthing Elephants: One Writer's Journey to a Book," *The Bridge* (publicity newsletter), Boyds Mills, March, 1994.
Weisman, Kay, review of *Extra Cheese, Please!, Booklist,* March 15, 1994, pp. 1368-69.

PFLIEGER, Pat 1955-

■ Personal

Surname is pronounced "*Flee*-ger"; born August 29, 1955, in Columbus, OH; daughter of William Leo (a fishery biologist) and Jo Ann (an administrative assistant; maiden name, Osborne) Pflieger. *Education:* University of Missouri, B.A., 1977; Eastern Michigan University, M.A., 1979; University of Minnesota, Ph.D., 1987.

■ Addresses

Home—201 Elm Ave., #3, Swarthmore, PA 19081.

■ Career

University of Minnesota, Twin Cities, teaching associate in composition, 1980-86, cataloguer for Hess Collection, 1982-86; Illinois State University, Normal, temporary assistant professor of children's literature in English department, 1987-88; West Chester University, West Chester, PA, assistant professor of children's literature in English department (tenured, 1993), 1988—.

■ Awards, Honors

Selection, Outstanding Reference Book, American Library Association, 1985, for *Reference Guide to Modern Fantasy for Children.*

■ Writings

A Reference Guide to Modern Fantasy for Children, Greenwood Press, 1984.
Beverly Cleary (biography), Twayne, 1991.
The Fog's Net (picturebook), illustrated by Ruth Gamper, Houghton, 1994.

Also author of children's story, "How Pete and Mirelda Went to Market," *Ladybug,* November, 1995. Contributor to scholarly books, including *Children's Periodicals of the United States,* edited by R. Gordon Kelly, Greenwood Press, 1984; *Twentieth-Century Children's Writers,* St. James Press, 1989; and *Twentieth-Century Young Adult Writers,* St. James Press, 1994; contributor to *Children's Literature Association Quarterly.* Also author of computer software, "The House at the Edge of Time," distributed by PC-SIG, disk #2769.

■ Work in Progress

Researching a collection of letters written by nineteenth-century American children.

■ Sidelights

Pat Pflieger has received praise for her first published picturebook. According to a critic for *Publishers Weekly, The Fog's Net* "shines with lyrical, polished prose" and "celebrates the courage of a resourceful heroine." Pflieger explained how she writes for children to *SATA:* "My works for adults are serious and scholarly works of literary analysis—a written version of what I do for a living as a professor of children's literature. But when I write for children, I write what I enjoyed reading when I was young: fairytales and stories in which the characters have exciting adventures. Not everything I write gets published, but I'm never sorry to have written it; I enjoy telling myself the stories, and it's all good practice. Besides—someday it might get published!"

■ Works Cited

Review of *The Fog's Net, Publishers Weekly,* August 8, 1994, p. 434.

■ For More Information See

PERIODICALS

Booklist, January 1, 1985, p. 646; September 15, 1994, p. 144.

School Library Journal, September, 1991, p. 192.*

*   *   *

PIERS, Robert
See ANTHONY, Piers

*   *   *

PITRE, Felix 1949-

■ Personal

Born March 28, 1949, in Catano, Puerto Rico; son of Felix Pitre Rivera and Petra (a housewife; maiden name, Diaz) Pitre; married Marion Lugo (a homemaker), September 22, 1974; children: Felix III, Brandon. *Education:* Hofstra University, B.A., 1971. *Politics:* Independent. *Religion:* Episcopalian. *Hobbies and other interests:* Bowling, computers, cooking, camping.

■ Addresses

Home—P.O. Box 235, Nanuet, NY 10954-0235.

■ Career

Urban Arts Corps, New York City, performer, 1968-69; The Family Repertory Company, New York City, performer, 1973-80; "Infinity Factory II," Public Broadcasting Service, New York City, performer, 1977-78; Performing Arts Foundation, Huntington, Long Island, NY, performer, 1979-81; "Latin American Folk-

FELIX PITRE

tales and Songs" (one-man show), Nanuet, NY, performer, 1982—; Arts Connection, New York City Department of Cultural Affairs, performer, 1985—; "A Peasant of El Salvador," Brattleboro, VT, performer, 1986; Young Audiences of New Jersey, performer, 1986—; Young Audiences of Connecticut, performer, 1987—. *Member:* American Federation of Television and Radio Artists, Actors Equity Association, Screen Actors Guild.

■ Writings

Juan Bobo and the Pig: A Puerto Rican Folktale, illustrated by Christy Hale, Lodestar, 1993.
(Adaptor) *Paco and the Witch: A Puerto Rican Folktale,* illustrated by Christy Hale, Lodestar, 1995.

Also author of *From Jibaros to Juan Bobo: Folklore of Puerto Rico* (a musical play), commissioned by the Discovery Theatre at the Smithsonian Museum of Art, 1993. *Paco and the Witch* is available in Spanish translation.

■ Sidelights

After graduating from the prestigious New York City High School for the Performing Arts in 1967, Felix Pitre pursued a career as an actor. "I started out ... performing in all three media—theatre, television, and films," he recalled for *SATA.* "After my two sons were born I began storytelling as a more 'dependable' source of income. My shows caught on and became my main area of work—leading me to the Brooklyn Academy of Music, the Kennedy Center in Washington, D.C., and the Smithsonian's Discovery Theatre." Pitre began a career as a children's book writer, he told *SATA,* when "I decided to submit one of my stories, *Juan Bobo and the Pig,* for publication and it was accepted by Lodestar."

"My storytelling has had the most effect on my writing," Pitre continued. "*Juan Bobo and the Pig* is written in the bilingual style I use in my programs which reflect Latin American folklore." *Juan Bobo and the Pig* begins when Juan Bobo's mother tells him to take care of the pig and leaves Bobo (Spanish for "fool") at home to go to church. The pig begins to squeal, and Bobo tries to calm it by feeding it pork chops and soda. When that does not work, he decides that the pig wants to follow his mother, Mami, and dresses it up in Mami's girdle and dress. The beautifully dressed pig, however, does not make it to church, and Mami returns home to find him rooting in the mud in her dress. The moral of the story, as Lauren Mayer of *School Library Journal* notes, is that when a person pretends to be someone she or he is not, people will say that the person looks like Juan Bobo's pig. According to a critic for *Kirkus Reviews,* the Spanish words in *Juan Bobo and the Pig* bring "color, cadence, and a painless language lesson" to the story; and in the opinion of a *Publishers Weekly* reviewer, *Juan Bobo and the Pig* is an "evocative debut."

RETOLD BY FELIX PITRE ● ILLUSTRATED BY CHRISTY HALE

Pitre's retelling of this Juan Bobo story has some decidedly modern twists. (Cover illustration by Christy Hale.)

After *Juan Bobo and the Pig* was accepted for publication, Pitre felt "inspired to write other stories," as he remarked to *SATA.* Among these stories is *Paco and the Witch,* which tells the story of a boy who must guess the name of a witch in order to escape her. Pitre told *SATA,* "I continue to work as a storyteller/singer and encourage the children I perform for to write stories and use storytelling as a vehicle to that end."

■ Works Cited

Review of *Juan Bobo and the Pig, Publishers Weekly,* July 12, 1993, p. 79.
Review of *Juan Bobo and the Pig, Kirkus Reviews,* August 15, 1993, p. 1078.
Mayer, Lauren, review of *Juan Bobo and the Pig, School Library Journal,* November, 1993, p. 102.

■ For More Information See

PERIODICALS

Booklist, October 15, 1993, p. 447.
Bulletin of the Center for Children's Books, May, 1995, p. 320.
New York Times Book Review, March 13, 1994, p. 20.
Publishers Weekly, May 29, 1995, p. 84.

Peeping and Sleeping

by Fran Manushkin ★ Illustrated by Jennifer Plecas

Jennifer Plecas's gentle pastel illustrations add to the mood of this nighttime story of a boy who discovers a frog-filled pond with his father.

PLECAS, Jennifer 1966-
(Jennifer Barrett)

■ Personal

Born March 3, 1966, in Washington, DC; daughter of James Edward (a behavioral pharmacologist) and Maura (a discharge planning coordinator; maiden name, Bird) Barrett; married Tomislav Plecas, November 24, 1991. *Education:* Attended Hamilton College, 1985-87, and University of the Arts, 1987-88; Moore College of Art and Design, B.F.A., 1991.

■ Addresses

Home and office—2104 Northwest Hidden Point Ct., Blue Springs, MO 64015.

■ Career

AR & T Animation Studio, Philadelphia, PA, animation assistant intern, 1988; Hallmark Cards, Kansas City, MO, artist, 1991-1993; freelance artist and writer, 1993—.

■ Awards, Honors

American Library Association notable book selection, 1994, for *Outside Dog,* by Charlotte Pomerantz.

■ Writings

(Self-illustrated; as Jennifer Barrett) *Kiki's New Sister,* Bantam, 1992.

ILLUSTRATOR

Betsy Byars, *The Seven Treasure Hunts,* HarperCollins, 1991.

Pamela Greenwood, *What About My Goldfish?*, Clarion, 1993.

Charlotte Pomerantz, *Outside Dog*, HarperCollins, 1993.

Fran Manushkin, *Peeping and Sleeping*, Clarion, 1994.

Pamela Greenwood, *I Found Mouse*, Clarion, 1994.

Sylvia Andrews, *Rattlebone Rock*, HarperCollins, 1995.

Barbara Joosse, *Snow Day*, Clarion, 1995.

Contributor of illustrations to periodicals, including *Ladybug*, *Spider*, and *Cricket*. *Kiki's New Sister* has been published in France.

■ Work in Progress

"Currently focusing on writing more."

■ Sidelights

Jennifer Plecas told *SATA* that she loves books. "I seem to have some genetic urge to roll my eyes and mind over words.... I love books because you can really have time with them. You can borrow or buy. You can skim or pore over, you can read in private or public. You can go on a huge binge at the library, and providing you at least return the spoils on time, you don't have to pay interest or any fees. Amazing."

"I imagine most of my maturation (not necessarily much to brag about) took place in the pages of books, moving through the eyes and thoughts of other writers and artists, swallowing their vision and experiences so that they felt like my own, allowing me to grow in ways impossible through my own living. Somehow to write and illustrate them seems to be a way to come into dialogue with those people who touched me."

Plecas remarked that "being able to write and illustrate" books "is a true joy and honor." She explained her love of writing and drawing to *SATA*: "As long as I can remember, I have always written and drawn. Before I could write real letters I spent hours scribbling long pages of my own dramatic, loopy scrawls full of 'real-looking' breaks in flow and crayoned or inked illustrations.

"A huge boost came with my fifth grade teacher, Mr. Caramella. His classroom had plants and a rocking chair, and on dark winter mornings he had lamps which he used instead of fluorescent lights—wooden carvings of children under the lamp shades. We did a lot of creative talking and working in that class. He had very round handwriting and he was always writing things like 'DYNAMITE!' and 'OUTSTANDING!' in huge letters on our papers. He put tons of pepper on his food. I have never had a happier time in school, and I wrote and drew like crazy that year. I have some of the books and papers I did for him still. Sometimes I feel I am floundering since that wonderful time, waiting for another teacher to go full force for. I suppose we have to be our own teachers at intervals, or perhaps more subtle or sophisticated learners."

R

STATON RABIN

RABIN, Staton 1958-

■ Personal

Name is pronounced "*Stay*-ton *Ray*-bin"; born July 19, 1958, in Brooklyn, New York; daughter of Gideon (public relations vice president for Seagram and children's book author) and Mury (a graphic artist and art therapist) Rabin. *Education:* Attended Oberlin College; New York University Tisch School of the Arts, B.F.A., 1980. *Politics:* Liberal Democrat. *Religion:* Jewish. *Hobbies and other interests:* Fruit trees, movies, American history, musicals, Elvis, dogs.

■ Addresses

Home—46 Storm St., Tarrytown, NY 10591. *Agent*—(film rights) Lynn Pleshette, Pleshette, Green and Sanders Literary Agency, 2700 North Beachwood Dr., Los Angeles, CA 90068.

■ Career

Children's book author, 1986—. Freelance story analyst for Warner Brothers Pictures, 1993—. *Member:* Society of Children's Book Writers and Illustrators.

■ Awards, Honors

Notable Children's Trade Book in the Field of Social Studies, Children's Book Council and National Council for Social Studies, and co-winner (with Greg Shed), first prize, Marion Vannett Ridgway Award, 1995, for *Casey Over There.*

■ Writings

Monster Myths: The Truth about Water Monsters, Franklin Watts, 1992.
Casey Over There, illustrated by Greg Shed, Harcourt, 1994.

Contributor of articles and stories to periodicals, including *School Magazine* (Australia), *Cricket, Pennywhistle Press, Children's Digest, Ranger Rick, Woman,* and *San Francisco Examiner.* Contributor of story to *Literacy Place* (CD-ROM), Scholastic, Inc., 1995.

■ Adaptations

Betsy and the Emperor, a work in progress, has been optioned for a film by Storyopolis.

■ Work in Progress

The Last 'O'O, a historical novel about Hawaii, for Detskasya Literatura (Soviet Commonwealth); *In Annie's Arms,* "a novella for middle readers about Abraham Lincoln and Ann Rutledge in New Salem"; *Betsy and the Emperor,* a young adult novel "about Napoleon's friendship with an English teenager on St. Helena."

■ Sidelights

Children's author Staton Rabin was named after her Russian great-grandfather, whose last name "was something like Statonofsky," she told *SATA.* She was exposed to both art and literature early in life. Her mother was a graphic artist who "wouldn't even put a milk carton on the dinner table because she thought it was aesthetically ugly." Her father, also an author of children's books, used Staton as his pen name before she was born. Rabin, however, attributes her interest in writing to her love of films. A freelance story analyst for movie studios, Rabin told *SATA:* "In a way, my ending up as a writer of children's books seems a natural outgrowth of my background in the film business. Both media combine words and pictures—and many of America's best movies (*The Wizard of Oz* for example) have been aimed at the young and the young at heart.

"My work for the movie studios helps me in my writing for kids because it keeps my critical faculties sharp, so I'm a tough 'editor' of my own writing. It also gives me a good sense of how tired and jaded professional 'readers' can be, and reminds me just how good a manuscript has to be to impress one of these people, whether at a film

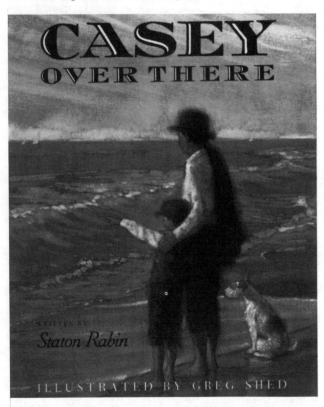

A young boy misses his brother, who is fighting in Europe during World War I, so he decides to write to Uncle Sam in this story inspired by the Persian Gulf War. (Cover illustration by Greg Shed.)

studio or a children's book publisher. New writers should be aware that if you send your book manuscript out to a publisher, you'd better be sure it's going to give an electric jolt to the staff member or freelancer who's going to be reading it."

Rabin started out writing nonfiction for children. She saw an ad in a newspaper for writers for a children's encyclopedia, and "auditioned" by writing an article about Alaska. She was hired for the job. "This job trained me to write in a way that a ten-year-old could fathom," she told *SATA.* "Best of all, I got to write about what interested me—all kinds of articles about American history, for example, from a biography of Lincoln to features about the Santa Fe Trail or the sinking of the Titanic."

In 1992, Franklin Watts published *Monster Myths: The Truth about Water Monsters.* In it, Rabin describes some of the scarier "water monsters," including sharks, killer whales, alligators, and piranhas. She reminds readers that some of the factors that make these creatures frightening are necessary to their survival in nature; she also notes that much of our fear is based on ignorance. Denia Hester, writing in *Booklist,* described it as "fascinating reading even as the myths are debunked."

It was during the Persian Gulf War that Rabin got the idea for writing her picture book, *Casey Over There.* As she told Christine Martin in an interview for the *1995 Children's Writer's & Illustrator's Market:* "It was the tug of war between my feelings of support for our soldiers and dismay and distress at our fighting that war that prompted me to write *Casey.* I felt that if I set the story during World War I instead of the present, it would give kids—and me—a safe emotional distance from the subject, to better be able to deal with it."

Casey Over There is the story of seven-year-old Aubrey, whose older brother Casey goes off to France to fight in World War I. Even as Aubrey plays games at home, such as kick the can and flattening pennies on the trolley tracks, he thinks of Casey at war. When he writes Uncle Sam a letter, he gets a reply from none other than president Woodrow Wilson. Scenes of Aubrey's everyday life in 1917 Brooklyn are juxtaposed with scenes of Casey's wartime ordeals overseas. The book received a starred review from a *Publishers Weekly* contributor who stated that it was an "excellent picture-book introduction to the topic of war and its effect on families."

"There's a real prejudice among some publishers against historical fiction," Rabin told *SATA.* "One editor told me 'Kids aren't interested in anything that doesn't take place in their own back yard.' I don't believe kids don't like historical fiction. I was a kid once, and I did.

"My advice for beginning writers is this: Read, and re-read picture books (if that's your category of interest) until you learn their rhythm and the way transitions are used to accommodate page-turns. Learn how to construct a plot (study movies and screenplays) and don't submit a book that doesn't have one. Learn each publisher's taste by looking at their catalog. Make sure your manuscript has about the right number of words, chapters (if applicable) and pages, and is aimed at a specific reading level/age group. Don't worry about the vocabulary you use in your books; it's the length of the sentences, and not the complexity of the words that determines reading level—despite what so-called experts may tell you. Children can understand tough words from context—or they can ask adults what a mystifying word means and thereby learn a new word. Give your book a succinct, intriguing but not mysterious-sounding title. The title should indicate what the book is about, but not give away the whole game. Be courteous to editors. Call them if they haven't replied to your manuscript after three months because polite nagging, up to a point, will get you a quicker response.

"The best advice I ever had about writing was from a screenwriter named Ian Hunter, who said writing is just a job, like digging ditches. Aspiring writers glamorize writing too much. It's just hard work, no mystique."

■ Works Cited

Review of *Casey Over There, Publishers Weekly*, March 14, 1994, pp. 72-73.
Hester, Denia, review of *Monster Myths: The Truth about Water Monsters, Booklist*, December 15, 1992, pp. 732-33.
Martin, Christine, interview with Staton Rabin, *1995 Children's Writer's & Illustrator's Market*, Writer's Digest Books, 1995.

■ For More Information See

PERIODICALS

Appraisal: Science Books for Young People, winter, 1993, p. 44.
Children's Book Review Service, spring, 1994, p. 138.
School Library Journal, May, 1994, p. 103.
Science Books & Film, August, 1993, p. 181.

*   *   *

ROBEL, S. L.
See FRAUSTINO, Lisa Rowe

*   *   *

ROBINSON, Barbara (Webb) 1927-

■ Personal

Born October 24, 1927, in Portsmouth, OH; daughter of Theodore L. and Grace (Mooney) Webb; married John F. Robinson, 1949; children: Carolyn, Marjorie. *Education:* Allegheny College, B.A., 1948.

BARBARA ROBINSON

■ Addresses

Home—2063 Fox Creek Rd., Berwyn, PA 19132.

■ Career

Freelance writer.

■ Awards, Honors

Breadloaf fellow, 1962; Georgia Children's Book Award, University of Georgia College of Education, 1976, Young Hoosier Book Award, Association for Indiana Media Educators, 1978, Emphasis on Reading Award, Alabama State Department of Education, 1980-81, and Maud Hart Lovelace Book Award, Friends of the Minnesota Valley Regional Library, 1982, all for *The Best Christmas Pageant Ever;* Outstanding Pennsylvania Author, Pennsylvania School Librarians Association, 1985.

■ Writings

Across from Indian Shore, Lothrop, 1962.
Trace through the Forest, Lothrop, 1965.
The Fattest Bear in the First Grade, illustrated by Cyndy Szekeres, Random House, 1969.
The Best Christmas Pageant Ever, illustrated by Judith Gwyn Brown, Harper, 1972.
Temporary Time, Temporary Places, Harper, 1982.

The Best Christmas Pageant Ever (play adaptation of book of the same title; produced at the Children's Theater, Seattle, WA), Samuel French, 1982.

The Best Christmas Pageant Ever (television screenplay adaptation of book of the same title), Schaefer-Karpf, 1983.

My Brother Louis Measures Worms, and Other Louis Stories, illustrated by Marc Simont, Harper, 1988.

The Best School Year Ever, HarperCollins, 1994.

Contributor of short stories to magazines, including *McCall's, Good Housekeeping, Redbook, Ladies' Home Journal,* and *Toronto Star Weekly.*

■ Sidelights

Zany characters whose actions become more and more outrageous as their stories progress fill the pages of Barbara Robinson's children's books. The six children who make up the Herdman family, appearing in both *The Best Christmas Pageant Ever* and *The Best School Year Ever,* are considered by one of their classmates as "absolutely the worst kids in the history of the world." And the family described in *My Brother Louis Measures Worms, and Other Louis Stories,* which includes the narrators Mary Elizabeth and Louis, continuously finds itself in mayhem due to some sort of miscommunication.

Robinson introduced the Herdman children in her 1972 work *The Best Christmas Pageant Ever,* which was also adapted into a play and a television script. Learning that there is free food available at Sunday School, the Herdmans show up, which leads to their involvement in the upcoming Christmas pageant. Imogene Herdman threatens her way into the part of Mary, and her siblings follow her example, each landing their own role. Despite the chaotic rehearsals, the Herdmans are benevolent toward the audience on the night of the actual pageant. "Although there is a touch of sentiment at the end ... the story otherwise romps through the festive preparations with comic relish," observed a *Bulletin of the Center for Children's Books* reviewer.

The sequel to *The Best Christmas Pageant Ever,* published over two decades later in 1994, covers a much broader scope. *The Best School Year Ever* is narrated by Beth Bradley, a sixth-grade classmate of Imogene who is faced with the assignment of coming up with compliments for everyone in her class. While trying to find something nice to say about Imogene, Beth relates some of the outrageous stunts the Herdman children have pulled over the years. Included in these activities are the painting of a baby's head and then charging admission for others to see the "tattooed" baby, an attempt to wash their cat at a laundromat, and the placing of frogs in the Town Hall water cooler. It is after Imogene rescues a boy whose head is stuck in the school bike rack (she tapes his ears to his head and then covers it with margarine) that Beth finds the right words with the help of her father—"resourceful" and "creative" among them. A *Publishers Weekly* reviewer noted that the readers "who have laughed out loud at Robinson's

In this sequel to *The Best Christmas Pageant Ever,* the Herdman children are at their old antics once again, but Beth Bradley discovers they might have some admirable traits after all. (Cover illustration by Michael Deas.)

uproarious 1972 novel,... will enthusiastically welcome the return of the six cigar-smoking Herdman kids." "The Herdmans will delight readers," a *Kirkus Reviews* contributor said confidently.

The stories contained in *My Brother Louis Measures Worms, and Other Louis Stories* have more to do with misunderstanding than mischievous behavior. It is the parents of Mary Elizabeth and Louis who most often have trouble understanding each other, and this is at the core of the crazy mix-ups that occur. Mother, who is just a little bit odd, has a hard time explaining what she wants, so Father loses his patience and ends up pulling crazy stunts like pushing a visiting child into a family reunion picture and telling Mary Elizabeth that Marcella is really the name on her birth certificate. Compared to the wacky family members around them, Mary Elizabeth and Louis seem quiet and subdued. Hanna B. Zeiger concluded in her *Horn Book* review of *My Brother Louis Measures Worms* that "Barbara Robinson has created a funny, lively family whose unique, slightly off-center approach to life provides some very entertaining reading."

■ Works Cited

Review of *The Best Christmas Pageant Ever, Bulletin of the Center for Children's Books,* December, 1972, p. 63.

Review of *The Best School Year Ever, Kirkus Reviews,* July 15, 1994, pp. 993-94.

Review of *The Best School Year Ever, Publishers Weekly,* July 4, 1994, p. 64.

Robinson, Barbara, *The Best Christmas Pageant Ever,* Harper, 1972.

Zeiger, Hanna B., review of *My Brother Louis Measures Worms, and Other Louis Stories, Horn Book,* January/February, 1989, pp. 74-75.

■ For More Information See

PERIODICALS

Booklist, November 15, 1965, p. 332.

Bulletin of the Center for Children's Books, July, 1970, pp. 184-85.

Horn Book, August, 1965, p. 388.

Kirkus Reviews, July 15, 1988, p. 1064.

Quill & Quire, September, 1994, p. 75.

School Library Journal, April, 1982.

* * *

ROOT, Betty

■ Personal

Education: Diploma (child psychology), University of Birmingham, England, 1956; awarded M.B.E., 1987.

■ Addresses

Home—5 Kelburne Close, Winnersh, Near Wokingham, Berkshire R941 5JG, England.

■ Career

Berkshire Local Education Authority, England, primary school teacher, 1950-55, remedial advisor, 1955-60; University of Reading, Reading, England, lecturer in education, 1961-68, senior lecturer in Arts and Humanities in Education department, and director of the Reading and Language Information Centre, 1968-90.

■ Awards, Honors

Honorary M.Phil., 1991.

■ Writings

(Editor with Sue Brownhill) *Starting Point: Books for the Illiterate Adult and Older Reluctant Reader,* National Book League, 1975.

Starters Blue Dictionary, MacDonald, 1982.

Starters Green Dictionary, MacDonald, 1982.

Starters Red Dictionary, MacDonald, 1982.

(Editor) *Forty Reading Games to Make and Play,* Macmillan, 1983.

Getting Ready, Puffin, 1985.

Word Building, Puffin, 1985.

(Editor) *Resources for Reading: Does Quality Count,* Macmillan, 1987.

Purnell's Illustrated Children's Dictionary, Purnell, 1988.

Chambers First Picture Dictionary, illustrated by Rosemary McMullen, Chambers, 1989.

Help Your Child Learn to Read, Osborne, 1989.

Dictionary, Simon & Schuster, 1992.

My First Dictionary, illustrated by Jonathan Langley, Dorling Kindersley, 1993.

Three Hundred First Words, photographs by Geoff Dann, Barron's Educational Series, 1993.

Also author of: four nature books for Ginn; four "Roundabout" stories for Arnold; twenty-four "Skyways" stories for Collins; four "Music and Mime" stories with records for Arnold; eight "Early Reading" computer programs for Macmillan; and sixty reading games for Ginn, Arnold, Collins, and Jolly Learning. Author of numerous academic papers in journals; author and director of two videos, *Children Learning to Read* and *Nobody Heard Me Read Today,* University of Reading. Consultant to television reading series, Granada; senior editorial consultant for early reading publications, Ginn, Puffin, and Macmillan. *Three Hundred First Words* was published in French as *Three Hundred First Words: Premiers Mots,* and Spanish as *Three Hundred First Words: Palabras Primeras,* both by Barron's Educational Series, 1993.

■ Sidelights

Betty Root is an author and reading consultant who, for more than twenty years, was the director of the Reading and Language Information Centre at the University of Reading in England. She is well known for her resource books for parents and teachers to help children learn to read, and for her dictionaries for young readers.

Root's first dictionaries for children just beginning to read were published in 1982. The *Starters Red Dictionary, Starters Blue Dictionary,* and *Starters Green Dictionary* earned praise for their departure from the standard dictionary format. They were instead divided by subject matter about which young children might be writing—for instance, "my family," "the park," and "shopping." Carolyn O'Grady commented in her review for the *Times Educational Supplement* that it was "obvious that a great deal of thought" had gone into these dictionaries, and that they were "both carefully structured and beautifully produced."

Root has contributed to several volumes dedicated to helping children build learning skills in school and at home. *Forty Reading Games to Make and Play, Getting Ready,* and *Word Building* are designed to encourage and enhance basic skills through a variety of games and activities. Angela Anning, reviewing *Forty Reading Games to Make and Play* for the *Times Educational Supplement,* called it a "useful resource for any staff room."

Games and activities teaching dictionary skills, memory, spelling, and deduction are also a feature of Root's 1993 work, *My First Dictionary*. A *Publishers Weekly* reviewer called the volume a "visual treat for youngsters," while a *Booklist* critic deemed it a "valuable learning tool for the pre- and beginning reader."

■ Works Cited

Anning, Angela, review of *Forty Reading Games to Make and Play*, *Times Educational Supplement*, March 11, 1983, p. 47.

Review of *My First Dictionary, Publishers Weekly,* July 19, 1993, p. 254.

Review of *My First Dictionary, Booklist,* December 1, 1993, p. 716.

O'Grady, Carolyn, review of *Starters Red Dictionary, Starters Blue Dictionary,* and *Starters Green Dictionary, Times Educational Supplement,* May 13, 1983, p. 30.

■ For More Information See

PERIODICALS

Junior Bookshelf, April, 1989, 75.
Library Talk, November, 1992, p. 47.
School Librarian, December, 1982, p. 327; March, 1986, p. 38; fall, 1989, p. 18.
School Library Journal, November, 1992, p. 135; January, 1994, p. 110.
Times Educational Supplement, March 20, 1987, p. 48.

*   *   *

ROSEN, Michael (Wayne) 1946-

■ Personal

Born May 7, 1946, Harrow, Middlesex, England; son of Harold (a professor) and Connie Ruby (a college lecturer; maiden name, Isakovsky) Rosen. *Education:* Attended Middlesex Hospital Medical School, 1964-65; attended Wadham College, Oxford, 1965-69; attended National Film School, 1973-76. *Politics:* Socialist. *Religion:* Atheist. *Hobbies and other interests:* Watching Arsenal F.C.

■ Addresses

Agent—Charles Walker, Peters, Fraser and Dunlop, 503/4 The Chambers, Chelsea Harbour, London SW10 0XF, England.

■ Career

Writer, poet, playwright, and broadcaster. Has appeared regularly on British Broadcasting Company (BBC) television and radio shows, including *Meridian Books, Treasure Islands,* and *Best Worlds. Member:* National Union of Journalists.

■ Awards, Honors

Best Original Full-Length Play Award, *Sunday Times* National Union of Students Drama Festival, 1968, for *Backbone;* Poetry Award, *Signal,* 1982, for *You Can't Catch Me!;* Other Award, *Children's Book Bulletin,* 1983, for *Everybody Here;* Smarties' Best Children's Book of the Year Award and *Boston Globe-Horn Book* Award, both 1990, and Japanese Picture Book Award, 1991, all for *We're Going On a Bear Hunt;* Cuffies Award for best anthology, *Publishers Weekly,* 1992, and Best Book Award, National Association of Parenting Publications, 1993, for *Poems for the Very Young.*

■ Writings

Once There Was a King Who Promised He Would Never Chop Anyone's Head Off, illustrated by Kathy Henderson, Deutsch, 1976.

The Bakerloo Flea, illustrated by Quentin Blake, Longman, 1979.

(Reteller) *A Cat and Mouse Story,* illustrated by William Rushton, Deutsch, 1982.

Nasty!, illustrated by Amanda Macphail, Longman, 1982, revised edition, Puffin, 1984.

You're Thinking about Doughnuts, illustrated by Tony Pinchuck, Deutsch, 1987.

Beep Beep! Here Come—The Horribles, illustrated by John Watson, Walker, 1988.

Norma and the Washing Machine, illustrated by David Hingham, Deutsch, 1988.

The Class Two Monster, illustrated by Maggie King, Heinemann, 1989.

We're Going on a Bear Hunt, illustrated by Helen Oxenbury, Walker, 1989, Aladdin, 1992.

(Reteller) *The Wicked Tricks of Till Owlyglass,* illustrated by Fritz Wegner, Walker, 1989.

The Golem of Old Prague, illustrated by Val Biro, Deutsch, 1990.

(Reteller) *Little Rabbit Foo Foo,* illustrated by Arthur Robins, Simon & Schuster, 1990.

The Royal Huddle [and] *The Royal Muddle,* illustrated by Colin West, Macmillan, 1990.

Clever Cakes, Walker, 1991.

The Deadman Tapes, Lion Tracks, 1991.

(Reteller) *How the Animals Got Their Colours: Animal Myths from around the World,* illustrated by John Clementson, Harcourt, 1991.

Burping Bertha, Andersen, 1993.

(Reteller) *How Giraffe Got Such a Long Neck ... and Why Rhino Is So Grumpy,* illustrated by Clementson, Dial, 1993.

Moving, illustrated by Sophy Williams, Viking, 1993.

Songbird Story, illustrated by Jill Dow, F. Lincoln, 1993.

The Arabian Frights and Other Gories, illustrated by Chris Fisher, Scholastic, 1994.

(Reteller) *Crow and Hawk: A Traditional Pueblo Indian Story,* illustrated by Clementson, Harcourt, 1995.

Even Stevens, F.C., Collins, 1995.

POETRY, VERSE, AND JOKE COLLECTIONS

Mind Your Own Business, illustrated by Quentin Blake, Deutsch, 1974.

(With Roger McGough) *You Tell Me,* illustrated by Sara Midda, Kestrel, 1979.

Wouldn't You Like to Know, illustrated by Blake, Penguin, 1981.

You Can't Catch Me!, illustrated by Blake, Deutsch, 1981.

Quick, Let's Get Out of Here, illustrated by Blake, Deutsch, 1983.

Bloody L.I.A.R.S., illustrated by Alan Gilbey, privately printed, 1984.

How to Get Out of the Bath and Other Problems, illustrated by Graham Round, Scholastic, 1984.

Don't Put Mustard in the Custard, illustrated by Blake, Deutsch, 1985.

Hairy Tales and Nursery Crimes, illustrated by Alan Baker, Deutsch, 1985.

Under the Bed, illustrated by Blake, Walker, 1986.

When Did You Last Wash Your Feet?, illustrated by Pinchuck, Deutsch, 1986.

The Hypnotiser, illustrated by Andrew Tiffen, Deutsch, 1988.

Silly Stories (jokes), illustrated by Mik Brown, Kingfisher, 1988.

Freckly Feet and Itchy Knees, illustrated by Sami Sweeten, Collins, Doubleday, 1990.

Never Mind!, BBC, 1990.

Who Drew on the Baby's Head, Deutsch, 1991.

Mind the Gap, Scholastic, 1992.

Nuts about Nuts, Collins, 1993.

Off the Wall: A Very Silly Story Book, illustrated by Mik Brown, Larousse Kingfisher Chambers, 1994.

"SCRAPBOOK" SERIES; POETRY AND PROSE COLLECTIONS; ILLUSTRATED BY QUENTIN BLAKE

Smelly Jelly Smelly Fish, Prentice-Hall, 1986.

Under the Bed, Prentice-Hall, 1986.

Hard-Boiled Legs, Prentice-Hall, 1987.

Spollyollydiddlytiddlyitis, Walker, 1987, published as *Down at the Doctors,* Simon & Schuster, 1987.

EDITOR

Everybody Here (miscellany), Bodley Head, 1982.

(With Susanna Steele), *Inky Pinky Ponky: Children's Playground Rhymes,* illustrated by Dan Jones, Granada, 1982.

(With David Jackson) *Speaking to You,* Macmillan, 1984.

(With Joan Griffiths) *That'd Be Telling,* Cambridge University Press, 1985.

The Kingfisher Book of Children's Poetry, Kingfisher, 1985.

A Spider Bought a Bicycle, and Other Poems for Young Children, illustrated by Inga Moore, Kingfisher, 1986.

The Kingfisher Book of Funny Stories, illustrated by Tony Blundell, Kingfisher, 1988.

Experiences (contains *The Attic: Fear, The Oar: Friendship, The Tree: Imagination, The Formula: Intelligence, Isabel: Shyness,* and *The Nose: Lying*), Firefly, 1989.

MICHAEL ROSEN

Tell Tales (contains *Peter Pan, Aladdin, Alice in Wonderland, Cinderella, Goldilocks and the Three Bears, Hansel and Gretel, Little Red Riding Hood, The Little Tin Soldier, The Princess and the Pea, Sinbad the Sailor,* and *Snow White*), Firefly, 1989-90.

Culture Shock, Viking, 1990.

Goodies and Daddies: An A-Z Guide to Fatherhood, Murray, 1991.

Give Me Shelter, Bodley Head, 1991.

A World of Poetry, Kingfisher, 1991.

(With David Widgery), *The Chatto Book of Dissent,* Chatto & Windus, 1991.

Mini Beasties, illustrated by Baker, Firefly, 1991, published as *Itsy-Bitsy Beasties: Poems from around the World,* Carolrhoda Books, 1992.

Rude Rhymes, Signet, 1992.

Sonsense Nongs, illustrated by Shoo Rayner, Black, 1992.

(With Jill Burridge) *Treasure Islands II: An Adult Guide to Children's Writers,* BBC Books, 1992.

South and North, East and West: The Oxfam Book of Children's Stories, Walker/Candlewick, 1992.

Action Replay, illustrated by Andrzej Krauze, Viking, 1993.

The Kingfisher Book of Children's Poetry, illustrated by Alice Englander, Kingfisher, 1993.

Poems for the Very Young, illustrated by Bob Graham, Kingfisher, 1993.

Rude Rhymes II, Signet, 1994.

Penguin Book of Childhood, Penguin, 1994.

Pilly Soems, illustrated by Rayner, Black, 1994.

OTHER

Backbone (first produced at Oxford University, 1967; produced on the West End at Royal Court Theatre, London, England, February, 1968), Faber, 1968.

Stewed Figs (play), first produced in Edinburgh at the University of Durham, 1968.

Regis Debray (radio play), first produced on BBC-Radio 4, 1971.

I See a Voice (on poetry), Thames Television-Hutchinson, 1981.

Did I Hear You Write?, illustrated by Pinchuck, Deutsch, 1989.

Rap with Rosen, Longmans, 1995.

The Best of Michael Rosen, RDR Books, 1995.

Also author of a retelling of von Chamisso's version of a Faust tale, *The Man with No Shadow*. Writer of television series, including *The Juice Job,* Thames TV, 1981, 1984; *You Tell Me,* Thames TV, 1982; *Everybody Here,* Channel 4, 1982; *Black and White and Read All Over,* Channel 4, 1984; and *Talk Write Read,* Central TV, 1986. Contributor of drama features for radio and articles to *New Statesman*.

■ Work in Progress

This Is Our House, illustrated by Bob Graham, for Walker.

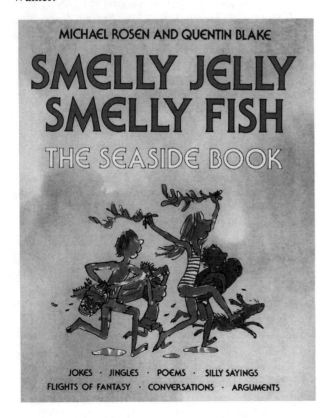

Rosen takes us to the beach, as we follow Nat and his sister Anna on a series of little adventures and daydreams. (Cover illustration by Quentin Blake.)

■ Sidelights

As *School Librarian* critic Margaret Meek proclaimed, anyone "who has seen Michael Rosen on TV, at work with children in school," or reading to children "testifies to his Pied Piper magic with words." Rosen's love of words, his talent for combining them in fresh and exciting ways, and his delightful ability to speak the words of a child in the way a child would speak them has made him one of England's most popular children's poets.

Rosen's love of words is reflected in his enthusiasm for writing, collecting, and sometimes piecing together anecdotes, jokes, songs, folktales, fairytales, vignettes, and nonsense verse, which he has published in informal poetry collections and *Action Replay* and *That'd Be Telling*. Rosen's habit of collecting stories—or parts of them—is apparent in his novels like *You're Thinking about Doughnuts* and *The Deadman Tapes,* which contain several stories within the larger plot. Rosen once told *SATA* that some "people are worried about whether what I write is 'poetry.' If they are worried, let them call it something else, for example, 'stuff.'"

Rosen realized the importance of pursuing his own style after reading James Joyce's unconventional novel, *Portrait of the Artist as a Young Man,* as a teenager. He told an interviewer for *Language Matters,* "That book really came home to me. It was really quite extraordinary, because for the first time I realized that you could actually play around with different ways of saying something. So, for example, you could do a stream of consciousness or you could write about things that happened to you when you were six, and you could do it in the voice of a child of six. So I became absolutely fascinated by this idea and I started to write a few things of that sort."

In college, Rosen developed an interest in performance and theater and wrote a play that was performed at the Royal Court in London. Later, when he noticed the poems his mother selected for a British Broadcasting Corporation show she helped produce, Rosen decided to write poems for radio and television programs. Although Rosen's poems made the air waves, it took a little longer for them to find a home on the printed page. As Rosen said in *Language Matters,* publishers rejected his submissions, "saying that 'Children don't like poems written from the child's point of view.'" Then, according to Rosen, "Pam Royds, from [publisher] Andre Deutsch, saw them and they said 'What lovely fun!,' 'Tremendous!' and so they married me to [illustrator] Quentin Blake, and that's how *Mind Your Own Business* came about."

Since the publication of that first poetry collection in 1974, Rosen's reputation for writing nonsense verse and humorous dialogue has grown. He is especially known for the childlike voice of his poetry, which, as he pointed out in *Language Matters,* is uncommon. While "plenty of people have written about their childhood, they haven't written about it in the kind of speaking voice

"You can't catch me, GRUMBLE PUMP PUMP."
"I'm very, very, very slow but when I'm quick

I'LL GET YOU . . .

I've got you
I've got you
and I'll never let you go."

The ordinary is shown to be extraordinary in Rosen's 1981 poetry collection, *You Can't Catch Me!* **(Illustration by** Quentin Blake.)

that is totally accessible to a child, so that they can read it out loud."

According to *Times Educational Supplement* critic Edward Blishen, reviewing *You Can't Catch Me!* and *Wouldn't You Like to Know,* some of Rosen's first collections, the poet's talent lies in his ability to show "how far from being ordinary are the most ordinary of events." Such events are the subjects of the collection of untitled, humorous poems in *You Can't Catch Me!* In the poems in this book, a father and child tease one another, the joy of sailing is pondered, and the fear of the dark is contemplated. Noting the compatibility of Quentin Blake's illustrations with Rosen's verse, a reviewer for *Junior Bookshelf* concluded that *You Can't Catch Me!* is a "gorgeous book." Like the poems in *You Can't Catch Me!,* those in *Wouldn't You Like to Know* focus on relationships, fears, and simple joys.

Similarly, the free-verse poems in *Quick, Let's Get Out of Here* recall the events, episodes, and special moments of childhood, and describe fights, birthday parties, tricks, and schemes. As Helen Gregory related in *School Library Journal,* Rosen evokes emotions ranging from the "hysteria of silly joking" to "the agony of breaking a friend's toy." *Horn Book* contributor Ann A. Flowers remarked that, with its "irrepressible" and "outrageous" poems, *Quick, Let's Get Out of Here* is a "far cry from Christopher Robin."

Rosen's ability to bring smiles to the faces of his young readers manifests itself in collections of silly verses, songs, fairytales, and folktales as well as in his poetry. *Freckly Feet and Itchy Knees* presents a list of body parts, describes their owners, and explains their functions in rhythmic verse. Rosen contemplates the nose: "I'm talking about noses/ wet noses/ warty noses/ sleepy noses/ when someone dozes." Before the end of the book, children are encouraged to wiggle and jiggle their own body parts. In the words of Diane Roback and Richard Donahue in *Publishers Weekly, Freckly Feet and Itchy Knees* is "always lighthearted" and "ideal for reading aloud." *Nuts about Nuts* is another list of things described in verse. This time, the focus is on food: sweets like ice cream, cake, and honey as well as staples like bread, eggs, nuts, and rice are, as a *Junior Bookshelf* critic noted, "celebrated and examined."

The works in *Sonsense Nongs,* eight ballads, parodies, and silly songs written by Rosen with contributions from children, are meant to be sung out loud. According to a *Junior Bookshelf* reviewer, *Sonsense Nongs* may help children gain a "deeper understanding of language as well as much fun and laughter." Children may also sing the words to *Little Rabbit Foo Foo,* which is based on the old children's finger-play song in which Little Rabbit Foo Foo bops his helpless victims on the head. Judith Sharman testified in *Books For Keeps* that her son found *Little Rabbit Foo Foo* so charming that she

Diapering a baby is one of many occasions for some lighthearted poetry in Rosen's 1983 collection, *Quick, Let's Get Out of Here.* (Illustration by Quentin Blake.)

had to "sneak" the book away from him while he slept to write her review of it.

Many children will recognize the story in *We're Going on a Bear Hunt* from the children's song. Eager to find a bear, a young family wades through mud, water, grass, and snow, and braves the dangers of a forest, a river, and a cave. As they meet each obstacle, they sing "We can't go over it. We can't go under it. Oh, no! We've got to go through it!" and make their way through the muck with joyful noises ranging from "swishy swashy" to "squelch squelch." When the family finally finds the bear, he scares them so much that they turn around and hurry back through each obstacle. As Elizabeth S. Watson commented in *Horn Book*, Rosen's text has "a driving rhythm" and "new sounds" that give the familiar tale added "sparkle."

The fables in *Hairy Tales and Nursery Crimes* are written in verse and lampoon traditional fairy tales. For example, Rosen's version of Hansel and Gretel begins, "Once a plum time, in the middle of a forest, there lived a poor wood-/nutter and his woof. They lived in a little wooden sausage with their two/children, Handsel and Gristle." In the opinion of George Szirtes, expressed in his *Times Literary Supplement* review, the jokes in these fables "are improved in the telling aloud. Hansel's pocketful of stones ... become a rocket full of phones." According to *School Librarian* reviewer Colin Walter, however, the book is "not for hearing, and therein lies its secret and appeal."

Rosen's treatment of folktales is tempered by his respect for their origins. His version of an Eastern and Southern African *porquoi* tale, *How Giraffe Got Such a Long Neck ... and Why Rhino Is So Grumpy,* according to *School Library Journal* contributor Lee Bock, is "lively" and "bright." This story tells how Giraffe, an originally

Searching for a bear might be more fun than actually finding one in *We're Going on a Bear Hunt*, based on the children's song. (Illustration by Helen Oxenbury.)

In this retelling of an East African story, Rhino arrives too late to receive the magical potion that gives Giraffe the ability to reach the leaves in the trees. (Cover illustration by John Clementson.)

small beast, and Rhino implore Man to help them survive the drought. Although Man instructs Giraffe and Rhino to visit him the next day for help reaching the leaves high in the trees, Rhino does not arrive on time, and Giraffe eats his portion of Man's remedy as well as her own. As a result, Giraffe's neck grows long. Rhino, who feels cheated, only grows grumpy.

The Golem of Old Prague is a collection of stories concerning the legendary Rabbi Loeb of Prague. The stories tell how Rabbi Loeb creates a Golem, a huge, strong, but mindless creature, out of clay and gives him life. With the help of the powerful and loyal Golem, Rabbi Loeb ensures the Jewish community's survival as they are persecuted by the monk Thaddeus. Writing in *Books for Your Children*, S. Williams concluded that *The Golem of Old Prague* "gives insight to Jewish thinking, customs, and way of life" in sixteenth-century Prague.

South and North, East and West: The Oxfam Anthology of Children's Stories, a collection of twenty-five stories, includes tales from Cyprus, Korea, the Dominican Republic, Bangladesh, China, Jamaica, Malta, Vietnam, and England. Betsy Hearne, writing in *Bulletin of the Center for Children's Books,* found these retellings to be "fresh and colloquial." The royalties from *South and North, East and West* benefit Oxfam, an international organization that establishes self-help development programs in countries disrupted by natural or man-made disasters.

Rosen's work for older children and teenagers frequently addresses serious issues. His poetry collection, *When Did You Last Wash Your Feet?*, for example, deals with topics from racism to terminal illness. *Mind the Gap*, a collection Sue Rogers described in *School Librarian* as "brilliant," features "comic, sad," and "controversial" poems, including one that recalls the past as the narrator's mother is dying. *Books for Keeps* critic Adrian Jackson advised librarians to buy many copies: "Teenagers will love it." In *Culture Shock*, a collection of poems Rosen selected from around the world, racism, sexism, love, and hate are also concerns.

Like his poetry, Rosen's fiction for older children often develops around episodes and anecdotes, calls upon his performer's love of dialogue, and insightfully expresses the perspectives of protagonist. *Nasty!* is a collection of stories narrated by a talkative Cockney cleaning woman known as the Bakerloo Flea Woman. She tells the story of the giant Bakerloo flea, recalls how wasps plagued the people on the East End of London one winter, and remembers how they dealt with the mice that invaded their homes. Although it is a short novel, *You're Thinking about Doughnuts* contains several stories told from strange perspectives. Frank, who is just eight years old, must wait in the dark halls of the museum where his mother works every Friday night. One night, the exhibits, including a skeleton, a space suit, a few Greek statues, and a stuffed tiger, come alive. As these exhibits tell Frank about their lives before they were taken to the quiet museum, asserts Tom Lewis in *School Librarian*, Rosen thoughtfully questions the "honesty and integrity of an institutional building like a museum."

Rosen's novel, *The Deadman Tapes*, also presents a series of stories within a larger plot. When Paul Deadman plays some tapes he has found in the attic of his new house, he is introduced to the voices and stories of eight teens. With occasional interruptions from Paul, these stories make up the text of *The Deadman Tapes*. Like some of Rosen's more serious poetry, they deal with various social problems that many teenagers face.

Rosen also enjoys sharing the techniques that have made him a successful children's writer. He has published books on writing, including *Did I Hear You Write?*, and visits schools and libraries. Rosen even revealed one of the secret's of his unique style to *Language Matters:* "What I try to do in my mind is to go back and write about my feelings when I was ten .... I write about my experience using the voice of a ten year old. I write in that voice, using what I know as a performer will work, knowing, that is, what children can take off a page."

■ Works Cited

Blishen, Edward, "Nonsense Not Nauseous," *Times Educational Supplement*, November 20, 1981, p. 34.

Bock, Lee, review of *How Giraffe Got Such a Long Neck ... and Why Rhino Is So Grumpy*, *School Library Journal*, October, 1993, pp. 121-22.

Flowers, Ann A., review of *Quick, Let's Get Out of Here*, *Horn Book*, June, 1984, p. 345.

Gregory, Helen, review of *Quick, Let's Get Out of Here*, *School Library Journal*, October, 1984, p. 161.

Hearne, Betsy, review of *South and North, East and West*, *Bulletin of the Center for Children's Books*, December, 1992, pp. 121-22.

"An Interview with Michael Rosen," *Language Matters*, Centre for Language in Primary Education, 1983.

Jackson, Adrian, review of *Mind the Gap*, *Books for Keeps*, September, 1992, p. 13.

Lewis, Tom, review of *You're Thinking about Doughnuts*, *School Librarian*, May, 1988, p. 59.

Meek, Margaret, review of *Did I Hear You Write?*, *School Librarian*, August, 1989, p. 128.

Review of *Nuts about Nuts*, *Junior Bookshelf*, June, 1993, p. 100.

Roback, Diane, and Richard Donahue, review of *Freckly Feet and Itchy Knees*, *Publishers Weekly*, June 8, 1990, p. 54.

Rogers, Sue, review of *Mind the Gap*, *School Librarian*, November, 1992, p. 156.

Sharman, Judith, review of *Little Rabbit Foo Foo*, *Books for Keeps*, May, 1992, p. 11.

Review of *Sonsense Nongs*, *Junior Bookshelf*, October, 1992, p. 201.

Szirtes, George, review of *Hairy Tales and Nursery Crimes*, *Times Literary Supplement*, March 8, 1985, p. 270.

Walter, Colin, review of *Hairy Tales and Nursery Crimes*, *School Librarian*, March, 1985, p. 40.

Watson, Elizabeth S., review of *We're Going on a Bear Hunt*, *Horn Book*, December, 1989, p. 765.

Williams, S., review of *The Golem of Old Prague*, *Books for Your Children*, spring, 1991, p. 24.

Review of *You Can't Catch Me!*, *Junior Bookshelf*, February, 1982, p. 22.

■ For More Information See

BOOKS

Nettell, Stephanie, editor, *Meet the Authors*, Scholastic, 1994.

Powling, Chris, *What It's Like to be Michael Rosen*, Ginn, 1990.

Styles, M., and H. Cook, editors, *There's a Poet Behind You*, ArcBlack, 1988.

PERIODICALS

Books for Keeps, May, 1981; July, 1988.

Books for Your Children, autumn/winter, 1991, p. 24.

Junior Bookshelf, June, 1993, p. 93; June, 1995, pp. 93-94.

Publishers Weekly, October 25, 1993, p. 62.

School Librarian, August, 1988, p. 100; November, 1990, p. 148; August, 1991, p. 112; May, 1993, p. 71.

School Library Journal, December, 1992, p. 127; January, 1994, p. 110; June, 1995, p. 104.

Times Educational Supplement, April 28, 1995.

TOM ROSS

ROSS, Tom 1958-

■ Personal

Born May 15, 1958, in Albuquerque, NM; son of
George (a psychiatrist) and Helen (a nurse; maiden
name, Lewis) Ross; married Elizabeth Hahn (an artist),
November, 1990; children: Aaron. *Education:* Columbia
College, B.A., 1981; Columbia School of Arts, M.F.A.,
1981. *Politics:* Democrat. *Religion:* Jewish.

■ Addresses

Office—Hahn Ross Gallery, 409 Canyon Rd. #1, Santa
Fe, NM 87501. *Agent*—Alice Martel, The Martel Agency, 555 Fifth Ave., New York, NY 10014.

■ Career

Hahn Ross Gallery, Santa Fe, NM, artist and gallery
owner, 1989—. Founding board member of non-profit
"Earth's Birthday" project.

■ Writings

(With Clifford Ross and Lisa Werenko, and illustrator)
  It Zwibble, the Star Touched Dinosaur, Scholastic,
  1986.
Eggbert, the Slightly Cracked Egg, illustrated by Rex
  Barron, Putnam, 1994.
Irma, the Flying Bowling Ball, Putnam, in press.

ILLUSTRATOR

Clifford Ross and Lisa Werenko, *It Zwibble and the Big
  Birthday Party,* Scholastic, 1988.
Ross and Werenko, *It Zwibble and the Greatest Clean
  Up Ever,* Scholastic, 1991.

Ross and Werenko, *It Zwibble and the Hunt for the Rain
  Forest,* Scholastic, 1992.

■ Work in Progress

A Pig in a Blanket, a pop-up book; a CD-ROM version
of *Eggbert, the Slightly Cracked Egg.*

■ Sidelights

Tom Ross told *SATA,* "People frequently ask me, 'How
did I come up with the idea for *Eggbert, the Slightly
Cracked Egg*?' I wish I could give a simple answer and
remember a specific moment when the whole idea for
the book came to me. But in reality the story evolved
over a few years and my original manuscript is very
different from the final published version. I can, however, look back and see how certain events and circum-
stances shaped the story.

"Tucked back in a part of my brain, I think I subcons-
ciously remember being disturbed as a child that 'all the
King's horses and all the King's men' were unable to put
Humpty Dumpty back together again. So perhaps my
own desire to put him back together again was the initial
seed to the *Eggbert* concept."

Eggbert is the story of a slightly cracked denizen of the
refrigerator who amuses its other inhabitants with his
paintings. But when they discover his cracks, Eggbert is
evicted because of his defect. At first, Eggbert tries to
disguise his cracks, but he soon discovers—and begins
to celebrate in paint—things around him that have
beautiful cracks, including the Liberty Bell and the
Grand Canyon. A contributor in *Kirkus Reviews* praised
Ross for having created a "vivacious Humpty Dumpty
look-alike" and for setting him in "an inviting world
that's as bright as new paint."

The seed for writing *Eggbert* was cultivated from Ross's
own lifelong feelings of being somewhat different from
the "norm." "At first I viewed my own eccentricities as
being weaknesses or disabilities," he told *SATA.* "As a
kid and a teenager, more than anything, I wanted to fit
in and be just like everybody else. It wasn't until after
college and recovering from a serious illness that I began
to realize that those things that set one apart can
actually be the source of one's strengths. 'Being different' allows one to experience a unique perspective
unavailable to the 'average Egg.'

"Strangely enough, shortly after I first started working
on the story line for *Eggbert,* I ended up getting hit by a
car while crossing a busy street in Los Angeles. Not only
did I break my leg, but two weeks later I fell down a
flight of stairs and broke my arm. It is funny how in
more ways than one my life seems to parallel with
Eggbert's. Maybe life is 'what it is all cracked up to be.'"

■ Works Cited

Review of *Eggbert, the Slightly Cracked Egg, Kirkus
  Reviews,* February 15, 1994, p. 233.

■ For More Information See

PERIODICALS

Children's Book Review Service, April, 1994, p. 102.
Publishers Weekly, January 16, 1987, p. 73; January 24, 1994, p. 54.
School Library Journal, May, 1994, p. 104.

* * *

ROZAKIS, Laurie E. 1952-

■ Personal

Born July 20, 1952, in New York, NY; daughter of Werner J. (an engineer) and Erna (an art teacher; maiden name, Easton) Neu; married Robert H. Rozakis (executive director of production, DC Comics, *Mad Magazine*), April 5, 1974; children: Charles Lawrence, Samantha Jill. *Education:* Hofstra University, B.A., 1973, M.A., 1975; State University of New York, Stony Brook, Ph.D., 1984. *Hobbies and other interests:* Reading, walking, swimming, travel, theater, socializing, cooking.

■ Addresses

Home—62 Sunset Ave., Farmingdale, NY 11735.

■ Career

Commack Schools, Commack, NY, English teacher, 1973-84; Hofstra University, Hempstead, NY, adjunct assistant professor of English, 1979-86; State University of New York at Farmingdale, associate professor of English and humanities, 1986—. Writer, 1973—. President of board of trustees, Farmingdale Public Library. *Member:* Modern Language Association, American Association of University Women, National Educational Association, National Council of Teachers of English, Women in Literature and Life Assembly.

■ Awards, Honors

Farmingdale College Foundation Faculty Merit Award, 1991; The State University of New York Chancellor's Award for Excellence in Teaching, 1994.

■ Writings

FOR CHILDREN

Steven Jobs: Computer Genius, Rourke Enterprises, 1993.
Mary Kay: Cosmetics Queen, Rourke Enterprises, 1993.
Celebrate! Holidays around the World, Learning Works, 1993.
Teen Pregnancy: Why Are Kids Having Babies?, Twenty-First Century Books, 1993.
Magic Johnson: Basketball Immortal, Rourke Enterprises, 1993.
Jeana Yeager and Dick Rutan: Flying Non-Stop around the World, illustrated by Jerry Harston, Blackbirch Press, 1994.

LAURIE E. ROZAKIS

Matthew Henson and Robert Peary: The Race for the North Pole, illustrated by Tom Foty, Blackbirch Press, 1994.
Bill Hanna and Joe Barbera: Yabba-Dabba-Doo!, illustrated by Dick Smolinski, Blackbirch Press, 1994.
Homelessness: Can We Solve the Problem?, Twenty-First Century Books, 1995.

EDUCATIONAL

Advanced Placement Examination in English: Composition and Literature, Prentice Hall, 1986, 3rd edition, 1993.
College English Placement and Proficiency Examinations, ARCO, 1988.
(With Sally Martin) *Verbal Workbook for the New ACT,* ARCO, 1988.
(With Martin) *English Workbook for the New ACT,* ARCO, 1990.
Random House Guide to Grammar Usage and Punctuation, Random House, 1991.
Power Vocabulary Pocket Guide, Random House, 1991.
Reproducibles, Activities, and Ideas to Develop Critical Thinking for the Middle and Upper Grades, Scholastic Professional Books, 1991.
Reproducibles, Activities, and Ideas to Develop Critical Thinking for the Primary Grades, Scholastic Professional Books, 1992.
Laura Ingalls Wilder: Activities Based on Research from the Laura Ingalls Wilder Homes and Museums, Scholastic Professional Books, 1993.

Merriam-Webster's Rules of Order, Merriam-Webster, 1994.

Appreciating Poetry, Prentice Hall/Macmillan, 1995.

Power Reading, Prentice Hall/Macmillan, 1995.

■ Sidelights

Laurie E. Rozakis told *SATA,* "In retrospect, I suppose that I've always been a writer, scribbling loopy crayon messages as a toddler, writing gossipy notes as a teenager, and typing dense letters in college. English was my best subject, but I never imagined making writing a career: I had never met a real live writer and could not believe that people actually made a living as word-smiths. As a child and teenager, I did what was expected of me in and out of school. During the day I took a full load of advanced classes and participated in various extracurricular activities. In the late afternoon, I went to charm school, ballet classes, and music lessons (failures all); took sewing, art, and ice skating lessons (modest successes). I could cook and test like a whiz—proving both when I aced the test that made me Betty Crocker Homemaker of the Year in high school—and did well enough overall to earn a full academic scholarship to Hofstra, a respectable Long Island university. I earned a degree in English and secondary education with various honors and promptly took a job teaching in a local high school. And just as fast started writing letters again.

In one of several biographies about partnerships, Rozakis profiles the successful cooperation of two famous cartoonists. (Cover illustration by Dick Smolinski.)

"My writing remained purely epistolary until 1981, when I was home for four months after the birth of my first child. Casting about for something to fill the time between burping and bathing my son, I decided to write a review book for the Advanced Placement Exam in English. I wish I could recount exactly when the lighting bolt hit, but I wasn't even teaching an AP English class that semester. Most likely, someone had passed an offhand remark in the teacher's room about the need for such a book, the remark germinated for a few years and sprouted that sultry June when I was busy shuffling gears. Regardless, with the boundless confidence of the novice, I created a Table of Contents, resurrected and updated my resume, wrote a cover letter, and sent the bundle to every single possible publisher listed in *Literary Market Place.* The post office thought this was a brilliant idea; it was not until much later that I cued into the idea of targeting an audience and saving on stamps.

"Who bought the manuscript? ARCO—the very first name on the list. My editors at this test-prep division of Simon & Schuster/Paramount proved both patient and kind, gently initiating me into the mysteries of the book biz. The book has since gone into its third revision and printing, and I've done a handful of other books for them as well, include *The New GED, College English Placement and Proficiency Exam, Reading Power: Getting Started, Verbal Workbook for the ACT* (with Sally Martin), and *Power Reading!*

"I returned to teaching in September of 1981, and writing was far back on the burner as I taught, completed my Ph.D., and took care of home and hearth. In 1984 the earth shifted once again, as I was laid off from the high school due to declining enrollment, finished my Ph.D., and birthed our second child, a daughter. Although a year later I took a job teaching English in the State University of New York, I began to feel an almost physical need to write. Suddenly, letters weren't enough; I needed to write something solid to sink my teeth into. The contacts I had made with ARCO helped me begin to publish more and in greater variety, as did some friendships I had made with a handful of extraordinarily talented and generous writers. Soon, I was doing a wide variety of educational materials, including work for McClanahan and Company; Prentice Hall; McDougal, Littel, and Company; Scholastic; Macmillan; and Random House. I love the challenge of figuring out each project and focusing on a different audience. Most of my writing has been in English, language arts, multicultural education, social studies, test prep, and writing, but I've also written large math and science projects. Recently, I completed a series of biographies, including *Dick Rutan and Jeana Yeager, Mary Kay, Magic Johnson, Henson and Peary,* and *Hanna and Barbera.* They were a special treat.

"I'm a compulsive writer, often losing track of time when my imagination catches fire. As a result, I usually continue to write long after midnight, always with a rapier-sharp #2 pencil behind my right ear, a cup of tepid, murky tea on the bookshelf, and the radio droning 'oldies but goodies' in the background. I never use the pencil, know enough to shun the tea, and rarely remember the words to any song, but that's the routine. The first draft usually comes easily to me, but it's all smoke and mirrors, for I write, rewrite, and rewrite again. I'd polish *this* entry until the next millennium, if I could! Words, like people, have rhythms and personalities, tastes and textures. I want more than meaning—I want the beat. Will you remember this phrase, suck on it like a ripe cherry, play with the pit in your mouth for half an hour? Will it linger on your tongue like the last sweet cold lick of the cherry icepop you shared with your younger sister on those sweltering August nights? If so, I've done my job well."

■ For More Information See

PERIODICALS

Booklist, July, 1994, p. 1939.
Book Report, January, 1988, p. 36.
Children's Bookwatch, August, 1994, p. 3.
Instructor, February, 1993, p. 45.
School Library Journal, February, 1994, p. 116; July, 1994, p. 108.

*   *   *

RUBIN, Susan Goldman 1939-

■ Personal

Born March 14, 1939, in New York, NY; daughter of Abraham (a manufacturing jeweler) and Julia (a homemaker; maiden name, Berlin) Moldof; married Hubert M. Goldman (a physician), June, 1959 (divorced, 1976); married Michael B. Rubin (a real estate broker), December 30, 1978; children: (first marriage) Katie Goldman Kolpas, John, Peter; (second marriage) Andrew. *Education:* Oberlin College, B.A. (with honors), 1959; graduate study at the University of California at Los Angeles, 1961-62, attended extension program, 1980-91. *Politics:* Democrat. *Religion:* Jewish. *Hobbies and other interests:* Jogging, cooking, life drawing, going to movies and theater.

■ Addresses

Home—6330 Sycamore Meadows Dr., Malibu, CA 90265. *Agent*—Andrea Brown, P.O. Box 429, El Granada, CA 94018-0429.

■ Career

Children's book writer and illustrator, 1975—; freelance writer of educational filmstrips, 1975-78. California State University Department of Continuing Education, Northridge, CA, instructor, 1977-86; University of California Extension School Writer's Program, Los Angeles, CA, instructor, 1986—. *Member:* Society for Children's Book Writers and Illustrators, PEN, Authors Guild, Authors League of America, Southern California Council on Literature for Children and Young People.

SUSAN GOLDMAN RUBIN

■ Awards, Honors

National Endowment for the Humanities Travel to Collections Grant, 1993, for research on a juvenile biography on Frank Lloyd Wright; International Reading Association Young Adults' Choice, 1995, for *Emily Good as Gold.*

■ Writings

(And illustrator) *Grandma Is Somebody Special,* A. Whitman, 1976.
(And illustrator) *Cousins Are Special,* A. Whitman, 1978.
(And illustrator) *Grandpa and Me Together,* A. Whitman, 1980.
Walk with Danger (young adult mystery), Silhouette Books, 1986.
The Black Orchid (young adult mystery), Crosswinds, 1988.
Emily Good as Gold (middle grade novel), Browndeer/Harcourt, 1993.
The Rainbow Fields, illustrated by Heather Preston, Enchante Publishing, 1993.
Frank Lloyd Wright (biography; "First Impressions" series), Abrams, 1994.

Also author of educational filmstrips for McGraw-Hill, BFA, and Pied Piper Productions; author of a story published in *Highlights for Children*. Editorial assistant for *Designers West,* Los Angeles, CA, 1991-92. *Walk with Danger* was published in Italy, 1987, and France, 1990; *The Black Orchid* was published in Spain, 1988, and France, 1988.

■ Work in Progress

Emily in Love, a companion book to *Emily Good as Gold,* Browndeer/Harcourt, 1996; *Margaret Burke-White* for the "First Impressions" series, Abrams, 1996; *Hank's Shadow,* a middle grade novel set in Venice, California, in 1949, "about the brother of a teenage boy who comes down with polio."

■ Sidelights

Susan Goldman Rubin spent her childhood in New York City and attended the famous High School of Music and Art in New York City as a teenager. She told *SATA* that she "dreamt of becoming an artist and illustrating children's books. However, when I moved to California as a young wife and mother, I couldn't easily go back to New York to show my portfolio and try to get illustrating assignments. So I began writing my own stories to give myself something to illustrate. When I sent my picture book dummies to editors, I found, to my great surprise, that they were as interested in my writing as my artwork. With their rejection letters came suggestions for revisions, and I started taking writing classes at UCLA Extension to learn my craft. I published my first story in *Highlights for Children.*

"A few years later I finally published my first picture book, *Grandma Is Somebody Special,* which I also illustrated. More books about my family followed. My two young adult novels, *Walk with Danger* and *The Black Orchid,* both mysteries, grew from incidents I read about in the newspaper. My biography of Frank Lloyd Wright stemmed from my desire to introduce young readers to architecture as an art form, and to acquaint them with the life and career of one of the most innovative architects of the twentieth century.

"*Emily Good as Gold* developed from an educational filmstrip that I made with my husband. We researched and photographed at a special school for handicapped children in Los Angeles, and I was deeply moved by the students I met. I felt that our filmstrip would only scratch the surface in terms of changing people's negative attitudes toward those who are disabled. I thought a middle grade novel featuring a heroine who is mentally retarded would be more effective."

Like many adolescent girls, the protagonist in *Emily Good as Gold* is proud of the changes taking place in her body and longs to be respected as a young woman. Yet Emily is developmentally disabled and thinks that her "head doesn't work right." Along with the rest of the family, Emily's father is reluctant to inform her about relationships between young men and women. He is afraid that Emily will not be able to handle the perils of adolescence, warns her to be careful of boys, and refuses

Although her father worries about her because she is mentally handicapped, thirteen-year-old Emily Gold proves to him that she can exercise good judgment when it comes to choices about sex in this sensitive story. (Cover illustration by Ellen Thompson.)

to let her wear earrings or to let her dress like the girls in the teenage magazines she reads.

When Emily attends a camp for the mentally disabled, a friend informs her about sex: "Fun is when you kiss naked and everything." Emily is disgusted by this revelation, but she is even more upset to discover that her older brother, Tom, is getting married. She prepares herself to hate her new sister-in-law, Phyllis. It is Phyllis, however, who finally explains sex and relationships with boys to Emily. When Tom and Phyllis have a baby, Emily wants one too. As a result, Emily's father becomes even more protective of her. Emily gradually learns how to tell the difference between well-meaning boys and malicious ones, but not without a struggle. She allows a boy to lead her into the basement and is attacked and must fight to get away. Also, two boys try to lure Emily into their car, yet this time she eludes them. Finally, Emily begins to develop a relationship with Donny, a student in her special education class, and her father admits that she "has a good head" on her shoulders.

Some reviewers of *Emily Good as Gold* appreciated Rubin's treatment of sex and the developmentally disabled—a subject which has been neglected in children's literature. A *Booklist* critic commented that Rubin "handles the subject with sensitivity and taste," and Cindy Darling Codell wrote in *School Library Journal* that *Emily Good as Gold* is "a gem of a book for changing perceptions." Some children also found Rubin's work rewarding. As the author told *SATA*, she "was thrilled to get fan mail from readers who wrote that they liked Emily, identified with her, and now feel differently about kids with disabilities." Rubin is writing "another book about Emily showing how Emily copes with the regular world as she struggles to become an independent young woman."

Rubin has fulfilled her childhood dream of illustrating books, and suggests to "aspiring writers and illustrators to follow their passionate interests, find their own voices, and never give up."

■ Works Cited

Codell, Cindy Darling, review of *Emily Good as Gold, School Library Journal,* October, 1993, p. 152.
Review of *Emily Good as Gold, Booklist,* November 1, 1993, p. 514.
Rubin, Susan Goldman, *Emily Good as Gold,* Browndeer/Harcourt, 1993.

■ For More Information See

PERIODICALS

Bulletin of the Center for Children's Books, November, 1993, p. 97.
Children's Bookwatch, December, 1993, p. 6.
Kirkus Reviews, October 1, 1993, p. 1279.
Publishers Weekly, October 25, 1993, p. 64.

*   *   *

RUELLE, Karen Gray 1957-

■ Personal

Born June 17, 1957, in Maryland; daughter of Edward (an engineer) and Barbara (an artist; maiden name, Ampolsey) Gray; married Lee Gray Ruelle (an artist), September 18, 1988; children: Nina Sophia. *Education:* University of Michigan, B.G.S. (with distinction), 1979, M.L.S., 1980. *Religion:* Jewish.

■ Addresses

Office—c/o Sterling Publishing, 387 Park Ave. S., New York, NY 10016-8810.

KAREN GRAY RUELLE

■ Career

Library Journal, New York City, assistant editor, 1980-83; *Publishers Weekly,* New York City, associate editor, 1983-85; English-Speaking Union, New York City, librarian, 1985-90; freelance editor and writer.

■ Awards, Honors

First runner-up, *Partners and Crimes* (bookstore) writing competition, 1994.

■ Writings

75 Fun Things to Make and Do By Yourself, illustrated by Sandy Haight, Sterling, 1993.

Contributor of book reviews to *Library Journal, Publishers Weekly,* and *Kirkus Reviews,* and of articles to *Stamford Advocate/Greenwich Time.*

■ Work in Progress

A picture book series, novels, board books.

■ Sidelights

Karen Gray Ruelle told *SATA:* "When I was growing up, I wanted to be a writer and I also wanted to be an artist. Since it never occurred to me that I could be both as an adult, I was in a state of constant conflict about what I would be when I grew up. Then a dear friend suggested that I write and illustrate children's books. A great fog lifted, and I've been pursuing that dream ever since!

"I've never had a problem coming up with ideas. My life is filled with little stories, made-up and real. I'm the kind of person who sees the humorous and ironic side of everything, and I'm forever imagining shapes and personalities in everything I see. A fire hydrant is a strange creature breaking through the concrete sidewalk; trees express powerful emotions with their branched arms; birds actually talk; houses listen. And I love the music of language. So it makes sense that I like to put these things down, as pictures and stories.

"My mother, the artist, showed me that the world is filled with magic and beauty; my dad, the humorist and engineer, showed me the funny side of life and that anything was possible. Both raised my brother and me to believe that we could do anything and they instilled in us a sense of fun and enjoyment. We travelled a lot when I was growing up—moving back and forth across the Atlantic several times—so I often feel as though I belong nowhere, which is to say that I belong everywhere, and home can be anywhere. This is a liberating state of mind, meaning that anything is, indeed, possible. On the other hand, I've also always felt a bit lost, looking for that place called home, and so this motivates me to keep the search going.

"I've always been an avid reader, a flashlight-under-the-covers-at-night kind of person. In fact, for a while I was a librarian, just so that I could be surrounded by books. (I thought of myself as not only a Keeper of the Books, but also as a kind of Private Investigator of Information, answering all sorts of odd and fascinating reference questions.) From a very young age, I started making up my own little books. The first was about penguins and how to dress them up for various special occasions—I think I was six years old at the time! I keep coming back to making up books. It's the only place where I do feel completely at home—with my writing and drawing and painting, making up little stories that develop often from a single image or phrase or sound.

"My first book, *75 Fun Things to Make and Do By Yourself,* evolved quite naturally. I must have the sensibilities of a ten-year-old because it was easy for me to think from that viewpoint. Brainstorming to come up with projects for the book was an extremely creative time for me, and soon my apartment was filled with a jumble of materials, half-finished projects, junk everywhere. From the midst of this constructive chaos, the book emerged. I like to think that my book is not only a useful resource of activities and projects, but that it also motivates independent and creative thinking in its readers. In addition, I hope the informal, anecdotal tone reads like a storybook, almost a documentation of the development of the creative process.

"Discipline has always been difficult for me. When I have less time to work on my writing and art, the need to focus becomes imperative. Having a child has helped me concentrate on being more productive—I have no choice but to focus during the brief time allotted to my work in the studio. My mother taught me how important it is to give yourself studio time. My husband, an artist as well, concurs, and has been supportive of my need to have a private and personal workspace.

"It's a joy to see my stories and pictures amuse my daughter. I strive to make my work both entertaining and moving. My goal is to combine sweetness and humor without making my work too sentimental or goofy.

"Tomorrow is my studio day. I'll start off with my usual cup of tea and then immerse myself in the world of a bear-like creature named Harry and his younger sister, Samantha. Perhaps something I see on my way to the studio will appear in one of Harry and Samantha's adventures. Later in the day, I'll work on making stories and pictures fit together, juggling and trying out different combinations to attain the simplicity and rhythm that I like. Maybe next week I'll work on the mid-grade novel I've begun, or perhaps I'll take out that adult novel I began some years ago. So many ideas, so much work, and not nearly enough time in which to do it all!"

■ For More Information See

PERIODICALS

Booklist, March 15, 1994.

*   *   *

RUMBAUT, Hendle 1949-

■ Personal

Surname is pronounced "Room-*bow*"; born Helen Elizabeth Livingston Pendleton, October 8, 1949, in Deland, FL; daughter of William Biklen Pendleton (an attorney, judge, and farmer) and Edith Marie Pendleton Rankin (an artist; maiden name, Cottom); married Carlos Alberto Rumbaut (a computer programmer), July 7, 1970 (divorced, 1978); married (common law) Michael E. Ambrose (a writer, editor, and publisher of *Argonaut* magazine), 1983; children: Sasha Rumbaut. *Education:* University of Kansas, B.A., 1971; graduate study at Washburn University, 1971. *Politics:* Democrat. *Religion:* Christian. *Hobbies and other interests:* Reading, music, photography, playing piano, things French, staring at the sea.

■ Addresses

Home—2208 Saratoga Dr., Austin, TX 78733. *Office*—Austin Public Library, 800 Guadalupe St., Austin, TX 78701; and P.O. Box 2287, Austin, TX

78768. *Agent*—Shawna McCarthy, Scovil Chichak Galen Literary Agency, Inc., 381 Park Ave. S., Suite 1020, New York, NY 10016.

■ Career

Writer, reporter, photographer, proofreader, and copyeditor for numerous newspapers and magazines, including *Argonaut, The Avenue, Global Parenting, Lawrence Daily Journal-World,* and *Westlake Picayune,* 1965-91; Austin Public Library, Austin, TX, public information specialist, marketing and public information division, 1974—; Permanent Press/Second Chance Publishing, Sag Harbor, NY, copy editor, 1991—; has also worked variously as a clerk/typist, camp counselor, French tutor, translator, and day care teacher. *Exhibitions:* Exhibitor at group show, Austin History Center art exhibit, 1987; one-woman photography exhibit, Westbank Community Library, 1991. *Member:* Authors Guild, Authors League of America, Society of Children's Book Writers and Illustrators, University of Kansas Alumni Association, PEN Center West, Texas Photographic Society, Austin Writers and Illustrators for Children, Austin Writers' League, Phi Beta Kappa, Pi Delta Phi.

■ Awards, Honors

Junior Year Abroad Program Scholarship in Bordeaux, France, University of Kansas, 1969; Book for the Teen Age selection, 1995, New York Public Library, Office of Young Adult Services, and Recommended Book for Reluctant Readers selection, 1995, American Library Association, both for *Dove Dream.*

■ Writings

Dove Dream, Houghton, 1994.

Also contributor of short stories to periodicals, including *Word & Image: The Illustrated Journal, Chiron Review,* and *Lone Star Literary Quarterly;* has had a play and short story published at the Phobia Society of America national conference, Rockville, MD, fall, 1987; contributed an essay to *S.A., An Opinionated Journal of Opinionated Essays,* fall, 1991, and a short story in *Women and Food: Eating Our Hearts Out,* Crossing Press, 1993. Author of the unpublished works, *Babes at Sea* (adult novel), *Love Steps* and *The Hungry Secret* (young adult novels), *Pinky the Poodle* and *The Sunday Cookies* (picture books). Coauthor (with Rodney Rincon) of *The Critic* (a screenplay) and the book for the musical *Spring Forward/Fall Back,* to be produced at the University of Texas at Austin.

Also editor (selected) of *Central Texas Library System Media Catalog,* Austin Public Library, 1990; *Counting What You Do: A Guide to Collecting and Reporting Public Library Statistics,* Texas State Library, 1992. Photographs published in *Austin Child* magazine, August, 1992, and *Mas* magazine, July/August, 1991.

■ Work in Progress

Junie Blue, an adult novel; short stories for adults and children; researching Native American history, Catholic saints and traditions, life in a Catholic monastery in the late 1960s, Haskell Indian Institute in the 1950s and 1960s, and the American Indian Movement.

■ Sidelights

Dove Dream, Hendle Rumbaut's first published novel, is a coming-of-age story that, in the words of a *Publishers Weekly* reviewer, "succeeds in paying tribute to Native American philosophies." In *Dove Dream,* thirteen-year-old Eleanor Derrysaw describes a summer spent with her divorced aunt Anna. The summer begins when Eleanor's parents, who are on the verge of divorce themselves, send her to stay with Anna in rural Kansas. Eleanor appreciates her aunt's carefree attitude and spontaneity, especially as it contrasts with the despairing moods of her alcoholic father and disabled mother. Aunt Anna nicknames Eleanor "Dove," gets her a job at the diner where she works, and teaches her how to drive. Her aunt treats her like an adult and tells Dove about her relationship with Troy, a Cheyenne man. It is not long before Dove develops enough independence to begin a relationship with her first boyfriend. As the summer progresses, Dove explores her surroundings and searches her soul. When she finds letters from her late grandmother explaining how the family's Chickasaw heritage was almost completely devastated, she decides

HENDLE RUMBAUT

to learn more about her Native American and Irish background. Finally, Dove sets out on an Ojibway vision quest and fasts for days in the desert.

In an interview with Rumbaut for the *Westlake Picayune,* Kim Pyle pointed out that *Dove Dream* "is set in the early 1960s, a time she [Rumbaut] knows from her own childhood. But in a symbolic sense, it is a time that parallels Dove's coming-of-age with America's own evolution.... To adults, the summer of 1963 will recall the last days of innocence before President John F. Kennedy's assassination." According to *School Library Journal* critic Rita Soltan, the "strong characterization of the narrator," Dove, along with the "good development" of Anna's character, makes *Dove Dream* "an enjoyable read."

Rumbaut told *SATA* that she began her writing career because she is "in love with words. I have always loved the feel of them in my mouth, the way they look on the page, diagramming them on a chalk board, the pleasure of printing or typing. My mother read to my brother and me every night before we went to bed, and my grandmother turned me into a great speller. In junior high I started writing seriously, and at age sixteen I had a weekly review column, 'Raves & Reviews,' in the *Lawrence Daily Journal-World,* covering cultural events at Lawrence High School. I was editor of the yearbook and have been a reporter and copy editor for various newspapers and magazines. (Journalism helped my fiction writing by keeping me grounded in the 'five W's'—who, what, where, when, and why—and forced me to write under short deadlines instead of waiting around for inspiration).

"For five years I worked in a bookstore and loved the company of books. I hungered to see my own name on a cover someday. In the 1980s I collaborated on a book for a musical to be produced by the University of Texas (it was cast and in rehearsal, but the song-writing side of the thing fell through at the last minute, alas). As my daughter got older, I started writing more, and by the time she left for college, my writing really took off. I got some short stories for adults and children published, a few essays, and then a novel, *Dove Dream.*"

Rumbaut explained that she wrote *Dove Dream* to "tell the story that was emerging. I had not thought of the story before I sat down that day to write. It was a warm sunny day, with popcorn clouds and a warm breeze. An image came to me of the same kind of day, with a Native American girl and her aunt driving on a dirt road through golden Kansas wheat fields. They were in a red Chevy convertible, and there was a special excitement in the air. I decided to follow these characters and see what they were up to. I got inside their heads, spoke their words, and felt their emotions. Soon a plot was shaping up, and I knew how it would end, though not exactly how they would get there."

Rumbaut takes her inspiration from a variety of sources. She told *SATA* that the works of Anne Tyler, Louise Erdrich, Gabriel Garcia Marquez, Isabel Al-

A young teen experiences a summer of self-discovery while living with her aunt in Kansas during the year 1963 in Rumbaut's first novel. (Cover illustration by Gwen Frankfeldt.)

lende, Judy Blume, Bobbie Ann Mason, Eudora Welty, Colette, Max Steele, and Ludwig Bemelmans have influenced her own work as a writer. "Their words are trustworthy, true, clear, magical, transporting, tasty as nectar." Rumbaut also noted that she finds "ideas everywhere: scraps of overheard conversations, newspaper articles, TV, dreams, memories, fantasies, obituaries, photos. There's no lack of ideas. As someone said, you could be placed in a sensory deprivation tank at an early age and never run out of ideas to write about. I believe that." To help her recall the pieces of information that interest her, Rumbaut keeps "folders of ideas, details, titles, characters, settings, images, scraps of dialogue, weird facts, names, odors, sounds, tastes."

Rumbaut explained her work habits when writing: "I usually see a character in my mind or hear one line of dialogue. It vibrates with possibilities and haunts me; something is about to happen, or has just happened. I sit down and go with it, just start writing and trusting that something will come out. For the first draft I use a pencil and paper, writing outdoors if possible, in a blue canvas chair I bought at K Mart. Sitting under my live oaks with the birds and the sky and the breeze, I am in my favorite 'office,' though I can also write in noisy places, with people around. My creative ideas usually come in the early to late afternoon; after dark I shut down, except for editing or proofing. I get in a time warp when I write. Suddenly it's too dark to see. The sun has gone down, there's a chill in the air, and I may have acquired some mosquito bites.

"Creating whole new worlds is exhilarating. The characters feel as real as people I know. After freewriting for several pages, I consider forming a general shape to the work, if it's a novel. I try to solve sticky places in the plot beforehand, so the writing will go more easily, but endless surprises pop up in every story. I don't force myself to write chapters sequentially, but often write the ones that interest me the most first. Writing is like doing a big puzzle. It helps to have a high degree of tolerance for ambiguity until all the pieces are put together.

"I avoid talking about the story or showing it to anyone until I have written it down. It's like a little seed germinating that needs protection. By sharing it too soon with others, you can kill it. People will inject their ideas, turn it upside down, convince you it isn't even worth writing about. Or you may get your satisfaction from talking the story instead of writing the story, which is okay unless you want to be a writer."

Rumbaut advises aspiring writers: "Write your heart out. Be bold. Read the best writers. Be still and listen. Don't write up or down to people. Don't worry what your mother might think. Never correct until you have it all down . . . . Be present with your words. Trust your stories, and know that you're the only one who can write them. Write what excites you, not what's trendy. After a story has been rejected, send it off to the next market on your list and forget about it; get on to the next thing. Go wherever the writing takes you, even if it's scary."

■ Works Cited

Review of *Dove Dream, Publishers Weekly,* March 28, 1994, p. 97.

Pyle, Kim, "Author's Memories Become Novel Idea," *Westlake Picayune* (Austin, TX), May 11, 1994, p. 9.

Soltan, Rita, review of *Dove Dream, School Library Journal,* May, 1994, pp. 134-35.

■ For More Information See

PERIODICALS

Kirkus Reviews, May 1, 1994, p. 636.

S

St. ANTOINE, Sara L. 1966-

■ Personal

Born July 26, 1966, in Ann Arbor, MI; daughter of
Theodore J. and Elizabeth L. St. Antoine. *Education:*
Williams College, B.A., 1988; Yale University, M.S.,
1993. *Hobbies and other interests:* Running, hiking,
piano playing, outdoor adventuring, waffle-making.

■ Addresses

Home and office—Washington, DC. *Agent*—c/o Bantam Books, 1540 Broadway, New York, NY 10036.

■ Career

Environmental Law Institute, Washington, DC, associate editor, 1988-89; National Wildlife Federation,
Washington, DC, project editor in School Programs
division, 1989-91; World Wildlife Fund, Washington,
DC, education consultant, 1993—; Echoing Green
Foundation, Washington, DC, public service fellow,
1993-95; American Association for the Advancement of
Science, Washington, DC, writer for children's science
radio drama, 1995—. Conservation International, research associate, 1991-92. *Member:* Sierra Club, DC-
Environmental Education Coalition.

■ Writings

Dress Code Mess, illustrated by Dave Henderson, Bantam, 1992.
The Green Musketeers and the Fabulous Frogs, Bantam,
1994.
*The Green Musketeers and the Incredible Energy Esca-
pade,* Bantam, 1994.

Also author of short story published in *Ranger Rick*
magazine; contributor to *The Biophilia Hypothesis,*
edited by Stephen J. Kellert and Edward O. Wilson,
Island Press, 1993.

The Green Musketeers set out to get their school to
save energy, but they face opposition when their plans
threaten the big school party. (Cover illustration by
Bob Larkin.)

■ Work in Progress

A third *Green Musketeers* story; a novel set in Northern
Michigan; curricula designed to develop children's
"sense of place."

225

▪ Sidelights

Sara L. St. Antoine told *SATA:* "When I was six, I made a portrait of myself as an adult. It reads, 'I am going to be an author and an illustrator,' and features a grown-up me seated at a desk writing, 'The bear went through the woods.' Delusions of art talent aside, it wasn't a bad forecast!

"After writing stories and poems with wild enthusiasm as a child, then working in the environmental field as an adult, I finally realized I could do both at once. My revelation inspired my first two books, about a group of kids called the Green Musketeers.

"Like many kids today, the Green Musketeers are concerned about the world around them. Their adventures will, I hope, help kids think and care about the environment. But most of all, I hope they inspire kids to get outside and create their own adventures. I don't think kids need to learn about global catastrophes to grow up to be concerned citizens. Much better to do what kids do best—play, explore, and fall in love with the wilder corners of their own home.

"My current projects have brought me to Washington, DC, where I am working to help kids develop a sense of place wherever they live. When I'm not writing, I'm usually reading novels and nature literature, taking runs and long walks, and seeking out the places in this city where the trees and birds still insist on making a statement."

* * *

SAINT JAMES, Synthia 1949-

▪ Personal

Born February 11, 1949, in Los Angeles, CA. *Education:* Self-taught artist/writer.

▪ Addresses

Home—P.O. Box 27683, Los Angeles, CA 90027.

▪ Career

Artist, 1969—; owner of Atelier Saint James (print publisher). Has worked as an actress, freelance writer, publicist, accountant, and tax consultant. *Exhibitions:* Works exhibited at solo shows in New York City, Charlotte, NC, Salt Lake City, UT, Los Angeles, Pasadena, Burbank, Westwood, and Santa Barbara, CA; works exhibited at group shows in Paris, France, Seoul, South Korea, Quebec, Canada, New York City, Los Angeles, Chicago, and Washington, DC. Works commissioned by major organizations and corporations, including the House of Seagram, the National Bar Association, *Essence* Magazine, Kayser-Roth/Maybelline, AT&T Alliance of Black Employees, Children's Institute International, UNICEF, the Mark Taper Forum, South State

SYNTHIA SAINT JAMES

Cooperative Library System, Los Angeles Public Library, and the Los Angeles Cultural Affairs Department.

▪ Writings

(Self-illustrated) *The Gifts of Kwanzaa,* Albert Whitman, 1994.

ILLUSTRATOR

Phyllis Gershator, adaptor, *Tukama Tootles the Flute: A Tale from St. Thomas,* Orchard Books, 1994.
Cheryl Chapman, *Snow on Snow on Snow,* Dial Books, 1994.
Marcia K. Vaughan, *Tingo Tango Mango Tree,* Silver, Burdett & Ginn, 1994.
Walter Dean Myers, *How Mr. Monkey Saw the Whole World,* Doubleday, 1995.

Also illustrator of more than thirty book covers, including *Waiting to Exhale* by Terry McMillan and children's books by Angela Shelf Medearis, Angela Johnson, and Barbara Ann Porte. Creator of designs appearing on over eighty greeting cards, including several for UNICEF, as well as licensed images appearing on T-shirts, magnets, boxes, gift bags, deck cards, puzzles, calendars, and mugs.

▪ Work in Progress

Illustrating *Neeny Coming . . . Neeny Going,* for Bridgewater; writing and illustrating a book, for Albert Whitman; creating characters and other artwork for a CD-ROM for Dream Connections.

■ **Sidelights**

Synthia Saint James told *SATA:* "One of the most beautiful things about painting is the actual sharing of the artwork visually with others, and what a pleasure it is now to be sharing more closely with children by way of children's picture books. The process of creating the images to bring the words to life is amazing in itself, and quite a task—but very rewarding once the challenge is met."

■ **For More Information See**

PERIODICALS

American Visions, October, 1992, pp. 34-36.
Caribe News, March 7, 1995.
Charlotte Observer, February 14, 1993, pp. 1F, 2F.
Essence, January, 1995.
Publishers Weekly, August 8, 1994; September 19, 1994.
School Library Journal, October, 1994.
U.S. Art, January/February, 1993.
Vibe, June, 1995.

*   *   *

SAWYER, Kem Knapp 1953-

■ **Personal**

Born June 11, 1953, in New York, NY; daughter of John E. and Evelyn (Kem) Knapp; married Jon Sawyer (a journalist), 1974; children: Kate, Eve, Ida. *Education:* Yale University, B.A., 1974.

■ **Addresses**

Home—2915 Porter St. N.W., Washington, DC 20008.

■ **Career**

Writer; teacher.

■ **Writings**

The National Foundation on the Arts and the Humanities (part of the "Know Your Government" series), Chelsea House, 1989.
The U.S. Arms Control and Disarmament Agency (part of the "Know Your Government" series), Chelsea House, 1990.
Lucretia Mott: Friend of Justice, illustrated by Leslie Carow, Discovery Enterprises, 1991.
Marjory Stoneman Douglas: Guardian of the Everglades, illustrated by Carow, Discovery Enterprises, 1994.
Refugees: Seeking a Safe Haven, Enslow, 1995.

■ **Work in Progress**

A work on the underground railroad (historical fiction).

■ **Sidelights**

Kem Knapp Sawyer told *SATA:* "For as long as I can remember I wanted to be a writer. I was lying in bed one night at the age of nine; when my mother came in to say good-night, I told her I wanted to be a writer. You would have thought I had just revealed the most private thought—the deepest, darkest secret. Of course she wasn't supposed to tell anyone and she wasn't supposed to bring it up or ever remind me what I had told her. I don't know why it had to be such a big secret, but it did. I didn't have many secrets then, but it seemed pretty daring to want to be a writer. I guess I didn't do that many daring things. My sister and I did on occasion crawl out onto the fire escape—forbidden territory on Waverly Place in New York City where I grew up. We took the cats with us and ate peanut-butter-and-jelly sandwiches and opened a can of real tuna—not cat food—for the cats. But that was about it in the daring secret category.

"I like writing about people whose lives are not very well known. I tend to spend much time in libraries uncovering little-known facts. In working on my book on the underground railroad, I've discovered events that happened a hundred and fifty years ago and have long been forgotten. But they are stories worth telling. And some are stories that must be told."

KEM KNAPP SAWYER

■ For More Information See

PERIODICALS

Booklist, January 1, 1990, p. 898; October 15, 1990, p. 432.
School Library Journal, June, 1990, p. 143; October, 1991, p. 134; December, 1993, p. 130.
Voice of Youth Advocates, February, 1990, p. 363.

*   *   *

SCHMID, Eleonore 1939-

■ Personal

Born March 15, 1939, in Lucerne, Switzerland; daughter of Josef and Elise (Wunderli) Schmid; married Aja Iskander Schmidlin (a painter), 1969 (divorced, 1973); children: Caspar Iskander. *Education:* School of Arts and Crafts, Lucerne, Switzerland, degree in graphics, 1961.

■ Addresses

Office—c/o Nord-Sued Books, Industriestrasse 837, CH-8625, Gossau, Zurich, Switzerland.

■ Career

Writer and illustrator of children's books. Worked in graphics in Zurich, Switzerland, 1961-64, in Paris, France, 1965, and in New York City, 1965-68.

■ Awards, Honors

Awards of excellence from societies of illustrators in New York, Bologna, and Bratislava.

■ Writings

SELF-ILLUSTRATED

(With Etienne Delessert) *The Tree,* Quist, 1966.
(With Delessert) *The Endless Party,* Quist, 1967.
Horns Everywhere, Quist, 1968.
Tonia: The Mouse with the White Stone and What Happened on Her Way to See Uncle Tobias, translated by Lone Thygesen-Blecher, Putnam, 1974 (originally published as *Tonia: Die Maus mit dem weissen Stein und was ihr begegnete auf der Reise zu Onkel Tobias,* Betz, 1970).
Little Black Lamb, Blackie, 1977 (originally published as *Das schwarze Schaf,* Nord-Sued Verlag, 1976).
My Cat Smokey, Blackie, 1979 (originally published as *Mein Kaetzchen Sebastian,* Nord-Sued Verlag, 1978).
Cats' Tales: Feline Fairy Tales from around the World, North-South Books, 1985 (originally published as *Maerchenkatzen-Kaetzenmaerchen,* Nord-Sued Verlag, 1981).
Sweet, Sour, Juicy, Burke, 1985 (originally published as *Suess, Sauer, Saftig,* Nord-Sued Verlag, 1985).

Seeds, Nuts, Kernels, Burke, 1985 (originally published as *Wo ist der kleinste Kern,* Nord-Sued Verlag, 1985).
Raw, Cooked, Spicy, Burke, 1985 (originally published as *Geschalt und Geschnitten,* Nord-Sued Verlag, 1985).
Farm Animals, North-South Books, 1985 (originally published as *Kennst du uns?,* Nord-Sued Verlag, 1985).
Alone in the Caves, North-South Books, 1986 (originally published as *Allein in der Hohle,* Nord-Sued Verlag, 1986).
Wake Up, Dormouse, Santa Claus Is Here, translation by Elizabeth D. Crawford, North-South Books, 1989 (originally published as *Wach auf, Siebenschlaefer, Sankt Nikolaus ist da,* Nord-Sued Verlag, 1989).
The Water's Journey, North-South Books, 1990 (originally published as *Eine Wasserreise,* Nord-Sued Verlag, 1990).
The Story of Christmas: From the Gospel According to Luke, Nord-Sued Verlag/North-South Books, 1990.
The Air around Us, translation by J. Alison James, North-South Books, 1992 (originally published as *Winde wehen, vom Lufthauch bis zum Sturm,* Nord-Sued Verlag, 1992).

ELEONORE SCHMID
WAKE UP, DORMOUSE,
SANTA CLAUS IS HERE
NORTH-SOUTH BOOKS

Gus the dormouse is determined not to let his urge to hibernate cause him to miss Santa Claus's yearly visit in Schmid's 1988 story. (Cover illustration by the author.)

The Living Earth, North-South Books, 1994 (originally published as *Erde lebt,* Nord-Sued Verlag, 1994).

ILLUSTRATOR

Hans Baumann, *Fenny: The Desert Fox,* adapted from the German by J. J. Curle, Pantheon, 1970.

James Kruess, *Die Geschichte vom grossen A,* Thienemann, 1972.

Robert Louis Stevenson, *Treasure Island,* McKay, 1977.

Marcel Ayme, *Les contes bleus du chat perche,* Gallimard, 1978.

Les contes rouges du chat perche, Gallimard, 1978.

Chantal de Marolles, *The Lonely Wolf,* North-South Books, 1986 (originally published as *Machs gut, Kleiner Wolf,* Nord-Sued Verlag, 1979).

Jerzy Andrzejewski, *Der goldene Fuchs,* Huber Verlag, 1979.

Silja Walter, *Eine kleine Bibel,* Huber Verlag, 1980.

La Vue, Gallimard, 1981.

Le Chene, Gallimard, 1982.

Fritz Seuft, *Unter dem Wiehnachtsfaern,* Huber Verlag, 1982.

Jacob Grimm and Wilhelm Grimm, *The Tree Feathers,* Creative Education, 1984 (originally published as *Die drei Federn,* Middelhanre, 1984).

Regine Schindler, *A Miracle of Sarah,* translated by Renate A. Lass Porter, Abingdon, 1984 (originally published as ... *und Sarah Lacht,* Kaufmann Verlag, 1984).

Schindler, *Christophorus,* Kaufmann Verlag, 1985.

Schindler, *Jesus teilt das Brot,* Kaufmann Verlag, 1986.

Schindler, *Napoleon the Donkey,* North-South Books, 1988 (originally published as *Der Esel Napoleon*).

Heinrich Wiesner, *Jaromir in einer mittelalterlichen Stadt: Schuelerroman,* Zytglogge, 1990.

Andrienne Soutter-Perrot, *The Oak,* adapted and edited from the French by Kitty Benedict, Creative Education, 1993.

■ Work in Progress

New illustrations and children's books.

■ Sidelights

The works of Eleonore Schmid, a prolific illustrator and writer, span a variety of genres, from board books for very young children to elaborately illustrated picture books that present both clever tales and scientific facts. *Farm Animals,* published in 1986, introduces very young children to the various barnyard animals through large, colorful drawings in a board book format. A later work, *Wake Up, Dormouse, Santa Claus Is Here,* becomes more involved as Schmid presents the tale of Gus the dormouse, who longs to meet Santa Claus. And some of Schmid's more recent works, including *The Water's Journey* and *The Living Earth,* use the picture book format to focus on the more scientific and serious topics that concern the earth and its various components. The most consistent element of these various works, however, is Schmid's striking illustrations, which stretch across and fill the pages.

Though an accurate description of the cycle of water on our planet, Schmid's drawings make this 1989 work much more than just a science book for the young. (Cover illustration by the author.)

Such illustrations can be found in *Horns Everywhere* and *Cats' Tales: Feline Fairy Tales from around the World,* which are among the many books in which Schmid features animals. The first, *Horns Everywhere,* concerns the hunt through a dark forest for a mysterious pig that possesses horns. It is the young boy Ivan who originally sights the pig during a walk with his grandfather; and upon hearing his story, the rest of the town sets out to find the horned pig. Schmid shows just how different people's fantasies and imaginations can be with her fifteen double-page spreads of what the horned pig might look like. *Cats' Tales* is a collection of folk tales from around the world that feature felines. "Here, it is the illustrations that are memorable: there are exquisite fine details of settings, humans, animals and objects," remarks a *Junior Bookshelf* reviewer.

Among the other memorable animal characters created by Schmid are two mice: Tonia and Gus. *Tonia: The Mouse with the White Stone and What Happened on Her Way to See Uncle Tobias,* published in 1970, follows the young mouse of the title as she travels to Nut Meadow for a visit with her Uncle Tobias. During the course of this journey, Tonia meets a spider, a telegram-delivering rabbit, an evil rat, and several other characters, each with their own stories to tell. A *Publishers Weekly* reviewer asserts that the details in *Tonia* "will prove entrancing to the young." Gus, featured in *Wake Up, Dormouse, Santa Claus Is Here,* is a dormouse who misses meeting Santa Claus every year because of his hibernation. Trying unsuccessfully to stay awake, Gus enlists the help of a squirrel, who promises to wake him when Santa arrives. Though the squirrel forgets, a friendly owl comes through and Gus is able to join the other animals for a visit with Santa. Ethel R. Twichell, writing in *Horn Book,* observes that the "large, softly colored illustrations" fill the pages and are "warm with autumn's preparations and hushed under the chill of winter."

The elements of the earth that contribute to these seasons and support Schmid's animals are explained in some of the author's more recent picture books: *The Water's Journey, The Air around Us,* and *The Living Earth.* In these books Schmid depicts the water cycle as it flows from mountains to eventually reach the oceans, the different forms and qualities of the air as it flows over the earth, and the interactions of plants and animals in relation to the earth's surface. In her *School Library Journal* review of *The Water's Journey,* Kathy Piehl relates: "Each two-page spread is a well-crafted painting that invites viewers to delight in the natural world." Piehl similarly praises *The Living Earth,* writing that Schmid's illustrations "of panoramic views and poetic language emphasize the wonder and beauty of the natural world."

■ Works Cited

Review of *Cats' Tales: Feline Fairy Tales from around the World, Junior Bookshelf,* February, 1986, p. 20.
Piehl, Kathy, review of *The Water's Journey, School Library Journal,* November, 1990, p. 98.
Piehl, Kathy, review of *The Living Earth, School Library Journal,* December, 1994, p. 102.
Review of *Tonia: The Mouse with the White Stone and What Happened on Her Way to See Uncle Tobias, Publishers Weekly,* April 8, 1974, p. 83.
Twichell, Ethel R., review of *Wake Up, Dormouse, Santa Claus Is Here, Horn Book,* January/February, 1990, pp. 56-57.

■ For More Information See

PERIODICALS

Booklist, December 15, 1992, pp. 741-42.
Horn Book, June, 1980, pp. 280-81.
Library Journal, October, 1968, p. 145.
New York Times Book Review, August 4, 1969, p. 20.
School Library Journal, March, 1986, p. 158; October, 1989, p. 44; December, 1992, p. 107.
Wilson Library Bulletin, December, 1988, p. 88.*

SHERRY, Clifford J. 1943-

■ Personal

Born January 16, 1943, in Chicago, IL; son of Clifford W. and Dorothy B. (Kohout) Sherry; married Nancy Cunningham, May 3, 1969; children: Christopher J., Jason W., Lori Beth. *Education:* Roosevelt University, B.S., 1968; Illinois Institute of Technology, M.S., 1974, Ph.D., 1976. *Politics:* "Independent-Conservative." *Religion:* Christian. *Hobbies and other interests:* Wine making, bee keeping.

■ Addresses

Office—8305 Hawkes Rd., Bldg. 1182, San Antonio, TX 78235.

■ Career

University of Illinois Medical School, Urbana-Champaign, IL, pharmacology research associate, 1969-75; Texas A & M University, College Station, TX, assistant professor of biology, 1975-82; Bio Feedback and Stress Management Consultants, Bryan, TX, therapist, 1983-89; Words Plus, Bryan and San Antonio, TX, writer, 1985—; Systems Research Laboratory, San Antonio, senior scientist, 1989—. *Member:* Spina Bifida Association of America (Bryan/College Station chapter), Brazos Valley March of Dimes (board member, 1979-84; chair, 1981-82).

■ Writings

The Mathematics of Technical Analysis, Probus, 1992.
Animal Rights: A Reference Handbook, ABC-Clio, 1994.
Drugs and Eating Disorders (young adult), Rosen, 1994.
Inhalants (young adult), Rosen, 1994.
The New Science of Technical Analysis, Probus, 1994.
Opportunities in Medical Imaging Careers (young adult), VGM Career Horizons, 1994.

Contributor of articles to scientific journals and mainstream periodicals.

■ Work in Progress

Over-the-Counter Drug Abuse (young adult), in press for Rosen; *Trader Psychology,* for Probus; and *Contemporary World Issues: Endangered Species.*

■ Sidelights

Clifford J. Sherry told *SATA:* "I have been a scientist for almost thirty years and most of my early writing focused on professional articles. I now have papers in more than thirty different refereed scientific journals, such as *Brain Research, The International Journal of Neuroscience,* and *Experientia.* I also have articles in a wide variety of magazines, such as *The Left Hander Magazine, Bestways, National Guard,* and *American Fire Journal.*

"Most of my scientific articles have focused on either neurophysiology (the study of the electrical activity of the nervous system), pharmacology (the study of the effects of drugs), or reproductive behavior/physiology. In attempting to understand how the nervous system processes information, I developed a series of statistical techniques. One day while browsing at the library I found a book dealing with the stock market and how people decide when to buy and sell stocks. I felt that these people (they are called technicians) might be interested in my statistical techniques. I soon discovered a magazine called *Technical Analysis of Stocks and Commodities* and began publishing a series of articles dealing with these statistical techniques in it. Questions about these articles helped me to decide to publish my first book, *The Mathematics of Technical Analysis* (Probus, 1992). My second book for Probus, *The New Science of Technical Analysis,* was published in 1994. I am currently writing a third book for them.

"I believe that drug abuse is one of the leading problems facing our society. As a psychopharmacologist, I believe that it is important for me to share information about drugs. This led to several books for Rosen Publishing Group. They include *Drugs and Eating Disorders* and *Inhalants,* which were released in 1994, and I have just completed a book, *Over-the-Counter Drug Abuse* for them.

"One of my young associates and I are currently working on a comic book and I have begun working on my first novel."

*   *   *

SHLICHTA, Joe 1968-

■ Personal

Born December 21, 1968, in Long Beach, CA. *Education:* Attended Otis Art Institute, 1987-89, and Cornish College of the Arts, 1992-93.

■ Addresses

Home—525 Henry St. #2, Brooklyn, NY 11231.

■ Career

Children's book illustrator.

■ Illustrator

Pleasant DeSpain, *33 Multicultural Tales to Tell,* August House, 1993.
DeSpain, *11 Turtle Tales to Tell,* August House, 1994.
DeSpain, *Strongheart Jack and the Beanstalk,* August House, 1995.
DeSpain, *11 Nature Tales to Tell,* August House, 1995.

JOE SHLICHTA

■ Sidelights

Joe Shlichta told *SATA:* "I grew up in San Pedro, California. I decided to be a surfer. However, in high school I changed my mind and became a painter. But a twist of fate and a need for money led me to illustrate a book for Pleasant DeSpain.

"I hope that illustration will enable me to quit my job. As I always say: The only thing worse than being unemployed is being employed."

*   *   *

SHUKEN, Julia 1948-

■ Personal

Born September 2, 1948, in California; daughter of John E. (an engineer) and Julia C. (a registered nurse; maiden name, Holleran) Carey; married David J. Shuken (an architect), August 8, 1981. *Education:* California State University at Fullerton, B.A., 1970; University of Redlands, M.A., 1981; studied at University of Texas at Arlington. *Politics:* Conservative. *Religion:* Evangelical Christian. *Hobbies and other interests:* Travel, anthropology.

■ Addresses

Home—18 Filare, Irvine, CA 92720-2578.

■ Career

Yorba Linda Star, Yorba Linda, CA, editor; technical editor in biomedical and aerospace industries; freelance writer.

■ Awards, Honors

Third Place, *Christianity Today* Critics Choice Award for fiction, 1994, for *Day of the East Wind.*

■ Writings

Day of the East Wind, Crossway Books, 1993.

Also author of *Songs in the House of Pilgrimage,* Crossway Books. *Day of the East Wind* has been translated into German.

■ Work in Progress

Researching the history and ethnology of (formerly Soviet) Georgia.

■ Sidelights

"As an artist," Julia Shuken told *SATA,* "I strive to translate the beauty around me into my chosen media—story. What story, either true or fictional, can do in a way no other art form can, is portray moral beauty. Love, courage, integrity are shuttled into the weft of human life as characters move and act in real or imagined history."

Shuken's first published novel, *Day of the East Wind,* blends fiction with historical fact, yet, as Mindy Belz commented in *World,* the work "seems strangely contemporary" given the turmoil among various ethnic groups in the region today. *Day of the East Wind* tells the story of Piotr, a Molokan serving as a Russian soldier, beginning in 1905. The Molokans, an unorthodox sect of Christian pacifists, must decide how to defend themselves when Muslims begin to fight Christians, and the Azerbaijanis battle with the Armenians. When the Tsar in Moscow attempts to bring order to the Transcaucasian region, Piotr's family urges him to desert the Tsar's army and travel to America. Piotr hesitates, but soon realizes that he has no choice but to begin the dangerous pilgrimage his parents have suggested. As he does so, Belz related, Piotr also makes a "harrowing spiritual journey." In exile in the United States, wrote Belz, he finally "discovers why he needs Jesus Christ."

Day of the East Wind has received favorable critical recognition. The book was selected by *Inklings* contributor Ed Veith as one of nine recommended works that "demonstrate some of the latest developments in contemporary fiction," and it received third prize in the Critics Choice fiction category from *Christianity Today.*

Shuken became fascinated with the Molokans' story in the early 1980s. After beginning research on the group and their persecution, she met and married David Shuken, a Molokan descendant, and based the character of Piotr on his grandfather. She told *SATA* that she admires "writers like Tolstoy, Dostoevski, Solzhenitsyn, and Chekhov" for their "ability to reach deeply into the human soul—echo the hollowness, reflect the brilliance, and forgive the frailties." "I look to them," she explained, "not for technique, but for an attitude of heart and mind that enables them to truly see people and enflesh them in words with wisdom and humanity."

■ Works Cited

Belz, Mindy, review of *Day of the East Wind, World,* November 6, 1993, pp. 20-21.

■ For More Information See

PERIODICALS

Inklings, spring, 1994, p. 7.
Voice of Youth Advocates, February, 1994, p. 373.

*   *   *

SLAUGHTER, Hope 1940-

■ Personal

Born December 29, 1940, in Deadwood, SD; daughter of Archie L. (a geologist) and Phebe M. (a homemaker; maiden name, Johnson) Slaughter; married D. Parker, August 6, 1961 (divorced, 1970); married Travis L. Bryant (a businessman), September 14, 1971; children: (second marriage) Glenda (stepdaughter), Derrik (stepson), Justin. *Education:* Macalester College, St. Paul, MN, B.A.; California Lutheran University, Thousand Oaks, CA, elementary teaching credential. *Politics:* Conservative. *Religion:* Protestant. *Hobbies and other interests:* Gardening, reading, skiing, hiking, traveling.

HOPE SLAUGHTER

■ Addresses

Home—P.O. Box 454, Big Sur, CA 93920. *Office*—c/o Pippin Press, 229 East 85th St., P.O. Box 92, Gracie Station, New York, NY 10028. *Electronic mail*—TLBDHB, or DHopey (America Online).

■ Career

Writer. Third-grade teacher, Oxnard, CA, 1968-71. *Member:* Society of Children's Book Writers and Illustrators, Southern California Council on Literature for Children and Young People, Santa Barbara Writers for Children.

■ Writings

PICTURE BOOKS

Plato's Fine Feathers, illustrated by David Shearer, Red Hen Press, 1984.
The Deeeeelicious Dragon, illustrated by Rhonda H. Heaney, Red Hen Press, 1986.
A Cozy Place, illustrated by Susan Torrence, Red Hen Press, 1990.

OTHER

Windmill Hill (juvenile novel), Newfield Publications (Weekly Reader Book Club edition), 1992, illustrated by Edward Frascino, Pippin Press, 1993.
Buckley and Wilberta (easy reader), illustrated by Susan Torrence, Red Hen Press, in press.

Also contributor of short stories to *Trails, Teen Power,* and *Highlights for Children,* and of poems to *P.E.O. Record, Santa Barbara's Child Life,* and *Byline.*

■ Work in Progress

Springtime on Windmill Hill (sequel to *Windmill Hill*); *Fernwood* and *The Beyond,* both fantasy; *Hey! C.J.!* and *Trouble in the Trailblazers,* both middle-grade contemporary; *One Hot Summer,* for young adults; miscellaneous short stories and poems.

■ Sidelights

"Since I can remember I have loved books, and always dreamed of being an author," Hope Slaughter told *SATA.* "Writing books is, however, more difficult than I had ever imagined when I began about fifteen years ago. The most difficult aspect of writing is the persistence and patience it requires, two qualities which demand daily attention.

"It was my great good fortune to grow up the middle child and only daughter of loving, caring, hardworking parents who passed on a legacy of solid values and unconditional love and support. My father and his sister were the first of his family to graduate from college, overcoming many obstacles to do so. Education was valued highly, books were revered, and there was always bedtime reading, one of my fondest memories of both my parents. I think reading to a child is one of the most important developmental things a parent can do.

"I think it was also fortunate in some ways that I grew up before television came to our small town in the mountains. We didn't get our first TV set until I was entering high school. We listened to radio, read books, played games as a family, and in longer summer evenings played ball, or went fishing or picnicking. Radio shows and books didn't supply instant visual characters. You had to imagine them, create them in your mind. The ability to imagine is certainly essential in writing fantasy, which is my favorite.

"I feel it's terribly important for everyone to have something they passionately want to do—something challenging, that requires constant effort and growth. For me, this is writing. The thought that my writing might ignite any of that passion in children is the ultimate reward."

■ For More Information See

PERIODICALS

Booklist, June 1, 1991, p. 1882.
Horn Book Guide, July-December, 1993, p. 70.
School Library Journal, September, 1993, pp. 235-36.

*   *   *

SNELLING, Dennis (Wayne) 1958-

■ Personal

Born January 16, 1958, in Stockton, CA; son of Donald Erwin and Leona Boyreta (a homemaker; maiden name, Rich) Snelling; married Linda Lee Jones (a homemaker), April 23, 1983; children: Tyler Steven, Garrett Donald, Andrea Michelle. *Education:* Attended Modesto Junior College, 1975-77; San Diego State University, B.S. (telecommunications and film), 1980; Chapman University, California State teaching credential, 1993. *Politics:* Republican. *Religion:* Protestant. *Hobbies and other interests:* Baseball history, American history, presidential politics, biography, the Civil War.

■ Addresses

Home—700 Brook Vale Dr., Modesto, CA 95355. *Office*—Modesto City Schools, 426 Locust St., Modesto, CA 95351.

■ Career

Accountant for Stanislaus County, Modesto, CA, 1981-87, and Modesto City Schools, Modesto, 1987—. Also serves as controller for the Salida Area Public Facilities Financing Agency, and for the Schools Infrastructure Financing Agency. *Member:* Society for American Baseball Research, Pacific Coast League Historical Society, California Association of School Business Officials.

■ Writings

A Glimpse of Fame (baseball history), McFarland, 1993.
The Pacific Coast League: A Statistical History (baseball history), McFarland, 1995.

■ Work in Progress

The Coast League, an anecdotal and photographic look at the Pacific Coast League; *The Adventures of Baseball's First Punk Rock Pitcher,* anecdotes and reminiscences of former big league pitcher Lowell Palmer.

■ Sidelights

Dennis Snelling told *SATA,* "I have always been fascinated by the stories behind events and everyday people. The famous are boring to me; I've heard all of their stories before and they rarely relate to you and me. In *A Glimpse of Fame,* my first book, I attempted to present a side of baseball not normally written about. Through research and interviews with fifteen different individuals, I wanted to show athletic life through the eyes of those who had to wrestle with the larger issues of success and failure—the pitcher who struck out twenty-seven batters in a minor league game and suffered a career-ending injury, the player who begins to doubt his own talent, the family pressures that build on a stalled career." Snelling reported that the idea for his book was also partly inspired by the character of "Moonlight" Graham in the film *Field of Dreams,* which he saw shortly after his father's death and just prior to the birth of his second son.

"I enjoy writing books because of the freedom one has," Snelling told *SATA.* "I've been lucky with my first two projects in that I've been able to do what I've wanted. The best advice I can give to young authors is to write. It's like exercising—in the same way that you will be in better physical shape the more you exercise, writing improves with practice. Don't be discouraged if your first writings aren't very good. Take the time to analyze what is wrong—and right—about your work. And it *is* work! You have to take it seriously, or no one else will. You'll run into a lot of people who will say, 'I've always wanted to write, but I just don't have the time.' If you really want to write, you will find the time.

"The great thing for me about writing nonfiction is that I get the opportunity to learn more about subjects in which I'm interested. Authors should choose to write about things that interest them. While not an original utterance by any means, it is nonetheless true that if an author is not interested in his subject, the reader won't be either."

■ For More Information See

PERIODICALS

Booklist, June 1 and 15, 1993, p. 1769.
Choice, November, 1993, p. 497.

SPEREGEN, Devra Newberger 1964-
(Debra Adams, Devra Newberger)

■ Personal

Born July 23, 1964, in Queens, NY; daughter of Joel (an engineer) and Shirley (a writer; maiden name, Feldman) Newberger; married Adam Speregen (a retail manager), October 31, 1991; children: Jordan Daniel. *Education:* State University of New York at Binghamton, B.A., 1986; attended Tel Aviv University, Israel, three semesters. *Religion:* Jewish. *Hobbies and other interests:* Gardening, walking, people.

■ Addresses

Home and office—69-10 108th St. #3M, Forest Hills, NY 11375.

■ Career

Welsh Publishing Group, New York City, editorial assistant, 1986-87; Prestige Publications, New York City, associate editor, 1987-88; Scholastic, Inc., New York City, managing editor, 1988-1992; Disney Press,

When Stephanie meets her pen pal for the first time, it turns out to be a huge disappointment in this third book in Speregen's "Full House Stephanie" series.

New York City, editor, 1992. Freelance writer for publishers, including Scholastic, Troll Associates, and Pocket Books, 1989—.

■ Writings

BIOGRAPHIES

Joe Montana, Scholastic, 1991.
Michael Jordan, Scholastic, 1992.
(Under name Devra Newberger) *Don Mattingly,* Scholastic, 1992.
Jason Priestley, Scholastic, 1992.
Gabrielle Carteris, Scholastic, 1992.
Jennie Garth, Scholastic, 1992.
Yoni Netanyahu: Hero at Entebbe, Jewish Publication Society, 1994.

Also author of *Macaulay Culkin: Star of Home Alone,* Parachute Press, and *The Magic of Paula Abdul,* Scholastic.

FICTION

(With mother, Shirley Newberger) *Arielle and the Hanukkah Surprise,* illustrated by Lena Schiffman, Scholastic, 1992.
Scary Stories to Drive You Batty, Troll Associates, 1994.

Also adapter of *The Secret Garden/Adapted for Young Readers,* Kidsbooks.

"FULL HOUSE STEPHANIE" SERIES

Phone Call from a Flamingo, Pocket Books, 1993.
Hip Hop 'til You Drop, Pocket Books, 1994.
P.S. Friends Forever, Pocket Books, 1995.
Back to School Cool, Pocket Books, 1995.

MEDIA BOOKS

Team USA: 1992 Summer Olympics' Dream Team, Scholastic, 1992.
Full House Family Scrapbook, Scholastic, 1992.
Blossom's Family Scrapbook, Scholastic, 1993.

Also author of *The Heat Is On,* Scholastic; *Nickelodeon's Fifteen Series: Battle of the Bands,* Putnam; *Full House Flip Book* and *Full House Poster Book,* Creative Media Applications; *The Stars of Beverly Hills, 90210, Star Magic, Good Guys, Bad Guys, New Kids on the Block: In Concert, Kid Power, Superstars,* and *The Stars of Full House,* all Publications International.

ACTIVITY, PUZZLE, AND JOKE BOOKS

Author of *Dennis the Menace Activity Book,* Troll Associates, and *All About Dinosaurs, In the Sky, Celebrity Date Book, Superstar Puzzle Book, The Book of Awards, Coast to Coast: Fun Facts about the Fifty States, My Super Summer Scrapbook, Holiday Fun Activity Book,* and *Fun Facts Word Searches,* all for Scholastic.

■ Sidelights

Devra Newberger Speregen told *SATA:* "I enjoy writing for children, mostly fiction and biographies. Recently I became interested in writing Judaica-themed children's

books. I lived in Israel for a year and a half and grew up in a traditional Jewish-American family. Another area of interest is in media-related books for kids, books that tie into movies and television or biographies about celebrities. This interest stems from my four-year stint as managing editor of Scholastic's *Dynamite Magazine.*

"Someday I hope to edit a teen-type entertainment magazine, or write for *Sesame Street.* But I am currently happy working from home and spending time with my baby son."

*   *   *

STRANGER, Joyce
See WILSON, Joyce M(uriel Judson)

*   *   *

STREET, Janet Travell 1959-

■ Personal

Born April 20, 1959, in Nashville, TN; daughter of Edward Hunt Street (an architect) and Virginia Gordon Powell (an artist). *Education:* University of Georgia, B.F.A., 1982. *Hobbies and other interests:* Equestrian/dressage riding.

They had safety clothes for riding bicycles— and even costumes for their little dinosaur dolls!

Street's flamboyant illustrations of dinosaurs wearing fantastical clothing add support to Allen L. Sirois's theory in *Dinosaur Dress Up* that dinos became extinct because of their obsession with fashions.

■ Addresses

Home and office—3 River Rd., South Deerfield, MA 01373.

■ Career

Bradford Communications, Hickory, NC, graphic designer, 1983-85; Sunshine Art Studio, Springfield, MA, graphic designer, 1985-86; Valley Advocate, Hatfield, MA, graphic designer, 1986-89; freelance illustrator. *Member:* Western Massachusetts Illustrators Group.

■ Awards, Honors

New York Times Best Children's Book citation, for *One Day, Two Dragons.*

■ Illustrator

Eugene Field, *The Gingham Dog and the Calico Cat,* Philomel, 1990.
Lynne Bertrand, *One Day, Two Dragons,* Clarkson Potter, 1992.
Al Sirois, *Dinosaur Dress Up,* Tambourine, 1992.
Jane Yolen, *Raining Cats and Dogs,* Harcourt, 1993.
Yolen, *Animal Fare: Zoological Nonsense Poems,* Harcourt, 1994.
Liz Rosenberg, *Mama Goose: A New Mother Goose,* Philomel, 1994.
Marilee Robin Burton, *One Little Chickadee,* Tambourine, 1994.
Bertrand, *Dragon Naps,* Viking, 1995.*

* * *

SWAIN, Gwenyth 1961-

■ Personal

Born June 29, 1961, in Columbus, IN; daughter of G. Henry, Jr. (a home builder) and Margaret (a homemaker; maiden name, Coman) Swain. *Education:* Grinnell College, B.A., 1983; attended Indiana University, 1983-84; Mills College, M.A., 1986. *Religion:* Society of Friends (Quaker).

■ Addresses

Home—2534 37th Ave. S., Minneapolis, MN 55406. *Office*—Carolrhoda Books, 241 1st Ave. N., Minneapolis, MN 55401.

■ Career

Children's book author. *Fine Print* magazine, San Francisco, CA, circulation manager, 1987-88; Hungry Mind bookstore, St. Paul, MN, clerk, 1989-90; Carolrhoda Books, Minneapolis, MN, editor, 1990—. Volunteer tutor for Literacy Volunteers of America, 1992—. *Member:* Society of Children's Book Writers and Illustrators, Minnesota Center for Book Arts, Indiana Historical Society.

■ Awards, Honors

National Merit Scholar, Phi Beta Kappa.

■ Writings

Indiana, Lerner, 1992.
Pennsylvania, Lerner, 1994.
(With Minnesota Center for Book Arts) *Bookworks: Making Books by Hand,* Carolrhoda Books, 1995.

■ Work in Progress

The Road to Seneca Falls: A Story about Elizabeth Cady Stanton, for Carolrhoda Books, due in 1996 or 1997; conducting research on Harriet Quimby and the Johnstown Flood.

■ Sidelights

Gwenyth Swain told *SATA:* "I write nonfiction, primarily on historical topics. My fascination with the stories behind important events and people in the past dates back to courses I took as a history major at Grinnell College."

■ For More Information See

PERIODICALS
School Library Journal, August, 1994, p. 163.

* * *

SWANN, Ruth Rice 1920-

■ Personal

Born December 5, 1920, in Sumter, SC; daughter of Henry Wardsworth (a school teacher) and Anna (a school teacher; maiden name, Goldsmith) Rice; married Edwin Everette Swann (a brick mason), June 12, 1948; children: Madeline. *Education:* Hampton University, B.S., 1941; Virginia State University, M.S., 1960. *Religion:* Protestant. *Hobbies and other interests:* Traveling, researching African history, needlework, herb gardening.

■ Addresses

Home—1612 Hungary Rd., Richmond, VA 23228.

■ Career

Finley High School, Chester, SC, home economics teacher, 1941-45; Russell Grove High School, Amelia, VA, home economics teacher, 1945-47; Central Intelligence Agency, Washington, DC, administrative assistant, 1949-51; Richmond Public School, Richmond, VA, school cafeteria manager, 1954-59; Richmond Social Service Bureau, Richmond, social worker, 1959-64; Mosby Middle School, Richmond, home economics teacher, 1964-86. VIP volunteer at Richmond Public Schools; volunteer at Richmond Public Schools Media

RUTH RICE SWANN

and Technology Department. Sunday school and nursery teacher, and monthly newsletter editor, All Souls Presbyterian Church; financial secretary of Begonia Garden Club. Member of Petersburg educational advisory committee, J.C. Penney Company, Richmond home economics education advisory committee, Craft advisory committee for clothing services. *Member:*

Middleton Civic Association (secretary), Phi Delta Kappa.

■ Awards, Honors

Outstanding Staff Member of the Year, Mosby Middle School, 1978-79; Dedication of Mosby Stinger Yearbook, Mosby Middle School, 1979-80; Outstanding Vocational Education Teacher, Richmond Public Schools, 1981; Outstanding Sponsor, Mosby Movie Makers, 1981-82; Candidate for State Teacher of the Year, 1984.

■ Writings

A History of Black Africans to A.D. 1400, Vantage Press, 1993.

Also American history reviewer for *America's Past and Promise,* Houghton, 1995.

■ Work in Progress

Research in East Africa on early African history and culture.

■ Sidelights

Ruth Rice Swann told *SATA:* "My trip to four countries in East Africa—Kenya, Tanzania, Ethiopia, and Zimbabwe—in September, 1994, was very rewarding. I not only saw a dozen prehistoric and ancient sites of African civilization and culture, but had the opportunity to spend time with some Maasai tribal families in their village. They are recognized by the red togas they wear and their cattle, which determines their wealth. They have changed little over the generations, and they are great environmentalists—giving back to the earth what they take and killing animals only if they threaten them or their cattle. In fact, they can communicate with wild animals."

T

TALBOTT, Hudson 1949-

■ Personal

Born July 11, 1949, in Louisville, KY; son of Peyton (a mortgage loan officer) and Mildred (a dress shop manager; maiden name, Pence) Talbott. *Education:* Attended University of Cincinnati; Tyler School of Art, B.F.A. *Politics:* Democrat. *Religion:* Siddha Yoga.

■ Addresses

Home—119 5th Ave. #500, New York, NY 10003; and Rte. 1, Box 168, Leeds, NY 12451.

■ Career

Freelance illustrator, New York City, 1974-86, for clients including the Metropolitan Museum of Art, Museum of Modern Art, Bloomingdale's Department

HUDSON TALBOTT

(From left to right) Dweeb, Rex, Woog, and Elsa are brought to life in the 1993 Universal
animated feature of Talbott's book, *We're Back! A Dinosaur's Story.*

Store, Harper & Row (publishing house), and Paper
Moon Graphics; children's book author and illustrator,
1986—. Member of board of directors of Art Awareness
(a nonprofit arts-presenting organization), Lexington,
NY. Speaker at conferences and workshops. Consultant
for *We're Back! A Dinosaur's Story,* a feature-length
animated film made by Steven Spielberg, based on
Talbott's book of same title. *Member:* Society of Children's Book Writers and Illustrators.

■ **Awards, Honors**

Library of Congress Children's Book of the Year cita-
tion, 1987, *Parents'* Magazine Best Book of 1987
citation, Georgia Children's Picture Storybook Award,
University of Georgia College of Education, 1991, and
International Readers Association Children's Choice
Award, all for *We're Back! A Dinosaur's Story;* Nevada
Young Reader's Award, 1991.

■ **Writings**

SELF-ILLUSTRATED

How to Show Grown-ups the Museum, Museum of
    Modern Art, 1986.
We're Back! A Dinosaur's Story, Crown, 1987.
(Adapter) *Into the Woods* (from Stephen Sondheim and
    James Lapine's play), Crown, 1988.
Going Hollywood! A Dinosaur's Dream, Crown, 1989.
The Lady at Liberty, Avon Books, 1991.
King Arthur: The Sword in the Stone, Morrow, 1991.

Your Pet Dinosaur: An Owner's Manual, Morrow, 1992.
King Arthur and the Round Table, Morrow, 1995.

■ **Adaptations**

We're Back! A Dinosaur's Story was adapted into a full-
length animated feature film by Steven Spielberg for
Universal, 1993.

■ **Work in Progress**

Coauthoring *The Jungle Diary of Alex Winters* with
Mark Greenberg, for Putnam, due in fall, 1996; *Excali-
bur,* the third book in the "Tales of King Arthur" series,
for Morrow, 1996; illustrations for *Robin Hood,* for
Morrow; *A Tale for the Telling* (tentative title), for the
Children's Book-of-the-Month Club; *Pendragon,* ani-
mated television series based on book *King Arthur: The
Sword in the Stone,* in development for Universal;
Finder's Keepers, a live action television series, in
development at Universal.

■ **Sidelights**

Hudson Talbott, creator of a band of educated dinosaurs that are time-warped into the twentieth century,
began his career as a freelance illustrator. It was only
after David Allender, an editor at Crown, saw one of
Talbott's dinosaur calendars and contacted him that he
contemplated writing a book of his own. Once encouraged, though, he rose to the challenge. "I've always

believed that the creative impulse is inherent in all of us," Talbott explains to *SATA*, "and that 'talent' really depends on whether this urge is encouraged or suppressed. From my point of view my 'gift' isn't so much my technical skills—nothing too unusual about that—but the love and support I was given by parents who saw my potential. Despite their own interests lying elsewhere (sports, mostly) they allowed my artistic self-expression to flourish, and in so doing, fostered my belief in myself—a belief that I had something to say, and something worth saying.

"Getting to the heart of that belief has fueled a journey through a number of art forms—painting, sculpture, graphic and fashion design, and illustration, to name a few. My pursuit seems to have found its most accommodating venue thus far in the world of children's books. It feels like a natural fit because of what I bring to it, as well as what it opens up for me. I've always told stories through pictures; now I'm discovering how to paint with words."

This evolution from artist to author led Talbott to write his first word painting, *We're Back! A Dinosaur's Story*. In this tale, a Tyrannosaurus Rex relates how he, along with other prehistoric creatures, is given Mega-Mind pills by a spaceship of aliens conducting experiments. This Brain Grain enables all the creatures to learn languages and other advanced skills. They are then all transported to twentieth-century New York City just in time for the Macy's Thanksgiving Day Parade. When it is realized that the dinosaurs are not really floats in the parade, they are hunted down until Dr. Miriam Bleeb rescues them at the Museum of Natural History; she has them pose as exhibits. Betsy Hearne, writing in the *Bulletin of the Center for Children's Books,* asserts that Talbott's illustrations in *We're Back! A Dinosaur's Story* "have lots of cartoon appeal, with kooky humor in every action-packed page."

"The seven-year-old in me wrote that book," observes Talbott in an interview with Diane Roback for *Publishers Weekly.* "It was an integrated me: the adult me making the pictures, and the child writing it." This first experience with children's books was a good one for Talbott, and he has since continued his dinosaur tales, in addition to adapting the tales of others. "Making a children's book is like directing a movie," he continues in *Publishers Weekly.* "You figure out the angle, the script, the emotions. It's a much bigger and more encompassing project than designing notecards. It's more rewarding, more permanent. After all, a good children's book can have a lifetime effect on people."

This is the kind of effect Rex is striving for in Talbott's next dinosaur adventure, *Going Hollywood! A Dinosaur's Dream,* and in his how-to guide, *Your Pet Dinosaur: An Owner's Manual.* In the first book, Rex and the rest of the dinosaurs travel to Hollywood to star in a dinosaur movie being made on location at the La Brea tar pits. When he discovers that he is not to be the star, however, Rex's ego causes him to fall into the tar pit; it is only through this near-death experience that he

"Doctor" Rex gives advice on how to raise and care for your pet dinosaur in this humorous guide book. (Cover illustration by the author.)

regains his senses. *Your Pet Dinosaur* also features Rex, but this time as Dr. Rex. He offers advice to prospective dinosaur owners, covering everything from childhood and training to the various breeds available. "Rex's madcap egocentric displays are given technicolor treatment in this lavish stream-of-consciousness romp," writes a *Publishers Weekly* contributor in a review of *Going Hollywood!* And Jeanne Marie Clancy maintains in her *School Library Journal* review of *Your Pet Dinosaur:* "This outrageous owner's manual is guaranteed to tickle readers' funny bones."

The act of writing these outrageous tales has given Talbott a chance to find out more about himself as an artist. He tells *SATA:* "Translating the sensibilities I've cultivated in visual media into language has revealed as much to me about myself as about the subject I'm addressing. Although I've always been rather instinctual in my work I feel the better I understand my own inner truth the more confidently I am able to convey its universality to my readers. In the end this is all we have to offer each other. I consider it a privilege to be given the opportunity to share *my* truth, and hope that my work reflects my gratitude."

■ Works Cited

Clancy, Jeanne Marie, review of *Your Pet Dinosaur: An Owner's Manual, School Library Journal,* May, 1993, p. 92.

Review of *Going Hollywood! A Dinosaur's Dream,*
  Publishers Weekly, November 10, 1989, p. 59.
Hearne, Betsy, review of *We're Back! A Dinosaur's*
  Story, Bulletin of the Center for Children's Books,
  December, 1987, p. 78.
Roback, Diane, "Flying Starts: New Faces of 1987,"
  Publishers Weekly, December 25, 1987, pp. 38-39.

■ For More Information See

PERIODICALS

Bulletin of the Center for Children's Books, November,
  1991, pp. 77-78; November, 1992, p. 90.
Kirkus Reviews, December 1, 1988, p. 1745.
Publishers Weekly, October 18, 1991, p. 60; August 3,
  1992, p. 72.
School Library Journal, September, 1987, p. 171; September, 1991, p. 273.

*   *   *

TODD, H. E.
See TODD, Herbert Eatton

*   *   *

TODD, Herbert Eatton 1908-1988
(H. E. Todd)

■ Personal

Born February 22, 1908, in London, England; died
February 25, 1988; son of Henry Graves (a headmaster)
and Minnie Elizabeth Todd; married Bertha Joyce
Hughes, 1936 (died, 1968); children: Jonathan (died,
1964), Mark, Stephen. *Education:* Attended Christ's
Hospital, Horsham, Sussex, England, 1919-25. *Religion:*
Church of England.

■ Career

Houlder Brothers Ltd., London, shipping clerk, 1925-
27; British Foreign and Colonial Corp., London, invest-
ment clerk, 1927-29; Bourne & Hollingsworth Ltd.,
London, hosiery underbuyer, 1929-31; F. G. Wigley &
Co. Ltd., London, salesman, 1931-47, director and sales
manager, 1947-69. Children's Book Week storyteller in
libraries and schools, beginning in 1953; broadcaster of
"Bobby Brewster" stories on radio and television;
broadcaster of children's musical programs. Performer
in local operatic productions, 1945-62. *Military service:*
Royal Air Force, 1940-45; became squadron leader.
Member: Berkhamsted Amateur Operatic and Dramatic
Society (choir master, 1948-52; chairman, 1956-60;
president, beginning 1961).

■ Awards, Honors

White Rose Award, 1971, for *Bobby Brewster and the
Ghost.*

■ Writings

FOR CHILDREN; UNDER NAME H. E. TODD

Bobby Brewster and the Winkers' Club, illustrated by
  Bryan Ward, Ward, 1949.
Bobby Brewster, illustrated by Buchanan, Brockhamp-
  ton Press, 1954.
Bobby Brewster—Bus Conductor, illustrated by Buchan-
  an, Brockhampton Press, 1954.
Bobby Brewster's Shadow, illustrated by Buchanan,
  Brockhampton Press, 1956.
Bobby Brewster's Bicycle, illustrated by Buchanan,
  Brockhampton Press, 1957.
Bobby Brewster's Camera, illustrated by Buchanan,
  Brockhampton Press, 1959.
Bobby Brewster's Wallpaper, illustrated by Buchanan,
  Brockhampton Press, 1961.
Bobby Brewster's Conker, illustrated by Buchanan,
  Brockhampton Press, 1963.
Bobby Brewster—Detective, illustrated by Buchanan,
  Brockhampton Press, 1964.
Bobby Brewster's Potato, illustrated by Buchanan,
  Brockhampton Press, 1964.
Bobby Brewster and the Ghost, illustrated by Buchanan,
  Brockhampton Press, 1966.
Bobby Brewster's Kite, illustrated by Buchanan, Brock-
  hampton Press, 1967.

HERBERT EATTON TODD

Bobby Brewster's Scarecrow, illustrated by Buchanan, Brockhampton Press, 1968.

Bobby Brewster's Torch, illustrated by Buchanan, Brockhampton Press, 1969.

Bobby Brewster's Balloon Race, illustrated by Buchanan, Brockhampton Press, 1970.

Bobby Brewster's First Magic, illustrated by Buchanan, Brockhampton Press, 1970.

Bobby Brewster's Typewriter, illustrated by Buchanan, Brockhampton Press, 1971.

Bobby Brewster's Bee, illustrated by Buchanan, Brockhampton Press, 1972.

Bobby Brewster's Wishbone, illustrated by Buchanan, Brockhampton Press, 1974.

Bobby Brewster's First Fun, illustrated by Buchanan, Brockhampton Press, 1974.

The Sick Cow, illustrated by Val Biro, Brockhampton Press, 1974, Children's Press, 1976.

Bobby Brewster's Bookmark, illustrated by Buchanan, Hodder & Stoughton, 1975.

George the Fire Engine, illustrated by Biro, Hodder & Stoughton, 1976, Children's Press, 1978.

Changing of the Guard, illustrated by Biro, Hodder & Stoughton, 1978.

The Roundabout Horse, illustrated by Biro, Hodder & Stoughton, 1978.

The Very, Very Long Dog, illustrated by Biro, Carousel, 1978.

Bobby Brewster's Tea-Leaves, illustrated by David Barnett, Hodder & Stoughton, 1979.

Here Comes Wordman!, illustrated by Biro, Carousel, 1979.

King of Beasts, illustrated by Biro, Hodder & Stoughton, 1979.

Santa's Big Sneeze, illustrated by Biro, Hodder & Stoughton, 1980.

The Crawly Crawly Caterpillar, illustrated by Biro, Carousel, 1981.

The Dial-a-Story Book, illustrated by Biro, Penguin, 1981.

Jungle Silver, illustrated by Biro, Hodder & Stoughton, 1981.

Bobby Brewster's Lamp Post, illustrated by Buchanan, Hodder & Stoughton, 1982.

Changing of the Guard; Wallpaper Holiday, illustrated by Lilian Buchanan, Penguin, 1982.

The Tiny, Tiny Tadpole, illustrated by Biro, Carousel, 1982.

The Scruffy Scruffy Dog, illustrated by Biro, Hodder & Stoughton, 1983.

The Tiger Who Couldn't Be Bothered, illustrated by Biro, Hodder & Stoughton, 1984.

The Clever Clever Cats, illustrated by Biro, Hodder & Stoughton, 1985.

Bobby Brewster's Hiccups, illustrated by Buchanan, Hodder & Stoughton, 1985.

Bobby Brewster's Old Van, illustrated by Barnett, Hodder & Stoughton, 1986.

The Silly Silly Ghost, illustrated by Biro, Hodder & Stoughton, 1987.

Bobby Brewster and the Magic Handyman, illustrated by Barnett, Hodder & Stoughton, 1987.

Bobby Brewster's Jigsaw Puzzle, illustrated by Biro, Hodder & Stoughton, 1988.

The Sleeping Policeman, illustrated by Biro, Hodder & Stoughton, 1988.

Musical works include *The Circus King, Blackbird Pie* (children's play) 1956, both with Capel Annand, and additional adult musical revues and children's musical programs produced by the British Broadcasting Corp., 1949-57. Todd's manuscripts are housed in the de Grummond Collection, University of Southern Mississippi, Hattiesburg.

■ Adaptations

A total of seven "Bobby Brewster" stories by Todd and "Gumdrop" stories by Biro were adapted into the videocassette *Tales of Bobby Brewster and More Adventures of Gumdrop,* Nutland Video Ltd., 1982.

■ Sidelights

Herbert Eaton Todd was a storyteller turned author, only because his stories were so well liked by his listeners that they convinced him to write them down. Over the course of his prolific career, Todd told thousands of stories to both children and adults at schools, libraries, and universities, as well as through the mediums of radio and television. More often than not, these stories revolved around the character of Bobby Brewster, an ordinary boy who encountered amazing and wondrous things. Antony Kamm, in an essay for

In this Bobby Brewster adventure, *The Sick Cow,* Bobby encounters a cow with a very unique medical condition. (Illustration by Val Biro.)

Twentieth-Century Children's Writers, explained the appeal of Todd's Bobby Brewster tales: "What is so good about the stories is that they are founded on everyday situations and everyday things .... Many of the situations are really funny. The stories have witty touches of detail, and they are told in public with the professional expertise, timing, and verve of many years' practice."

Todd once described Bobby Brewster for *SATA* as "a small boy nine years old who was three and a half [in 1942] when I started telling stories about him to my own sons. He is an ordinary boy who has the most extraordinary adventures with ordinary things. He has a round face, blue eyes, and a nose like a button—and he is part of me, part of my sons, and now part of the hundreds of thousands of children (girls as well as boys) who I meet every year."

The most common thread throughout Todd's Bobby Brewster stories is the magical powers that inanimate objects possess whenever Bobby is around. In *The Roundabout Horse,* for example, Bobby is able to make a wooden carousel horse's dream come true when he rides him in a horse race. The power of communicating with zoo animals is granted to Bobby in *King of Beasts* when a monkey winks at him and he winks back. *Bobby Brewster's Lamp Post* features a lamp post that can actually talk and a Christmas card with bells that really ring. And in *Bobby Brewster and the Magic Handyman,* a strange handyman shows up at the Brewster household one day, offering his unique services to the family for an

Bobby and his father must finish delivering presents on Christmas Eve when Santa comes down with a bad cold in this 1986 story. (Illustration by Val Biro.)

entire year. During the course of this year, garden tools magically dig on their own, different kinds of juices run out of the water taps, and ordinary brown paper thrown on the walls turns to patterned wallpaper. "The linked episodes run quickly and cheerfully for the delectation of young connoisseurs of practical nonsense," described Margery Fisher in her *Growing Point* review of *Bobby Brewster and the Magic Handyman.* Fisher similarly praised Todd's use of magical elements in her review of *Bobby Brewster's Lamp Post* by stating that the "everyday veracity and amusing fancy is as expert as ever."

When not writing about Bobby Brewster and his fabulous adventures, Todd concentrated on other characters, including several that are animals. Among these is Libby, the main character in *The Clever Clever Cats.* Libby is a well-educated cat who takes offense to the term "cat-burglar," which is being used to describe a neighborhood thief. Determined to protest the use of this word, Libby, along with several other cats from the neighborhood, starts a surveillance on houses that look to be prime targets for robbery. This effort flushes out the thief and drives him into the arms of the constable. Nigel Thomas asserted in *Books for Your Children* that *The Clever Clever Cats* is "an amusing tale" in which "the cats are delightfully characterised."

Another humorous animal tale, *The Tiger Who Couldn't Be Bothered,* concerns an animal of the jungle who is failing to live up to the expectations of the other animals because he is too lazy. This tiger could never frighten even the gentlest of creatures, and he is so dirty that his stripes are not even visible. One day, though, he manages to accidentally fall in the river and restore his appearance just in time to have his picture taken by passing photographers. When this picture makes it into an advertisement, the tiger is transformed into a glorious jungle beast. Jill Bennet maintained in her *Books for Keeps* review of *The Tiger Who Couldn't Be Bothered* that "Todd and Biro are a well-established partnership and this neatly constructed and drolly illustrated story should prove as popular."

All of Todd's books were also among the multitude of stories he told to numerous audiences; writing remained his second love throughout his career, which ended in 1988 with his death. He commented in 1978, as quoted in *Twentieth-Century Children's Writers:* "I do not claim to write stories of great literary merit, or to teach a lesson or point a moral. I write and tell stories simply for fun. And my stories are written in exactly the same language as I tell them, for *telling* stories was my first joy and I was only persuaded to write them because people seemed to enjoy hearing them."

■ Works Cited

Bennet, Jill, review of *The Tiger Who Couldn't Be Bothered, Books for Keeps,* June, 1987, p. 14.
Fisher, Margery, review of *Bobby Brewster's Lamp Post, Growing Point,* September, 1982, p. 3966.

Fisher, Margery, review of *Bobby Brewster and the Magic Handyman, Growing Point,* May, 1987, p. 4797.
Kamm, Antony, essay on H. E. Todd in *Twentieth-Century Children's Writers,* 4th edition, St. James Press, 1995.
Thomas, Nigel, review of *The Clever Clever Cats, Books for Your Children,* autumn, 1985, p. 16.

■ For More Information See

PERIODICALS

Booklist, July 1, 1976, p. 1529.
Emergency Librarian, November, 1981, p. 35.
Growing Point, September, 1978, p. 3396; March, 1980, p. 3665; May, 1982, pp. 3905-6; November, 1985, pp. 4516-17.
Junior Bookshelf, February, 1975, p. 27; April, 1979, p. 98; February, 1980, p. 23; April, 1981, p. 67; June, 1985, p. 124.
School Librarian, September, 1980, p. 271; September, 1982, p. 230; December, 1982, p. 347.
School Library Journal, September, 1980, p. 64.
Times Literary Supplement, February 26, 1982, p. 26; July 23, 1982, p. 796.*

*   *   *

TRIVIZAS, Eugene 1946-

■ Personal

Born September 8, 1946, in Athens, Greece; son of Nicolaos (a businessman) and Sophia Trivizas. *Education:* University of Athens, LL.B. 1969, B.Sc., 1973; University of London, LL.M., 1974; London School of Economics and Political Science, Ph.D., 1979.

■ Addresses

Home—26 Orsett Ter., London W2 6AJ, England. *Office*—Faculty of Letters, University of Reading, Whiteknights, Reading RG6 2AA, England.

■ Career

Barrister at Law. Lecturer in international and comparative criminology at University of Reading, and visiting professor in criminology and penology at Pantion University, Athens. Member of the Institute for the Study and Treatment of Offenders, England. *Military service:* Greek Navy, officer, 1969-72.

■ Writings

IN ENGLISH

The Three Little Wolves and the Big Bad Pig, illustrated by Helen Oxenbury, McElderry Books, 1993.

IN GREEK

To oneiro tou skiachtrou: to theatro me te mise aulaia (children's plays), Kollarou (Athens), 1984.
Ho eroteumenos pyrosvestes, Patake (Athens), 1992.

Greek author Trivizas turns the tables on a classic nursery tale—and throws in a few modern developments—in his first English-language picture book. (Cover illustration by Helen Oxenbury.)

He zographia tes Christinas: to vivlio pou den to diavaze kaneis, Psychogios (Athens), 1993.

Hoi peirates tes Kaminadas, Psychogios, 1993.

■ Work in Progress

Translating his books and theatre plays into English; researching female criminality, terrorism, and conformity and deviance in children's literature.

■ Sidelights

In *The Three Little Wolves and the Big Bad Pig,* Eugene Trivizas adds an ironic twist to a familiar fairy tale. Instead of three little pigs, he presents three soft and cuddly little wolves. And in place of the traditional Big Bad Wolf is a mean pig who goes to much greater lengths than the wolf ever did. Encouraged by their mother to go out on their own, the three little wolves industriously build their first house of bricks. When the Big Bad Pig is unable to blow the house down, he returns with a sledgehammer and demolishes it. Opting for a more stable design, the wolves next build a house of concrete. While at play after finishing their work, the wolves witness the pig approaching their new house with a pneumatic drill; they escape just in time. Work then begins on their third home, which is constructed of steel, iron, and plexiglas, and even includes a security system. When the pig destroys this house by blowing it up with dynamite, the wolves turn to nature, building their final house with flowers. The smell of the cherry blossoms, daffodils, pink roses, and marigolds stops the pig from blowing the house down, and he befriends the wolves, moving into the flower house with them.

"Eugene Trivizas' marauder is outsmarted, but he isn't cooked and eaten for supper," points out Linda Phillips Ashour in the *New York Times Book Review.* "This pig has been vanquished in the best, and perhaps, only way possible: through his own change of heart." Karen James, writing in *School Library Journal,* praises *The Three Little Wolves and the Big Bad Pig* for its "clever switch on the familiar counterparts" and concludes that children "will enjoy the turnabout, the narrow escapes, and the harmonious ending."

Eugene Trivizas described himself for *SATA:* "Eugene Trivizas is an explorer and inventor. He lives in the island of Fireworks with Asprojum his white elephant, Cynthia his parrot (who also doubles as an answering machine) and a green invisible kangaroo. The island has seven firework-volcanoes, a confetti-waterfall, a meadow of four-leafed clovers, and a cave full of secrets.

"Eugene has made a collection of things that have dropped out of fairy tales when no one was looking. He has a brick from the house that the three little wolves had built, the wick from Aladdin's lamp, a feather from the pillow that the princess slept on for a hundred years, a piece of the mirror that Snow White's mother used to own, and the eggshell from which the ugly duckling was hatched.

"Eugene is the inventor of chameleon paint. If you paint your bedroom with this paint, in the morning it has the colour of your last night's dream. If you dreamt about the sea it will be blue with white wavy stripes and if you dreamt about a field of poppies it will be green with red dots. Eugene has discovered Fruitopia, the Kingdom of Maximilian the Mini, Trainidad, the land of little trains, and he has found the eighth colour of the rainbow.

"When Eugene was six years old he had such a splendid birthday party and so many presents that he wished that he could have a birthday every day, day after day. His wish was fulfilled but in just three months he was 98 years of age. Since then he has been struggling to grow younger but it is much more difficult than growing older.

"His best friend is Captain Borfin the Whale Saver. Every now and then they sail the seven seas and save whales from whalers, puffins from puffin-hunters, princesses from dragons, and dragons from princesses."

■ Works Cited

Ashour, Linda Phillips, "Who's Afraid of the Big Bad Pig?," *New York Times Book Review,* November 14, 1993, p. 56.

James, Karen, review of *The Three Little Wolves and the Big Bad Pig, School Library Journal,* December, 1993, p. 95.

■ For More Information See

PERIODICALS

Australian Book Review, October, 1993, p. 68.

Bulletin of the Center for Children's Books, September, 1993, p. 3.

Junior Bookshelf, February, 1994, p. 20.

Magpies, May, 1994, p. 27.

Publishers Weekly, June 28, 1993, p. 77.

Spectator, December 11, 1993, p. 45.

V–W

Van ZYLE, Jon 1942-

■ Personal

Born November 9, 1942, in Petoskey, MI; son of Ruth Van Zyle; married Charlotte (a publisher), November 9, 1980; children: Michelle Kuhn, Robert David.

■ Addresses

Home—P.O. Box 518, Eagle River, AK 99577. *Agent*—Alaska Limited Editions, P.O. Box 770746, Eagle River, AK 99577; and Hadley House, 11001 Hampshire Ave. S., Minneapolis, MN 55438.

■ Career

Professional artist, 1975—. Organizer, race judge, and official artist for Hope 91, first intercontinental international sled dog race from Nome, Alaska, to Anadyr, Chukotka Region, USSR; official Iditarod Artist, 1979—. Artist for limited plate collections, Lenox China Inc., 1991—; clothing line, Arctic Circle Enterprises, Seattle, WA. *Exhibitions:* Has had several one-man art shows in galleries throughout the United States and Europe; Alaska's Artists, Capitol Rotunda, Washington, DC, 1983; Fry Art Museum, Seattle, WA, 1983, 1986, 1989, 1994; National Art exhibition of Alaskan Wildlife (Audubon Society), 1986, 1987, show judge, 1988; Artist of the Year, Milwaukee Sports/Wildlife Show, 1991; Pacific Rim Wildlife Art Show, Tacoma, WA, featured artist, 1990, 1992.

■ Illustrator

A. Allan Turner, editor, *The Iditarod Arctic Sports Medicine-Human Performance Guide,* American College of Sports Medicine, Alaska Regional Chapter, 1988, 2nd edition, 1989.
Carol Phillips, *Best of Alaska: The Art of Jon Van Zyle,* Epicenter Press, 1990.
Lew Friedman, *Iditarod Classics,* Epicenter Press, 1992.
Jonathan London, *The Eyes of Gray Wolf,* Chronicle Books, 1993.

London, *Honey Paw and Lightfoot,* Chronicle Books, 1994.
Debbie S. Miller, *A Caribou Journey,* Little, Brown, 1995.
Tim Jones, *Dog Heroes,* Epicenter Press, 1995.

■ Sidelights

Artist Jon Van Zyle gets his inspiration from Alaska. His completion of two Iditarod Trail Sled Dog Races, which cover more than twelve hundred miles between Anchorage and Nome, enabled him to create the commemorative poster series for the event, and he was named the official Iditarod artist in 1979.

In general, Van Zyle's art, for which he has received numerous awards, portrays the Alaskan people, natives and non-natives, and the landscape of the northern region. He and his wife, Charlotte, travel often to research and develop future projects. They reside near Eagle River with their Siberian Huskies.

*   *   *

WAKIN, Daniel (Joseph) 1961-

■ Personal

Born June 13, 1961, in New York, NY; son of Edward (a writer and professor) and Jeanette (a professor) Wakin; married Vera Haller (a journalist), August 1, 1992; children: Thomas Bernard. *Education:* Harvard University, B.A. (cum laude), 1983. *Hobbies and other interests:* Classical music, playing clarinet.

■ Addresses

Office—Associated Press, Piazza Grazioli 5, Roma 00186, Italy.

■ Career

Associated Press, New York City, general assignment reporter, courthouse correspondent, business writer, foreign desk editor, and foreign correspondent in Rome, Italy, 1983—.

■ Writings

(With father, Edward Wakin) *Photos That Made U.S. History,* Walker & Co., 1993.

■ Sidelights

Daniel Wakin explained the origins of *Photos That Made U.S. History* to *SATA:* "*Photos* began as a fun project over occasional lunches with my father. It was hatched, incubated, and nurtured at a wonderful fish restaurant, Dock's, on Manhattan's Upper West Side. Then we got down to serious work, dividing up the material and reading and critiquing each other's chapters."

* * *

WEINBERGER, Tanya 1939-

■ Personal

Born September 13, 1939, in San Francisco, CA; daughter of Drayton (a city planner) and Adya (a photographer; maiden name, Boratynski) Bryant; married Anthony Weinberger. *Education:* Attended Chouinard Art Institute for three years. *Politics:* "Variable."

■ Addresses

Office—82 Belmont St., Rochester, NY 14620. *Agent*—Marina Bryant, World Events, 4306 North Shallowford Rd., Chamblee, GA 30341.

■ Career

Animator, independent film and video producer in New York. *Exhibitions:* Works have appeared in museum shows and festivals in California, New York City, Quebec, Atlanta, Berlin, Los Angeles, San Francisco, and elsewhere, including the Museum of Modern Art and the Metropolitan Museum of Art.

■ Awards, Honors

Sinking Creek Film Festival award, 1983; Movies on a Shoestring award, 1983, 1984; Case Award, 1984; *Playboy Magazine* Grand Prize Award, 1984; First Hollywood Erotic Film Festival award, 1984; grand prize, National Computer Graphics Association (NCGA), 1986; grand prize, Cine Golden Eagle, 1986; Communicator of the Year, City of Rochester, NY, 1986; finalist, Monitor Award, 1986, 1987; Chicago International Festival of Children's Films awards, 1986, 1987; first prize, National Association of Vocational-Technical Education Communicators (NAVTEC), 1989; Golden Can Award, 1992; certificate of excellence, U.S. Film and Video Festival; merit award, Athens Video Festival.

■ Writings

(Self-illustrated) *Grace,* Longstreet Press, 1994.
(Self-illustrated) *Ms. Gravity,* Longstreet Press, 1995.

Also illustrator of books *Money Matters* and *The Littlest Spruce;* wrote and hosted instructional videotape, *Creating Animation on a Computer,* AIMS Media (Van Nuys, CA), 1986. Has written, designed, animated, and produced thirty-seven other films and videos for broadcast television which have appeared on HBO, Cinemax, Showtime, Playboy, Disney, MTV, Nickelodeon, PBS, and other networks.

■ Work in Progress

A novel/screenplay/musical for animated feature film *Cosmic Strings;* two books, *Teddyman* and *Quake,* awaiting publishers.

■ For More Information See

PERIODICALS

New York Times Book Review, September 25, 1994, p. 32.

* * *

WHEELER, Jody 1952-

■ Personal

Born February 20, 1952; daughter of Byrhl F. Jr. and Betty I. (a physical education teacher and union negotiator) Wheeler. *Education:* Elmira College, B.A.; has also attended the School of Visual Arts, the New School for Social Research.

■ Addresses

Office—375 South End Ave., #12T, New York, NY 10280.

■ Career

Writer and illustrator. Dial Press, New York City, worked as a design assistant and secretary for two years; owner of freelance illustration business, 1980—.

■ Illustrator

The City Mouse and the Country Mouse, Grosset & Dunlap, 1985.
The Night before Christmas, Ideals Publishing, 1988.
What a Teddy Bear Needs, Ladybird Books, 1989.
The Gift of the Magi, Ideals Publishing, 1990.
Very Scary Halloween, Scholastic, 1991.
The First Noel, Ideals Publishing, 1992.
An Old-Fashioned Thanksgiving, Ideals Publishing, 1993.
The Tea Party Book, Random House, 1994.
Wild Weather: Hurricane! Random House, 1994.

JODY WHEELER

Lorraine J. Hopping, *Wild Weather: Tornadoes!*, Scholastic, 1994.
Lost Little Bunny, Scholastic, 1995.
Tooth Fairy Magic, Scholastic, 1995.

Also illustrator of *My First Tools* series, Warner Books, 1988-90, and *The Very Scary Jack'O Lantern,* Scholastic. Illustrator for educational texts and magazines.

■ Sidelights

Jody Wheeler told *SATA:* "I developed a greater than average interest in children's books at an early age, having been influenced and encouraged by my great-aunt Opal Wheeler, a prolific writer of books for young readers in the 1950s. After being trained as a fine artist and art educator, I moved to Manhattan in 1977, and eventually turned to the field of publishing. I worked as a design assistant/secretary at Dial Press in the juvenile books division for two years before establishing my own free-lance illustration business in 1980. Since then I have enjoyed working on a variety of projects ranging from picture books to educational texts and magazines, greeting cards to coloring books."

WIATER, Stanley 1953-

■ Personal

Surname pronounced "*Wee*-otter"; born May 21, 1953, in Northampton, MA; son of Stanley and Ann (Misholovsky) Wiater; married Iris Arroyo (a social service directory), September 21, 1985; children: Tanya. *Education:* University of Massachusetts, B.A., 1975. *Politics:* Democrat. *Religion:* Catholic.

■ Addresses

Home and office—ShadoWind, Inc., 381 Upper Rd., Deerfield, MA 01342. *Agent*—John White, 60 Pound Ridge Rd., Cheshire, CT 06410.

■ Career

Freelance writer, 1975—; owner of corporation, ShadoWind, Inc. *Member:* National Writers Union, Horror Writers Association.

■ Awards, Honors

Winner of competition judged by Stephen King, 1980, for short story, "The Toucher"; Bram Stoker Award for superior achievement in nonfiction, Horror Writers Association, 1991, for *Dark Dreamers: Conversations with the Masters of Horror;* Master of Ceremonies, World Horror Convention III, 1993; Bram Stoker Award nomination, 1993, for *Dark Visions: Conversations with the Masters of the Horror Film;* Harvey Award

STANLEY WIATER

nomination and Eisner Award nomination, both 1994, for *Comic Book Rebels: Conversations with the Creators of the New Comics.*

■ Writings

(Editor) *Night Visions 7,* Dark Harvest, 1989.
Dark Dreamers: Conversations with the Masters of Horror, Underwood/Miller (limited edition), 1990, Avon Books, 1990.
The Official Teenage Mutant Ninja Turtles Treasury, Villard Books, 1991.
Dark Visions: Conversations with the Masters of the Horror Film, Avon Books, 1992.
(Editor) *After the Darkness,* Maclay & Associates, 1993.
(With Stephen R. Bissette) *Comic Book Rebels: Conversations with the Creators of the New Comics,* Donald I. Fine, 1993.
Mysteries of the Word, Crossroads Press, 1994.

Also author of original scripts for comic books, including *Teenage Mutant Ninja Turtles,* Archie Comics, 1992-94; *TMNT Universe Sourcebook,* Archie Comics, 1992-94; and *Teenage Mutant Ninja Turtles,* daily comic strip, 1993. Contributor of short story adaptations to *Goreshriek #5, Shriek #1,* and *Shriek #2.* Contributor to fiction anthologies, including *Masques II,* 1987, *Obsessions,* 1991, and *Voices from the Night,* 1994; contributor to nonfiction texts, including *The Star Trek Files: Where No Man Has Gone Before,* 1985, *The Robert Block Companion,* 1989, *Stephen King & Clive Barker: The Masters of the Macabre,* 1990, *Famous Monsters Chronicles,* 1991, *The Complete Stephen King Encyclopedia,* 1991, *James Herbert: By Horror Haunted,* 1992, and *Bizarre Bazaar III,* 1994. Contributor to newspapers and magazines, including *Valley Advocate, Amherst Record, Fate, Fangoria, Horrorstruck,* and *New Blood.* Wiater's stories and articles have been published in England, France, Spain, Mexico, Italy, and Germany.

■ Work in Progress

Jon Dark, Psychic Investigator: Wolves of Moordeth, a computer interactive game, for Animation Magic; "AlphaSaurs," a series of educational books for children using unique dinosaur characters to teach the alphabet.

■ Sidelights

Stanley Wiater told *SATA:* "Although I've spent most of my career writing in—and about—the horror genre, I find that the most appreciative audiences for this field are children and young people in general. Even better than most adults, they understand the healing and therapeutic values which tales of horror (which are little more than fairy tales for grown-ups) can provide to the attentive reader. As a young child, I distinctly recall actor Vincent Price being interviewed on television. When asked if scary movies and books had a negative effect on the youth of America, he replied without hesitation: 'Why, monsters are *good* for you!' I like to think my studies of the horror genre, and of the even less

respectable comic book medium, will help others to understand why monsters are, indeed, good for us all."

The actual creators of these monsters and heroes are the focus of Wiater's books *Dark Dreamers: Conversations with the Masters of Horror, Dark Visions: Conversations with the Masters of the Horror Film,* and *Comic Book Rebels: Conversations with the Creators of the New Comics.* In each work, Wiater interviews leaders in a particular field. Trends of both the past and present are explored in these interviews, and anecdotes, as well as philosophies, are related by the artists. Patrick S. Jones, reviewing *Dark Dreamers* in *Kliatt,* maintains that the work is "a fine collection for either leisure reading or use in research papers about any of these macabre masters." And in his review of *Dark Visions, Washington Post Book World* contributor Martin Morse Wooster asserts that "Wiater is an experienced interviewer," concluding that for "people who love horror movies, *Dark Visions* provides a good deal of chatty fun."

■ Works Cited

Jones, Patrick S., review of *Dark Dreamers: Conversations with the Masters of Horror, Kliatt,* January, 1991, p. 29.
Wooster, Martin Morse, review of *Dark Visions: Conversations with the Masters of the Horror Film, Washington Post Book World,* March 29, 1992, p. 8.

■ For More Information See

PERIODICALS

Kirkus Reviews, June 1, 1993, p. 712.
Locus, October, 1990, p. 31.
Publishers Weekly, June 21, 1993, p. 98.
Tribune Books (Chicago), February 2, 1992, p. 8.

*　　*　　*

WIENER, Lori 1956-

■ Personal

Born November 14, 1956, in New York, NY; daughter of Walter (a manufacturer) and Marilyn (an occupational therapist) Wiener; married Gary Brawerman (in retail), August 26, 1984; children: Marisa, Brett. *Education:* State University of New York, Buffalo, B.S. (magna cum laude), 1977; New York University, M.S.W., 1979, Ph.D., 1988. *Religion:* Jewish.

■ Addresses

Home—966 Coachway Ln., Annapolis, MD 21401. *Office*—National Cancer Institute, Bethesda, MD 20892.

■ Career

Nassau County Law Services, social worker, 1977-78; Jewish Board of Family and Children Services, clinical social worker in out-patient counseling clinic, 1978-79,

My brothers have H.I.V. I have three brothers. They all have H.I.V. It is really hard to see them go throw pain I Love my brothers alot I always take care of them when my mom cant I know that thier not going to die soon, but I'm still scared.

Candy, age 11

In *Be a Friend: Children Who Live with HIV Speak*, Wiener—along with Aprille Best and Philip A. Pizzo—collected telling illustrations like this one drawn by children suffering from the disease.

clinical social worker in a residential treatment center, 1979-82; private practice, New York City, 1981-85; Memorial Sloan-Kettering Cancer Center, clinical social worker, 1982-83, member of medical oncology unit, 1983-85, and implemented AIDS Psychosocial Support Program; clinical social worker, National Institutes of Health, 1986-89; National Cancer Institute, Bethesda, MD, coordinator of pediatric HIV psychosocial support program, 1989—. Member of advisory board, Ronald McDonald House, Washington, DC, 1987-89; cofounder and leader, Social Work AIDS Network (SWAN), 1987-91; member of board of directors, National Institutes of Health Children's Inn; member of medical advisory board, Pediatric AIDS Foundation, Los Angeles, CA; member of advisory board, Mother's Voices; former member of Health Service Professional Advisory Committee, U.S. Public Health Service, and Metropolitan Community AIDS Partnership Steering Committee, District of Columbia Hospital Association. Speaker and presenter at numerous conferences, hospitals, and symposiums. *Member:* National Association of Social Workers (board of directors, 1987-89), National Association of Clinical Social Workers, American Orthopsychiatric Association.

■ Awards, Honors

Clinical Center Honor Award, National Institutes of Health, 1988, 1991, 1992, and 1993; Clinical Center Cash Award, National Institutes of Health, 1989, 1990, and 1994; Bronze Telly Award, 1991, for video, *I Need a Friend: Kids Talk about the AIDS Virus;* Certificate of Merit Award, Intercom Chicago International Film Festival, and Cindy Award, Association of Visual Communicators, both for video, *Conducting an HIV Parent Support Group.*

■ Writings

(With Aprille Best and Philip A. Pizzo) *Be a Friend: Children Who Live with HIV Speak,* A. Whitman, 1994.

Also creator of videos, including *I Need a Friend: Kids Talk about the AIDS Virus* and *Conducting an HIV Parent Support Group.* Contributor to texts, including (with G. H. Christ) *AIDS: Diagnosis, Treatment, and Prevention,* 1985; (with S. P. Hersh) *Principles and Practices of Pediatric Oncology,* 1988; *Empowering Families for Better Health,* 1988; (with C. D. Fair and R. T. Granowsky) *The Expanding Face of AIDS,* 1993; (with Fair and Pizzo) *Hospice Care for Children,* 1993; (with others) *Pediatric AIDS: The Challenge of HIV Infection in Infants, Children, and Adolescents,* 2nd edition, 1994; and *Encyclopedia of Social Work,* 1995.

Editor, supplementary issue, *Journal of Developmental and Behavioral Pediatrics,* 1994. Reviewer for *AIDS Education and Prevention: An Interdisciplinary Journal.* Contributor to *Bear Essentials,* a quarterly newsletter of the pediatric branch of the National Cancer Institute, 1987-90. Also contributor to professional periodicals, including *Oncology Nursing Forum, Journal of Pediatrics, Hemophilia World, New England Journal of Medicine, Child and Adolescent Social Work Journal, Social Work, Social Work with Groups, Families in Society, American Journal of Orthopsychiatry, Journal of Developmental and Behavioral Pediatrics, Journal of HIV/AIDS Prevention and Education for Adolescents and Children,* and *Journal of Pediatric Psychology.*

■ Sidelights

The coordinator of the pediatric HIV support program at the National Cancer Institute, Lori Wiener is very close to the children who fill the pages of *Be a Friend: Children Who Live with HIV Speak.* These children, along with several adults, receive her support and expertise on a daily basis; Wiener is able to draw feelings and truths out of her patients in instances when others have failed. It is such truths that make up *Be a Friend,* which contains both writings and drawings done by children infected with the Human Immunodeficiency Virus (HIV) that leads to Acquired Immunodeficiency Syndrome, or AIDS. "Their words and drawings depict the inner world of children faced with a life threatening disease," explains Wiener in a letter to Albert Whitman and Company, the publisher of *Be a Friend.* "Their work has the capacity to teach others, children as well as adults, what AIDS is truly like to live with. Their words, in particular, provide invaluable lessons on life, death, and the importance of family."

Be a Friend is constructed to cover these very same life lessons. In the first section, "I Often Wonder," children finish this phrase with questions about acceptance by others and fears about their future and death. "Living with HIV," the middle portion of the book, deals with the day-to-day struggle of actually living with a disease that brings pain and the necessity of frequent medical assistance. And finally, "Family, Friends, and AIDS" reveals just how isolated these children are because of the societal stigma attached to their particular disease. The value of *Be a Friend,* writes Roger Sutton in the *Bulletin of the Center for Children's Books,* "lies in the way it will confront readers with how much like themselves and their families are the stories and feelings spoken here." And a *Publishers Weekly* reviewer asserts that *Be a Friend* is a "poignant collection" in which "the children express their emotions with wrenching candor."

The sadness prevalent to Wiener's work, evidenced in *Be a Friend,* does not result in depression for the author, however. "I truly believe I make a difference," Wiener maintains in an interview with Amy Goldstein for the *Washington Post.* "I help people so, in the time they have together . . . , they get to know each other in ways that most families don't. They really and truly appreciate life, because they don't know what tomorrow will bring. They don't know if they will have a tomorrow."

■ Works Cited

Review of *Be a Friend: Children Who Live with HIV Speak, Publishers Weekly,* January 24, 1994, pp. 55-56.
Goldstein, Amy, "Helping Children Who Live with AIDS," *Washington Post,* November 16, 1992, pp. A1, A13.
Sutton, Roger, review of *Be a Friend: Children Who Live with HIV Speak, Bulletin of the Center for Children's Books,* April, 1994, pp. 272-73.

*   *   *

WILKINS, Mary Huiskamp 1926-
(Mary Calhoun)

■ Personal

Born August 3, 1926, in Keokuk, IA; daughter of William Clark and Louisa Belle (Waples) Huiskamp; married James Franklin Calhoun (a reporter and photographer), September 3, 1948 (died August 12, 1961); married Leon Wilkins (an Episcopalian priest), November 8, 1962; children: (first marriage) Michael, Gregory. *Education:* University of Iowa, B.A. and certificate in journalism, 1948. *Religion:* Episcopalian. *Hobbies and other interests:* Hiking in the mountains, telling stories.

MARY HUISKAMP WILKINS

■ Addresses

Home—P.O. Box 719, Clark, CO 80428.

■ Career

Writer of books for young people. Worked in Keokuk (IA) Public Library, summers, 1943-45; reporter in Cedar Rapids, IA, 1947; *World-Herald,* Omaha, NE, reporter, 1948-49; *Gresham Outlook,* Gresham, OR, society editor, 1948-49. Member of board of trustees, Mount Vernon (WA) Public Library, 1960-61, and Rangely (CO) Public Library, 1966-70. Sunday School teacher for twenty-five years. *Member:* Authors Guild, Authors League of America, Society of Children's Book Writers and Illustrators.

■ Awards, Honors

Certificate of Achievement, Central Missouri State College; children's wing of Rangely (CO) Public Library named in her honor; Golden Kite Honor Book citation, Society of Children's Book Writers and Illustrators, 1979, Little Archer Award, University of Wisconsin, 1980, Colorado Children's Book Award, 1981, and Washington Children's Choice Picture Book Award, Washington Library Media Association, 1982, all for *Cross-Country Cat; School Library Journal* Best Books of the 1991 citation, California Young Readers Medal, 1994, and Maryland Children's Choice Award, 1994, all for *High-Wire Henry.*

■ Writings

FOR CHILDREN; UNDER NAME MARY CALHOUN

Making the Mississippi Shout, Morrow, 1957.
The Sweet Patootie Doll, Morrow, 1957.

The River-Minded Boy, illustrated by William R. Lohse, Morrow, 1958.
Wobble, the Witch Cat, illustrated by Roger Duvoisin, Morrow, 1958.
Houn' Dog, illustrated by Duvoisin, Morrow, 1959.
Katie John, illustrated by Paul Frame, Harper, 1960.
Depend on Katie John, illustrated by Paul Frame, Harper, 1961.
Cowboy Cal and the Outlaw, Morrow, 1961.
The Nine Lives of Homer C. Cat, Morrow, 1962.
The Hungry Leprechaun, Morrow, 1962.
Honestly, Katie John!, Harper, 1963.
The Witch of Hissing Hill, Morrow, 1964.
High Wind for Kansas, illustrated by W. T. Mars, Morrow, 1965.
The House of Thirty Cats, illustrated by Mary Chalmers, Harper, 1965.
The Thieving Dwarfs, illustrated by Janet McCaffery, Morrow, 1967.
The Runaway Brownie, illustrated by McCaffery, Morrow, 1967.
The Last Two Elves in Denmark, illustrated by McCaffery, Morrow, 1968.
The Goblin under the Stairs, illustrated by McCaffery, Morrow, 1968.
The Pixy and the Lazy Housewife, illustrated by McCaffery, Morrow, 1969.
The Traveling Ball of String, illustrated by McCaffery, Morrow, 1969.
Mermaid of Storms, illustrated by McCaffery, Morrow, 1970.
White Witch of Kynance (novel), Harper, 1970.
Magic in the Alley, illustrated by Wendy Watson, Atheneum, 1970.
Daisy, Tell Me!, illustrated by McCaffery, Morrow, 1971.
It's Getting Beautiful Now (novel), Harper, 1971.
Camels Are Meaner Than Mules, illustrated by Herman B. Vestal, Garrard, 1971.
The Flower Mother, illustrated by McCaffery, Morrow, 1972.
Three Kinds of Stubborn, illustrated by Edward Malsberg, Garrard, 1972.
Mrs. Dog's Own House, illustrated by McCaffery, Morrow, 1972.
The Battle of Reuben Robin and Kite Uncle John, illustrated by McCaffery, Morrow, 1973.
The Horse Comes First (novel), illustrated by John Gretzer, Atheneum, 1974.
Old Man Whickutt's Donkey, illustrated by Tomie de Paola, Parents Magazine Press, 1975.
Ownself (novel), Harper, 1975.
Medicine Show: Conning People and Making Them Like It (nonfiction), Harper, 1976.
Euphonia and the Flood, illustrated by Simms Taback, Parents Magazine Press, 1976.
(Adapter) *The Witch's Pig,* (based on a Cornish folk tale), illustrated by Lady McCrady, Morrow, 1977.
Jack the Wise and the Cornish Cuckoos, illustrated by McCrady, Parents Magazine Press, 1978.
Cross-Country Cat, illustrated by Erick Ingraham, Morrow, 1979, published in England as *Snow-Cat,* Gollancz, 1980.

The Witch Who Lost Her Shadow, illustrated by Trinka Hakes Noble, Harper, 1979.
Katie John and Heathcliff, Harper, 1980.
Audubon Cat, illustrated by Susan Bonners, Morrow, 1981.
Hot-Air Henry, illustrated by Ingraham, Morrow, 1981.
The Night the Monster Came, illustrated by Leslie Morrill, Morrow, 1982.
Big Sixteen, illustrated by Trina Schart Hyman, Morrow, 1983.
Jack and the Whoopee Wind, illustrated by Dick Gackenbach, Morrow, 1986.
Julie's Tree, Harper, 1988.
High-Wire Henry, illustrated by Ingraham, Morrow, 1991.
While I Sleep, illustrated by Ed Young, Morrow, 1992.
Henry the Sailor Cat, illustrated by Ingraham, Morrow, 1994.
Tonio's Cat, illustrated by Ed Martinez, Morrow, 1996.
Flood!, illustrated by Ingraham, Morrow, in press.

Contributor of fiction to magazines, including *Jack and Jill, Humpty Dumpty, Child Life,* and *Instructor.*

■ Sidelights

Mary Huiskamp Wilkins, who writes under the name Mary Calhoun, is a prolific writer of juvenile and young adult books whose themes stem, as she once reported to *SATA,* "from my enthusiasms." Calhoun appears to have an ample supply of such enthusiasms. There are her western historicals, which are often located along or near the Mississippi River, a region she has been familiar with since her youth. There are her tales of elfin spirits and witches—many of them set in England and Europe—inspired by her own love of nineteenth-century folklore. There are her "Katie John" books, which were "developed from my happy memories of childhood in the big old brick house my great-grandfather built on a bluff above the Mississippi," she told *SATA.* And there are her animal books, especially her "Henry the Cat" stories, which have not only won prizes but have also won Calhoun a new readership in the latter part of her career.

Spanning four decades, Calhoun began her career as a journalist in her native Iowa. Married at the age of twenty-two, she became a full-time mother and homemaker, as well as a volunteer at local libraries, until the publication of her first children's book in 1957, *Making the Mississippi Shout.* That book and 1958's *The River-Minded Boy* both were the outgrowth of her love for the river along which she had grown up in Keokuk, Iowa. "Beyond enthusiasm, a strong emotion seems to have impelled my most successful books," she wrote in a 1981 article for *The Writer.* It was such an emotion that inspired *Wobble, the Witch Cat* in 1958, when, on a whim, she first told her two preschool sons the story about a cat who was afraid to ride on a broom. In this case, Calhoun's emotion translated into what she called "a buoyancy of well-being and playfulness." A *Kirkus Reviews* critic considered the book to be a "thoroughly bewitching bit of cat-tailery."

When Wobble discovers he can't ride on Maggie the witch's broom because it's too slippery, he throws it out only to be further embarassed when Maggie drags out the magic vacuum cleaner. (Cover illustration by Roger Duvoisin.)

The emotion may also be love, as with the first of Calhoun's Katie John books for older children, in which she wrote of her love "for the big old house in which I grew up, the love brought fresh by a flood of home-sickness," she revealed in *The Writer.* In a day of suburban dwellings built to one plan, Calhoun decided to let her own children and others know what it felt like to grow up in such a home, one built by her own great-grandfather. *Katie John,* the book that came out of that impulse, tells the story of ten-year-old Katie John Tucker, who reluctantly spends the summer away from her friends in a huge old house in Missouri. But as she explores the secret nooks of the house with a new friend, Katie John finds surprises and excitement, endearing her to audiences enough to inspire several sequels over thirty years. "The headstrong lass is as realistically charming as any we've met in many books," Miriam James wrote in the *New York Times Book Review.* In the first sequel, *Depend on Katie John,* the Tuckers inherit the rambling old homestead and turn it into a rooming house, providing new responsibilities and adventures for Katie John. The story contains "a wide variety of characters, considerable humor, and the kind of family" story young children enjoy reading, Virginia Haviland noted in *Horn Book.* Calhoun followed these two successes with a third in the series in 1963, *Honestly,*

Katie John!, continuing the exploits of the young protagonist in the rambling home by the river.

The success of the Katie John books did not keep Calhoun from pursuing other enthusiasms in print. Already she had established two other themes or motifs that carry throughout her work: the American tall tale or western, and books about animals, especially cats. In the 1965 book *High Wind for Kansas,* she relates the story of Windwagon Jones, who invents a wind-powered wagon to make the trek West. It was based on real incidents and told "with sparkle and humor," according to Charlotte A. Gallant in *Library Journal,* while a *Kirkus Reviews* writer called it "a gusty tale told with a yarn spinner's twang." Turning again to her love of cats with *The House of Thirty Cats,* Calhoun tells the story of a lonely old woman and her feline-filled house who attracts a lonely neighbor girl, teaching her of life and friendship. With this book, Calhoun has written a "can't-fail offering for cat lovers," a *Publishers Weekly* reviewer declared.

Another of Calhoun's favorite sources of inspiration is European folklore, especially tales of the little ones, or elfin spirits. She first explored this subject with 1962's *The Hungry Leprechaun,* based on Celtic fairy lore, and with the publication of *The Thieving Dwarfs* in 1967 the author began a series of five books on similar themes. Based on a German tale, *The Thieving Dwarfs* tells the story of Karl, a farmer who tries to stop the little folk from stealing his wheat. He ends up making friends with them, but angry villagers succeed in driving the dwarfs away. The creatures do leave a pot of gold to pay for the Karl's crops, making for what *Kirkus Reviews* writer Barbara Bader called "a bittersweet story." Calhoun mined the vein of Celtic lore again with *The Runaway Brownie,* based on a tale from Scotland about Angus, a little half-man and half-beast brownie. Brownies are hard-working and honest fairy folk who attach them-selves one to a family and help around the house, but when Angus's greedy new master tries to bribe him to bring him riches, the offended brownie runs away. How the rest of the family tries to win him back makes up the rest of Angus's story.

Danish elves, known as "nisse," are the subject of *The Last Two Elves in Denmark.* The story of how the two elves end up battling each other is told with "verve and pace," according to Zena Sutherland in the *Bulletin of the Center for Children's Books.* Yorkshire, England, is the setting for Calhoun's fourth elfin book, *The Goblin under the Stairs,* in which the subject is a boggart, a hairy little man who hides himself beneath the stairs in a farmhouse and helps out the wife of the house in her cleaning chores. The woman's farmer husband, how-ever, does not like this visitor. The resulting conflict and eventual compromise creates a book told "with humor and spirit," as Ruth P. Bull and Betsy Hearne noted in *Booklist.* The final book in the elfin series is *The Pixy and the Lazy Housewife,* about another English house-wife, Bess, who tricks the pixies into cleaning her Devonshire house. The pixies, however, do not take kindly to being duped and plague Bess until she becomes industrious herself. "The most successful in the series," according to Bader in another *Kirkus Reviews* article, *The Pixy and the Lazy Housewife* is "pert and scrappy."

Throughout the 1970s Calhoun continued producing both juvenile and young adult books along the various themes and motifs she had already explored: folk tales involving witches and magic; tall tales and western sagas; and contemporary problem stories involving youthful protagonists. Additional books of folk tales and magic include *Mermaid of Storms, White Witch of Kynance,* and *Magic in the Alley*. With the novel *White Witch of Kynance,* Calhoun explored the conflict between reason and superstition, using young Jennet's experiences as a witch's apprentice trying to overcome her fear of demons. The setting of sixteenth-century Cornwall, England, is brought vividly to life by Calhoun, Jean Fritz noted in the *New York Times Book Review,* for the reader has the sense of "running across the moors, tiptoeing in midnight graveyards ... and tasting salt air." Mystery and magic are brought up to date in *Magic in the Alley,* in which the modern female protagonist, Cleery, is a believer in the elfin world and magic and has a chance to practice her beliefs when she discovers a magic box in an alleyway. Ethel L. Heins, writing in *Horn Book,* praised Calhoun not only for the well-crafted tale of fantasy, but also for the "highly individualized characters" and "delightful bits of practical, down-to-earth, unmagical wisdom."

Books such as *Camels Are Meaner Than Mules, Three Kinds of Stubborn, The Battle of Reuben Robin and Kite Uncle John,* and *Euphonia and the Flood* continue Calhoun's tall tales. All of these books are geared toward a read-aloud audience, are written in regional dialects, and explore themes as various as Missouri stubbornness and doing a thing well. Set in pre-Civil War days, *Camels Are Meaner Than Mules* tells of an amusing Army experiment in using camels as pack animals. *Three Kinds of Stubborn* shows three people using relentless determination to accomplish their goals. A conflict between a bird and a man over a kite string is the premise for *The Battle of Reuben Robin and Kite Uncle John,* which *Bulletin of the Center for Children's Books* contributor Sutherland called "a rollicking, lightweight, pleasant story." And in *Euphonia and the Flood,* Euphonia, her pet pig, and a broom follow floodwaters downstream, rescuing animals and seeing where the flood is going. Sutherland noted that this "breezy tall tale has humor, action, and some word play" and marks Calhoun as "a capable and experienced storyteller."

The 1971 novel *It's Getting Beautiful Now* was something of a departure for Calhoun, written from the point of view of a teenage boy and composed in montage form. Bert Tomlinson is a troubled senior in high school seeking approval from his often absent father and testing his limits with marijuana use and shoplifting. *The Horse Comes First* also tells the story from a boy's point of view. Randy Meister is a city kid spending the summer with his grandparents on their horse ranch. Throughout a summer of helping to train horses for harness racing, Randy learns a personal lesson about self-restraint in a story that is a "fast-moving blend of horse lore and local color," according to *Horn Book* critic Mary M. Burns.

With *Ownself,* Calhoun merges several motifs into one. Not only does she tell a historical tale—the time and setting is Missouri in the early 1900s—but she also deals with an adolescent problem as well as blending in a fair dose of fairy folk. The story tells of young Laurabelle, who feels bereft at the loss of her father's closeness since his conversion to a fervent, strict sect of Methodism. No longer do they share the joy they once had in reading the legends of their Welsh ancestors about folk and fairy lore. When Laurabelle conjures up one of the fairy folk, her father is livid and summons the preacher for an exorcism. The story ends with Laurabelle realizing that she can't change even the people she loves, so she must learn to accept herself and be her own person. "The action is explosive and often very humorous," a *Publishers Weekly* critic stated, while Haviland concluded in *Horn Book:* "Percipient in developing characters and their relationships, the author has written a story both subtle and powerful."

Cats have taken center stage in much of Calhoun's writing since 1979. Henry, the clever Siamese, was introduced in *Cross-Country Cat,* the story of a cat accidentally left behind after a skiing holiday. Henry uses a pair of cross-country skis fashioned by "the Kid" to catch up with his family and has several adventures along the way, outwitting a rabbit, a Steller's jay, and a coyote. Ann A. Flowers, writing in *Horn Book,* commented on Calhoun's "unusually strong narrative, told in a straight-faced, realistic way." Calhoun used her own cat as a model for Henry and blended her own joy at cross-country skiing into the writing. "In this book I wasn't trying to tell a moral story, and I worried a little about the theme," Calhoun explained in her article in *The Writer*. She came up with a "quick kicker ending"—where Henry is "rescued" by his family—and the result was a formula for success. "Calhoun's story races ... and keeps one in hair-curling suspense," wrote Jean F. Mercier in *Publishers Weekly*. The book proved popular with audiences and awards committees as well, earning a Golden Kite Honor Book citation.

More cats came along in *The Witch Who Lost Her Shadow*—the story of a healing witch who loses her cat and must learn to love a new one—and *Audubon Cat,* a feline so named because of her fondness for bird-watching. "Once again Calhoun has written a moving tale based on a strong theme," *School Library Journal* contributor Blair Christolon remarked about *The Witch Who Lost Her Shadow,* while *Publishers Weekly* reviewer Mercier called Hilda's adventures in *Audubon Cat* an "amusing, informative story of wildlife." Calhoun also returned to Katie John with a fourth installment in the girl's adventures—this after a hiatus of seventeen years. *Katie John and Heathcliff* finds Katie in the seventh grade and smitten with the idea of finding her own Heathcliff, having recently devoured Emily Bronte's classic novel *Wuthering Heights*. Filled with the hurts and crises of early adolescence, the book is both "believable and pleasant," according to Sutherland in the *Bulletin of the Center for Children's Books*. In addition to Katie John and cats, Calhoun also revisited folklore with *Big Sixteen,* an African-American folktale, and *Jack and the Whoopee Wind,* a Western tall tale.

It was Henry the Siamese, however, who demanded to have more of his adventures told, returning in *Hot-Air Henry, High-Wire Henry,* and *Henry the Sailor Cat.* The titles tell the story, and Henry the cat is put in some very un-cat-like situations involving hot-air balloons—another Calhoun enthusiasm—acrobatics, and nautical adventures. *School Library Journal* contributor Margaret L. Chatham declared the "exciting" adventure of *Hot-Air Henry* "a winner." *School Library Journal* included *High-Wire Henry* in its listing of Best Books of 1991, and a reviewer for that magazine found it a "high-spirited adventure" about Henry the cat feeling displaced by a new puppy. In another *Horn Book* article, Burns similarly praised the "skillfully narrated" story for combining with Erick Ingraham's illustrations to provide "a seamless and joyous experience." "Seamless" was also the word Caroline Ward used in *School Library Journal* to describe Henry's fourth adventure, *Henry the Sailor Cat.* The Siamese takes to sea and rescues his owner in this book, in which Calhoun "captures the lure of sailing," Ward noted.

In her article for *The Writer,* Calhoun delineated two magical aspects needed for the writer of children's

Henry the cat uses his expert balancing technique to save the family dog, even though he's jealous of the other pet, in Wilkins's 1991 story. (Cover illustration by Erick Ingraham.)

books: "a strong emotion and a desire to tell the story to certain children." Throughout her long writing career Calhoun has given her readers a swarm of unforgettable and lovable characters, translating into books that have long-lasting popularity; nearly thirty years after Katie John was first introduced to readers, for instance, Katherine Bruner wrote in *School Library Journal* that the "series continues to offer ... solid enjoyment" to children. Always following that two-fold precept, emotion and audience, Calhoun's various "enthusiasms," as she calls them, have translated into nearly fifty books and prompt a rewriting of the old saying that necessity is the mother of invention. In Calhoun's case, enthusiasm is the mother of creation.

■ Works Cited

Bader, Barbara, review of *The Thieving Dwarfs, Kirkus Reviews,* April 1, 1967, pp. 405-6.

Bader, Barbara, review of *The Pixy and the Lazy Housewife, Kirkus Reviews,* March 1, 1969, p. 233.

Bruner, Katharine, review of *Julie's Tree, School Library Journal,* August, 1988, p. 92.

Bull, Ruth P., and Betsy Hearne, review of *The Goblin under the Stairs, Booklist,* September 15, 1968, p. 112.

Burns, Mary M., review of *The Horse Comes First, Horn Book,* October, 1974, p. 136.

Burns, Mary M., review of *High-Wire Henry, Horn Book,* July-August, 1991, p. 445.

Henry saves his owners from a terrible storm at sea in this 1994 award-winner featuring Wilkins's frisky siamese hero. (Cover illustration by Erick Ingraham.)

Calhoun, Mary, "Developing the Picture Book Story," *The Writer,* July, 1981, pp. 16-18, 46.

Chatham, Margaret L., review of *Hot-Air Henry, School Library Journal,* November, 1981, p. 72.

Christolon, Blair, review of *The Witch Who Lost Her Shadow, School Library Journal,* September, 1979, p. 104.

Flowers, Ann A., review of *Cross-Country Cat, Horn Book,* August, 1979, pp. 404-5.

Fritz, Jean, review of *White Witch of Kynance, New York Times Book Review,* October 4, 1970, p. 30.

Gallant, Charlotte A., review of *High Wind for Kansas, Library Journal,* May 15, 1965, p. 2402.

Haviland, Virginia, review of *Depend on Katie John, Horn Book,* June, 1961, p. 264.

Haviland, Virginia, review of *Ownself, Horn Book,* June, 1975, pp. 265-66.

Heins, Ethel L., review of *Magic in the Alley, Horn Book,* June, 1970, p. 295.

Review of *High Wind for Kansas, Kirkus Reviews,* March 1, 1965, p. 238.

Review of *High-Wire Henry, School Library Journal,* December, 1991, p. 29.

Review of *The House of Thirty Cats, Publishers Weekly,* July 24, 1981, p. 149.

James, Miriam, review of *Katie John, New York Times Book Review,* April 3, 1960, p. 40.

Mercier, Jean F., review of *Cross-Country Cat, Publishers Weekly,* April 19, 1979, p. 110.

Mercier, Jean F., review of *Audubon Cat, Publishers Weekly,* March 6, 1981, p. 95.

Review of *Ownself, Publishers Weekly,* April 7, 1975, p. 81.

Sutherland, Zena, review of *The Last Two Elves in Denmark, Bulletin of the Center for Children's Books,* April, 1968, pp. 123-24.

Sutherland, Zena, review of *The Battle of Reuben Robin and Kite Uncle John, Bulletin of the Center for Children's Books,* January, 1974, p. 75.

Sutherland, Zena, review of *Euphonia and the Flood, Bulletin of the Center for Children's Books,* February, 1977, pp. 87-88.

Sutherland, Zena, review of *Katie John and Heathcliff, Bulletin of the Center for Children's Books,* October, 1980, pp. 27-28.

Ward, Caroline, review of *Henry the Sailor Cat, School Library Journal,* May, 1994, p. 89.

Review of *Wobble, the Witch Cat, Kirkus Reviews,* August 1, 1958, p. 90.

■ For More Information See

PERIODICALS

Bulletin of the Center for Children's Books, November, 1969, p. 55; September, 1975, p. 4; December, 1975, p. 59; March, 1977, p. 102; December, 1983, p. 63.

Christian Science Monitor, October 23, 1958, p. 18; May 12, 1960, p. 2B.

Horn Book, December, 1967, p. 741; February, 1984, pp. 41-42; October, 1994, p. 573.

Junior Bookshelf, December, 1980, p. 281.

Kirkus Reviews, January 15, 1960, p. 48; February 15, 1961; March 1, 1968, p. 253; June 15, 1969, p. 629; September 15, 1971, p. 1020; August 1, 1972, p. 856; November 1, 1981, p. 1337.

Library Journal, September 15, 1965, pp. 3786, 3788; May 15, 1970, pp. 1939, 1951; June 15, 1972, p. 2236; December 15, 1972, pp. 4085-86.

Publishers Weekly, August 30, 1971, p. 274; March 6, 1972, p. 63; April 23, 1982, p. 93; April 12, 1991, p. 57; April 4, 1994, p. 80.

School Library Journal, May, 1977, p. 49; April, 1978, p. 67; August, 1981, p. 53; December, 1982, p. 64; May, 1987, p. 82; August, 1988, p. 92; June, 1992, p. 89.

—Sketch by J. Sydney Jones

*   *   *

WILSON, Joyce M(uriel Judson) (Joyce Stranger)

■ Personal

Born May 26 in London, England; daughter of Ralph (an advertising manager) and Beryl Judson; married Kenneth Wilson, February 28, 1944; children: Andrew Bruce, Anne Patricia and Nicholas David (twins). *Education:* University College, B.Sc., 1942. *Religion:* Church of England.

JOYCE M. WILSON

■ Addresses

Agent—Aitken, Stone & Wylie, 29 Fernshaw Rd., London SW10 0TG, England.

■ Career

Imperial Chemical Industries, Manchester, England, research chemist, 1942-46. Lecturer and writer on dog training. *Member:* Society of Authors, Institute of Journalists, United Kingdom Registry of Canine Behaviourists, Society for the Study of Companion Animals, Canine Concern (honorary president), People and Dogs Society (honorary president).

■ Writings

FOR CHILDREN; UNDER PSEUDONYM JOYCE STRANGER

Wild Cat Island, illustrated by Joe Acheson, Methuen, 1961.
Circus All Alone, illustrated by Sheila Rose, Harrap, 1965.
Jason—Nobody's Dog, illustrated by Douglas Phillips, Dent, 1972.
The Honeywell Badger, illustrated by Douglas Phillips, Dent, 1972.
Paddy Joe, Collins, 1973.
The Hare at Dark Hollow, illustrated by Charles Pickard, Dent, 1973.
Trouble for Paddy Joe, Collins, 1973.
The Secret Herds: Animal Stories, illustrated by Douglas Reay, Dent, 1974.
Paddy Joe at Deep Hollow Farm, Collins, 1975.
The Fox at Drummer's Darkness, illustrated by William Geldart, Dent, 1976, Farrar, Straus, 1977.
The Wild Ponies, illustrated by Robert Rothero, Kaye and Ward, 1976.
Joyce Stranger's Book of Hanak's Animals (poetry), illustrated by Mirko Hanak, Dent, 1976.
Paddy Joe and Thomson's Folly, Pelham, 1979.
The Curse of Seal Valley, Dent, 1979.
Vet on Call, Carousel, 1981.
Double Trouble, Carousel, 1981.
Vet Riding High, Carousel, 1982.
No More Horses, Carousel, 1982.
Dial V.E.T., Carousel, 1982.
Marooned!, Kaye and Ward, 1982.
The Hound of Darkness, Dent, 1983.
Shadows in the Dark, Kaye and Ward, 1984.
The Family at Fools' Farm, Dent, 1985.
Spy, the No-Good Pup, Dent, 1989.
Midnight Magic, Lions, 1991.
Animal Park Trilogy, Lions, 1992.
The Runaway, Lions, 1992.
The Secret of Hunter's Keep, Lions, 1993.
The House of Secrets Trilogy, Lions, 1994.

FOR ADULTS; UNDER PSEUDONYM JOYCE STRANGER

The Running Foxes, Hammond, 1965, Viking, 1966.
Breed of Giants, Hammond, 1966, Viking, 1967.
Rex, Harvill Press, 1967, Viking, 1968.
Casey, Harvill Press, 1968, published as *Born to Trouble,* Viking, 1968.
Rusty, Harvill Press, 1969, published as *The Wind on the Dragon,* Viking, 1969.
One for Sorrow, Corgi, 1969.
Zara, Viking, 1970.
Chia, The Wildcat, Harvill Press, 1971.
Lakeland Vet, Viking, 1972.
Walk a Lonely Road, Harvill Press, 1973.
A Dog Called Gelert and Other Stories (short stories), Corgi, 1973.
Never Count Apples, Harvill Press, 1974.
Never Tell a Secret, Harvill Press, 1975.
Flash, Harvill Press, 1976.
Khazan, the Horse That Came Out of the Sea, Harvill Press, 1977.
A Walk in the Dark, Joseph, 1978.
The January Queen, Joseph, 1979.
The Stallion, Joseph, 1981.
The Monastery Cat and Other Stories (short stories), Corgi, 1982.
Josse, Joseph, 1983.
The Hounds of Hades, Joseph, 1985.
The Hills are Lonely, Souvenir, 1993.
Thursday's Child, Souvenir, 1994.
A Cry on the Wind, Souvenir, 1995.

OTHER; UNDER PSEUDONYM JOYCE STRANGER

Kym: The True Story of a Siamese Cat, Joseph, 1976, Coward McCann, 1977.
Two's Company, Joseph, 1977.
Three's a Pack, Joseph, 1980.
All about Your Pet Puppy, Pelham, 1980.
How to Own a Sensible Dog, Corgi, 1981.
Two for Joy, Joseph, 1982.
Stranger Than Fiction: The Biography of Elspeth Bryce-Smith, Joseph, 1984.
A Dog in a Million, Joseph, 1984.
Dog Days, Joseph, 1986.
Double or Quit, Joseph, 1987.

■ Sidelights

Joyce M. Wilson has written about animals and humans' relationships with animals for over thirty years under the pseudonym, Joyce Stranger. She studied to be a biologist, specializing in animal behavior. It is no surprise, therefore, that she calls the animal material in her books "autobiographical," written about animals she has known—horses she used to ride, hares that lived near her family in the middle of a city, or dogs she has owned. Stranger's books all promote the rewards of partnerships between human and animals. She commented in *Twentieth-Century Children's Writers,* "for many people, an animal can provide a harmony lacking in day-to-day relationships with people."

Many of her books, including *Jason—Nobody's Dog, Walk a Lonely Road,* and *Spy, the No-Good Pup,* explore the theme of friendship between humans and animals. Other books tell of humans who, intentionally or otherwise, mistreat animals. *The Honeywell Badger,* for instance, is the story of two young children who are so set upon having a badger for a pet that they ignore the consequences of trying to tame such an animal. In the 1973 book, *Trouble for Paddy Joe,* it is Paddy Joe's poor training of his pet Alsatian, Storm, that causes the animal to become lost in the Scottish wilderness.

Several of Stranger's books are told from the animal's point of view. *The Hare at Dark Hollow,* for example, is the story of how a hare adapts to changes in its natural surroundings. "*The Hare at Dark Hollow* came from a hare that lived near us in the middle of a housing estate," Stranger once told *SATA.* "She reared her family on a tiny playing field and fed in the gardens. There were hares there until we moved to Anglesey, yet the field was only about an acre in size. Another hare was on our caravan site and used to lurk and watch stock car racing. There are hares all over Manchester airport."

One of Stranger's literary strengths is her ability to appeal to a wide audience of adults and children. A review in *Junior Bookshelf* of *The Hound of Darkness* not only praised Stranger's "deep feeling for wild country and for nature in its harshest moods," but noted that it is "by no means a book for children alone, or even for them particularly."

Although Stranger's books concentrate on deepening human's understanding of animals' rights to exist, she does not go to extremes in defending animal rights. In *The Family at Fools' Farm,* for example, eighteen-year-old Jan is hampered in her attempts to keep her family together and make the farm profitable by the irresponsible activities of a group of animal rights activists. In what a critic in *Growing Point* called an "absorbing and stirring narrative," Stranger tells the story of Jan and her three younger siblings who are left orphans when their parents and brother are tragically killed by a terrorist bomb. The four Foyles and their elder brother's intended fiancee struggle with the hardships of farming and their own grief to keep the farm going, even after the neighbors have dubbed it "Fools' Farm." A reviewer in *Junior Bookshelf* stated that the book gives "an honest picture of what farming really means in daily repetitive hard work and disappointment when crops fail or animals are sick," but it also shows the joys and pleasures of "the fruition of plans followed out against all odds."

In the nineties, Stranger has continued writing stories for children that explore relationships both between family members and between humans and animals. In *Midnight Magic,* twelve-year-old Mandy has been thrown from a horse and is now afraid to ride again. Stranger incorporates much information about horses and horse training into the story when Mandy begins to take lessons from Kristy, an elderly horsewoman who helps Mandy get over her fear and learn to respond to each horse as an individual. In *Twentieth-Century Children's Writers,* Gwen Marsh called the book "a remarkable *tour de force* even from a writer whose feeling for animals has always been her greatest strength."

■ Works Cited

Review of *The Family at Fools' Farm, Growing Point,* November, 1985, p. 4524.

Review of *The Family at Fools' Farm, Junior Bookshelf,* December, 1985, p. 281.

Review of *The Hound of Darkness, Junior Bookshelf,* October, 1983, p. 215.

Marsh, Gwen, "Joyce Stranger," *Twentieth-Century Children's Writers,* 4th edition, edited by Laura Standley Berger, St. James Press, 1995, pp. 915-17.

■ For More Information See

PERIODICALS

Booklist, April 15, 1969, p. 944; July 15, 1977, p. 1731.

Junior Bookshelf, October, 1989, p. 245.

Kirkus Reviews, March 1, 1967, p. 300.

Magpies, September, 1992, p. 31.

New York Times Book Review, May 1, 1977, p. 44.

Publishers Weekly, March 28, 1977, p. 79.

School Librarian, June, 1986, p. 174; February, 1992, p. 21.

Times Educational Supplement, January 18, 1980, p. 41; July 17, 1981, p. 26.

Times Literary Supplement, November 23, 1973, p. 1430.

*   *   *

WOOG, Adam 1953-

■ Personal

Born August 17, 1953, in Seattle, WA; son of Alan H. Woog (an environmental forester) and Ronnie (Woog) Baumgarten (an artist; maiden name, Friedman); married Karen L. Kent (a geriatric psychotherapist), April 10, 1988; children: Leah Marie. *Education:* Fairhaven College and Simon Fraser University, B.A., 1975; Antioch University, M.A., 1980. *Hobbies and other interests:* Reading, hiking, beer-making, bread-making.

■ Addresses

Home and office—8016 Meridian Ave. N., Seattle, WA 98103.

■ Career

Free-lance writer, 1982—; *Kansai Time Out,* Kobe, Japan, music editor, 1982-84; International Christian University, Tokyo, Japan, writing instructor, 1984-86; Kodansha International, Tokyo, copy editor, 1984-86; *Seattle Times,* Seattle, WA, book reviewer, author, and interviewer, 1986—, jazz critic, 1986-90, staff reporter, 1987; *Seattle Home and Garden,* Seattle, contributing editor, 1989-91.

■ Awards, Honors

Writing Scholarship, Seattle Music and Art Foundation, 1970; Second Place, Lifestyles, Sigma Delta Chi

Awards, 1983, for "Let's Japan"; First Place, Columns, Sigma Delta Chi Awards, 1987, for "The Floating Life"; First Place, History, Washington Press Association Annual Communicator Competition, 1991, for *Sexless Oysters and Self-Tipping Hats; Harry Houdini* and *Louis Armstrong* were named to the New York Public Library Books for the Teen Age list, 1995.

■ Writings

FOR YOUNG PEOPLE

The United Nations ("Overview" series), Lucent, 1994.
Poltergeists: Opposing Viewpoints, 2nd edition ("Great Mysteries" series), Lucent, 1994.
Harry Houdini ("The Importance of ..." series), Lucent, 1995.
Louis Armstrong ("The Importance of ..." series), Lucent, 1995.

Also contributor to CD-ROM publications, including *Encarta* (CD-ROM Encyclopedia), Microsoft, 1993, and *The Magic Schoolbus Inside the Human Body* and *The Magic Schoolbus in Outer Space,* Microsoft/Scholastic, 1994.

FOR ADULTS

Sexless Oysters and Self-Tipping Hats: 100 Years of Invention in the Pacific Northwest, Sasquatch, 1991.

Poltergeists

ADAM WOOG

GREAT MYSTERIES
OPPOSING VIEWPOINTS

Woog introduces readers to the world of the noisy spirits who often seek out children as their victims in this 1995 work.

(With Harriet Baskas) *Atomic Marbles and Branding Irons: A Guide to Museums, Collections, and Roadside Curiosities in Washington and Oregon,* Sasquatch, 1993.

Also contributor to books, including *Handbook of Acoustic Ecology,* World Soundscape Project (Vancouver), 1974; *Japan,* Gaimusho (Tokyo), 1984; *1992 Fodor's Pacific North Coast Guide,* Random House; and *1993 Seattle Access,* HarperCollins. Contributor to inflight magazines for airlines including Aer Lingus, All Nippon, American, Cathay Pacific, Northwest, TWA, United, and USAir; contributor to periodicals, including *Chicago Tribune, San Francisco Chronicle, USA Today, Seattle Rocket,* and *Village Voice;* contributor to overseas publications, including *Hikari, Japan Times, Tokyo Journal, Asia 2000,* and *The Emigrant.*

■ Work in Progress

Duke Ellington, Billie Holiday, Amelia Earhart, Marilyn Monroe, The Beatles, and *Elvis Presley,* to be published by Lucent; a book on aging, cowritten with wife, Karen Kent; an adult biography of a musician/composer; a nonfiction adult book on fathers who stay home with their children and serve as primary parents.

■ Sidelights

Adam Woog told *SATA:* "I became a writer by default. My background and previous work experience had been in radio when, in 1980, I moved overseas. The interviewing skills I'd learned were then put to use as I began to freelance magazine and newspaper pieces, which I did full-time beginning in 1982.

"By the time I returned to my home town of Seattle in 1986, I had developed a specialty: writing for airline inflight magazines. I continued in this vein until my schedule and work habits received a rude shock: in December, 1990, my daughter Leah was born, and I became a full-time father (my wife Karen has a 'real' job—she's a geriatric psychotherapist).

"During my daughter's first year, I wrote my first book. Leah is now in part-time preschool, which means that (although I'm still the primary parent and full-time cook in our household) I get something like a twenty-hour work week. I have gradually weaned myself from the magazine world, and now spend my work time on book projects—all nonfiction, some for students and some for grown-ups. The subject matter has ranged from inventions to unusual museums, from Harry Houdini to Louis Armstrong. I love writing biography, and I find myself irresistibly drawn, over and over, to unusual topics."

■ For More Information See

PERIODICALS

Horn Book Guide, spring, 1994, p. 101.
Library Journal, March 1, 1993, p. 50.

Los Angeles Times Book Review, December 29, 1991, p. 10.
School Library Journal, March, 1994, p. 245.

*   *   *

WRIGHT, Courtni C(rump) 1950-

◉ Personal

Born June 24, 1950, in Washington, DC; daughter of J. Edward, Jr. (owner of a barber shop) and Sallie (a homemaker; maiden name, Robinson) Crump; married Grant S. Wright (a police officer), April 1, 1979; children: Ashley. *Education:* Trinity College, B.A., 1972; Johns Hopkins University, M.Ed., 1980. *Politics:* Democrat; "equity for African Americans in all aspects of American life, especially education and the arts." *Religion:* Episcopalian. *Hobbies and other interests:* Reading, research, and travel.

■ Addresses

Home and office—12612 Springloch Ct., Silver Spring, MD 20904.

■ Career

Teacher and author of children's books. C & P Telephone Company, Washington, DC, manager, 1972-86; Howard County Schools, Howard County, MD, English teacher, 1975-77; Grace Episcopal Day School, Kensington, MD, English teacher, 1987-90; National Cathedral School, Washington, DC, English teacher, 1990—.

■ Awards, Honors

National Endowment for the Humanities/Council for Basic Education fellowship, 1990, for independent study in the humanities; Best Books of 1994 citation, Society of School Librarians International, for *Jumping the Broom;* Teachers' Choice citation, International Reading Association, for *Journey to Freedom.*

■ Writings

Women of Shakespeare's Plays (adult nonfiction), University Press of America, 1993.
Journey to Freedom: A Story of the Underground Railroad, illustrated by Gershom Griffith, Holiday House, 1994.
Jumping the Broom, illustrated by Griffith, Holiday House, 1994.
Wagon Train: A Black Family's Westward Journey in 1865, illustrated by Griffith, 1995.

■ Work in Progress

Working on plays for children concerning African American issues and life; conducting research on Black soldiers in World War II.

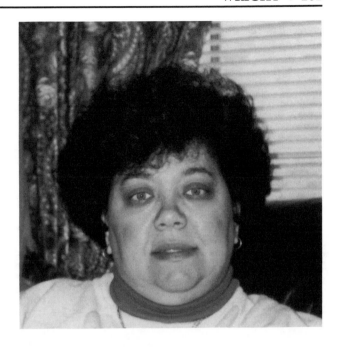

COURTNI C. WRIGHT

■ Sidelights

Courtni C. Wright told *SATA:* "I have wanted to be a writer for as long as I can remember. When I was in the sixth grade, I worked in the library as an aide. I longed to see my name on the spine of one of the many books I shelved every day. My plan was to write a popular best seller and make lots of money. However, after our son was born and I saw how few books there were in which African American children could see themselves portrayed or learn about our history, I decided to write children's books on the subject of African American history and life in general.

"I hope my work teaches children that African American people during slavery, after emancipation, and during the times of segregation lived rich lives filled with love and joy during times when society would rob them of the right to be individuals and deprive them of the freedoms enjoyed by others. Living under the hardships of slavery, African American people bonded and formed a sense of family and togetherness to share experiences and survive the evils of enslavement. During the time of segregation, when as a people we were forced to live under the dictates of 'separate but equal,' we found unity in working for equal rights. Today we still fight for equity in education, employment, and the arts.

"As a teacher I tell my students not to lose heart when revisions are demanded and to set aside time in their lives to write. I try to follow my own advice. For aspiring authors I feel that devoting time to the craft of writing is an excellent way of disciplining the mind. Even if I do not like the story that comes from the work, the act of creating flows more smoothly with practice. During school vacations, I dedicate a minimum of eight hours each day to either researching a topic for a book or doing some element of the writing process, either creating or revising. While teaching, I devote as much of my free time as possible to the creative process, often roughing in a manuscript and putting it aside for editing until later.

"My desire to be a writer was fed by works of African American women writers such as Ntozake Shange, Gwendolyn Brooks, Eloise Greenfield, Lorraine Hansberry, and Mildred Taylor, who blazed many trails, making it somewhat easier for me to follow. However, there is still much work to be done so that African American people can be more fully represented in literature and the arts as well as politics and education."